The doctor just performed a craniectomy.

There are 36 different code choices.

Now who's doing brain surgery?

Easy-to-use solutions that simplify today's complex coding practices.

Selecting the most appropriate codes requires a working knowledge of anatomy, terminology and the nuances of different procedures. Ingenix publications and software solutions translate these procedures into clear, understandable language, with accompanying illustrations and diagrams. By taking the guesswork out of billing, compliance and reimbursement, Ingenix helps you improve operational efficiency and add to your bottom line. In short, coding never has to be a headache again. Ingenix. Simplifying the complex business of health care.

To learn more, contact us at 1-800-INGENIX, or purchase online at www.ingenixonline.com

2004 Publications

2004 ICD-9-CM Code Books for Physicians

ICD-9-CM Professional for Physicians, Vols. 1 & 2

Softbound	Compact
Item No. 5583 **$74.95**	Item No. 5587 **$69.95**
Available: September 2003	Available: September 2003
ISBN: 1-56337-474-9	ISBN: 1-56337-475-7

ICD-9-CM Expert for Physicians, Vols. 1 & 2

Spiral	Binder
Item No. 5584 **$84.95**	**$144.95**
Available: September 2003	Item No. 3534
ISBN: 1-56337-476-5	

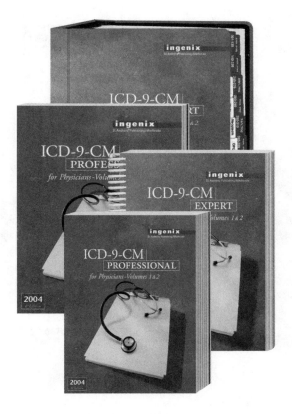

Our *ICD-9-CM for Physicians* offers easy access to pertinent coding and reimbursement information with its intuitive symbols and exclusive color coding. Plus detailed definitions and illustrations.

Professional and Expert editions feature:

- **New – AHA's** *Coding Clinic* **for ICD-9-CM references.**
- **New and Revised Code Symbols.**
- **Fourth or Fifth-digit Alerts.**
- **Complete Revised Official Coding Guidelines.**
- **Age and Sex Edits.**
- **Accurate and Clear Illustrations.**
- **Clinically Oriented Definitions.**
- **Medicare as Secondary Payer Indicators.**
- **Manifestation Code Alert.**
- **Other and Unspecified Diagnosis Alerts.**
- **V Code Symbols.** Primary and Secondary use only alerts.

The Expert editions also include these enhancements:

- **Special Reports Via E-mail.**
- **Code Tables.**
- **Valid Three-digit Category List.**

Expert Updateable Binder Subscriptions feature:

- **Three Updates a Year. (**Sept, Feb, and July)
  - Full text update with new code set in September.
  - February update with new illustrations, definitions, code edits, and AHA's *Coding Clinic* references.
  - July update newsletter with a preview of the new codes.

- **New—Summary of AHA's** *Coding Clinic* **Advice.** Quick look at the official advice on topics covered in the latest AHA's *Coding Clinics*.

100% Money Back Guarantee:
If our merchandise* ever fails to meet your expectations, please contact our Customer Service Department toll-free at 1.800.INGENIX (464.3649), option 1, for an immediate response.

*Software: Credit will be granted for unopened packages only.

2004 Publications

2004 ICD-9-CM Code Books for Hospitals

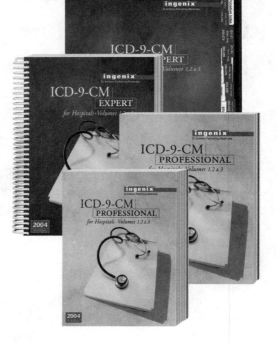

ICD-9-CM Professional for Hospitals, Vols. 1, 2, & 3

Softbound
Item No. 5586 **$84.95**
Available: September 2003
ISBN: 1-56337-478-1

Compact
Item No. 5588 **$79.95**
Available: September 2003
ISBN: 1-56337-479-X

ICD-9-CM Expert for Hospitals, Vols. 1, 2, & 3

Spiral
Item No. 5580 **$94.95**
Available: September 2003
ISBN: 1-56337-480-3

Binder
Item No. 3539 **$154.95**

These code books offer accurate and official code information integrated with all Medicare code edits crucial to appropriate reimbursement.

Professional and Expert editions feature:

- **New and Revised Code Symbols.**
- **Fourth or Fifth-digit Alerts.**
- **Complete Official Coding Guidelines**
- **Age and Sex Edits.**
- **AHA's** *Coding Clinic* **references.**
- **Illustrations and Definitions.**
- **Manifestation Code Alert**
- **Complex Diagnosis and Major Complication Alerts**
- **HIV Major Related Diagnosis Alert**
- **CC Principal Diagnosis Exclusion**
- **CC Diagnosis Symbol**
- **Crucial Medicare Procedure Code Edits**

Expert editions also include these enhancements:

- **Special Reports Via E-mail**
- **PDX/MDC/DRG List**
- **Pharmacological List**
- **Valid Three-Digit Category List**
- **CC Code List**

Expert Updateable Binder Subscriptions feature:

- **Three Updates a Year. (**Sept, Feb, and July)
  - Full text update with new code set in September.
  - February update with new illustrations, definitions, code edits, and AHA's *Coding Clinic* references.
  - July update newsletter with a preview of the new codes.
- **Summary of topics covered in the the latest AHA's** *Coding Clinic*

The Best Physicians' Current Procedural Terminology (CPT®) Reference in the Industry!

2004 CPT® Expert

Spiral bound **$89.95** Item No. 4531

Available: December 2003   ISBN: 1-56337-444-7

Compact **$79.95** Item No. 4532

Available December 2003   ISBN: 1-56337-445-5

Publisher's Note: CPT® Expert is not a replacement for the American Medical Association's CPT® 2003 Standard and Professional code books.

The CPT® Expert offers physicians' offices codes and icons denoting new, changed, and deleted language from the latest release (CPT® 2004), plus information that will help the coder find and use CPT® codes more easily. An extensive index, terms to know, and other additions help clarify the codes and speed assigning accurate codes. The product also provides valuable information about CPT® coding for Medicare Part B.

Inside you'll find:

- **New!** Crosswalk from CPT® to equivalent HCPCS codes helps Medicare billing

- **Exclusive** — Color Keys and Icons. Color keys reveal comprehensive NCCI edits, and icons denote Medicare, CLIA, and other common coding rules.

- **Exclusive** — Code-specific Definitions, Rules, and Tips pulled from the Medicare Carriers Manual and Coverage Issues Manual, among others.

- Complete—All 2004 CPT® codes and official, full descriptions

- 2004 Deleted codes with full descriptions and strike-outs to help you finish outstanding claims.

- ASC icon denoting ASC group.

- Color keys help you identify easily miscoded codes, unlisted codes, and codes not covered by Medicare

- Common icons from the AMA CPT® code book help you match information with the official book

- Simple, short introductions to each chapter describe how best to assure accuracy and speed claims

- Terms found in the nomenclature, defined, in glossary.

- Extensive, improved Index makes navigating easy.

- **Easy To Use.** Quick color references throughout, identifying unique nomenclature and rules, along with commonly misreported procedures that could impact your coding decisions.

- **Illustrated.** Detailed illustrations orient you to the procedures.

100% Money Back Guarantee:

If our merchandise* ever fails to meet your expectations, please contact our Customer Service Department toll-free at 1.800.INGENIX (464.3649), option 1, for an immediate response.

*Software: Credit will be granted for unopened packages only.

CPT is a registered trademark of the American Medical Association.

SAVE 5% when you order at www.ingenixonline.com (reference source code FOBW4)

or call toll-free 1.800.INGENIX (464.3649), option 1.

Also available from your medical bookstore or distributor.

2004 AMA CPT® Code Books

2004 CPT® Professional Edition

$82.95

Item No. 4438

Available November 2003   ISBN: 1-57947-421-7

2004 CPT® Standard Edition

$57.95

Item No. 4437

Available November 2003   ISBN: 1-57947-420-9

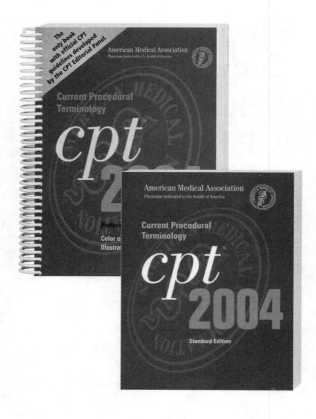

It's imperative that your office or facility has the latest official Physicians' Current Procedural Terminology (CPT®) codes. These AMA-published code books are comprehensive, informative, easy to use, and available in two formats—spiral and compact.

- **Stay Current.** Numerous code changes will impact coding accuracy and claims submission.

- **Reference Icon to AMA's CPT® Changes.** Find out where to get the facts about new additions and changes to CPT®codes.

- **Illustrations.** Procedural and anatomical illustrations to help visually confirm procedures being coded.

- **Easy Identification.** Color-coded keys make identifying section headings, coding changes, and coding alerts easier.

- **Thumb Tabs.** Pre-installed thumb-notch tabs for easy searches between sections.

CPT is a registered trademark of the American Medical Association.

St. Anthony Publishing/Medicode

Understand Each of the CPT® Code Changes found in CPT® 2004

2004 CPT® Changes: An Insider's View

$57.95

Item No. 4428

Available: November 2003

ISBN: 1-57947-423-3

Ingenix presents The American Medical Association's *CPT® Changes 2003: An Insider's View*, a must-have resource for AMA's CPT® Professional users. This book serves as a reference tool to understanding each of the Physicians' Current Procedural Terminology (CPT®) code changes found in CPT® 2004.

- **Includes every new, revised or deleted code change**—Listed along with a detailed rationale for the change. Guideline changes are also explained

- **Organized by CPT® code section and code number**—Find the codes that have changed easily and quickly.

- **Illustrated**—Illustrations help explain why changes were made and how to code new codes.

- **Clinical Examples** —Help you understand the practical application of the code.

- **Tabular review of 2004 changes** —Includes all new, revised, and deleted codes. See what changed in which codes at-a-glance.

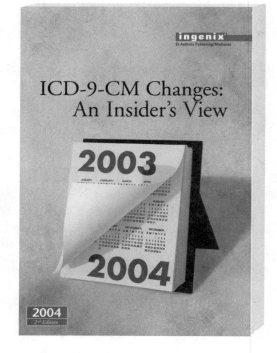

2004 Publications

St. Anthony Publishing/Medicode

Today's Most Comprehensive HCPCS Cross Coder

2004 HCPCS Cross Coder

$169.95

Available February 2004

Item No: 4525

ISBN: 1-56337-438-2

U se this reference to match HCPCS codes with ICD-9-CM Volumes I and III codes and check HCPCS claims to make sure the proper ICD-9-CM codes are listed.

- **Save time with a one-stop crosswalk for HCPCS codes to ICD-9-CM Volumes I and II codes.** Know which diagnoses your codes should match and link supplies and services with procedures.

- **Visualize the services you are coding.** Illustrations help orient you to the diagnoses, procedures, and supplies.

- **Avoid coding errors with visual information at your fingertips.** Icons alert coders to HCPCS Level II codes that have parallel Physicians' Current Procedural Terminology (CPT®) codes that may be preferred by private insurers.

- **Quickly reference medical, clinical, coding and reimbursement terms.** Easily grasp coding concepts and terminology, with a comprehensive glossary always at hand.

- **Convenient to use.** The softbound format allows it to lie flat on your desk while you work.

CPT is a registered trademark of the American Medical Association.

2004 Publications

Get Instant Answers to Your Tough Coding Questions

2004 Coders' Desk Reference for Procedures

2004 Coders' Desk Reference for HCPCS

2004 Coders' Desk Reference for Diagnoses

$119.95

ISBN No.	Item Description	Item No.	Available
1-56337-459-5	2004 Coders' Desk Reference for Procedures	5763	December 2003
1-56337-520-6	2004 Coders' Desk Reference for HCPCS	4974	December 2003
1-56337-503-6	2004 Coders' Desk Reference for Diagnoses	5765	September 2003

No matter how much experience you have using ICD-9-CM, Physicians' Current Procedural Terminology (CPT®) and HCPCS codes, there are always questions that hold up the billing process. And because billing errors can result in fines, you can't afford to guess... A staple for coders of all levels since 1995, *Coders' Desk Reference for Procedures* (formerly known as *Coders' Desk Reference*) has been providing the **RIGHT** answers to vexing coding questions. And now, Ingenix has added two additional must-have resources for ICD-9-CM and HCPCS coding—*Coders' Desk Reference for Diagnoses* and *Coders' Desk Reference for HCPCS*—creating an essential coding suite for every library.

Coders' Desk Reference for Procedures

- Curb claim denials or delays by using only updated CPT® codes and descriptions for more than 7,000 CPT® procedures.

- Improve your coding accuracy with lay descriptions of procedures and tests.

- Facilitate your coding with laboratory and radiology codes, along with lay descriptions for these complicated chapters.

Coders' Desk Reference for Diagnoses

- Submit claims with updated ICD-9-CM codes.

- Decrease coding time with the help of comprehensive lay descriptions of ICD-9-CM codes, along with clinical explanations of conditions, diseases and syndromes.

- Enhance your coding knowledge with explanatory clinical descriptions on using ICD-9-CM codes in DRGs.

Coders' Desk Reference for HCPCS

- Submit claims with updated HCPCS codes at your fingertips in a familiar format.

- Speed up your coding with comprehensive lay descriptions for HCPCS supply items and services.

- Learn the quickest way to bill and use HCPCS Level II codes successfully.

100% Money Back Guarantee:

If our merchandise* ever fails to meet your expectations, please contact our Customer Service Department toll-free at 1.800.INGENIX (464.3649), option 1, for an immediate response.

*Software: Credit will be granted for unopened packages only.

CPT is a registered trademark of the American Medical Association.

SAVE 5% when you order at www.ingenixonline.com (reference source code FOBW4)

or call toll-free 1.800.INGENIX (464.3649), option 1.

Also available from your medical bookstore or distributor.

2004 Publications

The International Source of the Best Available Evidence for Effective Health Care

Clinical Evidence and Clinical Evidence Concise

Clinical Evidence
$135.00   Item No: 1820   Available:
Now   ISSN: 1462-3846

Clinical Evidence Concise
$135.00   Item No: 1821   Available: Now   ISSN: 1475-9225

Clinical Evidence and *Clinical Evidence Concise* Package
$190.00   Item No: 1822   Available: Now

Published by the British Medical Journal, *Clinical Evidence* is an international research-based resource that pulls together some of the best available evidence for patient treatment based on common clinical interventions. *Clinical Evidence Concise* is a condensed, summary-sized version of this resource, complete with a mini CD-ROM that contains the complete content of *Clinical Evidence*. Derived from common questions of clinicians, with summaries of verification to answer them, both *Clinical Evidence* and *Clinical Evidence Concise* provide the most current evidence-based treatment plans available.

- **Comprehensive Coverage of Treatment Plans.** Findings from recent clinical interventions include topics like pancreatic cancer, seasonal allergic rhinitis, varicose veins, insomnia, and more!

- **Easy to use Formats to Select From.** Two versions are available to choose from—the complete, expanded version of *Clinical Evidence* or the compact, pocketbook-sized edition of *Clinical Evidence Concise* with a mini CD-ROM back-up.

- **Save Valuable Time and Energy Spent Doing Unnecessary Research.** The information in both *Clinical Evidence* and in *Clinical Evidence Concise* has been researched, validated, and summarized, so you don't need to spend the time searching for it on your own.

- **FREE! Additional Updates at No Additional Charge.** Get two updates a year—in June and in December—with *Clinical Evidence*. And, with your purchase of *Clinical Evidence* or *Clinical Evidence Concise*, you get FREE access to the latest ongoing clinical intervention information each month through the Internet.

100% Money Back Guarantee:
If our merchandise* ever fails to meet your expectations, please contact our Customer Service Department toll-free at 1.800.INGENIX (464.3649), option 1, for an immediate response.

*Software: Credit will be granted for unopened packages only.

SAVE 5% when you order at www.ingenixonline.com (reference source code FOBW4)

or call toll-free 1.800.INGENIX (464.3649), option 1.

Also available from your medical bookstore or distributor.

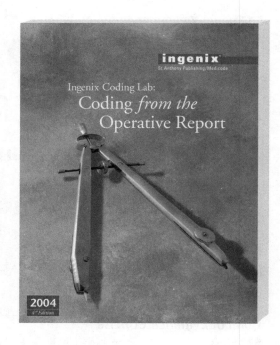

2004 Publications

St. Anthony Publishing/Medicode

The Most Comprehensive RBRVS Available

The Essential RBRVS

$199.95   Item No. 4334

$599.95   Data File (includes book) Item No. 4326

Available: December 2003   ISBN: 1-56337-497-8

The *Essential RBRVS* is a complete relative value schedule based on Medicare's RBRVS. CMS develops the RBRVS for the Medicare Physician Fee Schedule. The Medicare Physician Fee Schedule, however, is not a complete fee schedule. Medicare does not pay for some services and does not assign relative values for other services. Codes in the RBRVS not provided a RVU for Medicare are often referred to as "gap" codes. *The Essential RBRVS* provides all codes valued by CMS, as well as the codes not valued for Medicare. The valuation of "gap" codes provides a way to value services performed using one relative value scale.

This is a must-have tool for reimbursement disputes, contract negotiations, and determining accurate fees for Medicare or private payers.

- **RVUs for Physicians' Current Procedural Terminology (CPT®) Codes and HCPCS Level II Codes.** "Gap" codes are valued using the same methodology that CMS used to develop the Medicare Fee Schedule.

- **Three Values for Each CPT® Code.** Provides work, practice, and malpractice expense components for each procedure including "gap" codes, so you can evaluate and analyze the costs and effort associated with a service.

- **Comprehensive Relative Value Scale.** Save time by maintaining only one relative value scale for both Medicare and commercial claims.

- **Negotiate favorable managed care contracts by utilizing the same data used by many insurance companies.**

- **5 CEUs from AAPC**

- **HFMA Co-labeled Product.** Product has been reviewed by HFMA for quality, accuracy and practical use.

100% Money Back Guarantee:

If our merchandise* ever fails to meet your expectations, please contact our Customer Service Department toll-free at 1.800.INGENIX (464.3649), option 1, for an immediate response.

*Software: Credit will be granted for unopened packages only.

CPT is a registered trademark of the American Medical Association.

PUBLICATION ORDER AND FAX FORM

FOBA4

Customer No._____

Contact No._____

Purchase Order No._____
(Attach copy of Purchase Order)

Source Code_____

Contact Name _____

Title_____

Company_____

Specialty_____

Address _____
(no P.O. Boxes, please)

City_____ State_____ Zip_____

Phone (_____)_____
(in case we have questions about your order)

Fax (_____)_____

IMPORTANT: E-MAIL REQUIRED FOR ORDER CONFIRMATION AND SELECT PRODUCT DELIVERY.

E-mail _____

Ingenix respects your right to privacy. We will not sell or rent your e-mail address or fax number to anyone outside Ingenix and its business partners. If you would like to remove your name from Ingenix promotions, please call 1.800.INGENIX (464.3649), option 1.

Order Toll-Free
1.800.INGENIX
(464.3649), Option 1

Item #	Qty	Item Description	Price	Total
~~4025~~	~~1~~	~~(SAMPLE) DRG Guidebook~~	~~$89.95~~	~~$89.95~~

Shipping and Handling	
No. of Items	**Fee**
1	$10.95
2-4	$12.95
5-7	$14.95
8-10	$19.95
11+	Call

Sub Total _____

TX, UT, OH, and VA residents please add applicable sales tax _____

Shipping & handling (see chart)
(11 plus items, foreign, Canadian, AK, and HI orders, please call for shipping costs) _____

Total enclosed _____

Payment Options

☐ Check enclosed. (Make payable to Ingenix, Inc.)

☐ Charge my: ☐ MasterCard ☐ VISA ☐ AMEX ☐ Discover

Card # | | | | | | | | | | | | | | | | | | | Exp. Date: | | | | |
                                                                         MM   YR

☐ Bill Me P.O.#_____

Signature _____

EASY WAYS TO ORDER!

1 **MAIL** this order form with payment and/or purchase order to: **Ingenix, PO Box 27116, Salt Lake City, UT 84127-0116**.

2 **CALL** toll-free **1.800.INGENIX (464.3649), option 1** and mention the Source Code: **FOBA4**.

3 **FAX** this order form with credit card information and/or purchase order to **(801) 982-4033**.

4 **SHOP** on line at www.ingenixonline.com. Reference Source Code FOBW4 and save 5%.

100% Money Back Guarantee:

If our merchandise* ever fails to meet your expectations, please contact our Customer Service Department toll-free at 1.800.INGENIX (464.3649), option 1, for an immediate response.

*Software: Credit will be granted for unopened packages only.

FOBA4

St. Anthony Publishing/Medicode

Dear Ingenix Customer:

If you have not already responded, please help us keep you informed by e-mail of important news affecting *HCPCS*. Return this form by fax, mail, or e-mail.

Customer Number _____

Name _____

Department _____

Facility _____

Street Address _____

City _____ State _____ Zip _____

Telephone (____) _____ Fax (____) _____

E-mail address: _____

(Please write clearly)

I would like to receive product information and Web site updates via e-mail.

❏   Yes   ❏   No

I would like to receive new product and service offers, special promotions, and/or product discount information via e-mail.

❏   Yes   ❏   No

Return by fax to: 801.982.4033

Return by mail to: Product Manager, HCPCS
                         Ingenix, Inc.
                         2525 Lake Park Blvd
                         SLC, UT 84120

Return by e-mail to: brad.ericson@ingenix.com

St. Anthony Publishing/Medicode

HCPCS Level II
Expert

2004

15th edition

Publisher's Notice

The Ingenix *2004 HCPCS* is designed to be an accurate and authoritative source of information about this government coding system. Every effort has been made to verify the accuracy of the listings, and all information is believed reliable at the time of publication. Absolute accuracy cannot be guaranteed, however. This publication is made available with the understanding that the publisher is not engaged in rendering legal or other services that require a professional license. If you identify a correction or wish to share information, please email the Ingenix customer service department at customerservice@ingenix.com or fax us at 801.982.4033.

Acknowledgments

Brad Ericson, MPC, *Product Manager*
Elizabeth Boudrie, *Vice President, Publisher*
Lynn Speirs, *Senior Director, Publishing Services*
Sheri Poe Bernard, CPC, *Senior Product Director*
Kristin Hodkinson, RHIT, CPC, CPC-H, CIC, *Clinical/Technical Editor*
Wendy McConkie, CPC, CPC-H, *Clinical/Technical Editor*
Karen Kacher, RN, CPC, *Clinical/Technical Editor*
Regina Magnani, RHIT, *Clinical/Technical Editor*
Jean Parkinson, *Project Editor*
Kerrie Hornsby, *Desktop Publishing Manager*
Greg Kemp, *Desktop Publishing Specialist*

Continuing Education Units for AAPC Certified Members

This publication has prior approval by the American Academy of Professional Coders for continuing education units. Granting of prior approval in no way constitutes endorsement by AAPC of the publication content nor the publisher. Instructions to submit CEUs are available at www.aapc.com/education/ceus.htm

Technical Editors

Kristin Hodkinson, RHIT, CPC, CPC-H, CIC
Clinical/Technical Editor

Ms. Hodkinson has more than 10 years of experience in the health care profession including commercial insurance payers, health information management, and patient accounts. She has extensive background in both the professional and technical components of CPT/HCPCS and ICD-9-CM coding. Her areas of expertise include interventional radiology and cardiology, hospital chargemaster, and the Outpatient Prospective Payment System (OPPS). She recently served as the APC coordinator for a health care system in Florida. She is a member of the American Academy of Professional Coders (AAPC) and the American Health Information Management Association (AHIMA).

Wendy McConkie, CPC, CPC-H
Clinical/Technical Editor

Ms. McConkie has more than 20 years of experience in the health care field. She has extensive background in CPT/HCPCS and ICD-9-CM coding. She served several years as a coding consultant. Her areas of expertise include physician and hospital CPT coding assessments, chargemaster reviews, and the Outpatient Prospective Payment System (OPPS). She is a member of the American Academy of Professional Coders (AAPC).

Regina Magnani, RHIT
Clinical/Technical Editor

Ms. Magnani has 25 years of experience in the health care industry in both health information management and patient financial services. Her areas of expertise include patient financial services, CPT/HCPCS and ICD-9-CM coding, the Outpatient Prospective Payment System (OPPS), and chargemaster development and maintenance. She is an active member of the Healthcare Financial Management Association (HFMA), the American Health Information Management Association (AHIMA), and the American Association of Heathcare Administrative Management (AAHAM).

Karen Kachur, RN, CPC
Clinical/Technical Editor

Ms. Kachur is a Clinical/Technical Editor for Ingenix with expertise in CPT/HCPCS and ICD-9-CM coding, in addition to physician billing, compliance, and fraud and abuse. Prior to joining Ingenix, she worked for many years as a staff RN in a variety of clinical settings including medicine, surgery, intensive care, psychiatry, and geriatrics. Ms Kachur has served as assistant director of a hospital utilization management and quality assurance department. She also has extensive experience as a nurse reviewer for Blue Cross/Blue Shield.

Sheri Poe Bernard, CPC
Director of Essential Regulatory Products

Ms. Bernard has contributed to the development of coding products for Ingenix for more than 10 years, and her areas of expertise include ICD-9-CM and ICD-10 coding systems. A member of the National Advisory Board of the American Academy of Professional Coders, Ms. Bernard chairs its committee on ICD-10, and is a nationally-recognized speaker on ICD-10 coding systems. Prior to joining Ingenix, Ms. Bernard was a journalist specializing in business and medical writing and editing.

Brad Ericson, MPC
Product Manager

Brad Ericson has written and edited award-winning publications about health care and reimbursement for 25 years. He has developed several popular products and now manages products published under the Ingenix and AMA Press imprints. He holds degrees in journalism and professional communications.

Introduction

The HCPCS Level II national codes found in 2004 HCPCS include more than 4,000 codes and represent just one part of a larger, three-level coding system called HCPCS.

HCPCS (pronounced "hick-picks") is the acronym for the Healthcare Common Procedure Coding System. This system is a uniform method for health care providers and medical suppliers to report professional services, procedures, and supplies. Prior to the development of HCPCS in 1983, there was no uniform system for coding a procedure, service, or supply for reimbursement.

Blue Cross/Blue Shield created and required use of its own coding system; many other insurance companies created their own method of coding physician services and procedures. Despite the addition and subtraction of codes over the nearly 20-year history, the Centers for Medicare and Medicaid Services, or CMS (formerly the Health Care Financing Administration, or HCFA) has maintained the intentions of HCPCS, which is to:

- Meet the operational needs of Medicare/Medicaid
- Coordinate government programs by uniform application of CMS policies
- Allow providers and suppliers to communicate their services in a consistent manner
- Ensure the validity of profiles and fee schedules through standardized coding
- Enhance medical education and research by providing a vehicle for local, regional, and national utilization comparisons

Ingenix's HCPCS Level II products are compiled to facilitate the coding of supplies and services provided by physicians, therapists, home health, outpatient departments in hospitals, and other caregivers. The second level of HCPCS Level II includes such a broad spectrum of services and supplies—from patient transport to ostomy supplies, from chemotherapy drugs to durable medical equipment, and from new technologies to surgical procedures—it's often referred to as the "catch-all code system." Chapters differ by service, and some are specifically for use by dentists, Blue Cross, outpatient prospective payment system hospitals, and Medicaid.

Naturally, this proves confusing and the dynamic nature of the code set, which must be updated frequently to better serve various providers and payers, makes coding HCPCS Level II codes a difficult chore. Ingenix helps coders with a number of features, including:

- All the official HCPCS Level II codes and descriptions
- Ingenix expert coding tips and annotations
- New, changed, and deleted codes
- Medicare rules indicated by icon and color coding
- Medicare manual references and actual excerpts
- Ambulatory surgery center (ASC) group and ambulatory payment classification (APC) status codes
- Age and sex edits
- Quantity alerts for codes requiring that attention be paid to the number of items used
- Modifiers
- An enhanced index and table of drugs
- Choice of formats

In addition, *HCPCS Expert* customers may subscribe to an e-mail service to receive special reports when information in this book changes. Contact customer service at (800) INGENIX, option 1 to sign up.

Additional Copies

Contact the customer service department toll free at 1.800.INGENIX (464.3649), option 1 or access www.ingenixonline.com via your computer.

Use of Official Sources

Our HCPCS books are based on the CMS official 2004 update releases of HCPCS Level II codes, descriptions, and other relevant data. Other sources of information from which HCPCS codes and their usage are gleaned include

CMS's hospital Outpatient Prospective Payment System (OPPS), *Medicare Carriers Manual*, *Coverage Issues Manual*, Publication 100 sections, the Medicare physician fee schedule, and Ambulatory Surgical Center (ASC) rules.

Proprietary information in our HCPCS books includes annotations, age and sex edits, coding tips, an enhanced index and drug table, and other useful features.

Effective Dates for 2004

This new HCPCS Level II product is effective for dates of service beginning January 1, 2004. A three-month grace period still applies to discontinued HCPCS codes through March 2004. This grace period applies to claims received prior to April 1 2004, which include 2003 discontinued codes for dates of service January 1, 2004, through March 31, 2004. Carriers will accept both 2003 discontinued codes and valid 2004 codes from physicians, suppliers, and providers during the January–March 2004 grace period. The HCPCS grace period also applies to the durable medical equipment regional carriers (DMERCs). Ingenix has included codes from the November 2003 CMS Internet release as well as the temporary codes that were posted in October 2003. Ingenix offers an updateable HCPCS product for codes that were posted by CMS after November 1, 2003.

This 2004 HCPCS Level II includes additions, changes, and deletions released by CMS before November 2003 via the agency's public use files. Appropriate alterations have been made based on CMS program memos and transmittals, the October and November 2003 HCPCS temporary national coding decisions for 2004 documents, and addendum B of the outpatient prospective payment system (OPPS) update of November 2003; these are noted to promote accurate coding.

Because of the unstable nature of HCPCS Level II codes, everything has been done to include the latest information available at print time. Unfortunately, HCPCS Level II codes, their descriptions, and other related information change throughout the year. Consult the patient's payer and the CMS Web site to confirm the status of any HCPCS Level II code. The existence of a code does not imply coverage under any given payment plan.

What to Do If You Have Questions

If you have any questions, call our customer service department toll-free at 1.800.INGENIX (464.3649), option 1.

If you have comments on the content of this book, please e-mail them to customerservice@ingenix.com or fax them to (801) 982-2783.

HCPCS Levels of Codes

Each of the three HCPCS levels is a unique coding system. The levels I, II, and III are also known by the names shown here with the level numbers.

Level I—CPT

Level I is the American Medical Association's *Physician's Current Procedural Terminology* (CPT®). The Level I codes include five-digit codes and two-digit modifiers, both with descriptive terms for reporting services performed by health care providers. Level I codes and modifiers are described in detail in the CPT book. The AMA released its first edition of CPT in 1966 with the intention of simplifying the reporting of procedures or services rendered by physicians or health care providers under their supervision. Procedures are grouped within six major sections: evaluation and management (E/M), anesthesiology, surgery, radiology, pathology and laboratory, and medicine. The major sections are divided into subsections according to body part, service, or diagnosis (e.g., mouth, amputation, or septal defect).

Level II—HCPCS National Codes

The CPT book does not contain all the codes needed to report medical services and supplies, and CMS developed the second level of codes—those found in this book. In contrast to the five-digit codes found in Level I, national codes consist of one alphabetic character (a letter between A and V), followed by four digits. (All D codes are copyright by the American Dental Association.) They are grouped by the type of service or supply they represent and are updated annually by CMS with input from private insurance companies. Level II codes are required for reporting most medical services and supplies provided to Medicare and Medicaid patients and by most private payers.

Level II of HCPCS also contains modifiers, which are either alphanumeric or two letters in the range from A1 to VP. National modifiers can be used with all levels of HCPCS codes. The appendixes include a complete listing of Level II modifiers.

National permanent HCPCS Level II codes are maintained by the HCPCS National Panel. The National Panel is made up of representatives from the Blue Cross/Blue Shield Association (BCBSA), the Health Insurance Association of America (HIAA), and CMS. The panel is responsible for making decisions about additions, revisions, and deletions to the permanent national alphanumeric codes. These codes are for the use of all private and public health insurers. Contact CMS via www.cms.hhs.gov.

The permanent national codes serve the important function of providing a standardized coding system that is managed jointly by private and public insurers. It supplies a predictable set of uniform codes that provides a stable environment for claims submission and processing.

Level III—Local Codes

The third level contains codes assigned and maintained by individual state Medicare carriers. Like Level II, these codes begin with a letter (W through Z) followed by four numeric digits, but the most notable difference is that these codes are not common to all carriers. Individual carriers assign these codes to describe new procedures that are not yet available in Level I or II. These codes can be introduced on an as-needed basis throughout the year, but carriers must send written notification to the physicians and suppliers in their area when these local codes are required. Reading and implementing the information received from these carriers keeps providers up-to-date.

Level III (Local) modifiers are assigned by individual Medicare carriers and are distributed to physicians and suppliers through carrier newsletters. The carrier may change, add, or delete these local modifiers as needed.

Elimination of HCPCS Level III Codes and Modifiers

The HCPCS Level III codes are just one part of a larger three-level coding system that will soon become a two-level coding system. The Health Insurance Portability and Accountability Act (HIPAA) requires that there be standardized procedure coding. To meet this requirement, all HCPCS Level III codes/modifiers need to be eliminated by December 31, 2003. The Federal Register on August 17, 2000 (65 FR 50312) published regulations to provide for the elimination of Level III local codes by October 2002. The elimination of local codes is currently on hold as a result of section 532(a) of BIPA, which directs CMS to maintain and continue the use of local codes through December 31, 2003.

Unapproved local procedure and modified codes required that a request for approval be submitted to the regional office representative by April 1, 2002. The regional offices were required to submit any requests they received for a temporary national code to be received by the central office by May 1, 2002. All unapproved local procedure and modifier codes were to be deleted by October 16, 2002. The deadline for requests for temporary national codes, including a justification for any temporary national codes that have been requested and approved as the result of the Medicare contractors' clean-up effort of HCPCS Level II procedure codes/modifiers, will be January 1, 2004.

To compensate for the loss in local reporting, a greater number of codes are available on the national level. For example, in 2001 there was a 35 percent increase in the number of Level II codes (from 3,204 to 4,145), owing in part to the increasing number of codes in the recently added S and C categories. Private payers have in the past two years created nearly 200 S codes, and the government will be creating national codes to replace local HCPCS Level III codes.

More information about C codes and the development of categories for determining transitional pass-through payment devices is found later in this book.

Organization

The Ingenix 2004 *HCPCS Expert* contains mandated changes and new codes for use as of January 1, 2004. Deleted codes have also been indicated and cross-referenced to active codes when possible. New codes have been added to the appropriate sections, eliminating the time-consuming step of looking in two places for a code. However, keep in mind that the information in this book is a reproduction of the 2004 HCPCS; additional information on coverage issues may have been provided to carriers after publication. All carriers periodically update their systems and records throughout the year.

To make this year's HCPCS book even more useful, we included codes noted in addendum B of the November 2003 outpatient prospective payment system (OPPS) update as published in the *Federal Register* and from program memorandums through 2003 that include codes not discussed in other CMS documents. The sources for these codes are noted in blue beneath the description.

Index

Since HCPCS is organized by code number rather than by service or supply name, the index enables the coder to locate any code without looking through individual ranges of codes. Just look up the medical or surgical supply, service, orthotic, prosthetic, or generic or brand name drug in question to find the appropriate codes. This index also refers to many of the brand names by which these items are known.

Table of Drugs and Cross-Referencing

Our HCPCS provides three ways to cross-reference from brand name to generic drugs. In the listing of codes, brand name items are included after the generic name. The brand names listed are examples only and may not include all products available for that type of drug. Our table of drugs lists A codes, several C codes, all J codes, a few K codes, many S codes, and several Q codes under generic drug names with amount, route of administration, and code numbers. Brand name drugs are also listed in the table with a reference to the appropriate generic drug.

Color-coded Coverage Instructions

The Ingenix HCPCS Level II code book provides colored symbols for each coverage and reimbursement instruction. A legend to these symbols is provided on the bottom of each two-page spread.

Red Color Bar	Codes that are not covered by or are invalid for Medicare are covered by a red bar. The pertinent *Coverage Issues Manual* (CIM) and *Medicare Carriers Manual* (MCM) reference numbers are also given explaining why a particular code is not covered. These numbers refer to appendix 4, where we have listed the CIM and MCM references.
Yellow Color Bar	Issues that are left to "carrier discretion" are covered with a yellow bar. Contact the carrier for specific coverage information on those codes.
Blue Color Bar	A blue bar for "special coverage instructions" over a code means that special coverage instructions apply to that code. These special instructions are also typically given in the form of CIM and MCM reference numbers. The appendixes provide the full text of the cited CIM and MCM references.
☑	Many codes in HCPCS report quantities that may not coincide with quantities available in the marketplace. For instance, a HCPCS code for a surgical mask reports 20 masks, but the product is generally sold in a box of 100; "5" must be indicated in the quantity box on the CMS claim form to ensure proper reimbursement. This symbol (boxed checkmark) indicates that care should be taken to verify quantities in this code.

2004 *HCPCS Expert* uses the AMA's CPT book conventions to indicate new, revised, and deleted codes.

- A black circle (●) precedes a new code.
- A black triangle (▲) precedes a code with revised terminology or rules.
- Codes deleted from the 2004 active codes appear with a strike-out.

Notes

A few of the subsections, headings, or codes have special instructions that apply only to them. The term "NOTE" sometimes, but not always, is used to identify these instructions. Some notes are found following the subsection, heading, or code to which they apply. Others appear as part of a description in a heading or code, separated by a comma or dash or placed within parentheses.

Unlisted Procedures

CMS does not use consistent terminology when a code for a specific procedure is not listed. The code description may include any of the following terms: unlisted, not otherwise classified (NOC), unspecified, unclassified, other and miscellaneous. When coding this type of procedure, check with your Medicare carrier in case a specific HCPCS Level III code is available. If one is not available, the appropriate unlisted procedure code should be used and a special report should be submitted with the claim.

Age and Sex Edits

Age and sex edits help identify supplies and procedures Medicare and commercial payers may consider appropriate for a patient of a certain age or gender. Icons to the right of the code description are intuitive and keyed at the bottom of each page.

P	Pediatrics:	Years 0 – 10
A	Adult:	Years 11 – 99
M	Maternity:	Years 12 – 50

Gender is indicated by the following icons:

♀ Female

♂ Male

ASC Groupings

Codes designated as being paid by ambulatory surgery center groupings are denoted in the HCPCS Level II code book by the group number.

APC Status Indicators

A - X APC Status Indicators

Status indicators identify how individual HCPCS Level II codes are paid or not paid under the OPPS. The same status indicator is assigned to all the codes within an APC. Consult the payer or resource to learn which CPT codes fall within various APCs.

A   Indicates services that are paid under some other method such as the DMEPOS fee schedule or the physician fee schedule

C   Indicates inpatient services that are not paid under the OPPS

E   Indicates services for which payment is not allowed under the OPPS. In some instances, the service is not covered by Medicare. In other instances, Medicare does not use the code in question but does use another code to describe the service

F   Indicates corneal tissue acquisition costs, which are paid separately

G   Indicates a current drug or biological for which payment is made under the transitional pass-through

H   Indicates a device for which payment is made under the transitional pass-through

K   Indicates non-pass-through drugs and biologicals. Effective July 1, 2001, copayments for these items and the service of the administration of the items are aggregated and may not exceed the inpatient hospital deductible.

N   Indicates services that are incidental, with payment packaged into another service or APC group

P   Indicates services paid only in partial hospitalization programs

S   Indicates significant procedures for which payment is allowed under the hospital OPPS but to which the multiple procedure reduction does not apply

T   Indicates surgical services for which payment is allowed under the hospital OPPS. Services with this payment indicator are the only ones to which the multiple procedure payment reduction applies.

V   Indicates medical visits for which payment is allowed under the hospital OPPS

X   Indicates ancillary services for which payment is allowed under the hospital OPPS

Appendixes

The following is a list of the appendixes in the Ingenix HCPCS Level II code book.

Appendix 1: Modifiers

Under certain situations, procedures have been altered by a specific circumstance. Modifiers are required to adequately report the procedure. Appendix 1 contains an introduction and a complete listing of modifiers used with HCPCS Level II codes.

Appendix 2: Abbreviations and Acronyms

A complete list of all abbreviations and acronyms for the current year is provided in a summary format.

Appendix 3: Table of Drugs

The brand names are listed in alphabetical order and will refer to the appropriate specific generic drug for correct code assignment by route of administration and dosage.

Appendix 4: Medicare Coverage Issues Manual (CIM) and Medicare Carriers Manual (MCM) References

To make it easier to understand the coverage issues associated with certain codes, we have provided the coverage guidelines for HCPCS Level II codes using the *Medicare Coverage Issues Manual* (CIM) and the *Medicare Carriers Manual* (MCM), which are published by CMS.

Appendix 5: Companies Accepting HCPCS Level II Codes

The information is based on our surveys sent to individual payers. It is always best to verify coverage with the carrier before submitting a claim.

Appendix 6: HCPCS Codes for which CPT Codes Should be Reported

Some HCPCS codes are to be reported using another code. Find out which ones are affected.

Appendix 7: New, Changed, and Deleted HCPCS Codes for 2004

This appendix lists all new, changed, and deleted HCPCS codes as of November 7, 2003, effective January 1, 2004.

Appendix 8: Medicare and Commercial National Average Payment

We provide a table representing commercial and Medicare national average payment for services and supplies reported using HCPCS Level II codes.

Coders should keep in mind, however, that the insurance companies and government do not base payment solely on what was done for the patient. They need to know why the services were performed. In addition to using the HCPCS coding system for procedures and supplies, coders must also use the ICD-9-CM coding system to denote the diagnosis. This book will not discuss ICD-9-CM codes, which can be found in a current ICD-9-CM code book for diagnosis codes.

How to Use HCPCS Level II

To locate a HCPCS Level II code, follow these steps:

1. Identify the services or procedures the patient received.

    Example:

    Patient receives flexible sigmoidoscopy for colorectal cancer screening.

2. Look up the appropriate term in the index.

    Example:

    > **Screening**
    > prostate

    Coding Tip: Coders who are unable to find the procedure or service in the index can look in the table of contents for the type of procedure or device to narrow the code choices. Also, coders should remember to check the unlisted procedure guidelines for additional choices.

3. Assign a tentative code.

    Example:

    Codes G0103

    Coding Tip: To the right of the terminology, there may be a single code or multiple codes, a cross-reference or an indication that the code has been deleted. Tentatively assign all codes listed.

4. Locate the code or codes in the appropriate section. When multiple codes are listed in the index, be sure to read the narrative of all codes listed to find the appropriate code based on the service performed.

    Example:

    > **G0103 Prostate cancer screening; prostate specific antigen test (PSA), total**

5. Check for color bars, symbols, notes, and references.

    Example:

    > Ⓐ **G0103 Prostate cancer screening; prostate specific antigen test (PSA), total** ♂
    > **MED: CIM 50-55, MCM 4182**

6. Review the appendixes for the reference definitions and other guidelines for coverage issues that apply.

7. Determine whether any modifiers should be used.

8. Assign the code.

    Example:

    The code assigned is G0103.

Coding Standards

Levels of Use

Coders may find that the same procedure is coded at two or even three levels. Which code is correct? There are certain rules to follow if this should occur. First, if there is an overlap between a local code and either a CPT or Level II code, use the local code—it has the highest priority.

When both a CPT and a HCPCS Level II code have virtually identical narratives for a procedure or service, the CPT code should be used. If, however, the narratives are not identical (for example, the CPT code narrative is generic, whereas the HCPCS Level II code is specific), the Level II code should be used.

Be sure to check for a national or local code when a CPT code description contains an instruction to include additional information, such as describing specific medication. For example, when billing Medicare or Medicaid for supplies, avoid using CPT code 99070, supplies and materials (except spectacles), provided by the physician over and above those usually included with the office visit or other services rendered (list drugs, trays, supplies, or materials provided). There are many HCPCS Level II codes that specify supplies in more detail.

Special Reports

Submit a special report with the claim when a new, unusual, or variable procedure is provided or a modifier is used. Include the following information:

*   A copy of the appropriate report (e.g., operative, x-ray), explaining the nature, extent, and need for the procedure
*   Documentation of the medical necessity of the procedure
*   Documentation of the time and effort necessary to perform the procedure

Bariatric
bed, E0302-E0304
surgery, S2085

Barium enema, G0106
cancer screening, G0120

Barrier
4x4, A4372
adhesion, C1765
with flange, A4373

Baseball finger splint, A4570

Basiliximab, Q2019

Bath chair, E0240

Bathtub
heat unit, E0249
stool or bench, E0245
transfer rail, E0246
wall rail, E0241, E0242

Battery, L7360, L7364
blood glucose monitor, A4254
charger, L7362, L7366
hearing device, V5266
infusion pump, A4632
lithium, L7367
charger, L7368
replacement
ear pulse generator, A4638
external defibrillator, K0607
external infusion pump, K0601-K0605
TENS, A4630
ventilator, A4611-A4613

Bayer chemical reagent strips, box of 100 glucose/ketone urine test strips, A4250

BCG live, intravesical, J9031

BCW 600, manual wheelchair, K0007

BCW Power, power wheelchair, K0014

BCW recliner, manual wheelchair, K0007

B-D alcohol swabs, box, A4245

B-D disposable insulin syringes, up to 1cc, per syringe, A4206

B-D lancets, per box of 100, A4258

Bebax, foot orthosis, L3160

Becaplermin gel, S0157

Becker, hand prosthesis
Imperial, L6840
Lock Grip, L6845
Plylite, L6850

Betamethasone, J7622-J7624

Bed
air fluidized, E0194
accessory, E0315
cradle, any type, E0280
drainage bag, bottle, A4357, A5102
extra size for bariatric patients, E0302-E0304
hospital, E0250-E0270
full electric, home care, without mattress, E0297
manual, without mattress, E0293
safety enclosure frame/canopy, E0316
semi-electric, without mattress, E0295
pan, E0275, E0276
Moore, E0275
rail, E0305, E0310
safety enclosure frame/canopy, hospital bed, E0316

Behavior management, dental care, D9920

Behavioral health, H0002-H0030
day treatment, H2013
per hour, H2012

Bell-Horn
prosthetic shrinker, L8440-L8465
sacrocinch, L0510, L0610

Belt
adapter, A4421

Belt — *continued*
extremity, E0945
Little Ones Sur-Fit pediatric, A4367
ostomy, A4367
pelvic, E0944
wheelchair, E0978, E0979

Bena-D (10, 50), J1200

Benadryl, J1200

Benahist (10, 50), J1200

Ben-Allergin-50, J1200

Bench, bathtub (*see also* **Bathtub**), E0245

Benesch boot, L3212-L3214

Benoject (-10, -50), J1200

Bentyl, J0500

Benztropine, J0515

Berkeley shell, foot orthosis, L3000

Berubigen, J3420

Betadine, A4246
swabs/wipes, A4247

Betalin 12, J3420

Betameth, J0704

Betamethasone
acetate and betamethasone sodium phosphate, J0702
sodium phosphate, J0704

Betaseron, J1830

Bethanechol chloride, J0520

Bicarbonate concentration for hemodialysis, A4706-A4707

Bicillin, Bicillin C-R, Bicillin C-R 900/300, and Bicillin L-A, J0530-J0580

BiCNU, J9050

Bifocal, glass or plastic, V2200-V2299

Bilirubin (phototherapy) light, E0202

Binder
extremity, nonelastic, A4465
lumbar-sacral-orthosis (LSO), A4462, L0500, L0510

Bioengineered dermal or epidermal graft, Q0182

Biofeedback device, E0746

Bio Flote alternating air pressure pump, pad system, E0181, E0182

Biologic materials, dental, D4265

Biologics, unclassified, J3590

Biopsy
hard tissue, dental, D7285
soft tissue, dental, D7286

Biperiden lactate, J0190

Birth control pills, S4993

Birthing classes, S9436-S9439, S9442

Bite disposable jaw locks, E0700

Bitewing radiographs, D0270-D0277

Bitolterol mesylate, inhalation solution
concentrated, J7628
unit dose, J7629

Bivalirudin, J0583

Bleaching, dental
external, per arch, D9972
external, per tooth, D9973
internal, per tooth, D9974

Blenoxane, J9040

Bleomycin sulfate, J9040

Blood
Congo red, P2029
glucose monitor, A4258, E0607
with voice synthesizer, E2100

Blood — *continued*
glucose monitor — *continued*
with integrated lancing system, E2101
glucose test strips, A4253
leak detector, dialysis, E1560
leukocyte poor, P9016
mucoprotein, P2038
pressure equipment, A4660, A4663, A4670
pump, dialysis, E1620
strips, A4253
supply, P9010-P9022
testing supplies, A4770
transfusion, home, S9538
tubing, A4750, A4755
leukocytes reduced, P9051-P9056
CMV-negative, P9051, P9053, P9055

Bock, hand prosthesis, L6875, L6880

Bock Dynamic, foot prosthesis, L5972

Bock, Otto (*see* **Otto Bock**)

Body jacket
lumbar-sacral orthosis (spinal), L0500-L0565, L0600, L0610
scoliosis, L1300, L1310

Body sock, L0984

Body Wrap
foam positioners, E0191
therapeutic overlay, E0199

Bond or cement, ostomy, skin, A4364

Bone tissue excision, dental, D7471-D7490

Boot
pelvic, E0944
surgical, ambulatory, L3260
walking
non-pneumatic, L4386
pneumatic, L4360

Bortezomib, C9207, S0115

Boston type spinal orthosis, L1200

Botulinum toxin
type A, J0585
type B, J0587

Brachytherapy
prostate, G0261
radioelements, Q3001
source, C1716-C1720, C2616
yttrium-90, C2616

Brake attachment, wheeled walker, E0159

Breas PV10, E0601

Breast
exam (with pelvice exam), G0101
mammography, G0202-G0206
milk processing, T2101
prosthesis, L8000-L8035, L8600
adhesive skin support, A4280
skin support, S8433
pump, E0602-E0604
supplies, A4281-A4286

Breathing circuit, A4618

Brethine, J3105

Bricanyl subcutaneous, J3105

Bridge
recement, D6930
repair, by report, D6980

Brief, incontinence
adult, A4525-A4528
child, A4531-A4532
youth, A4534

Brompheniramine maleate, J0945

Broncho-Cath endobronchial tubes, with CPAP system, E0601

Bruxism appliance, D9940

Buck's, traction
  frame, E0870
  stand, E0880

Budesonide, J7626, J7633

Bulb for therapeutic light box, A4634

Bumetanide, S0171

Bupivicaine, S0020

Buprenorphine hydrochloride, J0592

Bupropion HCl, S0106

Burn garment, A6501, A6512

Bus, nonemergency, A0110

Busulfan, injection, C1178

Butorphanol tartrate, J0595

Butorphanolt tartrate nasal spray, S0012

Cabergoline, Q2001

Caffeine citrate, J0706

Calcijex, J0635

Calcimar, J0630

Calcitonin-salmon, J0630

Calcitriol, J0636

Calcium
  disodium edetate, J0600
  disodium versenate, J0600
  EDTA, J0600
  gluconate, J0610
  glycerophosphate and calcium lactate,
    J0620
  lactate and calcium glycerophosphate,
    J0620
  leucovorin, J0640

Calibrator solution, A4256

Calphosan, J0620

Camisole, post mastectomy, S8460

CAMP
  thoracolumbar support, L0300

Camping therapy, T2036-T2037

Camptosar, J9206

Canavan disease, genetic test, S3851

Cancer screening
  breast exam, G0101
  barium enema, G0122
  cervical exam, G0101
  colorectal, G0104-G0106, G0120-G0122
  prostate, G0102-G0103

Cane, E0100, E0105
  accessory, A4636, A4637
  Easy-Care quad, E0105
  quad canes, E0105
  Quadri-Poise, E0105
  wooden canes, E0100

Canister
  disposable, used with suction pump,
    A7000
  non-disposable, used with suction pump,
    A7001

Cannula
  fistula, set (for dialysis), A4730
  nasal, A4615
  tracheostomy, A4623

Canolith, repositioning, S9092

Capecitabine, oral, J8520, J8521

Carbocaine with Neo-Cobefrin, J0670

Carbon filter, A4680

Carboplatin, J9045

Cardia event, recorder implantable,
  E0616

Cardiokymography, Q0035

Cardiovascular services, M0300-M0301

**Cardioverter defibrillator pulse
  generator,** G0297
  dual chamber
    insertion, G0300
    repositioning, G0300
  single chamber
    insertion, G0298-G0299

Carelet safety lancet, A4258

Carex
  adjustable bath/shower stool, E0245
  aluminum crutches, E0114
  cane, E0100
  folding walker, E0135
  shower bench, E0245

Carmustine, J9050

Carnitor, J1955

Case presentation, dental, D9459

Case management, T1016-T1017
  per month, T2022

Casec, enteral nutrition, B4155

Cash, spinal orthosis, L0370

Caspofungin acetate, J0637

Cast
  dental diagnostic study models, D0470
  diagnostic, dental, D0470
  gauntlet, Q4013-Q4016
  hand restoration, L6900-L6915
  hip spica, Q4025-Q4028
  long arm, Q4005-Q4008
  materials, special, A4590
  padding, (not separately reimbursable
    from the casting procedure or
    casting supplies codes)
    Delta-Rol™ Cast Padding
    Sof-Rol™ Cast Padding
    Specialist™ 100 Cotton Cast Padding
    Specialist™ Cast Padding
  plaster, A4580, L2122
  post and core, dental, D2952
    each additional, D2953
  short arm, Q4009-Q4012
  shoulder, Q4003-Q4004
  supplies, A4580, A4590, Q4050
    Delta-Cast™ Elite™ Casting Material,
      A4590
    Delta-Lite™ Conformable Casting
      Tape, A4590
    Delta-Lite™ C-Splint™ Fibreglass
      Immobilizer, A4590
    Delta-Lite™ "S" Fibreglass Casting
      Tape, A4590
    Flashcast™ Elite™ Casting Material,
      A4590
    Orthoflex™ Elastic Plaster Bandages,
      A4580
    Orthoplast™ Splints (and Orthoplast™
      II Splints), A4590
    Specialist™ J-Splint™ Plaster Roll
      Immobilizer
    Specialist™ Plaster Bandages, A4580
    Specialist™ Plaster Roll Immobilizer,
      A4580
    Specialist™ Plaster Splints, A4580
  thermoplastic, L2106, L2126

Caster, wheelchair, E0997, E0998, K0099

Catheter, A4300-A4365
  anchoring device, A4333, A4334
    percutaneous, A5200
  cap, disposable (dialysis), A4860
  external collection device, A4326-A4330,
    A4348
  implantable access, A4301
  implantable intraspinal, E0785
  indwelling, A4338-A4346
  insertion tray, A4354
  intermittent, with insertion supplies,
    A4353
  irrigation supplies, A4319, A4355
  lubricant, A4332
  male, external, A4324, A4325

Catheter — *continued*
  oropharyngeal suction, A4628
  pleural, A7042
  trachea (suction), A4609-A4610, A4624

CBC, G0306-G0307

Cefadyl, J0710

Cefazolin sodium, J0690

Cefepime HCl, J0692

Cefizox, J0715

Cefotaxime sodium, J0698

Cefotetan disodium, S0074

Cefoxitin, J0694

Ceftazidime, J0713

Ceftizoxime soduim, J0715

Ceftriaxone sodium, J0696

Ceftoperazone, S0021

Cefuroxime sodium, J0697

Celestone phosphate, J0704

Cellular therapy, M0075

Cel-U-Jec, J0704

Cement, ostomy, A4364

Cenacort
  A-40, J3301
  Forte, J3302

Centrifuge, for dialysis, E1500

Cephalin floculation, blood, P2028

Cephalothin sodium, J1890

Cephapirin sodium, J0710

Ceredase, J0205

Cerezyme, J1785

Certified nurse assistant, S9122

Cerubidine, J9150

Cerumen removal, G0268

Cervical
  collar, L0120, L0130, L0140, L0150
  halo, L0810-L0830
  head harness/halter, E0942
  helmet, L0100, L0110
    Softop, leather protective, L0110
  orthosis, L0100-L0200
  traction equipment, not requiring frame,
    E0855

Cervical cap contraceptive, A4261

**Cervical-thoracic-lumbar-sacral orthosis
  (CTLSO)**, L0700, L0710, L1000

Chair
  adjustable, dialysis, E1570
  lift, E0627
  rollabout, E1031
  shower or bath, E0240
  sitz bath, E0160-E0162

Challenger manual wheelchair, K0009

Champion 1000 manual wheelchair,
  K0004

Champion 30000, manual wheelchair,
  K0005

Chealamide, J3520

Chelation therapy, M0300
  home infusion, administration, S9355

CheckMate Plus blood glucose monitor,
  E0607

Chemical endarterectomy, M0300

Chemistry and toxicology tests, P2028-
  P3001

Chemodenervation, vocal cord, S2341

Chemotherapy
  dental, D4381

Cophene-B, J0945

Coping, dental, D6975

Copying fee, medical records, S9981-S9982

Core buildup, dental, D2950, D6973

Corgonject-5, J0725

Corn, trim or remove, S0390

Corneal tissue processing, V2785

Coronary artery bypass surgery, direct
with coronary arterial grafts, only
single, S2205
two grafts, S2206
with coronary arterial and venous grafts
single, each, S2208
two arterial and single venous, S2209
with coronary venous grafts, only
single, S2207

Coronoidectomy, dental, D7991

Corset, spinal orthosis, L0970-L0976

Corticotropin, J0800

Cortrosyn, J0835

Corvert, J1742

Cosmegen, J9120

Cosyntropin, J0835

Cotranzine, J0780

Cough stimulation device, E0482

Counseling for control of dental disease, D1310, D1320

Cover, wound
alginate dressing, A6196-A6198
collagen dressing, A6020
foam dressing, A6209-A6214
hydrocolloid dressing, A6234-A6239
hydrogel dressing, A6242-A6248
specialty absorptive dressing, A6251-A6256

CPAP (continuous positive airway pressure) device, E0601
chin strap, A7036
face mask, A7030-A7031
filter, K0188-K0189
headgear, A7035
humidifier, K0268, E0561-E0562
nasal application accessories, A7032-A7034
oral interface, A7044
supplies, E0470-E0472, E0561-E0562
tubing, A7037

Cradle, bed, E0280

Crisis intervention, H2011, T2034

Criticare HN, enteral nutrition, B4153

Cromolyn sodium, inhalation solution, unit dose, J7631

Crown
composite resin, D2390
lengthening, D4249
recementation, D2920
repair, D2980

Crowns
as retainer for FPD, D6720-D6792
implant/abutment supported, D6058-D6067
implant/abutment supported retainer for FPD, D6720-D6792
individual restoration, D2710-D2799
prefabricated, D2930-D2933
provisional, D2799
temporary (fractured tooth), D2970

Crutch
substitute, E0118

Crutches, E0110-E0116
accessories, A4635-A4637, K0102
aluminum, E0114
articulating, spring assisted, E0117

Crutches — *continued*
forearm, E0111
Ortho-Ease, E0111
underarm, other than wood, pair, E0114
Quikfit Custom Pack, E0114
Red Dot, E0114
underarm, wood, single, E0113
Ready-for-use, E0113
wooden, E0112

Cryoprecipitate, each unit, P9012

Cryopreservation of cells, G0265

Cryosurgery
renal tumors, S2090-S2091

Crysticillin (300 A.S., 600 A.S.), J2510

CTLSO, L1000-L1120, L0700, L0710

Cuirass, E0457

Cultured analogous chondrocytes, S2113

Culture sensitivity study, P7001

Curasorb, alginate dressing, A6196-A6199

Curettage, apical, perpendicular, D3410-D3426

Cushion
decubitus care, E0190

Cushion, wheelchair, E0962-E0965, E0977
AK addition, L5648
BK addition, L5646
Geo-Matt, E0964
High Profile Therapeutic Dry Flotation, 4-inch, E0965
Low Profile Therapeutic Dry Flotation, 2-inch, E0963

Customized item (in addition to code for basic item), S1002

Custom Masterhinge™ Hip Hinge 3, L2999

Cyanocobalamin cobalt, C1079, Q3012

Cycler
disposable set, A4671

Cycler dialysis machine, E1594

Cyclophosphamide, J9070-J9092
lyophilized, J9093-J9097
oral, J8530

Cyclosporine, J7502, J7515, J7516

Cylinder tank carrier, K0104

Cystourethroscopy
for ute…eral calculi, S2070

Cytarabine, J9110

Cytarabine liposome, J9098

Cytarabine 100, J9100

CytoGam, J0850

Cytologic
sample collection, dental, D7287
smears, dental, D0480

Cytomegalovirus immune globulin (human), J0850

Cytopathology, screening, G0123, G0124, G0141, G0143-G0148

Cytosar-U, J9100

Cytovene, J1570

Cytoxan, J8530, J9070-J9097

Darbepoetin alpha
ESRD, Q4054
non-ESRD, Q0137

Dacarbazine, J9130, J9140

Daclizumab, J7513

Dactinomycin, J9120

Dalalone, J1100

Dalfopristin, J2270

Dalteparin sodium, J1645

Darbepoetin alpha, J0880
ESRD Q4054
non-ESRD Q0137

Daunorubicin citrate, J9151
HCl, J9150

DaunoXome, J9151

Day Treads slippers, E0690

DDAVP, J2597

Debridement
endodontic, D3221
periodontal, D4355

Decadron, J1100

Decadron-LA, J1094

Decadron Phosphate, J1100

Deca-Durabolin, J2320-J2322

Decaject, J1100

Decaject-LA, J1094

Decolone
-50, J2320
-100, J2321

De-Comberol, J1060

Decompression, vertebral axial, S9090

Decubitus care equipment, E0180-E0199
cushion or pillow, E0190
mattress
AquaPedic Sectional Gel Flotation, E0196
Iris Pressure Reduction/Relief, dry, E0184
PressureGuard II, air, E0186
TenderFlo II, E0187
TenderGel II, E0196
pressure pads, overlays, E0197-E0199
Body Wrap, E0199
Geo-Matt, E0199
Iris, E0199
PressureKair, E0197
Richfoam Convoluted and Flat, E0199
pressure pads, with pumps, E0180, E0181
Bio Flote, E0181
KoalaKair, E0181
protectors
Heel or elbow, E0191
Body Wrap Foam Positioners, E0191
Pre-Vent, E0191
pump, E0182
Bio Flote, E0182
Pillo, E0182
TenderCloud, E0182
wheelchair cushion, E0964
Geo-Matt, E0964
High Profile Therapeutic Dry Flotation, 4-inch, E0965
Low Profile Therapeutic Dry Flotation, 2-inch, E0963

Deferoxamine mesylate, J0895

Dehist, J0945

Dehydroergotamine mesylate, J1110

Deionizer, water purification system, E1615

Deladumone (OB), J0900

Delatest, J3120

Delatestadiol, J0900

Delatestryl, J3120, J3130

Delestrogen, J0970

Delivery/set-up/dispensing, A9901

Delta-Cortef, J7510

Index

Foot   INDEX   Hallux prosthetic implant

Foot, soles
 Masterfoot™ Walking Cast Sole, L3649
 Solo™ Cast Sole, L3540

Footdrop splint, L4398

Footplate, E0175, E0970

Footwear, orthopedic, L3201-L3265

Forearm crutches, E0110, E0111

Fortaz, J0713

Fortex, alginate dressing, A6196-A6199

Foscarnet sodium, J1455

Foscavir, J1455

Fosphenytoin, Q2009

Fosphenytoin sodium, S0078

Foster care, H0041-H0042

Four Poster, fracture frame, E0946

Four-pronged finger splint, A4570

Fracture
 bedpan, E0276
 frame, E0920, E0930, E0946-E0948
 orthosis, L2108-L2136, L2102-L2136,
  L3980-L3986
 orthotic additions, L3995
 Specialist™ Pre-Formed Humeral
  Fracture Brace, L3980

Fractures, dental, treatment
 alveolus, D7670, D7770
 malar/zygomatic arch
  incision, D7650-D7660
  surgical incision, D7750-D7760
 mandible
  compound closed reduction, D7740
  compound open reduction, D7730
  simple closed reduction, D7640
  simple open reduction, D7630
 maxilla
  compound closed reduction, D7720
  compound open reduction, D7710
  simple closed reduction, D7620
  simple open reduction, D7610

Fragmin, J1645

Frame
 meaning spectacles, V2020, V2025
  sales tax, S9999
 safety, for hospital bed, E0316

FreAmine HBC, parenteral nutrition,
 B5100

Frejka, hip orthosis, L1600
 replacement cover, L1610

Frenectomy/frenotomy (frenulectomy),
 D7960

FUDR, J9200

Fulvestrant, C9120, J9395

Fungizone, J0285

Furomide MD, J1940

Furosemide, J1940

Gadolinium, A4647

Gallium Ga 67, Q3002

Gamastan, J1460

Gamma globulin, J1460

Gamulin RH, J2790

Ganciclovir
 implant, J7310
 sodium, J1570

Ganirelix acetate, S0132

Garamycin, J1580

Gas system
 compressed, E0424, E0425
 gaseous, E0430, E0431, E0441, E0443
 liquid, E0434-E0440, E0442, E0444

Gastric bypass, S2085

**Gastric electrical stimulation device,
 implantation**, S2213

Gastric suction pump, E2000

Gastrostomy/jejunostomy tubing, B4086

Gastrostomy tube, B4086

Gatifloxacin, J1590

Gaucher disease, genetic test, S3848

Gauzem A6216-A6230, A6266
 impregnated, A6222-A6230, A6266
 nonimpregnated, A6216, A6221, A6402
 pads, A6216-A6230, A6402-A6404
  Johnson & Johnson, A6402
  Kendall, A6402
  Moore, A6402

Gel
 conductive, A4558
 pressure pad, E0178, E0185, E0196
 sheet, dermal or epidermal, A6025

Gemcitabine HCl, J9201

Gemtuzumab ozogamicin, J9300

GemZar, J9201

Genetic testing, S3818-S3853

Genmould™ Creamy Plaster, A4580

Gentamicin (sulfate), J1580

Gentran, J7100, J7110

Geo-Matt
 therapeutic overlay, E0199
 wheelchair cushion, E0964

Geronimo PR, power wheelchair, K0011

Gerval Protein, enteral nutrition, B4155

Gestational home visit
 for diabetes, S9214
 for hypertension, S9211
 for preeclampsia, S9213

GIFT, S4013

Gingiva, pericoronal, removal, D7971

Gingivectomy/gingivoplasty, D4210-
 D4211

Glass ionomer (resin restoration), D2330-
 D2394

Glasses
 air conduction, V5070
 binaural, V5120-V5150
 bone conduction, V5080
 frames, V2020, V2025
 hearing aid, V5150, V5190, V5230
 lens, V2100-V2499, V2610, V2718,
  V2730, V2755, V2770, V2780

Glatiramer acetate, J1595

Glaucoma screening, G0117-G0118

Global fee, urgent care center, S9083

Gloves
 dialysis, A4927
 non-sterile, A4927
 sterile, A4930

Glucagon HCl, J1610

Glucometer
 II blood glucose meter, E0607
 II blood glucose test strips, box of 50,
  A4253
 3 blood glucose meter, E0607
 3 blood glucose test strips, box of 50,
  A4253

Glucose
 monitor device, continuous, noninvasive,
  S1030-S1031
 test strips, A4253, A4772

Glukor, J0725

Gluteal pad, L2650

Glycopyrrolate, inhalation solution
 concentrated, J7642
 unit dose, J7643

Gold
 foil dental, D2310-D2430
 sodium thiomalate, J1600

**Gold Probe Single-Use Electrohemostasis
 catheter**, C2600

**Goldthwaite apron-front, sacroiliac
 orthosis**, L0620

Gomco
 aspirators, E0600

Gonadorelin HCl, J1620

Gonic, J0725

Goserelin acetate implant (*see also*
 Implant), J9202

Grab bar, trapeze, E0910, E0940

Grade-aid, wheelchair, E0974

Gradient pressure aids, S8421-S8429

Graft, dental
 bone replacement, D4263-D4264
 maxillofacial soft/hard tissue, D7955
 ridge augmentation, D7950
 soft tissue, D4270-D4273

Granisetron HCl, J1626, Q0166, S0091

Gravity traction device, E0941

Gravlee jet washer, A4470

Greissing, foot prosthesis, L5978

Guided tissue regeneration, dental,
 D4266-D4267

**Guilford multiple-post collar, cervical
 orthosis**, L0190

**Gynecare VERSAPOINT Resectoscopic
 System Bipolar Electrode**, C1329

Gynogen, J1380, J1390
 L.A. (10, 20, 40), J0970, J1380, J1390

H-Tron Plus insulin pump, E0784

H. Weniger finger orthosis
 cock-up splint, L3914
 combination Oppenheimer
  with
   knuckle bender no. 13, L3950
   reverse knuckle no. 13B, L3952
 composite elastic no. 10, L3946
 dorsal wrist no. 8, L3938
  with outrigger attachment no. 8A,
   L3940
 finger extension, with clock spring no. 5,
  L3928
 finger extension, with wrist support no.
  5A, L3930
 finger knuckle bender no. 11, L3948
 knuckle bender splint type no. 2, L3918
 knuckle bender, two segment no. 2B,
  L3922
 knuckle bender with outrigger no. 2,
  L3920
 Oppenheimer, L3924
 Palmer no. 7, L3936
 reverse knuckle bender no. 9, L3942
  with outrigger no. 9A, L3944
 safety pin, modified no. 6A, L3934
 safety pin, spring wire no. 6, L3932
 spreading hand no. 14, L3954
 Thomas suspension no. 4, L3926

Haberman feeder, S8265

Habilitation, T2012-T2021

Hair analysis (excluding arsenic), P2031

Haldol, J1630
 decanoate (-50, -100), J1631

Hallus-valgus dynamic splint, L3100

Hallux prosthetic implant, L8642

Haloperidol, J1630
  decanoate, J1631

Halo procedures, L0810-L0860

Halter, cervical head, E0942

Hand restoration, L6900-L6915
  partial prosthesis, L6000-L6020
  orthosis (WHFO), E1805, E1825, L3800-
    L3805, L3900-L3954
  rims, wheelchair, E0967

Handgrip (cane, crutch, walker), A4636

Harness, E0942, E0944, E0945

Harvest
  bone marrow, G0267
  multivisceral organs, cadaver donor,
    S2055
  peripheral stem cell, G0267, S2150

Harvey arm abduction orthosis, L3960

Headgear (for CPAP device), K0185

Health club membership, S9970

Hearing devices, L8614, V5008-V5299
  accessories/supplies, V5267
  analog, V5242-V5251
  battery, V5266
  digital, V5250-V5261
  dispensing fee, V5241
  ear mold/insert, V5264-V5265
  ear impression, V5275
  NOS, V5728

Heat
  application, E0200-E0239
  lamp, E0200, E0205
  pad, E0210, E0215, E0217, E0218,
    E0238, E0249
  units, E0239
    Hydroacollator, mobile, E0239
    Thermalator T-12-M, E0239

Heater (nebulizer), E1372

Heating pad, Dunlap, E0210
  for peritoneal dialysis, E0210

Heel
  elevator, air, E0370
  loop/holder, E0951
  pad, L3480, L3485
  protector, E0191
  shoe, L3430-L3485
  stabilizer, L3170

Helicopter, ambulance (*see also*
  Ambulance), A0431

Helmet
  cervical, L0100, L0110
  with face guard, E0701

Hematopoietic hormone administration,
  S9537

Hemalet lancet device, A4258

Hemin, Q2011

Hemi-wheelchair, E1083-E1086

Hemipelvectomy prosthesis, L5280

Hemisection, dental, D3920

Hemodialysis
  acetate concentrate, A4708
  acid solution, A4709
  bicarbonate concentrate, A4706-A4707
  drain bag/bottle, A4911
  machine, E1590
  mask, surgical, A4928
  protamine sulfate, A4802
  surgical mask, A4928
  tourniquet, A4929

Hemodialyzer, portable, E1635

Hemofil M, J7190

Hemophilia clotting factor, J7190-J7198

Hemophilia clotting factor, NOC, J7199

Hemostats, for dialysis, E1637

Hemostix, A4773

Heparin
  infusion pump (for dialysis), E1520
  lock flush, J1642
  sodium, J1644

HepatAmine, parenteral nutrition, B5100

Hepatic-aid, enteral nutrition, B4154

Hepatitis B immune globulin, C9105

Hep-Lock (U/P), J1642

Herceptin, J9355

Hexadrol phosphate, J1100

Hexalite, A4590

Hexior power wheelchair, K0014

**High Frequency chest wall oscillation
equipment**, A7025-A7026, E0483

**High Profile therapeutic dry flotation
cushion**, E0965

High risk area requiring escort, S9381

Hip
  Custom Masterhinge™ Hip Hinge 3,
    L2999
  disarticulation prosthesis, L5250, L5270
  Masterhinge™ Hip Hinge 3, L2999
  orthosis (HO), L1600-L1686

Hip-knee-ankle-foot orthosis (HKAFO),
  L2040-L2090

Histaject, J0945

Histerone (-50, -100), J3140

Histrelin acetate, Q2020

HIV-1 antibody testing, S3645

HKAFO, L2040-L2090

HN2, J9230

Holder
  heel, E0951
  toe, E0952

Hole cutter tool, A4421

Hollister
  belt adapter, A4421
  closed pouch, A5051, A5052
  colostomy/ileostomy kit, A5061
  drainable pouches, A5061
    with flange, A5063
  medical adhesive, A4364
  pediatric ostomy belt, A4367
  remover, adhesive, A4455
  stoma cap, A5055
  skin barrier, A4362, A5122
  skin cleanser, A4335
  skin conditioning creme, A4335
  skin gel protective dressing wipes, A5119
  stoma cap, A5055
  two-piece pediatric ostomy system,
    A5054, A5063, A5073
  urostomy pouch, A5071, A5072

Home health
  aide, S9122, T1030-T1031
    home health setting, G0156
  care
    certified nurse assistant, S9122,
      T1021
    home health aide, S9122, T1021
    nursing care, S9122-S9124, T1030-
      T1031
    re-certification, G0179-G0180
  gestational
    assessment, T1028
    delivery suppies, S8415
    diabetes, S9214
    hypertension, S9211
    pre-eclampsia, S9213
    preterm labor, S9208-S9209
  hydration therapy, S9373-S9379
  infusion therapy, S9325-S9379, S9494-
    S9497, S9537-S9810
  nursing services, S9212-S9213
  postpartum hypertension, S9212

Home health — continued
  services of
    clinical social worker, G0155
    occupational therapist, G0152
    physical therapist, G0151
    skilled nurse, G0154
    speech/language pathologist, G0153
  transfusion, blood products, S9538

Home uterine monitor, S9001

Hosmer
  baby mitt, L6870
  child hand, mechanical, L6872
  forearm lift, assist unit only, L6635
  gloves, above hands, L6890, L6895
  hand prosthesis, L6868
  hip orthotic joint, post-op, L1685
  hook
    with
      neoprene fingers, #8X, L6740
      neoprene fingers, #88X, L6745
      plastisol, #10P, L6750
    #5, L6705
    #5X, L6710
    #5XA, L6715
    child, L6755, L6765
    small adult, L6770
    stainless steel #8, L6735
      with neopren, L6780
    work, #3, L6700
      for use with tools, #7, L6725
      with lock, #6, L6720
      with wider opening, L6730
  passive hand, L6868
  soft, passive hand, L6865

Hospice
  care, S9126, T2041-T2046
  referral visit, S0255

Hospital call, dental, D9420

Hot water bottle, E0220

H-Tron insulin pump, E0784

Houdini security suit, E0700

House call, dental, D9410

Housing, supported, H0043-H0044

Hoyer patient lifts, E0621, E0625, E0630

Hudson
  adult multi-vent "venturi" style mask,
    A4620
  nasal cannula, A4615
  oxygen supply tubing, A4616
  UC-BL type shoe insert, L3000

Humalog, J1815, J1817, S5550

Human insulin, J1815, J1817

**Human serum albumin with
octafluoropropane**, C9202

Humidifier, E0550-E0560, S8182-S8183
  water chamber, A7046

Humulin insulin, J1815, J1817

Hyaluronidase, J3470

Hyate, J7191

Hybolin
  decanoate, J2321

Hycamtin, J9350

Hydralazine HCl, J0360

Hydrate, J1240

Hydration therapy, S9373-S9379

Hydraulic patient lift, E0630

Hydrochlorides of opium alkaloids,
  J2480

Hydrocollator, E0225, E0239

Hydrocolloid dressing, A6234-A6241

Hydrocortisone
  acetate, J1700
  sodium phosphate, J1710
  sodium succinate, J1720

Hydrocortone
acetate, J1700
phosphate, J1710

Hydrogel dressing, A6242-A6248

Hydromorphone, J1170, S0092

Hydroxyurea, S0176

Hydroxyzine HCl, J3410
pamoate, Q0177-Q0178

Hylan G-F 20, J7320

Hyoscyamine sulfate, J1980

Hyperbaric oxygen chamber, topical, A4575

Hyperstat IV, J1730

Hypertonic saline solution, J7130

Hypo-Let lancet device, A4258

Hypothermia
intragastric, M0100

HypRho-D, J2790

Hyrexin-50, J1200

Hyzine-50, J3410

Ibutilide fumarate, J1742

Ice cap or collar, E0230

Idamycin, J9211

Idarubicin HCl, J9211

Ifex, J9208

Ifosfamide, J9208

IL-2, J9015

Iletin insulin, J1815, J1817, S5552

Ilfeld, hip orthosis, L1650

Images, oral/facial, D0350

Imaging coil, MRI, C1770

Imatinib, S0088

Imiglucerase, J1785

Imitrex, J3030

Immune globulin IV, J1562, J1563, J1564

Immunosuppressive drug, not otherwise classified, J7599

Impacted tooth, removal, D7220-D7241

Implant
access system, A4301
aqueous shunt, L8612
auditory device
brainstem, S2235
middle ear, S2230
breast, L8600
cochlear, L8614, L8619
collagen, urinary tract, L8603
condrocytes in knee, S2113
contraceptive, A4260
dental
chin, D7995
endodontic, D3460
endosteal/endosseous, D6010, D6020
eposteal/subperiosteal, D6040
facial, D7995
maintenance, D6080
other implant service, D6052-6079
supported prosthetics, D6053-D6079
removal, D6100
repair, D6090, D6095
transosteal/tenosseous, D6050
ganciclovir, J7310
gastric electrical stimulation device, S2213
gastric stimulation, S2213
goserelin acetate, J9202
hallux, L8642
infusion pump, E0782, E0783
injectable bulking agent, urinary tract, L8606

Implant — *continued*
joint, L8630, L8641, L8658
lacrimal duct, A4262, A4263
levonorgestral, A4260
maintenance procedures, D6080, D6100
maxillofacial, D5913-D5937
medication pellet(s), subcutaneous, S2190
metacarpophalangeal joint, L8630
metatarsal joint, L8641
neurostimulator, pulse generator or receiver, E0755, E0756
Norplant, A4260
not otherwise specified, L8699
ocular, L8610
ossicular, L8613
osteogenesis stimulator, E0749
percutaneous access system, A4301
removal, dental, D6100
repair, dental, D6090
vascular access portal, A4300
vascular graft, L8670
Yttrium-90, S2095
Zoladex, J9202

Implantation/reimplantation, tooth, D7270
intentional reimplantation, D3470

Impregnated gauze dressing, A6222-A6230

Imuran, J7500, J7501

Inapsine, J1790

Incontinence
appliances and supplies, A4310, A4521-A4538, A5051-A5093, A5102-A5114, A5119-A5200
brief
adult, A4525-4528
child, A4531-A4532
youth, A4534
diaper
adult, A4521-A4524
child, A4529-A4530
service, A4538
youth, A4533
treatment system, E0740
under pad, A4537
underwear, A4536

Inderal, J1800

Indium/111
capromab pendetide, A9507
ibritumomab tiuxetan, A9522
oxyquinoline, C1091
pentetate disodium, C1092
satumomab pendetide, A4642

Indwelling catheter insertion, G0002

Infant safety, CPR, training, S9447

Infed, J1750

Infergen, J9212

Infliximab injection, J1745

Infusion, G0258
pump
ambulatory, with administrative equipment, E0781
epoprostenol, K0455
heparin, dialysis, E1520
implantable, E0782, E0783
implantable, refill kit, A4220
insulin, E0784
mechanical, reusable, E0779, E0780
supplies, A4221, A4222, A4230-A4232
Versa-Pole IV, E0776
therapy, home, S9347, S9497-S9504

Inhalation solution (*see also* drug name), J7608-J7799

Injectable bulking agent, urinary tract, L8606

Injection (*see also* **drug name**), J0120-J7506
busulfan, C1178

Injection — *continued*
contrast material, during MRI, A4643
dental service, D9610, D9630
metatarsal neuroma, S2135
procedure
sacroiliac joint, G0254-G0260
supplies for self-administered, A4211

Inlay, dental
fixed partial denture retainers
metallic, D6545-D6615
porcelain/ceramic, D6548-D6609
metallic, D2510-D2530
porcelain/ceramic, D2610-2630
recement inlay, D2910
intentional replantation, D3470, D7270
resin-based composite, D2650-D2652

Innovar, J1810

Insert
convex, for ostomy, A5093
diabetic, for shoe, A5502-A5511

Insertion
tray, A4310-A4316

Insulin, J1815, J1817
delivery device other than pump, S5565-S5571
home infusion administration, S9353
intermediate acting, S5552
long acting, S5553
NPH, S5552, J1815
rapid onset, S5550-S5551

Insulin pump, external, E0784

Intal, J7631

Interdigital neuritis injection, S2135

Intergrilin injection, J1327

Interferon
Alfa, J9212-J9215
Alfacon-1, J9212
Beta-1a, J1825, Q3025-Q3026
Beta-1b, J1830
Gamma, J9216
home injection, S9559

Intermittent
peritoneal dialysis system, E1592
positive pressure breathing (IPPB) machine, E0500

Interphalangeal joint, prosthetic implant, L8658

Interscapular thoracic prosthesis
endoskeletal, L6570
upper limb, L6350-L6370

Intrafallopian transfer
complete cycle, gamete, S4013
complete cycle, zygote, S4014
donor egg cycle, S4023
incomplete cycle, S4017

Intraocular lenses, V2630-V2632, Q1001-Q1005
new technology
category 1, Q1001
category 2, Q1002
category 3, Q1003
category 4, Q1004
category 5, Q1005

Intraoral radiographs, D0210-D0240

Intrauterine device
copper contraceptive, J7300
other, S4989
Progestacert, S4989

Intravaginal culture, S4036

Intravenous sedation/analgesia, dental
first 30 minutes, D9241
each additional 15 minutes, D9242

Intron A, J9214

Iodine I-123, A9516

Iodine I-131
　albumin, A9524
　iobenguane sulfate, A9508, C1045
　sodium iodide, A9517, A9603

Iodine swabs/wipes, A4247

IPD
　supply kit, A4905
　system, E1592

IPPB machine, E0500

Ipratropium bromide
　0.2%, J7645
　inhalation solution, unit dose, J7644

Irinotecan, J9206

Iris Preventix pressure relief/reduction mattress, E0184

Iris therapeutic overlays, E0199

IRM ankle-foot orthosis, L1950

Irodex, J1750

Iron
　dextran, J1750
　sucrose, J1756

Irrigation
　solution, A4319

Irrigation/evacuation system, bowel
　control unit, E0350
　disposable supplies for, E0352

Irrigation supplies, A4320, A4322, A4323, A4355, A4397-A4400
　Solution, A4319
　Surfit
　　irrigation sleeve, A4397
　　night drainage container set, A5102
　Visi-flow irrigator, A4398, A4399

Isocaine HCl, J0670

Isocal, enteral nutrition, B4150
　HCN, B4152

Isoetharine
　inhalation solution
　　concentrated, J7648
　　unit dose, J7649

Isolates, B4150, B4152

Isoproterenol HCl, inhalation solution
　concentrated, J7658
　unit dose, J7659

Isotein, enteral nutrition, B4153

Isuprel, J7658-J7659

Itraconazole, J1835

IUD, J7300

IV pole, E0776, K0105

J-cell battery, replacement for blood glucose monitor, A4254

Jace tribrace, L1832

Jacket
　body (LSO) (spinal), L0500-L0565
　scoliosis, L1300, L1310

Jenamicin, J1580

Johnson's orthopedic wrist hand cock-up splint, L3914

Johnson's thumb immobilizer, L3800

Joint reconstruction, dental, D7838

Kabikinase, J2995

Kaleinate, J0610

Kaltostat, alginate dressing, A6196-A6199

Kanamycin sulfate, J1840, J1850

Kantrex, J1840, J1850

Kartop Patient Lift, toilet or bathroom (*see also* **Lift**), E0625

Keflin, J1890

Kefurox, J0697

Kefzol, J0690

Kenaject -40, J3301

Kenalog (-10,-40), J3301

Keratectomy photorefractive, S0810

Keratoprosthesis, C1818

Kestrone-5, J1435

Keto-Diastix, box of 100 glucose/ketone urine test strips, A4250

Ketorolac thomethamine, J1885

Key-Pred
　-25,-50, J2650

K-Flex, J2360

Kidney
　ESRD supply, A4656-A4927
　system, E1510
　wearable artificial, E1632

Kingsley gloves, above hands, L6890

Kits
　enteral feeding supply (syringe) (pump) (gravity), B4034-B4036
　fistula cannulation (set), A4730
　parenteral nutrition, B4220-B4224
　surgical dressing (tray), A4550
　tracheostomy, A4625

Klebcil, J1840, J1850

Knee
　Adjustabrace™ 3, L2999
　disarticulation, prosthesis, L5150-L5160
　immobilizer, L1830
　joint, miniature, L5826
　Knee-O-Prene™ Hinged Knee Sleeve, L1810
　Knee-O-Prene™ Hinged Wraparound Knee Support, L1810
　orthosis (KO), E1810, L1800-L1885
　locks, L2405-L2425
　Masterbrace™ 3, L2999
　Masterhinge Adjustabrace™ 3, L2999
　Performance Wrap™ (KO), L1825

Knee-ankle-foot orthosis (KAFO), L2000-L2039, L2122-L2136

Knee-O-Prene™ Hinged Knee Sleeve, L1810

Knee-O-Prene™ Hinged Wraparound Knee Support, L1810

Knight apron-front, spinal orthosis, L0520

KnitRite
　prosthetic
　　sheath, L8400-L8415
　　sock, L8420-L8435
　　stump sock, L8470-L8485

KoalaKair mattress overlay, with pump, E0180

Kodel clavicle splint, L3660

Kogenate, J7192

Konakion, J3430

Konyne-HT, J7194

K-Y Lubricating Jelly, A4402, A4332

Kyphoplasty, S2362-S2362

Kyphosis pad, L1020, L1025

Kytril, J1626

Labor care (not resulting in delivery), S4005

Laboratory tests
　chemistry, P2028-P2038

Laboratory tests — *continued*
　microbiology, P7001
　miscellaneous, P9010-P9615, Q0111-Q0115
　toxicology, P3000-P3001, Q0091

Lacrimal duct implant
　permanent, A4263
　temporary, A4262

Lactated Ringer's infusion, J7120

LAE 20, J0970, J1380, J1390

Laetrile, J3570

Lancet, A4258, A4259

Lanoxin, J1160

Laparoscopy
　bariatric surgery, S2085

Laronidase, C9209

Laryngectomy
　tube, A7520-A7522

Larynx, artificial, L8500

Laser
　application, S8948
　assisted uvulopalatoplasty (LAUP) S2080
　in situ keratomileusis, S0800
　myringotomy, S2225

Laser skin piercing device, for blood collection, E0620
　replacement lens, A4257

Lasix, J1940

LAUP, S2080

Lead, environmental, home evaluation, T1029

Lederle, J8610

LeFort
　I osteotomy, D7946-D7947
　II osteotomy, D7948-D7949
　III osteotomy, D7948-D7949

Leg
　bag, A4358, A5112
　extensions for walker, E0158
　Nextep™ Contour™ Lower Leg Walker, L2999
　Nextep™ Low Silhouette™ Lower Leg Walkers, L2999
　rest, elevating, K0195
　rest, wheelchair, E0990
　strap, A5113, A5114, K0038, K0039

Legg Perthes orthosis, L1700-L1755

Lens
　aniseikonic, V2118, V2318
　contact, V2500-V2599
　eye, S0504-S0508, S0580-S0590, V2100-V2615, V2700-V2799
　intraocular, V2630-V2632
　low vision, V2600-V2615
　mirror coating, V2761
　occupational multifoca, V2786
　polarization, V2762
　polycarbonate, V2784
　progressive, V2781
　skin piercing device, replacement, A4257
　tint, V2744
　　addition, V2745

Lente insulin, J1815, S5552

Lenticular lens
　bifocal, V2221
　single vision, V2121
　trifocal, V2321

Lepirudin, Q2021

Lerman Minerva spinal orthosis, L0174

Lesions, surgical excision, dental, D7410-D7465

Leucovorin calcium, J0640

Leukocyte
　poor blood, each unit, P9016

Leuprolide acetate, J9217, J9218, J1950

Leuprolide acetate implant, J9219

Leustatin, J9065

Levamisole HCl, S0177

Levaquin I.U., J1956

Levine, stomach tube, B4086

Levocarnitine, J1955

Levo-Dromoran, J1960

Levofloxacin, J1956

Levonorgestrel, contraceptive implants and supplies, A4260, J7302

Levorphanol tartrate, J1960

Librium, J1990

Lidocaine HCl for intravenous infusion, J2001

Lifescan lancets, box of 100, A4259

Lifestand manual wheelchair, K0009

Lifestyle modification program, coronary heart disease, S0340-S0342

Lift
combination, E0637
patient, and seat, E0621-E0635
  Hoyer
    Home Care, E0621
    Partner All-Purpose, hydraulic, E0630
    Partner Power Multifunction, E0625
shoe, L3300-L3334
standing frame system, E0638

Lift-Aid patient lifts, E0621

Light box, E0203

Lincocin, J2010

Lincomycin HCl, J2010

Lioresal, J0475, C9009

Liquaemin sodium, J1644

Lispro insulin, S5551

Lithium battery for blood glucose monitor, A4254

Lithrotripsy, gallstones, S9034

Little Ones
drainable pouch, A5063
mini-pouch, A5054
one-piece custom drainable pouch, A5061
one-piece custom urostomy pouch, A5071
pediatric belt, A4367
pediatric urine collector, A4335
urostomy pouch, transparent, A5073

Lively, knee-ankle-foot orthosis, L2038

LMD, 10%, J7100

Lobectomy, lung, donor, S2061

Localized osteitis, dry socket, D9110, D9930

Lodging
recipient, escort nonemergency transport, A0180, A0200
transplant-related, S9975

Lomustine, S0178

Lonalac powder, enteral nutrition, B4150

Lorazepam, J2060

Lovenox, J1650

Low Profile therapeutic dry flotation cushion, E0964

Lower limb, prosthesis, addition, L5968

LPN services, T1003

LSO, L0500-L0565

Lubricant, A4332, A4402

Lufyllin, J1180

Lumbar
criss-cross (LSO), L0500
EZ Fit LSO, L0500
flexion, L0540
pad, L1030, L1040
-sacral orthosis (LSO), L0500-L0565

Luminal sodium, J2560

Lung volume reduction surgery services, G0302-G0305

Lunelle, J1056

Lupron, J9218
depot, J1950

LVRS services, G0302-G0305

Lymphedema therapy, S8950

Lymphocyte immune globulin, J7504, J7511

Macausland apron-front, spinal orthosis, L0530

Madamist II medication compressor/nebulizer, E0570

Magnacal, enteral nutrition, B4152

Magnesium sulphate, J3475

Magnetic
resonance angiography, C8901-C8914, C8918-C8920
resonance imaging, low field, S8042
source imaging, S8035

Maintenance contract, ESRD, A4890

Malar bone, fracture repair, D7650, D7750, D7760

Malibu cervical turtleneck safety collar, L0150

Malocclusion correction, D8000-D8999

Mammogram
computer analysis, S8075

Mammography, G0202-G0206

Management
disease, S0317

Mandible, fracture, D7630-D7640, D7730-D7740

Mannitol, J2150

Mapping, topographic brain, S8040

Marmine, J1240

Maryland bridge (resin-bonded fixed prosthesis)
pontic, D6210-D6252
retainer/abutment, D6545

Mask
oxygen, A4620
surgical, for dialysis, A4928

Mastectomy
bra, L8002
camisole, S8460
form, L8020
prosthesis, L8000-L8039, L8600
sleeve, L8010

Masterbrace™ 3, L2999

Masterfoot™ Walking Cast Sole, L3649

Masterhinge Adjustabrace™ 3, L2999

Masterhinge™ Elbow Brace 3, L3999

Masterhinge™ Hip Hinge 3, L2999

Masterhinge™ Shoulder Brace 3, L3999

Mattress
air pressure, E0176, E0186, E0197
alternating pressure, E0277
  pad, Bio Flote, E0181
  pad, KoalaKair, E0181

Mattress — *continued*
AquaPedic Sectional, E0196
decubitus care, E0196
dry pressure, E0184
flotation, E0184
gel pressure, E0196
hospital bed, E0271, E0272
  non-powered, pressure reducing, E0373
Iris Preventix pressure relief/reduction, E0184
Overlay, E0371-E0372
TenderFlor II, E0187
TenderGel II, E0196
water pressure, E0177, E0187, E0198
  powered, pressure reducing, E0277

Maxilla, fracture, D7610-D7620, D7710-D7720

Maxillofacial dental procedures, D5911-D5999

MCP, multi-axial rotation unit, L5986

MCT Oil, enteral nutrition, B4155

Meals, adults in treatment, T1010

Mechlorethamine HCl, J9230

Medical and surgical supplies, A4206-A6404

Medical conference, S0220-S0221

Medical food, S9435

Medical records copying fee, S9981-S9982

Medi-Jector injection device, A4210

MediSense 2 Pen blood glucose monitor, E0607

Medralone
40, J1030
80, J1040

Medrol, J7509

Medroxyprogesterone acetate, J1055
with estradiol cypionate, J1056

Mefoxin, J0694

Megestrol acetate, S0179

Melphalan HCl, J9245
oral, J8600

Menotropins, S0122

Mental health
assessment, H0031
hospitalization, H0035
peer services, H0038
self-help, H0038
service plan, H0032
services, NOS, H0046
supportive treatment, H0026-H0037

Mepergan (injection), J2180

Meperidine, J2175
and promethazine, J2180

Mepivacaine HCl, J0670

Mercaptopurine, S0108

Meritene, enteral nutrition, B4150
powder, B4150

Meropenem, J2185

Mesna, J9209

Mesnex, J9209

Metabolically active tissue, Q0184

Metabolism error, food supplement, S9434

Metacarpophalangeal joint prosthesis, L8630

Metaproterenol
inhalation solution
  concentrated, J7668
  unit dose, J7669

Metaraminol bitartrate, J0380

Metatarsal joint, prosthetic implant, L8641

Metatarsal neuroma injection, S2135

Meter, bath conductivity, dialysis, E1550

Methadone HCl, J1230

Methergine, J2210

Methocarbamol, J2800

Methotrexate, oral, J8610
  sodium, J9250, J9260

Methyldopate HCl, J0210

Methylergonovine maleate, J2210

Methylprednisolone
  acetate, J1020-J1040
  oral, J7509
  sodium succinate, J2920, J2930

Metoclopramide HCl, J2765

Metronidazole, S0030

Meunster Suspension, socket prosthesis, L6110

Miacalcin, J0630

Microabrasion, enamel, D9970

Microbiology test, P7001

Midazolam HCl, J2250

Micro-Fine
  disposable insulin syringes, up to 1cc, per syringe, A4206
  lancets, box of 100, A4259

Microcapillary tube, A4651
  sealant, A4652

Microlipids, enteral nutrition, B4155

Microspirometer, S8190

Mileage, ambulance, A0380, A0390

Milk, breast
  processing, T2101

Milrinone lactate, J2260

Milwaukee spinal orthosis, L1000

Minerva, spinal orthosis, L0700, L0710

Mini-bus, nonemergency transportation, A0120

Minimed
  3 cc syringe, A4232
  506 insulin pump, E0784
  insulin infusion set with bent needle wings, each, A4231
  Sof-Set 24" insulin infusion set, each, A4230

Minoxidil, S0139

Miscellaneous, A9150-A9600

Mitomycin, J9280-J9291

Mitoxantrone HCl, J9293

Mobilite hospital beds, E0293, E0295, E0297

Moducal, enteral nutrition, B4155

Moisture exchanger for use with invasive mechanical ventilation, A4483

Moisturizer, skin, A6250

Monarc-M, J7190

Monitor
  apnea, E0618
  blood glucose, E0607
    Accu-Check, E0607
    Tracer II, E0607
  blood pressure, A4670
  pacemaker, E0610, E0615
  ventilator, E0450

Monoclonal antibodies, J7505

Monoject disposable insulin syringes, up to 1cc, per syringe, A4206

Monojector lancet device, A4258

Morphine sulfate, J2270, J2271, S0093
  sterile, preservative-free, J2275

Moulage, facial, D5911-D5912

Mouth exam, athletic, D9941

Mouthpiece (for respiratory equipment), A4617

Moxifloxacin, J2280

M-Prednisol-40, J1030
  -80, J1040

MRI
  contrast material, A4643
  low field, S8042

Mucoprotein, blood, P2038

Multifetal pregnancy reduction, ultrasound guidance, S8055

Multiple post collar, cervical, L0180-L0200

Multipositional patient support system, E0636

Muscular dystrophy, genetic test, S3853

Muse, J0275

Mutamycin, J9280

Mycophenolate mofetil, J7517

Mylotarg, J9300

Myochrysine, J1600

Myolin, J2360

Myotomy, D7056

Myotonic muscular dystrophy, genetic test, S3853

Myringotomy, S2225

Nafcillin sodium, S0032

Nail trim, G0127, S0390

Nalbuphine HCl, J2300

Naloxone HCl, J2310

Nandrobolic L.A., J2321

Nandrolone
  decanoate, J2320-J2322

Narrowing device, wheelchair, E0969

Narcan, J2310

Nasahist B, J0945

Nasal
  application device (for CPAP device), A7032-A7034
  vaccine inhalation, J3530

Nasogastric tubing, B4081, B4082

Navelbine, J9390

ND Stat, J0945

Nebcin, J3260

Nebulizer, E0570-E0585
  aerosol compressor, E0571
  aerosol mask, A7015
  aerosols, E0580
    Airlife Brand Misty-Neb, E0580
    Power-Mist, E0580
    Up-Draft Neb-U-Mist, E0580
    Up-Mist hand-held nebulizer, E0580
  compressor, with, E0570
    Madamist II medication compressor/nebulizer, E0570
    Pulmo-Aide compressor/nebulizer, E0570
    Schuco Mist nebulizer system, E0570

Nebulizer — continued
  corrugated tubing
    disposable, A7010, A7018
    non-disposable, A7011
  distilled water, A7018
  drug dispensing fee, E0590
  filter
    disposable, A7013
    non-disposable, A7014
  heater, E1372
  large volume
    disposable, prefilled, A7008
    disposable, unfilled, A7007
  not used with oxygen
    durable glass, A7017
  pneumatic, administration set, A7003, A7005, A7006
  pneumatic, nonfiltered, A7004
  portable, E0570
  small volume, E0574
  spacer or nebulizer, S8100
    with mask, S8101
  sterile water/saline, A7020
  ultrasonic, dome and mouthpiece, A7016
  ultrasonic, reservoir bottle non-disposable, A7009
  water, A7018-A7020
  water collection device large volume nebulizer, A7012
    distilled water, A7018
    sterile water, A7020

NebuPent, J2545

Needle, A4215
  any size, A4656
  non-coring, A4212
  with syringe, A4206-A4209

Negative pressure wound therapy
  canister set, A6551
  dressing set, A6550
  pump, E2402

Nembutal sodium solution, J2515

Neocyten, J2360

Neo-Durabolic, J2320-J2322

Neomax knee support, L1800

Neoplasms, dental, D7410-D7465

Neoquess, J0500

Neosar, J9070-J9092

Neostigmine methylsulfate, J2710

Neo-Synephrine, J2370

NephrAmine, parenteral nutrition, B5000

Nesacaine MPF, J2400

Nesiritide, J2324

Neulasta, J2505

Neumega, J2355

Neurolysis
  foot, S2135

Neuromuscular stimulator, E0745
  ambulation of spinal cord injured, K0600

Neuro-Pulse, E0720

Neurostimulator
  implantable
    pulse generator, E0756
    receiver, E0757
  patient programmer, C1787, E0754

Neutrexin, J3305

Newington
  Legg Perthes orthosis L1710
  mobility frame, L1500

Newport Lite hip orthosis, L1685

Nextep™ Contour™ Lower Leg Walker, L2999

Nextep™ Low Silhouette™ Lower Leg Walkers, L2999

Nicotine
  gum, S4995
  patches, S4990-S4991

Niemann-Pick disease, genetic test, S3849

Nightguard, D9940

Nipent, J9268

Nitric oxide, for hypoxic respiratory failure in neonate, S1025

Nitrogen mustard, J9230

Nitrous oxide, dental analgesia, D9230

Nonchemotherapy drug, oral, J8499

Noncovered services, A9270, G0293-G0294

Nonemergency transportation, A0080-A0210

Nonimpregnated gauze dressing, A6216, A6221, A6402, A6404

Non-intravenous conscious sedation, dental, D9248

Nonmetabolic active tissue, Q0183

Nonprescription drug, A9150

Nonthermal pulsed high frequency radiowaves treatment device, E0761

Nordryl, J1200

Norflex, J2360

Norplant System contraceptive, A4260

Northwestern Suspension, socket prosthesis, L6110

Not otherwise classified drug, J3490, J7599, J7699, J7799, J8499, J8999, J9999, Q0181

Novantrone, J9293

Novo Nordisk insulin, J1815, J1817

Novo Seven, Q0187

NPH insulin, J1815, S5552

Nubain, J2300

NuHope
  adhesive, 1 oz bottle with applicator, A4364
  adhesive, 3 oz bottle with applicator, A4364
  cleaning solvent, 4 oz bottle, A4455
  cleaning solvent, 16 oz bottle, A4455
  extra long adhering tape strips (100/pkg), A4454
  extra long pink adhering tape strips (100/pkg), A4454
  extra wide adhering tape strips (100/pkg), A4454
  extra wide pink adhering tape strips (100/pkg), A4454
  hole cutter tool, A4421
  regular adhering tape strips (100/pkg), A4454
  regular pink adhering tape strips (100/pkg), A4454
  thinning solvent, A4454

Numorphan H.P., J2410

Nursing care, in home
  licensed practical nurse, S9124
  registered nurse, S9123

Nursing home visit, dental, D9410

Nursing services, S9211-S9212, T1000-T1004

Nutri-Source, enteral nutrition, B4155

Nutrition
  counseling
    dental, D1310, D1320
    dietary, S9452
  enteral infusion pump, B9000, B9002
  enteral formulae, B4150-B4156

Nutrition — *continued*
  parenteral infusion pump, B9004, B9006
  parenteral solution, B4164-B5200

Nutritional counseling, dietition visit, S9470

NYU, hand prosthesis, child, L6872

Observation care for CHF, chest pain or asthma, G0244

Obturator prosthesis
  definitive, D5932
  dental
    postsurgical, D5932
    refitting, D5933
    surgical, D5931
  interim, D5936
  surgical, D5931

Occipital/mandibular support, cervical, L0160

Occlusal
  adjustment, dental, D9951-D9952
  guard, dental, D9940
  orthotic device, D7877

Occlusion/analysis, D9950

Occlusion device placement, G0264

Occupational multifocal lens, V2786

Occupational therapist
  home health setting, G0152

Occupational therapy, S9129

Octafluoropropane with human serum albumin, C9202

Octreotide
  intramuscular form, J2353
  subcutaneous or intravenous form, J2354

Ocular prosthetic implant, L8610

Ocularist evaluation, S9105

Oculinum, J0585

Odansetron HCl, J2405, Q0179

Odontoplasty (enameloplasty), D9971

Office service, M0064

Offobock cosmetic gloves, L6895

O-Flex, J2360

Ofloxacin, S0034

Ohio Willow
  prosthetic sheath
    above knee, L8410
    below knee, L8400
    upper limb, L8415
  prosthetic sock, L8420-L8435
  stump sock, L8470-L8485

Omalizumab, S0107

Omnipen-N, J0290

Oncaspar, J9266

Oncoscint, A4642

Oncovin, J9370

Ondanestron HCl, S0181

One-Button foldaway walker, E0143

One Touch
  Basic blood glucose meter, E0607
  Basic test strips, box of 50, A4253
  Profile blood glucose meter, E0607

Onlay, dental
  fixed partial denture retainer, metallic, D6602, D6615
  metallic, D2542-D2544
  porcelain/ceramic, D2642-D2644
  resin-based composite, D2662, D2664

O & P Express
  above knee, L5210

O & P Express — *continued*
  ankle-foot orthosis with bilateral uprights, L1990
  anterior floor reaction orthosis, L1945
  below knee, L5105
  elbow disarticulation, L6200
  hip disarticulation, L5250
  hip-knee-ankle-foot orthosis, L2080
  interscapular thoracic, L6370
  Legg Perthes orthosis, Scottish Rite, L1730
  Legg Perthes orthosis, Patten, L1755
  knee-ankle-foot orthosis, L2000, L2010, L2020, L2036
  knee disarticulation, L5150, L5160
  partial foot, L5000, L5020
  plastic foot drop brace, L1960
  supply/accessory/service, L9900

Oppenheimer, wrist-hand-finger orthosis, L3924

Operculectomy, D7971

Oprelvekin, J2355

Osteotomy, periacetabular, S2115

Oral and maxillofacial surgery, D7000-D7999

Oral examination, D0120-D0160

Oral hygiene instruction, D1330

Oral interpreter or sign language services, T1013

Oral orthotic treatment for sleep apnea, S8260

Oral pathology
  accession of tissue, D0472-D0474
  bacteriologic studies, D0415
  cytology, D0480
  other oral pathology procedures, D0502

Oraminic II, J0945

Orcel, C9200

Ormazine, J3230

Oropharyngeal suction catheter, A4628

Orphenadrine, J2360

Orphenate, J2360

Orthodontics, D8000-D8999

Ortho-Ease forearm crutches, E0111

Orthoflex™ Elastic Plaster Bandages, A4580

Orthoguard hip orthosis, L1685

Orthomedics
  ankle-foot orthosis, L1900
  pediatric hip abduction splint, L1640
  plastic foot drop brace, L1960
  single axis shoe insert, L2180
  ultralight airplane arm abduction splint, L3960
  upper extremity fracture orthosis
    combination, L3986
    humeral, L3980
    radius/ulnar, L3982

Orthomerica
  below knee test socket, L5620
  pediatric hip abduction splint, L1640
  plastic foot drop brace, L1960
  single axis shoe insert, L2180
  upper extremity fracture orthosis
    humeral, L3980
    radius/ulnar, L3982
  wrist extension cock-up, L3914

Orthopedic devices, E0910-E0948
  cervical
    Diskard head halters, E0942
    Turtle Neck safety collars, E0942

Orthopedic shoes
  arch support, L3040-L3100
  footwear, L3201-L3265
  insert, L3000-L3030
  lift, L3300-L3334

Parenteral nutrition — *continued*
solution, B4164-B5200
supplies, not otherwise classified, B9999
supply kit, B4220, B4222

Parenting class, S9444
infant safety, S9447

Paricalcitol, J2501

Parking fee, nonemergency transport, A0170

Partial dentures
fixed
implant/adjustment-supported
retainers, D6068-D6077
pontic, D6210-D6252
retainers, D6545-D6792
removable, D5211-D5281

PASRR, T2010-T2011

Paste, conductive, A4558

Pathology and laboratory tests, miscellaneous, P9010-P9615

Patten Bottom, Legg Perthes orthosis, L1755

Pavlik harness, hip orthosis, L1650

Peak expiratory flow meter, S8110

Peak flow meter, portable, S8096

Pediatric hip abduction splint
Orthomedics, L1640
Orthomerica, L1640

PEFR, peak expiratory flow rate meter, A4614

Pegfilgrastrim, J2505

Pegademase bovine, Q2012

Pegaspargase, J9266

Peg-L-asparaginase, J9266

Pelvic and breast exam, G0101

Pelvic belt/harness/boot, E0944

Penicillin G
benzathine and penicillin G procaine,
J0530-J0580
potassium, J2540
procaine, aqueous, J2510

Penlet lancet device, A4258

Penlet II lancet device, A4258

Pentamidine isethionate, J2545, S0080

Pentastarch, Q2013

Pentazocine HCl, J3070

Pentobarbital sodium, J2515

Pentostatin, J9268

Percussor, E0480

Percutaneous
access system, A4301
lumbar discectomy probe, C2314

Perflexane lipic microspheres, C9203

Perflutren lipid microsphere, C9112

Performance Wrap™ (KO), L1825

Periapical service, D3410-D3470

Periodontal procedures, D4000-D4999

Periradicular/apicoectomy, D3410-D3426

Perlstein, ankle-foot orthosis, L1920

Permapen, J0560-J0580

Peroneal strap, L0980

Peroxide, A4244

Perphenazine, J3310, Q0175-Q0176

Persantine, J1245

Personal care services, T1019-T1020

Pessary, A4561-A4562

PET imaging
breast, G0252-G0254
colorectal, G0213-G0215
esophageal, G0226-G0228
lung, G0125, G0210-G0212
lymphoma, G0220-G0222
metabolic bain imaging, G0229-G0230
myocardial perfusion, G0030-G0047
regional, G0125, G0223-G0225, G0234
thyroid, G0296
whole body, G0125, G0210-G0228,
G0230-G0234

Pfizerpen, J2540
A.S., J2510

PGE₁, J0270

Phamacologicals, dental, D9610, D9630

Pharmacy services, S9430

Pharmaplast disposable insulin syringes, per syringe, A4206

Phelps, ankle-foot orthosis, L1920

Phenazine (25, 50), J2550

Phenergan, J2550

Phenobarbital sodium, J2560

Phentolamine mesylate, J2760

Phenylephrine HCl, J2370

Phenytoin sodium, J1165

Philadelphia™ tracheotomy cervical collar, L0172

Philly™ One-piece™ Extrication collar, L0150

PHisoHex solution, A4246

Photofrin, J9600

Photographs, dental, diagnostic, D0350

Phototherapy
home visit service (bili-lite), S9098
keratectomy (PKT), S0812
light, E0202

Physical exam for college, S0622

Physical therapy, S8990

Physical therapy/therapist
home health setting, G0151, S9131

Phytonadione, J3430

Pillo pump, E0182

Pillow
abduction, E1399
decubitus care, E0190

Pin retention, per tooth, D2951

Pinworm examination, Q0113

Piperacillin sodium, S0081

Pit and fissure sealant, D1351

Pitocin, J2590

Planing, dental root, D0350

Plasma
frozen, P9058-P9060
multiple donor, pooled, frozen, P9023
protein fraction, P9048
single donor, fresh frozen, P9017

Plastazote, L3002, L3252, L3253, L3265,
L5654-L5658

Plaster
bandages
Orthoflex™ Elastic Plaster Bandages,
A4580
Specialist™ Plaster Bandages, A4580
Genmould™ Creamy Plaster, A4580
Specialist™ J-Splint™ Plaster Roll
Immobilizer, A4580
Specialist™ Plaster Roll Immobilizer,
A4580
Specialist™ Plaster Splints, A4580

Platelet
concentrate, each unit, P9019
rich plasma, each unit, P9020

Platelets, P9032-P9040, P9052-P9053

Platform, for home blood glucose monitor, A4255

Platform attachment
forearm crutch, E0153
walker, E0154

Platinol, J9060, J9062

Pleural catheter, A7042
drainage bottle, A7043

Plicamycin, J9270

Plumbing, for home ESRD equipment, A4870

Pneumatic
appliance, E0655-E0673, L4350-L4380
compressor, E0650-E0652, E0675
splint, L4350-L4380
tire, wheelchair, E0953

Pneumatic nebulizer
administration set
small volume
filtered, A7006
non-filtered, A7003
non-disposable, A7005
small volume, disposable, A7004

Pneumococcal conjugate vaccine, S0195

Polaris, E0601

Polaris Lt, E0601

Polocaine, J0670

Polycillin-N, J0290

Polycose, enteral nutrition,
liquid, B4155
powder, B4155

Pontics, D5281, D6210-D6252

Poor blood, each unit, P9016

Porfimer, J9600

Pork insulin, J1815, J1817

Portable
equipment transfer, R0070-R0076
hemodialyzer system, E1635
nebulizer, E0570
x-ray equipment, Q0092

Portagen Powder, enteral nutrition,
B4150

Posey restraints, E0700

Positive airway pressure device supply,
A7046

Post-coital examination, Q0115

Post and core, dental, D2952-D2954,
D2957, D6970-D6972, D6976-D6977

Post, removal, dental, D2955

Postural drainage board, E0606

Potassium
chloride, J3480
hydroxide (KOH) preparation, Q0112

Pouch
Active Life convex one-piece urostomy,
A4421
closed, A4387, A5052
drainable, A4388-A4389, A5061
fecal collection, A4330
Little Ones Sur-fit mini, A5054
ostomy, A4375-A4378, A4387-A4391,
A5051-A5054, A5061-A5063,
A4416-A4420, A4423-A4434
pediatric, drainable, A5061
Pouchkins pediatric ostomy system,
A5061, A5062, A5073
Sur-Fit, drainable, A5063
urinary, A4379-A4383, A4391, A5071-
A5075

Pouch — *continued*
  urosotomy, A5073

Power mist nebulizer, E0580

Pralidoxime chloride, J2730

Precision attachment, dental, D5862, D6950

Precision, enteral nutrition
  HN, B4153
  Isotonic, B4153
  LR, B4156

Predalone-50, J2650

Predcor (-25, -50), J2650

Predicort-50, J2650

Prednisolone
  acetate, J2650
  oral, J7506, J7510

Prednisone, J7506

Predoject-50, J2650

Prefabricated crown, D2930-D2933

Prefabricated post and core, dental,
  D2954, D6972
  each additional (same tooth), D2957,
    D6977

Pregnancy care, H1000-H1005

Pregnyl, J0725

Premarin IV, J1410

Premium knee sleeve, L1830

Prenatal care, H1000-H1005

Preparatory prosthesis, L5510-L5595

Prescription drug, (*see also* **Table of
  Drugs**) J3490, J7140, J8499
  chemotherapy, J7150, J8999, J9999
  nonchemotherapy, J8499

Pressure
  alarm, dialysis, E1540
  pad, E0176-E0199

PressureGuard II, E0186

PressureKair mattress overlay, E0197

Prestige blood glucose monitor, E0607

Pre-Vent heel & elbow protector, E0191

Prevention, developmental delay, H2037

Preventive
  dental procedures, D1000-D1550
  foot care, S0390

Preview treatment planning software,
  C9708

Primacor, J2260

Primaxin, J0743

Priscoline HCl, J2670

Probe
  cryoablation, C2618
  oximeter, A4606
  percutaneous lumbar discectomy, C2614

Procainamide HCl, J2690

Procarbazine HCl, S0182

Processing
  breast milk, T2101

Prochlorperazine, J0780, Q0164-Q0165
  oral, S0183

Procrit, Q0136

Procuren, S9055

Profasi HP, J0725

Profilnine Heat-Treated, J7194

Progesterone, J2675

Prograf, J7507, J7508

Prolastin, J0256

Proleukin, J9015

Prolixin decanoate, J2680

Prolotherapy, M0076

Promazine HCl, J2950

Promethazine HCl, J2550, Q0169-Q0170

Promethazine and meperdine, J2180

Promix, enteral nutrition, B4155

Pronation/supination device, forearm,
  E1802

Pronestyl, J2690

Propac, enteral nutrition, B4155

Prophylaxis, dental, D1110, D1120

Proplex (-T and SX-T), J7194

Propranolol HCl, J1800

Prorex (-25, -50), J2550

Prostaglandin E$_1$, J0270

Prostaphlin, J2700

Prosthesis
  adhesive, used for facial
    remover, A4365
  auricular, D5914
  breast, L8000-L8035, L8600
  cranial, D5924
  dental, fixed, D6210-D6999
  dental, removable, D5110-D5899
  eye, L8610, V2623-V2629
  finger joint, L8659
  fitting, L5400-L5460, L6380-L6388
  grasper, L6881
  hand, L6000-L6020
  hemifacial, L8044
  implants, L8600-L8699
  larynx, L8500, L8505
  lower extremity, L5700-L5999, L8642
  mandibular resection, D5934-D5935
  maxiofacial, provided by a nonphysician,
    L8040-L8048
  metacarpal, L8631
  midfacial, K0441, L8041
  miscellaneous service, L8499
  nasal, K0440
  nasal septal, K0447, L8047
  obturator, D5931-D5933, D5936
  ocular, D5916
  orbital, D5915
  palatal, D5954-D5959
  partial facial, K0446, L8046
  repair, K0449, L7520
  repair or modification, maxillofacial,
    L8048-L8049
  socks (shrinker, sheath, stump sock),
    L8400-L8480
  tracheoesophageal, L8511-L8514
  tracheostomy speaking, L8501
  unspecified maxillofacial, L8048
  upper extremity, L6000-L6915
  upper facial, K0443-L8043
  vacuum erection system, L7900

Prosthetic additions
  lower extremity, L5610-L5999
  upper extremity, L6600-L7274

Prosthetic shrinker, L8440-L8465

Prosthodontic procedures
  fixed, D6200-D6999
  implant-supported, D6055-D6079
  maxillofacial, D5900-D5999
  pediatric partial denture, D6985
  removable, D5000-D5999

Prostigmin, J2710

Prostin VR Pediatric, J0270

Protamine sulfate, J2720, A4802

Protectant, skin, A6250

Protector, heel or elbow, E0191

Protirelin, J2725

Protopam chloride, J2730

Proventil, J7618-J7619

Provisional, dental
  single crown, D2799
  retainer crown (FPD), D6793

Prozine-50, J2950

Psychiatric care, H0036-H0037, H2013-
  H2014

PTK, S0812

Pulmo-Aide compressor
  nebulizer, E0570

Pulp cap, D3110, D3120

Pulp capping, D3110, D3120

Pulp sedation, D2940

Pulp vitality test, D0460

Pulpal debridement, D3221

Pulpal therapy, on primary teeth,
  D3230, D3240

Pulpotomy, D3220
  vitality test, D0460

Pulse generator,
  ear E2120
    battery, A4638

Pump
  alternating pressure pad, E0182
  ambulatory infusion, E0781
  ambulatory insulin, E0784
  Bio Flote alternating pressure pad,
    E0182
  blood, dialysis, E1620
  breast, E0602-E0604
    supplies, A4281-A4286
  Broncho-Cath endobronchial tubes, with
    CPAP, E0601
  enteral infusion, B9000, B9002
    supply, K0552
  gastric suction, E2000
  Gomco lightweight mobile aspirator,
    E0600
  Gomco portable aspirator, E0600
  heparin infusion, E1520
  implantable infusion, E0782, E0783
  implantable infusion, refill kit, A4220
  infusion
    supplies, A4230-A4232
  insulin, external, E0784
    instruction, S9145
  negative pressure wound therapy, E2402
  parenteral infusion, B9004, B9006,
    K0455
  Pillo alternating pressure pad, E0182
  speech aid, D5952-D5953, D5960
  suction
    CPAP, E0601
    gastric, E2000
    portable, E0600
  TenderCloud alternating pressure pad,
    E0182
  water circulating pad, E0217, E0218,
    E0236

Purification system, E1610, E1615

Purified pork insulin, J1815, J1817

Pyeloscopy
  for ureteral calculi, S2070

Pyridoxine HCl, J3415

Quad cane, E0105

Quadri-Poise canes, E0105

Quelicin, J0330

**Quick Check blood glucose test strips,
  box of 50**, A4253

Quick release restraints, E0700

Quikfit crutch, E0114

Quik-Fold Walkers, E0141, E0143

Quinoprestin, J2770

Rack/stand, oxygen, E1355

Radiation, dental
    carrier, D5983
    cone locator, D5985
    shield, D5984

Radiation therapy, intraoperative, S8049

Radioelements for brachytherapy, Q3001

Radiofrequency transmitter, sacral root
    neurostimulator, replacement,
    E0759

Radiograph, dental, D0210-D0340

Radioimmunoscintigraphy, S8080

Radiology service, R0070-R0076

Radiopharmaceutical
    ammonia N-13, A9526
    cobaltous chloride, C9013
    diagnostic imaging agent, A4641, A4642,
        A9500-A9505
    I-131 tositumomab, A9533-A9534,
        C1081
    indium I-111 satumomab pendetide,
        A4642
    sodium iodide I-131, A9528-A9531
    technetium Tc 99m
        albumin aggregated, A9519
        arcitumomab, C1122
        depreotide, A9511
        disofenin, A9510
        exametazime, A9521
        glucepatate, Q3006
        mebrofenin, A9513
        medronate, A9503
        mertiatide, Q3005
        oxidronate, Q3009
        pentetate, A9515
        pertechnetate, A9512
        pyrophosphate, A9515
        sestamibi, A9500
        sulfur colloid, A9520
        tetrofosmin, A9502
        vicisate, Q3003
    therapeutic, A9600

Rail
    bathtub, E0241, E0242, E0246
    bed, E0305, E0310
    toilet, E0243

Rancho hip action, hip orthosis, L1680

Rasburicase, J2783

Rascal, power wheelchair, K0010

Ready-For-Use wooden crutches, E0113

Reassessment, nutrition therapy, G0270-
    G0271

Recement
    crown, D2920
    inlay, D2910

Reciprocating peritoneal dialysis system,
    E1630

Recombinant
    ankle splints, L4392-L4398
    DNA insulin, J1815, J1817

Recombinate, J7192

Red blood cells, P9038-P9040

Red blood cells, each unit, P9021, P9022

Red Dot
    crutches, E0114
    folding walkers, E0135, E0143

Redisol, J3420

Regitine, J2760

Reglan, J2765

Regular insulin, J1815

Regulator, oxygen, E1353

Rehabilitation
    vestibular, S9476

Rehabilitation program, H2001

Rehabilitation service
    juveniles, H2033
    mental health clubhouse, H2030-H2031
    psychosocial, H2017-H2018
    substance abuse, H2034-H2036
    supported employment, H2023-H2024

Reimplantation, dental
    accidentally evulsed, D7270
    intentional, D3470

Relefact TRH, J2725

Remicade, J1745

RemRes, E0601

REMStar, E0601

Renacidin, Q2004

RenAmin, parenteral nutrition, B5000

Renu, enteral nutrition, B4150

ReoPro, TRH, J0130

Repair
    contract, ERSD, A4890
    dental, D2980, D3351-D3353, D5510-
        D5630, D6090, D6980, D7852,
        D7955
    diaphragmatic hernia, S2400
    durable medical equipment, E1340
    hearing aid, V5014, V5336
    home dialysis equipment, A4890
    orthotic, L4000-L4130
    prosthetic, L7500, L7510, L7520
    skilled technical, E1340

Replacement
    battery, A4254, A4630, A4631
        ear pulse generator, A4638
    handgrip for cane, crutch, walker A4636
    ostomy filters, A4421
    tip for cane, crutch, walker, A4637
    underarm pad for crutch, A4635

Repositioning device, mandibular, S8262

Rep-Pred
    40, J1030
    80, J1040

ResCap headgear, A7035

Reservoir
    metered dose inhaler, A4627

Residential care, T2032-T2033

Resin dental restoration, D2330-D2394

Resipiradyne II Plus pulmonary
    function/ventilation monitor,
    E0450

ResMed Sb Elite, E0601

RespiGam, J1565

Respiratory syncytial virus immune
    globulin, J1565

Respiratory therapy, G0237-G0238

Respite care, T1005
    in home, S9125
    not in home, H0045

Restorations, dental
    amalgam, D2140-D2161
    gold foil, D2410-D2430
    resin-based composite, D2330-D2394
    inlay/onlay, D2510-D2664, D6600-
        D6615

Restorative dental work, D2000-D2999

Restraint
    any type, E0710
    belts
        Posey, E0700
        Secure-All, E0700
    Bite disposable jaw locks, E0700
    body holders
        Houdini security suit, E0700
        Quick Release, one piece, E0700
        Secure-All, one piece, E0700
        System2 zippered, E0700
        UltraCare vest-style

Restraint — continued
    body holders — continued
        with sleeves, E0700
    hand
        Secure-All finger control mit, E0700
    limb holders
        Posey, E0700
        Quick Release, E0700
        Secure-All, E0700
    pelvic
        Secure-All, E0700

Retail therapy item, miscellaneous,
    T1999

Retainers, dental
    fixed partial denture, D6545-D6792
    implant/abutment supported, D6068-
        D6077
    orthodontic, D8680

Retinal device, intraoperative, C1784

Retinal exam for diabetes, S3000

Retinal tamponade, C1814

Retinoblastoma, genetic test, S3841

Retrieval device, insertable, C1773

Retrograde dental filling, D3430

Rhesonativ, J2790

Rheumatrex, J8610

Rho(D) immune globulin, human, J2790,
    J2792
    minidose, J2788

RhoGAM, J2790

Rib belt
    thoracic, L0210, L0220
    Don-Joy, L0210

Rice ankle splint, L1904

Richhfoam convoluted & flat overlays,
    E0199

Ride Lite 200, Ride Lite 9000, manual
    wheelchair, K0004

Ridge augmentation/sinus lift, dental,
    D7950

Rimso, J1212

Ringer's lactate infusion, J7120

Ring, ostomy, A4404

Rituxan, J9310

Rituximab, J9310

Riveton, foot orthosis, L3140, L3150

RN services, T1002

Road Savage power wheelchair, K0011

Road Warrior power wheelchair, K0011

Robaxin, J2800

Robin-Aids, prosthesis
    hand, L6855, L6860
    partial hand, L6000-L6020

Rocephin, J0696

Rocking bed, E0462

Rollabout chair, E1031

Root canal therapy, D3310-D3353

Root planning and scaling, dental,
    D4341

Root removal, dental, D7140, D7250

Root resection/amputation, dental,
    D3450

Ropivacaine hydrochloride, J2795

Roux-en-Y gastroenterostomy, S2085

RSV immune globulin, J1565

Rubex, J9000

Rubramin PC, J3420

Sabre power wheelchair, K0011

Source — *continued*
  brachytherapy — *continued*
    Iodine 125, C1718
    non-high dose rate Iridium 192,
      C1719
    Palladium 103, C1720
    Yttrium-90, C2616

Spacer
  interphalangeal joint, L8658

Space maintainer, dental, D1510-D1550

Sparine, J2950

Spasmoject, J0500

Specialist™ Ankle Foot Orthosis, L1930

Specialist™ Closed-Back Cast Boot,
  L3260

Specialist™ 100 Cotton Cast Padding,
  (not separately reimbursable from the
  casting procedure or casting supplies
  codes)

Specialist™ Cast Padding, (not separately
  reimbursable from the casting
  procedure or casting supplies codes)

Specialist™ Gaitkeeper™ Boot, L3260

Specialist™ Health/Post Operative Shoe,
  A9270

Specialist™ Heel Cups, L3485

Specialist™ Insoles, L3510

**Specialist™ J-Splint™ Plaster Roll
  Immobilizer**, A4580

Specialist™ Open-Back Cast Boot, L3260

Specialist™ Orthopaedic Stockinet, (not
  separately reimbursable from the
  casting procedure or casting supplies
  codes)

Specialist™ Plaster Bandages, A4580

Specialist™ Plaster Roll Immobilizer,
  A4580

Specialist™ Plaster Splints, A4580

**Specialist™ Pre-Formed Humeral
  Fracture Brace**, L3980

**Specialist™ Pre-Formed Ulnar Fracture
  Brace**, L3982

Specialist™ Thumb Orthosis, L3800

**Specialist™ Tibial Pre-formed Fracture
  Brace**, L2116

**Specialist™ Toe Insert for Specialist™
  Closed-Back Cast Boot and
  Specialist™ Health/Post Operative
  Shoe**, A9270

Specialist™ Wrist/Hand Orthosis, L3999

Specialist™ Wrist-Hand-Thumb-orthosis,
  L3999

Specialty absorptive dressing, A6251-
  A6256

Spectacles, S0504-S0510, S0516-S0518

Spectinomycin HCl, J3320

Speech aid
  pediatric, D5952
  adult, D5953

Speech and language pathologist
  home health setting, G0153

Speech assessment, V5362-V5364
  Speech Generating Device
    software, E2511
    supplies, E2500-E2599

Speech therapy, S9128

Spenco shoe insert, foot orthosis, L3001

Sperm procurement, S4026, S4030-S4031
  donor service, S4025

Sphygmomanometer/blood pressure,
  A4660

Spinal orthosis
  anterior-posterior, L0530
  anterior-posterior-lateral, L0520, L0550-
    L0565
  Boston type, L1200
  cervical, L0100-L0200
  cervical-thoracic-lumbar-sacral orthosis
    (CTLSO), L0700, L0710, L1000
  DME, K0114-K0116
  halo, L0810-L0830
  lumbar flexion, L0540
  lumbar-sacral (LSO), L0500-L0565
  Milwaukee, L1000
  multiple post collar, L0180-L0200
  sacroilliac, L0600-L0620
  scoliosis, L1000, L1200, L1300-L1499
  torso supports, L0900-L0999

Spirometer, electronic, S8190

Splint, A4570, L3100, L4350-L4380
  ankle, L4392-L4398, S8451
  digit, prefabricated, S8450
  dynamic, E1800, E1805, E1810, E1815
  elbow, S8452
  footdrop, L4398
  long arm, Q4017-Q4020
  long leg, Q4041-Q4044
  Orthoplast™ Splints (and Orthoplast™ II
    Splints), A4590
  pneumatic, L4350
  short arm, Q4021-Q4024
  short leg, Q4045-Q4046
  Specialist™ Plaster Splints, A4580
  supplies, Q4051
  Thumb-O-Prene™ Splint, L3999
  toad finger, A4570
  wrist, S8451
  Wrist-O-Prene™ Splint, L3800

Splinting, dental
  commissure, D5987
  provisional, D4320-D4321
  surgical, D5988

Spoke protectors, each, K0065

Sports supports hinged knee support,
  L1832

Stainless steel crown, D2930-D2931,
  D2933

Standing frame system, E0638

Star Lumen tubing, A4616

Steeper, hand prosthesis, L6868, L6873

Steindler apron-front, spinal orthosis,
  L0340

Sten, foot prosthesis, L5972

Stent, in dentistry, D5982

Stent placement, transcatheter
  intracoronary, G0290-G0291
  intravascular, S2211

Stereotactic radiosurgery, G0242-G0243,
  G0251

Sterile cefuroxime sodium, J0697

Sterile water, A4216-A4217

Stilphostrol, J9165

Stimulated intrauterine insemination,
  S4035

Stimulation
  electrical, G0281-G0283
  electromagnetic, G0295

Stimulation, gastric electrical implant,
  S2213

Stimulators
  cough, device, E0482
  electric, supplies, A4595
  neuromuscular, E0744, E0745
  osteogenesis, electrical, E0747-E0749
  salivary reflex, E0755
  ultrasound, E0760

Stocking
  Delta-Net™ Orthopaedic Stockinet, (not
    separately reimbursable from the
    casting procedure or casting
    supplies codes)
  gradient compression, L8100-L8239
  Specialist™ Orthopaedic Stockinet, (not
    separately reimbursable from the
    casting procedure or casting
    supplies codes)

Stoma
  cap, A5055
  catheter, A5082
  cone, A4399
  plug, A5081

Stomach tube, B4083

Stomahesive
  paste, K0138
  powder, K0139
  skin barrier, A4362, A5122
  sterile wafer, A4362
  strips, A4362

Storm Arrow power wheelchair, K0014

Storm Torque power wheelchair, K0011

Streptase, J2995

Streptokinase, J2995

Streptomycin sulfate, J3000

Streptozocin, J9320

Stress breaker, in dentistry, D6940

Stress management class, S9454

Strip(s)
  blood, A4253
  glucose test, A4253, A4772
  Nu-Hope
    adhesive, 1 oz bottle with applicator,
      A4364
    adhesive, 3 oz bottle with applicator,
      A4364
    extra long adhering tape strips
      (100/pkg), A4454
    extra long pink adhering tape strips
      (100/pkg), A4454
    extra wide adhering tape strips
      (100/pkg), A4454
    extra wide pink adhering tape strips
      (100/pkg) , A4454
    regular adhering tape strips
      (100/pkg), A4454
    regular pink adhering tape strips
      (100/pkg), A4454
  urine reagent, A4250

Strontium-89 chloride, A9600

Study, gastrointestinal fat absorption,
  S3708

Stump sock, L8470-L8485

Stylet, A4212

Sublimaze, J3010

Substance abuse treatment, T1006-T1012
  childcare during, T1009
  couples counseling, T1006
  family counseling, T1006
  meals during, T1010
  skills development, T1012
  treatment plan, T1007

Succinylcholine chloride, J0330

Sucostrin, J0330

Suction pump
  portable, E0600

Sulfamethoxazole and trimethoprim,
  S0039

Sullivan
  CPAP, E0601

Sumacal, enteral nutrition, B4155

Sumatriptan succinate, J3030

Sunglass frames, S0518

Water chamber
humidifier, A7046

Wedges, shoe, L3340-L3420

Wehamine, J1240

Wehdryl, J1200

Weight management class, S9449

Wellcovorin, J0640

Wet mount, Q0111

Wheel attachment, rigid pickup walker, E0155

Wheelchair, E0950-E1298, K0001-K0108
accessories, E0192, E0950-E1001, E1065, E2203-E2399
cushions, E0963-E0965
High Profile, 4-inch, E0965
Low Profile, 2-inch, E0963
tray, E0950
Visi, E0950
amputee, E1170-E1200
bearings, any type, K0452
component or accessory, NOS, K0108
heavy-duty
shock absorber, E1015-E1016
Tracer, E1280, E1285, E1290, E1295
lightweight, E1240-E1270
Ez Lite, E1250
Tracer, E1240, E1250, E1260, E1270
manual, adult, E1161
accessories, E2201-E2204, E2300-E2399
motorized, E1210-E1213
narrowing device, E0969
pediatric, E1231-E1238
integrated seating system, E1012-1013
modification, E1011
support, E10025-1027
power, accessories, E2300-E2399
reclining back, E1014
residual limb support, E1020
specially sized, E1220-E1230
support, E1020
tire, E0996, E0999, E1000
transfer board or device, E0972
transport chair, E1037-E1038
van, nonemergency, A0130, S0209
youth, E1091

WHFO, with inflatable air chamber, L3807

Whirlpool equipment, E1300-E1310

WHO, wrist extension, L3914

Wig, S8095

Wilcox apron-front, spinal orthosis, L0520

Williams, spinal orthosis, L0540

Win RhoSD, J2792

Wipes, A4245, A4247
Allkare protective barrier, A5119

WIZZ-ard manual wheelchair, K0006

Wound
cleanser, A6260
cover
alginate dressing, A6196-A6198
collagen dressing, A6021-A6024
foam dressing, A6209-A6214
hydrocolloid dressing, A6234-A6239
hydrogel dressing, A6242-A6248
packing strips, A6407
specialty absorptive dressing, A6251-A6256
warming card, E0232
warming device, E0231
non-contact warming cover, A6000
dental, D7910-D7912
filler
alginate, A6199
foam, A6215
hydrocolloid, A6240-A6241
hydrogel, A6242-A6248
not elsewhere classified, A6261-A6262
healing
other growth factor preparation, S9055
Procuren, S9055
packing strips, A6407
pouch, A6154
warming device, E0231
cover, A6000
warming card, E0232
therapy
negative pressure
supplies, A6550-A6551

Wrap
abdominal aneurysm, M0301

Wrist
brace, cock-up, L3908
disarticulation prosthesis, L6050, L6055
hand/finger orthosis (WHFO), E1805, E1825, L3800-L3954
Specialist™ Pre-Formed Ulnar Fracture Brace, L3982
Specialist™ Wrist/Hand Orthosis, L3999
Specialist™ Wrist-Hand-Thumb-orthosis, L3999
Splint, lace-up, L3800
Wrist-O-Prene™ Splint, L3800

Wycillin, J2510

Wydase, J3470

Xcaliber power wheelchair, K0014

Xenon Xe 133, Q3004

X-ray equipment, portable, Q0092, R0070, R0075

Y set tubing for peritoneal dialysis, A4719

Yttrium 90
ibritumomab tiuxeton, A9523
microsphere
brachytherapy, C2616
procedure, S2095

Zantac, J2780

Zalcitabine, S0141

Zenapax, J7513

Zetran, J3360

Zidovudine, J3485

ZIFT, S4014

Zinacef, J0697

Zinecard, J1190

Ziprasidone mesylate, J3486

Zithromax
I.V., J0456
oral, Q0144

Zofran, J2405

Zoladex, J9202

Zoledronic acid, J3487

Zolicef, J0690

Zosyn, J2543

Zygomatic arch, fracture treatment, D7650, D7660, D7750, D7760

Zyvok, J2020

TRANSPORTATION SERVICES INCLUDING AMBULANCE *A0000-A0999*

This code range includes ground and air ambulance, nonemergency transportation (taxi, bus, automobile, wheelchair van), and ancillary transportation-related fees.

Ambulance Origin and Destination modifiers used with Transportation Service codes are single-digit modifiers used in combination in boxes 12 and 13 of CMS form 1491. The first digit indicates the transport's place of origin, and the destination is indicated by the second digit. The modifiers most commonly used are:

D   Diagnostic or therapeutic site other than 'P' or 'H'

E   Residential, domiciliary, custodial facility (nursing home, not skilled nursing facility)

G   Hospital-based dialysis facility (hospital or hospital-related)

H   Hospital

I   Site of transfer (for example, airport or helicopter pad) between types of ambulance

J   Non-hospital-based dialysis facility

N   Skilled nursing facility (SNF)

P   Physician's office (includes HMO non-hospital facility, clinic, etc.)

R   Residence

S   Scene of accident or acute event

X   Intermediate stop at physician's office enroute to the hospital (includes HMO non-hospital facility, clinic, etc.) Note: Modifier X can only be used as a designation code in the second position of a modifier.

See Q3019, Q3020, and S0215. For Medicaid, see T codes and T modifiers.

Claims for transportation services fall under the jurisdiction of the local carrier.

E   **A0021**   **Ambulance service, outside state per mile, transport (Medicaid only)**
     Cross-reference A0430

A0080   **Non-emergency transportation, per mile — vehicle provided by volunteer (individual or organization), with no vested interest**

A0090   **Non-emergency transportation, per mile — vehicle provided by individual (family member, self, neighbor) with vested interest**

A0100   **Non-emergency transportation; taxi**

A0110   **Nonemergency transportation and bus, intra- or interstate carrier**

A0120   **Non-emergency transportation: mini-bus, mountain area transports, or other transportation systems**

A0130   **Nonemergency transportation: wheelchair van**

A0140   **Nonemergency transportation and air travel (private or commercial), intra- or interstate**

A0160   **Nonemergency transportation: per mile — caseworker or social worker**

A0170   **Transportation ancillary: parking fees, tolls, other**

A0180   **Nonemergency transportation: ancillary: lodging — recipient**

A0190   **Nonemergency transportation: ancillary: meals — recipient**

A0200   **Nonemergency transportation: ancillary: lodging — escort**

A0210   **Nonemergency transportation: ancillary: meals — escort**

▲   **A0225**   **Ambulance service, neonatal transport, base rate, emergency transport, one way**

A0380   **BLS mileage (per mile)**
     Cross-reference A0425

A0382   **BLS routine disposable supplies**

A0384   **BLS specialized service disposable supplies; defibrillation (used by ALS ambulances and BLS ambulances in jurisdictions where defibrillation is permitted in BLS ambulances)**

A0390   **ALS mileage (per mile)**
     Cross-reference A0425

A0392   **ALS specialized service disposable supplies; defibrillation (to be used only in jurisdictions where defibrillation cannot be performed by BLS ambulances)**

A0394   **ALS specialized service disposable supplies; IV drug therapy**

A0396   **ALS specialized service disposable supplies; esophageal intubation**

A0398   **ALS routine disposable supplies**

WAITING TIME TABLE

	UNITS		TIME
1	1/2	to	1 hr.
2	1	to	1 1/2 hrs.
3	1 1/2	to	2 hrs.
4	2	to	2 1/2 hrs.
5	2 1/2	to	3 hrs.
6	3	to	3 1/2 hrs.
7	3 1/2	to	4 hrs.
8	4	to	4 1/2 hrs.
9	4 1/2	to	5 hrs.
10	5	to	5 1/2 hrs.

A0420   **Ambulance waiting time (ALS or BLS), one-half (1/2) hour increments**

A0422   **Ambulance (ALS or BLS) oxygen and oxygen supplies, life sustaining situation**

A0424   **Extra ambulance attendant, ground (ALS or BLS) or air (fixed or rotary winged); (requires medical review)**
     Pertinent documentation to evaluate medical appropriateness should be included when this code is reported.

A0425   **Ground mileage, per statute mile**

A0426   **Ambulance service, advanced life support, non-emergency transport, level 1 (ALS 1)**

A0427   **Ambulance service, advanced life support, emergency transport, level 1 (ALS 1 — emergency)**

A0428   **Ambulance service, basic life support, non-emergency transport (BLS)**

A0429   **Ambulance service, basic life support, emergency transport (BLS — emergency)**

A0430   **Ambulance service, conventional air services, transport, one way (fixed wing)**

A0431 Ambulance service, conventional air services, transport, one way (rotary wing)

A0432 Paramedic intercept (PI), rural area, transport furnished by a volunteer ambulance company which is prohibited by state law from billing third party payers

A0433 Advanced life support, level 2 (ALS 2)

A0434 Specialty care transport (SCT)

A0435 Fixed wing air mileage, per statute mile

A0436 Rotary wing air mileage, per statute mile

● A0800 Ambulance transport provided between the hours of 7 p.m. and 7 a.m.

E A0888 Non-covered ambulance mileage, per mile (e.g., for miles traveled beyond closest appropriate facility)
MED: MCM 2125

A A0999 Unlisted ambulance service
Determine if an alternative HCPCS Level II code or a CPT code better describes the service being reported. This code should be used only if a more specific code is unavailable.
MED: MCM 2120.1, MCM 2125

MEDICAL AND SURGICAL SUPPLIES *A4000-A8999*

This section covers a wide variety of medical, surgical, and some durable medical equipment (DME) related supplies and accessories. DME-related supplies, accessories, maintenance, and repair required to ensure the proper functioning of this equipment is generally covered by Medicare under the prosthetic devices provision.

MISCELLANEOUS SUPPLIES

These codes are to be filed with the Medicare local carrier, unless otherwise noted (if incident to a physicians' services, not separately billable). unless they represent incidental service or supplies which are referred to the DME regional carrier.

☑ A4206 Syringe with needle, sterile 1 cc, each
This code specifies a 1 cc syringe but is also used to report 3/10 cc or 1/2 cc syringes.

☑ A4207 Syringe with needle, sterile 2 cc, each

☑ A4208 Syringe with needle, sterile 3 cc, each

☑ A4209 Syringe with needle, sterile 5 cc or greater, each

A4210 Needle-free injection device, each
Sometimes covered by commercial payers with preauthorization and physician letter stating need (e.g., for insulin injection in young children). Medicare jurisdiction: DME regional carrier.
MED: CIM 60-9

A4211 Supplies for self-administered injections
When a drug that is usually injected by the patient (e.g., insulin or calcitonin) is injected by the physician, it is excluded from Medicare coverage unless administered in an emergency situation (e.g., diabetic coma).
MED: MCM 2049

A4212 Non coring needle or stylet with or without catheter

A4213 Syringe, sterile, 20 cc or greater, each
Medicare jurisdiction: DME regional carrier.

A4214 Sterile saline or water, 30 cc vial

E A4215 Needles only, sterile, any size, each
Medicare jurisdiction: DME regional carrier.

● A ☑ A4216 Sterile water/saline, 10 ml
MED: MCM 2049

● A ☑ A4217 Sterile water/saline, 500 ml
MED: MCM 2049

A4220 Refill kit for implantable infusion pump
Implantable infusion pumps are covered by Medicare for 5-FUdR therapy for unresected liver or colorectal cancer and for opioid drug therapy for intractable pain. They are not covered by Medicare for heparin therapy for thromboembolic disease. Report drugs separately.
MED: CIM 60-14

A4221 Supplies for maintenance of drug infusion catheter, per week (list drug separately)
Medicare jurisdiction: DME regional carrier.

A4222 Supplies for external drug infusion pump, per cassette or bag (list drug separately)
Medicare jurisdiction: DME regional carrier.

☑ A4230 Infusion set for external insulin pump, nonneedle cannula type
Covered by some commercial payers as ongoing supply to preauthorized pump. Medicare jurisdiction: DME regional carrier.
MED: CIM 60-14

☑ A4231 Infusion set for external insulin pump, needle type
Covered by some commercial payers as ongoing supply to preauthorized pump. Medicare jurisdiction: DME regional carrier.
MED: CIM 60-14

E ☑ A4232 Syringe with needle for external insulin pump, sterile, 3cc
Covered by some commercial payers as ongoing supply to preauthorized pump. Medicare jurisdiction: DME regional carrier.
MED: CIM 60-14

☑ A4244 Alcohol or peroxide, per pint
Medicare jurisdiction: DME regional carrier.

☑ A4245 Alcohol wipes, per box
Medicare jurisdiction: DME regional carrier.

☑ A4246 Betadine or pHisoHex solution, per pint
Medicare jurisdiction: DME regional carrier.

☑ A4247 Betadine or iodine swabs/wipes, per box
Medicare jurisdiction: DME regional carrier.

● N ☑ A4248 Chlorhexidine containing antiseptic, 1 ml

E ☑ A4250 Urine test or reagent strips or tablets (100 tablets or strips)
Medicare jurisdiction: DME regional carrier.
MED: MCM 2100

Note: Codes A4253-A4256 are for home blood glucose monitors. For supplies for End Stage Renal Disease (ESRD)/dialysis, see codes A4651-A4929 (Some codes in this range do not specify ESRD/dialysis, verify coverage with your carrier). For DME items for ESRD, see codes E1500-E1699.

☑ A4253 Blood glucose test or reagent strips for home blood glucose monitor, per 50 strips
Medicare covers glucose strips for diabetic patients using home glucose monitoring devices prescribed by their physicians. Medicare jurisdiction: DME regional carrier.
MED: CIM 60-11

☑ A4254 Replacement battery, any type, for use with medically necessary home blood glucose monitor owned by patient, each
Medicare covers glucose strips for diabetic patients using home glucose monitoring devices prescribed by their physicians. Medicare jurisdiction: DME regional carrier.
MED: CIM 60-11

| Special Coverage Instructions | Noncovered by Medicare | Carrier Discretion | ☑ Quantity Alert | ● New Code | ▲ Revised Code |

2 — A Codes   M Maternity   A Adult   P Pediatrics   A-X APC Status Indicator   *2004 HCPCS*

☑ **A4255** Platforms for home blood glucose monitor, 50 per box
Some Medicare carriers cover monitor platforms for diabetic patients using home glucose monitoring devices prescribed by their physicians. Medicare jurisdiction: DME regional carrier. Some commercial payers also provide this coverage to non-insulin dependent diabetics.
MED: CIM 60-11

A4256 Normal, low, and high calibrator solution/chips
Some Medicare carriers cover calibration solutions or chips for diabetic patients using home glucose monitoring devices prescribed by their physicians. Medicare jurisdiction: DME regional carrier. Some commercial payers also provide this coverage to non-insulin dependent diabetics.
MED: CIM 60-11

☑ **A4257** Replacement lens shield cartridge for use with laser skin piercing device, each

☑ **A4258** Spring-powered device for lancet, each
Some Medicare carriers cover lancing devices for diabetic patients using home glucose monitoring devices prescribed by their physicians. Medicare jurisdiction: DME regional carrier. Some commercial payers also provide this coverage to non-insulin dependent diabetics.
MED: CIM 60-11

☑ **A4259** Lancets, per box of 100
Medicare covers lancets for diabetic patients using home glucose monitoring devices prescribed by their physicians. Medicare jurisdiction: DME regional carrier. Some commercial payers also provide this coverage to non-insulin dependent diabetics.
MED: CIM 60-11

A4260 Levonorgestrel (contraceptive) implants system, including implants and supplies ♀
Covered by some commercial payers. Always report concurrent to the implant procedure. Use this code for Norplant.
MED: Medicare Statute: 1862a1A

A4261 Cervical cap for contraceptive use ♀
MED: Medicare Statute: 1862a1

N ☑ **A4262** Temporary, absorbable lacrimal duct implant, each
Always report concurrent to the implant procedure.

N ☑ **A4263** Permanent, long-term, nondissolvable lacrimal duct implant, each
Always report concurrent to the implant procedure.
MED: MCM 15030

A ☑ **A4265** Paraffin, per pound
Medicare jurisdiction: DME regional carrier.
MED: CIM 60-9

A4266 Diaphragm for contraceptive use ♀

☑ **A4267** Contraceptive supply, condom, male, each ♂

☑ **A4268** Contraceptive supply, condom, female, each ♀

☑ **A4269** Contraceptive supply, spermicide (e.g., foam, gel), each A

☑ **A4270** Disposable endoscope sheath, each

A4280 Adhesive skin support attachment for use with external breast prosthesis, each A ♀

A4281 Tubing for breast pump, replacement M ♀

A4282 Adapter for breast pump, replacement M ♀

A4283 Cap for breast pump bottle, replacement M ♀

A4284 Breast shield and splash protector for use with breast pump, replacement M ♀

A4285 Polycarbonate bottle for use with breast pump, replacement M ♀

A4286 Locking ring for breast pump, replacement M ♀

E ☑ **A4290** Sacral nerve stimulation test lead, each

VASCULAR CATHETERS

N **A4300** Implantable access catheter, (e.g., venous, arterial, epidural subarachnoid, or peritoneal, etc.) external access
MED: MCM 2130

N **A4301** Implantable access total catheter, port/reservoir (e.g., venous, arterial, epidural, subarachnoid, peritoneal, etc.)

A4305 Disposable drug delivery system, flow rate of 50 ml or greater per hour

A4306 Disposable drug delivery system, flow rate of 5 ml or less per hour

INCONTINENCE APPLIANCES AND CARE SUPPLIES
Covered by Medicare when the medical record indicates incontinence is permanent, or of long and indefinite duration.

Medicare claims fall under the jurisdiction of the DME regional carrier for a permanent condition, and under the local carrier when provided in the physician's office for a temporary condition.

A4310 Insertion tray without drainage bag and without catheter (accessories only)
MED: MCM 2130

A4311 Insertion tray without drainage bag with indwelling catheter, Foley type, two-way latex with coating (Teflon, silicone, silicone elastomer or hydrophilic, etc.)
MED: MCM 2130

A4312 Insertion tray without drainage bag with indwelling catheter, Foley type, two-way, all silicone
MED: MCM 2130

A4313 Insertion tray without drainage bag with indwelling catheter, Foley type, three-way, for continuous irrigation
MED: MCM 2130

A4314 Insertion tray with drainage bag with indwelling catheter, Foley type, two-way latex with coating (Teflon, silicone, silicone elastomer or hydrophilic, etc.)
MED: MCM 2130

A4315 Insertion tray with drainage bag with indwelling catheter, Foley type, two-way, all silicone
MED: MCM 2130

A4316 Insertion tray with drainage bag with indwelling catheter, Foley type, three-way, for continuous irrigation
MED: MCM 2130

~~A4319~~ ~~Sterile water irrigation solution, 1000 ml~~

A4320 Irrigation tray with bulb or piston syringe, any purpose
MED: MCM 2130

A4321 Therapeutic agent for urinary catheter irrigation
MED: MCM 2130

☑ **A4322** Irrigation syringe, bulb or piston, each
MED: MCM 2130

Medical and Surgical Supplies

A4323 — A4372

~~A4323 Sterile saline irrigation solution, 1000 ml.~~

☑ **A4324** Male external catheter, with adhesive coating, each ♂
MED: MCM 2130

☑ **A4325** Male external catheter, with adhesive strip, each ♂
MED: MCM 2130

▲ ☑ **A4326** Male external catheter specialty type with integral collection chamber, each ♂
MED: MCM 2130

☑ **A4327** Female external urinary collection device; metal cup, each ♀
MED: MCM 2130

☑ **A4328** Female external urinary collection device; pouch, each ♀
MED: MCM 2130

☑ **A4330** Perianal fecal collection pouch with adhesive, each
MED: MCM 2130

☑ **A4331** Extension drainage tubing, any type, any length, with connector/adaptor, for use with urinary leg bag or urostomy pouch, each
MED: MCM 2130

☑ **A4332** Lubricant, individual sterile packet, for insertion of urinary catheter, each
MED: MCM 2130

☑ **A4333** Urinary catheter anchoring device, adhesive skin attachment, each
MED: MCM 2130

☑ **A4334** Urinary catheter anchoring device, leg strap, each
MED: MCM 2130

A4335 Incontinence supply; miscellaneous
MED: MCM 2130

☑ **A4338** Indwelling catheter; Foley type, two-way latex with coating (Teflon, silicone, silicone elastomer, or hydrophilic, etc.), each
MED: MCM 2130

☑ **A4340** Indwelling catheter; specialty type, (e.g., coudé, mushroom, wing, etc.), each
MED: MCM 2130

☑ **A4344** Indwelling catheter, Foley type, two-way, all silicone, each
MED: MCM 2130

☑ **A4346** Indwelling catheter; Foley type, three-way for continuous irrigation, each
MED: MCM 2130

☑ **A4347** Male external catheter with or without adhesive, with or without anti-reflux device; per dozen ♂
MED: MCM 2130

A4348 Male external catheter with integral collection compartment, extended wear, each (e.g., 2 per month) ♂
MED: MCM 2130

☑ **A4351** Intermittent urinary catheter; straight tip, with or without coating (Teflon, silicone, silicone elastomer, or hydrophilic, etc.), each
MED: MCM 2130

☑ **A4352** Intermittent urinary catheter; coude (curved) tip, with or without coating (Teflon, silicone, silicone elastomeric, or hydrophilic, etc.), each
MED: MCM 2130

A4353 Intermittent urinary catheter, with insertion supplies
MED: MCM 2130

A4354 Insertion tray with drainage bag but without catheter
MED: MCM 2130

☑ **A4355** Irrigation tubing set for continuous bladder irrigation through a three-way indwelling Foley catheter, each
MED: MCM 2130

EXTERNAL URINARY SUPPLIES

Medicare claims fall under the jurisdiction of the DME regional carrier for a permanent condition, and under the local carrier when provided in the physician's office for a temporary condition.

☑ **A4356** External urethral clamp or compression device (not to be used for catheter clamp), each
MED: MCM 2130

☑ **A4357** Bedside drainage bag, day or night, with or without anti-reflux device, with or without tube, each
MED: MCM 2130

☑ **A4358** Urinary drainage bag, leg or abdomen, vinyl, with or without tube, with straps, each
MED: MCM 2130

☑ **A4359** Urinary suspensory without leg bag, each
MED: MCM 2130

OSTOMY SUPPLIES

Medicare claims fall under the jurisdiction of the DME regional carrier for a permanent condition, and under the local carrier when provided in the physician's office for a temporary condition.

☑ **A4361** Ostomy faceplate, each
MED: MCM 2130

☑ **A4362** Skin barrier; solid, four by four or equivalent; each
MED: MCM 2130

☑ **A4364** Adhesive, liquid, or equal, any type, per ounce
MED: MCM 2130

☑ **A4365** Adhesive remover wipes, any type, per 50
MED: MCM 2130

● Ⓐ ☑ **A4366** Ostomy vent, any type, each

☑ **A4367** Ostomy belt, each
MED: MCM 2130A

Ⓔ ☑ **A4368** Ostomy filter, any type, each

Ⓐ ☑ **A4369** Ostomy skin barrier, liquid (spray, brush, etc), per oz
MED: MCM 2130

☑ **A4371** Ostomy skin barrier, powder, per oz
MED: MCM 2130

☑ **A4372** Ostomy skin barrier, solid 4x4 or equivalent, with built-in convexity, each
MED: MCM 2130

| Special Coverage Instructions | Noncovered by Medicare | Carrier Discretion | ☑ Quantity Alert | ● New Code | ▲ Revised Code |

☑ **A4373** Ostomy skin barrier, with flange (solid, flexible or accordion), with built-in convexity, any size, each
MED: MCM 2130

☑ **A4375** Ostomy pouch, drainable, with faceplate attached, plastic, each
MED: MCM 2130

☑ **A4376** Ostomy pouch, drainable, with faceplate attached, rubber, each
MED: MCM 2130

☑ **A4377** Ostomy pouch, drainable, for use on faceplate, plastic, each
MED: MCM 2130

☑ **A4378** Ostomy pouch, drainable, for use on faceplate, rubber, each
MED: MCM 2130

☑ **A4379** Ostomy pouch, urinary, with faceplate attached, plastic, each
MED: MCM 2130

☑ **A4380** Ostomy pouch, urinary, with faceplate attached, rubber, each
MED: MCM 2130

☑ **A4381** Ostomy pouch, urinary, for use on faceplate, plastic, each
MED: MCM 2130

☑ **A4382** Ostomy pouch, urinary, for use on faceplate, heavy plastic, each
MED: MCM 2130

☑ **A4383** Ostomy pouch, urinary, for use on faceplate, rubber, each
MED: MCM 2130

☑ **A4384** Ostomy faceplate equivalent, silicone ring, each
MED: MCM 2130

☑ **A4385** Ostomy skin barrier, solid 4x4 or equivalent, extended wear, without built-in convexity, each
MED: MCM 2130

☑ **A4387** Ostomy pouch, closed, with barrier attached, with built-in convexity (one piece), each
MED: MCM 2130

☑ **A4388** Ostomy pouch, drainable, with extended wear barrier attached, (one piece), each
MED: MCM 2130

☑ **A4389** Ostomy pouch, drainable, with barrier attached, with built-in convexity (one piece), each
MED: MCM 2130

☑ **A4390** Ostomy pouch, drainable, with extended wear barrier attached, with built-in convexity (1 piece), each
MED: MCM 2130

☑ **A4391** Ostomy pouch, urinary, with extended wear barrier attached (1 piece), each
MED: MCM 2130

☑ **A4392** Ostomy pouch, urinary, with standard wear barrier attached, with built-in convexity (1 piece), each
MED: MCM 2130

☑ **A4393** Ostomy pouch, urinary, with extended wear barrier attached, with built-in convexity (1 piece), each
MED: MCM 2130

☑ **A4394** Ostomy deodorant for use in ostomy pouch, liquid, per fluid ounce
MED: MCM 2130

☑ **A4395** Ostomy deodorant for use in ostomy pouch, solid, per tablet
MED: MCM 2130

A4396 Ostomy belt with peristomal hernia support
MED: MCM 2130

☑ **A4397** Irrigation supply; sleeve, each
MED: MCM 2130

☑ **A4398** Ostomy irrigation supply; bag, each
MED: MCM 2130

A4399 Ostomy irrigation supply; cone/catheter, including brush
MED: MCM 2130

A4400 Ostomy irrigation set
MED: MCM 2130

☑ **A4402** Lubricant, per ounce
MED: MCM 2130

☑ **A4404** Ostomy ring, each
MED: MCM 2130

☑ **A4405** Ostomy skin barrier, non-pectin based, paste, per ounce
MED: MCM 2130

☑ **A4406** Ostomy skin barrier, pectin-based, paste, per ounce
MED: MCM 2130

☑ **A4407** Ostomy skin barrier, with flange (solid, flexible, or accordion), extended wear, with built-in convexity, 4 x 4 inches or smaller, each
MED: MCM 2130

☑ **A4408** Ostomy skin barrier, with flange (solid, flexible or accordion), extended wear, with built-in convexity, larger than 4 x 4 inches, each
MED: MCM 2130

☑ **A4409** Ostomy skin barrier, with flange (solid, flexible or accordion), extended wear, without built-in convexity, 4 x 4 inches or smaller, each
MED: MCM 2130

☑ **A4410** Ostomy skin barrier, with flange (solid, flexible or accordion), extended wear, without built-in convexity, larger than 4 x 4 inches, each
MED: MCM 2130

☑ **A4413** Ostomy pouch, drainable, high output, for use on a barrier with flange (2 piece system), with filter, each
MED: MCM 2130

☑ **A4414** Ostomy skin barrier, with flange (solid, flexible or accordion), without built-in convexity, 4 x 4 inches or smaller, each
MED: MCM 2130

☑ **A4415** Ostomy skin barrier, with flange (solid, flexible or accordion), without built-in convexity, larger than 4x4 inches, each
MED: MCM 2130

● ☑ **A4416** Ostomy pouch, closed, with barrier attached, with filter (one piece), each

● ☑ **A4417** Ostomy pouch, closed, with barrier attached, with built-in convexity, with filter (one piece), each

● ☑ **A4418** Ostomy pouch, closed; without barrier attached, with filter (one piece), each

● ☑ **A4419** Ostomy pouch, closed; for use on barrier with non-locking flange, with filter (two piece), each

● ☑ **A4420** Ostomy pouch, closed; for use on barrier with locking flange (two piece), each

Ⓐ **A4421** Ostomy supply; miscellaneous
Determine if an alternative HCPCS Level II code better describes the supply being reported. This code should be used only if a more specific code is unavailable.
MED: MCM 2130

Ⓐ **A4422** Ostomy absorbent material (sheet/pad/crystal packet) for use in ostomy pouch to thicken liquid stomal output, each
MED: MCM 2130

● ☑ **A4423** Ostomy pouch, closed; for use on barrier with locking flange, with filter (two piece), each

● ☑ **A4424** Ostomy pouch, drainable, with barrier attached, with filter (one piece), each

● ☑ **A4425** Ostomy pouch, drainable; for use on barrier with non-locking flange, with filter (two piece system), each

● ☑ **A4426** Ostomy pouch, drainable; for use on barrier with locking flange (two piece system), each

● ☑ **A4427** Ostomy pouch, drainable; for use on barrier with locking flange, with filter (two piece system), each

● ☑ **A4428** Ostomy pouch, urinary, with extended wear barrier attached, with faucet-type tap with valve (one piece), each

● ☑ **A4429** Ostomy pouch, urinary, with barrier attached, with built-in convexity, with faucet-type tap with valve (one piece), each

● ☑ **A4430** Ostomy pouch, urinary, with extended wear barrier attached, with built-in convexity, with faucet-type tap with valve (one piece), each

● ☑ **A4431** Ostomy pouch, urinary; with barrier attached, with faucet-type tap with valve (one piece), each

● ☑ **A4432** Ostomy pouch, urinary; for use on barrier with non-locking flange, with faucet-type tap with valve (two piece), each

● ☑ **A4433** Ostomy pouch, urinary; for use on barrier with locking flange (two piece), each

● ☑ **A4434** Ostomy pouch, urinary; for use on barrier with locking flange, with faucet-type tap with valve (two piece), each

ADDITIONAL MISCELLANEOUS SUPPLIES

Ⓐ ☑ **A4450** Tape, non-waterproof, per 18 square inches
See also code A4452.
MED: MCM 2130

Ⓐ ☑ **A4452** Tape, waterproof, per 18 square inches
See also code A4450.
MED: MCM 2130

Ⓐ ☑ **A4455** Adhesive remover or solvent (for tape, cement or other adhesive), per ounce
MED: MCM 2130

Ⓔ **A4458** Enema bag with tubing, reusable

Ⓐ **A4462** Abdominal dressing holder, each
Dressings applied by a physician are included as part of the professional service. Surgical dressings obtained by the patient to perform homecare as prescribed by the physician are covered.
MED: MCM 2079

A4465 Nonelastic binder for extremity
Medicare jurisdiction: DME regional carrier.

A4470 Gravlee jet washer
The Gravlee jet washer is a disposable device used to detect endometrial cancer. It is covered only in patients exhibiting clinical symptoms or signs suggestive of endometrial disease. Medicare jurisdiction: local carrier.
MED: CIM 50-4, MCM 2320

A4480 VABRA aspirator   ♀
The VABRA aspirator is a disposable device used to detect endometrial cancer. It is covered only in patients exhibiting clinical symptoms or signs suggestive of endometrial disease. Medicare jurisdiction: local carrier.
MED: CIM 50-10, MCM 2320

☑ **A4481** Tracheostoma filter, any type, any size, each
MED: MCM 2130

A4483 Moisture exchanger, disposable, for use with invasive mechanical ventilation
Medicare jurisdiction: DME regional carrier.
MED: MCM 2130

☑ **A4490** Surgical stocking above knee length, each
MED: CIM 60-9, MCM 2079, MCM 2100

☑ **A4495** Surgical stocking thigh length, each
MED: CIM 60-9, MCM 2079, MCM 2100

☑ **A4500** Surgical stocking below knee length, each
MED: CIM 60-9, MCM 2079, MCM 2100

☑ **A4510** Surgical stocking full-length, each
MED: CIM 60-9, MCM 2079, MCM 2100

☑ **A4521** Adult-sized incontinence product, diaper, small size, each Ⓐ
MED: CIM 60-9

☑ **A4522** Adult-sized incontinence product, diaper, medium size, each Ⓐ
MED: CIM 60-9

☑ **A4523** Adult-sized incontinence product, diaper, large size, each Ⓐ
MED: CIM 60-9

☑ **A4524** Adult-sized incontinence product, diaper, extra large size, each Ⓐ
MED: CIM 60-9

☑ **A4525** Adult-sized incontinence product, brief, small size, each Ⓐ
MED: CIM 60-9

☑ **A4526** Adult-sized incontinence product, brief, medium size, each Ⓐ
MED: CIM 60-9

☑ **A4527** Adult-sized incontinence product, brief, large size, each
MED: CIM 60-9

☑ **A4528** Adult-sized incontinence product, brief, extra-large size, each
MED: CIM 60-9

☑ **A4529** Child-sized incontinence product, diaper, small/medium size, each
MED: CIM 60-9

☑ **A4530** Child-sized incontinence product, diaper, large size, each
MED: CIM 60-9

☑ **A4531** Child-sized incontinence product, brief, small/medium size, each
MED: CIM 60-9

☑ **A4532** Child-sized incontinence product, brief, large size, each
MED: CIM 60-9

☑ **A4533** Youth-sized incontinence product, diaper, each
MED: CIM 60-9

☑ **A4534** Youth-sized incontinence product, brief, each
MED: CIM 60-9

☑ **A4535** Disposable liner/shield for incontinence, each
See also codes A4537; A4554.
MED: CIM 60-9

☑ **A4536** Protective underwear, washable, any size, each
See also codes A4525-A4528; A45231-A4554.
MED: CIM 60-9

☑ **A4537** Under pad, reusable/washable, any size, each
For disposable under pads all sizes (e.g., Chux's) see A4554.
MED: CIM 60-9

▲ **A4538** Diaper, reusable, provided by a diaper service, each diaper
MED: CIM 60-9

E **A4550** Surgical trays
Medicare jurisdiction: local carrier.
MED: MCM 15030

E ☑ **A4554** Disposable underpads, all sizes (e.g., Chux's)
Medicare jurisdiction: DME regional carrier.
MED: CIM 60-9, MCM 2130

☑ **A4556** Electrodes (e.g., Apnea monitor), per pair

☑ **A4557** Lead wires (e.g., Apnea monitor), per pair

A4558 Conductive paste or gel

N **A4561** Pessary, rubber, any type   A ♀
Medicare jurisdiction: DME regional carrier.

N **A4562** Pessary, non rubber, any type   A ♀
Medicare jurisdiction: DME regional carrier.

A **A4565** Slings
Dressings applied by a physician are included as part of the professional service. Surgical dressings obtained by the patient to perform homecare as prescribed by the physician are covered. Medicare jurisdiction: DME regional carrier.

N **A4570** Splint
Dressings applied by a physician are included as part of the professional service. Medicare jurisdiction: DME regional carrier.
MED: MCM 2079

E **A4575** Topical hyperbaric oxygen chamber, disposable
Medicare jurisdiction: DME regional carrier.
MED: CIM 35-10

N **A4580** Cast supplies (e.g., plaster)
Dressings applied by a physician are included as part of the professional service. Medicare jurisdiction: local carrier.
MED: MCM 2079

N **A4590** Special casting material (e.g., fiberglass)
Dressings applied by a physician are included as part of the professional service. Medicare jurisdiction: local carrier.
MED: MCM 2079

A **A4595** Electrical stimulator supplies, 2 lead, per month, (e.g. tens, nmes)
MED: CIM 45-25

A **A4606** Oxygen probe for use with oximeter device, replacement

A ☑ **A4608** Transtracheal oxygen catheter, each
Medicare jurisdiction: DME regional carrier.

A ☑ **A4609** Tracheal suction catheter, closed system, for less than 72 hours of use, each

A ☑ **A4610** Tracheal suction catheter, closed system, for 72 or more hours of use, each

SUPPLIES FOR OXYGEN AND RELATED RESPIRATORY EQUIPMENT

A4611 Battery, heavy duty; replacement for patient-owned ventilator
Medicare jurisdiction: DME regional carrier.

A4612 Battery cables; replacement for patient-owned ventilator
Medicare jurisdiction: DME regional carrier.

A4613 Battery charger; replacement for patient-owned ventilator
Medicare jurisdiction: DME regional carrier.

A4614 Peak expiratory flow rate meter, hand held

A4615 Cannula, nasal
MED: CIM 60-4, MCM 3312

☑ **A4616** Tubing (oxygen), per foot
MED: CIM 60-4, MCM 3312

A4617 Mouthpiece
MED: CIM 60-4, MCM 3312

A4618 Breathing circuits
MED: CIM 60-4, MCM 3312

A4619 Face tent
MED: CIM 60-4, MCM 3312

A4620 Variable concentration mask
MED: CIM 60-4, MCM 3312

~~A4621~~ ~~Tracheostomy mask or collar~~

~~A4622~~ ~~Tracheostomy or laryngectomy tube~~

▲ **A4623** Tracheostomy, inner cannula
MED: CIM 65-16, MCM 2130

☑ **A4624** Tracheal suction catheter, any type other than closed system, each

A4625 Tracheostomy care kit for new tracheostomy
MED: MCM 2130

☑ **A4626** Tracheostomy cleaning brush, each
MED: MCM 2130

A4627 Spacer, bag or reservoir, with or without mask, for use with metered dose inhaler
MED: MCM 2100

☑ **A4628** Oropharyngeal suction catheter, each

A4629 Tracheostomy care kit for established tracheostomy
MED: MCM 2130

SUPPLIES FOR OTHER DURABLE MEDICAL EQUIPMENT

☑ **A4630** Replacement batteries for medically necessary transcutaneous electrical nerve stimulator (TENS) owned by patient
Medicare jurisdiction: DME regional carrier.
MED: CIM 65-8

A4631 ~~Replacement, batteries for medically necessary electronic wheel chair owned by patient~~
See code E2360.

E **A4632** Replacement battery for external infusion pump, any type, each

A **A4633** Replacement bulb/lamp for ultraviolet light therapy system, each

A **A4634** Replacement bulb for therapeutic light box, tabletop model

☑ **A4635** Underarm pad, crutch, replacement, each
Medicare jurisdiction: DME regional carrier.
MED: CIM 60-9

☑ **A4636** Replacement, handgrip, cane, crutch, or walker, each
Medicare jurisdiction: DME regional carrier.
MED: CIM 60-9

☑ **A4637** Replacement, tip, cane, crutch, walker, each
Medicare jurisdiction: DME regional carrier.
MED: CIM 60-9

● ☒ ☑ **A4638** Replacement battery for patient-owned ear pulse generator, each

A **A4639** Replacement pad for infrared heating pad system, each

A **A4640** Replacement pad for use with medically necessary alternating pressure pad owned by patient
Medicare jurisdiction: DME regional carrier.
MED: CIM 60-9, MCM 4107.6

SUPPLIES FOR RADIOLOGIC PROCEDURES

N **A4641** Supply of radiopharmaceutical diagnostic imaging agent, not otherwise classified
Medicare jurisdiction: local carrier.
MED: MCM 15030

N ☑ **A4642** Supply of satumomab pendetide, radiopharmaceutical diagnostic imaging agent, per dose
Medicare jurisdiction: local carrier.
MED: MCM 15030

N **A4643** Supply of additional high dose contrast material(s) during magnetic resonance imaging, e.g., gadoteridol injection
Medicare jurisdiction: local carrier.
MED: MCM 15030

A4644 ~~Supply of low osmolar contrast material (100-199 mgs of iodine)~~

A4645 ~~Supply of low osmolar contrast material (200-299 mgs of iodine)~~

A4646 ~~Supply of low osmolar contrast material (300-399 mgs of iodine)~~

N **A4647** Supply of paramagnetic contrast material (e.g., gadolinium)
Medicare jurisdiction: local carrier.
MED: MCM 15022, MCM 15030

A **A4649** Surgical supply; miscellaneous
Determine if an alternative HCPCS Level II code better describes the supply being reported. This code should be used only if a more specific code is unavailable. Medicare jurisdiction: local carrier.

NOTE: Some supplies for ESRD/dialysis appear in range A4651-A4929. For glucose monitor/supplies see A4253-A4259. For DME items for ESRD see codes E1500-E1699 (Many codes found in this range no longer specify "ESRD/dialysis, verify coverage with your carrier").

☑ **A4651** Calibrated microcapillary tube, each
Not covered by or valid for Medicare
MED: MCM 4270

A4652 Microcapillary tube sealant
MED: MCM 4270

A ☑ **A4653** Peritoneal dialysis catheter anchoring device, belt, each

☑ **A4656** Needle, any size, each
MED: MCM 4270

☑ **A4657** Syringe, with or without needle, each
MED: MCM 4270

A4660 Sphygmomanometer/blood pressure apparatus with cuff and stethoscope
Medicare jurisdiction: DME regional carrier.
MED: MCM 4270

A4663 Blood pressure cuff only
Medicare jurisdiction: DME regional carrier.
MED: MCM 4270

A4670 Automatic blood pressure monitor
Medicare jurisdiction: DME regional carrier.
MED: CIM 50-42, MCM 4270

● E ☑ **A4671** Disposable cycler set used with cycler dialysis machine, each
MED: MCM 4270

● E ☑ **A4672** Drainage extension line, sterile, for dialysis, each
MED: MCM 4270

● E **A4673** Extension line with easy lock connectors, used with dialysis
MED: MCM 4270

● E ☑ **A4674** Chemicals/antiseptics solution used to clean/sterilize dialysis equipment, per 8 oz
MED: MCM 4270

☑ **A4680** Activated carbon filter for hemodialysis, each
Medicare jurisdiction: DME regional carrier.
MED: CIM 55-1, MCM 4270

☑ **A4690** Dialyzer (artificial kidneys), all types, all sizes, for hemodialysis, each
Medicare jurisdiction: DME regional carrier.
MED: MCM 4270

| Special Coverage Instructions | Noncovered by Medicare | Carrier Discretion | ☑ Quantity Alert | ● New Code | ▲ Revised Code |

8 — A Codes   M Maternity   A Adult   P Pediatrics   A-X APC Status Indicator   *2004 HCPCS*

☑ **A4706** Bicarbonate concentrate, solution, for hemodialysis, per gallon
MED: MCM 4270

☑ **A4707** Bicarbonate concentrate, powder, for hemodialysis, per packet
MED: MCM 4270

☑ **A4708** Acetate concentrate solution, for hemodialysis, per gallon
MED: MCM 4270

☑ **A4709** Acid concentrate, solution, for hemodialysis, per gallon
MED: MCM 4270

~~**A4712** Water, sterile, for injection, per 10 ml~~

☑ **A4714** Treated water (deionized, distilled, or reverse osmosis) for peritoneal dialysis, per gallon
Medicare jurisdiction: DME regional carrier.
MED: CIM 55-1, MCM 4270

A4719 Y set tubing for peritoneal dialysis
MED: MCM 4270

☑ **A4720** Dialysate solution, any concentration of dextrose, fluid volume greater than 249 cc, but less than or equal to 999 cc, for peritoneal dialysis
MED: MCM 4270

☑ **A4721** Dialysate solution, any concentration of dextrose, fluid volume greater than 999 cc, but less than or equal to 1999 cc, for peritoneal dialysis
MED: MCM 4270

☑ **A4722** Dialysate solution, any concentration of dextrose, fluid volume greater than 1999 cc, but less than or equal to 2999 cc, for peritoneal dialysis
MED: MCM 4270

☑ **A4723** Dialysate solution, any concentration of dextrose, fluid volume greater than 2999 cc, but less than or equal to 3999 cc, for peritoneal dialysis
MED: MCM 4270

☑ **A4724** Dialysate solution, any concentration of dextrose, fluid volume greater than 3999 cc, but less than or equal to 4999 cc, for peritoneal dialysis
MED: MCM 4270

☑ **A4725** Dialysate solution, any concentration of dextrose, fluid volume greater than 4999 cc, but less than or equal to 5999 cc, for peritoneal dialysis
MED: MCM 4270

☑ **A4726** Dialysate solution, any concentration of dextrose, fluid volume greater than 5999 cc
MED: MCM 4270

● ☑ **A4728** Dialysate solution, non-dextrose containing, 500 ml

☑ **A4730** Fistula cannulation set for hemodialysis, each
Medicare jurisdiction: DME regional carrier.
MED: MCM 4270

☑ **A4736** Topical anesthetic, for dialysis, per gm
MED: MCM 4270

☑ **A4737** Injectable anesthetic, for dialysis, per 10 ml
MED: MCM 4270

☑ **A4740** Shunt accessory, for hemodialysis, any type
Medicare jurisdiction: DME regional carrier.
MED: MCM 4270

☑ **A4750** Blood tubing, arterial or venous, for hemodialysis, each
Medicare jurisdiction: DME regional carrier.
MED: MCM 4270

☑ **A4755** Blood tubing, arterial and venous combined, for hemodialysis, each
Medicare jurisdiction: DME regional carrier.
MED: MCM 4270

☑ **A4760** Dialysate solution test kit, for peritoneal dialysis, any type, each
Medicare jurisdiction: DME regional carrier.
MED: MCM 4270

☑ **A4765** Dialysate concentrate, powder, additive for peritoneal dialysis, per packet
Medicare jurisdiction: DME regional carrier.
MED: MCM 4270

☑ **A4766** Dialysate concentrate, solution, additive for peritoneal dialysis, per 10 ml
MED: MCM 4270

☑ **A4770** Blood collection tube, vacuum, for dialysis, per 50
Medicare jurisdiction: DME regional carrier.
MED: MCM 4270

☑ **A4771** Serum clotting time tube, for dialysis, per 50
Medicare jurisdiction: DME regional carrier.
MED: MCM 4270

☑ **A4772** Blood glucose test strips, for dialysis, per 50
Medicare jurisdiction: DME regional carrier.
MED: MCM 4270

☑ **A4773** Occult blood test strips, for dialysis, per 50
Medicare jurisdiction: DME regional carrier.
MED: MCM 4270

☑ **A4774** Ammonia test strips, for dialysis, per 50
Medicare jurisdiction: DME regional carrier.
MED: MCM 4270

☑ **A4802** Protamine sulfate, for hemodialysis, per 50 mg
MED: MCM 4270

☑ **A4860** Disposable catheter tips for peritoneal dialysis, per 10
Medicare jurisdiction: DME regional carrier.
MED: MCM 4270

☑ **A4870** Plumbing and/or electrical work for home hemodialysis equipment
Medicare jurisdiction: DME regional carrier.
MED: MCM 4270

☑ **A4890** Contracts, repair and maintenance, for hemodialysis equipment
Medicare jurisdiction: DME regional carrier.
MED: MCM 2100.4

☑ **A4911** Drain bag/bottle, for dialysis, each

☑ **A4913** Miscellaneous dialysis supplies, not otherwise specified
Pertinent documentation to evaluate medical appropriateness should be included when this code is reported. Determine if an alternative HCPCS Level II code better describes the supplies being reported. This code should be used only if a more specific code is unavailable. Medicare jurisdiction: DME regional carrier.

Medical and Surgical Supplies

A4918 — A5503

☑ A4918 Venous pressure clamp, for hemodialysis, each
Medicare jurisdiction: DME regional carrier.

☑ A4927 Gloves, non-sterile, per 100
Medicare jurisdiction: DME regional carrier.

☑ A4928 Surgical mask, per 20
For ESRD see also codes A4650-A4999

A4929 Tourniquet for dialysis, each

Ⓐ A4930 Gloves, sterile, per pair

Ⓐ A4931 Oral thermometer, reusable, any type, each

Ⓔ A4932 Rectal thermometer, reusable, any type, each

ADDITIONAL OSTOMY SUPPLIES
Medicare claims fall under the jurisdiction of the DME regional carrier, unless otherwise noted.

☑ A5051 Ostomy pouch, closed; with barrier attached (one piece), each
MED: MCM 2130

☑ A5052 Ostomy pouch, closed; without barrier attached (one piece), each
MED: MCM 2130

☑ A5053 Ostomy pouch, closed; for use on faceplate, each
MED: MCM 2130

☑ A5054 Ostomy pouch, closed; for use on barrier with flange (two piece), each
MED: MCM 2130

A5055 Stoma cap
MED: MCM 2130

Ⓔ ☑ A5061 Ostomy pouch, drainable; with barrier attached, (one piece), each
MED: MCM 2130

☑ A5062 Ostomy pouch, drainable; without barrier attached (one piece), each
MED: MCM 2130

☑ A5063 Ostomy pouch, drainable; for use on barrier with flange (two piece system), each
MED: MCM 2130

☑ A5071 Ostomy pouch, urinary; with barrier attached (one piece), each
MED: MCM 2130

☑ A5072 Ostomy pouch, urinary; without barrier attached (one piece), each
MED: MCM 2130

☑ A5073 Ostomy pouch, urinary; for use on barrier with flange (two piece), each
MED: MCM 2130

A5081 Continent device; plug for continent stoma
MED: MCM 2130

A5082 Continent device; catheter for continent stoma
MED: MCM 2130

A5093 Ostomy accessory; convex insert
Medicare jurisdiction: local carrier.
MED: MCM 2130

ADDITIONAL INCONTINENCE APPLIANCES/SUPPLIES
Medicare claims fall under the jurisdiction of the DME regional carrier, unless otherwise noted.

☑ A5102 Bedside drainage bottle, with or without tubing, rigid or expandable, each
MED: MCM 2130

A5105 Urinary suspensory; with leg bag, with or without tube
MED: MCM 2130

A5112 Urinary leg bag; latex
MED: MCM 2130

☑ A5113 Leg strap; latex, replacement only, per set
MED: MCM 2130

☑ A5114 Leg strap; foam or fabric, replacement only, per set
MED: MCM 2130

SUPPLIES FOR EITHER INCONTINENCE OR OSTOMY APPLIANCES
For additional skin barrier codes see new codes A4405-A4415.

☑ A5119 Skin barrier; wipes, box per 50
MED: MCM 2130

☑ A5121 Skin barrier; solid, 6 x 6 or equivalent, each
MED: MCM 2130

☑ A5122 Skin barrier; solid, 8 x 8 or equivalent, each
MED: MCM 2130

A5126 Adhesive or non-adhesive; disk or foam pad
MED: MCM 2130

☑ A5131 Appliance cleaner, incontinence and ostomy appliances, per 16 oz.
MED: MCM 2130

A5200 Percutaneous catheter/tube anchoring device, adhesive skin attachment
MED: MCM 2130

DIABETIC SHOES, FITTING, AND MODIFICATIONS
According to Medicare, documentation from the prescribing physician must certify the diabetic patient has one of the following conditions: peripheral neuropathy with evidence of callus formation; history of preulcerative calluses; history of ulceration; foot deformity; previous amputation; or poor circulation. The footwear must be fitted and furnished by a podiatrist, pedorthist, orthotist, or prosthetist.

Medicare jurisdiction: DME regional carrier.

☑ A5500 For diabetics only, fitting (including follow-up) custom preparation and supply of off-the-shelf depth-inlay shoe manufactured to accommodate multi-density insert(s), per shoe
MED: MCM 2134

☑ A5501 For diabetics only, fitting (including follow-up) custom preparation and supply of shoe molded from cast(s) of patient's foot (custom molded shoe), per shoe
MED: MCM 2134

☑ A5503 For diabetics only, modification (including fitting) of off-the-shelf depth-inlay shoe or custom molded shoe with roller or rigid rocker bottom, per shoe
MED: MCM 2134

| ▨ Special Coverage Instructions | ▨ Noncovered by Medicare | ▨ Carrier Discretion | ☑ Quantity Alert | ● New Code | ▲ Revised Code |

10 — A Codes | Ⓜ Maternity | Ⓐ Adult | Ⓟ Pediatrics | Ⓐ-Ⓧ APC Status Indicator | *2004 HCPCS*

☑ **A5504** For diabetics only, modification (including fitting) of off-the-shelf depth-inlay shoe or custom molded shoe with wedge(s), per shoe
MED: MCM 2134

☑ **A5505** For diabetics only, modification (including fitting) of off-the-shelf depth-inlay shoe or custom molded shoe with metatarsal bar, per shoe
MED: MCM 2134

☑ **A5506** For diabetics only, modification (including fitting) of off-the-shelf depth-inlay shoe or custom molded shoe with off-set heel(s), per shoe
MED: MCM 2134

☑ **A5507** For diabetics only, not otherwise specified modification (including fitting) of off-the-shelf depth-inlay shoe or custom molded shoe, per shoe
MED: MCM 2134

☑ **A5508** For diabetics only, deluxe feature of off-the-shelf depth-inlay shoe or custom-molded shoe, per shoe
MED: MCM 2134

A5509 For diabetics only, direct formed, molded to foot with external heat source (i.e., heat gun) multiple density insert(s), prefabricated, per shoe
MED: MCM 2134

A5510 For diabetics only, direct formed, compression molded to patient's foot without external heat source, multiple-density insert(s) prefabricated, per shoe
MED: MCM 2134

A5511 For diabetics only, custom-molded from model of patient's foot, multiple density insert(s), custom-fabricated, per shoe
MED: MCM 2134

DRESSINGS

Medicare claims for A6021-A6404 fall under the jurisdiction of the local carrier if the supply or accessory is used for an implanted prosthetic device (e.g. pleural catheter) or implanted DME (e.g., infusion pump). Medicare claims for other uses of A6021-A6404 fall under the jurisdiction of the DME regional carrier. The jurisdiction for Medicare claims containing all other codes falls to the DME regional carrier, unless otherwise noted.

E **A6000** Non-contact wound warming wound cover for use with the non-contact wound warming device and warming card
MED: MCM 2303

A ☑ **A6010** Collagen based wound filler, dry form, per gram of collagen
MED: MCM 2079

A ☑ **A6011** Collagen based wound filler, gel/paste, per gram of collagen
MED: MCM 2079

☑ **A6021** Collagen dressing, pad size 16 sq. in. or less, each
MED: MCM 2079

☑ **A6022** Collagen dressing, pad size more than 16 sq. in. but less than or equal to 48 sq in, each
MED: MCM 2079

☑ **A6023** Collagen dressing, pad size more than 48 sq. in., each
MED: MCM 2079

☑ **A6024** Collagen dressing wound filler, per 6 in
MED: MCM 2079

▲ ☑ **A6025** Gel sheet for dermal or epidermal application, (e.g., silicone, hydrogel, other), each

☑ **A6154** Wound pouch, each
MED: MCM 2079

☑ **A6196** Alginate or other fiber gelling dressing, wound cover, pad size 16 sq in or less, each dressing
MED: MCM 2079

☑ **A6197** Alginate or other fiber gelling dressing, wound cover, pad size more than 16 sq in but less than or equal to 48 sq in, each dressing
MED: MCM 2079

☑ **A6198** Alginate or other fiber gelling dressing, wound cover, pad size more than 48 sq in, each dressing
MED: MCM 2079

☑ **A6199** Alginate or other fiber gelling dressing, wound filler, per 6 inches
MED: MCM 2079

☑ **A6200** Composite dressing, pad size 16 sq. in. or less, without adhesive border, each dressing
MED: MCM 2079

☑ **A6201** Composite dressing, pad size more than 16 sq. in. but less than or equal to 48 sq. in., without adhesive border, each dressing
MED: MCM 2079

☑ **A6202** Composite dressing, pad size more than 48 sq. in., without adhesive border, each dressing
MED: MCM 2079

☑ **A6203** Composite dressing, pad size 16 sq. in. or less, with any size adhesive border, each dressing
MED: MCM 2079

☑ **A6204** Composite dressing, pad size more than 16 sq. in. but less than or equal to 48 sq. in., with any size adhesive border, each dressing
MED: MCM 2079

☑ **A6205** Composite dressing, pad size more than 48 sq. in., with any size adhesive border, each dressing
MED: MCM 2079

☑ **A6206** Contact layer, 16 sq. in. or less, each dressing
MED: MCM 2079

☑ **A6207** Contact layer, more than 16 sq. in. but less than or equal to 48 sq. in., each dressing
MED: MCM 2079

☑ **A6208** Contact layer, more than 48 sq. in., each dressing
MED: MCM 2079

☑ **A6209** Foam dressing, wound cover, pad size 16 sq. in. or less, without adhesive border, each dressing
MED: MCM 2079

☑ **A6210** Foam dressing, wound cover, pad size more than 16 sq. in. but less than or equal to 48 sq. in., without adhesive border, each dressing
MED: MCM 2079

☑   A6211   Foam dressing, wound cover, pad size more then 48 sq. in., without adhesive border, each dressing
MED: MCM 2079

☑   A6212   Foam dressing, wound cover, pad size 16 sq. in. or less, with any size adhesive border, each dressing
MED: MCM 2079

☑   A6213   Foam dressing, wound cover, pad size more than 16 sq. in. but less than or equal to 48 sq. in., with any size adhesive border, each dressing
MED: MCM 2079

☑   A6214   Foam dressing, wound cover, pad size more than 48 sq. in., with any size adhesive border, each dressing
MED: MCM 2079

☑   A6215   Foam dressing, wound filler, per gram
MED: MCM 2079

☑   A6216   Gauze, non-impregnated, non-sterile, pad size 16 sq. in. or less, without adhesive border, each dressing
MED: MCM 2079

☑   A6217   Gauze, non-impregnated, non-sterile, pad size more than 16 sq. in. but less than or equal to 48 sq. in., without adhesive border, each dressing
MED: MCM 2079

☑   A6218   Gauze, non-impregnated, non-sterile, pad size more than 48 sq. in., without adhesive border, each dressing
MED: MCM 2079

☑   A6219   Gauze, non-impregnated, pad size 16 sq. in. or less, with any size adhesive border, each dressing
MED: MCM 2079

☑   A6220   Gauze, non-impregnated, pad size more than 16 sq. in. but less than or equal to 48 sq. in., with any size adhesive border, each dressing
MED: MCM 2079

☑   A6221   Gauze, non-impregnated, pad size more than 48 sq. in., with any size adhesive border, each dressing
MED: MCM 2079

☑   A6222   Gauze, impregnated with other than water, normal saline, or hydrogel, pad size 16 sq. in. or less, without adhesive border, each dressing
MED: MCM 2079

☑   A6223   Gauze, impregnated with other than water, normal saline, or hydrogel, pad size more than 16 sq. in. but less than or equal to 48 sq. in., without adhesive border, each dressing
MED: MCM 2079

☑   A6224   Gauze, impregnated with other than water, normal saline, or hydrogel, pad size more than 48 sq. in., without adhesive border, each dressing
MED: MCM 2079

☑   A6228   Gauze, impregnated, water or normal saline, pad size 16 sq. in. or less, without adhesive border, each dressing
MED: MCM 2079

☑   A6229   Gauze, impregnated, water or normal saline, pad size more than 16 sq. in. but less than or equal to 48 sq. in., without adhesive border, each dressing
MED: MCM 2079

☑   A6230   Gauze, impregnated, water or normal saline, pad size more than 48 sq. in., without adhesive border, each dressing
MED: MCM 2079

☑   A6231   Gauze, impregnated, hydrogel, for direct wound contact, pad size 16 sq. in. or less, each dressing
MED: MCM 2079

☑   A6232   Gauze, impregnated, hydrogel, for direct wound contact, pad size greater than 16 sq. in., but less than or equal to 48 sq. in., each dressing
MED: MCM 2079

☑   A6233   Gauze, impregnated, hydrogel for direct wound contact, pad size more than 48 sq. in., each dressing
MED: MCM 2079

☑   A6234   Hydrocolloid dressing, wound cover, pad size 16 sq. in. or less, without adhesive border, each dressing
MED: MCM 2079

☑   A6235   Hydrocolloid dressing, wound cover, pad size more than 16 sq. in. but less than or equal to 48 sq. in., without adhesive border, each dressing
MED: MCM 2079

☑   A6236   Hydrocolloid dressing, wound cover, pad size more than 48 sq. in., without adhesive border, each dressing
MED: MCM 2079

☑   A6237   Hydrocolloid dressing, wound cover, pad size 16 sq. in. or less, with any size adhesive border, each dressing
MED: MCM 2079

☑   A6238   Hydrocolloid dressing, wound cover, pad size more than 16 sq. in. but less than or equal to 48 sq. in., with any size adhesive border, each dressing
MED: MCM 2079

☑   A6239   Hydrocolloid dressing, wound cover, pad size more than 48 sq. in., with any size adhesive border, each dressing
MED: MCM 2079

☑   A6240   Hydrocolloid dressing, wound filler, paste, per fluid ounce
MED: MCM 2079

☑   A6241   Hydrocolloid dressing, wound filler, dry form, per gram
MED: MCM 2079

☑   A6242   Hydrogel dressing, wound cover, pad size 16 sq. in. or less, without adhesive border, each dressing
MED: MCM 2079

☑   A6243   Hydrogel dressing, wound cover, pad size more than 16 sq. in. but less than or equal to 48 sq. in., without adhesive border, each dressing
MED: MCM 2079

☑ **A6244** Hydrogel dressing, wound cover, pad size more than 48 sq. in., without adhesive border, each dressing
MED: MCM 2079

☑ **A6245** Hydrogel dressing, wound cover, pad size 16 sq. in. or less, with any size adhesive border, each dressing
MED: MCM 2079

☑ **A6246** Hydrogel dressing, wound cover, pad size more than 16 sq. in. but less than or equal to 48 sq. in., with any size adhesive border, each dressing
MED: MCM 2079

☑ **A6247** Hydrogel dressing, wound cover, pad size more than 48 sq. in., with any size adhesive border, each dressing
MED: MCM 2079

☑ **A6248** Hydrogel dressing, wound filler, gel, per fluid ounce
MED: MCM 2079

A6250 Skin sealants, protectants, moisturizers, ointments, any type, any size
Surgical dressings applied by a physician are included as part of the professional service. Surgical dressings obtained by the patient to perform homecare as prescribed by the physician are covered.
MED: MCM 2079

☑ **A6251** Specialty absorptive dressing, wound cover, pad size 16 sq. in. or less, without adhesive border, each dressing
MED: MCM 2079

☑ **A6252** Specialty absorptive dressing, wound cover, pad size more than 16 sq. in. but less than or equal to 48 sq. in., without adhesive border, each dressing
MED: MCM 2079

☑ **A6253** Specialty absorptive dressing, wound cover, pad size more than 48 sq. in., without adhesive border, each dressing
MED: MCM 2079

☑ **A6254** Specialty absorptive dressing, wound cover, pad size 16 sq. in. or less, with any size adhesive border, each dressing
MED: MCM 2079

☑ **A6255** Specialty absorptive dressing, wound cover, pad size more than 16 sq. in. but less than or equal to 48 sq. in., with any size adhesive border, each dressing
MED: MCM 2079

☑ **A6256** Specialty absorptive dressing, wound cover, pad size more than 48 sq. in., with any size adhesive border, each dressing
MED: MCM 2079

☑ **A6257** Transparent film, 16 sq. in. or less, each dressing
Surgical dressings applied by a physician are included as part of the professional service. Surgical dressings obtained by the patient to perform homecare as prescribed by the physician are covered. Use this code for Polyskin, Tegaderm, and Tegaderm HP.
MED: MCM 2079

☑ **A6258** Transparent film, more than 16 sq. in. but less than or equal to 48 sq. in., each dressing
Surgical dressings applied by a physician are included as part of the professional service. Surgical dressings obtained by the patient to perform homecare as prescribed by the physician are covered.
MED: MCM 2079

☑ **A6259** Transparent film, more than 48 sq. in., each dressing
Surgical dressings applied by a physician are included as part of the professional service. Surgical dressings obtained by the patient to perform homecare as prescribed by the physician are covered.
MED: MCM 2079

☑ **A6260** Wound cleansers, any type, any size
Surgical dressings applied by a physician are included as part of the professional service. Surgical dressings obtained by the patient to perform homecare as prescribed by the physician are covered.
MED: MCM 2079

☑ **A6261** Wound filler, gel/paste, per fluid ounce, not elsewhere classified
Surgical dressings applied by a physician are included as part of the professional service. Surgical dressings obtained by the patient to perform homecare as prescribed by the physician are covered.
MED: MCM 2079

☑ **A6262** Wound filler, dry form, per gram, not elsewhere classified
MED: MCM 2079

☑ **A6266** Gauze, impregnated, other than water, normal saline, or zinc paste, any width, per linear yard
Surgical dressings applied by a physician are included as part of the professional service. Surgical dressings obtained by the patient to perform homecare as prescribed by the physician are covered.
MED: MCM 2079

☑ **A6402** Gauze, non-impregnated, sterile, pad size 16 sq. in. or less, without adhesive border, each dressing
Surgical dressings applied by a physician are included as part of the professional service. Surgical dressings obtained by the patient to perform homecare as prescribed by the physician are covered.
MED: MCM 2079

☑ **A6403** Gauze, non-impregnated, sterile, pad size more than 16 sq. in. but less than or equal to 48 sq. in., without adhesive border, each dressing
Surgical dressings applied by a physician are included as part of the professional service. Surgical dressings obtained by the patient to perform homecare as prescribed by the physician are covered.
MED: MCM 2079

☑ **A6404** Gauze, non-impregnated, sterile, pad size more than 48 sq. in., without adhesive border, each dressing
MED: MCM 2079

● ☑ **A6407** Packing strips, non-impregnated, up to two inches in width, per linear yard

☑ **A6410** Eye pad, sterile, each
MED: MCM 2079

☑ **A6411** Eye pad, non-sterile, each
MED: MCM 2079

E ☑ **A6412** Eye patch, occlusive, each

A6421 ~~Padding bandage, non-elastic, non woven/non-knitted, width greater than or equal to 3 inches and less than 5 inches, per roll (at least 3 yards, unstretched)~~

A6422 ~~Conforming bandage, non-elastic, knitted/woven, non sterile, width greater than or equal to 3 inches and less than 5 inches per roll (at least 3 yards, unstretched)~~

Medical and Surgical Supplies

A6424 — A6550

A6424 ~~Conforming bandage, non-elastic, knitted/woven, non sterile, width greater than or equal to 5 inches, per roll (at least 3 yards, unstretched)~~

A6426 ~~Conforming bandage, non-elastic, knitted/woven, sterile width greater than or equal to 3 inches and less than 5 inches, per roll (at least 3 yards, unstretched)~~

A6428 ~~Conforming bandage, non-elastic, knitted/woven, sterile, width greater than or equal to 5 inches, per roll (at least 3 yards, unstretched)~~

A6430 ~~Light compression bandage, elastic, knitted/woven, load resistance less than 1.25 foot pounds at 50% maximum stretch, width greater than or equal to 3 inches and less than 5 inches, per roll (at least 3 yards, unstretched)~~

A6432 ~~Light compression bandage, elastic, knitted/woven, load resistance less than 1.25 foot pounds at 50% maximum stretch, width greater than or equal to 5 inches, per roll (at least 3 yards, unstretched)~~

A6434 ~~Moderate compression bandage, elastic, knitted/woven, load resistance of 1.25 to 1.34 foot pounds at 50% maximum stretch, width greater than or equal to 3 inches or less than 5 inches, per roll (at least 3 yards, unstretched)~~

A6436 ~~High compression bandage, elastic, knitted/woven, load resistance greater than or equal to 1.35 foot pounds at 50% maximum stretch, width greater than or equal to 3 inches and less than 5 inches, per roll (at least 3 yards, unstretched)~~

A6438 ~~Self adherent bandage, elastic, non knitted/non woven, load resistance greater than or equal to 0.55 foot pounds at 50% maximum stretch, width greater than or equal to 3 inches and less than 5 inches, per roll (at least 3 yards, unstretched)~~

A6440 ~~Zinc paste impregnated bandage, non elastic, knitted/woven, width greater than or equal to 3 inches and less than 5 inches, per roll (at least 10 yards, unstretched)~~

● ☑ A6441 Padding bandage, non-elastic, non-woven/non-knitted, width greater than or equal to three inches and less than five inches, per yard

● ☑ A6442 Conforming bandage, non-elastic, knitted/woven, non-sterile, width less than three inches, per yard

● ☑ A6443 Conforming bandage, non-elastic, knitted/woven, non-sterile, width greater than or equal to three inches and less than five inches, per yard

● ☑ A6444 Conforming bandage, non-elastic, knitted/woven, non-sterile, width greater than or equal to five inches, per yard

● ☑ A6445 Conforming bandage, non-elastic, knitted/woven, sterile, width less than three inches, per yard

● ☑ A6446 Conforming bandage, non-elastic, knitted/woven, sterile, width greater than or equal to three inches and less than five inches, per yard

● ☑ A6447 Conforming bandage, non-elastic, knitted/woven, sterile, width greater than or equal to five inches, per yard

● ☑ A6448 Light compression bandage, elastic, knitted/woven, width less than three inches, per yard

● ☑ A6449 Light compression bandage, elastic, knitted/woven, width greater than or equal to three inches and less than five inches, per yard

● ☑ A6450 Light compression bandage, elastic, knitted/woven, width greater than or equal to five inches, per yard

● ☑ A6451 Moderate compression bandage, elastic, knitted/woven, load resistance of 1.25 to 1.34 foot pounds at 50 percent maximum stretch, width greater than or equal to three inches and less than five inches, per yard

● ☑ A6452 High compression bandage, elastic, knitted/woven, load resistance greater than or equal to 1.35 foot pounds at 50 percent maximum stretch, width greater than or equal to three inches and less than five inches, per yard

● ☑ A6453 Self-adherent bandage, elastic, non-knitted/non-woven, width less than three inches, per yard

● ☑ A6454 Self-adherent bandage, elastic, non-knitted/non-woven, width greater than or equal to three inches and less than five inches, per yard

● ☑ A6455 Self-adherent bandage, elastic, non-knitted/non-woven, width greater than or equal to five inches, per yard

● ☑ A6456 Zinc paste impregnated bandage, non-elastic, knitted/woven, width greater than or equal to three inches and less than five inches, per yard

A6501 Compression burn garment, bodysuit (head to foot), custom fabricated
MED: MCM 2079

A6502 Compression burn garment, chin strap, custom fabricated
MED: MCM 2079

A6503 Compression burn garment, facial hood, custom fabricated
MED: MCM 2079

A6504 Compression burn garment, glove to wrist, custom fabricated
MED: MCM 2079

A6505 Compression burn garment, glove to elbow, custom fabricated
MED: MCM 2079

A6506 Compression burn garment, glove to axilla, custom fabricated
MED: MCM 2079

A6507 Compression burn garment, foot to knee length, custom fabricated
MED: MCM 2079

A6508 Compression burn garment, foot to thigh length, custom fabricated
MED: MCM 2079

A6509 Compression burn garment, upper trunk to waist including arm openings (vest), custom fabricated
MED: MCM 2079

A6510 Compression burn garment, trunk, including arms down to leg openings (leotard), custom fabricated
MED: MCM 2079

A6511 Compression burn garment, lower trunk including leg openings (panty), custom fabricated
MED: MCM 2079

A6512 Compression burn garment, not otherwise classified
MED: MCM 2079

● ☑ A6550 Dressing set for negative pressure wound therapy electrical pump, stationary or portable, each

| Special Coverage Instructions | Noncovered by Medicare | Carrier Discretion | ☑ Quantity Alert | ● New Code | ▲ Revised Code |

14 — A Codes   M Maternity   A Adult   P Pediatrics   A-X APC Status Indicator   *2004 HCPCS*

● ☑ **A6551** Canister set for negative pressure wound therapy electrical pump, stationary or portable, each

☑ **A7000** Canister, disposable, used with suction pump, each
Medicare jurisdiction: DME regional carrier.

☑ **A7001** Canister, non-disposable, used with suction pump, each
Medicare jurisdiction: DME regional carrier.

A7002 Tubing, used with suction pump, each
Medicare jurisdiction: DME regional carrier.

A7003 Administration set, with small volume nonfiltered pneumatic nebulizer, disposable
Medicare jurisdiction: DME regional carrier.

A7004 Small volume nonfiltered pneumatic nebulizer, disposable
Medicare jurisdiction: DME regional carrier.

A7005 Administration set, with small volume nonfiltered pneumatic nebulizer, non-disposable
Medicare jurisdiction: DME regional carrier.

A7006 Administration set, with small volume filtered pneumatic nebulizer
Medicare jurisdiction: DME regional carrier.

A7007 Large volume nebulizer, disposable, unfilled, used with aerosol compressor
Medicare jurisdiction: DME regional carrier.

A7008 Large volume nebulizer, disposable, prefilled, used with aerosol compressor
Medicare jurisdiction: DME regional carrier.

A7009 Reservoir bottle, non-disposable, used with large volume ultrasonic nebulizer
Medicare jurisdiction: DME regional carrier.

☑ **A7010** Corrugated tubing, disposable, used with large volume nebulizer, 100 feet
Medicare jurisdiction: DME regional carrier.

☑ **A7011** Corrugated tubing, non-disposable, used with large volume nebulizer, 10 feet
Medicare jurisdiction: DME regional carrier.

A7012 Water collection device, used with large volume nebulizer
Medicare jurisdiction: DME regional carrier.

A7013 Filter, disposable, used with aerosol compressor
Medicare jurisdiction: DME regional carrier.

A7014 Filter, non-disposable, used with aerosol compressor or ultrasonic generator
Medicare jurisdiction: DME regional carrier.

A7015 Aerosol mask, used with DME nebulizer
Medicare jurisdiction: DME regional carrier.

A7016 Dome and mouthpiece, used with small volume ultrasonic nebulizer
Medicare jurisdiction: DME regional carrier.

A7017 Nebulizer, durable, glass or autoclavable plastic, bottle type, not used with oxygen
Medicare jurisdiction: DME regional carrier.
MED: CIM 60-9

☑ **A7018** Water, distilled, used with large volume nebulizer, 1000 ml
Medicare jurisdiction: DME regional carrier.

~~**A7019** Saline solution, per 10 ml, metered dose dispenser, for use with inhalation drugs~~

~~**A7020** Sterile water or sterile saline, 1000 ml, used with large volume nebulizer~~

☑ **A7025** High frequency chest wall oscillation system vest, replacement for use with patient owned equipment, each

☑ **A7026** High frequency chest wall oscillation system hose, replacement for use with patient owned equipment, each

☑ **A7030** Full face mask used with positive airway pressure device, each

☑ **A7031** Face mask interface, replacement for full face mask, each

☑ **A7032** Replacement cushion for nasal application device, each

A7033 Replacement pillows for nasal application device, pair

A7034 Nasal interface (mask or cannula type) used with positive airway pressure device, with or without head strap

A7035 Headgear used with positive airway pressure device

A7036 Chinstrap used with positive airway pressure device

A7037 Tubing used with positive airway pressure device

A7038 Filter, disposable, used with positive airway pressure device

A7039 Filter, non disposable, used with positive airway pressure device

A7042 Implanted pleural catheter, each

A7043 Vacuum drainage bottle and tubing for use with implanted catheter

A7044 Oral interface used with positive airway pressure device, each

● ☑ **A7046** Water chamber for humidifier, used with positive airway pressure device, replacement, each
MED: CIM 60-17

☑ **A7501** Tracheostoma valve, including diaphragm, each
Medicare jurisdiction: DME regional carrier.
MED: MCM 2130

☑ **A7502** Replacement diaphragm/faceplate for tracheostoma valve, each
Medicare jurisdiction: DME regional carrier.
MED: MCM 2130

☑ **A7503** Filter holder or filter cap, reusable, for use in a tracheostoma heat and moisture exchange system, each
Medicare jurisdiction: DME regional carrier.
MED: MCM 2130

☑ **A7504** Filter for use in a tracheostoma heat and moisture exchange system, each
Medicare jurisdiction: DME regional carrier.
MED: MCM 2130

☑ **A7505** Housing, reusable without adhesive, for use in a heat and moisture exchange system and/or with a tracheostoma valve, each
Medicare jurisdiction: DME regional carrier.
MED: MCM 2130

☑ **A7506** Adhesive disc for use in a heat and moisture exchange system and/or with tracheostoma valve, any type each
Medicare jurisdiction: DME regional carrier.
MED: MCM 2130

☑ **A7507** Filter holder and integrated filter without adhesive, for use in a tracheostoma heat and moisture exchange system, each
Medicare jurisdiction: DME regional carrier.
MED: MCM 2130

☑ **A7508** Housing and integrated adhesive, for use in a tracheostoma heat and moisture exchange system and/or with a tracheostoma valve, each
Medicare jurisdiction: DME regional carrier.
MED: MCM 2130

☑ **A7509** Filter holder and integrated filter housing, and adhesive, for use as a tracheostoma heat and moisture exchange system, each
Medicare jurisdiction: DME regional carrier.
MED: MCM 2130

● ☑ **A7520** Tracheostomy/laryngectomy tube, non-cuffed, polyvinylchloride (PVC), silicone or equal, each

● ☑ **A7521** Tracheostomy/laryngectomy tube, cuffed, polyvinylchloride (PVC), silicone or equal, each

● ☑ **A7522** Tracheostomy/laryngectomy tube, stainless steel or equal (sterilizable and reusable), each

● ☑ **A7523** Tracheostomy shower protector, each

● ☑ **A7524** Tracheostoma stent/stud/button, each

● ☑ **A7525** Tracheostomy mask, each

● ☑ **A7526** Tracheostomy tube collar/holder, each

ADMINISTRATIVE, MISCELLANEOUS AND INVESTIGATIONAL *A9000-A9999*

This section of codes reports items such as nonprescription drugs, noncovered items/services, exercise equipment and, most notably, radiopharmaceutical diagnostic imaging agents.

E **A9150** Nonprescription drug
Medicare jurisdiction: local carrier.
MED: MCM 2050.5

A **A9270** Noncovered item or service
Medicare jurisdiction: local or DME regional carrier.
MED: MCM 2303

● **A9280** Alert or alarm device, not otherwise classified
MED: Medicare Statute: 1861

E **A9300** Exercise equipment
Medicare jurisdiction: DME regional carrier
MED: CIM 60-9, MCM 2100.1

N ☑ **A9500** Supply of radiopharmaceutical diagnostic imaging agent, technetium Tc 99m sestamibi, per dose
Use this code for Cardiolite. Medicare jurisdiction: local carrier.
MED: MCM 15022

N ☑ **A9502** Supply of radiopharmaceutical diagnostic imaging agent, technetium Tc 99m tetrofosmin, per unit dose
Medicare jurisdiction: local carrier.
MED: MCM 15022

N ☑ **A9503** Supply of radiopharmaceutical diagnostic imaging agent, Technetium Tc 99m, medronate, up to 30 millicurie
Medicare jurisdiction: local carrier.
MED: MCM 15022

N **A9504** Supply of radiopharmaceutical diagnostic imaging agent, technetium Tc 99m apcitide
Medicare jurisdiction: local carrier.
MED: MCM 15022

N ☑ **A9505** Supply of radiopharmaceutical diagnostic imaging agent, thallous chloride TL-201, per millicurie
Medicare jurisdiction: local carrier.
MED: MCM 15022

K ☑ **A9507** Supply of radiopharmaceutical diagnostic imaging agent, Indium In 111 capromab pendetide, per dose
Medicare jurisdiction: local carrier.
MED: MCM 15022

K ☑ **A9508** Supply of radiopharmaceutical diagnostic imaging agent, iobenguane sulfate I-131, per 0.5 millicurie
Medicare jurisdiction: DME regional carrier.
MED: MCM 15030

N ☑ **A9510** Supply of radiopharmaceutical diagnostic imaging agent, technetium Tc 99m disofenin, per vial
Medicare jurisdiction: DME regional carrier.
MED: MCM 15030

K ☑ **A9511** Supply of radiopharmaceutical diagnostic imaging agent, technetium TC 99m, depreotide, per millicurie

N ☑ **A9512** Supply of radiopharmaceutical diagnostic imaging agent, technetium Tc 99m pertechnetate, per mci

N ☑ **A9513** Supply of radiopharmaceutical diagnostic imaging agent, technetium Tc 99m mebrofenin, per mci

N ☑ **A9514** Supply of radiopharmaceutical diagnostic imaging agent, technetium Tc 99m pyrophosphate, per mci

N ☑ **A9515** Supply of radiopharmaceutical diagnostic imaging agent, technetium Tc 99m pentetate, per mci

N ☑ **A9516** Supply of radiopharmaceutical diagnostic imaging agent, I-123 sodium iodide capsule, per 100 uci

N ☑ **A9517** Supply of radiopharmaceutical therapeutic imaging agent, I-131 sodium iodide capsule, per mci

K ~~**A9518** Supply of radiopharmaceutical therapeutic imaging agent, i 131 sodium iodide solution, per uci~~
See code A9530.

N ☑ **A9519** Supply of radiopharmaceutical diagnostic imaging agent, technetium Tc 99m macroaggregated albumin, per mci

N ☑ **A9520** Supply of radiopharmaceutical diagnostic imaging agent, technetium Tc 99m sulfur colloid, per mci

K ☑ **A9521** Supply of radiopharmaceutical diagnostic imaging agent, technetium Tc 99m exametazine, per dose

N ☑ **A9522** Supply of radiopharmaceutical diagnostic imaging agent, indium-111 ibritumomab tiuxetan, per mci
MED: MCM 15022

N ☑ **A9523** Supply of radiopharmaceutical therapeutic imaging agent, yttrium 90 ibritumomab tiuxetan, per mci
MED: MCM 15022

N ☑ **A9524** Supply of radiopharmaceutical diagnostic imaging agent, iodinated I-131 serum albumin, 5 microcuries
MED: MCM 15022

● ☑ **A9525** Supply of low or iso-osmolar contrast material, 10 mg of iodine
MED: MCM 15022, MCM 15030

● ☑ **A9526** Supply of radiopharmaceutical diagnostic imaging agent, ammonia N-13, per dose
MED: CIM 50-36

● ☑ **A9528** Supply of radiopharmaceutical diagnostic agent, I-131 sodium iodide capsule, per millicurie

● ☑ **A9529** Supply of radiopharmaceutical diagnostic agent, I-131 sodium iodide solution, per millicurie

● ☑ **A9530** Supply of radiopharmaceutical therapeutic agent, I-131 sodium iodide solution, per millicurie

● ☑ **A9531** Supply of radiopharmaceutical diagnostic agent, I-131 sodium iodide, per microcurie (up to 100 microcuries)

● ☑ **A9532** Supply of radiopharmaceutical therapeutic agent, iodinated I-125, serum albumin, 5 microcuries

● ☑ **A9533** Supply of radiopharmaceutical diagnostic imaging agent, I-131 tositumomab, per millicurie

● ☑ **A9534** Supply of radiopharmaceutical therapeutic imaging agent, I-131 tositumomab, per millicurie

Ⓚ ☑ **A9600** Supply of therapeutic radiopharmaceutical, strontium-89 chloride, per millicurie
Medicare jurisdiction: local carrier.

Ⓚ ☑ **A9605** Supply of therapeutic radiopharmaceutical, Samarium Sm 153 lexidronamm, 50 millicurie
Medicare jurisdiction: DME regional carrier.

Ⓝ **A9699** Supply of radiopharmaceutical therapeutic imaging agent, not otherwise classified

Ⓔ **A9700** Supply of injectable contrast material for use in echocardiography, per study
MED: MCM 15360

Ⓐ **A9900** Miscellaneous DME supply, accessory, and/or service component of another HCPCS code
Medicare jurisdiction: local carrier if implanted DME; if other, regional carrier.

Ⓐ **A9901** DME delivery, set up, and/or dispensing service component of another HCPCS code
Medicare jurisdiction: local carrier if implanted DME; if other, regional carrier.

● **A9999** Miscellaneous DME supply or accessory, not otherwise specified

ENTERAL AND PARENTERAL THERAPY *B4000-B9999*
This section includes codes for supplies, formulae, nutritional solutions, and infusion pumps.

ENTERAL FORMULAE AND ENTERAL MEDICAL SUPPLIES
Certification of medical necessity is required for coverage. Submit a revision to the certification of medical necessity if the patient's daily volume changes by more than one liter; if there is a change in infusion method; or if there is a change from premix to home mix or parenteral to enteral therapy. Medicare claims fall under the jurisdiction of the DME regional carrier, unless otherwise noted.

B4034 Enteral feeding supply kit; syringe, per day
MED: CIM 65-10, MCM 2130, MCM 4450

B4035 Enteral feeding supply kit; pump fed, per day
MED: CIM 65-10, MCM 2130, MCM 4450

B4036 Enteral feeding supply kit; gravity fed, per day
MED: CIM 65-10, MCM 2130, MCM 4450

B4081 Nasogastric tubing with stylet
MED: CIM 65-10, MCM 2130, MCM 4450

B4082 Nasogastric tubing without stylet
MED: CIM 65-10, MCM 2130, MCM 4450

B4083 Stomach tube — Levine type
MED: CIM 65-10, MCM 2130, MCM 4450

B4086 Gastrostomy/jejunostomy tube, any material, any type, (standard or low profile), each

E **B4100** Food thickener, administered orally, per ounce

B4150 Enteral formulae; category I; semi-synthetic intact protein/protein isolates, administered through an enteral feeding tube, 100 calories = 1 unit
Use this code for Enrich, Ensure, Ensure HN, Ensure Powder, Isocal, Lonalac Powder, Meritene, Meritene Powder, Osmolite, Osmolite HN, Portagen Powder, Sustacal, Renu, Sustagen Powder, Travasorb.
MED: CIM 65-10, MCM 2130, MCM 4450

B4151 Enteral formulae; category I: natural intact protein/protein isolates, administered through an enteral feeding tube, 100 calories = 1 unit
Use this code for Compleat B, Vitaneed, Compleat B Modified.
MED: CIM 65-10, MCM 2130, MCM 4450

B4152 Enteral formulae; category II: intact protein/protein isolates (calorically dense), administered through an enteral feeding tube, 100 calories = 1 unit
Use this code for Magnacal, Isocal HCN, Sustacal HC, Ensure Plus, Ensure Plus HN.
MED: CIM 65-10, MCM 2130, MCM 4450

B4153 Enteral formulae; category III: hydrolyzed protein/amino acids, administered through an enteral feeding tube, 100 calories = 1 unit
Use this code for Criticare HN, Vivonex t.e.n. (Total Enteral Nutrition), Vivonex HN, Vital (Vital HN), Travasorb HN, Isotein HN, Precision HN, Precision Isotonic.
MED: CIM 65-10, MCM 2130, MCM 4450

B4154 Enteral formulae; category IV: defined formula for special metabolic need, administered through an enteral feeding tube, 100 calories = 1 unit
Use this code for Hepatic-aid, Travasorb Hepatic, Travasorb MCT, Travasorb Renal, Traum-aid, Tramacal, Aminaid.
MED: CIM 65-10, MCM 2130, MCM 4450

B4155 Enteral formulae; category V: modular components, administered through an enteral feeding tube, 100 calories = 1 unit
Use this code for Propac, Gerval Protein, Promix, Casec, Moducal, Controlyte, Polycose Liquid or Powder, Sumacal, Microlipids, MCT Oil, Nutri-source.
MED: CIM 65-10, MCM 2130, MCM 4450

B4156 Enteral formulae; category VI: standardized nutrients, administered through an enteral feeding tube, 100 calories = 1 unit
Use this code for Vivonex STD, Travasorb STD, Precision LR, Tolerex.
MED: CIM 65-10, MCM 2130, MCM 4450

PARENTERAL NUTRITION SOLUTIONS AND SUPPLIES

B4164 Parenteral nutrition solution; carbohydrates (dextrose), 50% or less (500 ml = 1 unit) — home mix
MED: CIM 65-10, MCM 2130, MCM 4450

B4168 Parenteral nutrition solution; amino acid, 3.5%, (500 ml = 1 unit) — home mix
MED: CIM 65-10, MCM 2130, MCM 4450

B4172 Parenteral nutrition solution; amino acid, 5.5% through 7%, (500 ml = 1 unit) — home mix
MED: CIM 65-10, MCM 2130, MCM 4450

B4176 Parenteral nutrition solution; amino acid, 7% through 8.5%, (500 ml = 1 unit) — home mix
MED: CIM 65-10, MCM 2130, MCM 4450

B4178 Parenteral nutrition solution; amino acid, greater than 8.5% (500 ml = 1 unit) — home mix
MED: CIM 65-10, MCM 2130, MCM 4450

B4180 Parenteral nutrition solution; carbohydrates (dextrose), greater than 50% (500 ml = 1 unit) — home mix
MED: CIM 65-10, MCM 2130, MCM 4450

B4184 Parenteral nutrition solution; lipids, 10% with administration set (500 ml = 1 unit)
MED: CIM 65-10, MCM 2130, MCM 4450

B4186 Parenteral nutrition solution; lipids, 20% with administration set (500 ml = 1 unit)
MED: CIM 65-10, MCM 2130, MCM 4450

☑ **B4189** Parenteral nutrition solution; compounded amino acid and carbohydrates with electrolytes, trace elements, and vitamins, including preparation, any strength, 10 to 51 grams of protein — premix
MED: CIM 65-10, MCM 2130, MCM 4450

☑ **B4193** Parenteral nutrition solution; compounded amino acid and carbohydrates with electrolytes, trace elements, and vitamins, including preparation, any strength, 52 to 73 grams of protein — premix
MED: CIM 65-10, MCM 2130, MCM 4450

☑ **B4197** Parenteral nutrition solution; compounded amino acid and carbohydrates with electrolytes, trace elements and vitamins, including preparation, any strength, 74 to 100 grams of protein — premix
MED: CIM 65-10, MCM 2130, MCM 4450

☑ **B4199** **Parenteral nutrition solution; compounded amino acid and carbohydrates with electrolytes, trace elements and vitamins, including preparation, any strength, over 100 grams of protein — premix**
MED: CIM 65-10, MCM 2130, MCM 4450

B4216 **Parenteral nutrition; additives (vitamins, trace elements, heparin, electrolytes) — home mix, per day**
MED: CIM 65-10, MCM 2130, MCM 4450

B4220 **Parenteral nutrition supply kit; premix, per day**
MED: CIM 65-10, MCM 2130, MCM 4450

B4222 **Parenteral nutrition supply kit; home mix, per day**
MED: CIM 65-10, MCM 2130, MCM 4450

B4224 **Parenteral nutrition administration kit, per day**
MED: CIM 65-10, MCM 2130, MCM 4450

B5000 **Parenteral nutrition solution; compounded amino acid and carbohydrates with electrolytes, trace elements, and vitamins, including preparation, any strength, renal — amirosyn RF, nephramine, renamine — premix**
Use this code for Amirosyn-RF, NephrAmine, RenAmin.
MED: CIM 65-10, MCM 2130, MCM 4450

B5100 **Parenteral nutrition solution; compounded amino acid and carbohydrates with electrolytes, trace elements, and vitamins, including preparation, any strength, hepatic — freamine HBC, hepatamine — premix**
Use this code for FreAmine HBC, HepatAmine.
MED: CIM 65-10, MCM 2130, MCM 4450

B5200 **Parenteral nutrition solution; compounded amino acid and carbohydrates with electrolytes, trace elements, and vitamins, including preparation, any strength, stress — branch chain amino acids — premix**
MED: CIM 65-10, MCM 2130, MCM 4450

ENTERAL AND PARENTERAL PUMPS
Submit documentation of the need for the infusion pump. Medicare will reimburse for the simplest model that meets the patient's needs.

B9000 **Enteral nutrition infusion pump — without alarm**
MED: CIM 65-10, MCM 2130, MCM 4450

B9002 **Enteral nutrition infusion pump — with alarm**
MED: CIM 65-10, MCM 2130, MCM 4450

B9004 **Parenteral nutrition infusion pump, portable**
MED: CIM 65-10, MCM 2130, MCM 4450

B9006 **Parenteral nutrition infusion pump, stationary**
MED: CIM 65-10, MCM 2130, MCM 4450

B9998 **NOC for enteral supplies**
MED: CIM 65-10, MCM 2130, MCM 4450

B9999 **NOC for parenteral supplies**
Determine if an alternative HCPCS Level II code better describes the supplies being reported. This code should be used only if a more specific code is unavailable.
MED: CIM 65-10, MCM 2130, MCM 4450

| Special Coverage Instructions | Noncovered by Medicare | Carrier Discretion | ☑ Quantity Alert | ● New Code | ▲ Revised Code |

20 — B Codes   M Maternity   A Adult   P Pediatrics   A-X APC Status Indicator   *2004 HCPCS*

OUTPATIENT PPS *C1000-C9999*

This section reports drugs, biologicals, and devices eligible for transitional pass-through payments for hospitals, and for items classified in new-technology ambulatory payment classifications (APCs) under the outpatient prospective payment system. These supplies can be billed in addition to the APC for ambulatory surgery center services when billing APCs to Medicare. Similar to all reimbursement requirements, Medicare makes transitional pass-through payments for a device only in conjunction with a procedure for its implantation or insertion. Consequently, a device will be considered medically necessary and eligible for a transitional pass-through payment only if the associated procedure is also medically necessary and payable under the outpatient prospective payment system.

CMS established categories for determining transitional pass-through payment devices, effective April 1, 2001, to meet the requirements of the Medicare, Medicaid, and SCHIP Benefits Improvement and Protection Act (BIPA). These new codes are also in the C series of HCPCS and are exclusively for use in billing for transitional pass-through payments. The introduction of categories does not affect payment methods. The transitional pass-through payment for a device will continue to be based on the charge on the individual bill, reduced to cost, and subject to a deduction that represents the cost of similar devices already included in the APC payment rate.

Each item previously determined to qualify fits in one of these categories. Other items may be billed using the category codes, even though CMS has not qualified them on an item-specific basis, as long as they:

- Meet the definition of a device that qualifies for transitional pass-through payments and other requirements and definitions

- Are described by the long descriptor associated with an active category code assigned by CMS

- Correlate with the definitions of terms and other general explanations issued by CMS to accompany coding assignments in this or subsequent instructions

- Have been approved by the Food and Drug Administration, if required. Some investigational devices have received an FDA investigational device exemption and may qualify.

- Are considered reasonable and necessary for the diagnosis or treatment of an illness or injury

- Are an integral part of the procedure

- Are used for one patient only, are single use, come in contact with human tissue, and are surgically implanted or inserted. They may or may not remain with the patient when the patient is released from the hospital.

- Cannot be taken as a depreciation, such as equipment, instruments, apparatuses, or implements

- Are not supplies used during the service or procedure, other than radiological site markers

- Are not materials such as biological or synthetics that are used to replace human skin

Future program memorandums will announce any new categories CMS develops. Keep in mind that the qualification of a device for transitional pass-through payments is temporary.

C1010 ~~Whole blood or red blood cells, leukoreduced, cmv negative, each unit~~
See code P9051.

C1011 ~~Platelet, hla matched leukoreduced, apheresis/pheresis, each unit~~
See code P9052.

C1015 ~~Platelets, pheresis, leukocyte reduced, cmv negative, irradiated, each unit~~
See code P9053.

C1016 ~~Whole blood or red blood cells, leukoreduced, frozen, deglycerol, washed, each unit~~
See code P9054.

C1017 ~~Platelet, leukoreduced, cmv negative, apheresis/pheresis, each unit~~
See code P9055.

C1018 ~~Whole blood, leukoreduced, irradiated, each unit~~
See code P9056.

C1020 ~~Red blood cells, frozen/deglycerolized/washed, leukocyte reduced, irradiated, each unit~~
See code P9057.

C1021 ~~Red blood cells, leukocyte reduced, cmv negative, irradiated, each unit~~
See code P9058.

C1022 ~~Plasma, frozen within 24 hours of collection, each unit~~
See code P9059.

N ☑ **C1079** Supply of radiopharmaceutical diagnostic imaging agent, cyanocobalamin Co 57/58, per 0.5 millicurie
MED: Medicare Statute: 1833(T)

● **C1080** Supply of radiopharmaceurical therapeutic imaging agent, I-131 tositumamab, per dose
Added as per final 2004 Outpatient Prospective Payment System rule. *Federal Register*, November 7, 2003.

● **C1081** Supply of radiopharmaceutical therapeutic imaging agent, I-131 tositumomab, per dose
Added as per final 2004 Outpatient Prospective Payment System rule. *Federal Register*, November 7, 2003.

● **C1082** Supply of radiopharmaceutical diagnostic imaging agent, indium-111 ibtitumomab tiuxetan, per dose
Added as per final 2004 Outpatient Prospective Payment System rule. *Federal Register*, November 7, 2003.

● **C1083** Supply of radiopharmaceutical therapeutic imaging agen, Yttrium 90 ibritumomab tiuxetan, per dose
Added as per final 2004 Outpatient Prospective Payment System rule. *Federal Register*, November 7, 2003.

T **C1088** Laser optic treatment system, Indigo Laseroptic Treatment System
MED: Medicare Statute: 1833(T)

K ☑ **C1091** Supply of radiopharmaceutical diagnostic imaging agent, Indium 111 oxyquinoline, per 0.5 millicurie
MED: Medicare Statute: 1833(T)

K ☑ **C1092** Supply of radiopharmaceutical diagnostic imaging agent, Indium 111 pentetate, per 0.5 millicurie
MED: Medicare Statute: 1833(T)

K **C1122** Supply of radiopharmaceutical diagnostic imaging agent, technetium Tc 99m arcitumomab, per vial
MED: Medicare Statute: 1833(T)

N **C1166** ~~Injection, cytarabine liposome, per 10 mg~~
See code J9110.

K **C1167** ~~Injection, epirubicin hydrochloride, 2 mg~~
See code J9178.

K ☑ **C1178** Injection, busulfan, per 6 mg
Use this code for Busulfex.
MED: Medicare Statute: 1833(T)

N **C1200** Supply of radiopharmaceutical diagnostic imaging agent, technetium Tc 99m sodium glucoheptonate, per vial
MED: Medicare Statute: 1833(T)

Outpatient PPS

C1201 — C9000

N   **C1201** Supply of radiopharmaceutical diagnostic imaging agent, technetium Tc 99m succimer, per vial
MED: Medicare Statute: 1833(T)

~~C1207 Octreotide acetate, 1 mg~~
This code was added and deleted in the same year.

S   **C1300** Hyperbaric oxygen under pressure, full body chamber, per 30 minute interval
MED: Medicare Statute: 1833(T)

K   **C1305** Apligraf, per 44 sq cm
MED: Medicare Statute: 1833(T)

▲ K   **C1716** Brachytherapy source, gold 198
MED: Medicare Statute: 1833(T)

▲ K   **C1718** Brachytherapy source, iodine 125
MED: Medicare Statute: 1833(T)

▲ K   **C1719** Brachytherapy source, non-high dose rate iridium 192
MED: Medicare Statute: 1833(T)

▲ K   **C1720** Brachytherapy source, palladium 103
MED: Medicare Statute: 1833(T)

H   **C1765** Adhesion barrier
MED: Medicare Statute: 1833(T)

~~C1774 Injection, darbepoetin alfa (for non-esrd use), per 1 mcg~~

K ☑   **C1775** Supply of radiopharmaceutical diagnostic imaging agent, fluorodeoxyglucose f18 (2-deoxy-2-[18f]fluoro-d-glucose), per dose (4-40 mci/ml)
MED: Medicare Statute: 1833(T)

H   **C1783** Ocular implant, aqueous drainage assist device
MED: Medicare Statute: 1833(T)

● H   **C1814** Retinal tamponade device, silicone oil

● H   **C1818** Integrated keratoprosthesis

●   **C1819** Tissue localization excision
Added as per final 2004 Outpatient Prospective Payment System rule, *Federal Register*, November 7, 2003

● H   **C1884** Embolization protective system
MED: Medicare Statute: 1833(T)

H   **C1888** Catheter, ablation, non-cardiac, endovascular (implantable)
MED: Medicare Statute: 1833(T)

H   **C1900** Lead, left ventricular coronary venous system
MED: Medicare Statute: 1833(T)

H   **C2614** Probe, percutaneous lumbar discectomy
MED: Medicare Statute: 1833(T)

▲ K   **C2616** Brachytherapy source, yttrium-90
MED: Medicare Statute: 1833(T)

H   **C2618** Probe, cryoablation
MED: Medicare Statute: 1833(T)

H ☑   **C2632** Brachytherapy solution, Iodine-125, per mci
MED: Medicare Statute: 1833(T)

S   **C8900** Magnetic resonance angiography with contrast, abdomen
MED: Medicare Statute: 1833(t)(2)

S   **C8901** Magnetic resonance angiography without contrast, abdomen
MED: Medicare Statute: 1833(t)(2)

S   **C8902** Magnetic resonance angiography without contrast followed by with contrast, abdomen
MED: Medicare Statute: 1833(t)(2)

S   **C8903** Magnetic resonance imaging with contrast, breast; unilateral
MED: Medicare Statute: 1833(t)(2)

S   **C8904** Magnetic resonance imaging without contrast, breast; unilateral
MED: Medicare Statute: 1833(t)(2)

S   **C8905** Magnetic resonance imaging without contrast followed by with contrast, breast; unilateral
MED: Medicare Statute: 1833(t)(2)

S   **C8906** Magnetic resonance imaging with contrast, breast; bilateral
MED: Medicare Statute: 1833(t)(2)

S   **C8907** Magnetic resonance imaging without contrast, breast; bilateral
MED: Medicare Statute: 1833(t)(2)

S   **C8908** Magnetic resonance imaging without contrast followed by with contrast, breast; bilateral
MED: Medicare Statute: 1833(t)(2)

S   **C8909** Magnetic resonance angiography with contrast, chest (excluding myocardium)
MED: Medicare Statute: 1833(t)(2)

S   **C8910** Magnetic resonance angiography without contrast, chest (excluding myocardium)
MED: Medicare Statute: 1833(t)(2)

S   **C8911** Magnetic resonance angiography without contrast followed by with contrast, chest (excluding myocardium)
MED: Medicare Statute: 1833(t)(2)

S   **C8912** Magnetic resonance angiography with contrast, lower extremity
MED: Medicare Statute: 1833(t)(2)

S   **C8913** Magnetic resonance angiography without contrast, lower extremity
MED: Medicare Statute: 1833(t)(2)

S   **C8914** Magnetic resonance angiography without contrast followed by with contrast, lower extremity
MED: Medicare Statute: 1833(t)(2)

● S   **C8918** Magnetic resonance angiography with contrast, pelvis
MED: Medicare Statute: 430 BIPA

● S   **C8919** Magnetic resonance angiography without contrast, pelvis
MED: Medicare Statute: 430 BIPA

● S   **C8920** Magnetic resonance angiography without contrast followed by with contrast, pelvis
MED: Medicare Statute: 430 BIPA

K   **C9000** Injection, sodium chromate Cr51, per 0.25 millicurie
See Radiology CPT code 73225.
MED: Medicare Statute: 1833(t)

Special Coverage Instructions   Noncovered by Medicare   Carrier Discretion   ☑ Quantity Alert   ● New Code   ▲ Revised Code

K   C9003 **Palivizumab-RSV-IgM, per 50 mg**
Use this code for Synagis.
MED: Medicare Statute: 1833(t)

N   C9007 **Baclofen Intrathecal Screening Kit (1 amp)**
Use this code for Lioresal Intrathecal.
MED: Medicare Statute: 1833(t)

N   C9008 **Baclofen Intrathecal Refill Kit, per 500 mcg**
MED: Medicare Statute: 1833(t)

▲ K   C9009 **Baclofen intrathecal refill kit, per 2000 mcg**
Use this code for Lioresal.
MED: Medicare Statute: 1833(t)

~~C0010~~ ~~Baclofen intrathecal refill kit, per 4000 mcg~~

N   C9013 **Supply of Co 57 cobaltous chloride, radiopharmaceutical diagnostic imaging agent**
MED: Medicare Statute: 1833(t)

N ☑ C9102 **Supply of radiopharmaceutical diagnostic imaging agent, 51 sodium chromate, per 50 millicurie**
MED: Medicare Statute: 1833(t)

N ☑ C9103 **Supply of radiopharmaceutical diagnostic imaging agent, sodium iothalamate I-125 injection, per 10 uCi**
MED: Medicare Statute: 1833(t)

K ☑ C9105 **Injection, hepatitis B immune globulin, per 1 ml**
Use this code for Bayhep B, H-BIG.
MED: Medicare Statute: 1833(t)

K ☑ C9109 **Injection, tirofiban HCl, 6.25 mg**
Use this code for Aggrastat.
MED: Medicare Statute: 1833(T)

~~C0111~~ ~~Injection, bivalirudin, 250 mg per vial~~
See code J0583.

G   C9112 **Injection, perflutren lipid microsphere, per 2 ml vial**
Use this code for Definity.
MED: Medicare Statute: 1833(t)

G   C9113 **Injection, pantoprazole sodium, per vial**
Use this code for Profonix.
MED: Medicare Statute: 1833(T)

~~C0116~~ ~~Injection, ertapenem sodium, per 1 gram vial~~
See code J1335.

~~C0110~~ ~~Injection, pegfilgrastim, per 6 mg single dose vial~~
See code J0560.

~~C0120~~ ~~Injection, fulvestrant, per 50 mg~~
See code J9395.

G   C9121 **Injection, argatroban, per 5 mg**
Use this code for Acova.
MED: Medicare Statute: 1833(T)

● ☑ C9123 **Transcyte, per 247 square centimeters**

G   C9200 **Orcel, per 36 sq cm**
Use this code for bilayered cellular matrix.
MED: Medicare Statute: 1833(T)

G ☑ C9201 **Dermagraft, per 37.5 sq cm**
Use this code for Dermal tissue of human origin. See also J7340, J7342, J7350.
MED: Medicare Statute: 1833(T)

● G ☑ C9202 **Injection, suspension of microspheres of human serum albumin with octafluoropropane, per 3 ml**

● G ☑ C9203 **Injection, perflexane lipid microspheres, per 10 ml vial**

~~C9204~~ ~~Injection, ziprasidone mesylate, per 20 mg~~

~~C9205~~ ~~Injection, oxaliplatin, per 5 mg~~

●   C9207 **Bortezomib, IV, per 3.5 mg**
Added as per final 2004 Outpatient Prospective Payment System rule, *Federal Register*, November 7, 2003

● ☑ C9208 **Injection, agalsidase beta, per 1 mg**

● ☑ C9209 **Injection, laronidase, per 2.9 mg**

●   C9210 **Palonosetron HCl, IV, per 0.25 mg (250 micrograms)**
Added as per final 2004 Outpatient Prospective Payment System rule, *Federal Register*, November 7, 2003

●   C9211 **Alefacept, IV, per 7.5 mg**
Added as per final 2004 Outpatient Prospective Payment System rule, *Federal Register*, November 7, 2003

●   C9212 **Alefacept, IM, per 7.5 mg**
Added as per final 2004 Outpatient Prospective Payment System rule, *Federal Register*, November 7, 2003

~~C9503~~ ~~Fresh frozen plasma, donor retested, each unit~~
See code P9060.

T   C9701 **Stretta System**
MED: Medicare Statute: 1833(T)

T   C9703 **Bard Endoscopic Suturing System**
MED: Medicare Statute: 1833(T)

T   C9711 **H.E.L.P. apheresis system**
MED: Medicare Statute: 1833(T)

DENTAL PROCEDURES *D0000-D9999*

The D, or dental, codes are a separate category of national codes. The Current Dental Terminology (CDT-4) code set is copyrighted by the American Dental Association (ADA). CDT-4 is included in HCPCS Level II. Decisions regarding the modification, deletion, or addition of CDT-4 codes are made by the ADA and not the national panel responsible for the administration of HCPCS.

The Department of Health and Human Services has an agreement with the AMA pertaining to the use of the CPT codes for physician services; it also has an agreement with the ADA to include CDT-4 as a set of HCPCS Level II codes for use in billing for dental services.

DIAGNOSTIC D0100-D0999

CLINICAL ORAL EVALUATION

All dental codes fall under the jurisdiction of the Medicare local carrier.

D0120 Periodic oral examination
This procedure is covered if its purpose is to identify a patient's existing infections prior to kidney transplantation.
MED: Medicare Statute: 1862A(12)

D0140 Limited oral evaluation — problem focused
MED: Medicare Statute: 1862A(12)

S **D0150** Comprehensive oral evaluation — new or established patient
This procedure is covered if its purpose is to identify a patient's existing infections prior to kidney transplantation.
MED: CIM 50-26, MCM 2136, MCM 2336

D0160 Detailed and extensive oral evaluation — problem focused, by report
Pertinent documentation to evaluate medical appropriateness should be included when this code is reported.
MED: Medicare Statute: 1862A(12)

D0170 Re-evaluation — limited, problem focused (Established patient; not post-operative visit)
MED: Medicare Statute: 1862a(12)

D0180 Comprehensive periodontal evaluation — new or established patient
See also equivalent CPT E&M codes.
MED: Medicare Statute: 1862a(12)

RADIOGRAPHS

D0210 Intraoral — complete series (including bitewings)
Cross-reference CPT 70320

☑ **D0220** Intraoral — periapical, first film
Cross-reference CPT 70300

☑ **D0230** Intraoral — periapical, each additional film
Cross-reference CPT 70310

S **D0240** Intraoral — occlusal film
MED: MCM 2136, MCM 2336

S ☑ **D0250** Extraoral — first film
MED: MCM 2136, MCM 2336

S ☑ **D0260** Extraoral — each additional film
MED: MCM 2136, MCM 2336

S ☑ **D0270** Bitewing — single film
MED: MCM 2136, MCM 2336

S ☑ **D0272** Bitewings — two films
MED: MCM 2136, MCM 2336

S ☑ **D0274** Bitewings — four films
MED: MCM 2136, MCM 2336

S ☑ **D0277** Vertical bitewings — 7 to 8 films
MED: MCM 2136, MCM 2336

D0290 Posterior-anterior or lateral skull and facial bone survey film
Cross-reference CPT 70150

D0310 Sialography
Cross-reference CPT 70390

D0320 Temporomandibular joint arthrogram, including injection
Cross-reference CPT 70332

D0321 Other temporomandibular joint films, by report
Cross-reference 76499

D0322 Tomographic survey
MED: CIM 50-26

D0330 Panoramic film
Cross-reference CPT 70320

D0340 Cephalometric film
Cross-reference CPT 70350

D0350 Oral/facial images (includes intra and extraoral images)
This code excludes conventional radiographs.

TEST AND LABORATORY EXAMINATIONS

D0415 Bacteriologic studies for determination of pathologic agents
This procedure is covered if its purpose is to identify a patient's existing infections prior to kidney transplantation.
MED: Medicare Statute: 1862 A(12)

D0425 Caries susceptibility tests
This procedure is covered by Medicare if its purpose is to identify a patient's existing infections prior to kidney transplantation.
MED: Medicare Statute: 1862 A(12)

S **D0460** Pulp vitality tests
This procedure is covered by Medicare if its purpose is to identify a patient's existing infections prior to kidney transplantation.
MED: CIM 50-26, MCM 2136, MCM 2336

E **D0470** Diagnostic casts
MED: Medicare Statute: 1862 a(12)

S **D0472** Accession of tissue, gross examination, preparation and transmission of written report
MED: CIM 50-26, MCM 2136, MCM 2336

S **D0473** Accession of tissue, gross and microscopic examination, preparation and transmission of written report
MED: CIM 50-26, MCM 2136, MCM 2336

S **D0474** Accession of tissue, gross and microscopic examination, including assessment of surgical margins for presence of disease, preparation and transmission of written report
MED: CIM 50-26, MCM 2136, MCM 2336

Dental Procedures

D0480 — D2530

[S] **D0480** **Processing and interpretation of cytologic smears, including the preparation and transmission of written report**
MED: CIM 50-26, MCM 2136, MCM 2336

[S] **D0502** **Other oral pathology procedures, by report**
Pertinent documentation to evaluate medical appropriateness should be included when this code is reported. This procedure is covered by Medicare if its purpose is to identify a patient's existing infections prior to kidney transplantation.
MED: CIM 50-26, MCM 2136, MCM 2336

[S] **D0999** **Unspecified diagnostic procedure, by report**
Determine if an alternative HCPCS Level II or a CPT code better describes the service being reported. This code should be used only if a more specific code is unavailable.
MED: CIM 50-26, MCM 2136, MCM 2336

PREVENTIVE D1000-D1999

DENTAL PROPHYLAXIS

D1110 **Prophylaxis — adult** [A]
MED: Medicare Statute: 1862 a(12)

D1120 **Prophylaxis — child** [P]
MED: Medicare Statute: 1862 a(12)

TOPICAL FLUORIDE TREATMENT (OFFICE PROCEDURE)

D1201 **Topical application of fluoride (including prophylaxis) — child** [P]
MED: Medicare Statute: 1862 a(12)

D1203 **Topical application of fluoride (prophylaxis not included) — child** [P]
MED: Medicare Statute: 1862 a(12)

D1204 **Topical application of fluoride (prophylaxis not included) — adult** [A]
MED: Medicare Statute: 1862 a(12)

D1205 **Topical application of fluoride (including prophylaxis) — adult** [A]
MED: Medicare Statute: 1862 a(12)

OTHER PREVENTIVE SERVICES

D1310 **Nutritional counseling for control of dental disease**
MED: MCM 2300

D1320 **Tobacco counseling for the control and prevention of oral disease**
MED: MCM 2300

D1330 **Oral hygiene instructions**
MED: MCM 2300

☑ **D1351** **Sealant — per tooth**
MED: Medicare Statute: 1862 a(12)

SPACE MAINTENANCE (PASSIVE APPLIANCES)

[S] **D1510** **Space maintainer — fixed-unilateral**
MED: MCM 2336

[S] **D1515** **Space maintainer — fixed-bilateral**
MED: MCM 2336, MCM 2136

[S] **D1520** **Space maintainer — removable-unilateral**
MED: MCM 2336, MCM 2136

[S] **D1525** **Space maintainer — removable-bilateral**
MED: MCM 2336, MCM 2136

[S] **D1550** **Recementation of space maintainer**
MED: MCM 2336, MCM 2136

☑ **D2140** **Amalgam-one surface, primary or permanent**
MED: Medicare Statute: 1862 a(12)

☑ **D2150** **Amalgam-two surfaces, primary or permanent**
MED: Medicare Statute: 1862 a(12)

☑ **D2160** **Amalgam-three surfaces, primary or permanent**
MED: Medicare Statute: 1862 a(12)

☑ **D2161** **Amalgam-four or more surfaces, primary or permanent**
MED: Medicare Statute: 1862 a(12)

RESIN RESTORATIONS

☑ **D2330** **Resin-based composite — one surface, anterior**
MED: Medicare Statute: 1862 a(12)

☑ **D2331** **Resin-based composite — two surfaces, anterior**
MED: Medicare Statute: 1861 a(12)

☑ **D2332** **Resin-based composite — three surfaces, anterior**
MED: Medicare Statute: 1862 a(12)

☑ **D2335** **Resin-based composite — four or more surfaces or involving incisal angle (anterior)**
MED: Medicare Statute: 1862 a(12)

D2390 **Resin-based composite crown, anterior**
MED: Medicare Statute: 1862a(12)

D2391 **Resin-based composite — one surface, posterior**
MED: Medicare Statute: 1862a(12)

D2392 **Resin-based composite — two surfaces, posterior**
MED: Medicare Statute: 1862a(12)

D2393 **Resin-based composite — three surfaces, posterior**
MED: Medicare Statute: 1862a(12)

D2394 **Resin-based composite — four or more surfaces, posterior**
MED: Medicare Statute: 1862a(12)

GOLD FOIL RESTORATIONS

☑ **D2410** **Gold foil — one surface**
MED: Medicare Statute: 1862 a(12)

☑ **D2420** **Gold foil — two surfaces**
MED: Medicare Statute: 1862 a(12)

☑ **D2430** **Gold foil — three surfaces**
MED: Medicare Statute: 1862 a(12)

INLAY/ONLAY RESTORATIONS

☑ **D2510** **Inlay — metallic — one surface**
MED: Medicare Statute: 1862 a(12)

☑ **D2520** **Inlay — metallic — two surfaces**
MED: Medicare Statute: 1862 a(12)

☑ **D2530** **Inlay — metallic — three or more surfaces**
MED: Medicare Statute: 1862 a(12)

| Special Coverage Instructions | Noncovered by Medicare | Carrier Discretion | ☑ Quantity Alert | ● New Code | ▲ Revised Code |

26 — D Codes   [M] Maternity   [A] Adult   [P] Pediatrics   [A]-[X] APC Status Indicator   *2004 HCPCS*

☑ **D2542** Onlay — metallic — two surfaces
MED: Medicare Statute: 1862a(12)

☑ **D2543** Onlay — metallic — three surfaces
MED: Medicare Statute: 1862 a(12)

☑ **D2544** Onlay — metallic — four or more surfaces
MED: Medicare Statute: 1862 a(12)

☑ **D2610** Inlay — porcelain/ceramic — one surface
MED: Medicare Statute: 1862 a(12)

☑ **D2620** Inlay — porcelain/ceramic — two surfaces
MED: Medicare Statute: 1862 a(12)

☑ **D2630** Inlay — porcelain/ceramic — three or more surfaces
MED: Medicare Statute: 1862 a(12)

☑ **D2642** Onlay — porcelain/ceramic — two surfaces
MED: Medicare Statute: 1862 a(12)

☑ **D2643** Onlay — porcelain/ceramic — three surfaces
MED: Medicare Statute: 1862 a(12)

☑ **D2644** Onlay — porcelain/ceramic — four or more surfaces
MED: Medicare Statute: 1862 a(12)

☑ **D2650** Inlay — resin-based composite composite/resin — one surface
MED: Medicare Statute: 1862 a(12)

☑ **D2651** Inlay — resin-based composite composite/resin — two surfaces
MED: Medicare Statute: 1862 a(12)

☑ **D2652** Inlay — resin-based composite composite/resin — three or more surfaces
MED: Medicare Statute: 1862 a(12)

☑ **D2662** Onlay — resin-based composite composite/resin — two surfaces
MED: Medicare Statute: 1862 a(12)

☑ **D2663** Onlay — resin-based composite composite/resin — three surfaces
MED: Medicare Statute: 1862 a(12)

☑ **D2664** Onlay — resin-based composite composite/resin — four or more surfaces
MED: Medicare Statute: 1862 a(12)

CROWNS — SINGLE RESTORATION ONLY

D2710 Crown - resin (indirect)
MED: Medicare Statute: 1862a(12)

D2720 Crown — resin with high noble metal
MED: Medicare Statute: 1862a(12)

D2721 Crown — resin with predominantly base metal
MED: Medicare Statute: 1862a(12)

D2722 Crown — resin with noble metal
MED: Medicare Statute: 1862a(12)

D2740 Crown — porcelain/ceramic substrate
MED: Medicare Statute: 1862a(12)

D2750 Crown — porcelain fused to high noble metal
MED: Medicare Statute: 1862a(12)

D2751 Crown — porcelain fused to predominantly base metal
MED: Medicare Statute: 1862a(12)

D2752 Crown — porcelain fused to noble metal
MED: Medicare Statute: 1862a(12)

D2780 Crown — 3/4 cast high noble metal
MED: Medicare Statute: 1862a(12)

D2781 Crown — 3/4 cast predominately base metal
MED: Medicare Statute: 1862a(12)

D2782 Crown — 3/4 cast noble metal
MED: Medicare Statute: 1862a(12)

D2783 Crown — 3/4 porcelain/ceramic
MED: Medicare Statute: 1862a(12)

D2790 Crown — full cast high noble metal
MED: Medicare Statute: 1862a(12)

D2791 Crown — full cast predominantly base metal
MED: Medicare Statute: 1862a(12)

D2792 Crown — full cast noble metal
MED: Medicare Statute: 1862a(12)

D2799 Provisional crown
Do not use this code to report a temporary crown for routine prosthetic restoration.
MED: Medicare Statute: 1862a(12)

OTHER RESTORATIVE SERVICES

D2910 Recement inlay
MED: Medicare Statute: 1862a(12)

D2920 Recement crown
MED: Medicare Statute: 1862a(12)

D2930 Prefabricated stainless steel crown — primary tooth
MED: Medicare Statute: 1862a(12)

D2931 Prefabricated stainless steel crown — permanent tooth
MED: Medicare Statute: 1862a(12)

D2932 Prefabricated resin crown

D2933 Prefabricated stainless steel crown with resin window
MED: Medicare Statute: 1862a(12)

D2940 Sedative filling
MED: Medicare Statute: 1862a(12)

D2950 Core buildup, including any pins
MED: Medicare Statute: 1862a(12)

D2951 Pin retention — per tooth, in addition to restoration
MED: Medicare Statute: 1862a(12)

D2952 Cast post and core in addition to crown
MED: Medicare Statute: 1862a(12)

D2953 Each additional cast post — same tooth
Report in addition to code D2952.
MED: Medicare Statute: 1862a(12)

Dental Procedures

D2954 — D3450

D2954 Prefabricated post and core in addition to crown
MED: Medicare Statute: 1862a(12)

D2955 Post removal (not in conjunction with endodontic therapy)
MED: Medicare Statute: 1862a(12)

D2957 Each additional prefabricated post — same tooth
Report in addition to code D2954.
MED: Medicare Statute: 1862a(12)

D2960 Labial veneer (resin laminate) — chairside
MED: Medicare Statute: 1862a(12)

D2961 Labial veneer (resin laminate) — laboratory
MED: Medicare Statute: 1862a(12)

D2962 Labial veneer (porcelain laminate) — laboratory
MED: Medicare Statute: 1862a(12)

S   **D2970** Temporary crown (fractured tooth)
MED: MCM 2336, MCM 2136

E   **D2980** Crown repair, by report
Pertinent documentation to evaluate medical appropriateness should be included when this code is reported.
MED: Medicare Statute: 1862a(12)

S   **D2999** Unspecified restorative procedure, by report
Determine if an alternative HCPCS Level II code or a CPT code better describes the service being reported. This code should be used only if a more specific code is unavailable.
MED: MCM 2336, MCM 2136

ENDODONTICS D3000-D3999

PULP CAPPING

D3110 Pulp cap — direct (excluding final restoration)
MED: Medicare Statute: 1862a(12)

D3120 Pulp cap — indirect (excluding final restoration)
MED: Medicare Statute: 1862a(12)

PULPOTOMY

D3220 Therapeutic pulpotomy (excluding final restoration) — removal of pulp coronal to the dentinocemental junction and application of medicament
Do not use this code to report the first stage of root canal therapy.
MED: Medicare Statute: 1862a(12)

D3221 Pulpal debridement, primary and permanent teeth
MED: Medicare Statute: 1862a(12)

PULPAL THERAPY ON PRIMARY TEETH (INCLUDES PRIMARY TEETH WITH SUCCEDANEOUS TEETH AND PLACEMENT OF RESORBABLE FILLING)

D3230 Pulpal therapy (resorbable filling) — anterior, primary tooth (excluding final restoration)
MED: Medicare Statute: 1862a(12)

D3240 Pulpal therapy (resorbable filling) — posterior, primary tooth (excluding final restoration)
MED: Medicare Statute: 1862a(12)

ROOT CANAL THERAPY (INCLUDING TREATMENT PLAN, CLINICAL PROCEDURES, AND FOLLOW-UP CARE, INCLUDES PRIMARY TEETH WITHOUT SUCCEDANEOUS TEETH AND PERMANENT TEETH)

D3310 Anterior (excluding final restoration)
MED: Medicare Statute: 1862a(12)

D3320 Bicuspid (excluding final restoration)
MED: Medicare Statute: 1862a(12)

D3330 Molar (excluding final restoration)
MED: Medicare Statute: 1862a(12)

D3331 Treatment of root canal obstruction; non-surgical access
MED: Medicare Statute: 1862a(12)

D3332 Incomplete endodontic therapy; inoperable or fractured tooth
MED: Medicare Statute: 1862a(12)

D3333 Internal root repair of perforation defects
MED: Medicare Statute: 1862a(12)

D3346 Retreatment of previous root canal therapy — anterior
MED: Medicare Statute: 1862a(12)

D3347 Retreatment of previous root canal therapy — bicuspid
MED: Medicare Statute: 1862a(12)

D3348 Retreatment of previous root canal therapy — molar
MED: Medicare Statute: 1862a(12)

D3351 Apexification/recalcification — initial visit (apical closure/calcific repair of perforations, root resorption, etc.)
MED: Medicare Statute: 1862a(12)

D3352 Apexification/recalcification — interim medication replacement (apical closure/calcific repair of perforations, root resorption, etc.)
MED: Medicare Statute: 1862a(12)

D3353 Apexification/recalcification - final visit (includes completed root canal therapy — apical closure/calcific repair of perforations, root resorption, etc.)
MED: Medicare Statute: 1862a(12)

APICOECTOMY/PERIRADICULAR SERVICES

D3410 Apicoectomy/periradicular surgery — anterior
MED: Medicare Statute: 1862a(12)

D3421 Apicoectomy/periradicular surgery — bicuspid (first root)
MED: Medicare Statute: 1862a(12)

D3425 Apicoectomy/periradicular surgery — molar (first root)
MED: Medicare Statute: 1862a(12)

☑ **D3426** Apicoectomy/periradicular surgery (each additional root)
MED: Medicare Statute: 1862a(12)

☑ **D3430** Retrograde filling — per root
MED: Medicare Statute: 1862a(12)

☑ **D3450** Root amputation — per root
MED: Medicare Statute: 1862a(12)

Ⓢ D3460 **Endodontic endosseous implant**
MED: MCM 2336, MCM 2136

D3470 **Intentional reimplantation (including necessary splinting)**
MED: Medicare Statute: 1862a(12)

OTHER ENDODONTIC PROCEDURES

D3910 **Surgical procedure for isolation of tooth with rubber dam**
MED: Medicare Statute: 1862a(12)

D3920 **Hemisection (including any root removal), not including root canal therapy**
MED: Medicare Statute: 1862a(12)

D3950 **Canal preparation and fitting of preformed dowel or post**
MED: Medicare Statute: 1862a(12)

Ⓢ D3999 **Unspecified endodontic procedure, by report**
Determine if an alternative HCPCS Level II code or a CPT code better describes the service being reported. This code should be used only if a more specific code is unavailable.
MED: MCM 2336, MCM 2136

PERIODONTICS D4000-D4999

SURGICAL SERVICES (INCLUDING USUAL POSTOPERATIVE SERVICES)

☑ D4210 **Gingivectomy or gingivoplasty - four or more contiguous teeth or bounded teeth spaces, per quadrant**
See also CPT code in the Surgery section (41820).
Cross-reference CPT 41820

☑ D4211 **Gingivectomy or gingivoplasty - one to three teeth, per quadrant**
See also CPT code (64400-64530).
Cross-reference CPT

☑ D4240 **Gingival flap procedure, including root planing - four or more contiguous teeth or bounded teeth spaces, per quadrant**
MED: Medicare Statute: 1862a(12)

D4241 **Gingival flap procedure, including root planing — one to three teeth, per quadrant**
See also D4240.
MED: Medicare Statute: 1862a(12)

D4245 **Apically positioned flap**
MED: Medicare Statute: 1862a(12)

D4249 **Clinical crown lengthening — hard tissue**
MED: Medicare Statute: 1862a(12)

Ⓢ ☑ D4260 **Osseous surgery (including flap entry and closure) - four or more contiguous teeth or bounded teeth spaces, per quadrant**
MED: MCM 2136, MCM 2336

Ⓔ D4261 **Osseous surgery (including flap entry and closure) — one to three teeth, per quadrant**
See CPT code 41823.
MED: Medicare Statute: 1862a(12)

Ⓢ ☑ D4263 **Bone replacement graft — first site in quadrant**
MED: CIM 50-26, MCM 2336, MCM 2136

Ⓢ ☑ D4264 **Bone replacement graft — each additional site in quadrant (use if performed on same date of service as D4263)**
MED: CIM 50-26, MCM 2336, MCM 2136

D4265 **Biologic materials to aid in soft and osseous tissue regeneration**
MED: Medicare Statute: 1862a(12)

☑ D4266 **Guided tissue regeneration — resorbable barrier, per site**
MED: Medicare Statute: 1862a(12)

☑ D4267 **Guided tissue regeneration — nonresorbable barrier, per site (includes membrane removal)**
MED: Medicare Statute: 1862a(12)

Ⓢ ☑ D4268 **Surgical revision procedure, per tooth**
MED: MCM 2136, MCM 2336

Ⓢ D4270 **Pedicle soft tissue graft procedure**
MED: MCM 2336, MCM 2136

Ⓢ D4271 **Free soft tissue graft procedure (including donor site surgery)**
MED: MCM 2336, MCM 2136

Ⓢ D4273 **Subepithelial connective tissue graft procedures**
For tissue grafts, see CPT 15000 et seq.
MED: CIM 50-26, MCM 2136, MCM 2336

D4274 **Distal or proximal wedge procedure (when not performed in conjunction with surgical procedures in the same anatomical area)**
MED: Medicare Statute: 1862a(12)

D4275 **Soft tissue allograft**
For tissue grafts, see CPT 15000 et seq.
MED: Medicare Statute: 1862a(12)

D4276 **Combined connective tissue and double pedicle graft**
For tissue/pedicle grafts see CPT 15000 et seq.
MED: Medicare Statute: 1862a(12)

ADJUNCTIVE PERIODONTAL SERVICES

D4320 **Provisional splinting — intracoronal**
MED: Medicare Statute: 1862a(12)

D4321 **Provisional splinting — extracoronal**
MED: Medicare Statute: 1862a(12)

☑ D4341 **Periodontal scaling and root planing - four or more contiguous teeth or bounded teeth spaces, per quadrant**
MED: Medicare Statute: 1862a(12)

D4342 **Periodontal scaling and root planing — one to three teeth, per quadrant**
MED: Medicare Statute: 1862a(12)

Ⓢ D4355 **Full mouth debridement to enable comprehensive evaluation and diagnosis**
This procedure is covered by Medicare if its purpose is to identify a patient's existing infections prior to kidney transplantation. For debridement see CPT 11000 et seq.
MED: CIM 50-26, MCM 2136, MCM 2336

| Special Coverage Instructions | Noncovered by Medicare | Carrier Discretion | ☑ Quantity Alert | ● New Code | ▲ Revised Code |

Ⓢ   **D4381**   **Localized delivery of chemotherapeutic agents via a controlled release vehicle into diseased crevicular tissue, per tooth, by report**
Pertinent documentation to evaluate medical appropriateness should be included when this code is reported.
MED: CIM 50-26, MCM 2336, MCM 2136

OTHER PERIODONTAL SERVICES

D4910   **Periodontal maintenance**
MED: Medicare Statute: 1862a(12)

D4920   **Unscheduled dressing change (by someone other than treating dentist)**
MED: Medicare Statute: 1862a(12)

D4999   **Unspecified periodontal procedure, by report**
Determine if an alternative HCPCS Level II code or a CPT code better describes the service being reported. This code should be used only if a more specific code is unavailable.
MED: Medicare Statute: 1862a(12)

PROSTHODONTICS (REMOVABLE) D5000-D5899

COMPLETE DENTURES (INCLUDING ROUTINE POST DELIVERY CARE)

D5110   **Complete denture — maxillary**
MED: Medicare Statute: 1862a(12)

D5120   **Complete denture — mandibular**
MED: Medicare Statute: 1862a(12)

D5130   **Immediate denture — maxillary**
MED: Medicare Statute: 1862a(12)

D5140   **Immediate denture — mandibular**
MED: Medicare Statute: 1862a(12)

PARTIAL DENTURES (INCLUDING ROUTINE POST DELIVERY CARE)

D5211   **Maxillary partial denture — resin base (including any conventional clasps, rests and teeth)**
MED: Medicare Statute: 1862a(12)

D5212   **Mandibular partial denture — resin base (including any conventional clasps, rests and teeth)**
MED: Medicare Statute: 1862a(12)

D5213   **Maxillary partial denture — cast metal framework with resin denture bases (including any conventional clasps, rests and teeth)**
MED: Medicare Statute: 1862a(12)

D5214   **Mandibular partial denture — cast metal framework with resin denture bases (including any conventional clasps, rests and teeth)**
MED: Medicare Statute: 1862a(12)

D5281   **Removable unilateral partial denture — one piece cast metal (including clasps and teeth)**
MED: Medicare Statute: 1862a(12)

ADJUSTMENTS TO REMOVABLE PROSTHESES

D5410   **Adjust complete denture — maxillary**
MED: Medicare Statute: 1862a(12)

D5411   **Adjust complete denture — mandibular**
MED: Medicare Statute: 1862a(12)

D5421   **Adjust partial denture — maxillary**
MED: Medicare Statute: 1862a(12)

D5422   **Adjust partial denture — mandibular**
MED: Medicare Statute: 1862a(12)

REPAIRS TO COMPLETE DENTURES

D5510   **Repair broken complete denture base**
MED: Medicare Statute: 1862a(12)

D5520   **Replace missing or broken teeth — complete denture (each tooth)**
MED: Medicare Statute: 1862a(12)

REPAIRS TO PARTIAL DENTURES

D5610   **Repair resin denture base**
MED: Medicare Statute: 1862a(12)

D5620   **Repair cast framework**
MED: Medicare Statute: 1862a(12)

D5630   **Repair or replace broken clasp**
MED: Medicare Statute: 1862a(12)

☑   **D5640**   **Replace broken teeth — per tooth**
MED: Medicare Statute: 1862a(12)

D5650   **Add tooth to existing partial denture**
MED: Medicare Statute: 1862a(12)

D5660   **Add clasp to existing partial denture**
MED: Medicare Statute: 1862a(12)

D5670   **Replace all teeth and acrylic on cast metal framework (maxillary)**
MED: Medicare Statute: 1862a(12)

D5671   **Replace all teeth and acrylic on cast metal framework (mandibular)**
MED: Medicare Statute: 1862a(12)

DENTURE REBASE PROCEDURES

D5710   **Rebase complete maxillary denture**
MED: Medicare Statute: 1862a(12)

D5711   **Rebase complete mandibular denture**
MED: Medicare Statute: 1862a(12)

D5720   **Rebase maxillary partial denture**
MED: Medicare Statute: 1862a(12)

D5721   **Rebase mandibular partial denture**
MED: Medicare Statute: 1862a(12)

DENTURE RELINE PROCEDURES

D5730   **Reline complete maxillary denture (chairside)**
MED: Medicare Statute: 1862a(12)

D5731   **Reline complete mandibular denture (chairside)**
MED: Medicare Statute: 1862a(12)

D5740   **Reline maxillary partial denture (chairside)**
MED: Medicare Statute: 1862a(12)

D5741   **Reline mandibular partial denture (chairside)**
MED: Medicare Statute: 1862a(12)

D5750   Reline complete maxillary denture (laboratory)
MED: Medicare Statute: 1862a(12)

D5751   Reline complete mandibular denture (laboratory)
MED: Medicare Statute: 1862a(12)

D5760   Reline maxillary partial denture (laboratory)
MED: Medicare Statute: 1862a(12)

D5761   Reline mandibular partial denture (laboratory)
MED: Medicare Statute: 1862a(12)

OTHER REMOVABLE PROSTHETIC SERVICES

D5810   Interim complete denture (maxillary)
MED: Medicare Statute: 1862a(12)

D5811   Interim complete denture (mandibular)
MED: Medicare Statute: 1862a(12)

D5820   Interim partial denture (maxillary)
MED: Medicare Statute: 1862a(12)

D5821   Interim partial denture (mandibular)
MED: Medicare Statute: 1862a(12)

D5850   Tissue conditioning, maxillary
MED: Medicare Statute: 1862a(12)

D5851   Tissue conditioning, mandibular
MED: Medicare Statute: 1862a(12)

D5860   Overdenture — complete, by report
Pertinent documentation to evaluate medical appropriateness should be included when this code is reported.
MED: Medicare Statute: 1862a(12)

D5861   Overdenture — partial, by report
Pertinent documentation to evaluate medical appropriateness should be included when this code is reported.
MED: Medicare Statute: 1862a(12)

D5862   Precision attachment, by report
Pertinent documentation to evaluate medical appropriateness should be included when this code is reported.
MED: Medicare Statute: 1862a(12)

D5867   Replacement of replaceable part of semi-precision or precision attachment (male or female component)
MED: Medicare Statute: 1862a(12)

D5875   Modification of removable prosthesis following implant surgery
MED: Medicare Statute: 1862a(12)

D5899   Unspecified removable prosthodontic procedure, by report
Determine if an alternative HCPCS Level II code or a CPT code better describes the service being reported. This code should be used only if a more specific code is unavailable.
MED: Medicare Statute: 1862a(12)

MAXILLOFACIAL PROSTHETICS D5900-D5999

Ⓢ   **D5911**   Facial moulage (sectional)
MED: MCM 2130 A, MCM 2136

Ⓢ   **D5912**   Facial moulage (complete)
MED: MCM 2130 A

D5913   Nasal prosthesis
Cross-reference CPT 21087

D5914   Auricular prosthesis
See also CPT code in the Surgery section (21086).
Cross-reference CPT 21086

D5915   Orbital prosthesis
Cross-reference L8611

D5916   Ocular prosthesis
See also CPT code (21077, 65770, 66982-66985, 92330-92335, 92358, 92393).
Cross-reference V2623, V2629

D5919   Facial prosthesis
Cross-reference CPT 21088

D5922   Nasal septal prosthesis
Cross-reference CPT 30220

D5923   Ocular prosthesis, interim
Cross-reference CPT 92330

D5924   Cranial prosthesis
Cross-reference CPT 62143

D5925   Facial augmentation implant prosthesis
Cross-reference CPT 21208

D5926   Nasal prosthesis, replacement
Cross-reference CPT 21087

D5927   Auricular prosthesis, replacement
Cross-reference CPT 21086

D5928   Orbital prosthesis, replacement
Cross-reference CPT 67550

D5929   Facial prosthesis, replacement
Cross-reference CPT 21088

D5931   Obturator prosthesis, surgical
Cross-reference CPT 21079

D5932   Obturator prosthesis, definitive
Cross-reference CPT 21080

D5933   Obturator prosthesis, modification
Cross-reference CPT 21080

D5934   Mandibular resection prosthesis with guide flange
Cross-reference CPT 21081

D5935   Mandibular resection prosthesis without guide flange
Cross-reference CPT 21081

D5936   Obturator/prosthesis, interim
Cross-reference CPT 21079

D5937   Trismus appliance (not for TMD treatment)
MED: MCM 2130

D5951   Feeding aid
MED: MCM 2336, MCM 2130

D5952   Speech aid prosthesis, pediatric
Cross-reference CPT 21084

D5953   Speech aid prosthesis, adult
Cross-reference CPT 21084

D5954   Palatal augmentation prosthesis
Cross-reference CPT 21082

Dental Procedures

D5955   Palatal lift prosthesis, definitive
Cross-reference CPT 21083

D5958   Palatal lift prosthesis, interim
Cross-reference CPT 21083

D5959   Palatal lift prosthesis, modification
Cross-reference CPT 21083

D5960   Speech aid prosthesis, modification
Cross-reference CPT 21084

D5982   Surgical stent
For oral surgical stent see CPT code. Surgical stent.
Periodontal stent, skin graft stent, columellar stent.
Cross-reference CPT 21085

S   **D5983**   Radiation carrier
MED: MCM 2336, MCM 2136

S   **D5984**   Radiation shield
MED: MCM 2336, MCM 2136

S   **D5985**   Radiation cone locator
MED: MCM 2336, MCM 2136

E   **D5986**   Fluoride gel carrier
MED: Medicare Statute: 1862a(12)

S   **D5987**   Commissure splint
MED: MCM 2136, MCM 2336

E   **D5988**   Surgical splint. See also CPT.
See also CPT code (21085)
Cross-reference CPT

E   **D5999**   Unspecified maxillofacial prosthesis, by report
Determine if an alternative HCPCS Level II code or a CPT
code better describes the service being reported. This code
should be used only if a more specific code is unavailable.
Cross-reference CPT

IMPLANT SERVICES D6000-D6199

D6010   Surgical placement of implant body: endosteal implant
Cross-reference CPT 21248

D6020   Abutment placement or substitution: endosteal implant
Cross-reference CPT 21248

D6040   Surgical placement: eposteal implant
Cross-reference CPT 21245

D6050   Surgical placement: transosteal implant
Cross-reference CPT 21244

D6053   Implant/abutment supported removable denture for completely edentulous arch
MED: MCM 2136

D6054   Implant/abutment supported removable denture for partially edentulous arch
MED: MCM 2136

D6055   Dental implant supported connecting bar
MED: MCM 2136

D6056   Prefabricated abutment
MED: MCM 2136

D6057   Custom abutment
MED: MCM 2136

D6058   Abutment supported porcelain/ceramic crown
MED: MCM 2136

D6059   Abutment supported porcelain fused to metal crown (high noble metal)
MED: MCM 2136

D6060   Abutment supported porcelain fused to metal crown (predominantly base metal)
MED: MCM 2136

D6061   Abutment supported porcelain fused to metal crown (noble metal)
MED: MCM 2136

D6062   Abutment supported cast metal crown (high noble metal)
MED: MCM 2136

D6063   Abutment supported cast metal crown (predominantly base metal)
MED: MCM 2136

D6064   Abutment supported cast metal crown (noble metal)
MED: MCM 2136

D6065   Implant supported porcelain/ceramic crown
MED: MCM 2136

D6066   Implant supported porcelain fused to metal crown (titanium, titanium alloy, high noble metal)
MED: MCM 2136

D6067   Implant supported metal crown (titanium, titanium alloy, high noble metal)
MED: MCM 2136

D6068   Abutment supported retainer for porcelain/ceramic FPD
MED: MCM 2136

D6069   Abutment supported retainer for porcelain fused to metal FPD (high noble metal)
MED: MCM 2136

D6070   Abutment supported retainer for porcelain fused to metal FPD (predominately base metal)
MED: MCM 2136

D6071   Abutment supported retainer for porcelain fused to metal FPD (noble metal)
MED: MCM 2136

D6072   Abutment supported retainer for cast metal FPD (high noble metal)
MED: MCM 2136

D6073   Abutment supported retainer for cast metal FPD (predominately base metal)
MED: MCM 2136

D6074   Abutment supported retainer for cast metal FPD (noble metal)
MED: MCM 2136

D6075   Implant supported retainer for ceramic FPD
MED: MCM 2136

D6076   Implant supported retainer for porcelain fused to metal FPD (titanium, titanium alloy, or high noble metal)
MED: MCM 2136

D6077 Implant supported retainer for cast metal FPD (titanium, titanium alloy, or high noble metal)
MED: MCM 2136

D6078 Implant/abutment supported fixed denture for completely edentulous arch
MED: MCM 2136

D6079 Implant/abutment supported fixed denture for partially edentulous arch
MED: MCM 2136

D6080 Implant maintenance procedures, including removal of prosthesis, cleansing of prosthesis and abutments, reinsertion of prosthesis
MED: MCM 2136

D6090 Repair implant supported prosthesis, by report
Pertinent documentation to evaluate medical appropriateness should be included when this code is reported. See also CPT code (21299).
Cross-reference CPT 21299

D6095 Repair implant abutment, by report
Pertinent documentation to evaluate medical appropriateness should be included when this code is reported. See also CPT code (21299).

D6100 Implant removal, by report
Pertinent documentation to evaluate medical appropriateness should be included when this code is reported. See also CPT code (21299).
Cross-reference CPT 21299

D6199 Unspecified implant procedure, by report
Cross-reference CPT 21299

PROSTHODONTICS (FIXED) D6200-D6999

FIXED PARTIAL DENTURE PONTICS

D6210 Pontic — cast high noble metal
Each abutment and each pontic constitute a unit in a prosthesis. An alloy of at least 60 percent Gold (Au), Palladium (Pd), or Platinum (Pt) is considered a high noble metal.
MED: Medicare Statute: 1862a(12)

D6211 Pontic — cast predominantly base metal
Each abutment and each pontic constitute a unit in a prosthesis. An alloy of less than 25 percent Gold (Au), Palladium (Pd), or Platinum (Pt) is considered a base metal.
MED: Medicare Statute: 1862a(12)

D6212 Pontic — cast noble metal
Each abutment and each pontic constitute a unit in a prosthesis. An alloy of at least 25 percent Gold (Au), Palladium (Pd), or Platinum (Pt) is considered a noble metal.
MED: Medicare Statute: 1862a(12)

D6240 Pontic — porcelain fused to high noble metal
Each abutment and each pontic constitute a unit in a prosthesis. An alloy of at least 60 percent Gold (Au), Palladium (Pd), or Platinum (Pt) is considered a high noble metal.
MED: Medicare Statute: 1862a(12)

D6241 Pontic — porcelain fused to predominantly base metal
Each abutment and each pontic constitute a unit in a prosthesis. An alloy of less than 25 percent Gold (Au), Palladium (Pd), or Platinum (Pt) is considered a base metal.
MED: Medicare Statute: 1862a(12)

D6242 Pontic — porcelain fused to noble metal
Each abutment and each pontic constitute a unit in a prosthesis. An alloy of at least 60 percent Gold (Au), Palladium (Pd), or Platinum (Pt) is considered a high noble metal.
MED: Medicare Statute: 1862a(12)

D6245 Pontic — porcelain/ceramic
MED: MCM 2136

D6250 Pontic — resin with high noble metal
Each abutment and each pontic constitute a unit in a prosthesis. An alloy of at least 60 percent Gold (Au), Palladium (Pd), or Platinum (Pt) is considered a high noble metal.
MED: Medicare Statute: 1862a(12)

D6251 Pontic — resin with predominantly base metal
Each abutment and each pontic constitute a unit in a prosthesis. An alloy of less than 25 percent Gold (Au), Palladium (Pd), or Platinum (Pt) is considered a base metal.
MED: Medicare Statute: 1862a(12)

D6252 Pontic — resin with noble metal
Each abutment and each pontic constitute a unit in a prosthesis. An alloy of at least 25 percent Gold (Au), Palladium (Pd), or Platinum (Pt) is considered a noble metal.
MED: Medicare Statute: 1862a(12)

D6253 Provisional pontic
MED: Medicare Statute: 1862a(12)

D6545 Retainer — cast metal for resin bonded fixed prosthesis
MED: Medicare Statute: 1862a(12)

D6548 Retainer — porcelain/ceramic for resin bonded fixed prosthesis
MED: MCM 2136

D6600 Inlay-porcelain/ceramic, two surfaces
MED: MCM 2136

D6601 Inlay — porcelain/ceramic, three or more surfaces
MED: MCM 2136

D6602 Inlay — cast high noble metal, two surfaces
MED: MCM 2136

D6603 Inlay — cast high noble metal, three or more surfaces
MED: MCM 2136

D6604 Inlay — cast predominantly base metal, two surfaces
MED: MCM 2136

D6605 Inlay — cast predominantly base metal, three or more surfaces
MED: MCM 2136

D6606 Inlay — cast noble metal, two surfaces
MED: MCM 2136

D6607 Inlay — cast noble metal, three or more surfaces
MED: MCM 2136

D6608 Onlay — porcelain/ceramic, two surfaces
MED: MCM 2136

D6609 Onlay — porcelain/ceramic, three or more surfaces
MED: MCM 2136

D6610 Onlay — cast high noble metal, two surfaces
MED: MCM 2136

Dental Procedures

D6611 — D7111

D6611 Onlay — cast high noble metal, three or more surfaces
MED: MCM 2136

D6612 Onlay — cast predominantly base metal, two surfaces
MED: MCM 2136

D6613 Onlay — cast predominantly base metal, three or more surfaces
MED: MCM 2136

D6614 Onlay — cast noble metal, two surfaces
MED: MCM 2136

D6615 Onlay — cast noble metal, three or more surfaces
MED: MCM 2136

FIXED PARTIAL DENTURE RETAINERS — CROWNS

D6720 Crown — resin with high noble metal
An alloy of at least 60 percent Gold (Au), Palladium (Pd), or Platinum (Pt) is considered a high noble metal.
MED: Medicare Statute: 1862a(12)

D6721 Crown — resin with predominantly base metal
An alloy of less than 25 percent Gold (Au), Palladium (Pd), or Platinum (Pt) is considered a base metal.
MED: Medicare Statute: 1862a(12)

D6722 Crown — resin with noble metal
An alloy of at least 25 percent Gold (Au), Palladium (Pd), or Platinum (Pt) is considered a noble metal.
MED: Medicare Statute: 1862a(12)

D6740 Crown — porcelain/ceramic
MED: MCM 2136

D6750 Crown — porcelain fused to high noble metal
An alloy of at least 60 percent Gold (Au), Palladium (Pd), or Platinum (Pt) is considered a high noble metal.
MED: Medicare Statute: 1862a(12)

D6751 Crown — porcelain fused to predominantly base metal
An alloy of less than 25 percent Gold (Au), Palladium (Pd), or Platinum (Pt) is considered a base metal.
MED: Medicare Statute: 1862a(12)

D6752 Crown — porcelain fused to noble metal
An alloy of at least 25 percent Gold (Au), Palladium (Pd), or Platinum (Pt) is considered a noble metal.
MED: Medicare Statute: 1862a(12)

D6780 Crown — 3/4 cast high noble metal
An alloy of at least 60 percent Gold (Au), Palladium (Pd), or Platinum (Pt) is considered a high noble metal.
MED: Medicare Statute: 1862a(12)

D6781 Crown — 3/4 cast predominately base metal
An alloy of less than 25 percent Gold (Au), Palladium (Pd), or Platinum (Pt) is considered a base metal.
MED: MCM 2136

D6782 Crown — 3/4 cast noble metal
An alloy of at least 25 percent Gold (Au), Palladium (Pd), or Platinum (Pt) is considered a noble metal.
MED: MCM 2136

D6783 Crown — 3/4 porcelain/ceramic
MED: MCM 2136

D6790 Crown — full cast high noble metal
An alloy of at least 60 percent Gold (Au), Palladium (Pd), or Platinum (Pt) is considered a high noble metal.
MED: Medicare Statute: 1862a(12)

D6791 Crown — full cast predominantly base metal
An alloy of less than 25 percent Gold (Au), Palladium (Pd), or Platinum (Pt) is considered a base metal.
MED: Medicare Statute: 1862a(12)

D6792 Crown — full cast noble metal
An alloy of at least 25 percent Gold (Au), Palladium (Pd), or Platinum (Pt) is considered a noble metal.
MED: Medicare Statute: 1862a(12)

D6793 Provisional retainer crown
MED: Medicare Statute: 1862a(12)

OTHER FIXED PARTIAL DENTURE SERVICES

S **D6920** Connector bar
MED: CIM 50-26, MCM 2336, MCM 2136

D6930 Recement fixed partial denture
MED: Medicare Statute: 1862a(12)

D6940 Stress breaker
MED: Medicare Statute: 1862a(12)

D6950 Precision attachment
MED: Medicare Statute: 1862a(12)

D6970 Cast post and core in addition to fixed partial denture retainer
MED: Medicare Statute: 1862a(12)

D6971 Cast post as part of fixed partial denture retainer
MED: Medicare Statute: 1862a(12)

D6972 Prefabricated post and core in addition to fixed partial denture retainer
MED: Medicare Statute: 1862a(12)

D6973 Core build up for retainer, including any pins
MED: Medicare Statute: 1862a(12)

D6975 Coping — metal
MED: Medicare Statute: 1862a(12)

D6976 Each additional cast post — same tooth
Report this code in addition to codes D6970 or D6971.
MED: MCM 2136

D6977 Each additional prefabricated post — same tooth
Report this code in addition to code D6972.
MED: MCM 2136

D6980 Fixed partial denture repair, by report
Pertinent documentation to evaluate medical appropriateness should be included when this code is reported.
MED: Medicare Statute: 1862a(12)

D6985 Pediatric partial denture, fixed   P
MED: Medicare Statute: 1862a(12)

D6999 Unspecified, fixed prosthodontic procedure, by report
Determine if an alternative HCPCS Level II code or a CPT code better describes the service being reported. This code should be used only if a more specific code is unavailable.
MED: Medicare Statute: 1862a(12)

S **D7111** Coronal remnants — deciduous tooth
MED: MCM 2336

Ⓢ   **D7140** Extraction, erupted tooth or exposed root (elevation and/or forceps removal)
MED: MCM 2336

SURGICAL EXTRACTIONS (INCLUDES LOCAL ANESTHESIA AND ROUTINE POSTOPERATIVE CARE)

Ⓢ   **D7210** Surgical removal of erupted tooth requiring elevation of mucoperiosteal flap and removal of bone and/section of tooth
MED: MCM 2336, MCM 2136

Ⓢ   **D7220** Removal of impacted tooth — soft tissue
MED: MCM 2336, MCM 2136

Ⓢ   **D7230** Removal of impacted tooth — partially bony
MED: MCM 2336, MCM 2136

Ⓢ   **D7240** Removal of impacted tooth — completely bony
MED: MCM 2336, MCM 2136

Ⓢ   **D7241** Removal of impacted tooth — completely bony, with unusual surgical complications
MED: MCM 2336, MCM 2136

Ⓢ   **D7250** Surgical removal of residual tooth roots (cutting procedure)
MED: MCM 2336, MCM 2136

OTHER SURGICAL PROCEDURES

Ⓢ   **D7260** Orolantral fistula closure
MED: MCM 2336, MCM 2136

Ⓢ   **D7261** Primary closure of a sinus perforation
See equivalent CPT code for repair of mucous membranes.
MED: MCM 2336

D7270 Tooth reimplantation and/or stabilization of accidentally evulsed or displaced tooth
MED: Medicare Statute: 1862a(12)

D7272 Tooth transplantation (includes reimplantation from one site to another and splinting and/or stabilization)
MED: Medicare Statute: 1862a(12)

D7280 Surgical access of an unerupted tooth
MED: Medicare Statute: 1862a(12)

D7281 Surgical exposure of impacted or unerupted tooth to aid eruption
MED: Medicare Statute: 1862a(12)

D7282 Mobilization of erupted or malpositioned tooth to aid eruption
MED: Medicare Statute: 1862a(12)

D7285 Biopsy of oral tissue — hard (bone, tooth)
Cross-reference CPT 20220, 20225, 20240, 20245

D7286 Biopsy of oral tissue — soft (all others)
Cross-reference CPT 40808

D7287 Cytology sample collection

D7290 Surgical repositioning of teeth
MED: Medicare Statute: 1862a(12)

Ⓢ   **D7291** Transseptal fiberotomy/supra crestal fiberotomy, by report
Pertinent documentation to evaluate medical appropriateness should be included when this code is reported.
MED: MCM 2136, MCM 2336

ALVEOLOPLASTY — SURGICAL PREPARATION OF RIDGE FOR DENTURES

☑   **D7310** Alveoloplasty in conjunction with extractions — per quadrant
Cross-reference CPT 41874

☑   **D7320** Alveoloplasty not in conjunction with extractions — per quadrant
Cross-reference CPT 41870

VESTIBULOPLASTY

D7340 Vestibuloplasty — ridge extension (second epithelialization)
Cross-reference CPT 40840, 40842, 40843, 40844

D7350 Vestibuloplasty — ridge extension (including soft tissue grafts, muscle reattachments, revision of soft tissue attachment and management of hypertrophied and hyperplastic tissue)
Cross-reference CPT 40845

SURGICAL EXCISION OF REACTIVE INFLAMMATORY LESIONS (SCAR TISSUE OR LOCALIZED CONGENITAL LESIONS)

☑   **D7410** Excision of benign lesion up to 1.25 cm
Cross-reference CPT

D7411 Excision of benign lesion greater than 1.25 cm
See CPT codes in the surgical section (11440 & 40520)

D7412 Excision of benign lesion, complicated
See CPT code in the surgical section (10000 & 40000)

D7413 Excision of malignant lesion up to 1.25 cm
See CPT code in the surgical section (11442)

D7414 Excision of malignant lesion greater than 1.25 cm
See CPT codes in the surgical section (11442-11446)

D7415 Excision of malignant lesion, complicated
See CPT codes in the surgical section (11440-11446 with modifier 22 for complicated)

☑   **D7440** Excision of malignant tumor - lesion diameter up to 1.25 cm
Cross-reference CPT

☑   **D7441** Excision of malignant tumor - lesion diameter greater than 1.25 cm
Cross-reference CPT

☑   **D7450** Removal of benign odontogenic cyst or tumor-lesion diameter up to 1.25 cm
Cross-reference CPT

☑   **D7451** Removal of benign odontogenic cyst or tumor-lesion diameter greater than 1.25 cm
Cross-reference CPT

☑   **D7460** Removal of benign nonodontogenic cyst or tumor-lesion diameter up to 1.25 cm
Cross-reference CPT

☑   **D7461** Removal of benign nonodontogenic cyst or tumor-lesion diameter greater than 1.25 cm
Cross-reference CPT

Dental Procedures

D7465 — D7860

☑ **D7465** Destruction of lesion(s) by physical or chemical method, by report
Pertinent documentation to evaluate medical appropriateness should be included when this code is reported.
Cross-reference CPT 41850

☑ **D7471** Removal of lateral exostosis (maxilla or mandible)
Cross-reference CPT 21031, 21032

D7472 Removal of torus palatinus
See CPT code in the surgical section (21029, 21030, 21031)

D7473 Removal of torus mandibularis

D7485 Surgical reduction of osseous tuberosity

D7490 Radical resection of mandible with bone graft
Cross-reference CPT 21095

SURGICAL INCISION

D7510 Incision and drainage of abscess - intraoral soft tissue
Cross-reference CPT 41800

D7520 Incision and drainage of abscess - extraoral soft tissue
Cross-reference CPT 40800

D7530 Removal of foreign body from mucosa, skin, or subcutaneous alveolar tissue
Cross-reference CPT 41805, 41828

D7540 Removal of reaction-producing foreign bodies, musculoskeletal system
Cross-reference CPT 20520, 41800, 41806

D7550 Partial ostectomy/sequestrectomy for removal of non-vital bone
Cross-reference CPT 20999

D7560 Maxillary sinusotomy for removal of tooth fragment or foreign body
Cross-reference CPT 31020

TREATMENT OF FRACTURES — SIMPLE

D7610 Maxilla — open reduction (teeth immobilized, if present
Cross-reference CPT

D7620 Maxilla — closed reduction (teeth immobilized, if present)
Cross-reference CPT

D7630 Mandible — open reduction (teeth immobilized, if present)
Cross-reference CPT

D7640 Mandible — closed reduction (teeth immobilized, if present)
Cross-reference CPT

D7650 Malar and/or zygomatic arch — open reduction
Cross-reference CPT

D7660 Malar and/or zygomatic arch — closed reduction
Cross-reference CPT

D7670 Alveolus — closed reduction, may include stabilization of teeth
Cross-reference CPT

D7671 Alveolus — open reduction, may include stabilization of teeth

D7680 Facial bones — complicated reduction with fixation and multiple surgical approaches
Cross-reference CPT

TREATMENT OF FRACTURES — COMPOUND

D7710 Maxilla — open reduction
Cross-reference CPT 21346

D7720 Maxilla — closed reduction
Cross-reference CPT 21345

D7730 Mandible — open reduction
Cross-reference CPT 21461, 21462

D7740 Mandible — closed reduction
Cross-reference CPT 21455

D7750 Malar and/or zygomatic arch — open reduction
Cross-reference CPT 21360, 21365

D7760 Malar and/or zygomatic arch — closed reduction
Cross-reference CPT 21355

D7770 Alveolus — open reduction stabilization of teeth
Cross-reference CPT 21422

D7771 Alveolus, closed reduction stabilization of teeth
See CPT code in the surgical section (21421)

D7780 Facial bones — complicated reduction with fixation and multiple surgical approaches
Cross-reference CPT 21433, 21435, 21436

REDUCTION OF DISLOCATION AND MANAGEMENT OF OTHER TEMPOROMANDIBULAR JOINT DYSFUNCTIONS
Procedures which are an integral part of a primary procedure should not be reported separately.

D7810 Open reduction of dislocation
Cross-reference CPT 21490

D7820 Closed reduction of dislocation
Cross-reference CPT 21480

D7830 Manipulation under anesthesia
Cross-reference CPT 00190

D7840 Condylectomy
Cross-reference CPT 21050

D7850 Surgical discectomy, with/without implant
Cross-reference CPT 21060

D7852 Disc repair
Cross-reference CPT 21299

D7854 Synovectomy
Cross-reference CPT 21299

D7856 Myotomy
Cross-reference CPT 21299

D7858 Joint reconstruction
Cross-reference CPT 21242, 21243

D7860 Arthrotomy
MED: MCM 2336, MCM 2136

D7865 Arthroplasty
Cross-reference CPT 21240

D7870 Arthrocentesis
Cross-reference CPT 21060

D7871 Non-arthroscopic lysis and lavage
MED: Medicare Statute: 1862a(12)

D7872 Arthroscopy — diagnosis, with or without biopsy
Cross-reference CPT 29800

D7873 Arthroscopy — surgical: lavage and lysis of adhesions
Cross-reference CPT 29804

D7874 Arthroscopy — surgical: disc repositioning and stabilization
Cross-reference CPT 29804

D7875 Arthroscopy — surgical: synovectomy
Cross-reference CPT 29804

D7876 Arthroscopy — surgical: discectomy
Cross-reference CPT 29804

D7877 Arthroscopy — surgical: debridement
Cross-reference CPT 29804

D7880 Occlusal orthotic device, by report
Cross-reference CPT 21499

D7899 Unspecified TMD therapy, by report
Determine if an alternative HCPCS Level II code or a CPT code better describes the service being reported. This code should be used only if a more specific code is unavailable.
Cross-reference CPT 21499

REPAIR OF TRAUMATIC WOUNDS

☑ **D7910** Suture of recent small wounds up to 5 cm
Cross-reference CPT 12011, 12013

COMPLICATED SUTURING (RECONSTRUCTION REQUIRING DELICATE HANDLING OF TISSUES AND WIDE UNDERMINING FOR METICULOUS CLOSURE)

D7911 Complicated suture — up to 5 cm
Cross-reference CPT 12051, 12052

D7912 Complicated suture — greater than 5 cm
Cross-reference CPT 13132

OTHER REPAIR PROCEDURES

D7920 Skin graft (identify defect covered, location and type of graft)
Cross-reference CPT

S   **D7940** Osteoplasty — for orthognathic deformities
MED: MCM 2336, MCM 2136

D7941 Osteotomy — mandibular rami
Cross-reference CPT 21193, 21195, 21196

D7943 Osteotomy — mandibular rami with bone graft; includes obtaining the graft
Cross-reference CPT 21194

☑ **D7944** Osteotomy — segmented or subapical — per sextant or quadrant
Cross-reference CPT 21198, 21206

D7945 Osteotomy — body of mandible
Cross-reference CPT 21193, 21194, 21195, 21196

D7946 LeFort I (maxilla — total)
Cross-reference CPT 21147

D7947 LeFort I (maxilla — segmented)
Cross-reference CPT 21145, 21146

D7948 LeFort II or LeFort III (osteoplasty of facial bones for midface hypoplasia or retrusion) — without bone graft
Cross-reference CPT 21150

D7949 LeFort II or LeFort III — with bone graft
Cross-reference CPT

D7950 Osseous, osteoperiosteal, or cartilage graft of the mandible or facial bones — autogenous or nonautogenous, by report
Pertinent documentation to evaluate medical appropriateness should be included when this code is reported.
Cross-reference CPT 21247

D7955 Repair of maxillofacial soft and hard tissue defect
Cross-reference CPT 21299

D7960 Frenulectomy (frenectomy or frenotomy) — separate procedure
Cross-reference CPT 40819, 41010, 41115

☑ **D7970** Excision of hyperplastic tissue — per arch
Cross-reference CPT

D7971 Excision of pericoronal gingiva
Cross-reference CPT 41821

D7972 Surgical reduction of fibrous tuberosity
Cross-reference CPT 21029, 21030, 21031

D7980 Sialolithotomy
Cross-reference CPT 42330, 42335, 42340

D7981 Excision of salivary gland, by report
Pertinent documentation to evaluate medical appropriateness should be included when this code is reported.
Cross-reference CPT 42408

D7982 Sialodochoplasty
Cross-reference CPT 42500

D7983 Closure of salivary fistula
Cross-reference CPT 42600

D7990 Emergency tracheotomy
Cross-reference CPT 31605

D7991 Coronoidectomy
Cross-reference CPT 21070

D7995 Synthetic graft — mandible or facial bones, by report
Pertinent documentation to evaluate medical appropriateness should be included when this code is reported.
Cross-reference CPT 21299

D7996 Implant — mandible for augmentation purposes (excluding alveolar ridge), by report
Pertinent documentation to evaluate medical appropriateness should be included when this code is reported.
Cross-reference CPT 21299

Special Coverage Instructions   Noncovered by Medicare   Carrier Discretion   ☑ Quantity Alert   ● New Code   ▲ Revised Code

Dental Procedures

D7997 — D9420

D7997 Appliance removal (not by dentist who placed appliance), includes removal of archbar
MED: Medicare Statute: 1862a(12)

D7999 Unspecified oral surgery procedure, by report
Determine if an alternative HCPCS Level II code or a CPT code better describes the service being reported. This code should be used only if a more specific code is unavailable.
Cross-reference CPT 21299

ORTHODONTICS D8000-D8999

D8010 Limited orthodontic treatment of the primary dentition
MED: Medicare Statute: 1862a(12)

D8020 Limited orthodontic treatment of the transitional dentition
MED: Medicare Statute: 1862a(12)

D8030 Limited orthodontic treatment of the adolescent dentition
MED: Medicare Statute: 1862a(12)

D8040 Limited orthodontic treatment of the adult dentition
MED: Medicare Statute: 1862a(12)

D8050 Interceptive orthodontic treatment of the primary dentition
MED: Medicare Statute: 1862a(12)

D8060 Interceptive orthodontic treatment of the transitional dentition
MED: Medicare Statute: 1862a(12)

D8070 Comprehensive orthodontic treatment of the transitional dentition
MED: Medicare Statute: 1862a(12)

D8080 Comprehensive orthodontic treatment of the adolescent dentition
MED: Medicare Statute: 1862a(12)

D8090 Comprehensive orthodontic treatment of the adult dentition
MED: Medicare Statute: 1862a(12)

MINOR TREATMENT TO CONTROL HARMFUL HABITS

D8210 Removable appliance therapy
MED: Medicare Statute: 1862a(12)

D8220 Fixed appliance therapy
MED: Medicare Statute: 1862a(12)

OTHER ORTHODONTIC SERVICES

D8660 Pre-orthodontic treatment visit
MED: Medicare Statute: 1862a(12)

D8670 Periodic orthodontic treatment visit (as part of contract)
MED: Medicare Statute: 1862a(12)

D8680 Orthodontic retention (removal of appliances, construction and placement of retainer(s))
MED: Medicare Statute: 1862a(12)

D8690 Orthodontic treatment (alternative billing to a contract fee)
MED: Medicare Statute: 1862a(12)

D8691 Repair of orthodontic appliance
MED: Medicare Statute: 1862a(12)

D8692 Replacement of lost or broken retainer
MED: Medicare Statute: 1862a(12)

D8999 Unspecified orthodontic procedure, by report
Determine if an alternative HCPCS Level II code or a CPT code better describes the service being reported. This code should be used only if a more specific code is unavailable.
MED: Medicare Statute: 1862a(12)

ADJUNCTIVE GENERAL SERVICES D9110-D9999

UNCLASSIFIED TREATMENT

[N] **D9110** Palliative (emergency) treatment of dental pain — minor procedure
MED: MCM 2336, MCM 2136

ANESTHESIA

D9210 Local anesthesia not in conjunction with operative or surgical procedures
Cross-reference CPT 90784

D9211 Regional block anesthesia
Cross-reference CPT 01995

D9212 Trigeminal division block anesthesia
Cross-reference CPT 64400

D9215 Local anesthesia
Cross-reference CPT 90784

☑ **D9220** Deep sedation/general anesthesia — first 30 minutes
See also CPT code 00172-00176.
Cross-reference CPT

☑ **D9221** Deep sedation/general anesthesia — each additional 15 minutes
MED: MCM 2136, MCM 2336

[N] **D9230** Analgesia, anxiolysis, inhalation of nitrous oxide
MED: MCM 2136, MCM 2336

☑ **D9241** Intravenous conscious sedation/analgesia — first 30 minutes
See also CPT code 90784, 99141.

☑ **D9242** Intravenous conscious sedation/analgesia — each additional 15 minutes
See also CPT code 90784, 99141.

[N] **D9248** Non-intravenous conscious sedation

PROFESSIONAL CONSULTATION

D9310 Consultation (diagnostic service provided by dentist or physician other than practitioner providing treatment)
Cross-reference CPT

PROFESSIONAL VISITS

D9410 House/extended care facility call
Cross-reference CPT

D9420 Hospital call
See also CPT E & M codes
Cross-reference CPT

D9430 Office visit for observation (during regularly scheduled hours) — no other services performed
See also CPT E & M codes
Cross-reference CPT

D9440 Office visit — after regularly scheduled hours
Cross-reference CPT 99050

D9450 Case presentation, detailed and extensive treatment planning

DRUGS

D9610 Therapeutic drug injection, by report
Pertinent documentation to evaluate medical appropriateness should be included when this code is reported.
Cross-reference CPT 90784, 90788

S **D9630** Other drugs and/or medicaments, by report
Determine if an alternative HCPCS Level II code better describes the supplies being reported. This code should be used only if a more specific code is unavailable.
MED: MCM 2336, MCM 2136

MISCELLANEOUS SERVICES

D9910 Application of desensitizing medicament
MED: Medicare Statute: 1862a(12)

☑ **D9911** Application of desensitizing resin for cervical and/or root surface, per tooth
MED: Medicare Statute: 1862a(12)

D9920 Behavior management, by report
Pertinent documentation to evaluate medical appropriateness should be included when this code is reported.
MED: Medicare Statute: 1862a(12)

S **D9930** Treatment of complications (post-surgical) — unusual circumstances, by report
MED: MCM 2336, MCM 2136

S **D9940** Occlusal guard, by report
Pertinent documentation to evaluate medical appropriateness should be included when this code is reported.
MED: MCM 2336, MCM 2136

E **D9941** Fabrication of athletic mouthguard
See also CPT code (21089)
MED: Medicare Statute: 1862a(12)

S **D9950** Occlusion analysis — mounted case
MED: MCM 2336, MCM 2136

S **D9951** Occlusal adjustment — limited
MED: MCM 2336, MCM 2136

S **D9952** Occlusal adjustment — complete
MED: MCM 2336, MCM 2136

D9970 Enamel microabrasion
MED: Medicare Statute: 1862a(12)

☑ **D9971** Odontoplasty 1-2 teeth; includes removal of enamel projections
MED: Medicare Statute: 1862a(12)

☑ **D9972** External bleaching — per arch
MED: Medicare Statute: 1862a(12)

☑ **D9973** External bleaching — per tooth
MED: Medicare Statute: 1862a(12)

☑ **D9974** Internal bleaching — per tooth
MED: Medicare Statute: 1862a(12)

D9999 Unspecified adjunctive procedure, by report
Determine if an alternative HCPCS Level II or a CPT code better describes the service being reported. This code should be used only if a more specific code is unavailable.
Cross-reference CPT 21499

DURABLE MEDICAL EQUIPMENT *E0100-E9999*

E codes include durable medical equipment such as canes, crutches, walkers, commodes, decubitus care, bath and toilet aids, hospital beds, oxygen and related respiratory equipment, monitoring equipment, pacemakers, patient lifts, safety equipment, restraints, traction equipment, fracture frames, wheelchairs, and artificial kidney machines.

CANES

All E codes fall under the jurisdiction of the DME regional carrier unless otherwise noted.

E0100   Cane, includes canes of all materials, adjustable or fixed, with tip
White canes for the blind are not covered under Medicare.
MED: CIM 60-3, CIM 60-9, MCM 2100.1

E0105   Cane, quad or three-prong, includes canes of all materials, adjustable or fixed, with tips
MED: CIM 60-15, CIM 60-9, MCM 2100.1

CRUTCHES

☑ **E0110**   Crutches, forearm, includes crutches of various materials, adjustable or fixed, pair, complete with tips and handgrips
MED: CIM 60-9, MCM 2100.1

☑ **E0111**   Crutch, forearm, includes crutches of various materials, adjustable or fixed, each, with tip and handgrip
MED: CIM 60-9, MCM 2100.1

☑ **E0112**   Crutches, underarm, wood, adjustable or fixed, pair, with pads, tips and handgrips
MED: CIM 60-9, MCM 2100.1

☑ **E0113**   Crutch, underarm, wood, adjustable or fixed, each, with pad, tip and handgrip
MED: CIM 60-9, MCM 2100.1

E0114   Crutches, underarm, other than wood, adjustable or fixed, pair, with pads, tips and handgrips
MED: CIM 60-9, MCM 2100.1

E0116   Crutch, underarm, other than wood, adjustable or fixed, each, with pad, tip and handgrip
MED: CIM 60-9, MCM 2100.1

Ⓐ **E0117**   Crutch, underarm, articulating, spring assisted, each
MED: MCM 2100.1

● ☑ **E0118**   Crutch substitute, lower leg platform, with or without wheels, each

WALKERS

E0130   Walker, rigid (pickup), adjustable or fixed height
Medicare covers walkers if patient's ambulation is impaired.
MED: CIM 60-9, MCM 2100.1

E0135   Walker, folding (pickup), adjustable or fixed height
Medicare covers walkers if patient's ambulation is impaired.
MED: CIM 60-9, MCM 2100.1

● **E0140**   Walker, with trunk support, adjustable or fixed height, any type
MED: CIM 60-9, MCM 2100.1

▲ **E0141**   Walker, rigid, wheeled, adjustable or fixed height
Medicare covers walkers if patient's ambulation is impaired.
MED: CIM 60-9, MCM 2100.1

~~E0142~~   ~~Rigid walker, wheeled, with seat~~

▲ **E0143**   Walker, folding, wheeled, adjustable or fixed height
Medicare covers walkers if patient's ambulation is impaired.
MED: CIM 60-9, MCM 2100.1

▲ **E0144**   Walker, enclosed, four sided framed, rigid or folding, wheeled with posterior seat
MED: CIM 60-9, MCM 2100.1

~~E0145~~   ~~Walker, wheeled, with seat and crutch attachments~~

~~E0146~~   ~~Folding walker, wheeled, with seat~~

▲ **E0147**   Walker, heavy duty, multiple braking system, variable wheel resistance
Medicare covers safety roller walkers only in patients with severe neurological disorders or restricted use of one hand. In some cases, coverage will be extended to patients with a weight exceeding the limits of a standard wheeled walker.
MED: CIM 60-15, MCM 2100.1

E0148   Walker, heavy duty, without wheels, rigid or folding, any type, each

▲ **E0149**   Walker, heavy duty, wheeled, rigid or folding, any type

☑ **E0153**   Platform attachment, forearm crutch, each

☑ **E0154**   Platform attachment, walker, each

E0155   Wheel attachment, rigid pick-up walker, per pair seat attachment, walker

ATTACHMENTS

E0156   Seat attachment, walker

☑ **E0157**   Crutch attachment, walker, each

☑ **E0158**   Leg extensions for walker, per set of four (4)

☑ **E0159**   Brake attachment for wheeled walker, replacement, each

COMMODES

E0160   Sitz type bath or equipment, portable, used with or without commode
Medicare covers sitz baths if medical record indicates that the patient has an infection or injury of the perineal area and the sitz bath is prescribed by the physician.
MED: CIM 60-9

E0161   Sitz type bath or equipment, portable, used with or without commode, with faucet attachment(s)
Medicare covers sitz baths if medical record indicates that the patient has an infection or injury of the perineal area and the sitz bath is prescribed by the physician.
MED: CIM 60-9

E0162   Sitz bath chair
Medicare covers sitz baths if medical record indicates that the patient has an infection or injury of the perineal area and the sitz bath is prescribed by the physician.
MED: CIM 60-9

E0163   Commode chair, stationary, with fixed arms
Medicare covers commodes for patients confined to their beds or rooms, for patients without indoor bathroom facilities, and to patients who cannot climb or descend the stairs necessary to reach the bathrooms in their homes.
MED: CIM 60-9, MCM 2100.1

E0164   Commode chair, mobile, with fixed arms
Medicare covers commodes for patients confined to their beds or rooms, for patients without indoor bathroom facilities, and to patients who cannot climb or descend the stairs necessary to reach the bathrooms in their homes.
MED: CIM 60-9, MCM 2100.1

Durable Medical Equipment

E0165 — E0215

E0165 ~~Commode chair, stationary, with detachable arms~~

E0166 **Commode chair, mobile, with detachable arms**
Medicare covers commodes for patients confined to their beds or rooms, for patients without indoor bathroom facilities, and to patients who cannot climb or descend the stairs necessary to reach the bathrooms in their homes.
MED: CIM 60-9, MCM 2100.1

E0167 **Pail or pan for use with commode chair**
Medicare covers commodes for patients confined to their beds or rooms, for patients without indoor bathroom facilities, and to patients who cannot climb or descend the stairs necessary to reach the bathrooms in their homes.
MED: CIM 60-9

E0168 **Commode chair, extra wide and/or heavy duty, stationary or mobile, with or without arms, any type, each**

☑ E0169 **Commode chair with seat lift mechanism**

☑ E0175 **Foot rest, for use with commode chair, each**

DECUBITUS CARE EQUIPMENT

E0176 **Air pressure pad or cushion, nonpositioning**
MED: CIM 60-9

E0177 **Water pressure pad or cushion, nonpositioning**
MED: CIM 60-9

E0178 **Gel or gel-like pressure pad or cushion, nonpositioning**
MED: CIM 60-9

E0179 **Dry pressure pad or cushion, nonpositioning**
MED: CIM 60-9

E0180 **Pressure pad, alternating with pump**
Medicare covers pads if physicians supervise their use in patients who have decubitus ulcers or susceptibility to them. Prior authorization is required by Medicare for this item.
MED: CIM 60-9

E0181 **Pressure pad, alternating with pump, heavy duty**
Medicare covers pads if physicians supervise their use in patients who have decubitus ulcers or susceptibility to them. Prior authorization is required by Medicare for this item.
MED: CIM 60-9

E0182 **Pump for alternating pressure pad**
Medicare covers pads if physicians supervise their use in patients who have decubitus ulcers or susceptibility to them. Prior authorization is required by Medicare for this item.
MED: CIM 60-9

E0184 **Dry pressure mattress**
Medicare covers pads if physicians supervise their use in patients who have decubitus ulcers or susceptibility to them. Prior authorization is required by Medicare for this item.
MED: CIM 60-9

E0185 **Gel or gel-like pressure pad for mattress, standard mattress length and width**
Medicare covers pads if physicians supervise their use in patients who have decubitus ulcers or susceptibility to them. Prior authorization is required by Medicare for this item.
MED: CIM 60-9

E0186 **Air pressure mattress**
Medicare covers pads if physicians supervise their use in patients who have decubitus ulcers or susceptibility to them.
MED: CIM 60-9

E0187 **Water pressure mattress**
Medicare covers pads if physicians supervise their use in patients who have decubitus ulcers or susceptibility to them.
MED: CIM 60-9

E0188 **Synthetic sheepskin pad**
Medicare covers pads if physicians supervise their use in patients who have decubitus ulcers or susceptibility to them. Prior authorization is required by Medicare for this item.
MED: CIM 60-9

E0189 **Lambswool sheepskin pad, any size**
Medicare covers pads if physicians supervise their use in patients who have decubitus ulcers or susceptibility to them. Prior authorization is required by Medicare for this item.
MED: CIM 60-9

● E0190 **Positioning cushion/pillow/wedge, any shape or size**

☑ E0191 **Heel or elbow protector, each**

E0192 **Low pressure and positioning equalization pad, for wheelchair**
Medicare covers pads if physicians supervise their use in patients who have decubitus ulcers or susceptibility to them. Prior authorization and a written order is required by Medicare for this item.
MED: CIM 60-9

E0193 **Powered air flotation bed (low air loss therapy)**

E0194 **Air fluidized bed**
An air fluidized bed is covered by Medicare if the patient has a stage 3 or stage 4 pressure sore and, without the bed, would require institutionalization. A physician's prescription is required.
MED: CIM 60-19, Cross-reference Q0049

E0196 **Gel pressure mattress**
Medicare covers pads if physicians supervise their use in patients who have decubitus ulcers or susceptibility to them.
MED: CIM 60-9

E0197 **Air pressure pad for mattress, standard mattress length and width**
Medicare covers pads if physicians supervise their use in patients who have decubitus ulcers or susceptibility to them.
MED: CIM 60-9

E0198 **Water pressure pad for mattress, standard mattress length and width**
Medicare covers pads if physicians supervise their use in patients who have decubitus ulcers or susceptibility to them.
MED: CIM 60-9

E0199 **Dry pressure pad for mattress, standard mattress length and width**
Medicare covers pads if physicians supervise their use in patients who have decubitus ulcers or susceptibility to them.
MED: CIM 60-9

HEAT/COLD APPLICATION

E0200 **Heat lamp, without stand (table model), includes bulb, or infrared element**
MED: CIM 60-9, MCM 2100.1

E0202 **Phototherapy (bilirubin) light with photometer**

▲ E0203 **Therapeutic lightbox, minimum 10,000 lux, table top model**

E0205 **Heat lamp, with stand, includes bulb, or infrared element**
MED: CIM 60-9, MCM 2100.1

E0210 **Electric heat pad, standard**
MED: CIM 60-9

E0215 **Electric heat pad, moist**
MED: CIM 60-9

| Special Coverage Instructions | Noncovered by Medicare | Carrier Discretion | ☑ Quantity Alert | ● New Code | ▲ Revised Code |

42 — E Codes   Ⓜ Maternity   Ⓐ Adult   Ⓟ Pediatrics   Ⓐ-Ⓧ APC Status Indicator   *2004 HCPCS*

Durable Medical Equipment

E0217 — E0292

E0217 Water circulating heat pad with pump
MED: CIM 60-9

E0218 Water circulating cold pad with pump
MED: CIM 60-9

E0220 Hot water bottle

☑ **E0221** Infrared heating pad system

E0225 Hydrocollator unit, includes pads
MED: CIM 60-9, MCM 2210.3

E0230 Ice cap or collar

E **E0231** Non-contact wound warming device (temperature control unit, AC adapter and power cord) for use with warming card and wound cover
MED: MCM 2303

E **E0232** Warming card for use with the non-contact wound warming device and non-contact wound warming wound cover
MED: MCM 2303

E0235 Paraffin bath unit, portable (see medical supply code A4265 for paraffin)
MED: CIM 60-9, MCM 2210.3

E0236 Pump for water circulating pad
MED: CIM 60-9

E0238 Nonelectric heat pad, moist
MED: CIM 60-9

E0239 Hydrocollator unit, portable
MED: CIM 60-9, MCM 2210.3

● **E0240** Bath/shower chair, with or without wheels, any size
MED: CIM 60-9

BATH AND TOILET AIDS

☑ **E0241** Bathtub wall rail, each
MED: CIM 60-9, MCM 2100.1

E0242 Bathtub rail, floor base
MED: CIM 60-9, MCM 2100.1

☑ **E0243** Toilet rail, each
MED: CIM 60-9, MCM 2100.1

E0244 Raised toilet seat
MED: CIM 60-9

E0245 Tub stool or bench
MED: CIM 60-9

E0246 Transfer tub rail attachment

● **E0247** Transfer bench for tub or toilet with or without commode opening

● **E0248** Transfer bench, heavy duty, for tub or toilet with or without commode opening

A **E0249** Pad for water circulating heat unit
MED: CIM 60-9

HOSPITAL BEDS AND ACCESSORIES

E0250 Hospital bed, fixed height, with any type side rails, with mattress
MED: CIM 60-18, MCM 2100.1

E0251 Hospital bed, fixed height, with any type side rails, without mattress
MED: CIM 60-18, MCM 2100.1

E0255 Hospital bed, variable height, hi-lo, with any type side rails, with mattress
MED: CIM 60-18, MCM 2100.1

E0256 Hospital bed, variable height, hi-lo, with any type side rails, without mattress
MED: CIM 60-18, MCM 2100.1

E0260 Hospital bed, semi-electric (head and foot adjustment), with any type side rails, with mattress
MED: CIM 60-18, MCM 2100.1

E0261 Hospital bed, semi-electric (head and foot adjustment), with any type side rails, without mattress
MED: CIM 60-18, MCM 2100.1

E0265 Hospital bed, total electric (head, foot, and height adjustments), with any type side rails, with mattress
MED: CIM 60-18, MCM 2100.1

E0266 Hospital bed, total electric (head, foot, and height adjustments), with any type side rails, without mattress
MED: CIM 60-18, MCM 2100.1

E **E0270** Hospital bed, institutional type includes: oscillating, circulating and stryker frame, with mattress
MED: CIM 60-9

E0271 Mattress, inner spring
MED: CIM 60-18, CIM 60-9

E0272 Mattress, foam rubber
MED: CIM 60-18, CIM 60-9

E0273 Bed board
MED: CIM 60-9

E0274 Over-bed table
MED: CIM 60-9

E0275 Bed pan, standard, metal or plastic
Reusable, autoclavable bedpans are covered by Medicare for bed-confined patients.
MED: CIM 60-9

E0276 Bed pan, fracture, metal or plastic
Reusable, autoclavable bedpans are covered by Medicare for bed-confined patients.
MED: CIM 60-9

E0277 Powered pressure-reducing air mattress
MED: CIM 60-9

E0280 Bed cradle, any type

E0290 Hospital bed, fixed height, without side rails, with mattress
MED: CIM 60-18, MCM 2100.1

E0291 Hospital bed, fixed height, without side rails, without mattress
MED: CIM 60-18, MCM 2100.1

E0292 Hospital bed, variable height, hi-lo, without side rails, with mattress
MED: CIM 60-18, MCM 2100.1

Durable Medical Equipment

E0293 — E0442

E0293 Hospital bed, variable height, hi-lo, without side rails, without mattress
MED: CIM 60-18, MCM 2100.1

E0294 Hospital bed, semi-electric (head and foot adjustment), without side rails, with mattress
MED: CIM 60-18, MCM 2100.1

E0295 Hospital bed, semi-electric (head and foot adjustment), without side rails, without mattress
MED: CIM 60-18, MCM 2100.1

E0296 Hospital bed, total electric (head, foot, and height adjustments), without side rails, with mattress
MED: CIM 60-18, MCM 2100.1

E0297 Hospital bed, total electric (head, foot, and height adjustments), without side rails, without mattress
MED: CIM 60-18, MCM 2100.1

● **E0300** Pediatric crib, hospital grade, fully enclosed
MED: CIM 60-18

● **E0301** Hospital bed, heavy duty, extra wide, with weight capacity greater than 350 pounds, but less than or equal to 600 pounds, with any type side rails, without mattress
MED: CIM 60-18

● **E0302** Hospital bed, extra heavy duty, extra wide, with weight capacity greater than 600 pounds, with any type side rails, without mattress
MED: CIM 60-18

● **E0303** Hospital bed, heavy duty, extra wide, with weight capacity greater than 350 pounds, but less than or equal to 600 pounds, with any type side rails, with mattress
MED: CIM 60-18

● **E0304** Hospital bed, extra heavy duty, extra wide, with weight capacity greater than 600 pounds, with any type side rails, with mattress
MED: CIM 60-18

[A] **E0305** Bedside rails, half-length
MED: CIM 60-18

E0310 Bedside rails, full-length
MED: CIM 60-18

[E] **E0315** Bed accessory: board, table, or support device, any type
MED: CIM 60-9

E0316 Safety enclosure frame/canopy for use with hospital bed, any type

E0325 Urinal; male, jug-type, any material ♂
MED: CIM 60-9

E0326 Urinal; female, jug-type, any material ♀
MED: CIM 60-9

E0350 Control unit for electronic bowel irrigation/evacuation system

E0352 Disposable pack (water reservoir bag, speculum, valving mechanism and collection bag/box) for use with the electronic bowel irrigation/evacuation system

E0370 Air pressure elevator for heel

E0371 Nonpowered advanced pressure reducing overlay for mattress, standard mattress length and width

E0372 Powered air overlay for mattress, standard mattress length and width

E0373 Nonpowered advanced pressure reducing mattress

OXYGEN AND RELATED RESPIRATORY EQUIPMENT

[A] **E0424** Stationary compressed gaseous oxygen system, rental; includes container, contents, regulator, flowmeter, humidifier, nebulizer, cannula or mask, and tubing
For the first claim filed for home oxygen equipment or therapy, submit a certificate of medical necessity that includes the oxygen flow rate, anticipated frequency and duration of oxygen therapy, and physician signature. Medicare accepts oxygen therapy as medically necessary in cases documenting any of the following: erythocythemia with a hematocrit greater than 56 percent; a P pulmonale on EKG; or dependent edema consistent with congestive heart failure.
MED: CIM 60-4, MCM 4107.9

E0425 Stationary compressed gas system, purchase; includes regulator, flowmeter, humidifier, nebulizer, cannula or mask, and tubing
MED: CIM 60-4, MCM 4107.9

E0430 Portable gaseous oxygen system, purchase; includes regulator, flowmeter, humidifier, cannula or mask, and tubing
MED: CIM 60-4, MCM 4107.9

E0431 Portable gaseous oxygen system, rental; includes portable container, regulator, flowmeter, humidifier, cannula or mask, and tubing
MED: CIM 60-4, MCM 4107.9

E0434 Portable liquid oxygen system, rental; includes portable container, supply reservoir, humidifier, flowmeter, refill adaptor, contents gauge, cannula or mask, and tubing
MED: CIM 60-4, MCM 4107.9

[E] **E0435** Portable liquid oxygen system, purchase; includes portable container, supply reservoir, flowmeter, humidifier, contents gauge, cannula or mask, tubing, and refill adapter
MED: CIM 60-4, MCM 4107.9

[A] **E0439** Stationary liquid oxygen system, rental; includes container, contents, regulator, flowmeter, humidifier, nebulizer, cannula or mask, and tubing
MED: CIM 60-4, MCM 4107.9

[E] **E0440** Stationary liquid oxygen system, purchase; includes use of reservoir, contents indicator, regulator, flowmeter, humidifier, nebulizer, cannula or mask, and tubing
MED: CIM 60-4, MCM 4107.9

☑ **E0441** Oxygen contents, gaseous (for use with owned gaseous stationary systems or when both a stationary and portable gaseous system are owned), one month's supply = 1 unit
MED: CIM 60-4, MCM 4107.9

☑ **E0442** Oxygen contents, liquid (for use with owned liquid stationary systems or when both a stationary and portable liquid system are owned), one month's supply = 1 unit
MED: CIM 60-4, MCM 4107.9

☑ **E0443** Portable oxygen contents, gaseous (for use only with portable gaseous systems when no stationary gas or liquid system is used), one month's supply = 1 unit
MED: CIM 60-4, MCM 4107.9

☑ **E0444** Portable oxygen contents, liquid (for use only with portable liquid systems when no stationary gas or liquid system is used), one month's supply = 1 unit
MED: CIM 60-4, MCM 4107.9

E0445 Oximeter device for measuring blood oxygen levels non-invasively

E0450 Volume ventilator, stationary or portable, with backup rate feature, used with invasive interface (e.g., tracheostomy tube)
MED: CIM 60-9

E0454 Pressure ventilator with pressure control, pressure support and flow triggering features
MED: CIM 60-9

E0455 Oxygen tent, excluding croup or pediatric tents
MED: CIM 60-4, MCM 4107.9

E0457 Chest shell (cuirass)

E0459 Chest wrap

E0460 Negative pressure ventilator; portable or stationary
MED: CIM 60-9

E0461 Volume ventilator, stationary or portable, with backup rate feature, used with non-invasive interface
MED: CIM 60-9

E0462 Rocking bed, with or without side rails

● **E0470** Respiratory assist device, bi-level pressure capability, without backup rate feature, used with noninvasive interface, e.g., nasal or facial mask (intermittent assist device with continuous positive airway pressure device)
MED: CIM 60-9

● **E0471** Respiratory assist device, bi-level pressure capability, with back-up rate feature, used with noninvasive interface, e.g., nasal or facial mask (intermittent assist device with continuous positive airway pressure device)
MED: CIM 60-9

● **E0472** Respiratory assist device, bi-level pressure capability, with backup rate feature, used with invasive interface, e.g., tracheostomy tube (intermittent assist device with continuous positive airway pressure device)
MED: CIM 60-9

E0480 Percussor, electric or pneumatic, home model
MED: CIM 60-9

E **E0481** Intrapulmonary percussive ventilation system and related accessories
MED: CIM 60-21

E0482 Cough stimulating device, alternating positive and negative airway pressure

E0483 High frequency chest wall oscillation air-pulse generator system, (includes hoses and vest), each

E0484 Oscillatory positive expiratory pressure device, non-electric, any type, each

IPPB MACHINES

E0500 IPPB machine, all types, with built-in nebulization; manual or automatic valves; internal or external power source
MED: CIM 60-9

HUMIDIFIERS/COMPRESSORS/NEBULIZERS FOR USE WITH OXYGEN IPPB EQUIPMENT

E0550 Humidifier, durable for extensive supplemental humidification during IPPB treatments or oxygen delivery
MED: CIM 60-9

E0555 Humidifier, durable, glass or autoclavable plastic bottle type, for use with regulator or flowmeter
MED: CIM 60-9, MCM 4107.9

E0560 Humidifier, durable for supplemental humidification during IPPB treatment or oxygen delivery
MED: CIM 60-9

● **E0561** Humidifier, non-heated, used with positive airway pressure device

● **E0562** Humidifier, heated, used with positive airway pressure device

E0565 Compressor, air power source for equipment which is not self-contained or cylinder driven

E0570 Nebulizer, with compressor
MED: CIM 60-9, MCM 4107.9

E0571 Aerosol compressor, battery powered, for use with small volume nebulizer
MED: CIM 60-9

E0572 Aerosol compressor, adjustable pressure, light duty for intermittent use

E0574 Ultrasonic/electronic aerosol generator with small volume nebulizer

E0575 Nebulizer, ultrasonic, large volume
MED: CIM 60-9

E0580 Nebulizer, durable, glass or autoclavable plastic, bottle type, for use with regulator or flowmeter
MED: CIM 60-9, MCM 4107.9

E0585 Nebulizer, with compressor and heater
MED: CIM 60-9, MCM 4107.9

E0590 Dispensing fee covered drug administered through DME nebulizer suction pump, home model, portable

SUCTION PUMP/ROOM VAPORIZERS

E0600 Respiratory suction pump, home model, portable or stationary, electric
MED: CIM 60-9

E0601 Continuous airway pressure (CPAP) device
MED: CIM 60-17

E **E0602** Breast pump, manual, any type   M ♀

E0603 Breast pump, electric (AC and/or DC), any type   M ♀

E0604 Breast pump, heavy duty, hospital grade, piston operated, pulsatile vacuum suction/release cycles, vacuum regulator, supplies, transformer, electric (AC and/or DC)   M ♀

| Special Coverage Instructions | Noncovered by Medicare | Carrier Discretion | ☑ Quantity Alert | ● New Code | ▲ Revised Code |

Durable Medical Equipment

E0605 — E0694

[A] **E0605** Vaporizer, room type
MED: CIM 60-9

[A] **E0606** Postural drainage board
MED: CIM 60-9

MONITORING EQUIPMENT

E0607 Home blood glucose monitor
Medicare covers home blood testing devices for diabetic patients when the devices are prescribed by the patients' physicians. Many commercial payers provide this coverage to non-insulin dependent diabetics as well.
MED: CIM 60-11

PACEMAKER MONITOR

E0610 Pacemaker monitor, self-contained, checks battery depletion, includes audible and visible check systems
MED: CIM 60-7, CIM 50-1

E0615 Pacemaker monitor, self-contained, checks battery depletion and other pacemaker components, includes digital/visible check systems
MED: CIM 60-7, CIM 50-1

[N] **E0616** Implantable cardiac event recorder with memory, activator and programmer

[A] **E0617** External defibrillator with integrated electrocardiogram analysis

E0618 Apnea monitor, without recording feature

E0619 Apnea monitor, with recording feature

E0620 Skin piercing device for collection of capillary blood, laser, each

PATIENT LIFTS

E0621 Sling or seat, patient lift, canvas or nylon
MED: CIM 60-9

E0625 Patient lift, Kartop, bathroom or toilet
MED: CIM 60-9

E0627 Seat lift mechanism incorporated into a combination lift-chair mechanism
MED: CIM 60-8, MCM 4107.8, Cross-reference Q0080

E0628 Separate seat lift mechanism for use with patient owned furniture — electric
MED: CIM 60-8, MCM 4107.8, Cross-reference Q0078

E0629 Separate seat lift mechanism for use with patient owned furniture — nonelectric
MED: MCM 4107.8, Cross-reference Q0079

E0630 Patient lift, hydraulic, with seat or sling
MED: CIM 60-9

E0635 Patient lift, electric, with seat or sling
MED: CIM 60-9

E0636 Multipositional patient support system, with integrated lift, patient accessible controls

● **E0637** Combination sit to stand system, any size, with seat lift feature, with or without wheels

● **E0638** Standing frame system, any size, with or without wheels

PNEUMATIC COMPRESSOR AND APPLIANCES

E0650 Pneumatic compressor, nonsegmental home model
MED: CIM 60-16

E0651 Pneumatic compressor, segmental home model without calibrated gradient pressure
MED: CIM 60-16

E0652 Pneumatic compressor, segmental home model with calibrated gradient pressure
MED: CIM 60-16

E0655 Nonsegmental pneumatic appliance for use with pneumatic compressor, half arm
MED: CIM 60-16

E0660 Nonsegmental pneumatic appliance for use with pneumatic compressor, full leg
MED: CIM 60-16

E0665 Nonsegmental pneumatic appliance for use with pneumatic compressor, full arm
MED: CIM 60-16

E0666 Nonsegmental pneumatic appliance for use with pneumatic compressor, half leg
MED: CIM 60-16

E0667 Segmental pneumatic appliance for use with pneumatic compressor, full leg
MED: CIM 60-16

E0668 Segmental pneumatic appliance for use with pneumatic compressor, full arm
MED: CIM 60-16

E0669 Segmental pneumatic appliance for use with pneumatic compressor, half leg
MED: CIM 60-16

E0671 Segmental gradient pressure pneumatic appliance, full leg
MED: CIM 60-16

E0672 Segmental gradient pressure pneumatic appliance, full arm
MED: CIM 60-16

E0673 Segmental gradient pressure pneumatic appliance, half leg
MED: CIM 60-16

● **E0675** Pneumatic compression device, high pressure, rapid inflation/deflation cycle, for arterial insufficiency (unilateral or bilateral system)

E0691 Ultraviolet light therapy system panel, includes bulbs/lamps, timer and eye protection; treatment area two square feet or less

E0692 Ultraviolet light therapy system panel, includes bulbs/lamps, timer and eye protection, four foot panel

E0693 Ultraviolet light therapy system panel, includes bulbs/lamps, timer and eye protection, six foot panel

E0694 Ultraviolet multidirectional light therapy system in six foot cabinet, includes bulbs/lamps, timer and eye protection

---

SAFETY EQUIPMENT

E   **E0700**   Safety equipment (e.g., belt, harness or vest)

A   **E0701**   Helmet with face guard and soft interface material, prefabricated

RESTRAINTS

E   **E0710**   Restraint, any type (body, chest, wrist or ankle)

TRANSCUTANEOUS AND/OR NEUROMUSCULAR ELECTRICAL NERVE STIMULATORS — TENS

E0720   TENS, two lead, localized stimulation
While TENS is covered when employed to control chronic pain, it is not covered for experimental treatment, as in motor function disorders like MS. Prior authorization is required by Medicare for this item.
MED: CIM 35-20, CIM 35-46, MCM 4107.6

E0730   Transcutaneous electrical nerve stimulation device, four or more leads, for multiple nerve stimulation
While TENS is covered when employed to control chronic pain, it is not covered for experimental treatment, as in motor function disorders like MS. Prior authorization is required by Medicare for this item.
MED: CIM 35-20, CIM 35-46, MCM 4107.6

E0731   Form-fitting conductive garment for delivery of TENS or NMES (with conductive fibers separated from the patient's skin by layers of fabric)
MED: CIM 45-25

E0740   Incontinence treatment system, pelvic floor stimulator, monitor, sensor and/or trainer
MED: CIM 60.24

E0744   Neuromuscular stimulator for scoliosis

E0745   Neuromuscular stimulator, electronic shock unit
MED: CIM 35-77

E0746   Electromyography (EMG), biofeedback device
Biofeedback therapy is covered by Medicare only for re-education of specific muscles or for treatment of incapacitating muscle spasm or weakness. Medicare jurisdiction: local carrier.
MED: CIM 35-27

E0747   Osteogenesis stimulator, electrical, noninvasive, other than spinal applications
Medicare covers noninvasive osteogenic stimulation for nonunion of long bone fractures, failed fusion, or congenital pseudoarthroses.
MED: CIM 35-48

E0748   Osteogenesis stimulator, electrical, noninvasive, spinal applications
Medicare covers noninvasive osteogenic stimulation as an adjunct to spinal fusion surgery for patients at high risk of pseudoarthroses due to previously failed spinal fusion, or for those undergoing fusion of three or more vertebrae.
MED: CIM 35-48

N   **E0749**   Osteogenesis stimulator, electrical, surgically implanted
Medicare covers invasive osteogenic stimulation for nonunion of long bone fractures or as an adjunct to spinal fusion surgery for patients at high risk of pseudoarthroses due to previously failed spinal fusion, or for those undergoing fusion of three or more vertebrae.
MED: CIM 35-48

N   **E0752**   Implantable neurostimulator electrode, each
MED: CIM 65-8

A   **E0754**   Patient programmer (external) for use with implantable programmable neurostimulator pulse generator
MED: CIM 65-8

E   **E0755**   Electronic salivary reflex stimulator (intraoral/noninvasive)

N   **E0756**   Implantable neurostimulator pulse generator
Medicare jurisdiction: local carrier.
MED: CIM 65-8

N   **E0757**   Implantable neurostimulator radiofrequency receiver
Medicare jurisdiction: local carrier.
MED: CIM 65-8

A   **E0758**   Radiofrequency transmitter (external) for use with implantable neurostimulator radiofrequency receiver
Medicare jurisdiction: local carrier.
MED: CIM 65-8

A   **E0759**   Radiofrequency transmitter (external) for use with implantable sacral root neurostimulator receiver for bowel and bladder management, replacement

E   **E0760**   Osteogenesis stimulator, low intensity ultrasound, non-invasive
MED: CIM 35-48

E   **E0761**   Non-thermal pulsed high frequency radiowaves, high peak power electromagnetic energy treatment device

E   **E0765**   FDA approved nerve stimulator, with replaceable batteries, for treatment of nausea and vomiting

INFUSION SUPPLIES

E0776   IV pole

E0779   Ambulatory infusion pump, mechanical, reusable, for infusion 8 hours or greater

E0780   Ambulatory infusion pump, mechanical, reusable, for infusion less than 8 hours

E0781   Ambulatory infusion pump, single or multiple channels, electric or battery operated, with administrative equipment, worn by patient
Medicare jurisdiction: DME local or regional carrier. Bill Medicare claims for regional carrier when the infusion is initiated in the physician's office but the patient does not return during the same day of business.
MED: CIM 60-14

E0782   Infusion pump, implantable, non-programmable (includes all components, e.g., pump, catheter, connectors, etc.)
Medicare jurisdiction: local carrier.
MED: CIM 60-14

E0783   Infusion pump system, implantable, programmable (includes all components, e.g., pump, catheter, connectors, etc.)
Medicare jurisdiction: local carrier.
MED: CIM 60-14

A   **E0784**   External ambulatory infusion pump, insulin
Covered by some commercial payers with preauthorization.
MED: CIM 60-14

N   **E0785**   Implantable intraspinal (epidural/intrathecal) catheter used with implantable infusion pump, replacement
Medicare jurisdiction: local carrier.
MED: CIM 60-14

▨ Special Coverage Instructions   ▨ Noncovered by Medicare   ▨ Carrier Discretion   ☑ Quantity Alert   ● New Code   ▲ Revised Code

2004 HCPCS   ♀ Female Only   ♂ Male Only   123456789 ASC Groups   E Codes— 47

Durable Medical Equipment

E0786 — E0965

N   **E0786** Implantable programmable infusion pump, replacement (excludes implantable intraspinal catheter)
Medicare jurisdiction: local carrier.
MED: CIM 60-14

A   **E0791** Parenteral infusion pump, stationary, single or multichannel
MED: CIM 65-10, MCM 2130, MCM 4450

TRACTION — ALL TYPES

N   **E0830** Ambulatory traction device, all types, each
MED: CIM 60-9

TRACTION — CERVICAL

E0840 Traction frame, attached to headboard, cervical traction
MED: CIM 60-9

E0850 Traction stand, freestanding, cervical traction
MED: CIM 60-9

E0855 Cervical traction equipment not requiring additional stand or frame

TRACTION — OVERDOOR

E0860 Traction equipment, overdoor, cervical
MED: CIM 60-9

TRACTION — EXTREMITY

E0870 Traction frame, attached to footboard, extremity traction (e.g., Buck's)
MED: CIM 60-9

E0880 Traction stand, freestanding, extremity traction (e.g., Buck's)
MED: CIM 60-9

TRACTION — PELVIC

E0890 Traction frame, attached to footboard, pelvic traction
MED: CIM 60-9

E0900 Traction stand, freestanding, pelvic traction (e.g., Buck's)
MED: CIM 60-9

TRAPEZE EQUIPMENT, FRACTURE FRAME, AND OTHER ORTHOPEDIC DEVICES

E0910 Trapeze bars, also known as Patient Helper, attached to bed, with grab bar
MED: CIM 60-9

E0920 Fracture frame, attached to bed, includes weights
MED: CIM 60-9

E0930 Fracture frame, freestanding, includes weights
MED: CIM 60-9

E0935 Passive motion exercise device
MED: CIM 60-9

E0940 Trapeze bar, freestanding, complete with grab bar
MED: CIM 60-9

E0941 Gravity assisted traction device, any type
MED: CIM 60-9

E0942 Cervical head harness/halter

~~E0943 Cervical pillow~~

E0944 Pelvic belt/harness/boot

E0945 Extremity belt/harness

E0946 Fracture frame, dual with cross bars, attached to bed (e.g., Balken, Four Poster)
MED: CIM 60-9

E0947 Fracture frame, attachments for complex pelvic traction
MED: CIM 60-9

E0948 Fracture frame, attachments for complex cervical traction
MED: CIM 60-9

WHEELCHAIR ACCESSORIES
Note: See also K0001-K0109.

▲   **E0950** Wheelchair accessory, tray, each

▲   ☑   **E0951** Heel loop/holder, with or without ankle strap, each

▲   ☑   **E0952** Toe loop/holder, each

   ☑   **E0953** Pneumatic tire, each
See also K0067
MED: CIM 60-9

   ☑   **E0954** Semi-pneumatic caster, each
See also K0075
MED: CIM 60-9

●   ☑   **E0955** Wheelchair accessory, headrest, cushioned, prefabricated, including fixed mounting hardware, each

●   ☑   **E0956** Wheelchair accessory, lateral trunk or hip support, prefabricated, including fixed mounting hardware, each

●   ☑   **E0957** Wheelchair accessory, medial thigh support, prefabricated, including fixed mounting hardware, each

▲ A   **E0958** Manual wheelchair accessory, one-arm drive attachment, each
MED: CIM 60-9

▲   **E0959** Manual wheelchair accessory, adapter for amputee, each
MED: CIM 60-9

●   **E0960** Wheelchair accessory, shoulder harness/straps or chest strap, including any type mounting hardware

▲   **E0961** Manual wheelchair accessory, wheel lock brake extension (handle), each
MED: CIM 60-9

E0962 One-inch cushion, for wheelchair
MED: CIM 60-9

E0963 Two-inch cushion, for wheelchair
MED: CIM 60-9

E0964 Three-inch cushion, for wheelchair
MED: CIM 60-9

E0965 Four-inch cushion, for wheelchair
MED: CIM 60-9

▨ Special Coverage Instructions   ▨ Noncovered by Medicare   ▨ Carrier Discretion   ☑ Quantity Alert   ● New Code   ▲ Revised Code

48 — E Codes   M Maternity   A Adult   P Pediatrics   A-X APC Status Indicator   *2004 HCPCS*

▲   E0966   Manual wheelchair accessory, headrest extension, each
MED: CIM 60-9

▲   ☑   E0967   Manual wheelchair accessory, hand rim with projections, each
MED: CIM 60-9

Ⓐ   E0968   Commode seat, wheelchair
MED: CIM 60-9

E0969   Narrowing device, wheelchair
MED: CIM 60-9

E0970   No. 2 footplates, except for elevating legrest
See also K0037 and K0042
MED: CIM 60-9

E0971   Anti-tipping device, wheelchair
MED: CIM 60-9

▲ Ⓐ   E0972   Wheelchair accessory, transfer board or device, each

▲   E0973   Wheelchair accessory, adjustable height, detachable armrest, complete assembly, each
MED: CIM 60-9

▲   E0974   Manual wheelchair accessory, anti-rollback device, each

~~E0975 Reinforced seat upholstery, wheelchair~~
See code E0981.

~~E0976 Reinforced back, wheelchair, upholstery or other material~~
See code E0982.

E0977   Wedge cushion, wheelchair

▲   E0978   Wheelchair accessory, safety belt/pelvic strap, each
See also K0031

~~E0979 Belt, safety with velcro closure, wheelchair~~
See code E0978.

E0980   Safety vest, wheelchair

●   ☑   E0981   Wheelchair accessory, seat upholstery, replacement only, each

●   ☑   E0982   Wheelchair accessory, back upholstery, replacement only, each

●   E0983   Manual wheelchair accessory, power add-on to convert manual wheelchair to motorized wheelchair, joystick control

●   E0984   Manual wheelchair accessory, power add-on to convert manual wheelchair to motorized wheelchair, tiller control

●   E0985   Wheelchair accessory, seat lift mechanism

●   ☑   E0986   Manual wheelchair accessory, push-rim activated power assist, each

▲   ☑   E0990   Wheelchair accessory, elevating leg rest, complete assembly, each
MED: CIM 60-9

~~E0991 Upholstery seat~~
See code E0981.

▲   E0992   Manual wheelchair accessory, solid seat insert
MED: CIM 60-9

~~E0993 Back, upholstery~~
See code E0982.

☑   E0994   Armrest, each
MED: CIM 60-9

▲   ☑   E0995   Wheelchair accessory, calf rest/pad, each
MED: CIM 60-9

☑   E0996   Tire, solid, each
MED: CIM 60-9

E0997   Caster with fork
MED: CIM 60-9

E0998   Caster without fork
MED: CIM 60-9

E0999   Pneumatic tire with wheel
MED: CIM 60-9

E1000   Tire, pneumatic caster
See also K0074
MED: CIM 60-9

☑   E1001   Wheel, single
MED: CIM 60-9

●   E1002   Wheelchair accessory, power seating system, tilt only

●   E1003   Wheelchair accessory, power seating system, recline only, without shear reduction

●   E1004   Wheelchair accessory, power seating system, recline only, with mechanical shear reduction

●   E1005   Wheelchair accessory, power seating system, recline only, with power shear reduction

●   E1006   Wheelchair accessory, power seating system, combination tilt and recline, without shear reduction

●   E1007   Wheelchair accessory, power seating system, combination tilt and recline, with mechanical shear reduction

●   E1008   Wheelchair accessory, power seating system, combination tilt and recline, with power shear reduction

●   ☑   E1009   Wheelchair accessory, addition to power seating system, mechanically linked leg elevation system, including pushrod and leg rest, each

●   ☑   E1010   Wheelchair accessory, addition to power seating system, power leg elevation system, including leg rest, each

E1011   Modification to pediatric wheelchair, width adjustment package (not to be dispensed with initial chair)
MED: CIM 60-9

E1012   Integrated seating system, planar, for pediatric wheelchair
MED: CIM 60-9

E1013   Integrated seating system, contoured, for pediatric wheelchair
MED: CIM 60-9

E1014   Reclining back, addition to pediatric wheelchair
MED: CIM 60-9

E1015   Shock absorber for manual wheelchair, each
MED: MCM 60.9

E1016 Shock absorber for power wheelchair, each
MED: MCM 60.9

E1017 Heavy duty shock absorber for heavy duty or extra heavy duty manual wheelchair, each
MED: MCM 60.9

E1018 Heavy duty shock absorber for heavy duty or extra heavy duty power wheelchair, each
MED: MCM 60.9

● E1019 Wheelchair accessory, power seating system, heavy duty feature, patient weight capacity greater than 250 pounds and less than or equal to 400 pounds

E1020 Residual limb support system for wheelchair
MED: CIM 60-6

● E1021 Wheelchair accessory, power seating system, extra heavy duty feature, weight capacity greater than 400 pounds

E1025 Lateral thoracic support, non-contoured, for pediatric wheelchair, each (includes hardware)
MED: CIM 60-9

E1026 Lateral thoracic support, contoured, for pediatric wheelchair, each (includes hardware)
MED: CIM 60-9

E1027 Lateral/anterior support, for pediatric wheelchair, each (includes hardware)
MED: CIM 60-9

● E1028 Wheelchair accessory, manual swingaway, retractable or removable mounting hardware for joystick, other control interface or positioning accessory

● E1029 Wheelchair accessory, ventilator tray, fixed

● E1030 Wheelchair accessory, ventilator tray, gimbaled

ROLLABOUT CHAIR

Ⓐ E1031 Rollabout chair, any and all types with casters five inches or greater
MED: CIM 60-9

Ⓔ E1035 Multi-positional patient transfer system, with integrated seat, operated by care giver
MED: MCM 2100

E1037 Transport chair, pediatric size
MED: CIM 60-9

E1038 Transport chair, adult size
MED: CIM 60-9

WHEELCHAIRS — FULLY RECLINING

Ⓐ E1050 Fully reclining wheelchair; fixed full-length arms, swing-away, detachable, elevating legrests
MED: CIM 60-9

Ⓐ E1060 Fully reclining wheelchair; detachable arms, desk or full-length, swing-away, detachable, elevating legrests
MED: CIM 60-9

E1065 Power attachment (to convert any wheelchair to motorized wheelchair, e.g., Solo)
MED: CIM 60-9

~~E1066~~ ~~Battery charger~~
See code E2366.

~~E1060~~ ~~Deep cycle battery~~
See code E2360.

E1070 Fully reclining wheelchair; detachable arms, desk or full-length, swing-away, detachable footrests
MED: CIM 60-9

E1083 Hemi-wheelchair; fixed full-length arms, swing-away, detachable, elevating legrests
MED: CIM 60-9

E1084 Hemi-wheelchair; detachable arms, desk or full-length, swing-away, detachable, elevating legrests
MED: CIM 60-9

E1085 Hemi-wheelchair; fixed full-length arms, swing-away, detachable footrests
See also K0002
MED: CIM 60-9

E1086 Hemi-wheelchair; detachable arms, desk or full-length, swing-away, detachable footrests
See also K0002
MED: CIM 60-9

E1087 High-strength lightweight wheelchair; fixed full-length arms, swing-away, detachable, elevating legrests
MED: CIM 60-9

E1088 High-strength lightweight wheelchair; detachable arms, desk or full-length, swing-away, detachable, elevating legrests
MED: CIM 60-9

E1089 High-strength lightweight wheelchair; fixed-length arms, swing-away, detachable footrests
See also K0004
MED: CIM 60-9

E1090 High-strength lightweight wheelchair; detachable arms, desk or full-length, swing-away, detachable footrests
See also K0004
MED: CIM 60-9

E1092 Wide, heavy-duty wheelchair; detachable arms, desk or full-length, swing-away, detachable, elevating legrests
MED: CIM 60-9

E1093 Wide, heavy-duty wheelchair; detachable arms, desk or full-length arms, swing-away, detachable footrests
MED: CIM 60-9

WHEELCHAIR — SEMI-RECLINING

E1100 Semi-reclining wheelchair; fixed full-length arms, swing-away, detachable, elevating legrests
MED: CIM 60-9

E1110 Semi-reclining wheelchair; detachable arms, desk or full-length, elevating legrest
MED: CIM 60-9

| Special Coverage Instructions | Noncovered by Medicare | Carrier Discretion | ☑ Quantity Alert | ● New Code | ▲ Revised Code |

WHEELCHAIR — STANDARD

E1130   Standard wheelchair; fixed full-length arms, fixed or swing-away, detachable footrests
See also K0001
MED: CIM 60-9

E1140   Wheelchair; detachable arms, desk or full-length, swing-away, detachable footrests
See also K0001
MED: CIM 60-9

E1150   Wheelchair; detachable arms, desk or full-length, swing-away, detachable, elevating legrests
MED: CIM 60-9

E1160   Wheelchair; fixed full-length arms, swing-away, detachable, elevating legrests
MED: CIM 60-9

E1161   Manual adult size wheelchair, includes tilt in space

WHEELCHAIR — AMPUTEE

E1170   Amputee wheelchair; fixed full-length arms, swing-away, detachable, elevating legrests
MED: CIM 60-9

E1171   Amputee wheelchair; fixed full-length arms, without footrests or legrests
MED: CIM 60-9

E1172   Amputee wheelchair; detachable arms, desk or full-length, without footrests or legrests
MED: CIM 60-9

E1180   Amputee wheelchair; detachable arms, desk or full-length, swing-away, detachable footrests
MED: CIM 60-9

E1190   Amputee wheelchair; detachable arms, desk or full-length, swing-away, detachable, elevating legrests
MED: CIM 60-9

E1195   Heavy duty wheelchair; fixed full-length arms, swing-away, detachable, elevating legrests
MED: CIM 60-9

E1200   Amputee wheelchair; fixed full-length arms, swing-away, detachable footrests
MED: CIM 60-9

WHEELCHAIR — POWER

E1210   Motorized wheelchair; fixed full-length arms, swing-away, detachable, elevating legrests
MED: CIM 60-5, CIM 60-9

E1211   Motorized wheelchair; detachable arms, desk or full-length, swing-away, detachable, elevating legrests
MED: CIM 60-5, CIM 60-9

E1212   Motorized wheelchair; fixed full-length arms, swing-away, detachable footrests
See also K0010
MED: CIM 60-5, CIM 60-9

E1213   Motorized wheelchair; detachable arms, desk or full-length, swing-away, detachable footrests
See also K0010
MED: CIM 60-5, CIM 60-9

WHEELCHAIR — SPECIAL SIZE

E1220   Wheelchair; specially sized or constructed (indicate brand name, model number, if any, and justification)
MED: CIM 60-6

E1221   Wheelchair with fixed arm, footrests
MED: CIM 60-6

E1222   Wheelchair with fixed arm, elevating legrests
MED: CIM 60-6

E1223   Wheelchair with detachable arms, footrests
MED: CIM 60-6

E1224   Wheelchair with detachable arms, elevating legrests
MED: CIM 60-6

▲ **E1225**   Manual wheelchair accessory, semi-reclining back, (recline greater than 15 degrees, but less than 80 degrees), each
MED: CIM 60-6

▲ **E1226**   Manual wheelchair accessory, fully reclining back, each
See also K0028
MED: CIM 60-6

E1227   Special height arms for wheelchair
MED: CIM 60-6

E1228   Special back height for wheelchair
MED: CIM 60-6

Ⓐ **E1230**   Power operated vehicle (three- or four-wheel nonhighway), specify brand name and model number
Prior authorization is required by Medicare for this item.
MED: CIM 60-5, MCM 4107.6

E1231   Wheelchair, pediatric size, tilt-in-space, rigid, adjustable, with seating system
MED: CIM 60-9

E1232   Wheelchair, pediatric size, tilt-in-space, folding, adjustable, with seating system
MED: CIM 60-9

E1233   Wheelchair, pediatric size, tilt-in-space, rigid, adjustable, without seating system
MED: CIM 60-9

E1234   Wheelchair, pediatric size, tilt-in-space, folding, adjustable, without seating system
MED: CIM 60-9

E1235   Wheelchair, pediatric size, rigid, adjustable, with seating system
MED: CIM 60-9

E1236   Wheelchair, pediatric size, folding, adjustable, with seating system
MED: CIM 60-9

E1237   Wheelchair, pediatric size, rigid, adjustable, without seating system
MED: CIM 60-9

E1238   Wheelchair, pediatric size, folding, adjustable, without seating system
MED: CIM 60-9

Durable Medical Equipment

E1240 — E1620

WHEELCHAIR — LIGHTWEIGHT

E1240 Lightweight wheelchair; detachable arms, desk or full-length, swing-away, detachable, elevating legrest
MED: CIM 60-9

E1250 Lightweight wheelchair; fixed full-length arms, swing-away, detachable footrests
See also K0003
MED: CIM 60-9

E1260 Lightweight wheelchair; detachable arms, desk or full-length, swing-away, detachable footrests
See also K0003
MED: CIM 60-9

E1270 Lightweight wheelchair; fixed full-length arms, swing-away, detachable elevating legrests
MED: CIM 60-9

WHEELCHAIR — HEAVY-DUTY

E1280 Heavy-duty wheelchair; detachable arms, desk or full-length, elevating legrests
MED: CIM 60-9

E1285 Heavy-duty wheelchair; fixed full-length arms, swing-away, detachable footrests
See also K0006
MED: CIM 60-9

E1290 Heavy-duty wheelchair; detachable arms, desk or full-length, swing-away, detachable footrests
See also K0006
MED: CIM 60-9

E1295 Heavy-duty wheelchair; fixed full-length arms, elevating legrests
MED: CIM 60-9

E1296 Special wheelchair seat height from floor
MED: CIM 60-6

E1297 Special wheelchair seat depth, by upholstery
MED: CIM 60-6

E1298 Special wheelchair seat depth and/or width, by construction
MED: CIM 60-6

WHIRLPOOL — EQUIPMENT

E **E1300** Whirlpool, portable (overtub type)
MED: CIM 60-9

A **E1310** Whirlpool, nonportable (built-in type)
MED: CIM 60-9

REPAIRS AND REPLACEMENT SUPPLIES

A ☑ **E1340** Repair or nonroutine service for durable medical equipment requiring the skill of a technician, labor component, per 15 minutes
Medicare jurisdiction: local carrier if repair or implanted DME.
MED: MCM 2100.4

ADDITIONAL OXYGEN RELATED EQUIPMENT

E1353 Regulator
MED: CIM 60-4, MCM 4107.9

E1355 Stand/rack
MED: CIM 60-4

E1372 Immersion external heater for nebulizer
MED: CIM 60-4

▲ **E1390** Oxygen concentrator, single delivery port, capable of delivering 85 percent or greater oxygen concentration at the prescribed flow rate
MED: CIM 60-4

● ☑ **E1391** Oxygen concentrator, dual delivery port, capable of delivering 85 percent or greater oxygen concentration at the prescribed flow rate, each
MED: CIM 60-4

E1399 Durable medical equipment, miscellaneous
Determine if an alternative HCPCS Level II code better describes the equipment being reported. This code should be used only if a more specific code is unavailable. Medicare jurisdiction: local carrier if repair or implanted DME.

E1405 Oxygen and water vapor enriching system with heated delivery
MED: CIM 60-4, MCM 4107

E1406 Oxygen and water vapor enriching system without heated delivery
MED: CIM 60-4, MCM 4107

ARTIFICIAL KIDNEY MACHINES AND ACCESSORIES

For glucose monitors, see A4253-A4256. For supplies for ESRD, see procedure codes A4651-A4929.

E1500 Centrifuge, for dialysis

E1510 Kidney, dialysate delivery system kidney machine, pump recirculating, air removal system, flowrate meter, power off, heater and temp control with alarm, IV poles, pressure gauge, concentrate container

E1520 Heparin infusion pump for hemodialysis

E1530 Air bubble detector for hemodialysis, each, replacement

E1540 Pressure alarm for hemodialysis, each, replacement

E1550 Bath conductivity meter for hemodialysis, each

E1560 Blood leak detector for hemodialysis, each, replacement

E1570 Adjustable chair, for ESRD patients

☑ **E1575** Transducer protectors/fluid barriers, for hemodialysis, any size, per 10

E1580 Unipuncture control system for hemodialysis

E1590 Hemodialysis machine

E1592 Automatic intermittent peritoneal dialysis system

E1594 Cycler dialysis machine for peritoneal dialysis

E1600 Delivery and/or installation charges for hemodialysis equipment
MED: Medicaid suspend for medical review

E1610 Reverse osmosis water purification system, for hemodialysis
MED: CIM 55-1A

E1615 Deionizer water purification system, for hemodialysis
MED: CIM 55-1A

E1620 Blood pump for hemodialysis, replacement

E1625 Water softening system, for hemodialysis
MED: CIM 55-1B

E1630 Reciprocating peritoneal dialysis system

E1632 Wearable artificial kidney, each

● ☑ **E1634** Peritoneal dialysis clamps, each
MED: MCM 4270

E1635 Compact (portable) travel hemodialyzer system
MED: Medicaid suspend for medical review

☑ **E1636** Sorbent cartridges, for hemodialysis, per 10

☑ **E1637** Hemostats, each

☑ **E1639** Scale, each

E1699 Dialysis equipment, not otherwise specified
Determine if an alternative HCPCS Level II code better describes the equipment being reported. This code should be used only if a more specific code is unavailable. Pertinent documentation to evaluate medical appropriateness should be included when this code is reported.

JAW MOTION REHABILITATION SYSTEM AND ACCESSORIES

E1700 Jaw motion rehabilitation system
Medicare jurisdiction: local carrier.

☑ **E1701** Replacement cushions for jaw motion rehabilitation system, package of six
Medicare jurisdiction: local carrier.

☑ **E1702** Replacement measuring scales for jaw motion rehabilitation system, package of 200
Medicare jurisdiction: local carrier.

OTHER ORTHOPEDIC DEVICES

E1800 Dynamic adjustable elbow extension/flexion device, includes soft interface material

E1801 Bi-directional static progressive stretch elbow device with range of motion adjustment, includes cuffs

E1802 Dynamic adjustable forearm pronation/supination device, includes soft interface material

E1805 Dynamic adjustable wrist extension/flexion device, includes soft interface material

E1806 Bi-directional static progressive stretch wrist device with range of motion adjustment, includes cuffs

E1810 Dynamic adjustable knee extension/flexion device, includes soft interface material

E1811 Bi-directional progressive stretch knee device with range of motion adjustment, includes cuffs

E1815 Dynamic adjustable ankle extension/flexion, includes soft interface material

E1816 Bi-directional static progressive stretch ankle device with range of motion adjustment, includes cuffs

E1818 Bi-directional static progressive stretch forearm pronation/supination device with range of motion adjustment, includes cuffs

E1820 Replacement soft interface material, dynamic adjustable extension/flexion device

E1821 Replacement soft interface material/cuffs for bi-directional static progressive stretch device

E1825 Dynamic adjustable finger extension/flexion device, includes soft interface material

E1830 Dynamic adjustable toe extension/flexion device, includes soft interface material

E1840 Dynamic adjustable shoulder flexion/abduction/rotation device, includes soft interface material

Ⓐ **E1902** Communication board, non-electronic augmentative or alternative communication device

E2000 Gastric suction pump, home model, portable or stationary, electric

E2100 Blood glucose monitor with integrated voice synthesizer
MED: CIM 60-11

E2101 Blood glucose monitor with integrated lancing/blood sample
MED: CIM 60-11

● **E2120** Pulse generator system for tympanic treatment of inner ear endolymphatic fluid

● ☑ **E2201** Manual wheelchair accessory, nonstandard seat frame, width greater than or equal to 20 inches and less than 24 inches

● ☑ **E2202** Manual wheelchair accessory, nonstandard seat frame width, 24-27 inches

● ☑ **E2203** Manual wheelchair accessory, nonstandard seat frame depth, 20 to less than 22 inches

● ☑ **E2204** Manual wheelchair accessory, nonstandard seat frame depth, 22 to 25 inches

● **E2300** Power wheelchair accessory, power seat elevation system

● **E2301** Power wheelchair accessory, power standing system

● **E2310** Power wheelchair accessory, electronic connection between wheelchair controller and one power seating system motor, including all related electronics, indicator feature, mechanical function selection switch, and fixed mounting hardware

● **E2311** Power wheelchair accessory, electronic connection between wheelchair controller and two or more power seating system motors, including all related electronics, indicator feature, mechanical function selection switch, and fixed mounting hardware

● **E2320** Power wheelchair accessory, hand or chin control interface, remote joystick or touchpad, proportional, including all related electronics, and fixed mounting hardware

● **E2321** Power wheelchair accessory, hand control interface, remote joystick, nonproportional, including all related electronics, mechanical stop switch, and fixed mounting hardware

● **E2322** Power wheelchair accessory, hand control interface, multiple mechanical switches, nonproportional, including all related electronics, mechanical stop switch, and fixed mounting hardware

● **E2323** Power wheelchair accessory, specialty joystick handle for hand control interface, prefabricated

● **E2324** Power wheelchair accessory, chin cup for chin control interface

● **E2325** Power wheelchair accessory, sip and puff interface, nonproportional, including all related electronics, mechanical stop switch, and manual swingaway mounting hardware

● **E2326** Power wheelchair accessory, breath tube kit for sip and puff interface

Durable Medical Equipment

E1625 — E2326

Durable Medical Equipment

E2327 — E2599

● **E2327** Power wheelchair accessory, head control interface, mechanical, proportional, including all related electronics, mechanical direction change switch, and fixed mounting hardware

● **E2328** Power wheelchair accessory, head control or extremity control interface, electronic, proportional, including all related electronics and fixed mounting hardware

● **E2329** Power wheelchair accessory, head control interface, contact switch mechanism, nonproportional, including all related electronics, mechanical stop switch, mechanical direction change switch, head array, and fixed mounting hardware

● **E2330** Power wheelchair accessory, head control interface, proximity switch mechanism, nonproportional, including all related electronics, mechanical stop switch, mechanical direction change switch, head array, and fixed mounting hardware

● **E2331** Power wheelchair accessory, attendant control, proportional, including all related electronics and fixed mounting hardware

● ☑ **E2340** Power wheelchair accessory, nonstandard seat frame width, 20-23 inches

● ☑ **E2341** Power wheelchair accessory, nonstandard seat frame width, 24-27 inches

● ☑ **E2342** Power wheelchair accessory, nonstandard seat frame depth, 20 or 21 inches

● ☑ **E2343** Power wheelchair accessory, nonstandard seat frame depth, 22-25 inches

● **E2351** Power wheelchair accessory, electronic interface to operate speech generating device using power wheelchair control interface

● ☑ **E2360** Power wheelchair accessory, 22 NF non-sealed lead acid battery, each

● **E2361** Power wheelchair accessory, 22 NF sealed lead acid battery, each, (e.g. gel cell, absorbed glassmat)

● ☑ **E2362** Power wheelchair accessory, group 24 non-sealed lead acid battery, each

● ☑ **E2363** Power wheelchair accessory, group 24 sealed lead acid battery, each (e.g. gel cell, absorbed glassmat)

● ☑ **E2364** Power wheelchair accessory, U-1 non-sealed lead acid battery, each

● ☑ **E2365** Power wheelchair accessory, U-1 sealed lead acid battery, each (e.g. gel cell, absorbed glassmat)

● ☑ **E2366** Power wheelchair accessory, battery charger, single mode, for use with only one battery type, sealed or non-sealed, each

● ☑ **E2367** Power wheelchair accessory, battery charger, dual mode, for use with either battery type, sealed or non-sealed, each

● **E2399** Power wheelchair accessory, not otherwise classified interface, including all related electronics and any type mounting hardware

● **E2402** Negative pressure wound therapy electrical pump, stationary or portable

● ☑ **E2500** Speech generating device, digitized speech, using pre-recorded messages, less than or equal to 8 minutes recording time
MED: CIM 60-23

● ☑ **E2502** Speech generating device, digitized speech, using pre-recorded messages, greater than 8 minutes but less than or equal to 20 minutes recording time
MED: CIM 60-23

● ☑ **E2504** Speech generating device, digitized speech, using pre-recorded messages, greater than 20 minutes but less than or equal to 40 minutes recording time
MED: CIM 60-23

● ☑ **E2506** Speech generating device, digitized speech, using pre-recorded messages, greater than 40 minutes recording time
MED: CIM 60-23

● **E2508** Speech generating device, synthesized speech, requiring message formulation by spelling and access by physical contact with the device
MED: CIM 60-23

● **E2510** Speech generating device, synthesized speech, permitting multiple methods of message formulation and multiple methods of device access
MED: CIM 60-23

● **E2511** Speech generating software program, for personal computer or personal digital assistant
MED: CIM 60-23

● **E2512** Accessory for speech generating device, mounting system
MED: CIM 60-23

● **E2599** Accessory for speech generating device, not otherwise classified
MED: CIM 60-23

PROCEDURES/PROFESSIONAL SERVICES (TEMPORARY) *G0000-G9999*

The G codes are used to identify professional health care procedures and services that would otherwise be coded in CPT but for which there are no CPT codes.

PET SCAN MODIFIERS

CMS will no longer require the designation of the four PET scan modifiers (N, E, P, S) and has made the determination that no paper documentation needs to be submitted up front with PET scan claims. Documentation requirements such as physician referral and medical necessity determination are to be maintained by the provider as part of the beneficiary's medical record. Review the expanded coverage of PET scans and revised billing instructions. (PM AB-02-115 Aug. 2002)

G codes fall under the jurisdiction of the local carrier.

[A] **G0001** Routine venipuncture for collection of specimen(s)
See also new CPT code 36416. This code should be reported instead of 36415 on Medicare claims.

[L] **G0008** Administration of influenza virus vaccine when no physician fee schedule service on the same day

[L] **G0009** Administration of pneumococcal vaccine when no physician fee schedule service on the same day

[K] **G0010** Administration of hepatitis B vaccine when no physician fee schedule service on the same day

~~G0025~~ ~~Collagen skin test kit~~

This code was added and deleted in the same year.

[A] **G0027** Semen analysis; presence and/or motility of sperm excluding Huhner
Reinstated effective 01/01/04.

[S] **G0030** PET myocardial perfusion imaging, (following previous PET, G0030-G0047); single study, rest or stress (exercise and/or pharmacologic)
MED: CIM 50-36

[S] **G0031** PET myocardial perfusion imaging, (following previous PET, G0030-G0047); multiple studies, rest or stress (exercise and/or pharmacologic)
MED: CIM 50-36

[S] **G0032** PET myocardial perfusion imaging, (following rest SPECT, 78464); single study, rest or stress (exercise and/or pharmacologic)
MED: CIM 50-36

[S] **G0033** PET myocardial perfusion imaging, (following rest SPECT, 78464); multiple studies, rest or stress (exercise and/or pharmacologic)
MED: CIM 50-36

[S] **G0034** PET myocardial perfusion imaging, (following stress SPECT, 78465); single study, rest or stress (exercise and/or pharmacologic)
MED: CIM 50-36

[S] **G0035** PET myocardial perfusion imaging, (following stress SPECT, 78465); multiple studies, rest or stress (exercise and/or pharmacologic)
MED: CIM 50-36

[S] **G0036** PET myocardial perfusion imaging, (following coronary angiography, 93510-93529); single study, rest or stress (exercise and/or pharmacologic)
MED: CIM 50-36

[S] **G0037** PET myocardial perfusion imaging, (following coronary angiography, 93510-93529); multiple studies, rest or stress (exercise and/or pharmacologic)
MED: CIM 50-36

[S] **G0038** PET myocardial perfusion imaging, (following stress planar myocardial perfusion, 78460); single study, rest or stress (exercise and/or pharmacologic)
MED: CIM 50-36

[S] **G0039** PET myocardial perfusion imaging, (following stress planar myocardial perfusion, 78460); multiple studies, rest or stress (exercise and/or pharmacologic)
MED: CIM 50-36

[S] **G0040** PET myocardial perfusion imaging, (following stress echocardiogram, 93350); single study, rest or stress (exercise and/or pharmacologic)
MED: CIM 50-36

[S] **G0041** PET myocardial perfusion imaging, (following stress echocardiogram, 93350); multiple studies, rest or stress (exercise and/or pharmacologic)
MED: CIM 50-36

[S] **G0042** PET myocardial perfusion imaging, (following stress nuclear ventriculogram, 78481 or 78483); single study, rest or stress (exercise and/or pharmacologic)
MED: CIM 50-36

[S] **G0043** PET myocardial perfusion imaging, (following stress nuclear ventriculogram, 78481 or 78483); multiple studies, rest or stress (exercise and/or pharmacologic)
MED: CIM 50-36

[S] **G0044** PET myocardial perfusion imaging, (following rest ECG, 93000); single study, rest or stress (exercise and/or pharmacologic)
MED: CIM 50-36

[S] **G0045** PET myocardial perfusion imaging, (following rest ECG, 93000); multiple studies, rest or stress (exercise and/or pharmacologic)
MED: CIM 50-36

[S] **G0046** PET myocardial perfusion imaging, (following stress ECG, 93015); single study, rest or stress (exercise and/or pharmacologic)
MED: CIM 50-36

[S] **G0047** PET myocardial perfusion imaging, (following stress ECG, 93015); multiple studies, rest or stress (exercise and/or pharmacologic)
MED: CIM 50-36

[V] **G0101** Cervical or vaginal cancer screening; pelvic and clinical breast examination ♀
G0101 can be reported with an E/M code when a separately identifiable E/M service was provided.

[N] **G0102** Prostate cancer screening; digital rectal examination ♂
MED: CIM 50-55, MCM 4182

[A] **G0103** Prostate cancer screening; prostate specific antigen test (PSA), total ♂
MED: CIM 50-55, MCM 4182

S **G0104** Colorectal cancer screening; flexible sigmoidoscopy
Medicare covers colorectal screening for cancer via flexible sigmoidoscopy once every four years for patients 50 years or older.

T **G0105** Colorectal cancer screening; colonoscopy on individual at high risk ☑
An individual with ulcerative enteritis or a history of a malignant neoplasm of the lower gastrointestinal tract is considered at high-risk for colorectal cancer, as defined by CMS.

S **G0106** Colorectal cancer screening; alternative to G0104, screening sigmoidoscopy, barium enema
Medicare covers colorectal screening for cancer via barium enema once every four years for patients 50 years or older.

A **G0107** Colorectal cancer screening; fecal-occult blood test, 1-3 simultaneous determinations
Medicare covers colorectal screening for cancer via fecal-occult blood test once every year for patients 50 years or older.

A **G0108** Diabetes outpatient self-management training services, individual, per 30 minutes

A **G0109** Diabetes self-management training services, group session (2 or more), per 30 minutes

~~G0110~~ ~~Nett pulm rehab; education/skills training, individual~~

~~G0111~~ ~~Nett pulm rehab; education/skills training, group~~

~~G0112~~ ~~Nett pulm rehab; nutritional guidance, initial~~

~~G0113~~ ~~Nett pulm rehab; nutritional guidance, subsequent~~

~~G0114~~ ~~Nett pulm rehab; psychosocial consultation~~

~~G0115~~ ~~Nett pulm rehab; psychological testing~~

~~G0116~~ ~~Nett pulm rehab; psychosocial counselling~~

S **G0117** Glaucoma screening for high risk patients furnished by an optometrist or ophthalmologist

S **G0118** Glaucoma screening for high risk patient furnished under the direct supervision of an optometrist or ophthalmologist

S **G0120** Colorectal cancer screening; alternative to G0105, screening colonoscopy, barium enema

T **G0121** Colorectal cancer screening; colonoscopy on individual not meeting criteria for high risk ☑

▲ E **G0122** Colorectal cancer screening; barium enema

A **G0123** Screening cytopathology, cervical or vaginal (any reporting system), collected in preservative fluid, automated thin layer preparation, screening by cytotechnologist under physician supervision ♀
See also P3000-P3001.
MED: CIM 50-20

A **G0124** Screening cytopathology, cervical or vaginal (any reporting system), collected in preservative fluid, automated thin layer preparation, requiring interpretation by physician ♀
See also P3000-P3001.
MED: CIM 50-20

S **G0125** PET imaging regional or whole body; single pulmonary nodule
MED: CIM 50-36, MCM 4173

T **G0127** Trimming of dystrophic nails, any number
MED: MCM 2323, MCM 4120

E **G0128** Direct (face-to-face with patient) skilled nursing services of a registered nurse provided in a comprehensive outpatient rehabilitation facility, each 10 minutes beyond the first 5 minutes
MED: Medicare Statute: 1833(a)

P **G0129** Occupational therapy requiring the skills of a qualified occupational therapist, furnished as a component of a partial hospitalization treatment program, per day

X **G0130** Single energy x-ray absorptiometry (SEXA) bone density study, one or more sites; appendicular skeleton (peripheral) (e.g., radius, wrist, heel)
MED: CIM 50-44

E **G0141** Screening cytopathology smears, cervical or vaginal, performed by automated system, with manual rescreening, requiring interpretation by physician ♀

A **G0143** Screening cytopathology, cervical or vaginal (any reporting system), collected in preservative fluid, automated thin layer preparation, with manual screening and rescreening by cytotechnologist under physician supervision ♀

A **G0144** Screening cytopathology, cervical or vaginal (any reporting system), collected in preservative fluid, automated thin layer preparation, with screening by automated system, under physician supervision ♀

A **G0145** Screening cytopathology, cervical or vaginal (any reporting system), collected in preservative fluid, automated thin layer preparation, with screening by automated system and manual rescreening under physician supervision ♀

A **G0147** Screening cytopathology smears, cervical or vaginal, performed by automated system under physician supervision ♀

A **G0148** Screening cytopathology smears, cervical or vaginal, performed by automated system with manual rescreening ♀

G0151 Services of physical therapist in home health setting, each 15 minutes

G0152 Services of occupational therapist in home health setting, each 15 minutes

G0153 Services of speech and language pathologist in home health setting, each 15 minutes

G0154 Services of skilled nurse in home health setting, each 15 minutes

G0155 Services of clinical social worker in home health setting, each 15 minutes

G0156 Services of home health aide in home health setting, each 15 minutes

T **G0166** External counterpulsation, per treatment session
MED: CIM 35-74

~~G0167~~ ~~Hyperbaric oxygen treatment not requiring physician attendance, per treatment session~~

X **G0168** Wound closure utilizing tissue adhesive(s) only

S **G0173** Stereotactic radiosurgery, complete course of therapy in one session

V **G0175** Scheduled interdisciplinary team conference (minimum of three exclusive of patient care nursing staff) with patient present

---

P G0176 Activity therapy, such as music, dance, art or play therapies not for recreation, related to the care and treatment of patient's disabling mental health problems, per session (45 minutes or more)

P G0177 Training and educational services related to the care and treatment of patient's disabling mental health problems per session (45 minutes or more)

E G0179 Physician re-certification for Medicare-covered home health services under a home health plan of care (patient not present), including contacts with home health agency and review of reports of patient status required by physicians to affirm the initial implementation of the plan of care that meets patient's needs, per re-certification period

E G0180 Physician certification for Medicare-covered home health services under a home health plan of care (patient not present), including contacts with home health agency and review of reports of patient status required by physicians to affirm the initial implementation of the plan of care that meets patient's needs, per certification period

E G0181 Physician supervision of a patient receiving Medicare-covered services provided by a participating home health agency (patient not present) requiring complex and multidisciplinary care modalities involving regular physician development and/or revision of care plans, review of subsequent reports of patient status, review of laboratory and other studies, communication (including telephone calls) with other health care professionals involved in the patient's care, integration of new information into the medical treatment plan and/or adjustment of medical therapy, within a calendar month, 30 minutes or more

E G0182 Physician supervision of a patient under a Medicare-approved hospice (patient not present) requiring complex and multidisciplinary care modalities involving regular physician development and/or revision of care plans, review of subsequent reports of patient status, review of laboratory and other studies, communication (including telephone calls) with other health care professionals involved in the patient's care, integration of new information into the medical treatment plan and/or adjustment of medical therapy, within a calendar month, 30 minutes or more

T G0186 Destruction of localized lesion of choroid (for example, choroidal neovascularization); photocoagulation, feeder vessel technique (one or more sessions)

A G0202 Screening mammography, producing direct digital image, bilateral, all views

S G0204 Diagnostic mammography, producing direct digital image, bilateral, all views

S G0206 Diagnostic mammography, producing direct digital image, unilateral, all views

S G0210 PET imaging whole body; diagnosis; lung cancer, non-small cell
MED: CIM 50-36, MCM 4173

S G0211 PET imaging whole body; initial staging; lung cancer; non-small cell
MED: CIM 50-36, MCM 4173

S G0212 PET imaging whole body; restaging; lung cancer; non-small
MED: CIM 50-36, MCM 4173

S G0213 PET imaging whole body; diagnosis; colorectal
MED: CIM 50-36, MCM 4173

S G0214 PET imaging whole body; initial staging; colorectal
MED: CIM 50-36, MCM 4173

S G0215 PET imaging whole body; restaging; colorectal cancer
MED: CIM 50-36, MCM 4173

S G0216 PET imaging whole body; diagnosis; melanoma
MED: CIM 50-36, MCM 4173

S G0217 PET imaging whole body; initial staging; melanoma
MED: CIM 50-36, MCM 4173

S G0218 PET imaging whole body; restaging; melanoma
MED: CIM 50-36, MCM 4173

E G0219 PET imaging whole body; melanoma for non-covered indications
MED: CIM 50-36, MCM 4173

S G0220 PET imaging whole body; diagnosis; lymphoma
MED: CIM 50-36, MCM 4173

S G0221 PET imaging whole body; initial staging; lymphoma
MED: CIM 50-36, MCM 4173

S G0222 PET imaging whole body; restaging; lymphoma
MED: CIM 50-36, MCM 4173

S G0223 PET imaging whole body or regional; diagnosis; head and neck cancer; excluding thyroid and CNS cancers
MED: CIM 50-36, MCM 4173

S G0224 PET imaging whole body or regional; initial staging; head and neck cancer; excluding thyroid and CNS cancers
MED: CIM 50-36, MCM 4173

S G0225 PET imaging whole body or regional; restaging; head and neck cancer, excluding thyroid and CNS cancers
MED: CIM 50-36, MCM 4173

S G0226 PET imaging whole body; diagnosis; esophageal cancer
MED: CIM 50-36, MCM 4173

S G0227 PET imaging whole body; initial staging; esophageal cancer
MED: CIM 50-36, MCM 4173

S G0228 PET imaging whole body; restaging; esophageal cancer
MED: CIM 50-36, MCM 4173

S G0229 PET imaging; metabolic brain imaging for pre-surgical evaluation of refractory seizures
MED: CIM 50-36, MCM 4173

S G0230 PET imaging; metabolic assessment for myocardial viability following inconclusive SPECT study
MED: CIM 50-36, MCM 4173

S G0231 PET, whole body, for recurrence of colorectal or colorectal metastatic cancer; gamma cameras only
MED: CIM 50-36

S G0232 PET, whole body, for recurrence of lymphoma; gamma cameras only
MED: CIM 50-36

Procedures/Professional Services (Temporary)

G0233 — G0257

S **G0233** PET, whole body, for recurrence of melanoma; gamma cameras only
MED: CIM 50-36

S **G0234** PET, regional or whole body, for solitary pulmonary nodule following CT or for initial staging of pathologically diagnosed nonsmall cell lung cancer; gamma cameras only
MED: CIM 50-36

G0236 Digitization of film radiographic images with computer analysis for lesion detection, or computer analysis of digital mammogram for lesion detection, and further physician review for interpretation, diagnostic mammography (list separately in addition to code for primary procedure)
See CPT code 76082.

S **G0237** Therapeutic procedures to increase strength or endurance of respiratory muscles, face-to-face, one-on-one, each 15 minutes (includes monitoring)

S **G0238** Therapeutic procedures to improve respiratory function, other than described by G0237, one-on-one, face-to-face, per 15 minutes (includes monitoring)

S **G0239** Therapeutic procedures to improve respiratory function or increase strength or endurance of respiratory muscles, two or more individuals (includes monitoring)

S **G0242** Multi-source photon stereotactic radiosurgery (cobalt 60 multi-source converging beams) plan, including dose volume histograms for target and critical structure tolerances, plan optimization performed for highly conformal distributions, plan positional accuracy and dose verification, all lesions treated, per course of treatment

S **G0243** Multi-source photon stereotactic radiosurgery, delivery including collimator changes and custom plugging, complete course of treatment, all lesions

S **G0244** Observation care provided by a facility to a patient with CHF, chest pain, or asthma, minimum eight hours, maximum forty-eight hours

V **G0245** Initial physician evaluation and management of a diabetic patient with diabetic sensory neuropathy resulting in a loss of protective sensation (LOPS) which must include: (1) the diagnosis of lops, (2) a patient history, (3) a physical examination that consists of at least the following elements: (a) visual inspection of the forefoot, hindfoot and toe web spaces, (b) evaluation of a protective sensation, (c) evaluation of foot structure and biomechanics, (d) evaluation of vascular status and skin integrity, and (e) evaluation and recommendation of footwear, and (4) patient education
MED: CIM 50.81

V **G0246** Follow-up physician evaluation and management of a diabetic patient with diabetic sensory neuropathy resulting in a loss of protective sensation (LOPS) to include at least the following: (1) a patient history, (2) a physical examination that includes: (a) visual inspection of the forefoot, hindfoot and toe web spaces, (b) evaluation of protective sensation, (c) evaluation of foot structure and biomechanics, (d) evaluation of vascular status and skin integrity, and (e) evaluation and recommendation of footwear, and (3) patient education
MED: CIM 50.81

▲ T **G0247** Routine foot care by a physician of a diabetic patient with diabetic sensory neuropathy resulting in a loss of protective sensation (LOPS) to include, the local care of superficial wounds (i.e. superficial to muscle and fascia) and at least the following if present: (1) local care of superficial wounds, (2) debridement of corns and calluses, and (3) trimming and debridement of nails
MED: CIM 50.81

S **G0248** Demonstration, at initial use, of home INR monitoring for patient with mechanical heart valve(s) who meets Medicare coverage criteria, under the direction of a physician; includes: demonstrating use and care of the INR monitor, obtaining at least one blood sample, provision of instructions for reporting home INR test results, and documentation of patient ability to perform testing
MED: CIM 50.55

S **G0249** Provision of test materials and equipment for home INR monitoring to patient with mechanical heart valve(s) who meets Medicare coverage criteria; includes provision of materials for use in the home and reporting of test results to physician; per four tests
MED: CIM 50.55

E **G0250** Physician review, interpretation and patient management of home INR testing for a patient with mechanical heart valve(s) who meets other coverage criteria; per four tests (does not require face-to-face service)
MED: CIM 50.55

S **G0251** Linear accelerator based stereotactic radiosurgery, delivery including collimator changes and custom plugging, fractionated treatment, all lesions, per session, maximum five sessions per course of treatment

G0252 PET imaging, full and partial-ring pet scanners only, for initial diagnosis of breast cancer and/or surgical planning for breast cancer (e.g., initial staging of axillary lymph nodes)
MED: CIM 50-36

S **G0253** PET imaging for breast cancer, full and partial-ring pet scanners only, staging/restaging of local regional recurrence or distant metastases (i.e., staging/restaging after or prior to course of treatment)
MED: CIM 50-36

S **G0254** PET imaging for breast cancer, full and partial ring PET scanners only, evaluation of response to treatment, performed during course of treatment
MED: CIM 50-36

E **G0255** Current perception threshold/sensory nerve conduction test, (SNCT) per limb, any nerve
MED: CIM 50-57

T **G0256** Prostate brachytherapy using permanently implanted Palladium seeds, including transperitoneal placement of needles or catheters into the prostate, cystoscopy and application of permanent interstitial radiation source ♂

S **G0257** Unscheduled or emergency dialysis treatment for an ESRD patient in a hospital outpatient department that is not certified as an ESRD facility

☒   **G0258** Intravenous infusion during separately payable observation stay, per observation stay (must be reported with G0244)

Ⓝ   **G0259** Injection procedure for sacroiliac joint; arthrography

Ⓣ   **G0260** Injection procedure for sacroiliac joint; provision of anesthetic, steroid and/or other therapeutic agent and arthrography   Ⓘ

Ⓣ   **G0261** Prostate brachytherapy using permanently implanted iodine seeds, including transperineal placement of needles or catheters into the prostate, cystoscopy and application of permanent interstitial radiation source   ♂

~~**G0262** Small intestinal imaging; intraluminal, from ligament of treitz to the ileo-cecal valve, includes physician interpretation and report~~

See CPT code 91110.

Ⓝ   **G0263** Direct admission of patient with diagnosis of congestive heart failure, chest pain or asthma for observation services that meet all criteria for G0244

Ⓥ   **G0264** Initial nursing assessment of patient directly admitted to observation with diagnosis other than CHF, chest pain or asthma or patient directly admitted to observation with diagnosis of CHF, chest pain or asthma when the observation stay does not qualify for G0244

Ⓐ   **G0265** Cryopreservation, freezing and storage of cells for therapeutic use, each cell line

Ⓐ   **G0266** Thawing and expansion of frozen cells for therapeutic use, each aliquot

Ⓢ   **G0267** Bone marrow or peripheral stem cell harvest, modification or treatment to eliminate cell type(s) (e.g., t-cells, metastatic carcinoma)

☒   **G0268** Removal of impacted cerumen (one or both ears) by physician on same date of service as audiologic function testing

Ⓝ   **G0269** Placement of occlusive device into either a venous or arterial access site, post surgical or interventional procedure (e.g., angioseal plug, vascular plug)

Ⓐ   **G0270** Medical nutrition therapy; reassessment and subsequent intervention(s) following second referral in same year for change in diagnosis, medical condition or treatment regimen (including additional hours needed for renal disease), individual, face to face with the patient, each 15 minutes

Ⓐ   **G0271** Medical nutrition therapy, reassessment and subsequent intervention(s) following second referral in same year for change in diagnosis, medical condition, or treatment regimen (including additional hours needed for renal disease), group (2 or more individuals), each 30 minutes

~~**G0272** Naso/oro gastric tube placement, requiring physician's skill and fluoroscopic guidance (includes fluoroscopy, image documentation and report)~~

See CPT code 43752.

~~**G0273** Radiopharmaceutical biodistribution, single or multiple scans on one or more days, pre treatment planning for radiopharmaceutical therapy of non-hodgkin's lymphoma, includes administration of radiopharmaceutical (e.g., radiolabeled antibodies)~~

~~**G0274** Radiopharmaceutical therapy, non hodgkin's lymphoma, includes administration of radiopharmaceutical (.e.g. radiolabeled antibodies)~~

▲ Ⓝ   **G0275** Renal angiography, non-selective, one or both kidneys, performed at the same time as cardiac catheterization and/or coronary angiography, includes positioning or placement of any catheter in the abdominal aorta at or near the origins (ostia) of the renal arteries, injection of dye, flush aortogram, production of permanent images, and radiologic supervision and interpretation (List separately in addition to primary procedure)

▲ Ⓝ   **G0278** Iliac and/or femoral artery angiography, non-selective, bilateral or ipsilateral to catheter insertion, performed at the same time as cardiac catheterization and/or coronary angiography, includes positioning or placement of the catheter in the distal aorta or ipsilateral femoral or iliac artery, injection of dye, production of permanent images, and radiologic supervision and interpretation (List separately in addition to primary procedures)

Ⓐ   **G0279** Extracorporeal shock wave therapy; involving elbow epicondylitis

Ⓐ   **G0280** Extracorporeal shock wave therapy; involving other than elbow epicondylitis or plantar fasciitis

Ⓐ   **G0281** Electrical stimulation, (unattended), to one or more areas, for chronic Stage III and Stage IV pressure ulcers, arterial ulcers, diabetic ulcers, and venous stasis ulcers not demonstrating measurable signs of healing after 30 days of conventional care, as part of a therapy plan of care

Ⓔ   **G0282** Electrical stimulation, (unattended), to one or more areas, for wound care other than described in G0281

MED: MCM 35-98

Ⓐ   **G0283** Electrical stimulation (unattended), to one or more areas for indication(s) other than wound care, as part of a therapy plan of care

Ⓣ   **G0288** Reconstruction, computed tomographic angiography of aorta for surgical planning for vascular surgery

Ⓝ   **G0289** Arthroscopy, knee, surgical, for removal of loose body, foreign body, debridement/shaving of articular cartilage (chondroplasty) at the time of other surgical knee arthroscopy in a different compartment of the same knee

Ⓣ   **G0290** Transcatheter placement of a drug eluting intracoronary stent(s), percutaneous, with or without other therapeutic intervention, any method; single vessel

Ⓣ   **G0291** Transcatheter placement of a drug eluting intracoronary stent(s), percutaneous, with or without other therapeutic intervention, any method; each additional vessel

Ⓢ   **G0292** Administration(s) of experimental drug(s) only in a Medicare qualifying clinical trial (includes administration for chemotherapy and other types of therapy via infusion and/or other than infusion), per day

Ⓢ   **G0293** Noncovered surgical procedure(s) using conscious sedation, regional, general or spinal anesthesia in a Medicare qualifying clinical trial, per day

Ⓢ   **G0294** Noncovered procedure(s) using either no anesthesia or local anesthesia only, in a Medicare qualifying clinical trial, per day

Procedures/Professional Services (Temporary)

G0295 — G0320

E   **G0295** Electromagnetic stimulation, to one or more areas
Note: G0296 will not be implemented. Effective 04/01/2003.
MED: CIM 35-98

● S   **G0296** PET imaging, full and partial ring PET scanner only, for restaging of previously treated thyroid cancer of follicular cell origin following negative I-131 whole body scan

● T   **G0297** Insertion of single chamber pacing cardioverter defibrillator pulse generator

● T   **G0298** Insertion of dual chamber pacing cardioverter defibrillator pulse generator

● T   **G0299** Insertion or repositioning of electrode lead for single chamber pacing cardioverter defibrillator and insertion of pulse generator

● T   **G0300** Insertion or repositioning of electrode lead(s) for dual chamber pacing cardioverter defibrillator and insertion of pulse generator

● S ☑   **G0302** Pre-operative pulmonary surgery services for preparation for LVRS, complete course of services, to include a minimum of 16 days of services

● S ☑   **G0303** Pre-operative pulmonary surgery services for preparation for LVRS, 10 to 15 days of services

● S ☑   **G0304** Pre-operative pulmonary surgery services for preparation for LVRS, 1 to 9 days of services

● S ☑   **G0305** Post-discharge pulmonary surgery services after LVRS, minimum of 6 days of services

●   **G0306** Complete CBC, automated (HgB, HCT, RBC, WBC, without platelet count) and automated WBC differential count

●   **G0307** Complete CBC, automated (HgB, HCT, RBC, WBC; without platelet count)

●   **G0308** End Stage Renal Disease (ESRD) related services during the course of treatment, for patients under 2 years of age to include monitoring the adequacy of nutrition, assessment of growth and development, and counseling of parents; with 4 or more face-to-face physician visits per month
Added as per final 2004 Medicare Physician Fee Schedule. *Federal Register*, November 7, 2003.

●   **G0309** End Stage Renal Disease (ESRD) related services during the course of treatment, for patients under 2 years of age to include monitoring for the adequacy of nutrition, assessment of growth and development, and counseling of parents; with 2 or 3 face-to-face physician visits per month
Added as per final 2004 Medicare Physician Fee Schedule. *Federal Register*, November 7, 2003.

●   **G0310** End Stage Renal Disease (ESRD) related services during the course of treatment, for patients under 2 years of age to include monitoring for the adequacy of nutrition, assessment of growth and development, and counseling of parents; with 1 face–to-face meeting physician visit per month
Added as per final 2004 Medicare Physician Fee Schedule. *Federal Register*, November 7, 2003.

●   **G0311** End Stage Renal Disease (ESRD) related services during the course of treatment, for patients between 2 and 11 years of age to include monitoring for the adequacy of nutrition, assessment of growth and development, and counseling of parents; with 4 or more face-to-face physician visits per month
Added as per final 2004 Medicare Physician Fee Schedule. *Federal Register*, November 7, 2003.

●   **G0312** End Stage Renal Disease (ESRD) related services during the course of treatment, for patients between 2 and 11 years of age to include monitoring for the adequacy of nutrition, assessment of growth and development, and counseling of parents; with 2 or 3 face-to-face physician visits per month
Added as per final 2004 Medicare Physician Fee Schedule. *Federal Register*, November 7, 2003.

●   **G0313** End Stage Renal Disease (ESRD) related services during the course of treatment, for patients between 2 and 11 years of age to include monitoring for the adequacy of nutrition, assessment of growth and development, and counseling of parents; with 1 face-to-face physician visit per month
Added as per final 2004 Medicare Physician Fee Schedule. *Federal Register*, November 7, 2003.

●   **G0314** Ends Stage Renal Disease (ESRD) related services during the course of treatment for patients between 12 and 19 years of age to include monitoring for the adequacy of nutrition, assessment of growth and development, and counseling of parents; with 4 or more face-to-face physician visits per month
Added as per final 2004 Medicare Physician Fee Schedule. *Federal Register*, November 7, 2003.

●   **G0315** End Stage Renal Disease (ESRD related services during the course of treatment, for patients between 12 and 19 years of age to include monitoring for the adequacy of nutrition, assessment of growth and development, and counseling of parents; with 2 or 3 face-to-face physician visits per month
Added as per final 2004 Medicare Physician Fee Schedule. *Federal Register*, November 7, 2003.

●   **G0316** End Stage Renal Disease (ESRD) related services during the course of treatment, for patients between 12 and 19 years of age to include monitoring for the adequacy of nutrition, assessment of growth and development, and counseling of parents; with 1 face-to-face physician visit per month
Added as per final 2004 Medicare Physician Fee Schedule. *Federal Register*, November 7, 2003.

●   **G0317** End Stage Renal Disease (ESRD) related services during the course of treatment, for patients 20 years of age and over; with 4 or more face-to-face physician visits per month
Added as per final 2004 Medicare Physician Fee Schedule. *Federal Register*, November 7, 2003.

●   **G0318** End Stage Renal Disease (ESRD) related services during the course of treatment, for patients 20 years of age and over; with 2 or 3 face-to-face physician visits per month
Added as per final 2004 Medicare Physician Fee Schedule. *Federal Register*, November 7, 2003.

●   **G0319** End Stage Renal Disease (ESRD) related services during the course of treatment, for patients 20 years of age and over; with 1 face-to-face physician visit per month
Added as per final 2004 Medicare Physician Fee Schedule. *Federal Register*, November 7, 2003.

●   **G0320** End stage renal disease (ESRD) related services for home dialysis patients per full month; for patients under two years of age to include monitoring for adequacy of nutrition, assessment of growth and development, and counseling of parents
Added as per final 2004 Medicare Physician Fee Schedule. *Federal Register*, November 7, 2003.

●   G0321   End stage renal disease (ESRD) related services for home dialysis patients per full month; for patients two to eleven years of age to include monitoring for adequacy of nutrition, assessment of growth and development, and counseling of parents
Added as per final 2004 Medicare Physician Fee Schedule. *Federal Register*, November 7, 2003.

●   G0322   End stage renal disease (ESRD) related services for home dialysis patients per full month; for patients 12 to 19 years of age to include monitoring for adequacy of nutrition, assessment of growth and development, and counseling of parents
Added as per final 2004 Medicare Physician Fee Schedule. *Federal Register*, November 7, 2003.

●   G0323   End stage renal disease (ESRD) related services for home dialysis patients per full month; for patients 20 years of age and older.
Added as per final 2004 Medicare Physician Fee Schedule. *Federal Register*, November 7, 2003.

●   G0324   End stage renal disease (ESRD) related services for home dialysis (less than full month), per day; for patients under two years of age
Added as per final 2004 Medicare Physician Fee Schedule. *Federal Register*, November 7, 2003.

●   G0325   End stage renal disease (ESRD) related services for home dialysis (less than full month), per day; for patients between two and 11 years of age
Added as per final 2004 Medicare Physician Fee Schedule. *Federal Register*, November 7, 2003.

●   G0326   End stage renal disease (ESRD) related services for home dialysis (less than full month), per day; for patients between 12 and 19 years of age
Added as per final 2004 Medicare Physician Fee Schedule. *Federal Register*, November 7, 2003.

●   G0327   End stage renal disease (ESRD) related services for home dialysis (less than full month), per day; for patients 20 years of age and over
Added as per final 2004 Medicare Physician Fee Schedule. *Federal Register*, November 7, 2003.

●   G0328   Fecal blood screening immunoassay
Added as per final 2004 Medicare Physician Fee Schedule. *Federal Register*, November 7, 2003.

● S   G0338   Linear accelerator based stereotactic radiosurgery plan, including does volume histograms for target and critical structure tolerances, plan optimization performed for highly conformal distributions, plan postitional accuracy and does verification, all lesions treated, per course of treatment
Added as per final 2004 Outpatient Prospective Payment System rule. *Federal Register*, November 7, 2003

● S   G0339   Image guided robotic linear accelerator base stereotactic radiosurgery, complete course of therapy in one session, or first session of fractionated treatment
Added as per final 2004 Outpatient Prospective Payment System rule. *Federal Register*, November 7, 2003

● S   G0340   Image guided robotic linear accelerator based stereotactic radiosurgery, delivery including collimator changes and custom plugging, fractionated treatment, all lesions, per session, second through fifth sessions, maximum five sessions per course of treatment
Added as per final 2004 Outpatient Prospective Payment System rule. *Federal Register*, November 7, 2003

● S ☑   G3001   Administration and supply of tositumomab, 450 mg
Use this code for Bexxar.

    G9001   Coordinated care fee, initial rate

    G9002   Coordinated care fee, maintenance rate

    G9003   Coordinated care fee, risk adjusted high, initial

    G9004   Coordinated care fee, risk adjusted low, initial

    G9005   Coordinated care fee, risk adjusted maintenance

    G9006   Coordinated care fee, home monitoring

    G9007   Coordinated care fee, schedule team conference

    G9008   Coordinated care fee, physician coordinated care oversight services

    G9009   Coordinated care fee, risk adjusted maintenance, level 3

    G9010   Coordinated care fee, risk adjusted maintenance, level 4

    G9011   Coordinated care fee, risk adjusted maintenance, level 5

    G9012   Coordinated care fee, risk adjusted maintenance, other specified care management

A   G9016   Smoking cessation counseling, individual, in the absence of or in addition to any other evaluation and management service, per session (6-10 minutes) [demo project code only]

ALCOHOL AND DRUG ABUSE TREATMENT SERVICES
H0001-H2037
The H codes are used by those state Medicaid agencies that are mandated by state law to establish separate codes for identifying mental health services that include alcohol and drug treatment services.

H0001 Alcohol and/or drug assessment

H0002 Behavioral health screening to determine eligibility for admission to treatment program

H0003 Alcohol and/or drug screening; laboratory analysis of specimens for presence of alcohol and/or drugs

H0004 Behavioral health counseling and therapy, per 15 minutes

H0005 Alcohol and/or drug services; group counseling by a clinician

H0006 Alcohol and/or drug services; case management

H0007 Alcohol and/or drug services; crisis intervention (outpatient)

H0008 Alcohol and/or drug services; sub-acute detoxification (hospital inpatient)

H0009 Alcohol and/or drug services; acute detoxification (hospital inpatient)

H0010 Alcohol and/or drug services; sub-acute detoxification (residential addiction program inpatient)

H0011 Alcohol and/or drug services; acute detoxification (residential addiction program inpatient)

H0012 Alcohol and/or drug services; sub-acute detoxification (residential addiction program outpatient)

H0013 Alcohol and/or drug services; acute detoxification (residential addiction program outpatient)

H0014 Alcohol and/or drug services; ambulatory detoxification

H0015 Alcohol and/or drug services; intensive outpatient (treatment program that operates at least 3 hours/day and at least 3 days/week and is based on an individualized treatment plan), including assessment, counseling; crisis intervention, and activity therapies or education

H0016 Alcohol and/or drug services; medical/somatic (medical intervention in ambulatory setting)

H0017 Behavioral health; residential (hospital residential treatment program), without room and board, per diem

H0018 Behavioral health; short-term residential (non-hospital residential treatment program), without room and board, per diem

H0019 Behavioral health; long-term residential (non-medial, non-acute care in a residential treatment program where stay is typically longer than 30 days), without room and board, per diem

H0020 Alcohol and/or drug services; methadone administration and/or service (provision of the drug by a licensed program)

H0021 Alcohol and/or drug training service (for staff and personnel not employed by providers)

H0022 Alcohol and/or drug intervention service (planned facilitation)

H0023 Behavioral health outreach service (planned approach to reach a targeted population)

H0024 Behavioral health prevention information dissemination service (one-way direct or non-direct contact with service audiences to affect knowledge and attitude)

H0025 Behavioral health prevention education service (delivery of services with target population to affect knowledge, attitude and/or behavior)

H0026 Alcohol and/or drug prevention process service, community-based (delivery of services to develop skills of impactors)

H0027 Alcohol and/or drug prevention environmental service (broad range of external activities geared toward modifying systems in order to mainstream prevention through policy and law)

H0028 Alcohol and/or drug prevention problem identification and referral service (e.g., student assistance and employee assistance programs), does not include assessment

H0029 Alcohol and/or drug prevention alternatives service (services for populations that exclude alcohol and other drug use e.g., alcohol free social events)

H0030 Behavioral health hotline service

H0031 Mental health assessment, by non-physician

H0032 Mental health service plan development by non-physician

H0033 Oral medication administration, direct observation

H0034 Medication training and support, per 15 minutes

H0035 Mental health partial hospitalization, treatment, less than 24 hours

H0036 Community psychiatric supportive treatment, face-to-face, per 15 minutes

H0037 Community psychiatric supportive treatment program, per diem

H0038 Self-help/peer services, per 15 minutes

H0039 Assertive community treatment, face-to-face, per 15 minutes

H0040 Assertive community treatment program, per diem

H0041 Foster care, child, non-therapeutic, per diem

H0042 Foster care, child, non-therapeutic, per month

H0043 Supported housing, per diem

H0044 Supported housing, per month

H0045 Respite care services, not in the home, per diem

H0046 Mental health services, not otherwise specified

H0047 Alcohol and/or other drug abuse services, not otherwise specified
Replaces code T1011.

H0048 Alcohol and/or other drug testing: collection and handling only, specimens other than blood

H1000 Prenatal care, at-risk assessment M ♀

H1001 Prenatal care, at-risk enhanced service; antepartum management M ♀

H1002 Prenatal care, at risk enhanced service; care coordination M ♀

H1003 Prenatal care, at-risk enhanced service; education M ♀

H1004 Prenatal care, at-risk enhanced service; follow-up home visit M ♀

H1005 Prenatal care, at-risk enhanced service package (includes H1001-H1004) M ♀

Alcohol and Drug Abuse Treatment Services

H1010 — H2037

E **H1010** Non-medical family planning education, per session

E **H1011** Family assessment by licensed behavioral health professional for state defined purposes

E **H2000** Comprehensive multidisciplinary evaluation

E **H2001** Rehabilitation program, per 1/2 day

● **H2010** Comprehensive medication services, per 15 minutes

● **H2011** Crisis intervention service, per 15 minutes

● **H2012** Behavioral health day treatment, per hour

● **H2013** Psychiatric health facility service, per diem

● **H2014** Skills training and development, per 15 minutes

● **H2015** Comprehensive community support services, per 15 minutes

● **H2016** Comprehensive community support services, per diem

● **H2017** Psychosocial rehabilitation services, per 15 minutes

● **H2018** Psychosocial rehabilitation services, per diem

● **H2019** Therapeutic behavioral services, per 15 minutes

● **H2020** Therapeutic behavioral services, per diem

● **H2021** Community-based wrap-around services, per 15 minutes

● **H2022** Community-based wrap-around services, per diem

● **H2023** Supported employment, per 15 minutes

● **H2024** Supported employment, per diem

● **H2025** Ongoing support to maintain employment, per 15 minutes

● **H2026** Ongoing support to maintain employment, per diem

● **H2027** Psychoeducational service, per 15 minutes

● **H2028** Sexual offender treatment service, per 15 minutes

● **H2029** Sexual offender treatment service, per diem

● **H2030** Mental health clubhouse services, per 15 minutes

● **H2031** Mental health clubhouse services, per diem

● **H2032** Activity therapy, per 15 minutes

● **H2033** Multisystemic therapy for juveniles, per 15 minutes

● **H2034** Alcohol and/or drug abuse halfway house services, per diem

● **H2035** Alcohol and/or other drug treatment program, per hour

● **H2036** Alcohol and/or other drug treatment program, per diem

● **H2037** Developmental delay prevention activities, dependent child of client, per 15 minutes

DRUGS ADMINISTERED OTHER THAN ORAL METHOD
J0000-J9999

J codes include drugs that ordinarily cannot be self-administered, chemotherapy drugs, immunosuppressive drugs, inhalation solutions, and other miscellaneous drugs and solutions.

EXCEPTION: ORAL IMMUNOSUPPRESSIVE DRUGS
J codes fall under the jurisdiction of the DME Regional office for Medicare, unless incidental or otherwise noted.

N ☑ **J0120** Injection, tetracycline, up to 250 mg
Use this code for Achromycin, Sumycin.
MED: MCM 2049

K ☑ **J0130** Injection abciximab, 10 mg
Use this code for ReoPro.
MED: MCM 2049

N ☑ **J0150** Injection, adenosine, 6 mg (not to be used to report any adenosine phosphate compounds; instead use A9270)
Use this code for Adenocard.
MED: MCM 2049

~~J0151 Injection, adenosine, 90 mg (not to be used to report any adenosine phosphate compounds, instead use a9270)~~
See code J0152.

● ☑ **J0152** Injection, adenosine, 30 mg (not to be used to report any adenosine phosphate compounds; instead use A9270)

☑ **J0170** Injection, adrenalin, epinephrine, up to 1 ml ampule
Use this code for Adrenalin Chloride, Sus-Phrine.
MED: MCM 2049

☑ **J0190** Injection, biperiden lactate, per 5 mg
MED: MCM 2049

J0200 Injection, alatrofloxacin mesylate, 100 mg
Use this code for Trovan.
MED: MCM 2049.5

F ☑ **J0205** Injection, alglucerase, per 10 units
Use this code for Ceredase.
MED: MCM 2049

K ☑ **J0207** Injection, amifostine, 500 mg
Use this code for Ethyol.
MED: MCM 2049

N ☑ **J0210** Injection, methyldopate HCl, up to 250 mg
Use this code for Aldomet.
MED: MCM 2049

● ☑ **J0215** Injection, alefacept, 0.5 mg

F ☑ **J0256** Injection, alpha 1-proteinase inhibitor — human, 10 mg
Use this code for Prolastin.
MED: MCM 2049

☑ **J0270** Injection, alprostadil, 1.25 mcg (code may be used for Medicare when drug administered under direct supervision of a physician, not for use when drug is self-administered)
Use this code for Prostin VR Pediatric.
MED: MCM 2049

J0275 Alprostadil urethral suppository (code may be used for Medicare when drug administered under direct supervision of a physician, not for use when drug is self-administered)
Use this code for Muse.
MED: MCM 2049

☑ **J0280** Injection, aminophyllin, up to 250 mg
MED: MCM 2049

☑ **J0282** Injection, amiodarone HCl, 30 mg
Use this code for Cordarone IV.
MED: MCM 2049

☑ **J0285** Injection, amphotericin B, 50 mg
MED: MCM 2049

K ☑ **J0287** Injection, amphotericin B lipid complex, 10 mg
MED: MCM 2049

N ☑ **J0288** Injection, amphotericin B cholesteryl sulfate complex, 10 mg
Use this code for Amphotec.
MED: MCM 2049

N ☑ **J0289** Injection, amphotericin B liposome, 10 mg
Use this code for Ambisome.
MED: MCM 2049

☑ **J0290** Injection, ampicillin sodium, 500 mg
Use this code for Totacillin-N.
MED: MCM 2049

☑ **J0295** Injection, ampicillin sodium/sulbactam sodium, per 1.5 g
Use this code for Unasyn.
MED: MCM 2049

☑ **J0300** Injection, amobarbital, up to 125 mg
Use this code for Amytal.
MED: MCM 2049

☑ **J0330** Injection, succinylcholine chloride, up to 20 mg
Use this code for Anectine, Quelicin, Sucostrin.
MED: MCM 2049

N ☑ **J0350** Injection, anistreplase, per 30 units
Use this code for Eminase.
MED: MCM 2049

☑ **J0360** Injection, hydralazine HCl, up to 20 mg
Use this code for Apresoline.
MED: MCM 2049

☑ **J0380** Injection, metaraminol bitartrate, per 10 mg
Use this code for Aramine.
MED: MCM 2049

☑ **J0390** Injection, chloroquine HCl, up to 250 mg
Use this code for Aralen.
MED: MCM 2049

☑ **J0395** Injection, arbutamine HCl, 1 mg
MED: MCM 2049

☑ **J0456** Injection, azithromycin, 500 mg
Use this code for Zithromax.
MED: MCM 2049.5

☑ **J0460** Injection, atropine sulfate, up to 0.3 mg
MED: MCM 2049

☑ **J0470** Injection, dimercaprol, per 100 mg
Use this code for BAL in oil.
MED: MCM 2049

☑ **J0475** Injection, baclofen, 10 mg
Use this code for Lioresal.
MED: MCM 2049

E ☑ **J0476** Injection, baclofen, 50 mcg for intrathecal trial
Use this code for Lioresal for intrathecal trial.
MED: MCM 2049

☑ **J0500** Injection, dicyclomine HCl, up to 20 mg
Use this code for Bentyl, Antispas.
MED: MCM 2049

☑ **J0515** Injection, benztropine mesylate, per 1 mg
Use this code for Cogentin.
MED: MCM 2049

☑ **J0520** Injection, bethanechol chloride, mytonachol or Urecholine, up to 5 mg
Use this code for Urecholine.
MED: MCM 2049

☑ **J0530** Injection, penicillin G benzathine and penicillin G procaine, up to 600,000 units
Use this code for Bicillin C-R.
MED: MCM 2049

☑ **J0540** Injection, penicillin G benzathine and penicillin G procaine, up to 1,200,000 units
Use this code for Bicillin C-R, Bicillin C-R 900/300.
MED: MCM 2049

☑ **J0550** Injection, penicillin G benzathine and penicillin G procaine, up to 2,400,000 units
Use this code for Bicillin C-R.
MED: MCM 2049

☑ **J0560** Injection, penicillin G benzathine, up to 600,000 units
Use this code for Bicillin L-A, Permapen.
MED: MCM 2049

☑ **J0570** Injection, penicillin G benzathine, up to 1,200,000 units
Use this code for Bicillin L-A, Permapen.
MED: MCM 2049

☑ **J0580** Injection, penicillin G benzathine, up to 2,400,000 units
Use this code for Bicillin L-A, Permapen.
MED: MCM 2049

● ☑ **J0583** Injection, bivalirudin, 1 mg

K ☑ **J0585** Botulinum toxin type A, per unit
Use this code for Botox.
MED: MCM 2049

G ☑ **J0587** Botulinum toxin type B, per 100 units
Use this code for Myobloc.
MED: MCM 2049

N **J0592** Injection, buprenorphine hydrochloride, 0.1 mg
Use this code for Buprenix.
MED: MCM 2049

● ☑ **J0595** Injection, butorphanol tartrate, 1 mg

☑ **J0600** Injection, edetate calcium disodium, up to 1000 mg
Use this code for Calcium Disodium Versenate, Calcium EDTA).
MED: MCM 2049

☑ **J0610** Injection, calcium gluconate, per 10 ml
MED: MCM 2049

☑ **J0620** Injection, calcium glycerophosphate and calcium lactate, per 10 ml
Use this code for Calphosan.
MED: MCM 2049

☑ **J0630** Injection, calcitonin-salmon, up to 400 units
Use this code for Miacalcin.
MED: MCM 2049

N **J0636** Injection, calcitriol, 0.1 mcg
Use this code for Calcijex.
MED: MCM 2049

G **J0637** Injection, caspofungin acetate, 5 mg
Use this code for Cancidas.

N ☑ **J0640** Injection, leucovorin calcium, per 50 mg
MED: MCM 2049

☑ **J0670** Injection, mepivacaine HCl, per 10 ml
Use this code for Carbocaine, Polocaine, Isocaine HCl.
MED: MCM 2049

☑ **J0690** Injection, cefazolin sodium, 500 mg
Use this code for Ancef, Kefzol.
MED: MCM 2049

J0692 Injection, cefepime HCl, 500 mg
Use this code for Maxipime.

☑ **J0694** Injection, cefoxitin sodium, 1 g
Use this code for Mefoxin.
MED: MCM 2049

☑ **J0696** Injection, ceftriaxone sodium, per 250 mg
Use this code for Rocephin.
MED: MCM 2049

☑ **J0697** Injection, sterile cefuroxime sodium, per 750 mg
Use this code for Kefurox, Zinacef.
MED: MCM 2049

☑ **J0698** Cefotaxime sodium, per g
Use this code for Claforan.
MED: MCM 2049

☑ **J0702** Injection, betamethasone acetate and betamethasone sodium phosphate, per 3 mg
MED: MCM 2049

☑ **J0704** Injection, betamethasone sodium phosphate, per 4 mg
Use this code for Celestone Phosphate.

N **J0706** Injection, caffeine citrate, 5 mg
Use this code for Cafcit.

☑ **J0710** Injection, cephapirin sodium, up to 1 g
MED: MCM 2049

☑ **J0713** Injection, ceftazidime, per 500 mg
Use this code for Fortaz, Tazidime.
MED: MCM 2049

☑ **J0715** Injection, ceftizoxime sodium, per 500 mg
Use this code for Cefizox.
MED: MCM 2049

| ☐ Special Coverage Instructions | ☐ Noncovered by Medicare | ☐ Carrier Discretion | ☑ Quantity Alert | ● New Code | ▲ Revised Code |

66 — J Codes   M Maternity   A Adult   P Pediatrics   A-X APC Status Indicator   *2004 HCPCS*

☑ **J0720**   Injection, chloramphenicol sodium succinate, up to 1 g
Use this code for Chloromycetin Sodium Succinate.
MED: MCM 2049

☑ **J0725**   Injection, chorionic gonadotropin, per 1,000 USP units
Use this code for horex-5, Profasi HP, Pregnyl, Chorex-10.
MED: MCM 2049

☑ **J0735**   Injection, clonidine HCl, 1 mg
Use this code for Catapres.
MED: MCM 2049

☑ **J0740**   Injection, cidofovir, 375 mg
Use this code for Vistide.
MED: MCM 2049

☑ **J0743**   Injection, cilastatin sodium imipenem, per 250 mg
Use this code for Primaxin I.M., Primaxin I.V.
MED: MCM 2049

J0744   Injection, ciprofloxacin for intravenous infusion, 200 mg
Use this code for Cipro.

☑ **J0745**   Injection, codeine phosphate, per 30 mg
MED: MCM 2049

☑ **J0760**   Injection, colchicine, per 1 mg
MED: MCM 2049

☑ **J0770**   Injection, colistimethate sodium, up to 150 mg
Use this code for Coly-Mycin M.
MED: MCM 2049

☑ **J0780**   Injection, prochlorperazine, up to 10 mg
Use this code for Compazine.
MED: MCM 2049

☑ **J0800**   Injection, corticotropin, up to 40 units
MED: MCM 2049

☑ **J0835**   Injection, cosyntropin, per 0.25 mg
Use this code for Cortrosyn.
MED: MCM 2049

K ☑ **J0850**   Injection, cytomegalovirus immune globulin intravenous (human), per vial
MED: MCM 2049

▲ E **J0880**   Injection, darbepoetin alfa, 5 mcg
Use this code for Aranesp.

☑ **J0895**   Injection, deferoxamine mesylate, 500 mg
Use this code for Desferal.
MED: MCM 2049

☑ **J0900**   Injection, testosterone enanthate and estradiol valerate, up to 1 cc
Use this code for Andro-Estro 90-4, Androgyn L.A., Estra-Testrin, Valertest No. 1, Valertest No. 2.
MED: MCM 2049

☑ **J0945**   Injection, brompheniramine maleate, per 10 mg
Use this code for ND Stat.
MED: MCM 2049

☑ **J0970**   Injection, estradiol valerate, up to 40 mg
Use this code for Delestrogen, Estradiol L.A., Estradiol L.A. 20, Estradiol L.A. 40, Valergen 10, Valergen 20, Valergen 40, Estra-L 20, Estra-L 40.
MED: MCM 2049

☑ **J1000**   Injection, depo-estradiol cypionate, up to 5 mg
Use this code for Estradiol Cypionate, Estra-D, Estro-Cyp, Estroject L.A.
MED: MCM 2049

☑ **J1020**   Injection, methylprednisolone acetate, 20 mg
Use this code for Depo-Medrol.
MED: MCM 2049

☑ **J1030**   Injection, methylprednisolone acetate, 40 mg
Use this code for Depo-Medrol, depMedalone 40, M-Prednisol-40, Rep-Pred 40.
MED: MCM 2049

☑ **J1040**   Injection, methylprednisolone acetate, 80 mg
Use this code for Depo-Medrol, depMedalone 80, Medralone 80, M-Prednisol-80, Rep-Pred 80.
MED: MCM 2049

N **J1051**   Injection, medroxyprogesterone acetate, 50 mg
Use this code for Depo-Provera.
MED: MCM 2049

E ☑ **J1055**   Injection, medroxyprogesterone acetate for contraceptive use, 150 mg   ♀
Use this code for Depo-Provera.
MED: Medicare Statute: 1862A1

E **J1056**   Injection, medroxyprogesterone acetate/estradiol cypionate, 5 mg/25 mg   ♀
Use this code for Lunelle monthly contraceptive.

☑ **J1060**   Injection, testosterone cypionate and estradiol cypionate, up to 1 ml
Use this code for Depo-Testadiol, Andro/Fem.
MED: MCM 2049

☑ **J1070**   Injection, testosterone cypionate, up to 100 mg
Use this code for Depo-Testosterone, Depotest.
MED: MCM 2049

☑ **J1080**   Injection, testosterone cypionate, 1 cc, 200 mg
Use this code for Depo-Testosterone, Andro-Cyp 200, Andronate 200, depAndro 200, Depotest.
MED: MCM 2049

N **J1094**   Injection, dexamethasone acetate, 1 mg
Use this code for Dalalone L.A.
MED: MCM 2049

☑ **J1100**   Injection, dexamethosone sodium phosphate, 1 mg
Use this code for Cortastat, Dalalone.
MED: MCM 2049

☑ **J1110**   Injection, dihydroergotamine mesylate, per 1 mg
Use this code for D.H.E. 45.
MED: MCM 2049

☑ **J1120**   Injection, acetazolamide sodium, up to 500 mg
Use this code for Diamox.
MED: MCM 2049

☑ **J1160**   Injection, digoxin, up to 0.5 mg
Use this code for Lanoxin.
MED: MCM 2049

☑ **J1165**   Injection, phenytoin sodium, per 50 mg
Use this code for Dilantin.
MED: MCM 2049

☑ **J1170**   Injection, hydromorphone, up to 4 mg
Use this code for Dilaudid.
MED: MCM 2049

☑ **J1180**   Injection, dyphylline, up to 500 mg
Use this code for Lufyllin, Dilor.
MED: MCM 2049

Drugs Administered Other Than Oral Method   J0720 — J1180

K ☑ **J1190** Injection, dexrazoxane HCl, per 250 mg
Use this code for Zinecard.
MED: MCM 2049

☑ **J1200** Injection, diphenhydramine HCl, up to 50 mg
Use this code for Benadryl.
MED: MCM 2049

☑ **J1205** Injection, chlorothiazide sodium, per 500 mg
Use this code for Diuril Sodium.
MED: MCM 2049

☑ **J1212** Injection, DMSO, dimethyl sulfoxide, 50%, 50 ml
Use this code for Rimso. DMSO is covered only as a treatment of interstitial cystitis.
MED: CIM 45-23, MCM 2049

☑ **J1230** Injection, methadone HCl, up to 10 mg
Use this code for Dolophine HCl.
MED: MCM 2049

☑ **J1240** Injection, dimenhydrinate, up to 50 mg
MED: MCM 2049

N ☑ **J1245** Injection, dipyridamole, per 10 mg
Use this code for Persantine IV.
MED: MCM 15030, MCM 2049

N ☑ **J1250** Injection, dobutamine HCI, per 250 mg
Use this code for Dobutrex.
MED: MCM 2049

N ☑ **J1260** Injection, dolasetron mesylate, 10 mg
Use this code for Anzemet.
MED: MCM 2049

J1270 Injection, doxercalciferol, 1 mcg
Use this code for Hectorolc.

☑ **J1320** Injection, amitriptyline HCl, up to 20 mg
Use this code for Elavil.
MED: MCM 2049

N ☑ **J1325** Injection, epoprostenol, 0.5 mg
Use this code for Flolan. See K0455 for infusion pump for epoprosterol.
MED: MCM 2049

K ☑ **J1327** Injection, eptifibatide, 5 mg
Use this code for Integrilin.
MED: MCM 2049

● ☑ **J1330** Injection, ergonovine maleate, up to 0.2 mg
Medicare jurisdiction: local carrier. Use this code for Ergotrate Maleate.
MED: MCM 2049

● ☑ **J1335** Injection, ertapenem sodium, 500 mg

☑ **J1364** Injection, erythromycin lactobionate, per 500 mg
MED: MCM 2049

☑ **J1380** Injection, estradiol valerate, up to 10 mg
Use this code for Delestrogen, Duragen-20, Duragen-40, Estradiol L.A., Estradiol L.A. 20, Estradiol L.A. 40, Gynogen L.A. 10, Gynogen L.A. 20, Gynogen L.A. 40.
MED: MCM 2049

☑ **J1390** Injection, estradiol valerate, up to 20 mg
Use this code for Delestrogen, Estradiol L.A., Estradiol L.A. 20, Estradiol L.A. 40, Gynogen L.A. 10, Gynogen L.A. 20, Gynogen L.A. 40.
MED: MCM 2049

☑ **J1410** Injection, estrogen conjugated, per 25 mg
Use this code for Premarin Intravenous.
MED: MCM 2049

☑ **J1435** Injection, estrone, per 1 mg
Use this code for Theelin Aqueous, Estone 5, Kestrone 5.
MED: MCM 2049

N ☑ **J1436** Injection, etidronate disodium, per 300 mg
Use this code for Didronel.
MED: MCM 2049

N ☑ **J1438** Injection, etanercept, 25 mg (Code may be used for Medicare when drug administered under the direct supervision of a physician, not for use when drug is self-administered)
Use this code for Enbrel.
MED: MCM 2049

K ☑ **J1440** Injection, filgrastim (G-CSF), 300 mcg
Use this code for Neupogen.
MED: MCM 2049

K ☑ **J1441** Injection, filgrastim (G-CSF), 480 mcg
Use this code for Neupogen.
MED: MCM 2049

☑ **J1450** Injection, fluconazole, 200 mg
Use this code for Diflucan.
MED: MCM 2049.5

☑ **J1452** Injection, omivirsen sodium, intraocular, 1.65 mg
Use this code for Vitavene.
MED: MCM 2049.3

☑ **J1455** Injection, foscarnet sodium, per 1,000 mg
Use this code for Foscavir.
MED: MCM 2049

N ☑ **J1460** Injection, gamma globulin, intramuscular, 1 cc
MED: MCM 2049

☑ **J1470** Injection, gamma globulin, intramuscular, 2 cc
MED: MCM 2049

☑ **J1480** Injection, gamma globulin, intramuscular, 3 cc
MED: MCM 2049

☑ **J1490** Injection, gamma globulin, intramuscular, 4 cc
MED: MCM 2049

☑ **J1500** Injection, gamma globulin, intramuscular, 5 cc
MED: MCM 2049

☑ **J1510** Injection, gamma globulin, intramuscular, 6 cc
MED: MCM 2049

☑ **J1520** Injection, gamma globulin, intramuscular, 7 cc
MED: MCM 2049

☑ **J1530** Injection, gamma globulin, intramuscular, 8 cc
MED: MCM 2049

☑ **J1540** Injection, gamma globulin, intramuscular, 9 cc
MED: MCM 2049

☑ **J1550** Injection, gamma globulin, intramuscular, 10 cc
MED: MCM 2049

☑ **J1560** Injection, gamma globulin, intramuscular, over 10 cc
MED: MCM 2049

K ☑ **J1563** Injection, immune globulin, intravenous, 1 g
MED: MCM 2049

Special Coverage Instructions   Noncovered by Medicare   Carrier Discretion   ☑ Quantity Alert   ● New Code   ▲ Revised Code

K   **J1564** Injection, immune globulin, 10 mg
MED: MCM 2049

K ☑ **J1565** Injection, respiratory syncytial virus immune globulin, intravenous, 50 mg
MED: MCM 2049

N ☑ **J1570** Injection, ganciclovir sodium, 500 mg
Use this code for Cytovene.
MED: MCM 2049

☑ **J1580** Injection, Garamycin, gentamicin, up to 80 mg
Use this code for Gentamicin Sulfate.
MED: MCM 2049

☑ **J1590** Injection, gatifloxacin, 10 mg

● ☑ **J1595** Injection, glatiramer acetate, 20 mg
MED: MCM 2049

☑ **J1600** Injection, gold sodium thiomalate, up to 50 mg
Use this code for Myochrysine.
MED: MCM 2049

☑ **J1610** Injection, glucagon HCl, per 1 mg
Use this code for glucagon.
MED: MCM 2049

N ☑ **J1620** Injection, gonadorelin HCl, per 100 mcg
Use this code for Factrel.
MED: MCM 2049

N ☑ **J1626** Injection, granisetron HCl, 100 mcg
Use this code for Kytril.
MED: MCM 2049

☑ **J1630** Injection, haloperidol, up to 5 mg
Use this code for Haldol.
MED: MCM 2049

☑ **J1631** Injection, haloperidol decanoate, per 50 mg
Use this code for Haldol Decanoate-50.
MED: MCM 2049

☑ **J1642** Injection, heparin sodium, (heparin lock flush), per 10 units
Use this code for Hep-Lock, Hep-Lock U/P.
MED: MCM 2049

☑ **J1644** Injection, heparin sodium, per 1,000 units
MED: MCM 2049

☑ **J1645** Injection, dalteparin sodium, per 2500 IU
Use this code for Fragmin.
MED: MCM 2049

▲ N ☑ **J1650** Injection, enoxaparin sodium, 10 mg
Use this code for Lovenox.
MED: MCM 2049

N   **J1652** Injection, fondaparinux sodium, 0.5 mg
Use this code for Atrixtra.
MED: MCM 2049

N ☑ **J1655** Injection, tinzaparin sodium, 1000 IU
Use this code for Innohep.

N ☑ **J1670** Injection, tetanus immune globulin, human, up to 250 units
MED: MCM 2049

☑ **J1700** Injection, hydrocortisone acetate, up to 25 mg
Use this code for Hydrocortone Acetate.
MED: MCM 2049

☑ **J1710** Injection, hydrocortisone sodium phosphate, up to 50 mg
Use this code for Hydrocortone Phosphate.
MED: MCM 2049

☑ **J1720** Injection, hydrocortisone sodium succinate, up to 100 mg
Use this code for Solu-Cortef, A-Hydrocort.
MED: MCM 2049

☑ **J1730** Injection, diazoxide, up to 300 mg
Use this code for Hyperstat IV.
MED: MCM 2049

☑ **J1742** Injection, ibutilide fumarate, 1 mg
Use this code for Corvert.
MED: MCM 2049

K ☑ **J1745** Injection, infliximab, 10 mg
Use this code for Remicade.
MED: MCM 2049

N ☑ **J1750** Injection, iron dextran, 50 mg
Use this code for Infed.
MED: MCM 2049.5

N   **J1756** Injection, iron sucrose, 1 mg
Use this code for Venofer.

F ☑ **J1785** Injection, imiglucerase, per unit
Use this code for Cerezyme.
MED: MCM 2049

☑ **J1790** Injection, droperidol, up to 5 mg
Use this code for Inapsine.
MED: MCM 2049

☑ **J1800** Injection, propranolol HCl, up to 1 mg
Use this code for Inderal.
MED: MCM 2049

E ☑ **J1810** Injection, droperidol and fentanyl citrate, up to 2 ml ampule
MED: MCM 2049

N   **J1815** Injection, insulin, per 5 units
Use this code for Humalog, Humulin, Insulin Lispo.
MED: CIM 60-14, MCM 2049

N   **J1817** Insulin for administration through DME (i.e., insulin pump) per 50 units
Use this code for Humalog.

K ☑ **J1825** Injection, interferon beta-1a, 33 mcg
Use this code for Avonex.
MED: MCM 2049

K ☑ **J1830** Injection interferon beta-1b, 0.25 mg (code may be used for Medicare when drug administered under direct supervision of a physician, not for use when drug is self-administered)
MED: MCM 2049

☑ **J1835** Injection, itraconazole, 50 mg
Use this code for Sporonox IV.

☑ **J1840** Injection, kanamycin sulfate, up to 500 mg
Use this code for Kantrex, Klebcil.
MED: MCM 2049

☑ **J1850** Injection, kanamycin sulfate, up to 75 mg
Use this code for Kantrex.
MED: MCM 2049

| Special Coverage Instructions | Noncovered by Medicare | Carrier Discretion | ☑ Quantity Alert | ● New Code | ▲ Revised Code |

☑ **J1885** Injection, ketorolac tromethamine, per 15 mg
Use this code for Toradol.
MED: MCM 2049

☑ **J1890** Injection, cephalothin sodium, up to 1 g
Use this code for Cephalothin Sodium.
MED: MCM 2049

~~J1910 Injection, kutapressin, up to 2 ml~~

☑ **J1940** Injection, furosemide, up to 20 mg
Use this code for Lasix, Furomide M.D.
MED: MCM 2049

Ⓚ ☑ **J1950** Injection, leuprolide acetate (for depot suspension), per 3.75 mg
Use this code for Lupron Depot.
MED: MCM 2049

Ⓐ ☑ **J1955** Injection, levocarnitine, per 1 g
Use this code for Carnitor.
MED: MCM 2049

☑ **J1956** Injection, levofloxacin, 250 mg
Use this code for Levaquin.
MED: MCM 2049

☑ **J1960** Injection, levorphanol tartrate, up to 2 mg
MED: MCM 2049

J1980 Injection, hyoscyamine sulfate, up to 0.25 mg
Use this code for Levsin.

☑ **J1990** Injection, chlordiazepoxide HCl, up to 100 mg
Use this code for Librium.
MED: MCM 2049

~~J2000 Injection, lidocaine hcl, 50 cc~~

● ☑ **J2001** Injection, lidocaine HCl for intravenous infusion, 10 mg
MED: MCM 2049

☑ **J2010** Injection, lincomycin HCl, up to 300 mg
MED: MCM 2049

Ⓝ ☑ **J2020** Injection, linezolid, 200 mg
Use this code for Zyvox.

☑ **J2060** Injection, lorazepam, 2 mg
Use this code for Ativan.
MED: MCM 2049

☑ **J2150** Injection, mannitol, 25% in 50 ml

☑ **J2175** Injection, meperidine HCl, per 100 mg
Use this code for Demerol HCl.
MED: MCM 2049

☑ **J2180** Injection, meperidine and promethazine HCl, up to 50 mg
Use this code for Mepergan Injection.
MED: MCM 2049

● ☑ **J2185** Injection, meropenem, 100 mg

☑ **J2210** Injection, methylergonovine maleate, up to 0.2 mg
Use this code for Methergine.
MED: MCM 2049

☑ **J2250** Injection, midazolam HCl, per 1 mg
Use this code for Versed.
MED: MCM 2049

Ⓝ ☑ **J2260** Injection, milrinone lactate, 5 mg
Use this code for Primacor.
MED: MCM 2049

☑ **J2270** Injection, morphine sulfate, up to 10 mg
MED: MCM 2049

☑ **J2271** Injection, morphine sulfate, 100 mg
MED: CIM 60-14a, MCM 2049

Ⓝ ☑ **J2275** Injection, morphine sulfate (preservative-free sterile solution), per 10 mg
Use this code for Astramorph PF, Duramorph.
MED: CIM 60-14b, MCM 2049

● ☑ **J2280** Injection, moxifloxacin, 100 mg

☑ **J2300** Injection, nalbuphine HCl, per 10 mg
Use this code for Nubain.
MED: MCM 2049

☑ **J2310** Injection, naloxone HCl, per 1 mg
Use this code for Narcan.
MED: MCM 2049

☑ **J2320** Injection, nandrolone decanoate, up to 50 mg
Use this code for Deca-Durabolin, Hybolin Decanoate, Decolone-50, Neo-Durabolic.
MED: MCM 2049

☑ **J2321** Injection, nandrolone decanoate, up to 100 mg
Use this code for Deca-Durabolin, Hybolin Decanoate.
MED: MCM 2049

☑ **J2322** Injection, nandrolone decanoate, up to 200 mg
Use this code for Deca-Durabolin.
MED: MCM 2049

Ⓖ **J2324** Injection, nesiritide, 0.5 mg
Use this code for Natrecor.
MED: MCM 2049

~~J2352 Injection, octreotide acetate, 1 mg~~

● ☑ **J2353** Injection, octreotide, depot form for intramuscular injection, 1 mg

● ☑ **J2354** Injection, octreotide, non-depot form for subcutaneous or intravenous injection, 25 mcg

Ⓚ ☑ **J2355** Injection, oprelvekin, 5 mg
Use this code for Neumega.
MED: MCM 2049

☑ **J2360** Injection, orphenadrine citrate, up to 60 mg
Use this code for Norflex, Banflex, Orphenate.
MED: MCM 2049

☑ **J2370** Injection, phenylephrine HCl, up to 1 ml
Use this code for Neo-Synephrine.
MED: MCM 2049

☑ **J2400** Injection, chloroprocaine HCl, per 30 ml
Use this code for Nesacaine, Nesacaine-MPF.
MED: MCM 2049

Ⓝ ☑ **J2405** Injection, ondansetron HCl, per 1 mg
Use this code for Zofran.
MED: MCM 2049

Ⓝ ☑ **J2410** Injection, oxymorphone HCl, up to 1 mg
Use this code for Numorphan, Numorphan H.P.
MED: MCM 2049

Ⓚ ☑ **J2430** Injection, pamidronate disodium, per 30 mg
Use this code for Aredia.
MED: MCM 2049

☑ **J2440** Injection, papaverine HCl, up to 60 mg
MED: MCM 2049

| Special Coverage Instructions | Noncovered by Medicare | Carrier Discretion | ☑ Quantity Alert | ● New Code | ▲ Revised Code |

☑ **J2460** Injection, oxytetracycline HCl, up to 50 mg
Use this code for Terramycin IM.
MED: MCM 2049

Ⓝ **J2501** Injection, paricalcitol, 1 mcg
Use this code For Zemplar.
MED: MCM 2049

● ☑ **J2505** Injection, pegfilgrastim, 6 mg
Use this code for Neulasta.

☑ **J2510** Injection, penicillin G procaine, aqueous, up to 600,000 units
Use this code for Wycillin, Pfizerpen A.S.
MED: MCM 2049

☑ **J2515** Injection, pentobarbital sodium, per 50 mg
Use this code for Nembutal Sodium Solution.
MED: MCM 2049

☑ **J2540** Injection, penicillin G potassium, up to 600,000 units
Use this code for Pfizerpen.
MED: MCM 2049

☑ **J2543** Injection, piperacillin sodium/tazobactam sodium, 1 g/0.125 g (1.125 g)
Use this code for Zosyn.
MED: MCM 2049

Ⓐ ☑ **J2545** Pentamidine isethionate, inhalation solution, per 300 mg, administered through a DME
Use this code for Nebupent, PentacaRinat, Pentam 300.
MED: MCM 2049

☑ **J2550** Injection, promethazine HCl, up to 50 mg
Use this code for Phenergan, Prorex-25, Prorex-50.
MED: MCM 2049

☑ **J2560** Injection, phenobarbital sodium, up to 120 mg
Use this code for Luminal Sodium.
MED: MCM 2049

☑ **J2590** Injection, oxytocin, up to 10 units
Use this code for Pitocin.
MED: MCM 2049

☑ **J2597** Injection, desmopressin acetate, per 1 mcg
Use this code for DDAVP.
MED: MCM 2049

☑ **J2650** Injection, prednisolone acetate, up to 1 ml
Use this code for Key-Pred 25, Key-Pred 50, Predcor-25, Predcor-50, Predoject-50, Predalone-50.
MED: MCM 2049

☑ **J2670** Injection, tolazoline HCl, up to 25 mg
Use this code for Priscoline HCl.
MED: MCM 2049

J2675 Injection, progesterone, per 50 mg
MED: MCM 2049

☑ **J2680** Injection, fluphenazine decanoate, up to 25 mg
Use this code for Prolixin Decanoate.
MED: MCM 2049

☑ **J2690** Injection, procainamide HCl, up to 1 g
Use this code for Pronestyl.
MED: MCM 2049

☑ **J2700** Injection, oxacillin sodium, up to 250 mg
Use this code for Bactocill.
MED: MCM 2049

☑ **J2710** Injection, neostigmine methylsulfate, up to 0.5 mg
Use this code for Prostigmin.
MED: MCM 2049

☑ **J2720** Injection, protamine sulfate, per 10 mg
MED: MCM 2049

☑ **J2725** Injection, protirelin, per 250 mcg
MED: MCM 2049

☑ **J2730** Injection, pralidoxime chloride, up to 1 g
Use this code for Protopam Chloride.
MED: MCM 2049

☑ **J2760** Injection, phentolamine mesylate, up to 5 mg
Use this code for Regitine.
MED: MCM 2049

Ⓝ ☑ **J2765** Injection, metoclopramide HCl, up to 10 mg
Use this code for Reglan.
MED: MCM 2049

Ⓝ ☑ **J2770** Injection, quinupristin/dalfopristin, 500 mg (150/350)
Use this code for Synercid.
MED: MCM 2049

Ⓝ ☑ **J2780** Injection, ranitidine HCl, 25 mg
Use this code for Zantac.
MED: MCM 2049

● ☑ **J2783** Injection, rasburicase, 0.5 mg

Ⓚ **J2788** Injection, Rho d immune globulin, human, minidose, 50 mcg
Use this code for RhoGam, BAYRho-D, MICRhoGAM, HYPRho-D.
MED: MCM 2049

Ⓝ ☑ **J2790** Injection, Rho d immune globulin, human, full dose, 300 mcg
Use this code for Gamulin RH.
MED: MCM 2049

Ⓚ ☑ **J2792** Injection, Rho D immune globulin, intravenous, human, solvent detergent, 100 IU
Use this code for BAYRho-D, WINRho SDF.
MED: MCM 2049

☑ **J2795** Injection, ropivacaine HCl, 1 mg
Use this code for Naropin.

☑ **J2800** Injection, methocarbamol, up to 10 ml
Use this code for Robaxin.
MED: MCM 2049

☑ **J2810** Injection, theophylline, per 40 mg
MED: MCM 2049

Ⓝ ☑ **J2820** Injection, sargramostim (GM-CSF), 50 mcg
Use this code for Leukine.
MED: MCM 2049

☑ **J2910** Injection, aurothioglucose, up to 50 mg
Use this code for Solganal.
MED: MCM 2049

☑ **J2912** Injection, sodium chloride, 0.9%, per 2 ml
MED: MCM 2049

Ⓝ **J2916** Injection, sodium ferric gluconate complex in sucrose injection, 12.5 mg
Use this code for Ferrlecit.
MED: MCM 2049.2, MCM 2049.4

Drugs Administered Other Than Oral Method

J2920 — J3365

☑ **J2920** Injection, methylprednisolone sodium succinate, up to 40 mg
Use this code for Solu-Medrol, A-methaPred.
MED: MCM 2049

☑ **J2930** Injection, methylprednisolone sodium succinate, up to 125 mg
Use this code for Solu-Medrol, A-methaPred.
MED: MCM 2049

Ⓝ ☑ **J2940** Injection, somatrem, 1 mg
Use this code for Protropin.
MED: MCM 2049, Medicare Statute: 1861s2b

Ⓚ ☑ **J2941** Injection, somatropin, 1 mg
Use this code for Humatrope, Genotropin, Nutropin.
MED: MCM 2049, Medicare Statute: 1861s2b

Ⓝ ☑ **J2950** Injection, promazine HCl, up to 25 mg
MED: MCM 2049

Ⓚ ☑ **J2993** Injection, reteplase, 18.1 mg
Use this code for Retavase.
MED: MCM 2049

Ⓝ ☑ **J2995** Injection, streptokinase, per 250,000 IU
Use this code for Streptase.
MED: MCM 2049

Ⓝ ☑ **J2997** Injection, alteplase recombinant, 1 mg
Use this code for Activase.
MED: MCM 2049

Ⓝ ☑ **J3000** Injection, streptomycin, up to 1 g
Use this code for Streptomycin Sulfate.
MED: MCM 2049

Ⓝ ☑ **J3010** Injection, fentanyl citrate, 0.1 mg
Use this code for Sublimaze.
MED: MCM 2049

☑ **J3030** Injection, sumatriptan succinate, 6 mg (code may be used for Medicare when drug administered under the direct supervision of a physician, not for use when drug is self administered)
Use this code for Imitrex.
MED: MCM 2049

☑ **J3070** Injection, pentazocine, 30 mg
Use this code for Talwin.
MED: MCM 2049

Ⓚ ☑ **J3100** Injection, tenecteplase, 50 mg
Use this code for TNKase.

☑ **J3105** Injection, terbutaline sulfate, up to 1 mg
Use this code for Brethine. For terbutaline in inhalation solution, see K0525 and K0526.
MED: MCM 2049

☑ **J3120** Injection, testosterone enanthate, up to 100 mg
Use this code for Delatestryl.
MED: MCM 2049

☑ **J3130** Injection, testosterone enanthate, up to 200 mg
Use this code for Delatestryl.
MED: MCM 2049

☑ **J3140** Injection, testosterone suspension, up to 50 mg
MED: MCM 2049

☑ **J3150** Injection, testosterone propionate, up to 100 mg
MED: MCM 2049

☑ **J3230** Injection, chlorpromazine HCl, up to 50 mg
Use this code for Thorazine.
MED: MCM 2049

Ⓚ ☑ **J3240** Injection, thyrotropin alpha, 0.9 mg, provided in 1.1 mg vial
Use this code for Thyrogen.
MED: MCM 2049

Ⓚ ☑ **J3245** Injection, tirofiban HCl, 12.5 mg
Use this code for Aggrastat.
MED: MCM 2049

☑ **J3250** Injection, trimethobenzamide HCl, up to 200 mg
Use this code for Tigan.
MED: MCM 2049

☑ **J3260** Injection, tobramycin sulfate, up to 80 mg
Use this code for Nebcin.
MED: MCM 2049

☑ **J3265** Injection, torsemide, 10 mg/ml
Use this code for Demadex.
MED: MCM 2049

Ⓝ ☑ **J3280** Injection, thiethylperazine maleate, up to 10 mg
Use this code for Torecan.
MED: MCM 2049

☑ **J3301** Injection, triamcinolone acetonide, per 10 mg
Use this code for Kenalog-10, Kenalog-40, Triam-A. For triamcinolone in inhalation solution, see K0527 and K0528.
MED: MCM 2049

☑ **J3302** Injection, triamcinolone diacetate, per 5 mg
Use this code for Aristocort Intralesional, Aristocort Forte, Amcort, Cinolone, Trilone, Clinacort.
MED: MCM 2049

☑ **J3303** Injection, triamcinolone hexacetonide, per 5 mg
Use this code for Aristospan Intralesional, Aristospan Intra-articular.
MED: MCM 2049

Ⓚ ☑ **J3305** Injection, trimetrexate glucoronate, per 25 mg
Use this code for Neutrexin.
MED: MCM 2049

Ⓝ ☑ **J3310** Injection, perphenazine, up to 5 mg
MED: MCM 2049

Ⓖ **J3315** Injection, triptorelin pamoate, 3.75 mg
Use this code dor Trelstar LA.
MED: MCM 2049

☑ **J3320** Injection, spectinomycin dihydrochloride, up to 2 g
Use this code for Trobicin.
MED: MCM 2049

☑ **J3350** Injection, urea, up to 40 g
MED: MCM 2049

☑ **J3360** Injection, diazepam, up to 5 mg
Use this code for Valium.
MED: MCM 2049

☑ **J3364** Injection, urokinase, 5,000 IU vial
Use this code for Abbokinase Open-Cath.
MED: MCM 2049

Ⓝ ☑ **J3365** Injection, IV, urokinase, 250,000 IU vial
Use this code for Abbokinase.
MED: MCM 2049

Special Coverage Instructions   Noncovered by Medicare   Carrier Discretion   ☑ Quantity Alert   ● New Code   ▲ Revised Code

N ☑ **J3370** Injection, vancomycin HCl, 500 mg
MED: CIM 60-14, MCM 2049

K ☑ **J3395** Injection, verteporfin, 15 mg
Use this code for Visudyne.
MED: CIM 35-100, CIM 45-30

☑ **J3400** Injection, triflupromazine HCl, up to 20 mg
Use this code for Vesprin.
MED: MCM 2049

☑ **J3410** Injection, hydroxyzine HCl, up to 25 mg
Use this code for Vistaril,Hyzine-50.
MED: MCM 2049

● ☑ **J3411** Injection, thiamine HCl, 100 mg

● ☑ **J3415** Injection, pyridoxine HCl, 100 mg

☑ **J3420** Injection, vitamin B-12 cyanocobalamin, up to 1,000 mcg
MED: CIM 45-4, MCM 2049

☑ **J3430** Injection, phytonadione (vitamin K), per 1 mg
Use this code for AquaMephyton.
MED: MCM 2049

● ☑ **J3465** Injection, voriconazole, 10 mg
MED: MCM 2049

☑ **J3470** Injection, hyaluronidase, up to 150 units
Use this code for Wydase.
MED: MCM 2049

☑ **J3475** Injection, magnesium sulphate, per 500 mg
MED: MCM 2049

☑ **J3480** Injection, potassium chloride, per 2 mEq
MED: MCM 2049

☑ **J3485** Injection, zidovudine, 10 mg
Use this code for Retrovir.
MED: MCM 2049

● ☑ **J3486** Injection, ziprasidone mesylate, 10 mg

G **J3487** Injection, zoledronic acid, 1 mg
Use this code for Zometa.

N **J3490** Unclassified drugs
MED: MCM 2049

E ☑ **J3520** Edetate disodium, per 150 mg
Use this code for Endrate, Disotate. This drug is used in chelation therapy, a treatment for atherosclerosis that is not covered by Medicare.
MED: CIM 35-64, CIM 45-20

N **J3530** Nasal vaccine inhalation
MED: MCM 2049

E **J3535** Drug administered through a metered dose inhaler
MED: MCM 2050.5

E **J3570** Laetrile, amygdalin, vitamin B-17
The FDA has found Laetrile to have no safe or effective therapeutic purpose.
MED: CIM 45-10

N **J3590** Unclassified biologics

MISCELLANEOUS DRUGS AND SOLUTIONS

☑ **J7030** Infusion, normal saline solution, 1,000 cc
MED: MCM 2049

☑ **J7040** Infusion, normal saline solution, sterile (500 ml = 1 unit)
MED: MCM 2049

☑ **J7042** 5% dextrose/normal saline (500 ml = 1 unit)
MED: MCM 2049

☑ **J7050** Infusion, normal saline solution, 250 cc
MED: MCM 2049

☑ **J7051** Sterile saline or water, up to 5 cc
MED: MCM 2049

☑ **J7060** 5% dextrose/water (500 ml = 1 unit)
MED: MCM 2049

☑ **J7070** Infusion, D-5-W, 1,000 cc
MED: MCM 2049

☑ **J7100** Infusion, dextran 40, 500 ml
Use this code for Gentran, 10% LMD, Rheomacrodex.
MED: MCM 2049

☑ **J7110** Infusion, dextran 75, 500 ml
Use this code for Gentran 75.
MED: MCM 2049

☑ **J7120** Ringer's lactate infusion, up to 1,000 cc
MED: MCM 2049

☑ **J7130** Hypertonic saline solution, 50 or 100 mEq, 20 cc vial
MED: MCM 2049

K ☑ **J7190** Factor VIII (antihemophilic factor, human) per IU
Use this code for Monarc-M, Koate-HP.
Medicare jurisdiction: local carrier.
MED: MCM 2049

K ☑ **J7191** Factor VIII (anti-hemophilic factor (porcine)), per IU
Use this code for Hyate:C. Medicare jurisdiction: local carrier.
MED: MCM 2049

K ☑ **J7192** Factor VIII (antihemophilic factor, recombinant) per IU
Use this code for Recombinate, Kogenate, Helixate. Medicare jurisdiction: local carrier.
MED: MCM 2049

K ☑ **J7193** Factor IX (antihemophilic factor, purified, non-recombinant) per IU
Use this code for AlphaNine SD, mononine.
MED: MCM 2049

K ☑ **J7194** Factor IX complex, per IU
Use this code for Konyne-80, Profilnine Heat-Treated, Proplex T, Proplex SX-T. Medicare jurisdiction: local carrier.
MED: MCM 2049

K ☑ **J7195** Factor IX (antihemophilic factor, recombinant) per IU
Use this code for Benefix, Konyne 80, Profilnine SD, Proplex T.
MED: MCM 2049

K ☑ **J7197** Antithrombin III (human), per IU
Medicare jurisdiction: local carrier. Use this code for Throbate III, ATnativ.
MED: MCM 2049

Drugs Administered Other Than Oral Method

J7198 — J7621

J7198 Anti-inhibitor, per IU
Medicare jurisdiction: local carrier. Use this code for Autoplex T.
MED: CIM 45-24, MCM 2049

J7199 Hemophilia clotting factor, not otherwise classified
Medicare jurisdiction: local carrier.
MED: CIM 45-24, MCM 2049

J7300 Intrauterine copper contraceptive
Use this code for Paragard T380A. Medicare jurisdiction: local carrier.
MED: Medicare Statute: 1862A1

J7302 Levonorgestrel-releasing intrauterine contraceptive system, 52 mg
Use this code for Mirena.
MED: Medicare Statute: 1862a1

J7303 Contraceptive supply, hormone containing vaginal ring, each
MED: Medicare Statute: 1862.1

J7308 Aminolevulinic acid HCl for topical administration, 20%, single unit dosage form (354 mg)

J7310 Ganciclovir, 4.5 mg, long-acting implant
Use this code for Vitrasert.
MED: MCM 2049

J7317 Sodium hyaluronate, per 20 to 25 mg dose for intra-articular injection
Use this code for Hyalgan (20 mg), Supartz (25 mg).

J7320 Hylan G-F 20, 16 mg, for intra-articular injection
Use this code for Synvisc.

J7330 Autologous cultured chondrocytes, implant
Medicare jurisdiction: local carrier. Use this code for Carticel.

J7340 Dermal and epidermal tissue of human origin, with or without bioengineered or processed elements, with metabolically active elements, per square centimeter
Dermal tissue-not found in the drug table. Use this code for Dermagraft , Dermagraft TC. See also C9201 for Outpatient PPS.

J7342 Dermal tissue, of human origin, with or without other bioengineered or processed elements, with metabolically active elements, per square centimeter
Dermal Tissue, not found in the drug table. Use this code for Dermagraft , Dermagraft TC. See also C9201 for Outpatient PPS.

J7350 Dermal tissue of human origin, injectable, with or without other bioengineered or processed elements, but without metabolized active elements, per 10 mg
Dermal Tissue, not found in the drug table. Use this code for Dermagraft , Dermagraft TC. See also C9201 for Outpatient PPS.

J7500 Azathioprine, oral, 50 mg
Use this code for Imuran.
MED: MCM 2049.5

J7501 Azathioprine, parenteral, 100 mg
MED: MCM 2049

J7502 Cyclosporine, oral, 100 mg
Use this code for Neoral, Sandimmune.
MED: MCM 2049.5

J7504 Lymphocyte immune globulin, antithymocyte globulin, equine, parenteral, 250 mg
Use this code for Atgam.
MED: CIM 45-22, MCM 2049

J7505 Muromonab-CD3, parenteral, 5 mg
Use this code for Orthoclone OKT3.
MED: MCM 2049

J7506 Prednisone, oral, per 5 mg
Use this code for Deltasone meticorten orasone.
MED: MCM 2049.5

J7507 Tacrolimus, oral, per 1 mg
Use this code for Prograf.
MED: MCM 2049.5

J7508　Tacrolimus, oral, per 5 mg

J7509 Methylprednisolone, oral, per 4 mg
Use this code for Medrol.
MED: MCM 2049.5

J7510 Prednisolone, oral, per 5 mg
MED: MCM 2049.5

J7511 Lymphocyte immune globulin, antithymocyte globulin, rabbit, parenteral, 25 mg

J7513 Daclizumab, parenteral, 25 mg
Use this code for Zenapax.
MED: MCM 2049.5

J7515 Cyclosporine, oral, 25 mg
Use this code for Neoral, Sandimmune.

J7516 Cyclosporine, parenteral, 250 mg
Use this code for Neoral, Sandimmune.

J7517 Mycophenolate mofetil, oral, 250 mg
Use this code for CellCept.

J7520 Sirolimus, oral, 1 mg
Use this code for Rapamune.
MED: MCM 2049.5

J7525 Tacrolimus, parenteral, 5 mg
Use this code for Prograf.
MED: MCM 2049.5

J7599 Immunosuppressive drug, NOC
Determine if an alternative HCPCS Level II code better describes the service being reported. This code should be used only if a more specific code is unavailable.
MED: MCM 2049.5

INHALATION SOLUTIONS

J7608 Acetylcysteine, inhalation solution administered through DME, unit dose form, per g
Use this code for Mucomyst, Mucosil.
MED: MCM 2100.5

J7618 Albuterol, all formulations including separated isomers, inhalation solution administered through DME, concentrated form, per 1 mg (Albuterol) or per 0.5 mg (Levalbuterol)
MED: MCM 2100.5

J7619 Albuterol, all formulations including separated isomers, inhalation solution administered through DME, unit dose, per 1 mg (Albuterol) or per 0.5 mg (Levalbuterol)
MED: MCM 2100.5

J7621 Albuterol, all formulations, including separated isomers, up to 5 mg (albuterol) or 2.5 mg (levoalbuterol), and ipratropium bromide, up to 1 mg, compounded inhalation solution, administered through DME

Special Coverage Instructions　　　Noncovered by Medicare　　　Carrier Discretion　　☑ Quantity Alert　　● New Code　　▲ Revised Code

　　Ⓜ Maternity　　Ⓐ Adult　　Ⓟ Pediatrics　　Ⓐ-Ⓧ APC Status Indicator　　*2004 HCPCS*

☑ **J7622** Bethamethasone, inhalation solution administered through DME, unit dose form, per mg

☑ **J7624** Bethamethasone, inhalation solution administered through DME, unit dose form, per mg

☑ **J7626** Budesonide inhalation solution, administered through DME, unit dose form, 0.25 to 0.50 mg
Use this code for Pulmicort Respules.

☑ **J7628** Bitolterol mesylate, inhalation solution administered through DME, concentrated form, per mg
Use this code for Tornalate.
MED: MCM 2100.5

☑ **J7629** Bitolterol mesylate, inhalation solution administered through DME, unit dose form, per mg
Use this code for Tornalate.
MED: MCM 2100.5

☑ **J7631** Cromolyn sodium, inhalation solution administered through DME, unit dose form, per 10 mg
Use this code for Gastrocrom.
MED: MCM 2100.5

N **J7633** Budesonide, inhalation solution administered through DME, concentrated form, per 0.25 milligram
Use this code for Pumocort.

☑ **J7635** Atropine, inhalation solution administered through DME, concentrated form, per mg
MED: MCM 2100.5

☑ **J7636** Atropine, inhalation solution administered through DME, unit dose form, per mg
MED: MCM 2100.5

☑ **J7637** Dexamethasone, inhalation solution administered through DME, concentrated form, per mg
MED: MCM 2100.5

☑ **J7638** Dexamethasone, inhalation solution administered through DME, unit dose form, per mg
MED: MCM 2100.5

☑ **J7639** Dornase alpha, inhalation solution administered through DME, unit dose form, per mg
Use this code for Pulmozyme.
MED: MCM 2100.5

J7641 Flunisolide, inhalation solution administered through DME, unit dose, per mg

☑ **J7642** Glycopyrrolate, inhalation solution administered through DME, concentrated form, per mg
MED: MCM 2100.5

☑ **J7643** Glycopyrrolate, inhalation solution administered through DME, unit dose form, per mg
MED: MCM 2100.5

☑ **J7644** Ipratropium bromide, inhalation solution administered through DME, unit dose form, per mg
Use this code for Atrovent.
MED: MCM 2100.5

☑ **J7648** Isoetharine HCl, inhalation solution administered through DME, concentrated form, per mg
MED: MCM 2100.5

☑ **J7649** Isoetharine HCl, inhalation solution administered through DME, unit dose form, per mg
MED: MCM 2100.5

☑ **J7658** Isoproterenol HCl, inhalation solution administered through DME, concentrated form, per mg
MED: MCM 2100.5

☑ **J7659** Isoproterenol HCl, inhalation solution administered through DME, unit dose form, per mg
MED: MCM 2100.5

☑ **J7668** Metaproterenol sulfate, inhalation solution administered through DME, concentrated form, per 10 mg
Use this code for Alupent.
MED: MCM 2100.5

☑ **J7669** Metaproterenol sulfate, inhalation solution administered through DME, unit dose form, per 10 mg
Use this code for Alupent.
MED: MCM 2100.5

☑ **J7680** Terbutaline sulfate, inhalation solution administered through DME, concentrated form, per mg
Use this code for Brethine, Bricanyl.
MED: MCM 2100.5

☑ **J7681** Terbutaline sulfate, inhalation solution administered through DME, unit dose form, per mg
Use this code for Brethine.
MED: MCM 2100.5

☑ **J7682** Tobramycin, unit dose form, 300 mg, inhalation solution, administered through DME
Use this code for Tobi.
MED: MCM 2100.5

☑ **J7683** Triamcinolone, inhalation solution administered through DME, concentrated form, per mg
MED: MCM 2100.5

☑ **J7684** Triamcinolone, inhalation solution administered through DME, unit dose form, per mg
MED: MCM 2100.5

J7699 NOC drugs, inhalation solution administered through DME
MED: MCM 2100.5

J7799 NOC drugs, other than inhalation drugs, administered through DME
MED: MCM 2100.5

E **J8499** Prescription drug, oral, nonchemotherapeutic, NOS
MED: MCM 2049

N ☑ **J8510** Bulsulfan; oral, 2 mg
Use this code for Myleran.
MED: MCM 2049.5

K ☑ **J8520** Capecitabine, oral, 150 mg
Use this code for Xeloda.
MED: MCM 2049.5

E ☑ **J8521** Capecitabine, oral, 500 mg
Use this code for Xeloda.
MED: MCM 2049.5

N ☑ **J8530** Cyclophosphamide, oral, 25 mg
Use this code for Cytoxan.
MED: MCM 2049.5

K ☑ **J8560** Etoposide, oral, 50 mg
Use this code for VePesid.
MED: MCM 2049.5

Drugs Administered Other Than Oral Method　　J7622 — J8560

Chemotherapy Drugs

J8600 — J9165

N ☑ **J8600** Melphalan, oral 2 mg
Use this code for Alkeran.
MED: MCM 2049.5

N ☑ **J8610** Methotrexate, oral, 2.5 mg
Use this code for Rheumatrex Dose Pack.
MED: MCM 2049.5

K ☑ **J8700** Temozolomide, oral, 5 mg
Use this code for Temodar.
MED: MCM 2049.5C

E **J8999** Prescription drug, oral, chemotherapeutic, NOS
Determine if an alternative HCPCS Level II code better describes the service being reported. This code should be used only if a more specific code is unavailable.
MED: MCM 2049.5

CHEMOTHERAPY DRUGS *J9000-J9999*

These codes cover the cost of the chemotherapy drug only, not the administration. See also J8999.

N ☑ **J9000** Doxorubicin HCl, 10 mg
Use this code for Adriamycin PFS, Adriamycin RDF, Rubex.
MED: MCM 2049

K ☑ **J9001** Doxorubicin HCl, all lipid formulations, 10 mg
Use this code for Doxil.
MED: MCM 2049

G **J9010** Alemtuzumab, 10 mg
Use this code for Campath.
MED: Medicare Statute: 1833T

K ☑ **J9015** Aldesleukin, per single use vial
Use this code for Proleukin, IL-2.
MED: MCM 2049

G ☑ **J9017** Arsenic trioxide, 1 mg (Trisenox)
Use this code for Trisenox.

N ☑ **J9020** Asparaginase, 10,000 units
Use this code for Elspar.
MED: MCM 2049

N ☑ **J9031** BCG live (intravesical), per instillation
Use this code for Tice BCG, TheraCys.
MED: MCM 2049

K ☑ **J9040** Bleomycin sulfate, 15 units
Use this code for Blenoxane.
MED: MCM 2049

K ☑ **J9045** Carboplatin, 50 mg
Use this code for Paraplatin.
MED: MCM 2049

K ☑ **J9050** Carmustine, 100 mg
Use this code for BiCNU.
MED: MCM 2049

K ☑ **J9060** Cisplatin, powder or solution, per 10 mg
Use this code for Plantinol AQ.
MED: MCM 2049

E ☑ **J9062** Cisplatin, 50 mg
Use this code for Plantinol AQ.
MED: MCM 2049

K ☑ **J9065** Injection, cladribine, per 1 mg
Use this code for Leustatin.
MED: MCM 2049

N ☑ **J9070** Cyclophosphamide, 100 mg
Use this code for Cytoxan, Neosar.
MED: MCM 2049

☑ **J9080** Cyclophosphamide, 200 mg
Use this code for Cytoxan, Neosar.
MED: MCM 2049

☑ **J9090** Cyclophosphamide, 500 mg
Use this code for Cytoxan, Neosar.
MED: MCM 2049

☑ **J9091** Cyclophosphamide, 1 g
Use this code for Cytoxan, Neosar.
MED: MCM 2049

☑ **J9092** Cyclophosphamide, 2 g
Use this code for Cytoxan, Neosar.
MED: MCM 2049

N ☑ **J9093** Cyclophosphamide, lyophilized, 100 mg
Use this code for Cytoxan Lyophilized.
MED: MCM 2049

☑ **J9094** Cyclophosphamide, lyophilized, 200 mg
Use this code for Cytoxan Lyophilized.
MED: MCM 2049

☑ **J9095** Cyclophosphamide, lyophilized, 500 mg
Use this code for Cytoxan Lyophilized.
MED: MCM 2049

☑ **J9096** Cyclophosphamide, lyophilized, 1 g
Use this code for Cytoxan Lyophilized.
MED: MCM 2049

☑ **J9097** Cyclophosphamide, lyophilized, 2 g
Use this code for Cytoxan Lyophilized.
MED: MCM 2049

● ☑ **J9098** Cytarabine liposome, 10 mg

N ☑ **J9100** Cytarabine, 100 mg
Use this code for Cytosar-U.
MED: MCM 2049

E ☑ **J9110** Cytarabine, 500 mg
Use this code for Cytosar-U.
MED: MCM 2049

N ☑ **J9120** Dactinomycin, 0.5 mg
Use this code for Cosmegen.
MED: MCM 2049

N ☑ **J9130** Dacarbazine, 100 mg
Use this code for DTIC-Dome.
MED: MCM 2049

E ☑ **J9140** Dacarbazine, 200 mg
Use this code for DTIC-Dome.
MED: MCM 2049

K ☑ **J9150** Daunorubicin HCl, 10 mg
Use this code for Cerubidine.
MED: MCM 2049

K ☑ **J9151** Daunorubicin citrate, liposomal formulation, 10 mg
Use this code for Daunoxome.
MED: MCM 2049

K ☑ **J9160** Denileukin diftitox, 300 mcg
Use this code for Ontak.

K ☑ **J9165** Diethylstilbestrol diphosphate, 250 mg
Use this code for Stilphostrol.
MED: MCM 2049

Special Coverage Instructions   Noncovered by Medicare   Carrier Discretion   ☑ Quantity Alert   ● New Code   ▲ Revised Code

K ☑ **J9170** Docetaxel, 20 mg
Use this code for Taxotere.
MED: MCM 2049

● ☑ **J9178** Injection, epirubicin HCl, 2 mg

~~J9180~~ ~~Epirubicin hydrochloride, 50 mg~~

N ☑ **J9181** Etoposide, 10 mg
Use this code for VesPesid, Toposar.
MED: MCM 2049

E ☑ **J9182** Etoposide, 100 mg
Use this code for VesPesid, Toposar.
MED: MCM 2049

K ☑ **J9185** Fludarabine phosphate, 50 mg
Use this code for Fludara.
MED: MCM 2049

N ☑ **J9190** Fluorouracil, 500 mg
Use this code for Adrucil.
MED: MCM 2049

K ☑ **J9200** Floxuridine, 500 mg
Use this code for FUDR.
MED: MCM 2049

K ☑ **J9201** Gemcitabine HCl, 200 mg
Use this code for Gemzar.
MED: MCM 2049

K ☑ **J9202** Goserelin acetate implant, per 3.6 mg
Use this code for Zoladex.
MED: MCM 2049

K ☑ **J9206** Irinotecan, 20 mg
Use this code for Camptosar.
MED: MCM 2049

K ☑ **J9208** Ifosfamide, per 1 g
Use this code for Ifex.
MED: MCM 2049

K ☑ **J9209** Mesna, 200 mg
Use this code for Mesnex.
MED: MCM 2049

K ☑ **J9211** Idarubicin HCl, 5 mg
Use this code for Idamycin.
MED: MCM 2049

N ☑ **J9212** Injection, interferon Alfacon-1, recombinant, 1 mcg
Use this code for Infergen.
MED: MCM 2049

N ☑ **J9213** Interferon alfa-2A, recombinant, 3 million units
Use this code for Roferon-A.
MED: MCM 2049

N ☑ **J9214** Interferon alfa-2B, recombinant, 1 million units
Use this code for Intron A.
MED: MCM 2049

N ☑ **J9215** Interferon alfa-N3, (human leukocyte derived), 250,000 IU
Use this code for Alferon N.
MED: MCM 2049

K ☑ **J9216** Interferon gamma-1B, 3 million units
Use this code for Actimmune.
MED: MCM 2049

K ☑ **J9217** Leuprolide acetate (for depot suspension), 7.5 mg
Use this code for Lupron Depot, Eligard.
MED: MCM 2049

K ☑ **J9218** Leuprolide acetate, per 1 mg
Use this code for Lupron.
MED: MCM 2049

G ☑ **J9219** Leuprolide acetate implant, 65 mg
Use this code for Lupron Implant.
MED: MCM 2049

N ☑ **J9230** Mechlorethamine HCl, (nitrogen mustard), 10 mg
Use this code for Mustargen.
MED: MCM 2049

K ☑ **J9245** Injection, melphalan HCl, 50 mg
Use this code for Alkeran, L-phenylalanine mustard.
MED: MCM 2049

N ☑ **J9250** Methotrexate sodium, 5 mg
Use this code for Folex, Folex PFS, Methotrexate LPF.
MED: MCM 2049

E ☑ **J9260** Methotrexate sodium, 50 mg
Use this code Methotrexate LPF.
MED: MCM 2049

● ☑ **J9263** Injection, oxaliplatin, 0.5 mg

K ☑ **J9265** Paclitaxel, 30 mg
Use this code for Taxol.
MED: MCM 2049

K ☑ **J9266** Pegaspargase, per single dose vial
Use this code for Oncaspar, Peg-L-asparaginase.
MED: MCM 2049

K ☑ **J9268** Pentostatin, per 10 mg
Use this code for Nipent.
MED: MCM 2049

N ☑ **J9270** Plicamycin, 2.5 mg
Use this code for Mithacin.
MED: MCM 2049

K ☑ **J9280** Mitomycin, 5 mg
Use this code for Mitomycin.
MED: MCM 2049

☑ **J9290** Mitomycin, 20 mg
Use this code for Mitomycin.
MED: MCM 2049

☑ **J9291** Mitomycin, 40 mg
Use this code for Mitomycin.
MED: MCM 2049

K ☑ **J9293** Injection, mitoxantrone HCl, per 5 mg
Use this code for Navantrone.
MED: MCM 2049

F **J9300** Gemtuzumab ozogamicin, 5 mg
Use this code for Mylotarg.

K ☑ **J9310** Rituximab, 100 mg
Use this code for RituXan.
MED: MCM 2049

N ☑ **J9320** Streptozocin, 1 g
Use this code for Zanosar.
MED: MCM 2049

N ☑ **J9340** Thiotepa, 15 mg
Use this code for Thioplex.
MED: MCM 2049

Chemotherapy Drugs

J9350 — J9999

K ☑ **J9350** **Topotecan, 4 mg**
Use this code for Hycamtin.
MED: MCM 2049

K ☑ **J9355** **Trastuzumab, 10 mg**
Use this code for Herceptin.

K ☑ **J9357** **Valrubicin, intravesical, 200 mg**
Use this code for Valstar.
MED: MCM 2049

N ☑ **J9360** **Vinblastine sulfate, 1 mg**
Use this code for Velban.
MED: MCM 2049

N ☑ **J9370** **Vincristine sulfate, 1 mg**
MED: MCM 2049

☑ **J9375** **Vincristine sulfate, 2 mg**
MED: MCM 2049

☑ **J9380** **Vincristine sulfate, 5 mg**
MED: MCM 2049

K ☑ **J9390** **Vinorelbine tartrate, per 10 mg**
Use this code for Navelbine.
MED: MCM 2049

● ☑ **J9395** **Injection, fulvestrant, 25 mg**

K ☑ **J9600** **Porfimer sodium, 75 mg**
Use this code for Photofrin.
MED: MCM 2049

E **J9999** **NOC, antineoplastic drug**
Determine if an alternative HCPCS Level II code better
describes the service being reported. This code should be
used only if a more specific code is unavailable.
MED: CIM 45-16, MCM 2049

TEMPORARY CODES *K0000-K9999*

The K codes were established for use by the durable medical equipment regional carriers (DMERCs). The K codes are developed when the currently existing permanent national codes for supplies and certain product categories do not include the codes needed to implement a DMERC medical review policy.

K CODES ASSIGNED TO DURABLE MEDICAL EQUIPMENT

REGIONAL CARRIERS (DMERC)

WHEELCHAIR AND WHEELCHAIR ACCESSORIES

- K0001 Standard wheelchair
- K0002 Standard hemi (low seat) wheelchair
- K0003 Lightweight wheelchair
- K0004 High strength, lightweight wheelchair
- K0005 Ultralightweight wheelchair
- K0006 Heavy-duty wheelchair
- K0007 Extra heavy-duty wheelchair
- K0009 Other manual wheelchair/base
- K0010 Standard-weight frame motorized/power wheelchair
- K0011 Standard-weight frame motorized/power wheelchair with programmable control parameters for speed adjustment, tremor dampening, acceleration control and braking
- K0012 Lightweight portable motorized/power wheelchair
- K0014 Other motorized/power wheelchair base
- ☑ K0015 Detachable, nonadjustable height armrest, each
- K0016 ~~Detachable, adjustable height armrest, complete assembly, each~~
   See code E0973.
- ☑ K0017 Detachable, adjustable height armrest, base, each
- ☑ K0018 Detachable, adjustable height armrest, upper portion, each
- ☑ K0019 Arm pad, each
- ☑ K0020 Fixed, adjustable height armrest, pair
- K0022 ~~Reinforced back upholstery~~
   See code E0982.
- K0023 Solid back insert, planar back, single density foam, attached with straps
- K0024 Solid back insert, planar back, single density foam, with adjustable hook-on hardware
- K0025 ~~Hook on headrest extension~~
   See code E0966.
- K0026 ~~Back upholstery for ultralightweight or high strength lightweight wheelchair~~
   See code E0982.
- K0027 ~~Back upholstery for wheelchair type other than ultralightweight or high strength lightweight wheelchair~~
   See code E0982.
- K0028 ~~Manual, fully reclining back~~
   See code E1226.
- K0029 ~~Reinforced seat upholstery~~
   See code E0981.
- K0030 ~~Solid seat insert, planar seat, single density foam~~
   See code E0992.

- K0031 ~~Safety belt/pelvic strap, each~~
   See code E0978.
- K0032 ~~Seat upholstery for ultralightweight or high strength lightweight wheelchair~~
   See code E0981.
- K0033 ~~Seat upholstery for wheelchair type other than ultralightweight or high strength lightweight wheelchair~~
   See code E0981.
- K0035 ~~Heel loop with ankle strap, each~~
   See code E0951.
- K0036 ~~Toe loop, each~~
   See code E0952.
- ☑ K0037 High mount flip-up footrest, each
- ☑ K0038 Leg strap, each
- ☑ K0039 Leg strap, H style, each
- ☑ K0040 Adjustable angle footplate, each
- ☑ K0041 Large size footplate, each
- ☑ K0042 Standard size footplate, each
- ☑ K0043 Footrest, lower extension tube, each
- ☑ K0044 Footrest, upper hanger bracket, each
- K0045 Footrest, complete assembly
- ☑ K0046 Elevating legrest, lower extension tube, each
- ☑ K0047 Elevating legrest, upper hanger bracket, each
- K0048 ~~Elevating legrest, complete assembly~~
   See code E0990.
- K0049 ~~Calf pad, each~~
   See code E0995.
- K0050 Ratchet assembly
- ☑ K0051 Cam release assembly, footrest or legrest, each
- ☑ K0052 Swingaway, detachable footrests, each
- ☑ K0053 Elevating footrests, articulating (telescoping), each
- K0054 ~~Seat width of 10, 11, 12, 15, 17, or 20 for a high strength, lightweight or ultralightweight wheelchair~~
- K0055 ~~Seat depth of 15, 17, or 18 for a high strength, lightweight or ultralightweight wheelchair~~
- ☑ K0056 Seat height less than 17 inches or equal to or greater than 21 inches for a high strength, lightweight, or ultralightweight wheelchair
- K0057 ~~Seat width 19 or 20 for heavy duty or extra heavy duty chair~~
- K0058 ~~Seat depth 17 or 18 for motorized/power wheelchair~~
- ☑ K0059 Plastic coated handrim, each
- ☑ K0060 Steel handrim, each
- ☑ K0061 Aluminum handrim, each
- K0062 ~~Handrim with 8-10 vertical or oblique projections, each~~
   See code E0967.
- K0063 ~~Handrim with 12-16 vertical or oblique projections, each~~
   See code E0967.
- ☑ K0064 Zero pressure tube (flat free insert), any size, each
- ☑ K0065 Spoke protectors, each
- ☑ K0066 Solid tire, any size, each

Special Coverage Instructions | Noncovered by Medicare | Carrier Discretion | ☑ Quantity Alert | ● New Code | ▲ Revised Code

2004 HCPCS | ♀ Female Only | ♂ Male Only | ①②③④⑤⑥⑦⑧⑨ ASC Groups | K Codes — 79

Temporary Codes

K0067 — K0462

☑ **K0067** Pneumatic tire, any size, each

☑ **K0068** Pneumatic tire tube, each

☑ **K0069** Rear wheel assembly, complete, with solid tire, spokes or molded, each

☑ **K0070** Rear wheel assembly, complete with pneumatic tire, spokes or molded, each

☑ **K0071** Front caster assembly, complete, with pneumatic tire, each

☑ **K0072** Front caster assembly, complete, with semipneumatic tire, each

☑ **K0073** Caster pin lock, each

☑ **K0074** Pneumatic caster tire, any size, each

☑ **K0075** Semipneumatic caster tire, any size, each

☑ **K0076** Solid caster tire, any size, each

☑ **K0077** Front caster assembly, complete, with solid tire, each

☑ **K0078** Pneumatic caster tire tube, each

K0079 ~~Wheel lock extension, pair~~
See code E0961.

K0080 ~~Anti-rollback device, pair~~
See code E0974.

☑ **K0081** Wheel lock assembly, complete, each

K0082 ~~22-nf non-sealed lead acid battery, each~~
See code E2360.

K0083 ~~22-nf sealed lead acid battery, each (e.g., gel cell, absorbed glass mat)~~
See code E2361.

K0084 ~~Group 24 non-sealed lead acid battery, each~~
See code E2362.

K0085 ~~Group 24 sealed lead acid battery, each (e.g., gel cell, absorbed glass mat)~~
See code E2363.

K0086 ~~U-1 non-sealed lead acid battery, each~~
See code E2364.

K0087 ~~U-1 sealed lead acid battery, each (e.g., gel cell, absorbed glass mat)~~
See code E2365.

K0088 ~~Battery charger, single mode, for use with only one battery type, sealed or non-sealed~~
See code E2366.

K0089 ~~Battery charger, dual mode, for use with either battery type, sealed or non-sealed~~
See code E2367.

☑ **K0090** Rear wheel tire for power wheelchair, any size, each

☑ **K0091** Rear wheel tire tube other than zero pressure for power wheelchair, any size, each

☑ **K0092** Rear wheel assembly for power wheelchair, complete, each

☑ **K0093** Rear wheel zero pressure tire tube (flat free insert) for power wheelchair, any size, each

☑ **K0094** Wheel tire for power base, any size, each

☑ **K0095** Wheel tire tube other than zero pressure for each base, any size, each

☑ **K0096** Wheel assembly for power base, complete, each

☑ **K0097** Wheel zero-pressure tire tube (flat free insert) for power base, any size, each

K0098 Drive belt for power wheelchair

K0099 Front caster for power wheelchair

K0100 ~~Wheelchair adapter for amputee, pair (device used to compensate for transfer of weight due to lost limbs to maintain proper balance)~~
See code E0959.

☑ **K0102** Crutch and cane holder, each

K0103 ~~Transfer board, <25~~
See code E0972.

☑ **K0104** Cylinder tank carrier, each

☑ **K0105** IV hanger, each

☑ **K0106** Arm trough, each

K0107 ~~Wheelchair tray~~
See code E0950.

K0108 Other accessories

SPINAL ORTHOTICS

K0112 ~~Trunk support device, vest type, with inner frame, prefabricated~~

K0113 ~~Trunk support device, vest type, without inner frame, prefabricated~~

K0114 Back support system for use with a wheelchair, with inner frame, prefabricated

K0115 Seating system, back module, posterior-lateral control, with or without lateral supports, custom fabricated for attachment to wheelchair base

K0116 Seating system, combined back and seat module, custom fabricated for attachment to wheelchair base

K0195 Elevating legrest, pair (for use with capped rental wheelchair base)
MED: CIM 60-9

MISCELLANEOUS

K0268 ~~Humidifier, non-heated, used with positive airway pressure device~~
See code E0561.

E ☑ **K0415** Prescription antiemetic drug, oral, per 1 mg, for use in conjunction with oral anti-cancer drug, NOS
MED: MCM 2049.5c

E ☑ **K0416** Prescription antiemetic drug, rectal, per 1 mg, for use in conjunction with oral anti-cancer drug, NOS
MED: MCM 2049.5c

K0452 Wheelchair bearings, any type

▲ **K0455** Infusion pump used for uninterrupted parenteral administration of medication, (e.g., epoprostenol or treprostinol)
See J1325 for epoprostenol.
MED: CIM 60-14

K0460 ~~Power add-on, to convert manual wheelchair to motorized wheelchair, joystick control~~
See code E0983.

K0461 ~~Power add-on, to convert manual wheelchair to power-operated vehicle, tiller control~~
See code E0984.

K0462 Temporary replacement for patient owned equipment being repaired, any type
MED: MCM 5102.3

~~K0531 Humidifier, heated, used with positive airway pressure device~~

See code E0562.

~~K0532 Respiratory assist device, bi level pressure capability, without backup rate feature, used with noninvasive interface, e.g., nasal or facial mask (intermittent assist device with continuous positive airway pressure device)~~

See code E0470.

~~K0533 Respiratory assist device, bi level pressure capability, with backup rate feature, used with noninvasive interface, e.g., nasal or facial mask (intermittent assist device with continuous positive airway pressure device)~~

See code E0471.

~~K0534 Respiratory assist device, bi level pressure capacity, with back up rate feature, used with invasive interface, e.g., tracheostomy tube (intermittent assist device with continuous positive airway pressure device)~~

See code E0472.

~~K0538 Negative pressure wound therapy electrical pump, stationary or portable~~

See code E2402.

~~K0539 Dressing set for negative pressure wound therapy electrical pump, stationary or portable, each~~

See code A6550.

~~K0540 Canister set for negative pressure wound therapy electrical pump, stationary or portable, each~~

See code A6551.

~~K0541 Speech generating device, digitized speech, using pre recorded messages, less than or equal to 8 minutes recording time~~

See code E2500.

~~K0542 Speech generating device, digitized speech, using pre recorded messages, greater than 8 minutes recording time~~

See code E2502.

~~K0543 Speech generating device, synthesized speech, requiring message formulation by spelling and access by physical contact with the device~~

See code E2508.

~~K0544 Speech generating device, synthesized speech, permitting multiple methods of message formulation and multiple methods of device access~~

See code E2510.

~~K0545 Speech generating software program, for personal computer or personal digital assistant~~

See code E2511.

~~K0546 Accessory for speech generating device, mounting system~~

See code E2512.

~~K0547 Accessory for speech generating device, not otherwise classified~~

See code E2599.

~~K0549 Hospital bed, heavy duty, extra wide, with weight capacity greater than 350 pounds, but less than or equal to 600 pounds, with any type side rails, with mattress~~

See code E0303.

~~K0550 Hospital bed, extra heavy duty, extra wide, with weight capacity greater than 600 pounds, with any type side rails, with mattress~~

See code E0304.

● A ☑ **K0552** Supplies for external drug infusion pump, syringe type cartridge, sterile, each
MED: CIM 60-14

~~K0556 Addition to lower extremity, below knee/above knee, custom fabricated from existing mold or prefabricated, socket insert, silicone gel, elastomeric or equal, for use with locking mechanism~~

See code L5673.

~~K0557 Addition to lower extremity, below knee/above knee, custom fabricated from existing mold or prefabricated, socket insert, silicone gel, elastomeric or equal, not for use with locking mechanism~~

See code L5679.

~~K0558 Addition to lower extremity, below knee/above knee, custom fabricated socket insert for congenital or atypical traumatic amputee, silicone gel, elastomeric or equal, for use with or without locking mechanism, initial only (for other than initial, use code k0556 or k0557)~~

See code L5681.

~~K0559 Addition to lower extremity, below knee/above knee, custom fabricated socket insert for other than congenital or atypical traumatic amputee, silicone gel, elastomeric or equal, for use with or without locking mechanism, initial only (for other than initial, use code k0556 or k0557)~~

See code L5683.

~~K0560 Metacarpal phalangeal joint replacement, two pieces, metal (e.g., stainless steel or cobalt chrome), ceramic like material (e.g., pyrocarbon), for surgical implantation (all sizes, includes entire system)~~

See code L8631.

~~K0581 Ostomy pouch, closed, with barrier attached, with filter (1 piece), each~~

See code A4416.

~~K0582 Ostomy pouch, closed, with barrier attached, with built in convexity, with filter (1 piece), each~~

See code A4417.

~~K0583 Ostomy pouch, closed, without barrier attached, with filter (1 piece), each~~

See code A4418.

~~K0584 Ostomy pouch, closed, for use on barrier with flange, with filter (2 piece), each~~

See code A4419.

~~K0585 Ostomy pouch, closed, for use on barrier with locking flange (2 piece), each~~

See code A4420.

~~K0586 Ostomy pouch, closed, for use on barrier with locking flange, with filter (2 piece), each~~

See code A4423.

~~K0587 Ostomy pouch, drainable, with barrier attached, with filter (1 piece), each~~

See code A4424.

~~K0588 Ostomy pouch, drainable; for use on barrier with flange, with filter (2 piece system), each~~
See code A4425.

~~K0589 Ostomy pouch, drainable; for use on barrier with locking flange (2 piece system), each~~
See code A4426.

~~K0590 Ostomy pouch, drainable; for use on barrier with locking flange, with filter (2 piece system), each~~
See code A4427.

~~K0591 Ostomy pouch, urinary, with extended wear barrier attached, with faucet type tap with valve (1 piece), each~~
See code A4428.

~~K0592 Ostomy pouch, urinary, with barrier attached, with built in convexity, with faucet type tap with valve (1 piece), each~~
See code A4429.

~~K0593 Ostomy pouch, urinary, with extended wear barrier attached, with built in convexity, with faucet type tap with valve (1 piece), each~~
See code A4430.

~~K0594 Ostomy pouch, urinary; with barrier attached, with faucet type tap with valve (1 piece), each~~
See code A4431.

~~K0595 Ostomy pouch, urinary; for use on barrier with flange, with faucet type tap with valve (2 piece), each~~
See code A4432.

~~K0596 Ostomy pouch, urinary; for use on barrier with locking flange (2 piece), each~~
See code A4433.

~~K0597 Ostomy pouch, urinary; for use on barrier with locking flange, with faucet type tap with valve (2 piece), each~~
See code A4434.

● Ⓐ K0600 Functional neuromuscular stimulator, transcutaneous stimulation of muscles of ambulation with computer control, used for walking by spinal cord injured, entire system, after completion of training program
MED: CIM 35-77

● ☑ K0601 Replacement battery for external infusion pump owned by patient, silver oxide, 1.5 volt, each

● ☑ K0602 Replacement battery for external infusion pump owned by patient, silver oxide, 3 volt, each

● ☑ K0603 Replacement battery for external infusion pump owned by patient, alkaline, 1.5 volt, each

● ☑ K0604 Replacement battery for external infusion pump owned by patient, lithium, 3.6 volt, each

● ☑ K0605 Replacement battery for external infusion pump owned by patient, lithium, 4.5 volt, each

● K0606 Automatic external defibrillator, with integrated electrocardiogram analysis, garment type

● ☑ K0607 Replacement battery for automated external defibrillator, garment type only, each

● ☑ K0608 Replacement garment for use with automated external defibrillator, each

● ☑ K0609 Replacement electrodes for use with automated external defibrillator, garment type only, each

~~K0610 Peritoneal dialysis clamps, each~~
This code was added and deleted in the same year.

~~K0611 Disposable cycler set used with cycler dialysis machine, each~~
This code was added and deleted in the same year.

~~K0612 Drainage extension line, sterile, for dialysis, each~~
This code was added and deleted in the same year.

~~K0613 Extension line with easy lock connectors, used with dialysis~~
This code was added and deleted in the same year.

~~K0614 Chemicals/antiseptics solution used to clean/sterilize dialysis equipment, per 8 oz~~
This code was added and deleted in the same year.

~~K0615 Speech generating device, digitized speech, using pre-recorded messages, greater than 8 minutes but less than or equal to 20 minutes recording time~~
This code was added and deleted in the same year.

~~K0616 Speech generating device, digitized speech, using pre-recorded messages, greater than 20 minutes but less than or equal to 40 minutes recording time~~
This code was added and deleted in the same year.

~~K0617 Speech generating device, digitized speech, using pre-recorded messages, greater than 40 minutes recording time~~
This code was added and deleted in the same year.

● Ⓐ K0618 TLSO, sagittal-coronal control, modular segmented spinal system, two rigid plastic shells, posterior extends from the sacrococcygeal junction and terminates just inferior to the scapular spine, anterior extends from the symphysis pubis to the xiphoid, soft liner, restricts gross trunk motion in the sagittal and coronal planes, lateral strength is provided by overlapping plastic and stabilizing closures, includes straps and closures, prefabricated, includes fitting and adjustment

● Ⓐ K0619 TLSO, sagittal-coronal control, modular segmented spinal system, three rigid plastic shells, posterior extends from the sacrococcygeal junction and terminates just inferior to the scapular spine, anterior extends from the symphysis pubis to the xiphoid, soft liner, restricts gross trunk motion in the sagittal and coronal planes, lateral strength is provided by overlapping plastic and stabilizing closures, includes straps and closures, prefabricated, includes fitting and adjustment

● Ⓐ ☑ K0620 Tubular elastic dressing, any width, per linear yard

~~K0621 Gauze, packing strips, non-impregnated, up to 2 inches in width, per linear yard~~
This code was added and deleted in the same year.

~~K0622 Conforming bandage, non-elastic, knitted/woven, non-sterile width less than three inches, per roll~~
This code was added and deleted in the same year.

~~K0623 Conforming bandage, non-elastic, knitted/woven, sterile width less than three inches, per roll~~
This code was added and deleted in the same year.

~~K0624 Light compression bandage, elastic, knitted/woven, width less than 3 inches, per roll (at least 3 yards unstretched)~~
This code was added and deleted in the same year.

K0625 ~~Self adherent bandage, elastic, non-knitted/non-woven, load resistance greater than or equal to 0.55 foot-pounds at 50% maximum stretch, width less than 3 inches, per roll~~

This code was added and deleted in the same year.

K0626 ~~Self adherent bandage, elastic, non-knitted/non-woven, load resistance greater than or equal to 0.55 foot-pounds at 50% maximum stretch, width greater than or equal to 5 inches, per roll~~

This code was added and deleted in the same year.

ORTHOTIC PROCEDURES *L0000-L4999*

L codes include orthotic and prosthetic procedures and devices, as well as scoliosis equipment, orthopedic shoes, and prosthetic implants.

ORTHOTIC DEVICES — SPINAL

CERVICAL
Medicare claims for L codes fall under the jurisdiction of the DME regional carrier, unless otherwise noted.

☑ **L0100** Cranial orthosis (helmet), with or without soft interface, molded to patient model

☑ **L0110** Cranial orthosis (helmet), with or without soft-interface, non-molded

● **L0112** Cranial cervical orthosis, congenital torticollis type, with or without soft interface material, adjustable range of motion joint, custom fabricated

L0120 Cervical, flexible, nonadjustable (foam collar)

L0130 Cervical, flexible, thermoplastic collar, molded to patient

L0140 Cervical, semi-rigid, adjustable (plastic collar)

L0150 Cervical, semi-rigid, adjustable molded chin cup (plastic collar with mandibular/occipital piece)

L0160 Cervical, semi-rigid, wire frame occipital/mandibular support

L0170 Cervical, collar, molded to patient model

☑ **L0172** Cervical, collar, semi-rigid thermoplastic foam, two piece

☑ **L0174** Cervical, collar, semi-rigid, thermoplastic foam, two piece with thoracic extension

MULTIPLE POST COLLAR

L0180 Cervical, multiple post collar, occipital/mandibular supports, adjustable

L0190 Cervical, multiple post collar, occipital/mandibular supports, adjustable cervical bars (Somi, Guilford, Taylor types)

L0200 Cervical, multiple post collar, occipital/mandibular supports, adjustable cervical bars, and thoracic extension

THORACIC

L0210 Thoracic, rib belt

L0220 Thoracic, rib belt, custom fabricated

L0450 TLSO, flexible, provides trunk support, upper thoracic region, produces intracavitary pressure to reduce load on the intervertebral disks with rigid stays or panel(s), includes shoulder straps and closures, prefabricated, includes fitting and adjustment

L0452 TLSO, flexible, provides trunk support, upper thoracic region, produces intracavitary pressure to reduce load on the intervertebral disks with rigid stays or panel(s), includes shoulder straps and closures, custom fabricated

L0454 TLSO flexible, provides trunk support, extends from sacrococcygeal junction to above T-9 vertebra, restricts gross trunk motion in the sagittal plane, produces intracavitary pressure to reduce load on the intervertebral disks with rigid stays or panel(s), includes shoulder straps and closures, prefabricated, includes fitting and adjustment

L0456 TLSO, flexible, provides trunk support, thoracic region, rigid posterior panel and soft anterior apron, extends from the sacrococcygeal junction and terminates just inferior to the scapular spine, restricts gross trunk motion in the sagittal plane, produces intracavitary pressure to reduce load on the intervertebral disks, includes straps and closures, prefabricated, includes fitting and adjustment

L0458 TLSO, triplanar control, modular segmented spinal system, two rigid plastic shells, posterior extends from the sacrococcygeal junction and terminates just inferior to the scapular spine, anterior extends from the symphysis pubis to the xiphoid, soft liner, restricts gross trunk motion in the sagittal, coronal, and transverse planes, lateral strength is provided by overlapping plastic and stabilizing closures, includes straps and closures, prefabricated, includes fitting and adjustment

L0460 TLSO, triplanar control, modular segmented spinal system, two rigid plastic shells, posterior extends from the sacrococcygeal junction and terminates just inferior to the scapular spine, anterior extends from the symphysis pubis to the sternal notch, soft liner, restricts gross trunk motion in the sagittal, coronal, and transverse planes, lateral strength is provided by overlapping plastic and stabilizing closures, includes straps and closures, prefabricated, includes fitting and adjustment

L0462 TLSO, triplanar control, modular segmented spinal system, three rigid plastic shells, posterior extends from the sacrococcygeal junction and terminates just inferior to the scapular spine, anterior extends from the symphysis pubis to the sternal notch, soft liner, restricts gross trunk motion in the sagittal, coronal, and transverse planes, lateral strength is provided by overlapping plastic and stabilizing closures, includes straps and closures, prefabricated, includes fitting and adjustment

L0464 TLSO, triplanar control, modular segmented spinal system, four rigid plastic shells, posterior extends from sacrococcygeal junction and terminates just inferior to scapular spine, anterior extends from symphysis pubis to the sternal notch, soft liner, restricts gross trunk motion in sagittal, coronal, and transverse planes, lateral strength is provided by overlapping plastic and stabilizing closures, includes straps and closures, prefabricated, includes fitting and adjustment

L0466 TLSO, sagittal control, rigid posterior frame and flexible soft anterior apron with straps, closures and padding, restricts gross trunk motion in sagittal plane, produces intracavitary pressure to reduce load on intervertebral disks, includes fitting and shaping the frame, prefabricated, includes fitting and adjustment

L0468 TLSO, sagittal-coronal control, rigid posterior frame and flexible soft anterior apron with straps, closures and padding, extends from sacrococcygeal junction over scapulae, lateral strength provided by pelvic, thoracic, and lateral frame pieces, restricts gross trunk motion in sagittal, and coronal planes, produces intracavitary pressure to reduce load on intervertebral disks, includes fitting and shaping the frame, prefabricated, includes fitting and adjustment

Orthotic Procedures

L0470 — L0610

L0470 TLSO, triplanar control, rigid posterior frame and flexible soft anterior apron with straps, closures and padding, extends from sacrococcygeal junction to scapula, lateral strength provided by pelvic, thoracic, and lateral frame pieces, rotational strength provided by subclavicular extensions, restricts gross trunk motion in sagittal, coronal, and transverse planes, produces intracavitary pressure to reduce load on the intervertebral disks, includes fitting and shaping the frame, prefabricated, includes fitting and adjustment

L0472 TLSO, triplanar control, hyperextension, rigid anterior and lateral frame extends from symphysis pubis to sternal notch with two anterior components (one pubic and one sternal), posterior and lateral pads with straps and closures, limits spinal flexion, restricts gross trunk motion in sagittal, coronal, and transverse planes, includes fitting and shaping the frame, prefabricated, includes fitting and adjustment

L0476 TLSO, sagittal-coronal control, flexion compression jacket, two rigid plastic shells with soft liner, posterior extends from sacrococcygeal junction and terminates at or before the T9 vertebra, anterior extends from symphysis pubis to xiphoid, usually laced together on one side, restricts gross trunk motion in sagittal and coronal planes, allows free flexion and compression of the LS region, includes straps and closures, prefabricated, includes fitting and adjustment

L0478 TLSO, sagittal-coronal control, flexion compression jacket, two rigid plastic shells with soft liner, posterior extends from sacrococcygeal junction and terminates at or before the T9 vertebra, anterior extends from symphysis pubis to xiphoid, usually laced together on one side, restricts gross trunk motion in sagittal and coronal planes, allows free flexion and compression of LS region, includes straps and closures, custom fabricated

L0480 TLSO, triplanar control, one piece rigid plastic shell without interface liner, with multiple straps and closures, posterior extends from sacrococcygeal junction and terminates just inferior to scapular spine, anterior extends from symphysis pubis to sternal notch, anterior or posterior opening, restricts gross trunk motion in sagittal, coronal, and transverse planes, includes a carved plaster or CAD-CAM model, custom fabricated

L0482 TLSO, triplanar control, one piece rigid plastic shell with interface liner, multiple straps and closures, posterior extends from sacrococcygeal junction and terminates just inferior to scapular spine, anterior extends from symphysis pubis to sternal notch, anterior or posterior opening, restricts gross trunk motion in sagittal, coronal, and transverse planes, includes a carved plaster or CAD-CAM model, custom fabricated

L0484 TLSO, triplanar control, two piece rigid plastic shell without interface liner, with multiple straps and closures, posterior extends from sacrococcygeal junction and terminates just inferior to scapular spine, anterior extends from symphysis pubis to sternal notch, lateral strength is enhanced by overlapping plastic, restricts gross trunk motion in the sagittal, coronal, and transverse planes, includes a carved plaster or CAD-CAM model, custom fabricated

L0486 TLSO, triplanar control, two piece rigid plastic shell with interface liner, multiple straps and closures, posterior extends from sacrococcygeal junction and terminates just inferior to scapular spine, anterior extends from symphysis pubis to sternal notch, lateral strength is enhanced by overlapping plastic, restricts gross trunk motion in the sagittal, coronal, and transverse planes, includes a carved plaster or CAD-CAM model, custom fabricated

L0488 TLSO, triplanar control, one piece rigid plastic shell with interface liner, multiple straps and closures, posterior extends from sacrococcygeal junction and terminates just inferior to scapular spine, anterior extends from symphysis pubis to sternal notch, anterior or posterior opening, restricts gross trunk motion in sagittal, coronal, and transverse planes, prefabricated, includes fitting and adjustment

L0490 TLSO, sagittal-coronal control, one piece rigid plastic shell, with overlapping reinforced anterior, with multiple straps and closures, posterior extends from sacrococcygeal junction and terminates at or before the T9 vertebra, anterior extends from symphysis pubis to xiphoid, anterior opening, restricts gross trunk motion in sagittal and coronal planes, prefabricated, includes fitting and adjustment

LUMBAR-SACRAL ORTHOSIS (LSO)

FLEXIBLE

L0500 Lumbar-sacral-orthosis (LSO), flexible, (lumbo-sacral support)

L0510 LSO, flexible (lumbo-sacral support), custom fabricated

L0515 LSO, anterior-posterior control, with rigid or semi-rigid posterior panel, prefabricated

ANTERIOR-POSTERIOR-LATERAL CONTROL

L0520 LSO, anterior-posterior-lateral control (Knight, Wilcox types), with apron front

ANTERIOR-POSTERIOR CONTROL

L0530 LSO, anterior-posterior control (Macausland type), with apron front

LUMBAR FLEXION

L0540 LSO, lumbar flexion (Williams flexion type)

L0550 LSO, anterior-posterior-lateral control, molded to patient model

L0560 LSO, anterior-posterior-lateral control, molded to patient model, with interface material

L0561 LSO, anterior-posterior-lateral control, with rigid or semi-rigid posterior panel, prefabricated

L0565 LSO, anterior-posterior-lateral control, custom fitted

SACROILIAC

FLEXIBLE

L0600 Sacroiliac, flexible (sacroiliac surgical support)

L0610 Sacroiliac, flexible (sacroiliac surgical support), custom fabricated

SEMI-RIGID

L0620 Sacroiliac, semi-rigid (Goldthwaite, Osgood types), with apron front

CERVICAL-THORACIC-LUMBAR-SACRAL ORTHOSIS (CTLSO)

ANTERIOR-POSTERIOR-LATERAL CONTROL

L0700 CTLSO, anterior-posterior-lateral control, molded to patient model (Minerva type)

L0710 CTLSO, anterior-posterior-lateral control, molded to patient model, with interface material (Minerva type)

HALO PROCEDURE

L0810 Halo procedure, cervical halo incorporated into jacket vest

L0820 Halo procedure, cervical halo incorporated into plaster body jacket

L0830 Halo procedure, cervical halo incorporated into Milwaukee type orthosis

L0860 Addition to halo procedure, magnetic resonance image compatible system

● L0861 Addition to halo procedure, replacement liner/interface material

L0960 Torso support, postsurgical support, pads for postsurgical support

ADDITIONS TO SPINAL ORTHOSIS

L0970 TLSO, corset front

L0972 LSO, corset front

L0974 TLSO, full corset

L0976 LSO, full corset

L0978 Axillary crutch extension

☑ L0980 Peroneal straps, pair

☑ L0982 Stocking supporter grips, set of four (4)

☑ L0984 Protective body sock, each

L0999 Addition to spinal orthosis, NOS
Determine if an alternative HCPCS Level II code better describes the service being reported. This code should be used only if a more specific code is unavailable.

ORTHOTIC DEVICES — SCOLIOSIS PROCEDURES

The orthotic care of scoliosis differs from other orthotic care in that the treatment is more dynamic in nature and uses continual modification of the orthosis to the patient's changing condition. This coding structure uses the proper names - or eponyms - of the procedures because they have historic and universal acceptance in the profession. It should be recognized that variations to the basic procedures described by the founders/developers are accepted in various medical and orthotic practices throughout the country. All procedures include model of patient when indicated.

CERVICAL-THORACIC-LUMBAR-SACRAL ORTHOSIS (CTLSO) (MILWAUKEE)

L1000 CTLSO (Milwaukee), inclusive of furnishing initial orthosis, including model

L1005 Tension based scoliosis orthosis and accessory pads, includes fitting and adjustment

L1010 Addition to CTLSO or scoliosis orthosis, axilla sling

L1020 Addition to CTLSO or scoliosis orthosis, kyphosis pad

L1025 Addition to CTLSO or scoliosis orthosis, kyphosis pad, floating

L1030 Addition to CTLSO or scoliosis orthosis, lumbar bolster pad

L1040 Addition to CTLSO or scoliosis orthosis, lumbar or lumbar rib pad

L1050 Addition to CTLSO or scoliosis orthosis, sternal pad

L1060 Addition to CTLSO or scoliosis orthosis, thoracic pad

L1070 Addition to CTLSO or scoliosis orthosis, trapezius sling

L1080 Addition to CTLSO or scoliosis orthosis, outrigger

L1085 Addition to CTLSO or scoliosis orthosis, outrigger, bilateral with vertical extensions

L1090 Addition to CTLSO or scoliosis orthosis, lumbar sling

L1100 Addition to CTLSO or scoliosis orthosis, ring flange, plastic or leather

L1110 Addition to CTLSO or scoliosis orthosis, ring flange, plastic or leather, molded to patient model

☑ L1120 Addition to CTLSO, scoliosis orthosis, cover for upright, each

THORACIC-LUMBAR-SACRAL ORTHOSIS (TLSO) (LOW PROFILE)

L1200 TLSO, inclusive of furnishing initial orthosis only

L1210 Addition to TLSO, (low profile), lateral thoracic extension

L1220 Addition to TLSO, (low profile), anterior thoracic extension

L1230 Addition to TLSO, (low profile), Milwaukee type superstructure

L1240 Addition to TLSO, (low profile), lumbar derotation pad

L1250 Addition to TLSO, (low profile), anterior ASIS pad

L1260 Addition to TLSO, (low profile), anterior thoracic derotation pad

L1270 Addition to TLSO, (low profile), abdominal pad

☑ L1280 Addition to TLSO, (low profile), rib gusset (elastic), each

L1290 Addition to TLSO, (low profile), lateral trochanteric pad

OTHER SCOLIOSIS PROCEDURES

L1300 Other scoliosis procedure, body jacket molded to patient model

L1310 Other scoliosis procedure, postoperative body jacket

L1499 Spinal orthosis, not otherwise specified
Determine if an alternative HCPCS Level II code better describes the orthosis being reported. This code should be used only if a more specific code is unavailable.

THORACIC-HIP-KNEE-ANKLE ORTHOSIS (THKAO)

L1500 THKAO, mobility frame (Newington, Parapodium types)

L1510 THKAO, standing frame, with or without tray and accessories

L1520 THKAO, swivel walker

Orthotic Procedures

L1600 — L1901

ORTHOTIC DEVICES — LOWER LIMB

The procedures in L1600-L2999 are considered as "base" or "basic procedures" and may be modified by listing procedure from the "additions" sections and adding them to the base procedures.

HIP ORTHOSIS (HO) — FLEXIBLE

L1600 HO, abduction control of hip joints, flexible, Frejka type with cover, prefabricated, includes fitting and adjustment

L1610 HO, abduction control of hip joints, flexible, (Frejka cover only), prefabricated, includes fitting and adjustment ●

L1620 HO, abduction control of hip joints, flexible, (Pavlik harness), prefabricated, includes fitting and adjustment

L1630 HO, abduction control of hip joints, semi-flexible (Von Rosen type), custom fabricated

L1640 HO, abduction control of hip joints, static, pelvic band or spreader bar, thigh cuffs, custom fabricated

L1650 HO, abduction control of hip joints, static, adjustable (Ilfled type), prefabricated, includes fitting and adjustment

L1652 Hip orthosis, bilateral thigh cuffs with adjustable abductor spreader bar, adult size, prefabricated, includes fitting and adjustment, any type

L1660 HO, abduction control of hip joints, static, plastic, prefabricated, includes fitting and adjustment

L1680 HO, abduction control of hip joints, dynamic, pelvic control, adjustable hip motion control, thigh cuffs (Rancho hip action type), custom fabricated

L1685 HO, abduction control of hip joint, postoperative hip abduction type, custom fabricated

L1686 HO, abduction control of hip joint, postoperative hip abduction type, prefabricated, includes fitting and adjustments

L1690 Combination, bilateral, lumbo-sacral, hip, femur orthosis providing adduction and internal rotation control, prefabricated, includes fitting and adjustment

LEGG PERTHES

L1700 Legg Perthes orthosis, (Toronto type), custom fabricated

L1710 Legg Perthes orthosis, (Newington type), custom fabricated

L1720 Legg Perthes orthosis, trilateral, (Tachdijan type), custom fabricated

L1730 Legg Perthes orthosis, (Scottish Rite type), custom fabricated

L1750 Legg Perthes orthosis, Legg Perthes sling (Sam Brown type), prefabricated, includes fitting and adjustment

L1755 Legg Perthes orthosis, (Patten bottom type), custom fabricated

KNEE ORTHOSIS (KO)

L1800 KO, elastic with stays, prefabricated, includes fitting and adjustment

L1810 KO, elastic with joints, prefabricated, includes fitting and adjustment

L1815 KO, elastic or other elastic type material with condylar pad(s), prefabricated, includes fitting and adjustment

L1820 KO, elastic with condylar pads and joints, prefabricated, includes fitting and adjustment

L1825 KO, elastic knee cap, prefabricated, includes fitting and adjustment

L1830 KO, immobilizer, canvas longitudinal, prefabricated, includes fitting and adjustment

L1831 Knee orthosis, locking knee joint(s), positional orthosis, prefabricated, includes fitting and adjustment

L1832 KO, adjustable knee joints, positional orthosis, rigid support, prefabricated, includes fitting and adjustment

L1834 KO, without knee joint, rigid, custom fabricated

L1836 Knee orthosis, rigid, without joint(s), includes soft interface material, prefabricated, includes fitting and adjustment

L1840 KO, derotation, medial-lateral, anterior cruciate ligament, custom fabricated

▲ **L1843** Knee orthosis, single upright, thigh and calf, with adjustable flexion and extension joint, medial-lateral and rotation control, with or without varus/valgus adjustment, prefabricated, includes fitting and adjustment

▲ **L1844** Knee orthosis, single upright, thigh and calf, with adjustable flexion and extension joint, medial-lateral and rotation control, with or without varus/valgus adjustment, custom fabricated

L1845 KO, double upright, thigh and calf, with adjustable flexion and extension joint, medial-lateral and rotation control, prefabricated, includes fitting and adjustment

L1846 KO, double upright, thigh and calf, with adjustable flexion and extension joint, medial-lateral and rotation control, custom fabricated

L1847 KO, double upright with adjustable joint, with inflatable air support chamber(s), prefabricated, includes fitting and adjustment

L1850 KO, Swedish type, prefabricated, includes fitting and adjustment

L1855 KO, molded plastic, thigh and calf sections, with double upright knee joints, custom fabricated

L1858 KO, molded plastic, polycentric knee joints, pneumatic knee pads (CTI), custom fabricated

L1860 KO, modification of supracondylar prosthetic socket, custom fabricated (SK)

L1870 KO, double upright, thigh and calf lacers, with knee joints, custom fabricated

L1880 KO, double upright, nonmolded thigh and calf cuffs/lacers with knee joints, custom fabricated

~~**L1885** Knee orthosis, single or double upright, thigh and calf, with functional active resistance control, prefabricated, includes fitting and adjustment~~

See code E1810.

ANKLE-FOOT ORTHOSIS (AFO)

L1900 AFO, spring wire, dorsiflexion assist calf band, custom fabricated

L1901 Ankle orthosis, elastic, prefabricated, includes fitting and adjustment (e.g., neoprene, lycra)

L1902   AFO, ankle gauntlet, prefabricated, includes fitting and adjustment

L1904   AFO, molded ankle gauntlet, custom fabricated

L1906   AFO, multiligamentus ankle support, prefabricated, includes fitting and adjustment

● L1907   AFO, supramalleolar with straps, with or without interface/pads, custom fabricated

L1910   AFO, posterior, single bar, clasp attachment to shoe counter, prefabricated, includes fitting and adjustment

L1920   AFO, single upright with static or adjustable stop (Phelps or Perlstein type), custom fabricated

L1930   AFO, plastic or other material, prefabricated, includes fitting and adjustment

L1940   AFO, plastic or other material, custom-fabricated

L1945   AFO, molded to patient model, plastic, rigid anterior tibial section (floor reaction), custom fabricated

▲ L1950   AFO, spiral, (Institute of Rehabilitative Medicine type), plastic, custom-fabricated

● L1951   AFO, spiral, (Institute of Rehabilitative Medicine type), plastic or other material, prefabricated, includes fitting and adjustment

L1960   AFO, posterior solid ankle, plastic, custom fabricated

L1970   AFO, plastic, with ankle joint, custom fabricated

● L1971   AFO, plastic or other material with ankle joint, prefabricated, includes fitting and adjustment

L1980   AFO, single upright free plantar dorsiflexion, solid stirrup, calf band/cuff (single bar "BK" orthosis), custom fabricated

L1990   AFO, double upright free plantar dorsiflexion, solid stirrup, calf band/cuff (double bar "BK" orthosis), custom fabricated

KNEE-ANKLE-FOOT ORTHOSIS (KAFO) — OR ANY COMBINATION

L2000, L2020, L2036 are base procedures to be used with any knee joint, L2010 and L2030 are to be used only with no knee joint.

L2000   KAFO, single upright, free knee, free ankle, solid stirrup, thigh and calf bands/cuffs (single bar "AK" orthosis), custom fabricated

L2010   KAFO, single upright, free ankle, solid stirrup, thigh and calf bands/cuffs (single bar "AK" orthosis), without knee joint, custom fabricated

L2020   KAFO, double upright, free knee, free ankle, solid stirrup, thigh and calf bands/cuffs (double bar "AK" orthosis), custom fabricated

L2030   KAFO, double upright, free ankle, solid stirrup, thigh and calf bands/cuffs, (double bar "AK" orthosis), without knee joint, custom fabricated

L2035   KAFO, full plastic, static, (pediatric size), prefabricated, includes fitting and adjustment

L2036   KAFO, full plastic, double upright, free knee, custom fabricated

L2037   KAFO, full plastic, single upright, free knee, custom fabricated

L2038   KAFO, full plastic, without knee joint, multiaxis ankle, (Lively orthosis or equal), custom fabricated

L2039   KAFO, full plastic, single upright, poly-axial hinge, medial lateral rotation control, custom fabricated

TORSION CONTROL: HIP-KNEE-ANKLE-FOOT ORTHOSIS (HKAFO)

L2040   HKAFO, torsion control, bilateral rotation straps, pelvic band/belt, custom fabricated

L2050   HKAFO, torsion control, bilateral torsion cables, hip joint, pelvic band/belt, custom fabricated

L2060   HKAFO, torsion control, bilateral torsion cables, ball bearing hip joint, pelvic band/ belt, custom fabricated

L2070   HKAFO, torsion control, unilateral rotation straps, pelvic band/belt, custom fabricated

L2080   HKAFO, torsion control, unilateral torsion cable, hip joint, pelvic band/belt, custom fabricated

L2090   HKAFO, torsion control, unilateral torsion cable, ball bearing hip joint, pelvic band/belt, custom fabricated

FRACTURE ORTHOSIS

L2102   ~~Ankle foot orthosis, fracture orthosis, tibial fracture cast orthosis, plaster-type casting material, custom fabricated~~

L2104   ~~Ankle foot orthosis, fracture orthosis, tibial fracture cast orthosis, synthetic type casting material, custom fabricated~~

L2106   AFO, fracture orthosis, tibial fracture cast orthosis, thermoplastic type casting material, custom fabricated

L2108   AFO, fracture orthosis, tibial fracture cast orthosis, custom fabricated

L2112   AFO, fracture orthosis, tibial fracture orthosis, soft, prefabricated, includes fitting and adjustment

L2114   AFO, fracture orthosis, tibial fracture orthosis, semi-rigid, prefabricated, includes fitting and adjustment

L2116   AFO, fracture orthosis, tibial fracture orthosis, rigid, prefabricated, includes fitting and adjustment

L2122   ~~Knee ankle foot orthosis, fracture orthosis, femoral fracture cast orthosis, plaster type casting material, custom fabricated~~

L2124   ~~Knee ankle foot orthosis, fracture orthosis, femoral fracture cast orthosis, synthetic type casting material, custom fabricated~~

L2126   KAFO, fracture orthosis, femoral fracture cast orthosis, thermoplastic type casting material, custom fabricated

L2128   KAFO, fracture orthosis, femoral fracture cast orthosis, custom fabricated

L2132   KAFO, fracture orthosis, femoral fracture cast orthosis, soft, prefabricated, includes fitting and adjustment

L2134   KAFO, fracture orthosis, femoral fracture cast orthosis, semi-rigid, prefabricated, includes fitting and adjustment

L2136   KAFO, fracture orthosis, femoral fracture cast orthosis, rigid, prefabricated, includes fitting and adjustment

ADDITIONS TO FRACTURE ORTHOSIS

L2180   Addition to lower extremity fracture orthosis, plastic shoe insert with ankle joints

L2182   Addition to lower extremity fracture orthosis, drop lock knee joint

L1902 — L2182

Orthotic Procedures

L2184 — L2650

L2184 Addition to lower extremity fracture orthosis, limited motion knee joint

L2186 Addition to lower extremity fracture orthosis, adjustable motion knee joint, Lerman type

L2188 Addition to lower extremity fracture orthosis, quadrilateral brim

L2190 Addition to lower extremity fracture orthosis, waist belt

L2192 Addition to lower extremity fracture orthosis, hip joint, pelvic band, thigh flange, and pelvic belt

ADDITIONS TO LOWER EXTREMITY ORTHOSIS: SHOE-ANKLE-SHIN-KNEE

☑ **L2200** Addition to lower extremity, limited ankle motion, each joint

☑ **L2210** Addition to lower extremity, dorsiflexion assist (plantar flexion resist), each joint

☑ **L2220** Addition to lower extremity, dorsiflexion and plantar flexion assist/resist, each joint

L2230 Addition to lower extremity, split flat caliper stirrups and plate attachment

L2240 Addition to lower extremity, round caliper and plate attachment

L2250 Addition to lower extremity, foot plate, molded to patient model, stirrup attachment

L2260 Addition to lower extremity, reinforced solid stirrup (Scott-Craig type)

L2265 Addition to lower extremity, long tongue stirrup

L2270 Addition to lower extremity, varus/valgus correction ("T") strap, padded/lined or malleolus pad

L2275 Addition to lower extremity, varus/valgus correction, plastic modification, padded/lined

L2280 Addition to lower extremity, molded inner boot

L2300 Addition to lower extremity, abduction bar (bilateral hip involvement), jointed, adjustable

L2310 Addition to lower extremity, abduction bar, straight

L2320 Addition to lower extremity, nonmolded lacer

L2330 Addition to lower extremity, lacer molded to patient model

L2335 Addition to lower extremity, anterior swing band

L2340 Addition to lower extremity, pretibial shell, molded to patient model

L2350 Addition to lower extremity, prosthetic type, (BK) socket, molded to patient model, (used for "PTB," "AFO" orthoses)

L2360 Addition to lower extremity, extended steel shank

L2370 Addition to lower extremity, Patten bottom

L2375 Addition to lower extremity, torsion control, ankle joint and half solid stirrup

☑ **L2380** Addition to lower extremity, torsion control, straight knee joint, each joint

☑ **L2385** Addition to lower extremity, straight knee joint, heavy duty, each joint

☑ **L2390** Addition to lower extremity, offset knee joint, each joint

☑ **L2395** Addition to lower extremity, offset knee joint, heavy duty, each joint

L2397 Addition to lower extremity orthosis, suspension sleeve

ADDITIONS TO STRAIGHT KNEE OR OFFSET KNEE JOINTS

▲ ☑ **L2405** Addition to knee joint, lock; drop, stance or swing phase, each joint

☑ **L2415** Addition to knee lock with integrated release mechanism (bail, cable, or equal), any material, each joint

☑ **L2425** Addition to knee joint, disc or dial lock for adjustable knee flexion, each joint

☑ **L2430** Addition to knee joint, ratchet lock for active and progressive knee extension, each joint

☑ **L2435** Addition to knee joint, polycentric joint, each joint

L2492 Addition to knee joint, lift loop for drop lock ring

ADDITIONS: THIGH/WEIGHT BEARING — GLUTEAL/ISCHIAL WEIGHT BEARING

L2500 Addition to lower extremity, thigh/weight bearing, gluteal/ischial weight bearing, ring

L2510 Addition to lower extremity, thigh/weight bearing, quadri-lateral brim, molded to patient model

L2520 Addition to lower extremity, thigh/weight bearing, quadri-lateral brim, custom fitted

L2525 Addition to lower extremity, thigh/weight bearing, ischial containment/narrow M-L brim molded to patient model

L2526 Addition to lower extremity, thigh/weight bearing, ischial containment/narrow M-L brim, custom fitted

L2530 Addition to lower extremity, thigh/weight bearing, lacer, nonmolded

L2540 Addition to lower extremity, thigh/weight bearing, lacer, molded to patient model

L2550 Addition to lower extremity, thigh/weight bearing, high roll cuff

ADDITIONS: PELVIC AND THORACIC CONTROL

☑ **L2570** Addition to lower extremity, pelvic control, hip joint, Clevis type, two position joint, each

L2580 Addition to lower extremity, pelvic control, pelvic sling

☑ **L2600** Addition to lower extremity, pelvic control, hip joint, Clevis type, or thrust bearing, free, each

☑ **L2610** Addition to lower extremity, pelvic control, hip joint, Clevis or thrust bearing, lock, each

☑ **L2620** Addition to lower extremity, pelvic control, hip joint, heavy-duty, each

☑ **L2622** Addition to lower extremity, pelvic control, hip joint, adjustable flexion, each

☑ **L2624** Addition to lower extremity, pelvic control, hip joint, adjustable flexion, extension, abduction control, each

L2627 Addition to lower extremity, pelvic control, plastic, molded to patient model, reciprocating hip joint and cables

L2628 Addition to lower extremity, pelvic control, metal frame, reciprocating hip joint and cables

L2630 Addition to lower extremity, pelvic control, band and belt, unilateral

L2640 Addition to lower extremity, pelvic control, band and belt, bilateral

☑ **L2650** Addition to lower extremity, pelvic and thoracic control, gluteal pad, each

| Special Coverage Instructions | Noncovered by Medicare | Carrier Discretion | ☑ Quantity Alert | ● New Code | ▲ Revised Code |

90 — L Codes　　　M Maternity　　　A Adult　　　P Pediatrics　　　A-X APC Status Indicator　　　*2004 HCPCS*

L2660 Addition to lower extremity, thoracic control, thoracic band

L2670 Addition to lower extremity, thoracic control, paraspinal uprights

L2680 Addition to lower extremity, thoracic control, lateral support uprights

ADDITIONS: GENERAL

☑ **L2750** Addition to lower extremity orthosis, plating chrome or nickel, per bar

L2755 Addition to lower extremity orthosis, high strength, lightweight material, all hybrid lamination/prepreg composite, per segment

☑ **L2760** Addition to lower extremity orthosis, extension, per extension, per bar (for lineal adjustment for growth)

☑ **L2768** Orthotic side bar disconnect device, per bar

☑ **L2770** Addition to lower extremity orthosis, any material, per bar or joint

☑ **L2780** Addition to lower extremity orthosis, noncorrosive finish, per bar

☑ **L2785** Addition to lower extremity orthosis, drop lock retainer, each

L2795 Addition to lower extremity orthosis, knee control, full kneecap

L2800 Addition to lower extremity orthosis, knee control, kneecap, medial or lateral pull

L2810 Addition to lower extremity orthosis, knee control, condylar pad

L2820 Addition to lower extremity orthosis, soft interface for molded plastic, below knee section

L2830 Addition to lower extremity orthosis, soft interface for molded plastic, above knee section

☑ **L2840** Addition to lower extremity orthosis, tibial length sock, fracture or equal, each

☑ **L2850** Addition to lower extremity orthosis, femoral length sock, fracture or equal, each

☑ **L2860** Addition to lower extremity joint, knee or ankle, concentric adjustable torsion style mechanism, each

L2999 Lower extremity orthoses, NOS
Determine if an alternative HCPCS Level II code better describes the orthosis being reported. This code should be used only if a more specific code is unavailable.

ORTHOPEDIC SHOES

INSERTS

☑ **L3000** Foot insert, removable, molded to patient model, "UCB" type, Berkeley shell, each
MED: MCM 2323

☑ **L3001** Foot insert, removable, molded to patient model, Spenco, each
MED: MCM 2323

☑ **L3002** Foot insert, removable, molded to patient model, Plastazote or equal, each
MED: MCM 2323

☑ **L3003** Foot insert, removable, molded to patient model, silicone gel, each
MED: MCM 2323

☑ **L3010** Foot insert, removable, molded to patient model, longitudinal arch support, each
MED: MCM 2323

☑ **L3020** Foot insert, removable, molded to patient model, longitudinal/metatarsal support, each
MED: MCM 2323

☑ **L3030** Foot insert, removable, formed to patient foot, each
MED: MCM 2323

● ☑ **L3031** Foot, insert/plate, removable, addition to lower extremity orthosis, high strength, lightweight material, all hybrid lamination/prepreg composite, each

ARCH SUPPORT, REMOVABLE, PREMOLDED

☑ **L3040** Foot, arch support, removable, premolded, longitudinal, each
MED: MCM 2323

☑ **L3050** Foot, arch support, removable, premolded, metatarsal, each
MED: MCM 2323

☑ **L3060** Foot, arch support, removable, premolded, longitudinal/metatarsal, each
MED: MCM 2323

ARCH SUPPORT, NONREMOVABLE, ATTACHED TO SHOE

☑ **L3070** Foot, arch support, nonremovable, attached to shoe, longitudinal, each
MED: MCM 2323

☑ **L3080** Foot, arch support, nonremovable, attached to shoe, metatarsal, each
MED: MCM 2323

☑ **L3090** Foot, arch support, nonremovable, attached to shoe, longitudinal/metatarsal, each
MED: MCM 2323

L3100 Hallus-valgus night dynamic splint
MED: MCM 2323

ABDUCTION AND ROTATION BARS

L3140 Foot, abduction rotation bar, including shoes
MED: MCM 2323

L3150 Foot, abduction rotation bar, without shoes
MED: MCM 2323

L3160 Foot, adjustable shoe-styled positioning device

L3170 Foot, plastic heel stabilizer
MED: MCM 2323

ORTHOPEDIC FOOTWEAR

L3201 Orthopedic shoe, oxford with supinator or pronator, infant
MED: MCM 2323

L3202 Orthopedic shoe, oxford with supinator or pronator, child
MED: MCM 2323

L3203 Orthopedic shoe, oxford with supinator or pronator, junior
MED: MCM 2323

Orthotic Procedures

L3204 — L3420

L3204 Orthopedic shoe, hightop with supinator or pronator, infant
MED: MCM 2323

L3206 Orthopedic shoe, hightop with supinator or pronator, child
MED: MCM 2323

L3207 Orthopedic shoe, hightop with supinator or pronator, junior
MED: MCM 2323

☑ **L3208** Surgical boot, each, infant
MED: MCM 2079

☑ **L3209** Surgical boot, each, child
MED: MCM 2079

☑ **L3211** Surgical boot, each, junior
MED: MCM 2079

☑ **L3212** Benesch boot, pair, infant
MED: MCM 2079

☑ **L3213** Benesch boot, pair, child
MED: MCM 2079

☑ **L3214** Benesch boot, pair, junior
MED: MCM 2079

L3215 Orthopedic footwear, woman's shoes, oxford ♀
MED: Medicare Statute: 1862A8

L3216 Orthopedic footwear, woman's shoes, depth inlay ♀
MED: Medicare Statute: 1862A8

L3217 Orthopedic footwear, woman's shoes, hightop, depth inlay ♀
MED: Medicare Statute: 1862A8

L3219 Orthopedic footwear, man's shoes, oxford ♂
MED: Medicare Statute: 1862A8

L3221 Orthopedic footwear, man's shoes, depth inlay ♂
MED: Medicare Statute: 1862A8

L3222 Orthopedic footwear, man's shoes, hightop, depth inlay ♂
MED: Medicare Statute: 1862A8

Ⓐ **L3224** Orthopedic footwear, woman's shoe, oxford, used as an integral part of a brace (orthosis) ♀
MED: MCM 2323D

Ⓐ **L3225** Orthopedic footwear, man's shoe, oxford, used as an integral part of a brace (orthosis) ♂
MED: MCM 2323D

L3230 Orthopedic footwear, custom shoes, depth inlay
MED: MCM 2323

☑ **L3250** Orthopedic footwear, custom molded shoe, removable inner mold, prosthetic shoe, each
MED: MCM 2323

☑ **L3251** Foot, shoe molded to patient model, silicone shoe, each
MED: MCM 2323

☑ **L3252** Foot, shoe molded to patient model, Plastazote (or similar), custom fabricated, each
MED: MCM 2323

☑ **L3253** Foot, molded shoe Plastazote (or similar), custom fitted, each
MED: MCM 2323

L3254 Nonstandard size or width
MED: MCM 2323

L3255 Nonstandard size or length
MED: MCM 2323

L3257 Orthopedic footwear, additional charge for split size
MED: MCM 2323

☑ **L3260** Surgical boot/shoe, each
MED: MCM 2079

☑ **L3265** Plastazote sandal, each

SHOE MODIFICATION — LIFTS

☑ **L3300** Lift, elevation, heel, tapered to metatarsals, per inch
MED: MCM 2323

☑ **L3310** Lift, elevation, heel and sole, neoprene, per inch
MED: MCM 2323

☑ **L3320** Lift, elevation, heel and sole, cork, per inch
MED: MCM 2323

L3330 Lift, elevation, metal extension (skate)
MED: MCM 2323

☑ **L3332** Lift, elevation, inside shoe, tapered, up to one-half inch
MED: MCM 2323

☑ **L3334** Lift, elevation, heel, per inch
MED: MCM 2323

SHOE MODIFICATION — WEDGES

L3340 Heel wedge, SACH
MED: MCM 2323

L3350 Heel wedge
MED: MCM 2323

L3360 Sole wedge, outside sole
MED: MCM 2323

L3370 Sole wedge, between sole
MED: MCM 2323

L3380 Clubfoot wedge
MED: MCM 2323

L3390 Outflare wedge
MED: MCM 2323

L3400 Metatarsal bar wedge, rocker
MED: MCM 2323

L3410 Metatarsal bar wedge, between sole
MED: MCM 2323

L3420 Full sole and heel wedge, between sole
MED: MCM 2323

SHOE MODIFICATIONS — HEELS

L3430 Heel, counter, plastic reinforced
MED: MCM 2323

L3440 Heel, counter, leather reinforced
MED: MCM 2323

L3450 Heel, SACH cushion type
MED: MCM 2323

L3455 Heel, new leather, standard
MED: MCM 2323

L3460 Heel, new rubber, standard
MED: MCM 2323

L3465 Heel, Thomas with wedge
MED: MCM 2323

L3470 Heel, Thomas extended to ball
MED: MCM 2323

L3480 Heel, pad and depression for spur
MED: MCM 2323

L3485 Heel, pad, removable for spur
MED: MCM 2323

MISCELLANEOUS SHOE ADDITIONS

L3500 Orthopedic shoe addition, insole, leather
MED: MCM 2323

L3510 Orthopedic shoe addition, insole, rubber
MED: MCM 2323

L3520 Orthopedic shoe addition, insole, felt covered with leather
MED: MCM 2323

L3530 Orthopedic shoe addition, sole, half
MED: MCM 2323

L3540 Orthopedic shoe addition, sole, full
MED: MCM 2323

L3550 Orthopedic shoe addition, toe tap, standard
MED: MCM 2323

L3560 Orthopedic shoe addition, toe tap, horseshoe
MED: MCM 2323

L3570 Orthopedic shoe addition, special extension to instep (leather with eyelets)
MED: MCM 2323

L3580 Orthopedic shoe addition, convert instep to velcro closure
MED: MCM 2323

L3590 Orthopedic shoe addition, convert firm shoe counter to soft counter
MED: MCM 2323

L3595 Orthopedic shoe addition, March bar
MED: MCM 2323

TRANSFER OR REPLACEMENT

L3600 Transfer of an orthosis from one shoe to another, caliper plate, existing
MED: MCM 2323

L3610 Transfer of an orthosis from one shoe to another, caliper plate, new
MED: MCM 2323

L3620 Transfer of an orthosis from one shoe to another, solid stirrup, existing
MED: MCM 2323

L3630 Transfer of an orthosis from one shoe to another, solid stirrup, new
MED: MCM 2323

L3640 Transfer of an orthosis from one shoe to another, Dennis Browne splint (Riveton), both shoes
MED: MCM 2323

L3649 Orthopedic shoe, modification, addition or transfer, NOS
Determine if an alternative HCPCS Level II code better describes the service being reported. This code should be used only if a more specific code is unavailable.
MED: MCM 2323

ORTHOTIC DEVICES — UPPER LIMB

The procedures in this section are considered as "base" or "basic procedures" and may be modified by listing procedures from the "additions" sections and adding them to the base procedure.

SHOULDER ORTHOSIS (SO)

L3650 SO, figure of eight design abduction re- strainer, prefabricated, includes fitting and adjustment

L3651 Shoulder orthosis, single shoulder, elastic, prefabricated, includes fitting and adjustment (e.g., neoprene, lycra)

L3652 Shoulder orthosis, double shoulder, elastic, prefabricated, includes fitting and adjustment (e.g., neoprene, lycra)

L3660 SO, figure of eight design abduction restrainer, canvas and webbing, prefabricated, includes fitting and adjustment

L3670 SO, acromio/clavicular (canvas and webbing type), prefabricated, includes fitting and adjustment

L3675 SO, vest type abduction restrainer, canvas webbing type, or equal, prefabricated, includes fitting and adjustment

E **L3677** Shoulder orthosis, hard plastic, shoulder stabilizer, pre-fabricated, includes fitting and adjustment
MED: MCM 2130

ELBOW ORTHOSIS (EO)

L3700 EO, elastic with stays, prefabricated, includes fitting and adjustment

L3701 Elbow orthosis, elastic, prefabricated, includes fitting and adjustment (e.g., neoprene, lycra)

L3710 EO, elastic with metal joints, prefabricated, includes fitting and adjustment

L3720 EO, double upright with forearm/arm cuffs, free motion, custom fabricated

L3730 EO, double upright with forearm/arm cuffs, extension/flexion assist, custom fabricated

Orthotic Procedures

L3740 — L3950

L3740   EO, double upright with forearm/arm cuffs, adjustable position lock with active control, custom fabricated

L3760   Elbow orthosis, with adjustable position locking joint(s), prefabricated, includes fitting and adjustments, any type

L3762   Elbow orthosis, rigid, without joints, includes soft interface material, prefabricated, includes fitting and adjustment

WRIST-HAND-FINGER ORTHOSIS (WHFO)

L3800   WHFO, short opponens, no attachments, custom fabricated

L3805   WHFO, long opponens, no attachment, custom fabricated

L3807   WHFO, without joint(s), prefabricated, includes fitting and adjustments, any type

ADDITIONS

L3810   WHFO, addition to short and long opponens, thumb abduction ("C") bar

L3815   WHFO, addition to short and long opponens, second M.P. abduction assist

L3820   WHFO, addition to short and long opponens, I.P. extension assist, with M.P. extension stop

L3825   WHFO, addition to short and long opponens, M.P. extension stop

L3830   WHFO, addition to short and long opponens, M.P. extension assist

L3835   WHFO, addition to short and long opponens, M.P. spring extension assist

L3840   WHFO, addition to short and long opponens, spring swivel thumb

L3845   WHFO, addition to short and long opponens, thumb I.P. extension assist, with M.P. stop

L3850   WHO, addition to short and long opponens, action wrist, with dorsiflexion assist

L3855   WHFO, addition to short and long opponens, adjustable M.P. flexion control

L3860   WHFO, addition to short and long opponens, adjustable M.P. flexion control and I.P.

E   L3890   Addition to upper extremity joint, wrist or elbow, concentric adjustable torsion style mechanism, each

DYNAMIC FLEXOR HINGE, RECIPROCAL WRIST EXTENSION/FLEXION, FINGER FLEXION/EXTENSION

L3900   WHFO, dynamic flexor hinge, reciprocal wrist extension/flexion, finger flexion/extension, wrist or finger driven, custom fabricated

L3901   WHFO, dynamic flexor hinge, reciprocal wrist extension/flexion, finger flexion/extension, cable driven, custom fabricated

EXTERNAL POWER

▲   L3902   WHFO, external powered, compressed gas, custom fabricated

L3904   WHFO, external powered, electric, custom fabricated

OTHER WHFOS — CUSTOM FITTED

L3906   WHO, wrist gauntlet, molded to patient model, custom fabricated

L3907   WHFO, wrist gauntlet with thumb spica, molded to patient model, custom fabricated

L3908   WHO, wrist extension control cock-up, nonmolded, prefabricated, includes fitting and adjustment

L3909   Wrist orthosis, elastic, prefabricated, includes fitting and adjustment (e.g., neoprene, lycra)

L3910   WHFO, Swanson design, prefabricated, includes fitting and adjustment

L3911   Wrist hand finger orthosis, elastic, prefabricated, includes fitting and adjustment (e.g., neoprene, lycra)

L3912   HFO, flexion glove with elastic finger control, prefabricated, includes fitting and adjustment

L3914   WHO, wrist extension cock-up, prefabricated, includes fitting and adjustment

L3916   WHFO, wrist extension cock-up, with outrigger, prefabricated, includes fitting and adjustment

●   L3917   Hand orthosis, metacarpal fracture orthosis, prefabricated, includes fitting and adjustment

L3918   HFO, knuckle bender, prefabricated, includes fitting and adjustment

L3920   HFO, knuckle bender, with outrigger, prefabricated, includes fitting and adjustment

L3922   HFO, knuckle bender, two segment to flex joints, prefabricated, includes fitting and adjustment

L3923   HFO, without joint(s), prefabricated, includes fitting and adjustments, any type

L3924   WHFO, Oppenheimer, prefabricated, includes fitting and adjustment

L3926   WHFO, Thomas suspension, prefabricated, includes fitting and adjustment

L3928   HFO, finger extension, with clock spring, prefabricated, includes fitting and adjustment

L3930   WHFO, finger extension, with wrist support, prefabricated, includes fitting and adjustment

L3932   FO, safety pin, spring wire, prefabricated, includes fitting and adjustment

L3934   FO, safety pin, modified, prefabricated, includes fitting and adjustment

L3936   WHFO, Palmer, prefabricated, includes fitting and adjustment

L3938   WHFO, dorsal wrist, prefabricated, includes fitting and adjustment

L3940   WHFO, dorsal wrist, with outrigger attachment, prefabricated, includes fitting and adjustment

L3942   HFO, reverse knuckle bender, prefabricated, includes fitting and adjustment

L3944   HFO, reverse knuckle bender, with outrigger, prefabricated, includes fitting and adjustment

L3946   HFO, composite elastic, prefabricated, includes fitting and adjustment

L3948   FO, finger knuckle bender, prefabricated, includes fitting and adjustment

L3950   WHFO, combination Oppenheimer, with knuckle bender and two attachments, prefabricated, includes fitting and adjustment

◼ Special Coverage Instructions   ◼ Noncovered by Medicare   ◼ Carrier Discretion   ☑ Quantity Alert   ● New Code   ▲ Revised Code

94 — L Codes   ◼ Maternity   ◼ Adult   ◼ Pediatrics   ◼-◼ APC Status Indicator   *2004 HCPCS*

L3952   WHFO, combination Oppenheimer, with reverse knuckle and two attachments, prefabricated, includes fitting and adjustment

L3954   HFO, spreading hand, prefabricated, includes fitting and adjustment

☑ L3956   Addition of joint to upper extremity orthosis, any material; per joint

SHOULDER-ELBOW-WRIST-HAND ORTHOSIS (SEWHO)

ABDUCTION POSITION, CUSTOM FITTED

L3960   SEWHO, abduction positioning, airplane design, prefabricated, includes fitting and adjustment

L3962   SEWHO, abduction positioning, Erb's palsy design, prefabricated, includes fitting and adjustment

L3963   SEWHO, molded shoulder, arm, forearm, and wrist, with articulating elbow joint, custom fabricated

L3964   SEO, mobile arm support attached to wheelchair, balanced, adjustable, prefabricated, includes fitting and adjustment

L3965   SEO, mobile arm support attached to wheelchair, balanced, adjustable Rancho type, prefabricated, includes fitting and adjustment

L3966   SEO, mobile arm support attached to wheelchair, balanced, reclining, prefabricated, includes fitting and adjustment

L3968   SEO, mobile arm support attached to wheelchair, balanced, friction arm support (friction dampening to proximal and distal joints), prefabricated, includes fitting and adjustment

L3969   SEO, mobile arm support, monosuspension arm and hand support, overhead elbow forearm hand sling support, yoke type arm suspension support, prefabricated, includes fitting and adjustment

ADDITIONS TO MOBILE ARM SUPPORTS

L3970   SEO, addition to mobile arm support, elevating proximal arm

L3972   SEO, addition to mobile arm support, offset or lateral rocker arm with elastic balance control

L3974   SEO, addition to mobile arm support, supinator

FRACTURE ORTHOSIS

L3980   Upper extremity fracture orthosis, humeral, prefabricated, includes fitting and adjustment

L3982   Upper extremity fracture orthosis, radius/ulnar, prefabricated, includes fitting and adjustment

L3984   Upper extremity fracture orthosis, wrist, prefabricated, includes fitting and adjustment

L3985   Upper extremity fracture orthosis, forearm, hand with wrist hinge, custom fabricated

L3986   Upper extremity fracture orthosis, combination of humeral, radius/ulnar, wrist (example: Colles' fracture), custom fabricated

L3995   Addition to upper extremity orthosis, sock, fracture or equal, each

L3999   Upper limb orthosis, NOS

SPECIFIC REPAIR

L4000   Replace girdle for spinal orthosis (CTLSO or SO)

L4010   Replace trilateral socket brim

L4020   Replace quadrilateral socket brim, molded to patient model

L4030   Replace quadrilateral socket brim, custom fitted

L4040   Replace molded thigh lacer

L4045   Replace nonmolded thigh lacer

L4050   Replace molded calf lacer

L4055   Replace nonmolded calf lacer

L4060   Replace high roll cuff

L4070   Replace proximal and distal upright for KAFO

L4080   Replace metal bands KAFO, proximal thigh

L4090   Replace metal bands KAFO-AFO, calf or distal thigh

L4100   Replace leather cuff KAFO, proximal thigh

L4110   Replace leather cuff KAFO-AFO, calf or distal thigh

L4130   Replace pretibial shell

REPAIRS

☑ L4205   Repair of orthotic device, labor component, per 15 minutes
     MED: MCM 2100.4

L4210   Repair of orthotic device, repair or replace minor parts
     MED: MCM 2133, MCM 2100.4, MCM 2130D

▲ L4350   Ankle control orthosis, stirrup style, rigid, includes any type interface (e.g., pneumatic, gel), prefabricated, includes fitting and adjustment

▲ L4360   Walking boot, pneumatic, with or without joints, with or without interface material, prefabricated, includes fitting and adjustment

L4370   Pneumatic full leg splint, prefabricated, includes fitting and adjustment

L4380   Pneumatic knee splint, prefabricated, includes fitting and adjustment

▲ L4386   Walking boot, non-pneumatic, with or without joints, with or without interface material, prefabricated, includes fitting and adjustment

L4392   Replacement soft interface material, static AFO

L4394   Replace soft interface material, foot drop splint

L4396   Static ankle foot orthosis, including soft interface material, adjustable for fit, for positioning, pressure reduction, may be used for minimal ambulation, prefabricated, includes fitting and adjustment

L4398   Foot drop splint, recumbent positioning device, prefabricated, includes fitting and adjustment

Prosthetic Procedures

L5000 — L5570

PROSTHETIC PROCEDURES *L5000-L9999*

LOWER LIMB

The procedures in this section are considered as "base" or "basic procedures" and may be modified by listing items/procedures or special materials from the "additions" sections and adding them to the base procedure.

PARTIAL FOOT

L5000   Partial foot, shoe insert with longitudinal arch, toe filler

     MED: MCM 2323

L5010   Partial foot, molded socket, ankle height, with toe filler

     MED: MCM 2323

L5020   Partial foot, molded socket, tibial tubercle height, with toe filler

     MED: MCM 2323

ANKLE

L5050   Ankle, Symes, molded socket, SACH foot

L5060   Ankle, Symes, metal frame, molded leather socket, articulated ankle/foot

BELOW KNEE

L5100   Below knee, molded socket, shin, SACH foot

L5105   Below knee, plastic socket, joints and thigh lacer, SACH foot

KNEE DISARTICULATION

L5150   Knee disarticulation (or through knee), molded socket, external knee joints, shin, SACH foot

L5160   Knee disarticulation (or through knee), molded socket, bent knee configuration, external knee joints, shin, SACH foot

ABOVE KNEE

L5200   Above knee, molded socket, single axis constant friction knee, shin, SACH foot

☑ **L5210**   Above knee, short prosthesis, no knee joint ("stubbies"), with foot blocks, no ankle joints, each

☑ **L5220**   Above knee, short prosthesis, no knee joint ("stubbies"), with articulated ankle/foot, dynamically aligned, each

L5230   Above knee, for proximal femoral focal deficiency, constant friction knee, shin, SACH foot

HIP DISARTICULATION

L5250   Hip disarticulation, Canadian type; molded socket, hip joint, single axis constant friction knee, shin, SACH foot

L5270   Hip disarticulation, tilt table type; molded socket, locking hip joint, single axis constant friction knee, shin, SACH foot

HEMIPELVECTOMY

L5280   Hemipelvectomy, Canadian type; molded socket, hip joint, single axis constant friction knee, shin, SACH foot

L5301   Below knee, molded socket, shin, SACH foot, endoskeletal system

L5311   Knee disarticulation (or through knee), molded socket, external knee joints, shin, SACH foot, endoskeletal system

L5321   Above knee, molded socket, open end, SACH foot, endoskeletal system, single axis knee

L5331   Hip disarticulation, Canadian type, molded socket, endoskeletal system, hip joint, single axis knee, SACH foot

L5341   Hemipelvectomy, Canadian type, molded socket, endoskeletal system, hip joint, single axis knee, SACH foot

IMMEDIATE POSTSURGICAL OR EARLY FITTING PROCEDURES

☑ **L5400**   Immediate postsurgical or early fitting, application of initial rigid dressing, including fitting, alignment, suspension, and one cast change, below knee

☑ **L5410**   Immediate postsurgical or early fitting, application of initial rigid dressing, including fitting, alignment and suspension, below knee, each additional cast change and realignment

☑ **L5420**   Immediate postsurgical or early fitting, application of initial rigid dressing, including fitting, alignment and suspension and one cast change "AK" or knee disarticulation

☑ **L5430**   Immediate postsurgical or early fitting, application of initial rigid dressing, including fitting, alignment and suspension, "AK" or knee disarticulation, each additional cast change and realignment

L5450   Immediate postsurgical or early fitting, application of nonweight bearing rigid dressing, below knee

L5460   Immediate postsurgical or early fitting, application of nonweight bearing rigid dressing, above knee

INITIAL PROSTHESIS

L5500   Initial, below knee "PTB" type socket, non-alignable system, pylon, no cover, SACH foot, plaster socket, direct formed

L5505   Initial, above knee — knee disarticulation, ischial level socket, non-alignable system, pylon, no cover, SACH foot plaster socket, direct formed

PREPARATORY PROSTHESIS

L5510   Preparatory, below knee "PTB" type socket, non-alignable system, pylon, no cover, SACH foot, plaster socket, molded to model

L5520   Preparatory, below knee "PTB" type socket, non-alignable system, pylon, no cover, SACH foot, thermoplastic or equal, direct formed

L5530   Preparatory, below knee "PTB" type socket, non-alignable system, pylon, no cover, SACH foot, thermoplastic or equal, molded to model

L5535   Preparatory, below knee "PTB" type socket, non-alignable system, pylon, no cover, SACH foot, prefabricated, adjustable open end socket

L5540   Preparatory, below knee "PTB" type socket, non-alignable system, pylon, no cover, SACH foot, laminated socket, molded to model

L5560   Preparatory, above knee — knee disarticulation, ischial level socket, non-alignable system, pylon, no cover, SACH foot, plaster socket, molded to model

L5570   Preparatory, above knee — knee disarticulation, ischial level socket, non-alignable system, pylon, no cover, SACH foot, thermoplastic or equal, direct formed

L5580   Preparatory, above knee — knee disarticulation, ischial level socket, non-alignable system, pylon, no cover, SACH foot, thermoplastic or equal, molded to model

L5585   Preparatory, above knee — knee disarticulation, ischial level socket, non-alignable system, pylon, no cover, SACH foot, prefabricated adjustable open end socket

L5590   Preparatory, above knee — knee disarticulation, ischial level socket, non-alignable system, pylon, no cover, SACH foot, laminated socket, molded to model

L5595   Preparatory, hip disarticulation — hemipelvectomy, pylon, no cover, SACH foot, thermoplastic or equal, molded to patient model

L5600   Preparatory, hip disarticulation — hemipelvectomy, pylon, no cover, SACH foot, laminated socket, molded to patient model

ADDITIONS: LOWER EXTREMITY

L5610   Addition to lower extremity, endoskeletal system, above knee, hydracadence system

L5611   Addition to lower extremity, endoskeletal system, above knee — knee disarticulation, 4-bar linkage, with friction swing phase control

L5613   Addition to lower extremity, endoskeletal system, above knee — knee disarticulation, 4-bar linkage, with hydraulic swing phase control

L5614   Addition to lower extremity, endoskeletal system, above knee — knee disarticulation, 4-bar linkage, with pneumatic swing phase control

L5616   Addition to lower extremity, endoskeletal system, above knee, universal multiplex system, friction swing phase control

☑   L5617   Addition to lower extremity, quick change self-aligning unit, above or below knee, each

ADDITIONS: TEST SOCKETS

L5618   Addition to lower extremity, test socket, Symes

L5620   Addition to lower extremity, test socket, below knee

L5622   Addition to lower extremity, test socket, knee disarticulation

L5624   Addition to lower extremity, test socket, above knee

L5626   Addition to lower extremity, test socket, hip disarticulation

L5628   Addition to lower extremity, test socket, hemipelvectomy

L5629   Addition to lower extremity, below knee, acrylic socket

ADDITIONS: SOCKET VARIATIONS

L5630   Addition to lower extremity, Symes type, expandable wall socket

L5631   Addition to lower extremity, above knee or knee disarticulation, acrylic socket

L5632   Addition to lower extremity, Symes type, "PTB" brim design socket

L5634   Addition to lower extremity, Symes type, posterior opening (Canadian) socket

L5636   Addition to lower extremity, Symes type, medial opening socket

L5637   Addition to lower extremity, below knee, total contact

L5638   Addition to lower extremity, below knee, leather socket

L5639   Addition to lower extremity, below knee, wood socket

L5640   Addition to lower extremity, knee disarticulation, leather socket

L5642   Addition to lower extremity, above knee, leather socket

L5643   Addition to lower extremity, hip disarticulation, flexible inner socket, external frame

L5644   Addition to lower extremity, above knee, wood socket

L5645   Addition to lower extremity, below knee, flexible inner socket, external frame

▲   L5646   Addition to lower extremity, below knee, air, fluid, gel or equal, cushion socket

L5647   Addition to lower extremity, below knee, suction socket

▲   L5648   Addition to lower extremity, above knee, air, fluid, gel or equal, cushion socket

L5649   Addition to lower extremity, ischial containment/narrow M-L socket

L5650   Addition to lower extremity, total contact, above knee or knee disarticulation socket

L5651   Addition to lower extremity, above knee, flexible inner socket, external frame

L5652   Addition to lower extremity, suction suspension, above knee or knee disarticulation socket

L5653   Addition to lower extremity, knee disarticulation, expandable wall socket

ADDITIONS: SOCKET INSERT AND SUSPENSION

L5654   Addition to lower extremity, socket insert, Symes (Kemblo, Pelite, Aliplast, Plastazote or equal)

L5655   Addition to lower extremity, socket insert, below knee (Kemblo, Pelite, Aliplast, Plastazote or equal)

L5656   Addition to lower extremity, socket insert, knee disarticulation (Kemblo, Pelite, Aliplast, Plastazote or equal)

L5658   Addition to lower extremity, socket insert, above knee (Kemblo, Pelite, Aliplast, Plastazote or equal)

L5661   Addition to lower extremity, socket insert, multidurometer, Symes

L5665   Addition to lower extremity, socket insert, multidurometer, below knee

L5666   Addition to lower extremity, below knee, cuff suspension

L5668   Addition to lower extremity, below knee, molded distal cushion

L5670   Addition to lower extremity, below knee, molded supracondylar suspension ("PTS" or similar)

L5671   Addition to lower extremity, below knee/above knee suspension locking mechanism (shuttle, lanyard or equal), excludes socket insert

L5672   Addition to lower extremity, below knee, removable medial brim suspension

Special Coverage Instructions   Noncovered by Medicare   Carrier Discretion   ☑ Quantity Alert   ● New Code   ▲ Revised Code

Prosthetic Procedures

L5673 — L5812

●   **L5673**   Addition to lower extremity, below knee/above knee, custom fabricated from existing mold or prefabricated, socket insert, silicone gel, elastomeric or equal, for use with locking mechanism

L5674   Addition to lower extremity, below knee, suspension sleeve, any material, each

☑   **L5675**   Addition to lower extremity, below knee, suspension sleeve, heavy duty, any material, each

☑   **L5676**   Addition to lower extremity, below knee, knee joints, single axis, pair

☑   **L5677**   Addition to lower extremity, below knee, knee joints, polycentric, pair

☑   **L5678**   Addition to lower extremity, below knee joint covers, pair

●   **L5679**   Addition to lower extremity, below knee/above knee, custom fabricated from existing mold or prefabricated, socket insert, silicone gel, elastomeric or equal, not for use with locking mechanism

L5680   Addition to lower extremity, below knee, thigh lacer, nonmolded

●   **L5681**   Addition to lower extremity, below knee/above knee, custom fabricated socket insert for congenital or atypical traumatic amputee, silicone gel, elastomeric or equal, for use with or without locking mechanism, initial only (for other than initial, use code L5673 or L5679)

L5682   Addition to lower extremity, below knee, thigh lacer, gluteal/ischial, molded

●   **L5683**   Addition to lower extremity, below knee/above knee, custom fabricated socket insert for other than congenital or atypical traumatic amputee, silicone gel, elastomeric or equal, for use with or without locking mechanism, initial only (for other than initial, use code L5673 or L5679)

L5684   Addition to lower extremity, below knee, fork strap

L5686   Addition to lower extremity, below knee, back check (extension control)

L5688   Addition to lower extremity, below knee, waist belt, webbing

L5690   Addition to lower extremity, below knee, waist belt, padded and lined

L5692   Addition to lower extremity, above knee, pelvic control belt, light

L5694   Addition to lower extremity, above knee, pelvic control belt, padded and lined

☑   **L5695**   Addition to lower extremity, above knee, pelvic control, sleeve suspension, neoprene or equal, each

L5696   Addition to lower extremity, above knee or knee disarticulation, pelvic joint

L5697   Addition to lower extremity, above knee or knee disarticulation, pelvic band

L5698   Addition to lower extremity, above knee or knee disarticulation, Silesian bandage

L5699   All lower extremity prostheses, shoulder harness

REPLACEMENTS

L5700   Replacement, socket, below knee, molded to patient model

L5701   Replacement, socket, above knee/knee disarticulation, including attachment plate, molded to patient model

L5702   Replacement, socket, hip disarticulation, including hip joint, molded to patient model

L5704   Custom shaped protective cover, below knee

L5705   Custom shaped protective cover, above knee

L5706   Custom shaped protective cover, knee disarticulation

L5707   Custom shaped protective cover, hip disarticulation

ADDITIONS: EXOSKELETAL KNEE-SHIN SYSTEM

L5710   Addition, exoskeletal knee-shin system, single axis, manual lock

L5711   Addition, exoskeletal knee-shin system, single axis, manual lock, ultra-light material

L5712   Addition, exoskeletal knee-shin system, single axis, friction swing and stance phase control (safety knee)

L5714   Addition, exoskeletal knee-shin system, single axis, variable friction swing phase control

L5716   Addition, exoskeletal knee-shin system, polycentric, mechanical stance phase lock

L5718   Addition, exoskeletal knee-shin system, polycentric, friction swing and stance phase control

L5722   Addition, exoskeletal knee-shin system, single axis, pneumatic swing, friction stance phase control

L5724   Addition, exoskeletal knee-shin system, single axis, fluid swing phase control

L5726   Addition, exoskeletal knee-shin system, single axis, external joints, fluid swing phase control

L5728   Addition, exoskeletal knee-shin system, single axis, fluid swing and stance phase control

L5780   Addition, exoskeletal knee-shin system, single axis, pneumatic/hydra pneumatic swing phase control

L5781   Addition to lower limb prosthesis, vacuum pump, residual limb volume management and moisture evacuation system

L5782   Addition to lower limb prosthesis, vacuum pump, residual limb volume management and moisture evacuation system, heavy duty

COMPONENT MODIFICATION

L5785   Addition, exoskeletal system, below knee, ultra-light material (titanium, carbon fiber or equal)

L5790   Addition, exoskeletal system, above knee, ultra-light material (titanium, carbon fiber or equal)

L5795   Addition, exoskeletal system, hip disarticulation, ultra-light material (titanium, carbon fiber or equal)

ADDITIONS: ENDOSKELETAL KNEE-SHIN SYSTEM

L5810   Addition, endoskeletal knee-shin system, single axis, manual lock

L5811   Addition, endoskeletal knee-shin system, single axis, manual lock, ultra-light material

L5812   Addition, endoskeletal knee-shin system, single axis, friction swing and stance phase control (safety knee)

| Special Coverage Instructions | Noncovered by Medicare | Carrier Discretion | ☑ Quantity Alert | ● New Code | ▲ Revised Code |

L5814   Addition, endoskeletal knee-shin system, polycentric, hydraulic swing phase control, mechanical stance phase lock

L5816   Addition, endoskeletal knee-shin system, polycentric, mechanical stance phase lock

L5818   Addition, endoskeletal knee-shin system, polycentric, friction swing and stance phase control

L5822   Addition, endoskeletal knee-shin system, single axis, pneumatic swing, friction stance phase control

L5824   Addition, endoskeletal knee-shin system, single axis, fluid swing phase control

L5826   Addition, endoskeletal knee-shin system, single axis, hydraulic swing phase control, with miniature high activity frame

L5828   Addition, endoskeletal knee-shin system, single axis, fluid swing and stance phase control

L5830   Addition, endoskeletal knee-shin system, single axis, pneumatic/swing phase control

L5840   Addition, endoskeletal knee-shin system, 4-bar linkage or multiaxial, pneumatic swing phase control

L5845   Addition, endoskeletal knee-shin system, stance flexion feature, adjustable

L5846   Addition, endoskeletal knee-shin system, microprocessor control feature, swing phase only

L5847   Addition, endoskeletal knee-shin system, microprocessor control feature, stance phase

▲   L5848   Addition to endoskeletal, knee-shin system, hydraulic stance extension, dampening feature, with or without adjustability

L5850   Addition, endoskeletal system, above knee or hip disarticulation, knee extension assist

L5855   Addition, endoskeletal system, hip disarticulation, mechanical hip extension assist

L5910   Addition, endoskeletal system, below knee, alignable system

L5920   Addition, endoskeletal system, above knee or hip disarticulation, alignable system

L5925   Addition, endoskeletal system, above knee, knee disarticulation or hip disarticulation, manual lock

L5930   Addition, endoskeletal system, high activity knee control frame

L5940   Addition, endoskeletal system, below knee, ultra-light material (titanium, carbon fiber or equal)

L5950   Addition, endoskeletal system, above knee, ultra-light material (titanium, carbon fiber or equal)

L5960   Addition, endoskeletal system, hip disarticulation, ultra-light material (titanium, carbon fiber or equal)

L5962   Addition, endoskeletal system, below knee, flexible protective outer surface covering system

L5964   Addition, endoskeletal system, above knee, flexible protective outer surface covering system

L5966   Addition, endoskeletal system, hip disarticulation, flexible protective outer surface covering system

L5968   Addition to lower limb prosthesis, multiaxial ankle with swing phase active dorsiflexion feature

L5970   All lower extremity prostheses, foot, external keel, SACH foot

L5972   All lower extremity prostheses, flexible keel foot (Safe, Sten, Bock Dynamic or equal)

L5974   All lower extremity prostheses, foot, single axis ankle/foot

L5975   All lower extremity prosthesis, combination single axis ankle and flexible keel foot

L5976   All lower extremity prostheses, energy storing foot (Seattle Carbon Copy II or equal)

L5978   All lower extremity prostheses, foot, multi-axial ankle/foot

L5979   All lower extremity prostheses, multi-axial ankle, dynamic response foot, one piece system

L5980   All lower extremity prostheses, flex-foot system

L5981   All lower extremity prostheses, flex-walk system or equal

L5982   All exoskeletal lower extremity prostheses, axial rotation unit

▲   L5984   All endoskeletal lower extremity prosthesis, axial rotation unit, with or without adjustability

L5985   All endoskeletal lower extremity prostheses, dynamic prosthetic pylon

L5986   All lower extremity prostheses, multi-axial rotation unit ("MCP" or equal)

L5987   All lower extremity prosthesis, shank foot system with vertical loading pylon

L5988   Addition to lower limb prosthesis, vertical shock reducing pylon feature

L5989   Addition to lower extremity prosthesis, endoskeletal system, pylon with integrated electronic force sensors

L5990   Addition to lower extremity prosthesis, user adjustable heel height

L5995   Addition to lower extremity prosthesis, heavy duty feature (for patient weight > 300 lbs)

L5999   Lower extremity prosthesis, not otherwise specified
Determine if an alternative HCPCS Level II code better describes the prosthesis being reported. This code should be used only if a more specific code is unavailable.

UPPER LIMB

The procedures in L6000-L6590 are considered as "base" or "basic procedures" and may be modified by listing procedures from the "addition" sections. The base procedures include only standard friction wrist and control cable system unless otherwise specified.

PARTIAL HAND

L6000   Partial hand, Robin-Aids, thumb remaining (or equal)

L6010   Partial hand, Robin-Aids, little and/or ring finger remaining (or equal)

L6020   Partial hand, Robin-Aids, no finger remaining (or equal)

L6025   Transcarpal/metacarpal or partial hand disarticulation prosthesis, external power, self-suspended, inner socket with removable forearm section, electrodes and cables, two batteries, charger, myoelectric control of terminal device

| Special Coverage Instructions | Noncovered by Medicare | Carrier Discretion | ☑ Quantity Alert | ● New Code | ▲ Revised Code |

Prosthetic Procedures

L6050 — L6615

WRIST DISARTICULATION

L6050   Wrist disarticulation, molded socket, flexible elbow hinges, triceps pad

L6055   Wrist disarticulation, molded socket with expandable interface, flexible elbow hinges, triceps pad

BELOW ELBOW

L6100   Below elbow, molded socket, flexible elbow hinge, triceps pad

L6110   Below elbow, molded socket (Muenster or Northwestern suspension types)

L6120   Below elbow, molded double wall split socket, step-up hinges, half cuff

L6130   Below elbow, molded double wall split socket, stump activated locking hinge, half cuff

ELBOW DISARTICULATION

L6200   Elbow disarticulation, molded socket, outside locking hinge, forearm

L6205   Elbow disarticulation, molded socket with expandable interface, outside locking hinges, forearm

ABOVE ELBOW

L6250   Above elbow, molded double wall socket, internal locking elbow, forearm

SHOULDER DISARTICULATION

L6300   Shoulder disarticulation, molded socket, shoulder bulkhead, humeral section, internal locking elbow, forearm

L6310   Shoulder disarticulation, passive restoration (complete prosthesis)

L6320   Shoulder disarticulation, passive restoration (shoulder cap only)

INTERSCAPULAR THORACIC

L6350   Interscapular thoracic, molded socket, shoulder bulkhead, humeral section, internal locking elbow, forearm

L6360   Interscapular thoracic, passive restoration (complete prosthesis)

L6370   Interscapular thoracic, passive restoration (shoulder cap only)

IMMEDIATE AND EARLY POSTSURGICAL PROCEDURES

L6380   Immediate postsurgical or early fitting, application of initial rigid dressing, including fitting alignment and suspension of components, and one cast change, wrist disarticulation or below elbow

☑ **L6382**   Immediate postsurgical or early fitting, application of initial rigid dressing including fitting alignment and suspension of components, and one cast change, elbow disarticulation or above elbow

☑ **L6384**   Immediate postsurgical or early fitting, application of initial rigid dressing including fitting alignment and suspension of components, and one cast change, shoulder disarticulation or interscapular thoracic

☑ **L6386**   Immediate postsurgical or early fitting, each additional cast change and realignment

L6388   Immediate postsurgical or early fitting, application of rigid dressing only

ENDOSKELETAL: BELOW ELBOW

L6400   Below elbow, molded socket, endoskeletal system, including soft prosthetic tissue shaping

ENDOSKELETAL: ELBOW DISARTICULATION

L6450   Elbow disarticulation, molded socket, endoskeletal system, including soft prosthetic tissue shaping

ENDOSKELETAL: ABOVE ELBOW

L6500   Above elbow, molded socket, endoskeletal system, including soft prosthetic tissue shaping

ENDOSKELETAL: SHOULDER DISARTICULATION

L6550   Shoulder disarticulation, molded socket, endoskeletal system, including soft prosthetic tissue shaping

ENDOSKELETAL: INTERSCAPULAR THORACIC

L6570   Interscapular thoracic, molded socket, endoskeletal system, including soft prosthetic tissue shaping

L6580   Preparatory, wrist disarticulation or below elbow, single wall plastic socket, friction wrist, flexible elbow hinges, figure of eight harness, humeral cuff, Bowden cable control, "USMC" or equal pylon, no cover, molded to patient model

L6582   Preparatory, wrist disarticulation or below elbow, single wall socket, friction wrist, flexible elbow hinges, figure of eight harness, humeral cuff, Bowden cable control, "USMC" or equal pylon, no cover, direct formed

L6584   Preparatory, elbow disarticulation or above elbow, single wall plastic socket, friction wrist, locking elbow, figure of eight harness, fair lead cable control, "USMC" or equal pylon, no cover, molded to patient model

L6586   Preparatory, elbow disarticulation or above elbow, single wall socket, friction wrist, locking elbow, figure of eight harness, fair lead cable control, "USMC" or equal pylon, no cover, direct formed

L6588   Preparatory, shoulder disarticulation or interscapular thoracic, single wall plastic socket, shoulder joint, locking elbow, friction wrist, chest strap, fair lead cable control, "USMC" or equal pylon, no cover, molded to patient model

L6590   Preparatory, shoulder disarticulation or interscapular thoracic, single wall socket, shoulder joint, locking elbow, friction wrist, chest strap, fair lead cable control, "USMC" or equal pylon, no cover, direct formed

ADDITIONS: UPPER LIMB

The following procedures/modifications/components may be added to other base procedures. The items in this section should reflect the additional complexity of each modification procedure, in addition to the base procedure, at the time of the original order.

☑ **L6600**   Upper extremity additions, polycentric hinge, pair

☑ **L6605**   Upper extremity additions, single pivot hinge, pair

☑ **L6610**   Upper extremity additions, flexible metal hinge, pair

L6615   Upper extremity addition, disconnect locking wrist unit

---

| Special Coverage Instructions | Noncovered by Medicare | Carrier Discretion | ☑ Quantity Alert | ● New Code | ▲ Revised Code |

100 — L Codes   Ⓜ Maternity   Ⓐ Adult   Ⓟ Pediatrics   Ⓐ-Ⓧ APC Status Indicator   *2004 HCPCS*

☑ **L6616** Upper extremity addition, additional disconnect insert for locking wrist unit, each

▲ **L6620** Upper extremity addition, flexion/extension wrist unit, with or without friction

L6623 Upper extremity addition, spring assisted rotational wrist unit with latch release

L6625 Upper extremity addition, rotation wrist unit with cable lock

L6628 Upper extremity addition, quick disconnect hook adapter, Otto Bock or equal

L6629 Upper extremity addition, quick disconnect lamination collar with coupling piece, Otto Bock or equal

L6630 Upper extremity addition, stainless steel, any wrist

☑ **L6632** Upper extremity addition, latex suspension sleeve, each

L6635 Upper extremity addition, lift assist for elbow

L6637 Upper extremity addition, nudge control elbow lock

L6638 Upper extremity addition to prosthesis, electric locking feature, only for use with manually powered elbow

☑ **L6640** Upper extremity additions, shoulder abduction joint, pair

L6641 Upper extremity addition, excursion amplifier, pulley type

L6642 Upper extremity addition, excursion amplifier, lever type

☑ **L6645** Upper extremity addition, shoulder flexion-abduction joint, each

L6646 Upper extremity addition, shoulder joint, multipositional locking, flexion, adjustable abduction friction control, for use with body powered or external powered system

L6647 Upper extremity addition, shoulder lock mechanism, body powered actuator

L6648 Upper extremity addition, shoulder lock mechanism, external powered actuator

☑ **L6650** Upper extremity addition, shoulder universal joint, each

L6655 Upper extremity addition, standard control cable, extra

L6660 Upper extremity addition, heavy duty control cable

L6665 Upper extremity addition, Teflon, or equal, cable lining

L6670 Upper extremity addition, hook to hand, cable adapter

L6672 Upper extremity addition, harness, chest or shoulder, saddle type

▲ **L6675** Upper extremity addition, harness, (e.g. figure of eight type), single cable design

▲ **L6676** Upper extremity addition, harness, (e.g. figure of eight type), dual cable design

L6680 Upper extremity addition, test socket, wrist disarticulation or below elbow

L6682 Upper extremity addition, test socket, elbow disarticulation or above elbow

L6684 Upper extremity addition, test socket, shoulder disarticulation or interscapular thoracic

L6686 Upper extremity addition, suction socket

L6687 Upper extremity addition, frame type socket, below elbow or wrist disarticulation

L6688 Upper extremity addition, frame type socket, above elbow or elbow disarticulation

L6689 Upper extremity addition, frame type socket, shoulder disarticulation

L6690 Upper extremity addition, frame type socket, interscapular-thoracic

☑ **L6691** Upper extremity addition, removable insert, each

☑ **L6692** Upper extremity addition, silicone gel insert or equal, each

L6693 Upper extremity addition, locking elbow, forearm counterbalance

TERMINAL DEVICES

HOOKS

L6700 Terminal device, hook, Dorrance or equal, model #3
MED: MCM 2133

L6705 Terminal device, hook, Dorrance or equal, model #5
MED: MCM 2133

L6710 Terminal device, hook, Dorrance or equal, model #5X
MED: MCM 2133

L6715 Terminal device, hook, Dorrance or equal, model #5XA
MED: MCM 2133

L6720 Terminal device, hook, Dorrance or equal, model #6
MED: MCM 2133

L6725 Terminal device, hook, Dorrance or equal, model #7
MED: MCM 2133

L6730 Terminal device, hook, Dorrance or equal, model #7LO
MED: MCM 2133

L6735 Terminal device, hook, Dorrance or equal, model #8
MED: MCM 2133

L6740 Terminal device, hook, Dorrance or equal, model #8X
MED: MCM 2133

L6745 Terminal device, hook, Dorrance or equal, model #88X
MED: MCM 2133

L6750 Terminal device, hook, Dorrance or equal, model #10P
MED: MCM 2133

L6755 Terminal device, hook, Dorrance or equal, model #10X
MED: MCM 2133

L6765 Terminal device, hook, Dorrance or equal, model #12P
MED: MCM 2133

L6770 Terminal device, hook, Dorrance or equal, model #99X
MED: MCM 2133

Prosthetic Procedures

L6775 — L6940

L6775 Terminal device, hook, Dorrance or equal, model #555
MED: MCM 2133

L6780 Terminal device, hook, Dorrance or equal, model #SS555
MED: MCM 2133

L6790 Terminal device, hook, Accu hook or equal
MED: MCM 2133

L6795 Terminal device, hook, 2 load or equal
MED: MCM 2133

L6800 Terminal device, hook, APRL VC or equal
MED: MCM 2133

L6805 Terminal device, modifier wrist flexion unit
MED: MCM 2133

L6806 Terminal device, hook, TRS Grip, Grip III, VC, or equal
MED: MCM 2133

L6807 Terminal device, hook, Grip I, Grip II, VC, or equal
MED: MCM 2133

L6808 Terminal device, hook, TRS Adept, infant or child, VC, or equal
MED: MCM 2133

L6809 Terminal device, hook, TRS Super Sport, passive
MED: MCM 2133

L6810 Terminal device, pincher tool, Otto Bock or equal
MED: MCM 2133

HANDS

L6825 Terminal device, hand, Dorrance, VO
MED: MCM 2133

L6830 Terminal device, hand, APRL, VC
MED: MCM 2133

L6835 Terminal device, hand, Sierra, VO
MED: MCM 2133

L6840 Terminal device, hand, Becker Imperial
MED: MCM 2133

L6845 Terminal device, hand, Becker Lock Grip
MED: MCM 2133

L6850 Terminal device, hand, Becker Plylite
MED: MCM 2133

L6855 Terminal device, hand, Robin-Aids, VO
MED: MCM 2133

L6860 Terminal device, hand, Robin-Aids, VO soft
MED: MCM 2133

L6865 Terminal device, hand, passive hand
MED: MCM 2133

L6867 Terminal device, hand, Detroit Infant Hand (mechanical)   **P**
MED: MCM 2133

L6868 Terminal device, hand, passive infant hand, Steeper, Hosmer or equal   **P**
MED: MCM 2133

L6870 Terminal device, hand, child mitt
MED: MCM 2133

L6872 Terminal device, hand, NYU child hand
MED: MCM 2133

L6873 Terminal device, hand, mechanical infant hand, Steeper or equal
MED: MCM 2133

L6875 Terminal device, hand, Bock, VC
MED: MCM 2133

L6880 Terminal device, hand, Bock, VO
MED: MCM 2133

L6881 Automatic grasp feature, addition to upper limb prosthetic terminal device

L6882 Microprocessor control feature, addition to upper limb prosthetic terminal device
MED: MCM 2133

GLOVES FOR ABOVE HANDS

L6890 Terminal device, glove for above hands, production glove

L6895 Terminal device, glove for above hands, custom glove

HAND RESTORATION

L6900 Hand restoration (casts, shading and measurements included), partial hand, with glove, thumb or one finger remaining

L6905 Hand restoration (casts, shading and measurements included), partial hand, with glove, multiple fingers remaining

L6910 Hand restoration (casts, shading and measurements included), partial hand, with glove, no fingers remaining

L6915 Hand restoration (shading and measurements included), replacement glove for above

EXTERNAL POWER

BASE DEVICES

L6920 Wrist disarticulation, external power, self-suspended inner socket, removable forearm shell, Otto Bock or equal switch, cables, two batteries and one charger, switch control of terminal device

L6925 Wrist disarticulation, external power, self-suspended inner socket, removable forearm shell, Otto Bock or equal electrodes, cables, two batteries and one charger, myoelectronic control of terminal device

L6930 Below elbow, external power, self-suspended inner socket, removable forearm shell, Otto Bock or equal switch, cables, two batteries and one charger, switch control of terminal device

L6935 Below elbow, external power, self-suspended inner socket, removable forearm shell, Otto Bock or equal electrodes, cables, two batteries and one charger, myoelectronic control of terminal device

L6940 Elbow disarticulation, external power, molded inner socket, removable humeral shell, outside locking hinges, forearm, Otto Bock or equal switch, cables, two batteries and one charger, switch control of terminal device

Prosthetic Procedures

L6945 — L8020

L6945   Elbow disarticulation, external power, molded inner socket, removable humeral shell, outside locking hinges, forearm, Otto Bock or equal electrodes, cables, two batteries and one charger, myoelectronic control of terminal device

L6950   Above elbow, external power, molded inner socket, removable humeral shell, internal locking elbow, forearm, Otto Bock or equal switch, cables, two batteries and one charger, switch control of terminal device

L6955   Above elbow, external power, molded inner socket, removable humeral shell, internal locking elbow, forearm, Otto Bock or equal electrodes, cables, two batteries and one charger, myoelectronic control of terminal device

L6960   Shoulder disarticulation, external power, molded inner socket, removable shoulder shell, shoulder bulkhead, humeral section, mechanical elbow, forearm, Otto Bock or equal switch, cables, two batteries and one charger, switch control of terminal device

L6965   Shoulder disarticulation, external power, molded inner socket, removable shoulder shell, shoulder bulkhead, humeral section, mechanical elbow, forearm, Otto Bock or equal electrodes, cables, two batteries and one charger, myoelectronic control of terminal device

L6970   Interscapular-thoracic, external power, molded inner socket, removable shoulder shell, shoulder bulkhead, humeral section, mechanical elbow, forearm, Otto Bock or equal switch, cables, two batteries and one charger, switch control of terminal device

L6975   Interscapular-thoracic, external power, molded inner socket, removable shoulder shell, shoulder bulkhead, humeral section, mechanical elbow, forearm, Otto Bock or equal electrodes, cables, two batteries and one charger, myoelectronic control of terminal device

L7010   Electronic hand, Otto Bock, Steeper or equal, switch controlled

L7015   Electronic hand, System Teknik, Variety Village or equal, switch controlled

L7020   Electronic greifer, Otto Bock or equal, switch controlled

L7025   Electronic hand, Otto Bock or equal, myoelectronically controlled

L7030   Electronic hand, System Teknik, Variety Village or equal, myoelectronically controlled

L7035   Electronic greifer, Otto Bock or equal, myoelectronically controlled

L7040   Prehensile actuator, Hosmer or equal, switch controlled

L7045   Electronic hook, child, Michigan or equal, switch controlled

ELBOW

L7170   Electronic elbow, Hosmer or equal, switch controlled

L7180   Electronic elbow, Boston, Utah or equal, myoelectronically controlled

L7185   Electronic elbow, adolescent, Variety Village or equal, switch controlled

L7186   Electronic elbow, child, Variety Village or equal, switch controlled

L7190   Electronic elbow, adolescent, Variety Village or equal, myoelectronically controlled

L7191   Electronic elbow, child, Variety Village or equal, myoelectronically controlled

L7260   Electronic wrist rotator, Otto Bock or equal

L7261   Electronic wrist rotator, for Utah arm

L7266   Servo control, Steeper or equal

L7272   Analogue control, UNB or equal

L7274   Proportional control, 6-12 volt, Liberty, Utah or equal

BATTERY COMPONENTS

L7360   Six volt battery, Otto Bock or equal, each

L7362   Battery charger, six volt, Otto Bock or equal

L7364   Twelve volt battery, Utah or equal, each

L7366   Battery charger, twelve volt, Utah or equal

L7367   Lithium ion battery, replacement

L7368   Lithium ion battery charger

L7499   Upper extremity prosthesis, NOS

REPAIRS

L7500   Repair of prosthetic device, hourly rate
Medicare jurisdiction: local carrier if repair or implanted prosthetic device.
MED: MCM 2100.4, MCM 2130D, MCM 2133

L7510   Repair of prosthetic device, repair or replace minor parts
Medicare jurisdiction: local carrier if repair of implanted prosthetic device.
MED: MCM 2100.4, MCM 2130D, MCM 2133

☑   L7520   Repair prosthetic device, labor component, per 15 minutes
Medicare jurisdiction: local carrier if repair of implanted prosthetic device.

GENERAL

▲   L7900   Male vacuum erection system   Ⓐ ♂
This code is not noted as changed by CMS.

PROSTHESIS

L8000   Breast prosthesis, mastectomy bra   Ⓐ ♀
MED: MCM 2130 A

L8001   Breast prosthesis, mastectomy bra, with integrated breast prosthesis form, unilateral   Ⓐ ♀
MED: MCM 2130A

L8002   Breast prosthesis, mastectomy bra, with integrated breast prosthesis form, bilateral   Ⓐ ♀
MED: MCM 2130A

L8010   Breast prosthesis, mastectomy sleeve   Ⓐ ♀
MED: MCM 2130 A

L8015   External breast prosthesis garment, with mastectomy form, post-mastectomy   Ⓐ ♀
MED: MCM 2130

L8020   Breast prosthesis, mastectomy form   Ⓐ ♀
MED: MCM 2130 A

Prosthetic Procedures

L8030 — L8490

L8030 Breast prosthesis, silicone or equal ☒A ♀
MED: MCM 2130 A

L8035 Custom breast prosthesis, post mastectomy, molded to patient model ☒A ♀
MED: MCM 2130

L8039 Breast prosthesis, NOS ☒A ♀

L8040 Nasal prosthesis, provided by a non-physician

L8041 Midfacial prosthesis, provided by a non-physician

L8042 Orbital prosthesis, provided by a non-physician

L8043 Upper facial prosthesis, provided by a non-physician

L8044 Hemi-facial prosthesis, provided by a non-physician

L8045 Auricular prosthesis, provided by a non-physician

L8046 Partial facial prosthesis, provided by a non-physician

L8047 Nasal septal prosthesis, provided by a non-physician

L8048 Unspecified maxillofacial prosthesis, by report, provided by a non-physician

L8049 Repair or modification of maxillofacial prosthesis, labor component, 15 minute increments, provided by a non-physician

ELASTIC SUPPORTS

☑ L8100 Gradient compression stocking, below knee, 18-30 mmhg, each
MED: CIM 60-9, MCM 2133

☑ L8110 Gradient compression stocking, below knee, 30-40 mmhg, each
MED: MCM 2079

☑ L8120 Gradient compression stocking, below knee, 40-50 mmhg, each
MED: MCM 2079

☑ L8130 Gradient compression stocking, thigh length, 18-30 mmhg, each
MED: CIM 60-9, MCM 2133

☑ L8140 Gradient compression stocking, thigh length, 30-40 mmhg, each
MED: CIM 60-9, MCM 2133

☑ L8150 Gradient compression stocking, thigh length, 40-50 mmhg, each
MED: CIM 60-9, MCM 2133

☑ L8160 Gradient compression stocking, full length/chap style, 18-30 mmhg, each
MED: CIM 60-9, MCM 2133

☑ L8170 Gradient compression stocking, full length/chap style, 30-40 mmhg, each
MED: CIM 60-9, MCM 2133

☑ L8180 Gradient compression stocking, full length/chap style, 40-50 mmhg, each
MED: CIM 60-9, MCM 2133

☑ L8190 Gradient compression stocking, waist length, 18-30 mmhg, each
MED: CIM 60-9, MCM 2133

☑ L8195 Gradient compression stocking, waist length, 30-40 mmhg, each
MED: CIM 60-9, MCM 2133

☑ L8200 Gradient compression stocking, waist length, 40-50 mmhg, each
MED: CIM 60-9, MCM 2133

L8210 Gradient compression stocking, custom made
MED: CIM 60-9, MCM 2133

L8220 Gradient compression stocking, lymphedema
MED: CIM 60-9, MCM 2133

L8230 Gradient compression stocking, garter belt
MED: CIM 60-9, MCM 2133

L8239 Gradient compression stocking, NOS

TRUSSES

L8300 Truss, single with standard pad
MED: CIM 70-1, CIM 70-2, MCM 2133

L8310 Truss, double with standard pads
MED: CIM 70-1, CIM 70-2, MCM 2133

L8320 Truss, addition to standard pad, water pad
MED: CIM 70-1, CIM 70-2, MCM 2133

L8330 Truss, addition to standard pad, scrotal pad ♂
MED: CIM 70-1, CIM 70-2, MCM 2133

PROSTHETIC SOCKS

☑ L8400 Prosthetic sheath, below knee, each
MED: MCM 2133

☑ L8410 Prosthetic sheath, above knee, each
MED: MCM 2133

☑ L8415 Prosthetic sheath, upper limb, each
MED: MCM 2133

☑ L8417 Prosthetic sheath/sock, including a gel cushion layer, below knee or above knee, each

☑ L8420 Prosthetic sock, multiple ply, below knee, each
MED: MCM 2133

☑ L8430 Prosthetic sock, multiple ply, above knee, each
MED: MCM 2133

☑ L8435 Prosthetic sock, multiple ply, upper limb, each
MED: MCM 2133

☑ L8440 Prosthetic shrinker, below knee, each
MED: MCM 2133

☑ L8460 Prosthetic shrinker, above knee, each
MED: MCM 2133

☑ L8465 Prosthetic shrinker, upper limb, each
MED: MCM 2133

☑ L8470 Prosthetic sock, single ply, fitting, below knee, each
MED: MCM 2133

☑ L8480 Prosthetic sock, single ply, fitting, above knee, each
MED: MCM 2133

☑ L8485 Prosthetic sock, single ply, fitting, upper limb, each
MED: MCM 2133

L8490 Addition to prosthetic sheath/sock, air seal suction retention system

---

Special Coverage Instructions — Noncovered by Medicare — Carrier Discretion — ☑ Quantity Alert — ● New Code — ▲ Revised Code

104 — L Codes   M Maternity   A Adult   P Pediatrics   A-X APC Status Indicator   *2004 HCPCS*

L8499　Unlisted procedure for miscellaneous prosthetic services
Determine if an alternative HCPCS Level II or a CPT code better describes the service being reported. This code should be used only if a more specific code is unavailable.

PROSTHETIC IMPLANTS

INTEGUMENTARY SYSTEM

Ⓐ　L8500　Artificial larynx, any type
MED: CIM 65-5, MCM 2130

L8501　Tracheostomy speaking valve
MED: CIM 65-16

L8505　Artificial larynx replacement battery/accessory, any type

L8507　Tracheo-esophageal voice prosthesis, patient inserted, any type, each

L8509　Tracheo-esophageal voice prosthesis, inserted by a licensed health care provider, any type

L8510　Voice amplifier
MED: CIM 65-5

●　☑　L8511　Insert for indwelling tracheoesophageal prosthesis, with or without valve, replacement only, each

●　☑　L8512　Gelatin capsules or equivalent, for use with tracheoesophageal voice prosthesis, replacement only, per 10

●　☑　L8513　Cleaning device used with tracheoesophageal voice prosthesis, pipet, brush, or equal, replacement only, each

●　☑　L8514　Tracheoesophageal puncture dilator, replacement only, each

Ⓝ　L8600　Implantable breast prosthesis, silicone or equal　Ⓐ ♀
Medicare covers implants inserted in post-mastectomy reconstruction in a breast cancer patient. Always report concurrent to the implant procedure. Medicare jurisdiction: local carrier.
MED: CIM 35-47, MCM 2130

Ⓝ　☑　L8603　Injectable bulking agent, collagen implant, urinary tract, 2.5 ml syringe, includes shipping and necessary supplies
Medicare covers up to five separate collagen implant treatments in patients with intrinsic sphincter deficiency. Who have passed a collagen sensitivity test. Medicare jurisdiction: local carrier.
MED: CIM 65.9

Ⓝ　☑　L8606　Injectable bulking agent, synthetic implant, urinary tract, 1 ml syringe, includes shipping and necessary supplies
MED: CIM 65.9

HEAD: SKULL, FACIAL BONES, AND TEMPOROMANDIBULAR JOINT

Ⓝ　L8610　Ocular implant
Medicare jurisdiction: local carrier.
MED: MCM 2130

Ⓝ　L8612　Aqueous shunt
Medicare jurisdiction: local carrier.
MED: MCM 2130

Ⓝ　L8613　Ossicular implant
Medicare jurisdiction: local carrier.
MED: MCM 2130

Ⓝ　L8614　Cochlear device/system
A cochlear implant is covered by Medicare when the patient has bilateral sensorineural deafness. Medicare jurisdiction: local carrier.
MED: CIM 65-14, MCM 2130

Ⓐ　L8619　Cochlear implant external speech processor, replacement
Medicare jurisdiction: local carrier.
MED: CIM 65-14

UPPER EXTREMITY

Ⓝ　L8630　Metacarpophalangeal joint implant
Medicare jurisdiction: local carrier.
MED: MCM 2130

●　L8631　Metacarpal phalangeal joint replacement, two or more pieces, metal (e.g., stainless steel or cobalt chrome), ceramic-like material (e.g., pyrocarbon), for surgical implantation (all sizes, includes entire system)
MED: MCM 2130

LOWER EXTREMITY — JOINT: KNEE, ANKLE, TOE

Ⓝ　L8641　Metatarsal joint implant
Medicare jurisdiction: local carrier.
MED: MCM 2130

Ⓝ　L8642　Hallux implant
Medicare jurisdiction: local carrier.
MED: MCM 2130

MISCELLANEOUS MUSCULAR-SKELETAL

▲　Ⓝ　L8658　Interphalangeal joint spacer, silicone or equal, each
Medicare jurisdiction: local carrier.
MED: MCM 2130

●　L8659　Interphalangeal finger joint replacement, two or more pieces, metal (e.g., stainless steel or cobalt chrome), ceramic-like material (e.g., pyrocarbon) for surgical implantation, any size
MED: MCM 2130

CARDIOVASCULAR SYSTEM

Ⓝ　L8670　Vascular graft material, synthetic, implant
Medicare jurisdiction: local carrier.
MED: MCM 2130

GENERAL

Ⓝ　L8699　Prosthetic implant, not otherwise specified
Determine if an alternative HCPCS Level II or a CPT code better describes the service being reported. This code should be used only if a more specific code is unavailable. Medicare jurisdiction: local carrier.

Ⓐ　L9900　Orthotic and prosthetic supply, accessory, and/or service component of another HCPCS L code

---

MEDICAL SERVICES *M0000-M0301*

OTHER MEDICAL SERVICES

M codes include office services, cellular therapy, prolotherapy, intragastric hypothermia, IV chelation therapy, and fabric wrapping of an abdominal aneurysm (MNP).

M codes fall under the jurisdiction of the local carrier

  ☒   **M0064** **Brief office visit for the sole purpose of monitoring or changing drug prescriptions used in the treatment of mental psychoneurotic and personality disorders**
            MED: MCM 2476.3

  🅴   **M0075** **Cellular therapy**
            The therapeutic efficacy of injecting foreign proteins has not been established.
            MED: CIM 35-5

  🅴   **M0076** **Prolotherapy**
            The therapeutic efficacy of prolotherapy and joint sclerotherapy has not been established.
            MED: CIM 35-13

▲ 🅴   **M0100** **Intragastric hypothermia using gastric freezing**
            Code with caution: This procedure is considered obsolete.
            MED: CIM 35-65

CARDIOVASCULAR SERVICES

  🅴   **M0300** **IV chelation therapy (chemical endarterectomy)**
            Chelation therapy is considered experimental in the United States.
            MED: CIM 35-64

▲ 🅴   **M0301** **Fabric wrapping of abdominal aneurysm**
            Code with caution: This procedure has largely been replaced with more effective treatment modalities. Submit documentation.
            MED: CIM 35-34

Special Coverage Instructions   Noncovered by Medicare   Carrier Discretion   ☑ Quantity Alert   ● New Code   ▲ Revised Code

PATHOLOGY AND LABORATORY SERVICES *P0000-P9999*

P codes include chemistry, toxicology, and microbiology tests, screening Papanicolaou procedures, and various blood products.

CHEMISTRY AND TOXICOLOGY TESTS
P codes fall under the jurisdiction of the local carrier.

[A] **P2028** Cephalin floculation, blood
Code with caution: This test is considered obsolete. Submit documentation.
MED: CIM 50-34

[A] **P2029** Congo red, blood
Code with caution: This test is considered obsolete. Submit documentation.
MED: CIM 50-34

[E] **P2031** Hair analysis (excluding arsenic)
For hair analysis for arsenic see CPT codes 83015, 82175.
MED: CIM 50-24

[A] **P2033** Thymol turbidity, blood
Code with caution: This test is considered obsolete. Submit documentation.
MED: CIM 50-34

[A] **P2038** Mucoprotein, blood (seromucoid) (medical necessity procedure)
Code with caution: This test is considered obsolete. Submit documentation.
MED: CIM 50-34

PATHOLOGY SCREENING TESTS

[A] **P3000** Screening Papanicolaou smear, cervical or vaginal, up to three smears, by technician under physician supervision   [A] ♀
One Pap test is covered by Medicare every three years, unless the physician suspects cervical abnormalities and shortens the interval. See also G0123-G0124.
MED: CIM 50-20

[E] **P3001** Screening Papanicolaou smear, cervical or vaginal, up to three smears, requiring interpretation by physician   [A] ♀
One Pap test is covered by Medicare every three years, unless the physician suspects cervical abnormalities and shortens the interval. See also G0123-G0124.
MED: CIM 50-20

MICROBIOLOGY TESTS

[E] **P7001** Culture, bacterial, urine; quantitative, sensitivity study
Cross-reference CPT

MISCELLANEOUS

[K] ☑ **P9010** Blood (whole), for transfusion, per unit
MED: MCM 2455A

[E] ☑ **P9011** Blood (split unit), specify amount
MED: MCM 2455A

[K] ☑ **P9012** Cryoprecipitate, each unit
MED: MCM 2455 B

[K] ☑ **P9016** Red blood cells, leukocytes reduced, each unit
MED: MCM 2455 B

▲ [K] ☑ **P9017** Fresh frozen plasma (single donor), frozen within 8 hours of collection, each unit
MED: MCM 2455 B

[K] ☑ **P9019** Platelets, each unit
MED: MCM 2455 B

[K] ☑ **P9020** Platelet rich plasma, each unit
MED: MCM 2455 B

[K] ☑ **P9021** Red blood cells, each unit
MED: MCM 2455A

[K] ☑ **P9022** Red blood cells, washed, each unit
MED: MCM 2455A

[K] ☑ **P9023** Plasma, pooled multiple donor, solvent/detergent treated, frozen, each unit
MED: MCM 2455 B

[K] ☑ **P9031** Platelets, leukocytes reduced, each unit
MED: MCM 2455

[K] ☑ **P9032** Platelets, irradiated, each unit
MED: MCM 2455

[K] ☑ **P9033** Platelets, leukocytes reduced, irradiated, each unit
MED: MCM 2455

[K] ☑ **P9034** Platelets, pheresis, each unit
MED: MCM 2455

[K] ☑ **P9035** Platelets, pheresis, leukocytes reduced, each unit
MED: MCM 2455

[K] ☑ **P9036** Platelets, pheresis, irradiated, each unit
MED: MCM 2455

[K] ☑ **P9037** Platelets, pheresis, leukocytes reduced, irradiated, each unit
MED: MCM 2455

[K] ☑ **P9038** Red blood cells, irradiated, each unit
MED: MCM 2455

[K] ☑ **P9039** Red blood cells, deglycerolized, each unit
MED: MCM 2455

[K] ☑ **P9040** Red blood cells, leukocytes reduced, irradiated, each unit
MED: MCM 2455

[K] ☑ **P9041** Infusion, albumin (human), 5%, 50 ml

[K] ☑ **P9043** Infusion, plasma protein fraction (human), 5%, 50 ml
MED: MCM 2455B

[K] ☑ **P9044** Plasma, cryoprecipitate reduced, each unit
MED: MCM 2455.B

[K] ☑ **P9045** Infusion, albumin (human), 5%, 250 ml

[K] ☑ **P9046** Infusion, albumin (human), 25%, 20 ml

[K] ☑ **P9047** Infusion, albumin (human), 25%, 50 ml

[K] ☑ **P9048** Infusion, plasma protein fraction (human), 5%, 250 ml

[K] ☑ **P9050** Granulocytes, pheresis, each unit

● ☑ **P9051** Whole blood or red blood cells, leukocytes reduced, CMV-negative, each unit
MED: Medicare Statute 1833T

● ☑ **P9052** Platelets, HLA-matched leukocytes reduced, apheresis/pheresis, each unit
MED: Medicare Statute 1833T

Special Coverage Instructions   Noncovered by Medicare   Carrier Discretion   ☑ Quantity Alert   ● New Code   ▲ Revised Code

●   ☑   **P9053** Platelets, pheresis, leukocytes reduced, CMV-negative, irradiated, each unit
MED: Medicare Statute 1833T

●   ☑   **P9054** Whole blood or red blood cells, leukocytes reduced, frozen, deglycerol, washed, each unit
MED: Medicare Statute 1833T

●   ☑   **P9055** Platelets, leukocytes reduced, CMV-negative, apheresis/pheresis, each unit
MED: Medicare Statute 1833T

●   ☑   **P9056** Whole blood, leukocytes reduced, irradiated, each unit
MED: Medicare Statute 1833T

●   ☑   **P9057** Red blood cells, frozen/deglycerolized/washed, leukocytes reduced, irradiated, each unit
MED: Medicare Statute 1833T

●   ☑   **P9058** Red blood cells, leukocytes reduced, CMV-negative, irradiated, each unit
MED: Medicare Statute 1833T

●   ☑   **P9059** Fresh frozen plasma between 8-24 hours of collection, each unit
MED: Medicare Statute 1833T

●   ☑   **P9060** Fresh frozen plasma, donor retested, each unit
MED: Medicare Statute 1833T

Ⓐ   ☑   **P9603** Travel allowance one way in connection with medically necessary laboratory specimen collection drawn from homebound or nursing home bound patient; prorated miles actually travelled
MED: MCM 51141K

Ⓐ   ☑   **P9604** Travel allowance one way in connection with medically necessary laboratory specimen collection drawn from homebound or nursing home bound patient; prorated trip charge
MED: MCM 51141K

Ⓝ   **P9612** Catheterization for collection of specimen, single patient, all places of service
See also new CPT catheterization codes 51701-51703
MED: MCM 5114.1D

Ⓝ   **P9615** Catheterization for collection of specimen(s) (multiple patients)
See also new CPT catheterization codes 51701-51703
MED: MCM 51141D

Q CODES (TEMPORARY) *Q0000–Q9999*

New temporary Q codes to pay health care providers for the supplies used in creating casts were established to replace the removal of the practice expense for all HCPCS codes, including the CPT codes for fracture management and for casts and splints. Coders should continue to use the appropriate CPT code to report the work and practice expenses involved with creating the cast or splint; the temporary Q codes replace less specific coding for the casting and splinting supplies.

Q codes fall under the jurisdiction of the local carrier unless they represent an incidental service or are otherwise specified.

X   **Q0035** Cardiokymography
Covered only in conjunction with electrocardiographic stress testing in male patients with atypical angina or nonischemic chest pain, or female patients with angina.
MED: CIM 50-50

T   **Q0081** Infusion therapy, using other than chemotherapeutic drugs, per visit
MED: CIM 60-14

S   **Q0083** Chemotherapy administration by other than infusion technique only (e.g., subcutaneous, intramuscular, push), per visit

S ☑ **Q0084** Chemotherapy administration by infusion technique only, per visit
MED: CIM 60-14

S ☑ **Q0085** Chemotherapy administration by both infusion technique and other technique(s) (e.g., subcutaneous, intramuscular, push), per visit

~~Q0086 Physical therapy evaluation/treatment, per visit~~

T   **Q0091** Screening Papanicolaou smear; obtaining, preparing and conveyance of cervical or vaginal smear to laboratory   A ♀
One Pap test is covered by Medicare every three years, unless the physician suspects cervical abnormalities and shortens the interval. Q0091 can be reported with an E/M code when a separately identifiable E/M service is provided.
MED: CIM 50-20

N   **Q0092** Set-up portable x-ray equipment
MED: MCM 2070.4

A   **Q0111** Wet mounts, including preparations of vaginal, cervical or skin specimens   ♀

A   **Q0112** All potassium hydroxide (KOH) preparations
MED: Lab Certification - Mycology

A   **Q0113** Pinworm examination
MED: Lab Certification - Parasitology

A   **Q0114** Fern test
MED: Lab Certification - Routine Chemistry

A   **Q0115** Post-coital direct, qualitative examinations of vaginal or cervical mucous   A ♀
MED: Lab Certification - Hematology

K ☑ **Q0136** Injection, epoetin alpha, (for non ESRD use), per 1,000 units
This code is for EPO used to treat anemia in patients undergoing chemotherapy for non-myeloid malignancies. Use this code for Epogen, Procrit.
MED: MCM 2049

● ☑ **Q0137** Injection, darbepoetin alfa, 1 mcg (non-ESRD use)
This code is for EPO used to treat anemia in patients undergoing chemotherapy for non-myeloid malignancies. Use this code for Aranesp.
MED: MCM 4273.1

E   **Q0144** Azithromycin dihydrate, oral, capsules/powder, 1 gram
Use this code for Zithromax, Zithromax Z-PAK.

N   **Q0163** Diphenhydramine HCl, 50 mg, oral, FDA approved prescription anti-emetic, for use as a complete therapeutic substitute for an IV anti-emetic at time of chemotherapy treatment not to exceed a 48-hour dosage regimen
See also J1200. Medicare covers at the time of chemotherapy if regimen doesn't exceed 48 hours. Submit on the same claim as the chemotherapy.
MED: Medicare Statute: 4557

N   **Q0164** Prochlorperazine maleate, 5 mg, oral, FDA approved prescription anti-emetic, for use as a complete therapeutic substitute for an IV anti-emetic at the time of chemotherapy treatment, not to exceed a 48-hour dosage regimen
Medicare covers at the time of chemotherapy if regimen doesn't exceed 48 hours. Submit on the same claim as the chemotherapy. Medicare jurisdiction: DME regional carrier. Use this code for Compazine.
MED: Medicare Statute: 4557

E   **Q0165** Prochlorperazine maleate, 10 mg, oral, FDA approved prescription anti-emetic, for use as a complete therapeutic substitute for an IV anti-emetic at the time of chemotherapy treatment, not to exceed a 48-hour dosage regimen
Medicare covers at the time of chemotherapy if regimen doesn't exceed 48 hours. Submit on the same claim as the chemotherapy. Medicare jurisdiction: DME regional carrier. Use this code for Compazine.
MED: Medicare Statute: 4557

N   **Q0166** Granisetron HCl, 1 mg, oral, FDA approved prescription anti-emetic, for use as a complete therapeutic substitute for an IV anti-emetic at the time of chemotherapy treatment, not to exceed a 24-hour dosage regimen
Medicare covers at the time of chemotherapy if regimen doesn't exceed 48 hours. Submit on the same claim as the chemotherapy. Medicare jurisdiction: DME regional carrier. Use this code for Kytril.
MED: Medicare Statute: 4557

N   **Q0167** Dronabinol, 2.5 mg, oral, FDA approved prescription anti-emetic, for use as a complete therapeutic substitute for an IV anti-emetic at the time of chemotherapy treatment, not to exceed a 48-hour dosage regimen
Medicare covers at the time of chemotherapy if regimen doesn't exceed 48 hours. Submit on the same claim as the chemotherapy. Medicare jurisdiction: DME regional carrier. Use this code for Marinol.
MED: Medicare Statute: 4557

E   **Q0168** Dronabinol, 5 mg, oral, FDA approved prescription anti-emetic, for use as a complete therapeutic substitute for an IV anti-emetic at the time of chemotherapy treatment, not to exceed a 48-hour dosage regimen
Medicare jurisdiction: DME regional carrier. Use this code for Marinol.
MED: Medicare Statute: 4557

Q Codes (Temporary)

Q0169 — Q0181

N **Q0169** Promethazine HCl, 12.5 mg, oral, FDA approved prescription anti-emetic, for use as a complete therapeutic substitute for an IV anti-emetic at the time of chemotherapy treatment, not to exceed a 48-hour dosage regimen
Medicare covers at the time of chemotherapy if regimen doesn't exceed 48 hours. Submit on the same claim as the chemotherapy. Medicare jurisdiction: DME regional carrier. Use this code for Phenergan, Amergan.

MED: Medicare Statute: 4557

E **Q0170** Promethazine HCl, 25 mg, oral, FDA approved prescription anti-emetic, for use as a complete therapeutic substitute for an IV anti-emetic at the time of chemotherapy treatment, not to exceed a 48-hour dosage regimen
Medicare covers at the time of chemotherapy if regimen doesn't exceed 48 hours. Submit on the same claim as the chemotherapy. Medicare jurisdiction: DME regional carrier. Use this code for Phenergan, Amergan.

MED: Medicare Statute: 4557

N **Q0171** Chlorpromazine HCl, 10 mg, oral, FDA approved prescription anti-emetic, for use as a complete therapeutic substitute for an IV anti-emetic at the time of chemotherapy treatment, not to exceed a 48-hour dosage regimen
Medicare covers at the time of chemotherapy if regimen doesn't exceed 48 hours. Submit on the same claim as the chemotherapy. Medicare jurisdiction: DME regional carrier. Use this code for Thorazine.

MED: Medicare Statute: 4557

E **Q0172** Chlorpromazine HCl, 25 mg, oral, FDA approved prescription anti-emetic, for use as a complete therapeutic substitute for an IV anti-emetic at the time of chemotherapy treatment, not to exceed a 48-hour dosage regimen
Medicare covers at the time of chemotherapy if regimen doesn't exceed 48 hours. Submit on the same claim as the chemotherapy. Medicare jurisdiction: DME regional carrier. Use this code for Thorazine.

MED: Medicare Statute: 4557

N **Q0173** Trimethobenzamide HCl, 250 mg, oral, FDA approved prescription anti-emetic, for use as a complete therapeutic substitute for an IV anti-emetic at the time of chemotherapy treatment, not to exceed a 48-hour dosage regimen
Medicare covers at the time of chemotherapy if regimen doesn't exceed 48 hours. Submit on the same claim as the chemotherapy. Medicare jurisdiction: DME regional carrier. Use this code for Tebamide, T-Gen, Ticon, Tigan, Triban, Thimazide.

MED: Medicare Statute: 4557

N **Q0174** Thiethylperazine maleate, 10 mg, oral, FDA approved prescription anti-emetic, for use as a complete therapeutic substitute for an IV anti-emetic at the time of chemotherapy treatment, not to exceed a 48-hour dosage regimen
Medicare covers at the time of chemotherapy if regimen doesn't exceed 48 hours. Submit on the same claim as the chemotherapy. Medicare jurisdiction: DME regional carrier. Use this code for Torecan.

MED: Medicare Statute: 4557

N **Q0175** Perphenazine, 4 mg, oral, FDA approved prescription anti-emetic, for use as a complete therapeutic substitute for an IV anti-emetic at the time of chemotherapy treatment, not to exceed a 48-hour dosage regimen
Medicare covers at the time of chemotherapy if regimen doesn't exceed 48 hours. Submit on the same claim as the chemotherapy. Medicare jurisdiction: DME regional carrier. Use this code for Trilifon.

MED: Medicare Statute: 4557

E **Q0176** Perphenazine, 8mg, oral, FDA approved prescription anti-emetic, for use as a complete therapeutic substitute for an IV anti-emetic at the time of chemotherapy treatment, not to exceed a 48-hour dosage regimen
Medicare covers at the time of chemotherapy if regimen doesn't exceed 48 hours. Submit on the same claim as the chemotherapy. Medicare jurisdiction: DME regional carrier. Use this code for Trilifon.

MED: Medicare Statute: 4557

N **Q0177** Hydroxyzine pamoate, 25 mg, oral, FDA approved prescription anti-emetic, for use as a complete therapeutic substitute for an IV anti-emetic at the time of chemotherapy treatment, not to exceed a 48-hour dosage regimen
Medicare covers at the time of chemotherapy if regimen doesn't exceed 48 hours. Submit on the same claim as the chemotherapy. Medicare jurisdiction: DME regional carrier. Use this code for Vistaril.

MED: Medicare Statute: 4557

E **Q0178** Hydroxyzine pamoate, 50 mg, oral, FDA approved prescription anti-emetic, for use as a complete therapeutic substitute for an IV anti-emetic at the time of chemotherapy treatment, not to exceed a 48-hour dosage regimen
Medicare covers at the time of chemotherapy if regimen doesn't exceed 48 hours. Submit on the same claim as the chemotherapy.

MED: Medicare Statute: 4557

N **Q0179** Ondansetron HCl 8 mg, oral, FDA approved prescription anti-emetic, for use as a complete therapeutic substitute for an IV anti-emetic at the time of chemotherapy treatment, not to exceed a 48-hour dosage regimen
Medicare covers at the time of chemotherapy if regimen doesn't exceed 48 hours. Submit on the same claim as the chemotherapy. Medicare jurisdiction: DME regional carrier. Use this code for Zofran.

MED: Medicare Statute: 4557

N **Q0180** Dolasetron mesylate, 100 mg, oral, FDA approved prescription anti-emetic, for use as a complete therapeutic substitute for an IV anti-emetic at the time of chemotherapy treatment, not to exceed a 24-hour dosage regimen
Medicare covers at the time of chemotherapy if regimen doesn't exceed 24 hours. Submit on the same claim as the chemotherapy. Medicare jurisdiction: DME regional carrier. Use this code for Anzemet.

MED: Medicare Statute: 4557

E **Q0181** Unspecified oral dosage form, FDA approved prescription anti-emetic, for use as a complete therapeutic substitute for an IV anti-emetic at the time of chemotherapy treatment, not to exceed a 48-hour dosage regimen
Medicare covers at the time of chemotherapy if regimen doesn't exceed 48-hours. Submit on the same claim as the chemotherapy. Medicare jurisdiction: DME regional carrier.

MED: Medicare Statute: 4557

● ☑ **Q0182** Dermal and epidermal, tissue of non-human origin, with or without other bioengineered or processed elements, without metabolically active elements, per square centimeter

N ☑ **Q0183** Dermal tissue, of human origin, with and without other bioengineered or processed elements, but without metabolically active elements, per square centimeter

K ☑ **Q0187** Factor VIIa (coagulation factor, recombinant) per 1.2 mg ♂
Use this code for NovoSeven.
MED: MCM 2049

Q1001 New technology intraocular lens category 1 as defined in Federal Register notice, Vol. 65, date May 3, 2000

Q1002 New technology intraocular lens category 2 as defined in Federal Register notice, Vol. 65, dated May 3, 2000

Q1003 New technology intraocular lens category 3 as defined in Federal Register notice

Q1004 New technology intraocular lens category 4 as defined in Federal Register notice

Q1005 New technology intraocular lens category 5 as defined in Federal Register notice

N ☑ **Q2001** Oral, cabergoline, 0.5 mg
Use this code for Dostinex.
MED: MCM 2049.5

N ☑ **Q2002** Injection, Elliott's B solution, per ml
Use this code for Dextrose/electsol, IV.
MED: MCM 2049, Medicare Statute: 1861S2B

N ☑ **Q2003** Injection, aprotinin, 10,000 kiu
Use this code for Trasylol.
MED: MCM 2049, Medicare Statute: 1861S2B

N ☑ **Q2004** Irrigation solution for treatment of bladder calculi, for example renacidin, per 500 ml
Use this code for Renacidin.
MED: MCM 2049, Medicare Statute: 1861S2B

K ☑ **Q2005** Injection, corticorelin ovine triflutate, per dose
Use this code for Acthrel.
MED: MCM 2049, Medicare Statute: 1861S2B

K ☑ **Q2006** Injection, digoxin immune fab (ovine), per vial
Use this code for Digibind.
MED: MCM 2049, Medicare Statute: 1861S2B

N ☑ **Q2007** Injection, ethanolamine oleate, 100 mg
Use this code for Ethamolin.
MED: MCM 2049, Medicare Statute: 1861S2B

N ☑ **Q2008** Injection, fomepizole, 15 mg
Use this code for Antizol.
MED: MCM 2049, Medicare Statute: 1861S2B

N ☑ **Q2009** Injection, fosphenytoin, 50 mg
Use this code for Cerebryx.
MED: MCM 2049, Medicare Statute: 1861S2B

~~**Q2010** Injection, glatiramer acetate, per dose~~

K ☑ **Q2011** Injection, hemin, per 1 mg
Use this code for Panhematin.
MED: MCM 2049, Medicare Statute: 1861S2B

N ☑ **Q2012** Injection, pegademase bovine, 25 IU
Use this code for Adagen.
MED: MCM 2049, Medicare Statute: 1861S2B

N ☑ **Q2013** Injection, pentastarch, 10% solution, per 100 ml
Use this code for Pentaspan.
MED: MCM 2049, Medicare Statute: 1861S2B

N ☑ **Q2014** Injection, sermorelin acetate, 0.5 mg
Use this code for Geref diagnostic.
MED: MCM 2049, Medicare Statute: 1861S2B

K ☑ **Q2017** Injection, teniposide, 50 mg
Use this code for Vumon.
MED: MCM 2049, Medicare Statute: 1861S2B

N ☑ **Q2018** Injection, urofollitropin, 75 IU
Use this code for Fertinex.
MED: MCM 2049, Medicare Statute: 1861S2B

K ☑ **Q2019** Injection, basiliximab, 20 mg
Use this code for Simulect.
MED: MCM 2049

E ☑ **Q2020** Injection, histrelin acetate, 10 mg
Use this code for Supprelin.
MED: MCM 2049, Medicare Statute: 1861S2B

N ☑ **Q2021** Injection, lepirudin, 50 mg
Use this code for Refludan.
MED: MCM 2049, Medicare Statute: 1861S2B

K ☑ **Q2022** von Willebrand factor complex, human, per IU
MED: CIM 35.30, MCM 2049.5

K ☑ **Q3000** Supply of radiopharmaceutical diagnostic imaging agent, rubidium Rb-82, per dose

N ☑ **Q3001** Radioelements for brachytherapy, any type, each
MED: MCM 15022

N ☑ **Q3002** Supply of radiopharmaceutical diagnostic imaging agent, Gallium Ga 67, per millicurie
MED: MCM 15022

K ☑ **Q3003** Supply of radiopharmaceutical diagnostic imaging agent, technetium Tc 99m bicisate, per unit dose
MED: MCM 15022

N ☑ **Q3004** Supply of radiopharmaceutical diagnostic imaging agent, xenon Xe 133, per 10 millicurie
MED: MCM 15022

N ☑ **Q3005** Supply of radiopharmaceutical diagnostic imaging agent, technetium Tc 99m mertiatide, per millicurie
MED: MCM 15022

N ☑ **Q3006** Supply of radiopharmaceutical diagnostic imaging agent, technetium Tc 99m glucepatate, per 5 millicurie
MED: MCM 15022

N ☑ **Q3007** Supply of radiopharmaceutical diagnostic imaging agent, sodium phosphate P32, per millicurie
MED: MCM 15022

K ☑ **Q3008** Supply of radiopharmaceutical diagnostic imaging agent, indium 111 — in pentetreotide, per 3 millicurie
MED: MCM 15022

N ☑ **Q3009** Supply of radiopharmaceutical diagnostic imaging agent, technetium Tc 99m oxidronate, per millicurie
MED: MCM 15022

Q Codes (Temporary)

Q3010 — Q4046

N ☑ **Q3010** Supply of radiopharmaceutical diagnostic imaging agent, technetium Tc 99m — labeled red blood cells, per millicurie
MED: MCM 15022

K ☑ **Q3011** Supply of radiopharmaceutical diagnostic imaging agent, chromic phosphate P32 suspension, per millicurie
MED: MCM 15022

N ☑ **Q3012** Supply of oral radiopharmaceutical diagnostic imaging agent, cyanocobalamin cobalt Co57, per 0.5 millicurie
MED: MCM 15022

A **Q3014** Telehealth originating site facility fee

A **Q3019** ALS vehicle used, emergency transport, no ALS level services furnished

A **Q3020** ALS vehicle used, non-emergency transport, no ALS level service furnished

K **Q3025** Injection, interferon beta-1A, 11 mcg for intramuscular use
Use this code for Avonex. See also J1825.
MED: MCM 2049

N **Q3026** Injection, interferon beta-1A, 11 mcg for subcutaneous use
Use this code for Avonex. See also J1825.

● N **Q3031** Collagen skin test
MED: Proc Stat: B, CIM 65-9

Q4001 Casting supplies, body cast adult, with or without head, plaster   A

Q4002 Cast supplies, body cast adult, with or without head, fiberglass   A

Q4003 Cast supplies, shoulder cast, adult (11 years +), plaster   A

Q4004 Cast supplies, shoulder cast, adult (11 years +), fiberglass   A

Q4005 Cast supplies, long arm cast, adult (11 years +), plaster   A

Q4006 Cast supplies, long arm cast, adult (11 years +), fiberglass   A

Q4007 Cast supplies, long arm cast, pediatric (0-10 years), plaster   P

Q4008 Cast supplies, long arm cast, pediatric (0-10 years), fiberglass   P

Q4009 Cast supplies, short arm cast, adult (11 years +), plaster   A

Q4010 Cast supplies, short arm cast, adult (11 years +), fiberglass   A

Q4011 Cast supplies, short arm cast, pediatric (0-10 years), plaster   P

Q4012 Cast supplies, short arm cast, pediatric (0-10 years), fiberglass   P

Q4013 Cast supplies, gauntlet cast (includes lower forearm and hand), adult (11 years +), plaster   A

Q4014 Cast supplies, gauntlet cast (includes lower forearm and hand), adult (11 years +), fiberglass   A

Q4015 Cast supplies, gauntlet cast (includes lower forearm and hand), pediatric (0-10 years), plaster   P

Q4016 Cast supplies, gauntlet cast (includes lower forearm and hand), pediatric (0-10 years), fiberglass   P

Q4017 Cast supplies, long arm splint, adult (11 years +), plaster   A

Q4018 Cast supplies, long arm splint, adult (11 years +), fiberglass   A

Q4019 Cast supplies, long arm splint, pediatric (0-10 years), plaster   P

Q4020 Cast supplies, long arm splint, pediatric (0-10 years), fiberglass   P

Q4021 Cast supplies, short arm splint, adult (11 years +), plaster   A

Q4022 Cast supplies, short arm splint, adult (11 years +), fiberglass   A

Q4023 Cast supplies, short arm splint, pediatric (0-10 years), plaster   P

Q4024 Cast supplies, short arm splint, pediatric (0-10 years), fiberglass   P

Q4025 Cast supplies, hip spica (one or both legs), adult (11 years +), plaster   A

Q4026 Cast supplies, hip spica (one or both legs), adult (11 years +), fiberglass   A

Q4027 Cast supplies, hip spica (one or both legs), pediatric (0-10 years), plaster   P

Q4028 Cast supplies, hip spica (one or both legs), pediatric (0-10 years), fiberglass   P

Q4029 Cast supplies, long leg cast, adult (11 years +), plaster   A

Q4030 Cast supplies, long leg cast, adult (11 years +), fiberglass   A

Q4031 Cast supplies, long leg cast, pediatric (0-10 years), plaster   P

Q4032 Cast supplies, long leg cast, pediatric (0-10 years), fiberglass   P

Q4033 Cast supplies, long leg cylinder cast, adult (11 years +), plaster   A

Q4034 Cast supplies, long leg cylinder cast, adult (11 years +), fiberglass   A

Q4035 Cast supplies, long leg cylinder cast, pediatric (0-10 years), plaster   P

Q4036 Cast supplies, long leg cylinder cast, pediatric (0-10 years), fiberglass   P

Q4037 Cast supplies, short leg cast, adult (11 years +), plaster   A

Q4038 Cast supplies, short leg cast, adult (11 years +), fiberglass   A

Q4039 Cast supplies, short leg cast, pediatric (0-10 years), plaster   P

Q4040 Cast supplies, short leg cast, pediatric (0-10 years), fiberglass   P

Q4041 Cast supplies, long leg splint, adult (11 years +), plaster   A

Q4042 Cast supplies, long leg splint, adult (11 years +), fiberglass   A

Q4043 Cast supplies, long leg splint, pediatric (0-10 years), plaster   P

Q4044 Cast supplies, long leg splint, pediatric (0-10 years), fiberglass   P

Q4045 Cast supplies, short leg splint, adult (11 years +), plaster   A

Q4046 Cast supplies, short leg splint, adult (11 years +), fiberglass   A

Q4047   Cast supplies, short leg splint, pediatric (0-10 years), plaster   P

Q4048   Cast supplies, short leg splint, pediatric (0-10 years), fiberglass   P

Q4049   Finger splint, static

Q4050   Cast supplies, for unlisted types and materials of casts

Q4051   Splint supplies, miscellaneous (includes thermoplastics, strapping, fasteners, padding and other supplies)

~~Q4052~~   ~~Injection, octreotide, depot form for intramuscular injection, 1 mg~~

    See code J2353.

~~Q4053~~   ~~Injection, pegfilgrastim, 1 mg~~

    See code J2505.

● ☑ Q4054   Injection, darbepoetin alfa, 1 mcg (for ESRD on dialysis)
    Use this code for Aranesp.

● ☑ Q4055   Injection, epoetin alfa, 1000 units (for ESRD on dialysis)
    MED: MCM 4273.1

● ☑ Q4075   Injection, acyclovir, 5 mg

● ☑ Q4076   Injection, dopamine HCl, 40 mg

● ☑ Q4077   Injection, treprostinil, 1 mg

~~Q4078~~   ~~Supply of radiopharmaceutical diagnostic imaging agent, ammonia N-13, per dose~~

    See code A9526.

INJECTION CODES FOR EPOETIN ALPHA (EPO)

~~Q0020~~   ~~Injection of epo, per 1000 units, at patient hct of 20 or less~~

    See codes Q4054-Q4055.

~~Q0021~~   ~~Injection of epo, per 1000 units, at patient hct of 21~~

    See codes Q4054-Q4055.

~~Q0022~~   ~~Injection of epo, per 1000 units, at patient hct of 22~~

    See codes Q4054-Q4055.

~~Q0023~~   ~~Injection of epo, per 1000 units, at patient hct of 23~~

    See codes Q4054-Q4055.

~~Q0024~~   ~~Injection of epo, per 1000 units, at patient hct of 24~~

    See codes Q4054-Q4055.

~~Q0025~~   ~~Injection of epo, per 1000 units, at patient hct of 25~~

    See codes Q4054-Q4055.

~~Q0026~~   ~~Injection of epo, per 1000 units, at patient hct of 26~~

    See codes Q4054-Q4055.

~~Q0027~~   ~~Injection of epo, per 1000 units, at patient hct of 27~~

    See codes Q4054-Q4055.

~~Q0028~~   ~~Injection of epo, per 1000 units, at patient hct of 28~~

    See codes Q4054-Q4055.

~~Q0029~~   ~~Injection of epo, per 1000 units, at patient hct of 29~~

    See codes Q4054-Q4055.

~~Q0030~~   ~~Injection of epo, per 1000 units, at patient hct of 30~~

    See codes Q4054-Q4055.

~~Q0031~~   ~~Injection of epo, per 1000 units, at patient hct of 31~~

    See codes Q4054-Q4055.

~~Q0032~~   ~~Injection of epo, per 1000 units, at patient hct of 32~~

    See codes Q4054-Q4055.

~~Q0033~~   ~~Injection of epo, per 1000 units, at patient hct of 33~~

    See codes Q4054-Q4055.

~~Q0034~~   ~~Injection of epo, per 1000 units, at patient hct of 34~~

    See codes Q4054-Q4055.

~~Q0035~~   ~~Injection of epo, per 1000 units, at patient hct of 35~~

    See codes Q4054-Q4055.

~~Q0036~~   ~~Injection of epo, per 1000 units, at patient hct of 36~~

    See codes Q4054-Q4055.

~~Q0037~~   ~~Injection of epo, per 1000 units, at patient hct of 37~~

    See codes Q4054-Q4055.

~~Q0038~~   ~~Injection of epo, per 1000 units, at patient hct of 38~~

    See codes Q4054-Q4055.

~~Q0039~~   ~~Injection of epo, per 1000 units, at patient hct of 39~~

    See codes Q4054-Q4055.

~~Q0040~~   ~~Injection of epo, per 1000 units, at patient hct of 40 or above~~

    See codes Q4054-Q4055.

DIAGNOSTIC RADIOLOGY SERVICES *R0000-R5999*

R codes are used for the transportation of portable x-ray and/or EKG equipment.

R codes fall under the jurisdiction of the local carrier.

N ☑ **R0070** **Transportation of portable x-ray equipment and personnel to home or nursing home, per trip to facility or location, one patient seen**
Only a single, reasonable transportation charge is allowed for each trip the portable x-ray supplier makes to a location. When more than one patient is x-rayed at the same location, prorate the single allowable transport charge among all patients.

MED: MCM 2070.4, MCM 5244.B

N ☑ **R0075** **Transportation of portable x-ray equipment and personnel to home or nursing home, per trip to facility or location, more than one patient seen**
Only a single, reasonable transportation charge is allowed for each trip the portable x-ray supplier makes to a location. When more than one patient is x-rayed at the same location, prorate the single allowable transport charge among all patients.

MED: MCM 2070.4, MCM 5244.B

N ☑ **R0076** **Transportation of portable EKG to facility or location, per patient**
Only a single, reasonable transportation charge is allowed for each trip the portable EKG supplier makes to a location. When more than one patient is tested at the same location, prorate the single allowable transport charge among all patients.

MED: CIM 50-15, MCM 2070.1, MCM 2070.4

TEMPORARY NATIONAL CODES (NON-MEDICARE)
S0000-S9999

The S codes are used by the Blue Cross/Blue Shield Association (BCBSA) and the Health Insurance Association of America (HIAA) to report drugs, services, and supplies for which there are no national codes but for which codes are needed by the private sector to implement policies, programs, or claims processing. They are for the purpose of meeting the particular needs of the private sector. These codes are also used by the Medicaid program, but they are not payable by Medicare.

~~S0009~~   ~~Injection, butorphanol tartrate, 1 mg~~

☑ **S0012**   Butorphanol tartrate, nasal spray, 25 mg
Use this code for Stadol NS.

☑ **S0014**   Tacrine HCl, 10 mg
Use this code for Cognex.

☑ **S0016**   Injection, amikacin sulfate, 500 mg
Use this code for Amikin.

☑ **S0017**   Injection, aminocaproic acid, 5 grams
Use this code for Amicar.

☑ **S0020**   Injection, bupivicaine HCl, 30 ml
Use this code for Marcaine, Sensorcaine.

☑ **S0021**   Injection, ceftoperazone sodium, 1 gram
Use this code for Cefobid.

☑ **S0023**   Injection, cimetidine HCl, 300 mg
Use this code for Tagament HCl.

☑ **S0028**   Injection, famotidine, 20 mg
Use this code for Pepcid.

☑ **S0030**   Injection, metronidazole, 500 mg
Use this code for Flagyl IV RTU.

☑ **S0032**   Injection, nafcillin sodium, 2 grams
Use this code for Nallpen, Unipen.

☑ **S0034**   Injection, ofloxacin, 400 mg
Use this code for Floxin IV.

☑ **S0039**   Injection, sulfamethoxazole and trimethoprim, 10 ml
Use this code for Bactrim IV, Septra IV, SMZ-TMP, Sulfutrim.

☑ **S0040**   Injection, ticarcillin disodium and clavulanate potassium, 3.1 grams
Use this code for Timentin.

☑ **S0071**   Injection, acyclovir sodium, 50 mg
Use this code for Zovirax.

☑ **S0072**   Injection, amikacin sulfate, 100 mg
Use this code for Amikin.

☑ **S0073**   Injection, aztreonam, 500 mg
Use this code for Azactam.

☑ **S0074**   Injection, cefotetan disodium, 500 mg
Use this code for Cefotan.

☑ **S0077**   Injection, clindamycin phosphate, 300 mg
Use this code for Cleocin Phosphate.

☑ **S0078**   Injection, fosphenytoin sodium, 750 mg
Use this code for Cerebryx.

~~S0079~~   ~~Injection, octreotide acetate, 100 mcg (for doses over 1 mg use J2352 or C1207)~~

☑ **S0080**   Injection, pentamidine isethionate, 300 mg
Use this code for NebuPent, Pentam 300, Pentacarinat. See also code J2545.

☑ **S0081**   Injection, piperacillin sodium, 500 mg
Use this code for Pipracil.

☑ **S0088**   Imatinib 100 mg
Use this code for Gleevec.

☑ **S0090**   Sildenafil citrate, 25 mg   ▲
Use this code for Viagra.

☑ **S0091**   Granisetron hydrochloride, 1 mg (for circumstances falling under the Medicare statute, use Q0166)
Use this code for Kytril.

☑ **S0092**   Injection, hydromorphone hydrochloride, 250 mg (loading dose for infusion pump)
Use this code for Dilaudid. Hydromophone. See also J1170.

☑ **S0093**   Injection, morphine sulfate, 500 mg (loading dose for infusion pump)
Use this code for Duramorph, MS Contin, Morphine Sulfate. See also J2270, J2271, J2275.

☑ **S0104**   Zidovudine, oral 100 mg
See also J3485 for Retrovir.

☑ **S0106**   Bupropion HCl sustained release tablet, 150 mg, per bottle of 60 tablets
Use this code for Wellbutrin SR tablets.

● ☑ **S0107**   Injection, omalizumab, 25 mg

☑ **S0108**   Mercaptopurine, oral, 50 mg
Use this code for Purinethol oral.

☑ **S0114**   Injection, treprostinil sodium, 0.5 mg
Use this code for Remodulin. See also K0455.

● ☑ **S0115**   Bortezomib, 3.5 mg

☑ **S0122**   Injection, menotropins, 75 iu
Use this code for Humegon, Pergonal.

~~S0124~~   ~~Injection, urofollitropin, purified, 75 iu~~

☑ **S0126**   Injection, follitropin alfa, 75 iu
Use this code for Gonal-F.

☑ **S0128**   Injection, follitropin beta, 75 iu   ♀
Use this code for Follistim.

~~S0130~~   ~~Injection, chorionic gonadotropin, 5000 units~~

☑ **S0132**   Injection, ganirelix acetate, 250 mcg   ♀

~~S0135~~   ~~Injection, pegfilgrastim, 6 mg~~

● ☑ **S0136**   Clozapine, 25 mg

● ☑ **S0137**   Didanosine (ddi), 25 mg

● ☑ **S0138**   Finasteride, 5 mg   ♂
Use this code for Propecia (oral), Proscar (oral).

● ☑ **S0139**   Minoxidil, 10 mg
Use this code for Loniten (oral).

● ☑ **S0140**   Saquinavir, 200 mg
Use this code for Fortovase (oral).

● ☑ **S0141**   Zalcitabine (DDC), 0.375 mg
Use this code for Hivid (oral).

☑ **S0155**   Sterile dilutant for epoprostenol, 50 ml
Use this code for Flolan.

☑ **S0156**   Exemestane, 25 mg
Use this code for Aromasin.

☑ **S0157**   Becaplermin gel 0.01%, 0.5 gm
Use this code for Regraex Gel.

☑ **S0170**   Anastrozole, oral, 1mg
Use this code for Arimidex.

☑ **S0171**   Injection, bumetanide, 0.5 mg
Use this code for Bumex.

☑ **S0172**   Chlorambucil, oral, 2 mg
Use this code for Leukeran.

☑ **S0173**   Dexamethasone, oral, 4 mg
Use this code for Decadron, Dexone, Hexadrol.

☑ **S0174**   Dolasetron mesylate, oral 50 mg (for circumstances falling under the Medicare statute, use Q0180)
Use this code for Anzemet.

☑ **S0175**   Flutamide, oral, 125 mg
Use this code for Eulexin.

☑ **S0176**   Hydroxyurea, oral, 500 mg
Use this code for Droxia.

☑ **S0177**   Levamisole HCl, oral, 50 mg
Use this code for Ergamisol.

☑ **S0178**   Lomustine, oral, 10 mg
Use this code for Ceenu.

Special Coverage Instructions	Noncovered by Medicare	Carrier Discretion	☑ Quantity Alert	● New Code	▲ Revised Code

Temporary National Codes (Non-Medicare)

S0179 — S0621

☑ **S0179** Megestrol acetate, oral, 20 mg
Use this code for Megace.

☑ **S0181** Ondansetron HCl, oral, 4 mg (for circumstances falling under the Medicare statute, use Q0179)
Use this code for Zofran.

☑ **S0182** Procarbazine HCl, oral, 50 mg
Use this code for Matulane.

☑ **S0183** Prochlorperazine maleate, oral, 5 mg (for circumstances falling under the Medicare statute, use Q0164-Q0165)
Use this code for Compazine.

☑ **S0187** Tamoxifen citrate, oral, 10 mg
Use this code for Nolvadex.

☑ **S0189** Testosterone pellet, 75 mg

☑ **S0190** Mitepristone, oral, 200 mg   ♀
Use this code for Mifoprex 200 mg oral.

☑ **S0191** Misoprostol, oral, 200 mcg

~~**S0193** Injection, alefacept, 7.5 mg (includes dose packaging)~~

S0195 Pneumococcal conjugate vaccine, polyvalent, intramuscular, for children from five years to nine years of age who have not previously received the vaccine   P
Use this code for Pneumovax II.

S0199 Medically induced abortion by oral ingestion of medication including all associated services and supplies (e.g., patient counseling, office visits, confirmation of pregnancy by HCG, ultrasound to confirm duration of pregnancy, ultrasound to confirm completion of abortion) except drugs   A   ♀

S0201 Partial hospitalization services, less than 24 hours, per diem

S0207 Paramedic intercept, non-hospital based ALS service (non-voluntary), non-transport

S0208 Paramedic intercept, hospital-based ALS service (non-voluntary), non-transport

S0209 Wheelchair van, mileage, per mile

S0215 Non-emergency transportation; mileage, per mile
See also codes A0021-A0999 for transportation (per mile was added).

S0220 Medical conference by a physician with interdisciplinary team of health professionals or representatives of community agencies to coordinate activities of patient care (patient is present); approximately 30 minutes

S0221 Medical conference by a physician with interdisciplinary team of health professionals or representatives of community agencies to coordinate activities of patient care (patient is present); approximately 60 minutes

S0250 Comprehensive geriatric assessment and treatment planning performed by assessment team   A

S0255 Hospice referral visit (advising patient and family of care options) performed by nurse, social worker, or other designated staff

S0260 History and physical (outpatient or office) related to surgical procedure (List separately in addition to code for appropriate evaluation and management service)

S0302 Completed early periodic screening diagnosis and treatment (EPSDT) service (List in addition to code for appropriate evaluation and management service)

S0310 Hospitalist services (List separately in addition to code for appropriate evaluation and management service)

S0315 Disease management program; initial assessment and initiation of the program

▲ **S0316** Follow-up/reassessment

● ☑ **S0317** Disease management program; per diem

S0320 Telephone calls by a registered nurse to a disease management program member for monitoring purposes; per month

S0340 Lifestyle modification program for management of coronary artery disease, including all supportive services; first quarter/stage

S0341 Lifestyle modification program for management of coronary artery disease, including all supportive services; second or third quarter/stage

S0342 Lifestyle modification program for management of coronary artery disease, including all supportive services; fourth quarter/stage

S0390 Routine foot care; removal and/or trimming of corns, calluses and/or nails and preventive maintenance in specific medical conditions (e.g., diabetes), per visit
See also CPT code 11719-11721.

S0395 Impression casting of a foot performed by a practitioner other than the manufacturer of the orthotic

S0400 Global fee for extracorporeal shock wave lithotripsy treatment of kidney stone(s)
See CPT code 50590.

☑ **S0500** Disposable contact lens, per lens

☑ **S0504** Single vision prescription lens (safety, athletic, or sunglass), per lens

☑ **S0506** Bifocal vision prescription lens (safety, athletic, or sunglass), per lens

☑ **S0508** Trifocal vision prescription lens (safety, athletic, or sunglass), per lens

☑ **S0510** Non-prescription lens (safety, athletic, or sunglass), per lens

☑ **S0512** Daily wear specialty contact lens, per lens

☑ **S0514** Color contact lens, per lens

S0516 Safety eyeglass frames

S0518 Sunglasses frames

S0580 Polycarbonate lens (List this code in addition to the basic code for the lens)

S0581 Nonstandard lens (List this code in addition to the basic code for the lens)

S0590 Integral lens service, miscellaneous services reported separately

S0592 Comprehensive contact lens evaluation

S0601 Screening proctoscopy   ♂

S0605 Digital rectal examination, annual

S0610 Annual gynecological examination; new patient   ♀

S0612 Annual gynecological examination; established patient   ♀

S0620 Routine ophthalmological examination including refraction; new patient

S0621 Routine ophthalmological examination including refraction; established patient

---

S0622 Physical exam for college, new or established patient (List separately in addition to appropriate evaluation and management code)   A

S0630 Removal of sutures by a physician other than the physician who originally closed the wound

S0800 Laser in situ keratomileusis (LASIK)

S0810 Photorefractive keratectomy (PRK)

S0812 Phototherapeutic keratectomy (PTK)

S0820 Computerized corneal topography, unilateral

S0830 Ultrasound pachymetry to determine corneal thickness, with interpretation and report, unilateral

S1001 Deluxe item, patient aware (List in addition to code for basic item)

S1002 Customized item (List in addition to code for basic item)

S1015 IV tubing extension set

S1016 Non-PVC (polyvinyl chloride) intravenous administration set, for use with drugs that are not stable in PVC e.g., paclitaxel

S1025 Inhaled nitric oxide for the treatment of hypoxic respiratory failure in the neonate; per diem

S1030 Continuous noninvasive glucose monitoring device, purchase (for physician interpretation of data, use CPT code)

S1031 Continuous noninvasive glucose monitoring device, rental, including sensor, sensor replacement, and download to monitor (for physician interpretation of data, use CPT code)

S1040 Cranial remolding orthosis, rigid, with soft interface material, custom fabricated, includes fitting and adjustment(s)

S2053 Transplantation of small intestine, and liver allografts

S2054 Transplantation of multivisceral organs

S2055 Harvesting of donor multivisceral organs, with preparation and maintenance of allografts; from cadaver donor

S2060 Lobar lung transplantation

S2061 Donor lobectomy (lung) for transplantation, living donor

S2065 Simultaneous pancreas kidney transplantation

● **S2070** Cystourethroscopy, with ureteroscopy and/or pyeloscopy; with endoscopic laser treatment of ureteral calculi (includes ureteral catheterization)

S2080 Laser-assisted uvulopalatoplasty (LAUP)

● **S2085** Laparoscopy, gastric restrictive procedure, with gastric bypass for morbid obesity, with short limb (less than 100 cm) Roux-en-Y gastroenterostomy

● **S2090** Ablation, open, one or more renal tumor(s); cryosurgical

● **S2091** Ablation, percutaneous, one or more renal tumor(s); cryosurgical

● **S2095** Transcatheter occlusion or embolization for tumor destruction, percutaneous, any method, using yttrium-90 microspheres

S2102 Islet cell tissue transplant from pancreas; allogeneic

S2103 Adrenal tissue transplant to brain

S2107 Adoptive immunotherapy, i.e. development of specific anti-tumor reactivity (e.g., tumor-infiltrating lymphocyte therapy) per course of treatment

● **S2112** Arthroscopy, knee, surgical for harvesting of cartilage (chondrocyte cells)

S2113 Arthroscopy, knee, surgical for implantation of cultured analogous chondrocytes

S2115 Osteotomy, periacetabular, with internal fixation

● **S2120** Low density lipoprotein (LDL) apheresis using heparin-induced extracorporeal LDL precipitation

▲ **S2130** Endoluminal radiofrequency ablation of refluxing saphenous vein
For ligation of saphenous veins see appropriate CPT code.

S2135 Neurolysis, by injection, of metatarsal neuroma/interdigital neuritis, any interspace of the foot

S2140 Cord blood harvesting for transplantation, allogeneic

S2142 Cord blood-derived stem-cell transplantation, allogeneic

S2150 Bone marrow or blood-derived peripheral stem cell harvesting and transplantation, allogenic or autologous, including pheresis, high-dose chemotherapy, and the number of days of post-transplant care in the global definition (including drugs; hospitalization; medical, surgical, diagnostic and emergency services)

S2202 Echosclerotherapy

S2205 Minimally invasive direct coronary artery bypass surgery involving mini-thoracotomy or mini-sternotomy surgery, performed under direct vision; using arterial graft(s), single coronary arterial graft

S2206 Minimally invasive direct coronary artery bypass surgery involving mini-thoracotomy or mini-sternotomy surgery, performed under direct vision; using arterial graft(s), two coronary arterial grafts

S2207 Minimally invasive direct coronary artery bypass surgery involving mini-thoracotomy or mini-sternotomy surgery, performed under direct vision; using venous graft only, single coronary venous graft

S2208 Minimally invasive direct coronary artery bypass surgery involving mini-thoracotomy or mini-sternotomy surgery, performed under direct vision; using single arterial and venous graft(s), single venous graft

S2209 Minimally invasive direct coronary artery bypass surgery involving mini-thoracotomy or mini-sternotomy surgery, performed under direct vision; using two arterial grafts and single venous graft

S2211 Transcatheter placement of intravascular stent(s), carotid artery, percutaneous, unilateral (if performed bilaterally, use-50 modifier)

● **S2213** Implantation of gastric electrical stimulation device

● **S2225** Myringotomy, laser-assisted

● **S2230** Implantation of magnetic component of semi-implantable hearing device on ossicles in middle ear

● **S2235** Implantation of auditory brain stem implant

S2250 Uterine artery embolization for uterine fibroids   A ♀

S2260 Induced abortion, 17 to 24 weeks, any surgical method   M ♀

Temporary National Codes (Non-Medicare)

S2262 — S3845

S2262 Abortion for maternal indication, 25 weeks or greater   Ⓜ ♀

S2265 Abortion for fetal indication, 25-28 weeks   ♀

S2266 Abortion for fetal indication, 29-31 weeks   ♀

S2267 Abortion for fetal indication, 32 weeks or greater   Ⓜ ♀

S2300 Arthroscopy, shoulder, surgical; with thermally-induced capsulorrhaphy

S2340 Chemodenervation of abductor muscle(s) of vocal cord

S2341 Chemodenervation of adductor muscle(s) of vocal cord

S2342 Nasal endoscopy for post-operative debridement following functional endoscopic sinus surgery, nasal and/or sinus cavity(s), unilateral or bilateral

S2350 Diskectomy, anterior, with decompression of spinal cord and/or nerve root(s), including osteophytectomy; lumbar, single interspace

S2351 Diskectomy, anterior, with decompression of spinal cord and/or nerve root(s), including osteophytectomy; lumbar, each additional interspace (List separately in addition to code for primary procedure)

S2360 Percutaneous vertebroplasty, one vertebral body, unilateral or bilateral injection; cervical

S2361 Each additional cervical vertebral body (List separately in addition to code for primary procedure)

● **S2362** Kyphoplasty, one vertebral body, unilateral or bilateral injection

● ☑ **S2363** Kyphoplasty, one vertebral body, unilateral or bilateral injection; each additional vertebral body (List separately in addition to code for primary procedure)

S2370 Intradiscal electrothermal therapy, single interspace

☑ **S2371** Each additional interspace (List separately in addition to code for primary procedure)

S2400 Repair, congenital diaphragmatic hernia in the fetus using temporary tracheal occlusion, procedure performed in utero   Ⓜ ♀
Repair, congenital diaphragmatic hernia in the fetus using temporary tracheal occlusion, procedure performed in utero.

S2401 Repair, urinary tract obstruction in the fetus, procedure performed in utero   Ⓜ ♀

S2402 Repair, congenital cystic adenomatoid malformation in the fetus, procedure performed in utero   Ⓜ ♀

S2403 Repair, extralobar pulmonary sequestration in the fetus, procedure performed in utero   Ⓜ ♀

S2404 Repair, myelomeningocele in the fetus, procedure performed in utero   Ⓜ ♀

S2405 Repair of sacrococcygeal teratoma in the fetus, procedure performed in utero   Ⓜ ♀

S2409 Repair, congenital malformation of fetus, procedure performed in utero, not otherwise classified   Ⓜ ♀

S2411 Fetoscopic laser therapy for treatment of twin-to-twin transfusion syndrome   Ⓜ ♀

● **S3000** Diabetic indicator; retinal eye exam, dilated, bilateral

S3600 Stat laboratory request (situations other than S3601)

S3601 Emergency Stat laboratory charge for patient who is homebound or residing in a nursing facility

☑ **S3620** Newborn metabolic screening panel, includes test kit, postage and the laboratory tests specified by the state for inclusion in this panel (e.g., galactose; hemoglobin, electrophoresis; hydroxyprogesterone, 17-d; phenylanine (PKU); and thyroxine, total)   Ⓟ

● **S3625** Maternal serum triple marker screen including alpha-fetoprotein (AFP), estriol, and human chorionic gonadotropin (hCG)   Ⓜ ♀

S3630 Eosinophil count, blood, direct

S3645 HIV-1 antibody testing of oral mucosal transudate

S3650 Saliva test, hormone level; during menopause   Ⓐ ♀

S3652 Saliva test, hormone level; to assess preterm labor risk   Ⓜ ♀

S3655 Antisperm antibodies test (immunobead)   Ⓐ ♀

S3701 Immunoassay for nuclear matrix protein 22 (NMP-22), quantitative

S3708 Gastrointestinal fat absorption study

S3818 Complete gene sequence analysis; BRCA 1 gene

S3819 Complete gene sequence analysis; BRCA 2 gene

● **S3820** Complete BRCA1 and BRCA2 gene sequence analysis for susceptibility to breast and ovarian cancer

● **S3822** Single mutation analysis (in individual with a known BRCA1 or BRCA2 mutation in the family) for susceptibility to breast and ovarian cancer

● **S3823** Three-mutation BRCA1 and BRCA2 analysis for susceptibility to breast and ovarian cancer in Ashkenazi individuals

● **S3828** Complete gene sequence analysis; MLH1 gene

● **S3829** Complete gene sequence analysis; MLH2 gene

S3830 Complete MLH1 and MLH2 gene sequence analysis for hereditary nonpolyposis colorectal cancer (HNPCC) genetic testing

S3831 Single-mutation analysis (in individual with a known MLH1 and MLH2 mutation in the family) for hereditary nonpolyposis colorectal cancer (HNPCC) genetic testing

● **S3833** Complete APC gene sequence analysis for susceptibility to familial adenomatous polyposis (FAP) and attenuated FAP

● **S3834** Single-mutation analysis (in individual with a known APC mutation in the family) for susceptibility to familial adenomatous polyposis (FAP) and attenuated FAP

S3835 Complete gene sequence analysis for cystic fibrosis genetic testing

S3837 Complete gene sequence analysis for hemochromatosis genetic testing

● **S3840** DNA analysis for germline mutations of the ret proto-oncogene for susceptibility to multiple endocrine neoplasia type 2

● **S3841** Genetic testing for retinoblastoma

● **S3842** Genetic testing for von hippel-lindau disease

● **S3843** DNA analysis of the F5 gene for susceptibility to Factor V Leiden thrombophilia

● **S3844** DNA analysis of the connexin 26 gene (GJB2) for susceptibility to congenital, profound deafness

● **S3845** Genetic testing for alpha-thalassemia

- **S3846** Genetic testing for hemoglobin E beta-thalassemia
- **S3847** Genetic testing for Tay-Sachs disease
- **S3848** Genetic testing for Gaucher disease
- **S3849** Genetic testing for Niemann-Pick disease
- **S3850** Genetic testing for sickle cell anemia
- **S3851** Genetic testing for Canavan disease
- **S3852** DNA analysis for APOE epilson 4 allele for susceptibility to Alzheimer's disease
- **S3853** Genetic testing for myotonic muscular dystrophy

S3900 Surface electromyography (EMG)

S3902 Ballistocardiogram

S3904 Masters two step

S4005 Interim labor facility global (Labor occurring but not resulting in delivery) Ⓜ ♀

S4011 In vitro fertilization; including but not limited to identification and incubation of mature oocytes, fertilization with sperm, incubation of embryo(s), and subsequent visualization for determination of development Ⓜ ♀

S4013 Complete cycle, gamete intrafallopian transfer (GIFT), case rate Ⓜ ♀

S4014 Complete cycle, zygote intrafallopian transfer (ZIFT), case rate Ⓜ ♀

S4015 Complete in vitro fertilization cycle, not otherwise specified, case rate Ⓜ ♀

S4016 Frozen in vitro fertilization cycle, case rate ♀

S4017 Incomplete cycle, treatment cancelled prior to stimulation, case rate ♀

S4018 Frozen embryo transfer procedure cancelled before transfer, case rate ♀

S4020 In vitro fertilization procedure cancelled before aspiration, case rate ♀

S4021 In vitro fertilization procedure cancelled after aspiration, case rate ♀

S4022 Assisted oocyte fertilization, case rate ♀

S4023 Donor egg cycle, incomplete, case rate ♀

S4025 Donor services for in vitro fertilization (sperm or embryo), case rate Ⓐ

S4026 Procurement of donor sperm from sperm bank Ⓐ

S4027 Storage of previously frozen embryos

S4028 Microsurgical epididymal sperm aspiration (MESA) Ⓐ ♂

S4030 Sperm procurement and cryopreservation services; initial visit Ⓐ ♂

S4031 Sperm procurement and cryopreservation services; subsequent visit Ⓐ ♂

S4035 Stimulated intrauterine insemination (IUI), case rate ♀

S4036 Intravaginal culture (IVC), case rate ♀

S4037 Cryopreserved embryo transfer, case rate

S4040 Monitoring and storage of cryopreserved embryos, per 30 days

S4981 Insertion of levonorgestrel-releasing intrauterine system ♀

S4989 Contraceptive intrauterine device (e.g., Progestacert IUD), including implants and supplies ♀

☑ **S4990** Nicotine patches, legend

☑ **S4991** Nicotine patches, non-legend

S4993 Contraceptive pills for birth control ♀

S4995 Smoking cessation gum

☑ **S5000** Prescription drug, generic

☑ **S5001** Prescription drug, brand name

☑ **S5010** 5% dextrose and 45% normal saline, 1000 ml

☑ **S5011** 5% dextrose in lactated ringer's, 1000 ml

☑ **S5012** 5% dextrose with potassium chloride, 1000 ml

☑ **S5013** 5% dextrose/45% normal saline with potassium chloride and magnesium sulfate, 1000 ml

☑ **S5014** 5% dextrose/0.45% normal saline with potassium chloride and magnesium sulfate, 1500 ml

S5035 Home infusion therapy, routine service of infusion device (e.g., pump maintenance)

S5036 Home infusion therapy, repair of infusion device (e.g., pump repair)

S5100 Day care services, adult; per 15 minutes

S5101 Day care services, adult; per half day

S5102 Day care services, adult; per diem

S5105 Day care services, center-based; services not included in program fee, per diem

- ☑ **S5108** Home care training to home care client, per 15 minutes

- ☑ **S5109** Home care training to home care client, per session

S5110 Home care training, family; per 15 minutes

S5111 Home care training, family; per session

S5115 Home care training, non-family; per 15 minutes

S5116 Home care training, non-family; per session

S5120 Chore services; per 15 minutes

S5121 Chore services; per diem

S5125 Attendant care services; per 15 minutes

S5126 Attendant care services; per diem

S5130 Homemaker service, NOS; per 15 minutes

S5131 Homemaker service, NOS; per diem

S5135 Companion care, adult (e.g., IADL/ADL); per 15 minutes Ⓐ

S5136 Companion care, adult (e.g. IADL/ADL); per diem Ⓐ

S5140 Foster care, adult; per diem Ⓐ

S5141 Foster care, adult; per month Ⓐ

S5145 Foster care, therapeutic, child; per diem Ⓟ

S5146 Foster care, therapeutic, child; per month Ⓟ

S5150 Unskilled respite care, not hospice; per 15 minutes

S5151 Unskilled respite care, not hospice; per diem

S5160 Emergency response system; installation and testing

S5161 Emergency response system; service fee, per month (excludes installation and testing)

S5162 Emergency response system; purchase only

S5165 Home modifications; per service

S5170 Home delivered meals, including preparation; per meal

S5175 Laundry service, external, professional; per order

S5180 Home health respiratory therapy, initial evaluation

S5181 Home health respiratory therapy, NOS, per diem

S5185 Medication reminder services, non-face-to-face; per month

S5190 Wellness assessment, performed by non-physician

S5199 Personal care item, NOS, each

S5497 Home infusion therapy, catheter care/maintenance, not otherwise classified; includes administrative services, professional pharmacy services, care coordination, and all necessary supplies and equipment (drugs and nursing visits coded separately), per diem

S5498 Home infusion therapy, catheter care/maintenance, simple (single lumen), includes administrative services, professional pharmacy services, care coordination and all necessary supplies and equipment, (drugs and nursing visits coded separately), per diem

● **S5501** Home infusion therapy, catheter care/maintenance, complex (more than one lumen), includes administrative services, professional pharmacy services, care coordination, and all necessary supplies and equipment (drugs and nursing visits coded separately), per diem

S5502 Home infusion therapy, catheter care/maintenance, implanted access device, includes administrative services, professional pharmacy services, care coordination and all necessary supplies and equipment, (drugs and nursing visits coded separately), per diem (Use this code for interim maintenance of vascular access not currently in use)

S5517 Home infusion therapy, all supplies necessary for restoration of catheter patency or declotting

S5518 Home infusion therapy, all supplies necessary for catheter repair

S5520 Home infusion therapy, all supplies (including catheter) necessary for a peripherally inserted central venous catheter (PICC) line insertion

S5521 Home infusion therapy, all supplies (including catheter) necessary for a midline catheter insertion

S5522 Home infusion therapy, insertion of peripherally inserted central venous catheter (PICC), nursing services only (No supplies or catheter included)

S5523 Home infusion therapy, insertion of midline central venous catheter, nursing services only (No supplies or catheter included)

● ☑ **S5550** Insulin, rapid onset, 5 units

● ☑ **S5551** Insulin, most rapid onset (Lispro or Aspart); 5 units

● ☑ **S5552** Insulin, intermediate acting (NPH or lente); 5 units

● ☑ **S5553** Insulin, long acting; 5 units

● ☑ **S5560** Insulin delivery device, reusable pen; 1.5 ml size

● ☑ **S5561** Insulin delivery device, reusable pen; 3 ml size

● ☑ **S5565** Insulin cartridge for use in insulin delivery device other than pump; 150 units

● ☑ **S5566** Insulin cartridge for use in insulin delivery device other than pump; 300 units

● ☑ **S5570** Insulin delivery device, disposable pen (including insulin); 1.5 ml size

● ☑ **S5571** Insulin delivery device, disposable pen (including insulin); 3 ml size

S8004 Radioimmunopharmaceutical localization of targeted cells; whole body

S8030 Scleral application of tantalum ring(s) for localization of lesions for proton beam therapy

S8035 Magnetic source imaging

S8037 Magnetic resonance cholangiopancreatography (MRCP)

S8040 Topographic brain mapping

S8042 Magnetic resonance imaging (MRI), low-field

S8049 Intraoperative radiation therapy (single administration)

S8055 Ultrasound guidance for multifetal pregnancy reduction(s), technical component (only to be used when the physician doing the reduction procedure does not perform the ultrasound. Guidance is included in the CPT code for multifetal pregnancy reduction — 59866) Ⓜ ♀

● **S8075** Computer analysis of full-field digital mammogram and further physician review for interpretation, mammography (List separately in addition to code for primary procedure)

S8080 Scintimammography (radioimmunoscintigraphy of the breast), unilateral, including supply of radiopharmaceutical

S8085 Fluorine-18 fluorodeoxyglucose (F-18 FDG) imaging using dual-head coincidence detection system (non-dedicated PET scan)

S8092 Electron beam computed tomography (also known as ultrafast CT, cine CT)

S8095 Wig (for medically-induced or congenital hair loss)

S8096 Portable peak flow meter

☑ **S8097** Asthma kit (including but not limited to portable peak expiratory flow meter, instructional video, brochure, and/or spacer)

S8100 Holding chamber or spacer for use with an inhaler or nebulizer; without mask

S8101 Holding chamber or spacer for use with an inhaler or nebulizer; with mask

S8110 Peak expiratory flow rate (physician services)

● ☑ **S8120** Oxygen contents, gaseous, 1 unit equals 1 cubic foot

● ☑ **S8121** Oxygen contents, liquid, 1 unit equals 1 pound

~~**S8180** Tracheostomy shower protector~~

~~**S8181** Tracheostomy tube holder~~

S8182 Humidifier, heated, used with ventilator, non-servo-controlled

S8183 Humidifier, heated, used with ventilator, dual servo-controlled with temperature monitoring

S8185 Flutter device

S8186 Swivel adaptor

☑ **S8189** Tracheostomy supply, not otherwise classified

S8190 Electronic spirometer (or microspirometer)

S8210 Mucus trap

S8260 Oral orthotic for treatment of sleep apnea, includes fitting, fabrication, and materials

S8262 Mandibular orthopedic repositioning device, each

S8265 Haberman feeder for cleft lip/palate

☑ **S8415** Supplies for home delivery of infant Ⓜ ♀

S8420 Gradient pressure aid (sleeve and glove combination), custom made

---

▨ Special Coverage Instructions   ▨ Noncovered by Medicare   ▨ Carrier Discretion   ☑ Quantity Alert   ● New Code   ▲ Revised Code

124 — S Codes   Ⓜ Maternity   Ⓐ Adult   Ⓟ Pediatrics   Ⓐ-Ⓧ APC Status Indicator   *2004 HCPCS*

☑ **S8421** Gradient pressure aid (sleeve and glove combination), ready made

☑ **S8422** Gradient pressure aid (sleeve), custom made, medium weight

☑ **S8423** Gradient pressure aid (sleeve), custom made, heavy weight

☑ **S8424** Gradient pressure aid (sleeve), ready made

☑ **S8425** Gradient pressure aid (glove), custom made, medium weight

☑ **S8426** Gradient pressure aid (glove), custom made, heavy weight

☑ **S8427** Gradient pressure aid (glove), ready made

☑ **S8428** Gradient pressure aid (gauntlet), ready made

☑ **S8429** Gradient pressure exterior wrap

☑ **S8430** Padding for compression bandage, roll

☑ **S8431** Compression bandage, roll

☑ **S8450** Splint, prefabricated, digit (Specify digit by use of modifier)

☑ **S8451** Splint, prefabricated, wrist or ankle

☑ **S8452** Splint, prefabricated, elbow

● **S8460** Camisole, post-mastectomy

~~**S8470** Positioning device, stander, for use by patient who is unable to stand independently (e.g., cerebral palsy patient)~~

☑ **S8490** Insulin syringes (100 syringes, any size)

● ☑ **S8948** Application of a modality (requiring constant provider attendance) to one or more areas; low-level laser; each 15 minutes

S8950 Complex lymphedema therapy, each 15 minutes

● **S8990** Physical or manipulative therapy performed for maintenance rather than restoration

S8999 Resuscitation bag (for use by patient on artificial respiration during power failure or other catastrophic event)

S9001 Home uterine monitor with or without associated nursing services

S9007 Ultrafiltration monitor

S9015 Automated EEG monitoring

S9022 Digital subtraction angiography (use in addition to CPT code for the procedure for further identification)

S9024 Paranasal sinus ultrasound

S9025 Omnicardiogram/cardiointegram

S9034 Extracorporeal shockwave lithotripsy for gall stones
If performed with ERCP, use CPT code 43265.

S9055 Procuren or other growth factor preparation to promote wound healing

S9056 Coma stimulation per diem

S9061 Home administration of aerosolized drug therapy (e.g., pentamidine); administrative services, professional pharmacy services, care coordination, all necessary supplies and equipment (drugs and nursing visits coded separately), per diem

S9075 Smoking cessation treatment

S9083 Global fee urgent care centers

S9088 Services provided in an urgent care center (List in addition to code for service)

S9090 Vertebral axial decompression, per session

S9092 Canolith repositioning, per visit

S9098 Home visit, phototherapy services (e.g., Bili-lite), including equipment rental, nursing services, blood draw, supplies, and other services, per diem

S9109 Congestive heart failure telemonitoring, equipment rental, including telescale, computer system and software, telephone connections, and maintenance, per month

S9117 Back school, per visit

☑ **S9122** Home health aide or certified nurse assistant, providing care in the home; per hour

☑ **S9123** Nursing care, in the home; by registered nurse, per hour (use for general nursing care only, not to be used when CPT codes 99500-99602 can be used)

☑ **S9124** Nursing care, in the home; by licensed practical nurse, per hour

☑ **S9125** Respite care, in the home, per diem

☑ **S9126** Hospice care, in the home, per diem

☑ **S9127** Social work visit, in the home, per diem

☑ **S9128** Speech therapy, in the home, per diem

☑ **S9129** Occupational therapy, in the home, per diem

S9131 Physical therapy; in the home, per diem

☑ **S9140** Diabetic management program, follow-up visit to non-MD provider

☑ **S9141** Diabetic management program, follow-up visit to MD provider

S9145 Insulin pump initiation, instruction in initial use of pump (pump not included)

S9150 Evaluation by ocularist

S9208 Home management of preterm labor, including administrative services, professional pharmacy services, care coordination, and all necessary supplies or equipment (drugs and nursing visits coded separately), per diem (do not use this code with any home infusion per diem code) Ⓜ ♀

S9209 Home management of preterm premature rupture of membranes (PPROM), including administrative services, professional pharmacy services, care coordination, and all necessary supplies or equipment (drugs and nursing visits coded separately), per diem (do not use this code with any home infusion per diem code) Ⓜ ♀

S9211 Home management of gestational hypertension, includes administrative services, professional pharmacy services, care coordination and all necessary supplies and equipment (drugs and nursing visits coded separately); per diem (do not use this code with any home infusion per diem code) Ⓜ ♀

S9212 Home management of postpartum hypertension, includes administrative services, professional pharmacy services, care coordination, and all necessary supplies and equipment (drugs and nursing visits coded separately); per diem (do not use this code with any home infusion per diem code) ♀

S9213 Home management of preeclampsia, includes administrative services, professional pharmacy services, care coordination, and all necessary supplies and equipment (drugs and nursing services coded separately); per diem (do not use this code with any home infusion per diem code) Ⓜ ♀

▲ (revised code marker)

S9214 Home management of gestational diabetes, includes administrative services, professional pharmacy services, care coordination, and all necessary supplies and equipment (drugs and nursing visits coded separately); per diem (do not use this code with any home infusion per diem code)   Ⓜ ♀

S9325 Home infusion therapy, pain management infusion; administrative services, professional pharmacy services, care coordination, and all necessary supplies and equipment, (drugs and nursing visits coded separately), per diem (do not use this code with S9326, S9327 or S9328)

▲ **S9326** Home infusion therapy, continuous (twenty-four hours or more) pain management infusion; administrative services, professional pharmacy services, care coordination and all necessary supplies and equipment (drugs and nursing visits coded separately), per diem
This code is not noted as changed by CMS.

▲ **S9327** Home infusion therapy, intermittent (less than twenty-four hours) pain management infusion; administrative services, professional pharmacy services, care coordination, and all necessary supplies and equipment (drugs and nursing visits coded separately), per diem
This code is not noted as changed by CMS.

S9328 Home infusion therapy, implanted pump pain management infusion; administrative services, professional pharmacy services, care coordination, and all necessary supplies and equipment (drugs and nursing visits coded separately), per diem

S9329 Home infusion therapy, chemotherapy infusion; administrative services, professional pharmacy services, care coordination, and all necessary supplies and equipment (drugs and nursing visits coded separately), per diem (do not use this code with S9330 or S9331)

▲ **S9330** Home infusion therapy, continuous (twenty-four hours or more) chemotherapy infusion; administrative services, professional pharmacy services, care coordination, and all necessary supplies and equipment (drugs and nursing visits coded separately), per diem
This code is not noted as changed by CMS.

▲ **S9331** Home infusion therapy, intermittent (less than twenty-four hours) chemotherapy infusion; administrative services, professional pharmacy services, care coordination, and all necessary supplies and equipment (drugs and nursing visits coded separately), per diem
This code is not noted as changed by CMS.

● ☑ **S9335** Home therapy, hemodialysis; administrative services, professional pharmacy services, care coordination, and all necessary supplies and equipment (drugs and nursing services coded separately), per diem

S9336 Home infusion therapy, continuous anticoagulant infusion therapy (e.g., heparin), administrative services, professional pharmacy services, care coordination and all necessary supplies and equipment (drugs and nursing visits coded separately), per diem

▲ **S9338** Home infusion therapy, immunotherapy, administrative services, professional pharmacy services, care coordination, and all necessary supplies and equipment (drugs and nursing visits coded separately), per diem
This code is not noted as changed by CMS.

S9339 Home therapy; peritoneal dialysis, administrative services, professional pharmacy services, care coordination and all necessary supplies and equipment (drugs and nursing visits coded separately), per diem

S9340 Home therapy; enteral nutrition; administrative services, professional pharmacy services, care coordination, and all necessary supplies and equipment (enteral formula and nursing visits coded separately), per diem

S9341 Home therapy; enteral nutrition via gravity; administrative services, professional pharmacy services, care coordination, and all necessary supplies and equipment (enteral formula and nursing visits coded separately), per diem

S9342 Home therapy; enteral nutrition via pump; administrative services, professional pharmacy services, care coordination, and all necessary supplies and equipment (enteral formula and nursing visits coded separately), per diem

S9343 Home therapy; enteral nutrition via bolus; administrative services, professional pharmacy services, care coordination, and all necessary supplies and equipment (enteral formula and nursing visits coded separately), per diem

S9345 Home infusion therapy, anti-hemophilic agent infusion therapy (e.g., factor VIII); administrative services, professional pharmacy services, care coordination, and all necessary supplies and equipment (drugs and nursing visits coded separately), per diem

S9346 Home infusion therapy, alpha-1-proteinase inhibitor (e.g., Prolastin); administrative services, professional pharmacy services, care coordination, and all necessary supplies and equipment (drugs and nursing visits coded separately), per diem

S9347 Home infusion therapy, uninterrupted, long-term, controlled rate intravenous or subcutaneous infusion therapy (e.g. epoprostenol); administrative services, professional pharmacy services, care coordination, and all necessary supplies and equipment (drugs and nursing visits coded separately), per diem

S9348 Home infusion therapy, sympathomimetic/inotropic agent infusion therapy (e.g., Dobutamine); administrative services, professional pharmacy services, care coordination, all necessary supplies and equipment (drugs and nursing visits coded separately), per diem

S9349 Home infusion therapy, tocolytic infusion therapy; administrative services, professional pharmacy services, care coordination, and all necessary supplies and equipment (drugs and nursing visits coded separately), per diem   ♀

S9351 Home infusion therapy, continuous anti-emetic infusion therapy; administrative services, professional pharmacy services, care coordination, all necessary supplies and equipment (drugs and nursing visits coded separately), per diem

S9353 Home infusion therapy, continuous insulin infusion therapy; administrative services, professional pharmacy services, care coordination, and all necessary supplies and equipment (drugs and nursing visits coded separately), per diem

S9355 Home infusion therapy, chelation therapy; administrative services, professional pharmacy services, care coordination, and all necessary supplies and equipment (drugs and nursing visits coded separately), per diem

S9357 Home infusion therapy, enzyme replacement intravenous therapy; (e.g., Imiglucerase); administrative services, professional pharmacy services, care coordination, and all necessary supplies and equipment (drugs and nursing visits coded separately), per diem

S9359 Home infusion therapy, anti-tumor necrosis factor intravenous therapy; (e.g., Infliximab); administrative services, professional pharmacy services, care coordination, and all necessary supplies and equipment (drugs and nursing visits coded separately), per diem

S9361 Home infusion therapy, diuretic intravenous therapy; administrative services, professional pharmacy services, care coordination, and all necessary supplies and equipment (drugs and nursing visits coded separately), per diem

S9363 Home infusion therapy, anti-spasmotic intravenous therapy; administrative services, professional pharmacy services, care coordination, and all necessary supplies and equipment (drugs and nursing visits coded separately), per diem

▲ **S9364** Home infusion therapy, total parenteral nutrition (TPN); administrative services, professional pharmacy services, care coordination, and all necessary supplies and equipment including standard TPN formula (lipids, specialty amino acid formulas, drugs other than in standard formula and nursing visits coded separately), per diem (do not use with home infusion codes S9365-S9368 using daily volume scales)
This code is not noted as changed by CMS.

▲ **S9365** Home infusion therapy, total parenteral nutrition (TPN); one liter per day, administrative services, professional pharmacy services, care coordination, and all necessary supplies and equipment including standard TPN formula (lipids, specialty amino acid formulas, drugs other than in standard formula and nursing visits coded separately), per diem
This code is not noted as changed by CMS.

▲ **S9366** Home infusion therapy, total parenteral nutrition (TPN); more than one liter but no more than two liters per day, administrative services, professional pharmacy services, care coordination, and all necessary supplies and equipment including standard TPN formula (lipids, specialty amino acid formulas, drugs other than in standard formula and nursing visits coded separately), per diem
This code is not noted as changed by CMS.

▲ **S9367** Home infusion therapy, total parenteral nutrition (TPN); more than two liters but no more than three liters per day, administrative services, professional pharmacy services, care coordination, and all necessary supplies and equipment including standard tpn formula (lipids, specialty amino acid formulas, drugs other than in standard formula and nursing visits coded separately), per diem
This code is not noted as changed by CMS.

▲ **S9368** Home infusion therapy, total parenteral nutrition (TPN); more than three liters per day, administrative services, professional pharmacy services, care coordination, and all necessary supplies and equipment including standard TPN formula (lipids, specialty amino acid formulas, drugs other than in standard formula and nursing visits coded separately), per diem
This code is not noted as changed by CMS.

S9370 Home therapy, intermittent anti-emetic injection therapy; administrative services, professional pharmacy services, care coordination, and all necessary supplies and equipment (drugs and nursing visits coded separately), per diem

S9372 Home therapy; intermittent anticoagulant injection therapy (e.g., Heparin); administrative services, professional pharmacy services, care coordination, and all necessary supplies and equipment (drugs and nursing visits coded separately), per diem (do not use this code for flushing of infusion devices with Heparin to maintain patency)

S9373 Home infusion therapy, hydration therapy; administrative services, professional pharmacy services, care coordination, and all necessary supplies and equipment (drugs and nursing visits coded separately), per diem (do not use with hydration therapy codes S9374-S9377 using daily volume scales)

S9374 Home infusion therapy, hydration therapy; one liter per day, administrative services, professional pharmacy services, care coordination, and all necessary supplies and equipment (drugs and nursing visits coded separately), per diem

S9375 Home infusion therapy, hydration therapy; more than one liter but no more than two liters per day, administrative services, professional pharmacy services, care coordination, and all necessary supplies and equipment (drugs and nursing visits coded separately), per diem

S9376 Home infusion therapy, hydration therapy; more than two liters but no more than three liters per day, administrative services, professional pharmacy services, care coordination, and all necessary supplies and equipment (drugs and nursing visits coded separately), per diem

S9377 Home infusion therapy, hydration therapy; more than three liters per day, administrative services, professional pharmacy services, care coordination, and all necessary supplies (drugs and nursing visits coded separately), per diem

S9379 Home infusion therapy, infusion therapy, not otherwise classified; administrative services, professional pharmacy services, care coordination, and all necessary supplies and equipment (drugs and nursing visits coded separately), per diem

S9381 Delivery or service to high risk areas requiring escort or extra protection, per visit

S9401 Anticoagulation clinic, inclusive of all services except laboratory tests, per session

S9430 Pharmacy compounding and dispensing services

● **S9434** Modified solid food supplements for inborn errors of metabolism

S9435 Medical foods for inborn errors of metabolism

S9436 Childbirth preparation/lamaze classes, non-physician provider, per session

Temporary National Codes (Non-Medicare)

S9437 — S9558

S9437 Childbirth refresher classes, non-physician provider, per session   A

S9438 Cesarean birth classes, non-physician provider, per session   A

S9439 VBAC (vaginal birth after cesarean) classes, non-physician provider, per session   A

S9441 Asthma education, non-physician provider, per session

S9442 Birthing classes, non-physician provider, per session   A

S9443 Lactation classes, non-physician provider, per session   A

S9444 Parenting classes, non-physician provider, per session   A

S9445 Patient education, not otherwise classified, non-physician provider, individual, per session

S9446 Patient education, not otherwise classified, non-physician provider, group, per session

S9447 Infant safety (including CPR) classes, non-physician provider, per session

S9449 Weight management classes, non-physician provider, per session

S9451 Exercise classes, non-physician provider, per session

S9452 Nutrition classes, non-physician provider, per session

S9453 Smoking cessation classes, non-physician provider, per session

S9454 Stress management classes, non-physician provider, per session

S9455 Diabetic management program, group session

S9460 Diabetic management program, nurse visit

S9465 Diabetic management program, dietitian visit

S9470 Nutritional counseling, dietitian visit

S9472 Cardiac rehabilitation program, non-physician provider, per diem

S9473 Pulmonary rehabilitation program, non-physician provider, per diem

S9474 Enterostomal therapy by a registered nurse certified in enterostomal therapy, per diem

S9475 Ambulatory setting substance abuse treatment or detoxification services, per diem

● ☑ **S9476** Vestibular rehabilitation program, non-physician provider, per diem

S9480 Intensive outpatient psychiatric services, per diem

S9484 Crisis intervention mental health services, per hour ▲

S9485 Crisis intervention mental health services, per diem

S9490 Home infusion therapy, corticosteroid infusion; administrative services, professional pharmacy services, care coordination, and all necessary supplies and equipment (drugs and nursing visits coded separately), per diem

▲ **S9494** Home infusion therapy, antibiotic, antiviral, or antifungal therapy; administrative services, professional pharmacy services, care coordination, and all necessary supplies and equipment (drugs and nursing visits coded separately, per diem) (do not use this code with home infusion codes for hourly dosing schedules S9497-S9504)
This code is not noted as changed by CMS.

S9497 Home infusion therapy, antibiotic, antiviral, or antifungal therapy; once every three hours; administrative services, professional pharmacy services, care coordination, and all necessary supplies and equipment (drugs and nursing visits coded separately), per diem

S9500 Home infusion therapy, antibiotic, antiviral, or antifungal therapy; once every 24 hours; administrative services, professional pharmacy services, care coordination, and all necessary supplies and equipment (drugs and nursing visits coded separately), per diem

S9501 Home infusion therapy, antibiotic, antiviral, or antifungal therapy; once every 12 hours; administrative services, professional pharmacy services, care coordination, and all necessary supplies and equipment (drugs and nursing visits coded separately), per diem

S9502 Home infusion therapy, antibiotic, antiviral, or antifungal therapy; once every eight hours, administrative services, professional pharmacy services, care coordination, and all necessary supplies and equipment (drugs and nursing visits coded separately), per diem

S9503 Home infusion therapy, antibiotic, antiviral, or antifungal; once every six hours; administrative services, professional pharmacy services, care coordination, and all necessary supplies and equipment (drugs and nursing visits coded separately), per diem

S9504 Home infusion therapy, antibiotic, antiviral, or antifungal; once every four hours; administrative services, professional pharmacy services, care coordination, and all necessary supplies and equipment (drugs and nursing visits coded separately), per diem

S9529 Routine venipuncture for collection of specimen(s), single home bound, nursing home, or skilled nursing facility patient

▲ **S9537** Home therapy; hematopoietic hormone injection therapy (e.g., erythropoietin, G-CSF, GM-CSF); administrative services, professional pharmacy services, care coordination, and all necessary supplies and equipment (drugs and nursing visits coded separately), per diem
This code is not noted as changed by CMS.

S9538 Home transfusion of blood product(s); administrative services, professional pharmacy services, care coordination and all necessary supplies and equipment (blood products, drugs, and nursing visits coded separately), per diem

▲ **S9542** Home injectable therapy, not otherwise classified, including administrative services, professional pharmacy services, care coordination, and all necessary supplies and equipment (drugs and nursing visits coded separately), per diem
This code is not noted as changed by CMS.

~~**S9546** Home infusion of blood products, nursing services, per visit~~

▲ **S9558** Home injectable therapy; growth hormone, including administrative services, professional pharmacy services, care coordination, and all necessary supplies and equipment (drugs and nursing visits coded separately), per diem
This code is not noted as changed by CMS.

▲   S9559   Home injectable therapy, interferon, including administrative services, professional pharmacy services, care coordination, and all necessary supplies and equipment (drugs and nursing visits coded separately), per diem
This code is not noted as changed by CMS.

S9560   Home injectable therapy; hormonal therapy (e.g.; leuprolide, goserelin), including administrative services, professional pharmacy services, care coordination, and all necessary supplies and equipment (drugs and nursing visits coded separately), per diem

S9562   Home injectable therapy, palivizumab, including administrative services, professional pharmacy services, care coordination, and all necessary supplies and equipment (drugs and nursing visits coded separately), per diem

S9590   Home therapy, irrigation therapy (e.g. sterile irrigation of an organ or anatomical cavity); including administrative services, professional pharmacy services, care coordination, and all necessary supplies and equipment (drugs and nursing visits coded separately), per diem

~~S9802 Home infusion/specialty drug administration, nursing services; per visit (up to 2 hours)~~

~~S9803 Home infusion/specialty drug administration, nursing services; each additional hour (list separately in addition to code s9802)~~

~~S9806 Rn services in the infusion suite of the iv therapy provider, per visit~~

S9810   Home therapy; professional pharmacy services for provision of infusion, specialty drug administration, and/or disease state management, not otherwise classified, per hour (do not use this code with any per diem code)

▲   S9900   Services by authorized Christian Science practitioner for the process of healing, per diem; not to be used for rest or study; excludes in-patient services
This code is not noted as changed by CMS.

S9970   Health club membership, annual

S9975   Transplant related lodging, meals and transportation, per diem

S9981   Medical records copying fee, administrative

S9982   Medical records copying fee, per page

S9986   Not medically necessary service (patient is aware that service not medically necessary)

S9989   Services provided outside of the united states of america (List in addition to code(s) for services(s))

S9990   Services provided as part of a phase II clinical trial

S9991   Services provided as part of a phase III clinical trial

S9992   Transportation costs to and from trial location and local transportation costs (e.g., fares for taxicab or bus) for clinical trial participant and one caregiver/companion

S9994   Lodging costs (e.g., hotel charges) for clinical trial participant and one caregiver/companion

S9996   Meals for clinical trial participant and one caregiver/companion

S9999   Sales tax

NATIONAL T CODES ESTABLISHED FOR STATE MEDICAID AGENCIES *T1000-T9999*

The T codes are designed for use by Medicaid state agencies to establish codes for items for which there are no permanent national codes but for which codes are necessary to administer the Medicaid program (T codes are not used by Medicare but can be used by private insurers). This range of codes describes nursing and home health-related services, substance abuse treatment, and certain training-related procedures.

These codes are not valid for Medicare.

T1000 Private duty/independent nursing service(s) - licensed, up to 15 minutes

T1001 Nursing assessment/evaluation

T1002 RN services, up to 15 minutes

T1003 LPN/LVN services, up to 15 minutes

T1004 Services of a qualified nursing aide, up to 15 minutes

E   **T1005** Respite care services, up to 15 minutes

T1006 Alcohol and/or substance abuse services, family/couple counseling

T1007 Alcohol and/or substance abuse services, treatment plan development and/or modification

~~**T1008** Day treatment for individual alcohol and/or substance abuse services~~

T1009 Child sitting services for children of the individual receiving alcohol and/or substance abuse services

T1010 Meals for individuals receiving alcohol and/or substance abuse services (when meals not included in the program)

~~**T1011** Alcohol and/or substance abuse services, not otherwise classified~~

T1012 Alcohol and/or substance abuse services, skills development

T1013 Sign language or oral interpretive services, per 15 minutes

T1014 Telehealth transmission, per minute, professional services bill separately

T1015 Clinic visit/encounter, all-inclusive

T1016 Case management, each 15 minutes

T1017 Targeted case management, each 15 minutes

T1018 School-based individualized education program (IEP) services, bundled

● ☑ **T1019** Personal care services, per 15 minutes, not for an inpatient or resident of a hospital, nursing facility, ICF/MR or IMD, part of the individualized plan of treatment (code may not be used to identify services provided by home health aide or certified nurse assistant)

T1020 Personal care services, per diem, not for an inpatient or resident of a hospital, nursing facility, ICF/MR or IMD, part of the individualized plan of treatment (code may not be used to identify services provided by home health aide or certified nurse assistant)

T1021 Home health aide or certified nurse assistant, per visit

T1022 Contracted home health agency services, all services provided under contract, per day

T1023 Screening to determine the appropriateness of consideration of an individual for participation in a specified program, project or treatment protocol, per encounter

T1024 Evaluation and treatment by an integrated, specialty team contracted to provide coordinated care to multiple or severely handicapped children, per encounter

T1025 Intensive, extended multidisciplinary services provided in a clinic setting to children with complex medical, physical, mental and psychosocial impairments, per diem

T1026 Intensive, extended multidisciplinary services provided in a clinic setting to children with complex medical, physical, medical and psychosocial impairments, per hour

T1027 Family training and counseling for child development, per 15 minutes

T1028 Assessment of home, physical and family environment, to determine suitability to meet patient's medical needs

T1029 Comprehensive environmental lead investigation, not including laboratory analysis, per dwelling

T1030 Nursing care, in the home, by registered nurse, per diem

T1031 Nursing care, in the home, by licensed practical nurse, per diem

T1500 Diaper/incontinent pant, reusable/washable, any size, each

T1502 Administration of oral, intramuscular and/or subcutaneous medication by health care agency/professional, per visit

T1999 Miscellaneous therapeutic items and supplies, retail purchases, not otherwise classified; identify product in "remarks"

T2001 Non-emergency transportation; patient attendant/escort

T2002 Non-emergency transportation; per diem

T2003 Non-emergency transportation; encounter/trip

T2004 Non-emergency transport; commercial carrier, multi-pass

T2005 Non-emergency transportation; non-ambulatory stretcher van

T2006 Ambulance response and treatment, no transport

T2007 Transportation waiting time, air ambulance and non-emergency vehicle, one-half (1/2) hour increments

● ☑ **T2010** Preadmission screening and resident review (PASRR) level I identification screening, per screen

● **T2011** Preadmission screening and resident review (PASRR) level II evaluation, per evaluation

● ☑ **T2012** Habilitation, educational; waiver, per diem

● ☑ **T2013** Habilitation, educational, waiver; per hour

● ☑ **T2014** Habilitation, prevocational, waiver; per diem

● ☑ **T2015** Habilitation, prevocational, waiver; per hour

● ☑ **T2016** Habilitation, residential, waiver; per diem

● ☑ **T2017** Habilitation, residential, waiver; 15 minutes

● ☑ **T2018** Habilitation, supported employment, waiver; per diem

● ☑ **T2019** Habilitation, supported employment, waiver; per 15 minutes

● ☑ **T2020** Day habilitation, waiver; per diem

● ☑ **T2021** Day habilitation, waiver; per 15 minutes

● ☑ **T2022** Case management, per month

T2023 — T5999   National T Codes Established for State Medicaid Agencies

- ● ☑ **T2023** Targeted case management; per month
- ●   **T2024** Service assessment/plan of care development, waiver
- ●   **T2025** Waiver services; not otherwise specified (NOS)
- ● ☑ **T2026** Specialized childcare, waiver; per diem
- ● ☑ **T2027** Specialized childcare, waiver; per 15 minutes
- ●   **T2028** Specialized supply, not otherwise specified, waiver
- ●   **T2029** Specialized medical equipment, not otherwise specified, waiver
- ● ☑ **T2030** Assisted living, waiver; per month
- ● ☑ **T2031** Assisted living; waiver, per diem
- ● ☑ **T2032** Residential care, not otherwise specified (NOS), waiver; per month
- ● ☑ **T2033** Residential care, not otherwise specified (NOS), waiver; per diem
- ● ☑ **T2034** Crisis intervention, waiver; per diem
- ●   **T2035** Utility services to support medical equipment and assistive technology/devices, waiver
- ● ☑ **T2036** Therapeutic camping, overnight, waiver; each session
- ● ☑ **T2037** Therapeutic camping, day, waiver; each session
- ● ☑ **T2038** Community transition, waiver; per service
- ● ☑ **T2039** Vehicle modifications, waiver; per service
- ● ☑ **T2040** Financial management, self-directed, waiver; per 15 minutes
- ● ☑ **T2041** Supports brokerage, self-directed, waiver; per 15 minutes
- ● ☑ **T2042** Hospice routine home care; per diem
- ● ☑ **T2043** Hospice continuous home care; per hour
- ● ☑ **T2044** Hospice inpatient respite care; per diem
- ● ☑ **T2045** Hospice general inpatient care; per diem
- ● ☑ **T2046** Hospice long term care, room and board only; per diem
- ● ☑ **T2048** Behavioral health; long-term care residential (non-acute care in a residential treatment program where stay is typically longer than 30 days), with room and board, per diem
- ●   **T2101** Human breast milk processing, storage and distribution only
- ●   **T5001** Positioning seat for persons with special orthopedic needs, for use in vehicles
- ●   **T5999** Supply, not otherwise specified

VISION SERVICES *V0000-V2999*

These V codes include vision-related supplies, including spectacles, lenses, contact lenses, prostheses, intraocular lenses, and miscellaneous lenses.

FRAMES

V codes fall under the jurisdiction of the DME regional carrier, unless incident to other services or otherwise noted.

Ⓐ   **V2020**   Frames, purchases
           MED: MCM 2130

Ⓔ   **V2025**   Deluxe frame
           MED: MCM 3045.4

SPECTACLE LENSES

If procedure code 92390 or 92395 is reported, recode with the specific lens type listed below. For aphakic temporary spectacle correction, see 92358. See S0500-S0592 for temporary vision codes.

SINGLE VISION, GLASS, OR PLASTIC

☑   **V2100**   Sphere, single vision, plano to plus or minus 4.00, per lens

☑   **V2101**   Sphere, single vision, plus or minus 4.12 to plus or minus 7.00d, per lens

☑   **V2102**   Sphere, single vision, plus or minus 7.12 to plus or minus 20.00d, per lens

☑   **V2103**   Spherocylinder, single vision, plano to plus or minus 4.00d sphere, 0.12 to 2.00d cylinder, per lens

☑   **V2104**   Spherocylinder, single vision, plano to plus or minus 4.00d sphere, 2.12 to 4.00d cylinder, per lens

☑   **V2105**   Spherocylinder, single vision, plano to plus or minus 4.00d sphere, 4.25 to 6.00d cylinder, per lens

☑   **V2106**   Spherocylinder, single vision, plano to plus or minus 4.00d sphere, over 6.00d cylinder, per lens

☑   **V2107**   Spherocylinder, single vision, plus or minus 4.25 to plus or minus 7.00 sphere, 0.12 to 2.00d cylinder, per lens

☑   **V2108**   Spherocylinder, single vision, plus or minus 4.25d to plus or minus 7.00d sphere, 2.12 to 4.00d cylinder, per lens

☑   **V2109**   Spherocylinder, single vision, plus or minus 4.25 to plus or minus 7.00d sphere, 4.25 to 6.00d cylinder, per lens

☑   **V2110**   Spherocylinder, single vision, plus or minus 4.25 to 7.00d sphere, over 6.00d cylinder, per lens

☑   **V2111**   Spherocylinder, single vision, plus or minus 7.25 to plus or minus 12.00d sphere, 0.25 to 2.25d cylinder, per lens

☑   **V2112**   Spherocylinder, single vision, plus or minus 7.25 to plus or minus 12.00d sphere, 2.25d to 4.00d cylinder, per lens

☑   **V2113**   Spherocylinder, single vision, plus or minus 7.25 to plus or minus 12.00d sphere, 4.25 to 6.00d cylinder, per lens

☑   **V2114**   Spherocylinder, single vision sphere over plus or minus 12.00d, per lens

☑   **V2115**   Lenticular (myodisc), per lens, single vision

~~**V2116** Lenticular lens, nonaspheric, per lens, single vision~~

~~**V2117** Lenticular, aspheric, per lens, single vision~~

   V2118   Aniseikonic lens, single vision

●   **V2121**   Lenticular lens, per lens, single
           MED: MCM 2130.B

   V2199   Not otherwise classified, single vision lens

BIFOCAL, GLASS, OR PLASTIC

☑   **V2200**   Sphere, bifocal, plano to plus or minus 4.00d, per lens

☑   **V2201**   Sphere, bifocal, plus or minus 4.12 to plus or minus 7.00d, per lens

☑   **V2202**   Sphere, bifocal, plus or minus 7.12 to plus or minus 20.00d, per lens

☑   **V2203**   Spherocylinder, bifocal, plano to plus or minus 4.00d sphere, 0.12 to 2.00d cylinder, per lens

☑   **V2204**   Spherocylinder, bifocal, plano to plus or minus 4.00d sphere, 2.12 to 4.00d cylinder, per lens

☑   **V2205**   Spherocylinder, bifocal, plano to plus or minus 4.00d sphere, 4.25 to 6.00d cylinder, per lens

☑   **V2206**   Spherocylinder, bifocal, plano to plus or minus 4.00d sphere, over 6.00d cylinder, per lens

☑   **V2207**   Spherocylinder, bifocal, plus or minus 4.25 to plus or minus 7.00d sphere, 0.12 to 2.00d cylinder, per lens

☑   **V2208**   Spherocylinder, bifocal, plus or minus 4.25 to plus or minus 7.00d sphere, 2.12 to 4.00d cylinder, per lens

☑   **V2209**   Spherocylinder, bifocal, plus or minus 4.25 to plus or minus 7.00d sphere, 4.25 to 6.00d cylinder, per lens

☑   **V2210**   Spherocylinder, bifocal, plus or minus 4.25 to plus or minus 7.00d sphere, over 6.00d cylinder, per lens

☑   **V2211**   Spherocylinder, bifocal, plus or minus 7.25 to plus or minus 12.00d sphere, 0.25 to 2.25d cylinder, per lens

☑   **V2212**   Spherocylinder, bifocal, plus or minus 7.25 to plus or minus 12.00d sphere, 2.25 to 4.00d cylinder, per lens

☑   **V2213**   Spherocylinder, bifocal, plus or minus 7.25 to plus or minus 12.00d sphere, 4.25 to 6.00d cylinder, per lens

☑   **V2214**   Spherocylinder, bifocal, sphere over plus or minus 12.00d, per lens

☑   **V2215**   Lenticular (myodisc), per lens, bifocal

~~**V2216** Lenticular, nonaspheric, per lens, bifocal~~

~~**V2217** Lenticular, aspheric lens, bifocal~~

☑   **V2218**   Aniseikonic, per lens, bifocal

☑   **V2219**   Bifocal seg width over 28mm

☑   **V2220**   Bifocal add over 3.25d

●   **V2221**   Lenticular lens, per lens, bifocal
           MED: MCM 2130.B

   V2299   Specialty bifocal (by report)
           Pertinent documentation to evaluate medical appropriateness should be included when this code is reported.

TRIFOCAL, GLASS, OR PLASTIC

☑   **V2300**   Sphere, trifocal, plano to plus or minus 4.00d, per lens

☑   **V2301**   Sphere, trifocal, plus or minus 4.12 to plus or minus 7.00d per lens

☑   **V2302**   Sphere, trifocal, plus or minus 7.12 to plus or minus 20.00, per lens

---

Special Coverage Instructions   Noncovered by Medicare   Carrier Discretion   ☑ Quantity Alert   ● New Code   ▲ Revised Code

Vision Services

V2303 — V2629

☑ **V2303** Spherocylinder, trifocal, plano to plus or minus 4.00d sphere, 0.12 to 2.00d cylinder, per lens

☑ **V2304** Spherocylinder, trifocal, plano to plus or minus 4.00d sphere, 2.25 to 4.00d cylinder, per lens

☑ **V2305** Spherocylinder, trifocal, plano to plus or minus 4.00d sphere, 4.25 to 6.00 cylinder, per lens

☑ **V2306** Spherocylinder, trifocal, plano to plus or minus 4.00d sphere, over 6.00d cylinder, per lens

☑ **V2307** Spherocylinder, trifocal, plus or minus 4.25 to plus or minus 7.00d sphere, 0.12 to 2.00d cylinder, per lens

☑ **V2308** Spherocylinder, trifocal, plus or minus 4.25 to plus or minus 7.00d sphere, 2.12 to 4.00d cylinder, per lens

☑ **V2309** Spherocylinder, trifocal, plus or minus 4.25 to plus or minus 7.00d sphere, 4.25 to 6.00d cylinder, per lens

☑ **V2310** Spherocylinder, trifocal, plus or minus 4.25 to plus or minus 7.00d sphere, over 6.00d cylinder, per lens

☑ **V2311** Spherocylinder, trifocal, plus or minus 7.25 to plus or minus 12.00d sphere, 0.25 to 2.25d cylinder, per lens

☑ **V2312** Spherocylinder, trifocal, plus or minus 7.25 to plus or minus 12.00d sphere, 2.25 to 4.00d cylinder, per lens

☑ **V2313** Spherocylinder, trifocal, plus or minus 7.25 to plus or minus 12.00d sphere, 4.25 to 6.00d cylinder, per lens

☑ **V2314** Spherocylinder, trifocal, sphere over plus or minus 12.00d, per lens

☑ **V2315** Lenticular (myodisc), per lens, trifocal

~~**V2316** Lenticular nonaspheric, per lens, trifocal~~

~~**V2317** Lenticular, aspheric lens, trifocal~~

V2318 Aniseikonic lens, trifocal

☑ **V2319** Trifocal seg width over 28 mm

☑ **V2320** Trifocal add over 3.25d

● **V2321** Lenticular lens, per lens, trifocal
MED: MCM 2130.B

V2399 Specialty trifocal (by report)
Pertinent documentation to evaluate medical appropriateness should be included when this code is reported.

VARIABLE ASPHERICITY LENS, GLASS, OR PLASTIC

☑ **V2410** Variable asphericity lens, single vision, full field, glass or plastic, per lens

☑ **V2430** Variable asphericity lens, bifocal, full field, glass or plastic, per lens

V2499 Variable sphericity lens, other type

CONTACT LENS

If procedure code 92391 or 92396 is reported, recode with specific lens type listed below (per lens).

☑ **V2500** Contact lens, PMMA, spherical, per lens

☑ **V2501** Contact lens, PMMA, toric or prism ballast, per lens

☑ **V2502** Contact lens, PMMA, bifocal, per lens

☑ **V2503** Contact lens, PMMA, color vision deficiency, per lens

☑ **V2510** Contact lens, gas permeable, spherical, per lens

☑ **V2511** Contact lens, gas permeable, toric, prism ballast, per lens

☑ **V2512** Contact lens, gas permeable, bifocal, per lens

☑ **V2513** Contact lens, gas permeable, extended wear, per lens

☑ **V2520** Contact lens, hydrophilic, spherical, per lens
Hydrophilic contact lenses are covered by Medicare only for aphakic patients. Local carrier if incident to physician services.
MED: CIM 45-7, CIM 65-1

☑ **V2521** Contact lens, hydrophilic, toric, or prism ballast, per lens
Hydrophilic contact lenses are covered by Medicare only for aphakic patients. Local carrier if incident to physician services.
MED: CIM 45-7, CIM 65-1

☑ **V2522** Contact lens, hydrophilic, bifocal, per lens
Hydrophilic contact lenses are covered by Medicare only for aphakic patients. Local carrier if incident to physician services.
MED: CIM 45-7, CIM 65-1

☑ **V2523** Contact lens, hydrophilic, extended wear, per lens
Hydrophilic contact lenses are covered by Medicare only for aphakic patients.
MED: CIM 45-7, CIM 65-1

☑ **V2530** Contact lens, scleral, gas impermeable, per lens (for contact lens modification, see CPT Level I code 92325)
MED: CIM 45-7, CIM 65-1

☑ **V2531** Contact lens, scleral, gas permeable, per lens (for contact lens modification, see CPT Level I code 92325)
MED: CIM 65-3

V2599 Contact lens, other type
Local carrier if incident to physician services.

VISION AIDS

If procedure code 92392 is reported, recode with specific systems below.

V2600 Hand held low vision aids and other nonspectacle mounted aids

V2610 Single lens spectacle mounted low vision aids

V2615 Telescopic and other compound lens system, including distance vision telescopic, near vision telescopes and compound microscopic lens system

PROSTHETIC EYE

V2623 Prosthetic eye, plastic, custom
MED: MCM 2133

V2624 Polishing/resurfacing of ocular prosthesis

V2625 Enlargement of ocular prosthesis

V2626 Reduction of ocular prosthesis

V2627 Scleral cover shell
A scleral shell covers the cornea and the anterior sclera. Medicare covers a scleral shell when it is prescribed as an artificial support to a shrunken and sightless eye or as a barrier in the treatment of severe dry eye.
MED: CIM 65-3

V2628 Fabrication and fitting of ocular conformer

V2629 Prosthetic eye, other type

INTRAOCULAR LENSES

V2630 Anterior chamber intraocular lens
The IOL must be FDA-approved for reimbursement. Medicare payment for an IOL is included in the payment for ASC facility services. Medicare jurisdiction: local carrier.
MED: MCM 2130

V2631 Iris supported intraocular lens
The IOL must be FDA-approved for reimbursement. Medicare payment for an IOL is included in the payment for ASC facility services. Medicare jurisdiction: local carrier.
MED: MCM 2130

V2632 Posterior chamber intraocular lens
The IOL must be FDA-approved for reimbursement. Medicare payment for an IOL is included in the payment for ASC facility services. Medicare jurisdiction: local carrier.
MED: MCM 2130

MISCELLANEOUS

☑ **V2700** Balance lens, per lens

☑ **V2710** Slab off prism, glass or plastic, per lens

☑ **V2715** Prism, per lens

☑ **V2718** Press-on lens, Fresnell prism, per lens

☑ **V2730** Special base curve, glass or plastic, per lens

~~V2740 Tint, plastic, rose 1 or 2 per lens~~

~~V2741 Tint, plastic, other than rose 1 2, per lens~~

~~V2742 Tint, glass rose 1 or 2, per lens~~

~~V2743 Tint, glass other than rose 1 or 2, per lens~~

☑ **V2744** Tint, photochromatic, per lens
MED: MCM 2130B

● ☑ **V2745** Addition to lens, tint, any color, solid, gradient or equal, excludes photochromatic, any lens material, per lens
MED: MCM 2130.B

☑ **V2750** Antireflective coating, per lens
MED: MCM 2130B

☑ **V2755** U-V lens, per lens
MED: MCM 2130B

● **V2756** Eye glass case

☑ **V2760** Scratch resistant coating, per lens

● ☑ **V2761** Mirror coating, any type, solid, gradient or equal, any lens material, per lens
MED: MCM 2130.B

● ☑ **V2762** Polarization, any lens material, per lens
MED: MCM 2130.B

☑ **V2770** Occluder lens, per lens

☑ **V2780** Oversize lens, per lens

E ☑ **V2781** Progressive lens, per lens

● ☑ **V2782** Lens, index 1.54 to 1.65 plastic or 1.60 to 1.79 glass, excludes polycarbonate, per lens
MED: MCM 2130.B

● ☑ **V2783** Lens, index greater than or equal to 1.66 plastic or greater than or equal to 1.80 glass, excludes polycarbonate, per lens
MED: MCM 2130.B

● ☑ **V2784** Lens, polycarbonate or equal, any index, per lens
MED: MCM 2130.B

F **V2785** Processing, preserving and transporting corneal tissue
Medicare jurisdiction: local carrier.

● ☑ **V2786** Specialty occupational multifocal lens, per lens
MED: MCM 2130.B

N **V2790** Amniotic membrane for surgical reconstruction, per procedure
Medicare jurisdiction: local carrier.

● **V2797** Vision supply, accessory and/or service component of another HCPCS vision code

A **V2799** Vision service, miscellaneous
Level II, a local HCPCS Level III code or a CPT code better describes the service being reported. This code should be used only if a more specific code is unavailable.

HEARING SERVICES *V5000-V5999*
This range of codes describes hearing tests and related supplies and equipment, speech-language pathology screenings, and repair of augmentative communicative system.

Hearing services fall under the jurisdiction of the local carrier unless incidental or otherwise noted.

V5008 Hearing screening
MED: MCM 2320

V5010 Assessment for hearing aid
MED: Medicare Statute: 1862A7

V5011 Fitting/orientation/checking of hearing aid
MED: Medicare Statute: 1862A7

V5014 Repair/modification of a hearing aid
MED: Medicare Statute: 1862A7

V5020 Conformity evaluation
MED: Medicare Statute: 1862A7

V5030 Hearing aid, monaural, body worn, air conduction
MED: Medicare Statute: 1862A7

V5040 Hearing aid, monaural, body worn, bone conduction
MED: Medicare Statute: 1862A7

V5050 Hearing aid, monaural, in the ear
MED: Medicare Statute: 1862A7

V5060 Hearing aid, monaural, behind the ear
MED: Medicare Statute: 1862A7

V5070 Glasses, air conduction
MED: Medicare Statute: 1862A7

V5080 Glasses, bone conduction
MED: Medicare Statute: 1862A7

V5090 Dispensing fee, unspecified hearing aid
MED: Medicare Statute: 1862A7

V5095 Semi-implantable middle ear hearing prosthesis
Use this code for Vibrant Soundbridge Implantable Middle Ear Prosthesis.
MED: Medicare Statute: 1862A7

V5100 Hearing aid, bilateral, body worn
MED: Medicare Statute: 1862A7

V5110 Dispensing fee, bilateral
MED: Medicare Statute: 1862A7

V5120 Binaural, body
MED: Medicare Statute: 1862A7

Hearing Services

V5130 — V5273

V5130 Binaural, in the ear
MED: Medicare Statute: 1862A7

V5140 Binaural, behind the ear
MED: Medicare Statute: 1862A7

V5150 Binaural, glasses
MED: Medicare Statute: 1862A7

V5160 Dispensing fee, binaural
MED: Medicare Statute: 1862A7

V5170 Hearing aid, CROS, in the ear
MED: Medicare Statute: 1862A7

V5180 Hearing aid, CROS, behind the ear
MED: Medicare Statute: 1862A7

V5190 Hearing aid, CROS, glasses
MED: Medicare Statute: 1862A7

V5200 Dispensing fee, CROS
MED: Medicare Statute: 1862A7

V5210 Hearing aid, BICROS, in the ear
MED: Medicare Statute: 1862A7

V5220 Hearing aid, BICROS, behind the ear
MED: Medicare Statute: 1862A7

V5230 Hearing aid, BICROS, glasses
MED: Medicare Statute: 1862A7

V5240 Dispensing fee, BICROS
MED: Medicare Statute: 1862A7

V5241 Dispensing fee, monaural hearing aid, any type
MED: Medicare Statute: 1862A7

V5242 Hearing aid, analog, monaural, CIC (completely in the ear canal)
MED: Medicare Statute: 1862A7

V5243 Hearing aid, analog, monaural, ITC (in the canal)
MED: Medicare Statute: 1862A7

V5244 Hearing aid, digitally programmable analog, monaural, CIC
MED: Medicare Statute: 1862A7

V5245 Hearing aid, digitally programmable, analog, monaural, ITC
MED: Medicare Statute: 1862A7

V5246 Hearing aid, digitally programmable analog, monaural, ITE (in the ear)
MED: Medicare Statute: 1862A7

V5247 Hearing aid, digitally programmable analog, monaural, BTE (behind the ear)
MED: Medicare Statute: 1862A7

V5248 Hearing aid, analog, binaural, CIC
MED: Medicare Statute: 1862A7

V5249 Hearing aid, analog, binaural, ITC
MED: Medicare Statute: 1862A7

V5250 Hearing aid, digitally programmable analog, binaural, CIC
MED: Medicare Statute: 1862A7

V5251 Hearing aid, digitally programmable analog, binaural, ITC
MED: Medicare Statute: 1862A7

V5252 Hearing aid, digitally programmable, binaural, ITE
MED: Medicare Statute: 1862A7

V5253 Hearing aid, digitally programmable, binaural, BTE
MED: Medicare Statute: 1862A7

V5254 Hearing aid, digital, monaural, CIC
MED: Medicare Statute: 1862A7

V5255 Hearing aid, digital, monaural, ITC
MED: Medicare Statute: 1862A7

V5256 Hearing aid, digital, monaural, ITE
MED: Medicare Statute: 1862A7

V5257 Hearing aid, digital, monaural, BTE
MED: Medicare Statute: 1862A7

V5258 Hearing aid, digital, binaural, CIC
MED: Medicare Statute: 1862A7

V5259 Hearing aid, digital, binaural, ITC
MED: Medicare Statute: 1862A7

V5260 Hearing aid, digital, binaural, ITE
MED: Medicare Statute: 1862A7

V5261 Hearing aid, digital, binaural, BTE
MED: Medicare Statute: 1862A7

V5262 Hearing aid, disposable, any type, monaural
MED: Medicare Statute: 1862A7

☑ **V5263** Hearing aid, disposable, any type, binaural
MED: Medicare Statute: 1862A7

☑ **V5264** Ear mold/insert, not disposable, any type
MED: Medicare Statute: 1862A7

☑ **V5265** Ear mold/insert, disposable, any type
MED: Medicare Statute: 1862A7

☑ **V5266** Battery for use in hearing device
MED: Medicare Statute: 1862A7

☑ **V5267** Hearing aid supplies/accessories
MED: Medicare Statute: 1862A7

☑ **V5268** Assistive listening device, telephone amplifier, any type
MED: Medicare Statute: 1862A7

V5269 Assistive listening device, alerting, any type
MED: Medicare Statute: 1862A7

V5270 Assistive listening device, television amplifier, any type
MED: Medicare Statute: 1862A7

V5271 Assistive listening device, television caption decoder
MED: Medicare Statute: 1862A7

V5272 Assistive listening device, TDD
MED: Medicare Statute: 1862A7

V5273 Assistive listening device, for use with cochlear implant
MED: Medicare Statute: 1862A7

▲ | V5274 | **Assistive listening device, not otherwise specified**
This code is not noted as changed by CMS.
MED: Medicare Statute: 1862A7

| V5275 | **Ear impression, each**
MED: Medicare Statute: 1862A7

| V5298 | **Hearing aid, not otherwise classified**
MED: Medicare Statute: 1862A7

| V5299 | **Hearing service, miscellaneous**
Determine if an alternative HCPCS Level II or a CPT code
better describes the service being reported. This code should
be used only if a more specific code is unavailable.
MED: MCM 2320

SPEECH-LANGUAGE PATHOLOGY SERVICES

| V5336 | **Repair/modification of augmentative
communicative system or device (excludes adaptive
hearing aid)**
Medicare jurisdiction: DME regional carrier.
MED: Medicare Statute: 1862A7

▲ Ⓐ | V5362 | **Speech screening**
Medicare jurisdiction: local carrier.
MED: Medicare Statute: 42CFR41062

▲ Ⓐ | V5363 | **Language screening**
Medicare jurisdiction: local carrier.
MED: Medicare Statute: 42CFR41062

▲ Ⓐ | V5364 | **Dysphagia screening**
Medicare jurisdiction: local carrier.
MED: Medicare Statute: 42CFR41062

APPENDIX 1 — MODIFIERS

A1	Dressing for one wound
A2	Dressing for two wounds
A3	Dressing for three wounds
A4	Dressing for four wounds
A5	Dressing for five wounds
A6	Dressing for six wounds
A7	Dressing for seven wounds
A8	Dressing for eight wounds
A9	Dressing for nine or more wounds
AA	Anesthesia services performed personally by anesthesiologist
AD	Medical supervision by a physician: more than four concurrent anesthesia procedures
AH	Clinical psychologist
AJ	Clinical social worker
AM	Physician, team member service
AP	Determination of refractive state was not performed in the course of diagnostic ophthalmological examination
AS	Physician assistant, nurse practitioner, or clinical nurse specialist services for assistant at surgery
AT	Acute treatment (this modifier should be used when reporting service 98940, 98941, 98942)
AU	Item furnished in conjunction with a urological, ostomy, or tracheostomy supply
AV	Item furnished in conjunction with a prosthetic device, prosthetic or orthotic
AW	Item furnished in conjunction with a surgical dressing
AX	Item furnished in conjunction with dialysis services
BA	Item furnished in conjunction with parenteral enteral nutrition (PEN) services
BO	Orally administered nutrition, not by feeding tube
BP	The beneficiary has been informed of the purchase and rental options and has elected to purchase the item
BR	The beneficiary has been informed of the purchase and rental options and has elected to rent the item
BU	The beneficiary has been informed of the purchase and rental options and after 30 days has not informed the supplier of his/her decision
CA	Procedure payable only in the inpatient setting when performed emergently on an outpatient who expires prior to admission
CB	Service ordered by a renal dialysis facility (RDF) physician as part of the esrd beneficiary's dialysis benefit, is not part of the composite rate, and is separately reimbursable
CC	Procedure code change (use 'CC' when the procedure code submitted was changed either for administrative reasons or because an incorrect code was filed)
E1	Upper left, eyelid
E2	Lower left, eyelid
E3	Upper right, eyelid
E4	Lower right, eyelid
EJ	Subsequent claims for a defined course of therapy, e.g., EPO, Sodium Hyaluronate, Infliximab
EM	Emergency reserve supply (for ESRD benefit only)
EP	Service provided as part of medicaid early periodic screening diagnosis and treatment (EPSDT) program
ET	Emergency services
EY	No physician or other licensed health care provider order for this item or service
F1	Left hand, second digit
F2	Left hand, third digit
F3	Left hand, fourth digit
F4	Left hand, fifth digit
F5	Right hand, thumb
F6	Right hand, second digit
F7	Right hand, third digit
F8	Right hand, fourth digit
F9	Right hand, fifth digit
FA	Left hand, thumb
FP	Service provided as part of Medicaid Family Planning Program
G1	Most recent URR reading of less than 60
G2	Most recent URR reading of 60 to 64.9
G3	Most recent URR reading of 65 to 69.9
G4	Most recent URR reading of 70 to 74.9
G5	Most recent URR reading of 75 or greater
G6	ESRD patient for whom less than six dialysis sessions have been provided in a month
G7	Pregnancy resulted from rape or incest or pregnancy certified by physician as life threatening
G8	Monitored anesthesia care (MAC) for deep complex, complicated, or markedly invasive surgical procedure
G9	Monitored anesthesia care for patient who has history of severe cardio-pulmonary condition
GA	Waiver of liability statement on file
GB	Claim being re-submitted for payment because it is no longer covered under a global payment demonstration
GC	This service has been performed in part by a resident under the direction of a teaching physician
GE	This service has been performed by a resident without the presence of a teaching physician under the primary care exception
GF	Non-physician (e.g. nurse practitioner (NP), certified registered nurse anaesthetist (CRNA), certified registered nurse (CRN), clinical nurse specialist (CNS), physician assistant (PA)) services in a critical access hospital
GG	Performance and payment of a screening mammogram and diagnostic mammogram on the same patient, same day
GH	Diagnostic mammogram converted from screening mammogram on same day

GJ	"Opt out" physician or practitioner emergency or urgent service
GK	Actual item/service ordered by physician, item associated with GA or GZ modifier
GL	Medically unnecessary upgrade provided instead of standard item, no charge, no advance beneficiary notice (ABN)
GM	Multiple patients on one ambulance trip
GN	Services delivered under an outpatient speech language pathology plan of care
GO	Services delivered under an outpatient occupational therapy plan of care
GP	Services delivered under an outpatient physical therapy plan of care
GQ	Via asynchronous telecommunications system
GT	Via interactive audio and video telecommunication systems
GV	Attending physician not employed or paid under arrangement by the patient's hospice provider
GW	Service not related to the hospice patient's terminal condition
GY	Item or service statutorily excluded or does not meet the definition of any Medicare benefit
GZ	Item or service expected to be denied as not reasonable and necessary
H9	Court-ordered
HA	Child/adolescent program
HB	Adult program, non geriatric
HC	Adult program, geriatric
HD	Pregnant/parenting women's program
HE	Mental health program
HF	Substance abuse program
HG	Opioid addiction treatment program
HH	Integrated mental health/substance abuse program
HI	Integrated mental health and mental retardation/developmental disabilities program
HJ	Employee assistance program
HK	Specialized mental health programs for high-risk populations
HL	Intern
HM	Less than bachelor degree level
HN	Bachelors degree level
HO	Masters degree level
HP	Doctoral level
HQ	Group setting
HR	Family/couple with client present
HS	Family/couple without client present
HT	Multi-disciplinary team
HU	Funded by child welfare agency
HV	Funded state addictions agency

HW	Funded by state mental health agency
HX	Funded by county/local agency
HY	Funded by juvenile justice agency
HZ	Funded by criminal justice agency
JW	Drug amount discarded/not administered to any patient
K0	Lower extremity prosthesis functional level 0 - does not have the ability or potential to ambulate or transfer safely with or without assistance and a prosthesis does not enhance their quality of life or mobility.
K1	Lower extremity prosthesis functional level 1 - has the ability or potential to use a prosthesis for transfers or ambulation on level surfaces at fixed cadence. Typical of the limited and unlimited household ambulator.
K2	Lower extremity prosthesis functional level 2 - has the ability or potential for ambulation with the ability to traverse low level environmental barriers such as curbs, stairs or uneven surfaces. Typical of the limited community ambulator.
K3	Lower extremity prosthesis functional level 3 - has the ability or potential for ambulation with variable cadence. Typical of the community ambulator who has the ability to transverse most environmental barriers and may have vocational, therapeutic, or exercise activity that demands prosthetic utilization beyond simple locomotion.
K4	Lower extremity prosthesis functional level 4 - has the ability or potential for prosthetic ambulation that exceeds the basic ambulation skills, exhibiting high impact, stress, or energy levels, typical of the prosthetic demands of the child, active adult, or athlete.
KA	Add on option/accessory for wheelchair
KB	Beneficiary requested upgrade for ABN, more than 4 modifiers identified on claim
KH	DMEPOS item, initial claim, purchase or first month rental
KI	DMEPOS item, second or third month rental
KJ	DMEPOS item, parenteral enteral nutrition (PEN) pump or capped rental, months four to fifteen
KM	Replacement of facial prosthesis including new impression/moulage
KN	Replacement of facial prosthesis using previous master model
KO	Single drug unit dose formulation
KP	First drug of a multiple drug unit dose formulation
KQ	Second or subsequent drug of a multiple drug unit dose formulation
KR	Rental item, billing for partial month
KS	Glucose monitor supply for diabetic beneficiary not treated with insulin
KX	Specific required documentation on file
KZ	New coverage not implemented by managed care
LC	Left circumflex coronary artery
LD	Left anterior descending coronary artery
LL	Lease/rental (use the 'll' modifier when DME equipment rental is to be applied against the purchase price)

LR	Laboratory round trip
LS	FDA-monitored intraocular lens implant
LT	Left side (used to identify procedures performed on the left side of the body)
MS	Six month maintenance and servicing fee for reasonable and necessary parts and labor which are not covered under any manufacturer or supplier warranty
NR	New when rented (use the 'NR' modifier when DME which was new at the time of rental is subsequently purchased)
NU	New equipment
PL	Progressive addition lenses
Q2	HCFA/ORD demonstration project procedure/service
Q3	Live kidney donor surgery and related services
Q4	Service for ordering/referring physician qualifies as a service exemption
Q5	Service furnished by a substitute physician under a reciprocal billing arrangement
Q6	Service furnished by a locum tenens physician
Q7	One class A finding
Q8	Two class B findings
Q9	One class B and two class C findings
QA	FDA investigational device exemption
QB	Physician providing service in a rural HPSA
QC	Single channel monitoring
QD	Recording and storage in solid state memory by a digital recorder
QE	Prescribed amount of oxygen is less than 1 liter per minute (LPM)
QF	Prescribed amount of oxygen exceeds 4 liters per minute (LPM) and portable oxygen is prescribed
QG	Prescribed amount of oxygen is greater than 4 liters per minute (LPM)
QH	Oxygen conserving device is being used with an oxygen delivery system
QJ	Services/items provided to a prisoner or patient in state or local custody, however the state or local government, as applicable, meets the requirements in 42 CFR 411.4 (b)
QK	Medical direction of two, three, or four concurrent anesthesia procedures involving qualified individuals
QL	Patient pronounced dead after ambulance called
QM	Ambulance service provided under arrangement by a provider of services
QN	Ambulance service furnished directly by a provider of services
QP	Documentation is on file showing that the laboratory test(s) was ordered individually or ordered as a CPT-recognized panel other than automated profile codes 80002-80019, G0058, G0059, and G0060.
QQ	Claim submitted with a written statement of intent
QS	Monitored anesthesia care service

QT	Recording and storage on tape by an analog tape recorder
QU	Physician providing service in an urban HPSA
QV	Item or service provided as routine care in a medicare qualifying clinical trial
QW	CLIA waived test
QX	CRNA service: with medical direction by a physician
QY	Medical direction of one certified registered nurse anesthetist (CRNA) by an anesthesiologist
QZ	CRNA service: without medical direction by a physician
RC	Right coronary artery
RP	Replacement and repair-RP may be used to indicate replacement of DME, orthotic and prosthetic devices which have been in use for sometime. The claim shows the code for the part, followed by the 'RP' modifier and the charge for the part.
RR	Rental (use the 'RR' modifier when DME is to be rented)
RT	Right side (used to identify procedures performed on the right side of the body)
SA	Nurse practitioner rendering service in collaboration with a physician
SB	Nurse midwife
SC	Medically necessary service or supply
SD	Services provided by registered nurse with specialized, highly technical home infusion training
SE	State and/or federally-funded programs/services
SF	Second opinion ordered by a professional review organization (PRO) per section 9401, p.l. 99-272 (100% reimbursement - no Medicare deductible or coinsurance)
SG	Ambulatory surgical center (ASC) facility service
SH	Second concurrently administered infusion therapy
SJ	Third or more concurrently administered infusion therapy
SK	Member of high risk population (use only with codes for immunization)
SL	State supplied vaccine
SM	Second surgical opinion
SN	Third surgical opinion
SQ	Item ordered by home health
ST	Related to trauma or injury
SU	Procedure performed in physician's office (to denote use of facility and equipment)
SV	Pharmaceuticals delivered to patient's home but not utilized
T1	Left foot, second digit
T2	Left foot, third digit
T3	Left foot, fourth digit
T4	Left foot, fifth digit
T5	Right foot, great toe
T6	Right foot, second digit

T7	Right foot, third digit
T8	Right foot, fourth digit
T9	Right foot, fifth digit
TA	Left foot, great toe
TC	Technical component. Under certain circumstances, a charge may be made for the technical component alone. Under those circumstances the technical component charge is identified by adding modifier 'TC' to the usual procedure number. Technical component charges are institutional charges and not billed separately by physicians. However, portable x-ray suppliers only bill for technical component and should utilize modifier tc. The charge data from portable x-ray suppliers will then be used to build customary and prevailing profiles.
TD	RN
TE	LPN/LVN
TF	Intermediate level of care
TG	Complex/high tech level of care
TH	Obstetrical treatment/services, prenatal or postpartum
TJ	Program group, child and/or adolescent
TK	Extra patient or passenger, non-ambulance
TL	Early intervention/individualized family service plan (IFSP)
TM	Individualized education program (IEP)
TN	Rural/outside providers' customary service area
TP	Medical transport, unloaded vehicle
TQ	Basic life support transport by a volunteer ambulance provider
TR	School-based individualized education program (iep) services provided outside the public school district responsible for the student
TS	Follow-up service
TT	Individualized service provided to more than one patient in same setting
TU	Special payment rate, overtime
TV	Special payment rates, holidays/weekends
TW	Back-up equipment
U1	Medicaid level of care 1, as defined by each state
U2	Medicaid level of care 2, as defined by each state
U3	Medicaid level of care 3, as defined by each state
U4	Medicaid level of care 4, as defined by each state
U5	Medicaid level of care 5, as defined by each state
U6	Medicaid level of care 6, as defined by each state
U7	Medicaid level of care 7, as defined by each state
U8	Medicaid level of care 8, as defined by each state
U9	Medicaid level of care 9, as defined by each state
UA	Medicaid level of care 10, as defined by each state
UB	Medicaid level of care 11, as defined by each state
UC	Medicaid level of care 12, as defined by each state
UD	Medicaid level of care 13, as defined by each state

UE	Used durable medical equipment
UF	Services provided in the morning
UG	Services provided in the afternoon
UH	Services provided in the evening
UJ	Services provided at night
UK	Services provided on behalf of the client to someone other than the client (collateral relationship)
UN	Two patients served
UP	Three patients served
UQ	Four patients served
UR	Five patients served
US	Six or more patients served
VP	Aphakic patient

CMS will no longer require the designation of the four PET Scan modifiers (N, E, P, S) and has made the determination that no paper documentation needs to be submitted up front with PET scan claims. Documentation requirements such as physician referral and medical necessity determination are to be maintained by the provider as part of the beneficiary's medical record. Review the expanded coverage of PET Scans and revised billing instructions. (PM AB-02-115 August 7, 2002)

APPENDIX 2 — ABBREVIATIONS AND ACRONYMS

HCPCS ABBREVIATIONS AND ACRONYMS

The following abbreviations and acronyms are used in the HCPCS descriptions:

/	or
<	less than
<=	less than equal to
>	greater than
>=	greater than equal to
133Xe	xenon, isotope of mass 133
AC	alternating current
AFO	ankle-foot orthosis
AICC	anti-inhibitor coagulant complex
AK	above the knee
AKA	above knee amputation
ALS	advanced life support
AMP	ampule
ART	artery
ART	Arterial
ASC	ambulatory surgery center
ATT	attached
A-V	Arteriovenous
AVF	arteriovenous fistula
BICROS	bilateral routing of signals
BK	below the knee
BLS	basic life support
BP	blood pressure
BTE	behind the ear (hearing aid)
CAPD	continuous ambulatory peritoneal dialysis
Carb	carbohydrate
cc	cubic centimeter
CCPD	continuous cycling peritoneal analysis
CHF	congestive heart failure
CIC	completely in the canal (hearing aid)
CIM	Coverage Issue Manual
Clsd	closed
cm	centimeter
CMN	certificate of medical necessity
CMS	Centers for Medicare and Medicaid Services
CMV	Cytomegalovirus
Conc	concentrate
Conc	concentrated
Cont	continuous
CP	clinical psychologist
CPAP	continuous positive airway pressure
CPT	Current Procedural Terminology
CRF	chronic renal failure
CRNA	certified registered nurse anesthetist
CROS	contralateral routing of signals
CSW	clinical social worker
CT	computed tomography
CTLSO	cervical-thoracic-lumbar-sacral orthosis
cu	cubic
DC	direct current
DI	diurnal rhythm
Dx	diagnosis
DLI	donor leukocyte infusion
DME	durable medical equipment
DMEPOS	Durable Medical Equipment, Prosthestics, Orthotics and Other Supplies
DMERC	durable medical equipment regional carrier
DR	diagnostic radiology
DX	diagnostic
e.g.	for example
Ea	each
ECF	extended care facility
EEG	electroencephalogram
EKG	electrocardiogram
EMG	electromyography
EO	elbow orthosis
EP	electrophysiologic
EPO	epoetin alfa
EPSDT	early periodic screening, diagnosis and treatment
ESRD	end-stage renal disease
Ex	extended
Exper	experimental
Ext	external
F	french
FDA	Food and Drug Administration
FDG-PET	Positron emission with tomography with 18 fluorodeoxyglucose
Fem	female
FPD	fixed partial denture
Fr	french
ft	foot
G-CSF	filgrastim (granulocyte colony-stimulating factor)
gm	gram (g)
H2O	water
HCl	hydrochloric acid, hydrochloride
HCPCS	Healthcare Common Procedural Coding System
HCT, hct	hematocrit
HFO	hand-finger orthosis
HHA	home health agency
HI	high

HI-LO	high-low		mgs	milligrams
HIT	home infusion therapy		MHT	megahertz
HKAFO	hip-knee-ankle foot orthosis		ml	milliliter
HLA	human leukocyte antigen		mm	millimeter
HMES	heat and moisture exchange system		MRI	magnetic resonance imaging
HNPCC	Hereditary non-polyposis colorectal cancer		NA	sodium
HO	hip orthosis		NCI	National Cancer Institute
HPSA	health professional shortage area		NEC	not elsewhere classified
ip	interphalangeal		NG	nasogastric
I-131	Iodine 131		NH	nursing home
ICF	intermediate care facility		NMES	neuromuscular electrical stimulation
ICU	intensive care facility		NOC	not otherwise classified
IM	intramuscular		NOS	not otherwise specified
in	inch		O2	oxygen
INF	infusion		OBRA	Omnibus Budget Reconciliation Act
INH	inhalation solution		OMT	osteopathic manipulation therapy
INJ	injection		OPPS	outpatient prospective payment system
IOL	intraocular lens		OSA	obstructive sleep apnea
IPD	intermittent peritoneal dialysis		Ost	ostomy
IPPB	intermittent positive pressure breathing		OTH	other routes of administration
IT	intrathecal administration		oz	ounce
ITC	in the canal (hearing aid)		PA	physician's assistant
ITE	in the ear (hearing aid)		PAR	parenteral
IU	international units		PCA	patient controlled analgesia
IV	intravenous		PCH	pouch
IVF	in vitro fertilization		PEN	parenteral and enteral nutrition
KAFO	knee-ankle-foot orthosis		PENS	percutaneous electrical nerve stimulation
KO	knee orthosis		PET	positron emission tomography
KOH	potassium hydroxide		PHP	pre-paid health plan
L	left		PHP	physician hospital plan
LASIK	laser in situ keratomileusis		PI	paramedic intercept
LAUP	laser assisted uvulopalatoplasty		PICC	peripherally inserted central venous catheter
lbs	pounds		PKR	photorefractive keratotomy
LDL	low density lipoprotein		Pow	powder
Lo	low		PRO	peer review organization
LPM	liters per minute		PTB	patellar tendon bearing
LPN/LVN	Licensed Practical Nurse/Licensed Vocational Nurse		PTK	phototherapeutic keratectomy
LSO	lumbar-sacral orthosis		PVC	polyvinyl chloride
mp	metacarpophalangeal		R	right
mcg	microgram		Repl	replace
mCi	millicurie		RN	registered nurse
MCM	Medicare Carriers Manual		RP	retrograde pyelogram
MCP	metacarparpophalangeal joint		Rx	prescription
MCP	monthly capitation payment		SACH	solid ankle, cushion heel
mEq	milliequivalent		SC	subcutaneous
mg	milligram		SCT	specialty care transport

SEO	shoulder-elbow orthosis
SEWHO	shoulder-elbow-wrist-hand orthosis
SEXA	Single energy x-ray absorptiometry
SGD	speech generating device
SGD	sinus rhythm
SM	samarium
SNF	skilled nursing facility
SO	shoulder orthosis
Sol	solution
SQ	square
SR	screen
ST	standard
ST	sustained release
Syr	syrup
TABS	tablets
Tc	Technetium
Tc 99m	technetium isotope
TENS	transcutaneous electrical nerve stimulator
THKAO	thoracic-hip-knee-ankle orthosis
TLSO	thoracic-lumbar-sacral-orthosis
TM	temporomandibular
TMJ	temporomandibular joint
TPN	total parenteral nutrition
U	unit
VAR	various routes of administration
w	with
w/	with
w/o	with or without
WAK	wearable artificial kidney
wc	wheelchair
WHFO	wrist-hand-finger orthotic
Wk	week
wo	without
Xe	xenon (isotope mass of xenon 133)

APPENDIX 3 — TABLE OF DRUGS

INTRODUCTION AND DIRECTIONS

The *HCPCS 2003* Table of Drugs is designed to quickly and easily direct the user to drug names and their corresponding codes. Both generic and brand or trade names are alphabetically listed in the "Drug Name" column of the table. The associated A, C, J, K, Q, or S code is given only for the generic name of the drug. Brand or trade name drugs are cross-referenced to the appropriate generic drug name.

The "Amount" column lists the stated amount for the referenced generic drug as provided by CMS (formerly Health Care Financing Administration or HCFA). "Up to" listings are inclusive of all quantities up to and including the listed amount. All other listings are for the amount of the drug as listed. The editors recognize that the availability of some drugs in the quantities listed is dependent on many variables beyond the control of the clinical ordering clerk. The availability in your area of regularly used drugs in the most cost-effective quantities should be relayed to your third-party payers.

The "Route of Administration" column addresses the most common methods of delivering the referenced generic drug as described in current pharmaceutical literature. The official definitions for Level II drug codes generally describe administration other than by oral method. Therefore, with a handful of exceptions, oral-delivered options for most drugs are omitted from the Route of Administration column. The following abbreviations and listings are used in the Route of Administration column:

IA — Intra-arterial administration

IV — Intravenous administration

IM — Intramuscular administration

IT — Intrathecal

SC — Subcutaneous administration

INH — Administration by inhaled solution

INJ — Injection not otherwise specified

VAR — Various routes of administration

OTH — Other routes of administration

ORAL — Administered orally

Intravenous administration includes all methods, such as gravity infusion, injections, and timed pushes. When several routes of administration are listed, the first listing is simply the first, or most common, method as described in current reference literature. The "VAR" posting denotes various routes of administration and is used for drugs that are commonly administered into joints, cavities, tissues, or topical applications, in addition to other parenteral administrations. Listings posted with "OTH" alert the user to other administration methods, such as suppositories or catheter injections.

Please be reminded that the Table of Drugs, as well as all HCPCS Level II National definitions and listings, constitutes a post-treatment medical reference for billing purposes only. Although the editors have exercised all normal precautions to ensure the accuracy of the table and related material, the use of any of this information to select medical treatment is entirely inappropriate.

APPENDIX 3 — TABLE OF DRUGS

Drug Name	Route	Unit	Code
A-HYDROCORT	IV, IM, SC	50 mg	J1710
A-METHAPRED	IM, IV	125 mg	J2930
ABBOKINASE	IV	5,000 IU vial	J3364
ABBOKINASE, OPEN CATH	IV	250,000 IU vial	J3365
ACETAZOLAMIDE SODIUM	IM, IV	500 mg	J1120
ACETYLCYSTEINE, UNIT DOSE	INH	1 g	J7608
ACOVA	IV	5 mg	C9121
ACTH	IV, IM, SC	40 units	J0800
ACTHAR	IV, IM, SC	40 units	J0800
ACTHREL	IV	1 dose	Q2005
ACTIMMUNE	SC	3 million units	J9216
ACTIVASE	IV	1 mg	J2997
ACYCLOVIR SODIUM INJECTION	IV	50 mg	S0071
ADRENALIN CHLORIDE	SC, IM	1 ml amp	J0170
ADRENALIN, EPINEPHRINE	SC, IM	1 ml amp	J0170
ADRIAMYCIN PFS	IV	10 mg	J9000
ADRIAMYCIN RDF	IV	10 mg	J9000
ADRUCIL	IV	500 mg	J9190
AEROBID	INH	1 mg	J7641
AGALSIDASE BETA	INJ	1 mg	C9208
AGGRASTAT	INJ	12.5 mg	J3245
AGRATROBAN	IV	5 mg	C9121
AIRET	INH	1 mg or 5 mg	J7619
AKINETON	IM, IV	5 mg	J0190
ALATROFLOXACIN MESYLATE	IV	100 mg	J0200
ALBECET	IV	10 mg	J0287
ALBUTEROL	INH	5 mg	J7621
ALBUTEROL, CONCENTRATE	INH	1 mg	J7618
ALBUTEROL, UNIT DOSE	INH	1 mg or 5 mg	J7619
ALDESLEUKIN	IM, IV	1 vial	J9015
ALDOMET	IV	250 mg	J0210
ALEFACEPT	IV	0.5 mg	J0215
ALEMTUZUMAB	IV	10 mg	J9010
ALFERON N	IM	250,000 IU	J9215
ALGLUCERASE	IV	10 units	J0205
ALKABAN-AQ	IV	1 mg	J9360
ALKERAN	IV	50 mg	J9245
ALKERAN	ORAL	2 mg	J8600
ALPHA 1-PROTEINASE INHIBITOR, HUMAN	IV	10 mg	J0256
ALPHANINE SD	IV	1 IU	J7193
ALPROSTADIL	IV	1.25 mcg	J0270
ALPROSTADIL, URETHRAL SUPPOSITORY	OTHER	1 unit	J0275
ALTEPLASE RECOMBINANT	IV	1 mg	J2997
ALTEPLASE RECOMBINANT	IV	1 mg	J2997
ALUPENT, THROUGH DME, CONCENTRATE	INH	10 mg	J7668
ALUPENT, UNIT DOSE	INH	10 mg	J7669
AMBISOME	IV	10 mg	J0289
AMCORT	IM	5 mg	J3302
AMEVIVE	IM, IV	0.5 mg	J0215

Drug Name	Route	Unit	Code
AMICAR	5 G		IV
AMIFOSTINE	IV, INJ	500 mg	J0207
AMIKACIN SULFATE	IV, IM	100 mg	S0072
AMIKACIN SULFATE	IV, IM	500 mg	S0016
AMIKIN	IV, IM	100 mg	S0072
AMINOCAPROIC ACID	IV	5 g	S0017
AMINOLEVALINIC ACID HCL 20%	TOPICAL	354 mg	J7308
AMINOPHYLLINE/AMINOPHYLLIN	IV	250 mg	J0280
AMIODARONE HYDROCHLORIDE	IV	30 mg	J0282
AMITRIPTYLINE HCL	IM	20 mg	J1320
AMOBARBITAL	IM, IV	125 mg	J0300
AMPHOCIN	IV	50 mg	J0285
AMPHOTEC	IV	10 mg	J0288
AMPHOTERICIN B	IV	50 mg	J0285
AMPHOTERICIN B CHOLESTERYL SULFATE COMPLEX	IV	10 MG	
AMPHOTERICIN B LIPID COMPLEX	IV	10 mg	J0287
AMPHOTERICIN B LIPOSOME	IV	10 mg	J0289
AMPICILLIN SODIUM	IM, IV	500 mg	J0290
AMPICILLIN SODIUM/SULBACTAM SODIUM	IM, IV	1.5 gm	J0295
AMYTAL	IM, IV	125 MG	
ANCEF	IM, IV	500 mg	J0690
ANDREST 90-4	IM	1 cc	J0900
ANDRO L.A. 200	IM	200 mg	J3130
ANDRO-ESTRO 90-4	IM	1 cc	J0900
ANDROGYN L.A.	IM	1 cc	J0900
ANDROPOSITORY100	IM	100 mg	J3120
ANECTINE	IM, IV	20 mg	J0330
ANERGAN 50	IM, IV	50 mg	J2550
ANGIOMAX	IV	1 mg	J0583
ANISTREPLASE	IV	30 units	J0350
ANTAGON	SC	250 mcg	S0132
ANTI-INHIBITOR	IV	1 IU	J7198
ANTISPAS	IM	20 mg	J0500
ANTITHROMBIN III (HUMAN)	IV	1 IU	J7197
ANTIZOL	IV	1.5 MG	
ANZEMET	ORAL	100 mg	Q0180
APRESOLINE	IM, IV	20 mg	J0360
APROTININ	IV	10,000 kiu	Q2003
AQUAMEPHYTON	IM, SC, IV	1 mg	J3430
ARALEN HCL	IM	250 mg	J0390
ARAMINE	IV, IM, SC	10 mg	J0380
ARANESP	IV, SC	5 mcg	J0880
ARBUTAMINE HCL	IV	1 mg	J0395
AREDIA	IV	30 mg	J2430
ARESTIN	ORAL	250 mg	Q0173
ARGATROBAN	IV	5 mg	C9121
ARISTOCORT FORTE	IM	5 mg	J3302
ARISTOCORT INTRALESIONAL	IM	5 mg	J3302

Drug Name	Route	Unit	Code
ARISTOSPAN INTRAARTICULAR	VAR	5 mg	J3303
ARISTOSPAN INTRALESIONAL	VAR	5 mg	J3303
ARIXTRA	SC	0.5 mg	J1652
AROMASIN	ORAL	25 mg	S0156
ARSENIC TRIOXIDE	IV	1 mg	J9017
ASPARAGINASE	IV, IM	10,000 units	J9020
ASTRAMORPH PF	IT, IV, SC	100 mg	J2271
ATGAM	IV	250 mg	J7504
ATIVAN	IM, IV	2 mg	J2060
ATROPINE, CONCENTRATED	INH	1 mg	J7635
ATROPINE SULFATE	IV, IM, SC	0.3 mg	J0460
ATROPINE, UNIT DOSE	INH	1 mg	J7636
ATROVENT, THROUGH DME, UNIT DOSE)	INH	1 mg	J7644
AUROTHIOGLUCOSE	IM	50 mg	J2910
AUTOLOGOUS CULTURED CHONDROCYTES	OTH	implant	J7330
AUTOPLEX T	IV	1 IU	J7198
AVELOX	IV	100 mg	J2280
AVONEX	IM	11 mcg	Q3025
AVONEX	IM	33 mcg	J1825
AVONEX	SC	11 mcg	Q3026
AZACTAM	IV, INJ	500 mg	S0073
AZATHIOPRINE	ORAL	50 mg	J7500
AZATHIOPRINE, PARENTERAL	IV	100 mg	J7501
AZITHROMYCIN	IV	500 mg	J0456
AZITHROMYCIN DIHYDRATE	ORAL	1 g	Q0144
AZMACORT, THROUGH DME, UNIT DOSE	INH	1 mg	J7684
AZTREONAM	IV, INJ	500 mg	
BACLOFEN	IT	10 mg	J0475
BACLOFEN FOR INTRATHECAL TRIAL	IT	50 mcg	J0476
BACLOFEN INTRATHECAL REFILL KIT	IT	500 mcg	C9008
BACLOFEN INTRATHECAL SCREENING KIT	IT	1 amp	C9007
BACLOFEN REFILL KIT	IT	2000 mcg	C9009
BACTOCILL	IM, IV	250 mg	J2700
BACTRIM IV	IV	10 ml	S0039
BAL IN OIL	IM	100 mg	J0470
BANFLEX	IV, IM	60 mg	J2360
BASILIXIMAB	IV	20 mg	Q2019
BAYGAM	IV	10 mg	J1564
BCG	IV	1 vial	J9031
BECAPLERMIN GEL 0.01%	OTH	0.5 g	S0157
BENADRYL	IM, IV	50 mg	J1200
BENOJECT-50	IM, IV	50 mg	J1200
BENTYL	IM	20 mg	J0500
BENZTROPINE MESYLATE	IM, IV	1 mg	J0515
BETAMESTHASONE, UNIT DOSE	INH	1 mg	J7624
BETAMETH	IM, IV	4 mg	J0704
BETAMETHASONE ACETATE & BETAMETHASONE SODIUM PHOSPHATE	IM	3 mg of each	J0702
BETAMETHASONE SODIUM PHOSPHATE	IM, IV	4 mg	J0704

Drug Name	Route	Unit	Code
BETASERON	SC	0.25 mg	J1830
BETHANECHOL CHLORIDE	SC	5 mg	J0520
BICILLIN C-R	IM	1,200,000 units	J0570
BICILLIN C-R	IM	2,400,000 units	J0550
BICILLIN C-R	IM	3000, 000 units	J0530
BICILLIN C-R 900/300	IM	1,200,000 units	J0540
BICILLIN L-A	IM	2,400,000 units	J0580
BICILLIN L-A	IM	600,000 units	J0560
BICNU	IV	100 mg	J9050
BIPERIDEN LACTATE	IM, IV	5 mg	J0190
BITOLTEROL MESYLATE, CONCENTRATED	INH	1 mg	J7628
BITOLTEROL MESYLATE, UNIT DOSE	INH	1 mg	J7629
BIVALIRUDIN	IV	1 mg	J0583
BLENOXANE	IM, IV, SC	15 units	J9040
BLEOMYCIN SULFATE	IM, IV, SC	15 units	J9040
BOTOX	IM	1 unit	J0585
BOTULINUM TOXIN TYPE A	IM	1 unit	J0585
BOTULINUM TOXIN TYPE B	IM	100 units	J0587
BRETHINE	INH	1 mg	J7681
BRETHINE	INH	mg	J7680
BRETHINE	SC	1 mg	J3105
BRICANYL	SC	1 mg	J3105
BRICANYL, CONCENTRATED	INH	1 mg	J7680
BRICANYL, UNIT DOSE	INH	1 mg	J7681
BROMPHENIRAMINE MALEATE	IM, SC, IV	10 mg	J0945
BUDESONIDE, THROUGH DME, CONCENTRATED	INH	0.25 mg	J7633
BUDESONIDE, THROUGH DME, UNIT DOSE	INH	0.25-0.50 mg	J7626
BUPIVICAINE HCL	OTH	30 ml	S0020
BUPRENEX	IM, IV	0.1 mg	J0592
BUPRENORPHINE HYDROCHLORIDE	IM, IV	0.1 mg	J0592
BUPROPION HCL	ORAL	150 mg/bottle 60 tabs	S0106
BUSULFAN	IV	6 mg	C1178
BUSULFAN	ORAL	2 mg	J8510
BUTORPHANOL TARTRATE	INH	25 mg	S0012
BUTORPHANOL TARTRATE	IV	1 mg	J0595
BUTORPHANOL TARTRATE	NASAL SPRAY	25 mg	S0012
CABERGOLINE	ORAL	0.5 mg	Q2001
CAFCIT	IV	5 mg	J0706
CAFFEINE CITRATE	IV	5 mg	J0706
CALCIJEX	IM	0.1 mcg ampule	J0636
CALCIMAR	SC, IM	400 units	J0630
CALCITONIN-SALMON	SC, IM	400 units	J0630
CALCITRIOL	IM	0.1 mcg ampule	J0636
CALCIUM DISODIUM VERSENATE	IV	150 mg	J3520
CALCIUM DISODIUM VERSENATE	IV, SC, IM	1000 mg	J0600
CALCIUM EDTA	IV	150 mg	J3520
CALCIUM EDTA	IV, SC, IM	1000 mg	J0600
CALCIUM GLUCONATE	IV	10 ml	J0610

Appendixes

Drug Name	Route	Unit	Code
CALCIUM GLYCEROPHOSPHATE AND CALCIUM LACTATE	IM, SC	10 ml	J0620
CALPHOSAN	IM, SC	10 ml	J0620
CAMPATH	IV	10 mg	J9010
CAMPTOSAR	IV	20 mg	J9206
CANCIDAS	IV	5 mg	J0637
CAPECITABINE	ORAL	150 mg	J8520
CAPECITABINE	ORAL	500 mg	J8521
CARBOCAINE	VAR	10 ml	J0670
CARBOPLATIN	IV	50 mg	J9045
CARMUSTINE	IV	100 mg	J9050
CARNITOR	IV	per 1 gm	J1955
CARTICEL	OTH	implant	J7330
CASPOFUNGIN ACETATE	IV	5 mg	J0637
CATAPRES	VAR, ORAL	1 mg	J0735
CAVERJECT	IV	1.25 mcg	J0270
CEFADYL	IV, IM	1 g	J0710
CEFAZOLIN SODIUM	IV, IM	500 mg	J0690
CEFEPIME HCL	IM, IV	500 mg	J0692
CEFIZOX	IV, IM	500 mg	J0715
CEFOTAN	IV, IM	500 mg	S0074
CEFOTAXIME SODIUM	IV, IM	1 g	J0698
CEFOTETAN DISODIUM	IV, IM	500 mg	S0074
CEFOXITIN SODIUM	IV, IM	1 g	J0694
CEFTAZIDIME	IM, IV	500 mg	J0713
CEFTIZOXIME SODIUM	IV, IM	500 mg	J0715
CEFTRIAXONE SODIUM	IV, IM	250 mg	J0696
CEFUROXIME SODIUM	IM, IV	750 mg	J0697
CELESTONE PHOSPHATE	IM, IV	4 mg	J0704
CELESTONE SOLUSPAN	IM	3 mg of each	J0702
CELLCEPT	ORAL	250 mg	J7517
CEPHALOTHIN SODIUM	IM, IV	1 g	J1890
CEPHAPIRIN SODIUM	IV, IM	1 g	J0710
CERBYX	IV, IM	50 mg	Q2002
CEREBYX	IV, IM	50 mg	Q2009
CEREBYX	IV, IM	750 mg	S0078
CEREDASE	IV	10 units	J0205
CEREZYME	IV	unit	J1785
CERUBIDINE	IV	10 mg	J9150
CHLORAMPHENICOL SODIUM SUCCINATE	IV	1 g	J0720
CHLORDIAZEPOXIDE HCL	IM, IV	100 mg	J1990
CHLOROMYCETIN SODIUM SUCCINATE	IV	1 g	J0720
CHLOROPROCAINE HCL	VAR	30 ml	J2400
CHLOROQUINE HCL	IM	250 mg	J0390
CHLOROTHIAZIDE SODIUM	IV	500 mg	J1205
CHLORPROMAZINE HCL	IM, IV	50 mg	J3230
CHLORPROMAZINE HCL	ORAL	10 mg	Q0171
CHLORPROMAZINE HCL	ORAL	25 mg	Q0172
CHOREX	IM	1,000 USP units	J0725

Drug Name	Route	Unit	Code
CHOREX	IM	1,000 USP units	J0725
CHORIONIC GONADOTROPIN	IM	1,000 USP units	J0725
CHORIONIC GONADOTROPIN	IM	1,000 USP units	J0725
CHORON 10	IM	1,000 USP units	J0725
CHORON 10	IM	1,000 USP units	J0725
CIDOFOVIR	IV	375 mg	J0740
CILASTATIN SODIUM, IMIPENEM	IV, IM	250 mg	J0743
CIMETIDINE HYDROCHLORIDE	IV, IM	300 mg	S0023
CISPLATIN	IV	10 mg	J9060
CISPLATIN	IV	50 mg	J9062
CLADRIBINE	IV	1 mg	J9065
CLAFORAN	IV, IM	1 g	J0698
CLEOCIN PHOSPHATE	IV, IM	300 mg	S0077
CLINAGEN LA 40	IM	40 mg	J0970
CLINDAMYCIN PHOSPHATE	INJ	300 mg	S0077
CLONIDINE HCL	VAR, ORAL	1 mg	J0735
COBEX	IM, SC	1,000 mcg	J3420
CODEINE PHOSPHATE	IM, IV, SC	30 mg	J0745
COGENTIN	IM, IV	1 mg	J0515
COLCHICINE	IV	1 mg	J0760
COLHIST	IM, SC, IV	10 mg	J0945
COLISTIMETHATE SODIUM	IM, IV	150 mg	J0770
COLY-MYCIN M	IM, IV	150 mg	J0770
COMPAZINE	IM, IV	10 mg	J0780
CONTRACEPTIVE PILLS FOR BIRTH CONTROL	ORAL	-	S4993
COPAXONE	INJ	1 mg	J1595
COPPER CONTRACEPTIVE, INTRAUTERINE	OTH	-	J7300
CORDARONE IV	IV	30 mg	J0282
CORTASTAT	IM, IV	1 mg	J1100
CORTASTAT LA	IM, IV	1 mg	J1094
CORTICORELIN OVINE TRIFLUTATE	IV	1 dose	Q2005
CORTICORELIN OVINE TRIFLUTATE	IV	1dose	Q2005
CORTICOTROPIN	IV, IM, SC	40 units	J0800
CORTICOTROPIN	IV, IM, SC	40 units	J0800
CORTROSYN	IM, IV	per 0.25 mg	J0835
CORVERT	IV	1 mg	J1742
COSMEGEN	IV	0.5 mg	J9120
COSYNTROPIN	IM, IV	0.25 mg	J0835
CROMOLYN SODIUM, INHALATION SOLUTION	INH	10 mg	J7631
CYCLOPHOSPHAMIDE	IV	1 g	J9091
CYCLOPHOSPHAMIDE	IV	100 mg	J9070
CYCLOPHOSPHAMIDE	IV	2 g	J9092
CYCLOPHOSPHAMIDE	IV	200 mg	J9080
CYCLOPHOSPHAMIDE	IV	500 mg	J9090
CYCLOPHOSPHAMIDE, LYOPHILIZED	IV	1 g	J9096
CYCLOPHOSPHAMIDE, LYOPHILIZED	IV	100 mg	J9093
CYCLOPHOSPHAMIDE, LYOPHILIZED	IV	2 g	J9097
CYCLOPHOSPHAMIDE, LYOPHILIZED	IV	200 mg	J9094

Drug Name	Route	Unit	Code
CYCLOPHOSPHAMIDE, LYOPHILIZED	IV	500 mg	J9095
CYCLOPHOSPHAMIDE, ORAL	ORAL	25 mg	J8530
CYCLOSPORINE, ORAL	ORAL	100 mg	J7502
CYCLOSPORINE, ORAL	ORAL	25 mg	J7515
CYCLOSPORINE, PARENTERAL	IV	250 mg	J7516
CYTARABINE	SC, IV	100 mg	J9100
CYTARABINE	SC, IV	500 mg	J9110
CYTARABINE LIPOSOME	INJ	10 mg	J9098
CYTOMEGALOVIRUS IMMUNE GLOBULIN INTRAVENOUS (HUMAN)	IV	1 vial	J0850
CYTOSAR-U	SC, IV	10 mg	J9100
CYTOSAR-U	SC, IV	100 mg	J9100
CYTOSAR-U	SC, IV	500 mg	J9110
CYTOVENE	IV	500 mg	J1570
CYTOXAN	IV	100 mg	J9070
D.H.E. 45	IM, IV	1 mg	J1110
DACARBAZINE	IV	100 mg	J9130
DACARBAZINE	IV	200 mg	J9140
DACLIZUMAB	OTH	25 mg	J7513
DACTINOMYCIN	IV	0.5 mg	J9120
DALALONE	IM, IV	1 mg	J1100
DALALONE L.A.	IM IV	1 mg	J1094
DALTEPARIN SODIUM	SC	per 2500 IU	J1645
DARBEPOETIN ALFA	IV, SC	5 mcg	J0880
DARBEPOETIN ALFA	SC, IV	5 mcg	J0880
DAUNORUBICIN CITRATE, LIPOSOMAL FORMULATION	IV	10 mg	J9151
DAUNORUBICIN HCL	IV	10 mg	J9150
DAUNOXOME	IV	10 mg	J9151
DDAVP	IV, SC	1 mcg	J2597
DE-COMBEROL	IM	1 ml	J1060
DECA-DURABOLIN	IM	50 mg	J2320
DECADRON PHOSPHATE	IM, IV	1 mg	J1100
DECADRON-LA	IM, IV	1 mg	J1094
DECAJECT	IM, IV	1 mg	J1100
DECAJECT-L-A	IM, IV	1 mg	J1094
DEFEROXAMINE MESYLATE POWDER	IM, SC, IV	500 mg	J0895
DELADUMONE	IM	1 cc	J0900
DELADUMONE OB	IM	1 cc	J0900
DELATEST	IM	100 mg	J3120
DELATESTADIOL	IM	1 cc	J0900
DELATESTRYL	IM	200 mg	J3130
DELESTROGEN	IM	10 mg	J1380
DELESTROGEN	IM	40 mg	J0970
DELTA-CORTEF	ORAL	5 mg	J7510
DELTA-CORTEF	ORAL	any dose, 100 tabl	J7506
DELTASONE	ORAL	any dose, 100 tabl	J7506
DEMADEX	IV	10 mg/ml	J3265
DEMEROL HCL	IM, IV, SC	100 mg	J2175
DENILEUKIN DIFTITOX	IV	300 mcg	J9160

Drug Name	Route	Unit	Code
DEPANDRO 200	IM	1 cc, 200 mg	J1080
DEPANDROGYN	IM	1 ml	J1060
DEPGYNOGEN	IM	5 mg	J1000
DEPMEDALONE 40	IM	40 mg	J1030
DEPMEDALONE 80	IM	80 mg	J1040
DEPO-ESTRADIOL CYPIONATE	IM	5 mg	J1000
DEPO-MEDROL	IM	20 mg	J1020
DEPO-PROVERA	IM	50 mg	J1051
DEPO-TESTADIOL	IM	1 cc, 200 mg	J1080
DEPO-TESTADIOL	IM	1 ml	J1060
DEPO-TESTOSTERONE	IM	1 cc, 200 mg	J1080
DEPOANDRO 100	IM	100 mg	J1070
DEPOCYT	INJ	10 mg	J9098
DEPOGEN	IM	5 mg	J1000
DEPOTESTOGEN	IM	1 ml	J1060
DESFERAL MESYLATE	IV, SC	1 mcg	J2597
DEXAMETHASONE ACETATE	IM, IV	1 mg	J1094
DEXAMETHASONE, CONCENTRATE	INH	1 mg	J7637
DEXAMETHASONE SODIUM PHOSPHATE	IM, IV	.1 mg	J1100
DEXAMETHASONE, UNIT DOSE	INH	1 mg	J7638
DEXASONE	IM, IV	1 mg	J1100
DEXASONE L.A	IM, IV	1 mg	J1094
DEXFERRUM	INJ	50 mg	J1750
DEXONE LA	IM, IV	1 mg	J1094
DEXRAZOXANE HCL	IV	250 mg	J1190
DEXTRAN 40	IV	500 ml	J7100
DEXTRAN 75	IV	500 ml	J7110
DEXTROSE 5%/45% NS W/POTASSIUM CHLORIDE & MAGNESIUM SULFATE	IV	1000 ml	S5013, S5014
DEXTROSE 5% AND NORMAL SALINE 45%	IV	1000 ml	S5010
DEXTROSE 5% IN LACTATED RINGER'S	IV	1000 ml	S5011
DEXTROSE 5% IN WATER (D5W)	IV	1000 cc	J7070
DEXTROSE 5% WITH POTASSIUM CHLORIDE	IV	1000 ml	S5012
DEXTROSE/ELECTSOL	IV	1 ml	Q2002
DEXTROSE/NORMAL SALINE SOLUTION (5%)	IV	500 ml = 1 unit	J7042
DEXTROSE/WATER (5%)	IV	500 ml = 1 unit	J7060
DI-SPAZ	IM	20 mg	J0500
DIAMOX	IM, IV	500 mg	J1120
DIAMOX	IM, IV	500 mg	J1120
DIASTAT	IM, IV	5 mg	J3360
DIAZEPAM	IM, IV	5 mg	J3360
DIAZOXIDE	IV	300 mg	J1730
DICYCLOMINE HCL	IM	20 mg	J0500
DIDRONEL	IV	300 mg	J1436
DIETHYLSTILBESTROL DIPHOSPHATE	IV	250 mg	J9165
DIFLUCAN	INJ	200 mg	J1450
DIGIBIND	IV	1 vial	Q2006
DIGOXIN	IM, IV	0.5 mg	J1160

APPENDIX 3 — TABLE OF DRUGS

Drug Name	Route	Unit	Code	Drug Name	Route	Unit	Code
DIGOXIN IMMUNE FAB (OVINE)	IV	1 vial	Q2006	EDEX	IV	per 1.25 mcg	J0270
DIHYDROERGOTAMINE MESYLATE	IM, IV	1 mg	J1110	ELAVIL	IM	20 mg	J1320
DILANTIN	IM, IV	per 50 mg	J1165	ELITEK	IV	0.5 mg	J2783
DILAUDID	SC, IM, IV	4 mg	J1170	ELLENCE	IV	2 mg	J9178
DILAUDID BY DME	OTH	250 units	S0092	ELLIOTT'S B SOLUTION	IV	1 ml	Q2002
DILOR	IM	500 mg	J1180	ELOXATIN	IV	0.5 mg	J9263
DIMENHYDRINATE	IM, IV	50 mg	J1240	ELSPAR	IV, IM	10,000 units	J9020
DIMERCAPROL	IM	100 mg	J0470	EMINASE	IV	30 units	J0350
DIMETHYL SULFOXIDE50%	OTH	50 ml	J1212	ENBREL	INJ	25 mg	J1438
DINATE	IM, IV	50 mg	J1240	ENOXAPARIN SODIUM	SC	10 mg	J1650
DIPHENHYDRAMINE HCL	IM, IV	50 mg	J1200	EPINEPHRINE, ADRENALIN	SC, IM	1 ml amp	J0170
DIPYRIDAMOLE	IV	10 mg	J1245	EPIRUBICIN HCL	IV	2 mg	J9178
DIURIL SODIUM	IV	500 mg	J1205	EPOETIN ALPHA, FOR NON ESRD USE	IV, SC	1,000 units	Q0136
DIZAC	INJ	5 mg	J3360	EPOGEN FOR PATIENTS NOT ON DIALYSIS	IV, SC	1,000 units	Q0136
DME INSULIN FOR PUMP	OTH	50 units	J1817	EPOPROSTENOL		0.5 mg	J1325
DMSO, DIMETHYL SULFOXIDE 50%	OTH	50 ml	J1212	EPSOM SALTS	IV, IM	500 mg	J3475
DOBUTAMINE HCL	IV	250 mg	J1250	EPTIFIBATIDE	INJ	5 mg	J1327
DOBUTREX	QIV	250 mg	J1250	ERGONOVINE MALEATE	IM, IV	0.2 mg	J1330
DOCETAXEL		20 mg	J9170	ERGOTRATE MALEATE	IM, IV	0.2 mg	J1330
DOLASETRON MESYLATE	INJ	10 mg	J1260	ERTAPENEM SODIUM, INJECTION	IV	500 mg	J1335
DOLASETRON MESYLATE	ORAL	100 mg	Q0180	ERYTHROCIN	IV	500 mg	J1364
DOLASETRON MESYLATE INJECTION	IV	10 mg	J1260	ERYTHROMYCIN LACTOBIONATE	IV	500 mg	J1364
DOLOPHINE HCL	IM, SC	10 mg	J1230	ESTRADIOL VALERATE	IM	10 mg	J1380
DORNASE ALPHA, UNIT DOSE	INH	per mg	J7639	ESTRADIOL VALERATE	IM	20 mg	J1390
DOSTINEX	ORAL	0.5 mg	Q2001	ESTRADIOL VALERATE	IM	40 mg	J0970
DOXERCALCIFEROL	IV	1 mcg	J1270	ESTRO-CYP	IM	5 mg	J1000
DOXIL	IV	10 mg	J9001	ESTRO-L.A.	IM	5 mg	J1000
DOXORUBICIN HCL	IV	10 mg	J9000	ESTROGEN, CONJUGATED	IV, IM	25 mg	J1410
DOXORUBICIN HCL, ALL LIPID FORMULATIONS	IV	10 mg	J9001	ESTRONE	IM	1 mg	J1435
DRAMAMINE	IM, IV	50 mg	J1240	ESTRONE 5	IM	1 mg	J1435
DRAMANATE	IM, IV	50 mg	J1240	ETANERCEPT	INJ	25 mg	J1438
DRAMOJECT	IM, IV	50 mg	J1240	ETHAMOLIN	IV	100 mg	Q2007
DRONABINOL	ORAL	2.5 mg	Q0167	ETHANOLAMINE	IV	100 mg	Q2007
DRONABINOL	ORAL	5 mg	Q0168	ETHYOL	IV, INJ	500 mg	J0207
DROPERIDOL	IM, IV	5 mg	J1790	ETIDRONATE DISODIUM	IV	300 mg	J1436
DROPERIDOL AND FENTANYL CITRATE	IM, IV	2 ml amp	J1810	ETOPOSIDE	IV	10 mg	J9181
DRUG ADMINISTERED THROUGH A METERED DOSE INHALER	INH	-	J3535	ETOPOSIDE	IV	100 mg	J9182
DTIC-DOME	IV	200 mg	J9140	ETOPOSIDE	ORAL	50 mg	J8560
DUA-GEN L.A.	IM	1 cc	J0900	EVERONE	IM, SC	100 mg	J3120
DURA-ESTRIN	IM	5 mg	J1000	EXEMESTANE	ORAL	25 mg	S0156
DURACILLIN A.S.	IM	600,000 units	J2510	FACTOR, HEMOPHILIA CLOTTING, NOC	INJ	-	J7199
DURAMORPH	IM, IV, SC	10 mg	J2270	FACTOR IX	IV	1 IU	J7193
DURATEST-100	IM	100 mg	J1070	FACTOR IX	IV	1 IU	J7194
DURATEST-200	IM	1 cc, 200 mg	J1080	FACTOR IX	IV	1 IU	J7195
DURATESTRIN	IM	1 ml	J1060	FACTOR IX, NON-RECOMBINANT		1 IU	J7193
DYPHYLLINE	IM	500 mg	J1180	FACTOR IX, RECOMBINANT		1 IU	J7195
EDETATE CALCIUM DISODIUM	IV	150 mg	J3520	FACTOR VIIA	IV	1.2 mg	Q0187
EDETATE CALCIUM DISODIUM	IV, SC, IM	1000 mg	J0600	FACTOR VIII	IV	1 IU	J7190
				FACTOR VIII, PORCINE	IV	1 IU	J7191

Drug Name	Route	Unit	Code	Drug Name	Route	Unit	Code
FACTOR VIII, RECOMBINANT	IV	1 IU	J7192	GAMMA GLOBULIN	IM	greater than 10 cc	J1560
FACTREL	SC, IV	100 mcg	J1620	GAMMAGARD S/D	IV	10 mg	J1564
FAMOTIDINE, INJECTION	IV	20 mg	S0028	GAMMAR-P	IV	10 mg	J1564
FASLODEX	IV	25 mg	J9395	GAMULIN RH	IV	100 IU	J2792
FEIBA VH IMMUNO	IV	IU	J7198	GANCICLOVIR	OTH	4.5 mg	J7310
FENTANYL CITRATE	IM, IV	0.1 mg	J3010	GANCICLOVIR SODIUM	IV	500 mg	J1570
FERRLECIT	IV	12.5 mg	J2916	GANIRELIX ACETATE	SC	250 mcg	S0132
FERTINEX	SC	75 IU	Q2018	GARAMYCIN, GENTAMICIN	IM, IV	80 mg	J1580
FILGRASTIM	SC, IV	300 mcg	J1440	GASTROCROM	INH	10 mg	J7631
FILGRASTIM	SC, IV	480 mcg	J1441	GATIFLOXACIN	IV	10 mg	J1590
FLAGYL IV RTU	IV	500 mg	S0030	GEMCITABINE HCL	IV	200 mg	J9201
FLOLAN		1.5 mg	J1325	GEMTUZUMAB OZOGAMICIN	IV	5 mg	J9300
FLOXIN IV	IV	400 mg	S0034	GEMZAR	IV	200 mg	J9201
FLOXURIDINE	IV	500 mg	J9200	GENENTECH	IV	1 mg	J2997
FLUCONAZOLE	INJ	200 mg	J1450	GENESA	IV	1 mg	J0395
FLUDARA	IV	50 mg	J9185	GENOTROPIN	IM,SC	1 mg	J2941
FLUDARABINE PHOSPHATE	IV	50 mg	J9185	GENTAMICIN SULFATE	IM, IV	80 mg	J1580
FLUNISOLIDE,UNIT DOSE	INH	1 mg	J7641	GENTRAN	IV	500 ml	J7100
FLUOROURACIL	IV	500 mg	J9190	GENTRAN 75	IV	500 ml	J7110
FLUPHENAZINE DECANOATE	IM, SC	25 mg	J2680	GEODON	IV	10 mg	J3486
FOLEX	IV, IM, IT, IA	50 mg	J9260	GEREF DIAGNOSTIC	INJ	0.5 mg	Q2014
FOLLISTIM	SC, IM	75 IU	S0128	GESTEROL 50	IM	50 mg	J2675
FOLLITROPIN ALPHA	SC	75 IU	S0126	GLATIRAMER ACETATE, INJECTION	INJ	20 mg	J1595
FOLLITROPIN BETA	SC, IM	75 IU	S0128	GLEEVEC	INJ	100 mg	S0088
FOMEPIZOLE	IV	1.5 mg	Q2008	GLUCAGEN	SC, IM, IV	1 mg	J1610
FOMIVIRSEN SODIUM, INTRAOCULAR	OTH	1.65 mg	J1452	GLUCAGON HCL	SC, IM, IV	1 mg	J1610
FONDAPARINUX SODIUM	SC	0.5 mg	J1652	GLYCOPYRROLATE, CONCENTRATED	INH	1 mg	J7642
FORTAZ	IM, IV	500 mg	J0713	GLYCOPYRROLATE, UNIT DOSE	INH	1 mg	J7643
FOSCARNET SODIUM	IV	1,000 mg	J1455	GOLD SODIUM THIOMALATE	IM	50 mg	J1600
FOSCAVIR	IV	per 1,000 mg	J1455	GONADORELIN HCL	SC, IV	100 mcg	J1620
FOSPHENYTOIN SODIUM	IV, IM	50 mg	Q2009	GONAL-F	SC	75 IU	S0126
FOSPHENYTOIN SODIUM	IV, IM	750 mg	S0078	GOSERELIN ACETATE IMPLANT	SC	per 3.6 mg	J9202
FRAGMIN	SC	per 2500 IU	J1645	GRANISETRON HCL	IV	100 mcg	J1626
FUDR	IV	500 mg	J9200	GRANISETRON HCL	ORAL	1 mg	Q0166
FULVESTRANT INJECTION	IV	25 mg	J9395	GRANISETRON HYDROCHLORIDE	ORAL	1 mg	S0091
FUNGIZONE	IV	50 mg	J0285	GYNOGEN L.A.	IM	10 mg	J1380
FUROMIDE M.D.	IM, IV	20 mg	J1940	GYNOGEN L.A. 10	IM	10 mg	J1380
FUROSEMIDE	IM, IV	20 mg	J1940	GYNOGEN L.A. 20	IM	20 mg	J1390
GAMIMUNE N	IV	10 mg	J1564	GYNOGEN L.A. 40	IM	40 mg	J0970
GAMMA GLOBULIN	IM	1 cc	J1460	HALDOL	IM, IV	5 mg	J1630
GAMMA GLOBULIN	IM	10 cc	J1550	HALOPERIDOL	IM, IV	5 mg	J1630
GAMMA GLOBULIN	IM	2 cc	J1470	HALOPERIDOL DECANOATE	IM	50 mg	J1631
GAMMA GLOBULIN	IM	3 cc	J1480	HECTOROL	IV	1 mcg	J1270
GAMMA GLOBULIN	IM	4 cc	J1490	HELIXATE	IV	1 IU	J7192
GAMMA GLOBULIN	IM	5 cc	J1500	HEMIN	IV	1 mg	Q2011
GAMMA GLOBULIN	IM	6 cc	J1510	HEMOFIL M	IV	1 IU	J7190
GAMMA GLOBULIN	IM	7 cc	J1520	HEMOPHILIA CLOTTING FACTORS (E.G., ANTI-INHIBITORS)	IV	1 IU	J7198
GAMMA GLOBULIN	IM	8 cc	J1530	HEMOPHILIA CLOTTING FACTORS NOC	INJ	-	J7199
GAMMA GLOBULIN	IM	9 cc	J1540				

Drug Name	Route	Unit	Code
HEP-LOCK	IV	10 units	J1642
HEP-LOCK U/P	IV	10 units	J1642
HEPARIN SODIUM	IV	10 units	J1642
HEPARIN SODIUM	IV, SC	1,000 units	J1644
HERCEPTIN	IV	10 mg	J9355
HEXADROL PHOSPHATE	IM, IV	1 mg	J1100
HISTRELIN ACETATE	SC	10 mg	Q2020
HORMONE-INFUSED VAGINAL RING	OTH	unit	J7303
HUMALOG, THROUGH PUMP	OTH	50 units	J1817
HUMATE-P	IV	1 IU	Q2022
HUMATROPE	IM, SC	1 mg	J2941
HYALGAN	INJ	20-25 mg	J7317
HYALGAN	OTH	20 to 25 mg	J7317
HYALURONIDASE	SC, IV	150 units	J3470
HYATE:C (FACTOR VIII (PORCINE)	IV	1 unit	J7191
HYBOLIN DECANOATE	IM	100 mg	J2321
HYCAMTIN	IV	4 mg	J9350
HYDRALAZINE HCL	IV, IM	20 mg	J0360
HYDRATE	IM, IV	50 mg	J1240
HYDROCORTISONE ACETATE	IV, IM, SC	25 mg	J1700
HYDROCORTISONE SODIUM PHOSPHATE	IV, IM, SC	50 mg	J1710
HYDROCORTISONE SODIUM PHOSPHATE	IV, IM, SC	50 mg	J1710
HYDROCORTISONE SUCCINATE SODIUM	IV, IM, SC	100 mg	J1720
HYDROCORTONE ACETATE	IV, IM, SC	25 mg	J1700
HYDROCORTONE PHOSPHATE	IV, IM, SC	50 mg	J1710
HYDROCORTONE PHOSPHATE	IV, IM, SC	50 mg	J1710
HYDROMORPHONE HCL	SC, IM, IV	4 mg	J1170
HYDROMORPHONE HYDROCHLORIDE	DME INFUSE	250 units	S0092
HYDROXYZINE HCL	IM	25 mg	J3410
HYDROXYZINE PAMOATE	ORAL	25 mg	Q0177
HYDROXYZINE PAMOATE	ORAL	50 mg	Q0178
HYLAN G-F 20	INJ	20-25 mg	J7317
HYLAN G-F 20	OTH	16 mg	J7320
HYOSCYAMINE SULFATE	SC, IM, IV	0.25 mg	J1980
HYPER-TET	IM	250 units	J1670
HYPERSTAT IV	IV	300 mg	J1730
HYREXIN	IM, IV	50 mg	J1200
HYZINE-50	IM	25 mg	J3410
IBUTILIDE FUMARATE	IV	1 mg	J1742
IDAMYCIN	IV	5 mg	J9211
IDARUBICIN HCL	IV	5 mg	J9211
IFEX	IV	1 g	J9208
IFOSFAMIDE	IV	1 g	J9208
IL-2	IM, IV	1 vial	J9015
IMATINIB	INJ	100 mg	S0088
IMIGLUCERASE	IV	1 unit	J1785
IMITREX	SC	6 mg	J3030
IMMUNE GLOBULIN	IV	per 10 mg	J1564

Drug Name	Route	Unit	Code
IMMUNE GLOBULIN, ANTI-THYMOCYTE GLOBULIN	IV	250 mg	J7504
IMMUNE GLOBULIN, INTRAVENOUS INJECTION	IV	1 g	J1563
IMMUNE GLOBULIN, INTRAVENOUS INJECTION	IV	10 mg	J1564
IMMUNOSUPPRESSIVE DRUG, NOT OTHERWISE CLASSIFIED	-	-	J7599
IMURAN	IV	100 mg	J7501
INAPSINE	IM, IV	5 mg	J1790
INDERAL	IV	1 mg	J1800
INFED	INJ	50 mg	J1750
INFERGEN	IM	1 mcg	J9212
INFLIXIMAB	INJ	100 MG	
INNOHEP	SC	1000 IU	J1655
INNOVAR	IM, IV	2 ml ampule	J1810
INSULIN FOR PUMP	OTH	per 50 units	J1817
INTAL	INH	10 mg	J7631
INTEGRELIN	INJ	5 mg	J1327
INTERFERON ALFA-2A, RECOMBINANT	SC, IM	3 million units	J9213
INTERFERON ALFA-2B, RECOMBINANT	SC, IM	1 million units	J9214
INTERFERON ALFA-N3 (HUMAN LEUKOCYTE DERIVED)	IM	250,000 IU	J9215
INTERFERON ALFACON-1, RECOMBINANT	IM	1 mcg	J9212
INTERFERON BETA-1A	IM	11 mcg	Q3025
INTERFERON BETA-1A	IM	33 mcg	J1825
INTERFERON BETA-1A	SC	11 mcg	Q3026
INTERFERON BETA-1B	SC	0.25 mg	J1830
INTERFERON GAMMA-1B	SC	3 million units	J9216
INTERFERON GAMMA-1B	SC	3 million units	J9216
INTRAUTERINE COPPER CONTRACEPTIVE	OTH	-	J7300
INTRON-A	SC, IM	1 million units	J9214
INVANZ	IV	500 mg	J1335
IPRATOPIUM BROMIDE, THROUGH DME, UNIT DOSE	INH	1 mg	J7644
IRINOTECAN		20 mg	J9206
IRON DEXTRAN	INJ	50 mg	J1750
IRON SUCROSE	IM	1 mg	J1756
IRRIGATION SOLUTION FOR TX OF BLADDER CALCULI	OTH	per 50 ml	Q2004
ISOCAINE HCL	VAR	per 10 ml	J0670
ISOETHARINE HCL, CONCENTRATE	INH	1 mg	J7648
ISOETHARINE HCL, UNIT DOSE	INH	1 mg	J7649
ISOPROTERENOL HCL, CONCENTRATE	INH	1 mg	J7658
ISOPROTERENOL HCL, UNIT DOSE	INH	1 mg	J7659
ISUPREL (CONCENTRATE)	INH	1 mg	J7648
ISUPREL (UNIT DOSE)	INH	1 mg	J7659
ITRACONAZOLE	IV	50 mg	J1835
IVEEGAM, IVEEGAM-EN	IV	10 mg	J1564
JENAMICIN	IM, IV	80 mg	J1580
K-FERON	INJ	50 mg	J1750

Drug Name	Route	Unit	Code
KABIKINASE	IV	250,000 IU	J2995
KALEINATE	IV	10 ml	J0610
KANAMYCIN SULFATE	IM, IV	500 mg	J1840
KANAMYCIN SULFATE	IM, IV	75 mg	J1850
KANTREX	IM, IV	500 mg	J1840
KANTREX	IM, IV	75 mg	J1850
KEFLIN	IM, IV	1 g	J1890
KEFUROX	IM, IV	750 mg	J0697
KEFZO	IV, IM	500 mg	J0690
KENAJECT-40	IM	10 mg	J3301
KENALOG-10	IM	10 mg	J3301
KENALOG-40	IM	10 mg	J3301
KESTRONE 5	IM	1 mg	J1435
KETOROLAC TROMETHAMINE	IM, IV	15 mg	J1885
KEY-PRED 25	IM	1 ml	J2650
KEY-PRED 50	IM	1 ml	J2650
KOATE-HP)	IV	1 IU	J7190
KOGENATE)	IV	1 IU	J7190
KONAKION	IM, SC, IV	1mg	J3430
KONYNE 80	IV	1 IU	J7194
KONYNE 80	IV	1 IU	J7195
KYTRIL	ORAL	1 mg	Q0166
KYTRIL	ORAL	1 mg	S0091
LAETRILE, AMYGDALIN, VITAMIN B-17			J3570
LANOXIN	IM, IV	0.5 mg	J1160
LARONIDASE	INJ	2.9 mg	C9209
LASIX	IM, IV	20 mg	J1940
LEPIRUDIN	IV	50 mg	Q2021
LEUCOVORIN CALCIUM	IM, IV	per 50 mg	J0640
LEUKINE	IV	50 mcg	J2820
LEUPROLIDE ACETATE	IM	3.75 mg	J1950
LEUPROLIDE ACETATE	IM	7.5 mg	J9217
LEUPROLIDE ACETATE	IM	per 1 mg	J9218
LEUPROLIDE ACETATE IMPLANT	OTHR	65 mg	J9219
LEUSTATIN	IV	1 mg	J9065
LEVALBUTEROL HCL, CONCENTRATE	INH	0.5 mg	J7618
LEVALBUTEROL HCL, UNIT DOSE	INH	per 5 mg	J7619
LEVAQUIN	IV	250 mg	J1956
LEVO-DROMORAN	SC, IV	2 mg	J1960
LEVOCARNITINE	IV	per 1 gm	J1955
LEVOFLOXACIN	IV	250 mg	J1956
LEVONORGESTREL RELEASING INTRAUTERINE CONTRACEPTIVE	OTHR	52 mg	J7302
LEVORPHANOL TARTRATE	SC, IV	2 mg	J1960
LEVSIN	SC, IM, IV	0.25 mg	J1980
LEVULAN KERASTICK	TOPICAL	354 mg	J7308
LIBRIUM	IM, IV	100 mg	J1990
LIDOCAINE HCL	IV	10 mg	J2001
LINCOCIN	IV	300 mg	J2010

Drug Name	Route	Unit	Code
LINCOMYCIN HCL	IV	300 mg	J2010
LIORESAL	IT	10 mg	J0475
LIORESAL	IT	50 mcg	J0476
LIQUAEMIN SODIUM	IV, SC	1,000 units	J1644
LMD 10%	IV	500 ml	J7100
LORAZEPAM	IM, IV	2 mg	J2060
LOVENOX	SC	10 mg	J1650
LUFYLLIN	IM	500 mg	J1180
LUMINAL SODIUM	IM, IV	120 mg	J2560
LUNELLE MONTHLY CONTRACEPTIVE	IM	5mg/25mg	J1056
LUPRON	IM	1 mg	J9218
LUPRON	IM	3.75 mg	J1950
LUPRON	OTHR	65 mg	J9219
LUPRON DEPOT	IM	7.5 mg	J9217
LUPRON DEPOT-PED	IM	7.5 mg	J9217
LUTREPULSE	SC,IV	per 100 mcg	J1620
LYMPHOCYTE IMMUNE GLOBULIN, ANTI-THYMOCYTE GLOBULIN, EQUINE	IV	250 mg	J7504
LYMPHOCYTE IMMUNE GLOBULIN, ANTITHYMOCYTE GLOBULIN, RABBIT	IV	25 mg	J7511
MAGNESIUM SULFATE	IM, IV	500 mg	J3475
MANNITOL	IV	25% in 50 ml	J2150
MARCAINE	OTH	30 ml	S0020
MARINOL	ORAL	2.5 mg	Q0167
MAXIPIME	IM, IV	500 mg	J0692
MECHLORETHAMINE HCL	IV	10 mg	J9230
MEDIHALER-ISO	INH	1 mg	J7659
MEDRALONE 80	IM	80 mg	J1040
MEDROL	ORAL	4 mg	J7509
MEDROXYPROGESTERONE ACETATE	IM	150 mg	J1055
MEDROXYPROGESTERONE ACETATE	IM	50 mg	J1051
MEDROXYPROGESTERONE/ACETATE/ ESTRADIOL CYPIONATE	IM	5 mg/25mg	J1056
MEFOXIN	IV, IM	1 g	J0694
MELPHALAN HCL	IV	50 mg	J9245
MELPHALAN, ORAL	ORAL	2 mg	J8600
MENOJECT LA	IM	1 ml	J1060
MEPERGAN INJECTION	IM, IV	50 mg	J2180
MEPERIDINE AND PROMETHAZINE HCL	IM, IV	50 mg	J2180
MEPERIDINE HCL	IM, IV, SC	per 100 mg	J2175
MEPIVACAINE	VAR	per 10 ml	J0670
MERCAPTOPURINE	ORAL	50 mg	S0108
MEROPENEM	INJ	100 mg	J2185
MERREM IV	INJ	100 mg	J2185
MESNA	IV	200 mg	J9209
MESNEX	IV	200 mg	J9209
METAPROTERENOL, CONCENTRATE	INH	10 mg	J7668
METAPROTERENOL, UNIT DOSE	INH	10 mg	J7669
METARAMINOL BITARTRATE	IV, IM, SC	10 mg	J0380
METHADONE HCL	IM, SC	10 mg	J1230

APPENDIX 3 — TABLE OF DRUGS

Drug Name	Route	Unit	Code
METHERGINE		0.2 mg	J2210
METHOCARBAMOL	IV, IM	10 ml	J2800
METHOTREXATE LPF	IA, IM, IT, IV	5 mg	J9250
METHOTREXATE, ORAL	ORAL	2.5 mg	J8610
METHOTREXATE SODIUM	IA, IM, IT, IV	5 mg	J9250
METHOTREXATE SODIUM	IV, IM, IT, IA	50 mg	J9260
METHYLDOPATE HCL	IV	250 mg	J0210
METHYLERGONOVINE MALEATE		0.2 mg	J2210
METHYLPREDNISOLONE	ORAL	4 mg	J7509
METHYLPREDNISOLONE ACETATE	IM	20 mg	J1020
METHYLPREDNISOLONE ACETATE	IM	40 mg	J1030
METHYLPREDNISOLONE ACETATE	IM	80 mg	J1040
METHYLPREDNISOLONE SODIUM SUCCINATE	IM, IV	125 mg	J2930
METHYLPREDNISOLONE SODIUM SUCCINATE	IM, IV	125 mg	J2930
METHYLPREDNISOLONE SODIUM SUCCINATE	IM, IV	40 mg	J2920
METOCLOPRAMIDE HCL	IV	10 mg	J2765
METRONIDAZOLE INJECTION	IV	500 mg	S0030
MIACALCIN	SC, IM	400 units	J0630
MICRHOGAM	IM	50 mcg	J2788
MIDAZOLAM HCL	IM, IV	1 mg	J2250
MILRINONE LACTATE	IV	5 mg	J2260
MIRENA	OTHR	52 mg	J7302
MITHRACIN	IV	2,500 mcg	J9270
MITOMYCIN	IV	20 mg	J9290
MITOMYCIN	IV	40 mg	J9291
MITOMYCIN	IV	5 mg	J9280
MITOXANTRONE HCL	IV	5 mg	J9293
MONARC-M	IV	1 IU	J7190
MONOCLATE-P	IV	1 IU	J7190
MONOCLONAL ANTIBODIES	PAREN	5 mg/5 ml, 5 ml	J7505
MONONINE	IV	1 IU	J7193
MORPHINE SULFATE	IM, IV, SC	10 mg	J2270
MORPHINE SULFATE	IT, IV, SC	100 mg	J2271
MORPHINE SULFATE, PRESERVATIVE-FREE	SC, IM, IV	10 mg	J2275
MORPHINE SULFATE, THROUGH DME	OTH	500 mg	S0093
MOXIFLOXACIN	IV	100 mg	J2280
MS CONTIN	IT, IV, SC	100 mg	J2271
MUCOMYST	INH	1 g	J7608
MUCOMYST	INH	1 g	J7608
MUCOMYST, UNIT DOSE	INH	1 g	J7608
MUCOSIL	INH	1 g	J7608
MUCOSIL, UNIT DOSE	INH	1 g	J7608
MUCOSOL	INH	1 g	J7608
MUROMONAB-CD3	IV	5 mg	J7505
MUSE	IV	1.25 mcg	J0270
MUSTARGEN	IV	10 mg	J9230
MUTAMYCIN	IV	5 mg	J9280

Drug Name	Route	Unit	Code
MYCOPHENOLATE MOFETIL	ORAL	250 mg	J7517
MYLERAN	IV	6 mg	C1178
MYLERAN	ORAL	2 mg	J8510
MYLOBLOC	IM	100 units	J0587
MYLOTARG	IV	5 mg	J9300
MYOCHRYSINE	IM	50 mg	J1600
MYOLIN	IV, IM	60 mg	J2360
MYTONACHOL	SC	5 mg	J0520
NALBUPHINE HCL	IM, IV, SC	10 mg	J2300
NALOXONE HCL	IM, IV, SC	1 mg	J2310
NANDROLONE DECANOATE	IM	100 mg	J2321
NANDROLONE DECANOATE	IM	200 mg	J2322
NANDROLONE DECANOATE	IM	50 mg	J2320
NARCAN	IM, IV, SC	1 mg	J2310
NAROPIN	OTH	1 mg	J2795
NASAHIST B	IM, SC, IV	10 mg	J0945
NASAL VACCINE INHALATION	INH	-	J3530
NASALCROM	INH	10 mg	J7631
NASALIDE	INH	1 mg	J7641
NATRECOR	IV	0.5 mg	J2324
NAVELBINE	IV	10 mg	J9390
NEBCIN	IM, IV	80 mg	J3260
NEBUPENT	IM, IV	300 mg	S0080
NEBUPENT	INH	300 mg	J2545
NEMBUTAL SODIUM	IM, IV	50 mg	J2515
NEO-SYNEPHRINE	SC, IM, IV	1 ml	J2370
NEOCYTEN	IV, IM	60 mg	J2360
NEOQUESS	IM	20 mg	J0500
NEORAL	IV	250 mg	J7516
NEORAL	ORAL	25 mg	J7515
NEOSAR	IV	1 g	J9091
NEOSTIGMINE METHYLSULFATE	IM, IV, SC	0.5 mg	J2710
NESACAINE	VAR	30 ml	J2400
NESACAINE-MPF	VAR	30 ml	J2400
NESIRITIDE	IV	0.5 mg	J2324
NEULASTA	SQ	6 mg	J2505
NEUMEGA	INJ	5 mg	J2355
NEUPOGEN	SC, IV	300 mcg	J1440
NEUPOGEN	SC, IV	480 mcg	J1441
NEUTREXIN	IV	25 mg	J3305
NIPEN	IV	10 mg	J9268
NORFLEX	IV, IM	60 mg	J2360
NOT OTHERWISE CLASSIFIED DRUGS	-	-	J3490
NOT OTHERWISE CLASSIFIED DRUGS	INH	-	J7699
NOT OTHERWISE CLASSIFIED DRUGS	OTHER THAN INH	-	J7799
NOT OTHERWISE CLASSIFIED DRUGS, ANTI-EMETIC	ORAL	-	Q0181
NOT OTHERWISE CLASSIFIED DRUGS, ANTI-NEOPLASTIC	-	-	J9999

Drug Name	Route	Unit	Code
NOT OTHERWISE CLASSIFIED DRUGS, CHEMOTHERAPEUTIC	ORAL	-	J8999
NOT OTHERWISE CLASSIFIED DRUGS, IMMUNOSUPPRESSIVE	-	-	J7599
NOT OTHERWISE CLASSIFIED DRUGS, NONCHEMOTHERAPEUTIC	ORAL	-	J8499
NOVANTRONE	IV	5 mg	J9293
NOVOSEVEN	IV	1.2 mg	Q0187
NUBAIN	IM, IV, SC	per 10 mg	J2300
NUMORPHAN	IV, SC, IM	1 mg	J2410
NUMORPHAN H.P.	IV, SC, IM	1 mg	J2410
NUTROPIN	IM, SC	1 mg	J2941
OCTREOTIDE, DEPOT FORM	IM	1 mg	J2353
OCULINU	IM	1 unit	J0585
ODANSETRON HCL	IV	1 mg	J2405
OFLOXACIN, INJECTION	IV	400 mg	S0034
OMNIPEN-N	IM, IV	500 mg	J0290
ONCASPAR	IM, IV	1 vial	J9266
ONCOVIN	IV	1 mg	J9370
ONDANSETRON HCL	ORAL	8 mg	Q0179
ONTAK	IV	300 mcg	J9160
OPRELVEKIN	INJ	5 mg	J2355
ORMAZINE	IM, IV	50 mg	J3230
ORPHENADRINE CITRATE	IV, IM	60 mg	J2360
ORPHENATE	IV, IM	60 mg	J2360
ORTHOCLONE OKT 3	IV	5 mg	J7505
OSMITROL	IV	25% in 50 ml	J2150
OXACILLIN SODIUM	IM, IV	250 mg	J2700
OXALIPLATIN	IV	0.5 mg	J9263
OXYMORPHONE HCL	IV, SC, IM	1 mg	J2410
OXYTETRACYCLINE HCL	IM	50 mg	J2460
OXYTOCIN	IV, IM	10 units	J2590
PACLITAXEL	IV	30 mg	J9265
PALIVIZUMAB-RSV-IGM	IM	50 mg	C9003
PAMIDRONATE DISODIUM	IV	30 mg	J2430
PANGLOBULIN			J1564
PANGLOBULIN	IV	10 mg	J1564
PANHEMATIN	IV	1 mg	Q2001
PANMYCIN	IM, IV	250 mg	J0120
PAPAVERINE HCL	IV, IM	60 mg	J2440
PARAGARD T 380 A	OTH	1 unit	J7300
PARAPLATIN	IV	50 mg	J9045
PARICALCITOL	IM, IV	1 mcg	J2501
PARICALCITOL	IV	1 mcg	J2501
PAVAGEN TD	IM, IV	60 mg	J2440
PEG-L-ASPARAGINASE	IM, IV	1 vial	J9266
PEGADEMASE BOVINE	IM	25 IU	Q2012
PEGASPARGASE	IM, IV	1 vial	J9266
PEGFILGRASTIM	SQ	6 mg	J2505
PENICILLIN G BENZATHINE	IM	1,200,000 units	J0570

Drug Name	Route	Unit	Code
PENICILLIN G BENZATHINE	IM	2,400,000 units	J0580
PENICILLIN G BENZATHINE	IM	600,000 units	J0560
PENICILLIN G BENZATHINE AND PENICILLIN G PROCAINE	IM	1,200,000 units	J0540
PENICILLIN G BENZATHINE AND PENICILLIN G PROCAINE	IM	2,400,000 units	J0550
PENICILLIN G BENZATHINE AND PENICILLIN G PROCAINE	IM	600,000 units	J0530
PENICILLIN G POTASSIUM	IM, IV	600,000 units	J2540
PENICILLIN G PROCAINE, AQUEOUS	IM	600,000 units	J2510
PENTACARINAT	INH	300 mg	J2545
PENTACARINAT	IV, IM	300 mg	S0080
PENTAM 300	INH	300 mg	J2545
PENTAM 300	IV, IM	300 mg	S0080
PENTAMIDINE ISETHIONATE	IM, IV	300 mg	S0080
PENTAMIDINE ISETHIONATE	INH	300 mg	J2545
PENTASPAN	IV	100 ml	Q2013
PENTASTARCH, 10%	IV	100 ml	Q2013
PENTAZOCINE HCL	IM, SC, IV	30 mg	J3070
PENTOBARBITAL SODIUM	IM, IV	50 mg	J2515
PENTOSTATIN	IV	10 mg	J9268
PEPCID	IV	20 mg	S0028
PERFLEXANE LIPID MICROSPHERES	INJ	10 ml	C9203
PERMAPEN	IM	600,000 units	J0560
PERPHENAZINE	IM, IV	5 mg	J3310
PERPHENAZINE	ORAL	4 mg	Q0175
PERPHENAZINE	ORAL	8 mg	Q0176
PERSANTINE IV	IV	10 mg	J1245
PFIZERPEN	IM, IV	600,000 units	J2540
PFIZERPEN A.S.	IM	600,000 units	J2510
PGE1	IV	1.25 mcg	J0270
PHENAZINE 50	IM. IV	50 mg	J2550
PHENOBARBITAL SODIUM	IM, IV	120 mg	J2560
PHENTOLAMINE MESYLATE	IM, IV	5 mg	J2760
PHENYLEPHRINE HCL	SC, IM, IV	1 ml	J2370
PHENYTOIN SODIUM	IM, IV	50 mg	J1165
PHOTOFRIN	IV	75 mg	J9600
PHYLLOCONTIN	IV	250 mg	J0280
PHYTONADIONE	IM, SC, IV	1 mg	J3430
PIPERACILLIN SODIUM/TAZOBACTAM SODIUM	IV	1 g/0.125 g (1.125 g)	J2543
PIPERACILLIN/AZOBACTAM	IV	500 mg	S0081
PITOCIN	IV, IM	10 units	J2590
PLANTINOL AQ	IV	10 mg	J9060
PLANTINOL AQ	IV	50 mg	J9062
PLASMA, CYOPRECIPITATE REDUCED	IV	1 unit	P9044
PLASMA, POOLED MULTIPLE DONOR, FROZEN	IV	each unit	P9023
PLATINOL	IV	per 10 mg	J9060
PLICAMYCIN	IV	2,500 mcg	J9270
PNEUMONOCCAL CONJUGATE VACCINE	SC, IM	-	S0195

Drug Name	Route	Unit	Code
PNEUMOVAX II	SC, IM		S0195
POLOCAINE	VAR	10 ml	J0670
POLYCILLIN-N	IM, IV	500 mg	J0290
POLYGRAM	IV	10 mg	J1564
PORFIMER SODIUM		75 mg	J9600
POTASSIUM CHLORIDE	IV	2 mEq	J3480
PRALIDOXIME CHLORIDE	IV, IM, SC	1 g	J2730
PREDALONE-50	IM	1 ml	J2650
PREDCOR-25	IM	1 ml	J2650
PREDCOR-50	IM	1 ml	J2650
PREDICORT-50	IM	1 ml	J2650
PREDNISOLONE	ORAL	5 mg	J7510
PREDNISOLONE ACETATE	IM	1 ml	J2650
PREDNISONE	ORAL	any dose, 100 tab	J7506
PREDOJECT-50	IM	1 ml	J2650
PREGNYL	IM	1,000 USP units	J0725
PREGNYL	IM	1,000 USP units	J0725
PREMARIN INTRAVENOUS	IV, IM	25 mg	J1410
PRESCRIPTION ANTI-EMETIC FOR USE IN CONJUNCTION WITH ORAL ANTI-CANCER DRUG NOS	ORAL	-	K0415
PRESCRIPTION ANTIEMETIC DRUG, RECTAL, FOR USE IN CONJUNCTION WITH ORAL ANTICANCER DRUG, NOT OTHERWISE SPECIFIED	OTH	1 mg	K0416
PRESCRIPTION, CHEMOTHERAPEUTIC, NOT OTHERWISE SPECIFIED	ORAL	-	J8999
PRESCRIPTION DRUG BRAND NAME			S5001
PRESCRIPTION, DRUG, GENERIC			S5000
PRESCRIPTION, NONCHEMOTHERAPEUTIC, NOT OTHERWISE SPECIFIED	ORAL	-	J8999
PRIMACOR	IV	5 mg	J2260
PRIMAXIN I.M.	IV, IM	250 mg	J0743
PRIMAXIN I.V.	IV, IM	250 mg	J0743
PRISCOLINE HCL	IV	25 mg	J2670
PROCAINAMIDE HCL	IM, IV	1 g	J2690
PROCHLORPERAZINE	IM, IV	10 mg	J0780
PROCHLORPERAZINE MALEATE	ORAL	10 mg	Q0165
PROCHLORPERAZINE MALEATE	ORAL	5 mg	Q0164
PROCRIT, NONESRD USE	IV,SC	1,000 units	Q0136
PROFASI HP	IM	1,000 USP units	J0725
PROFASI HP	IM	1,000 USP units	J0725
PROFERDEX	INJ	50 mg	J1750
PROFILNINE HEAT-TREATED	IV	1 IU	J7195
PROGESTAJECT	IM	50 mg	J2675
PROGESTERONE	IM	50 mg	J2675
PROGRAF	IV	5 mg	J7525
PROGRAF	ORAL	1 mg	J7507
PROKINE	IV	50 mcg	
PROLASTIN	IV	10 mg	J0256
PROLEUKIN	IM, IV	vial	J9015

Drug Name	Route	Unit	Code
PROLIXIN DECANOATE	IM, SC	25 mg	
PROMAZINE HCL	IM	25 mg	J2950
PROMETHAZINE HCL	IM, IV	50 mg	J2550
PROMETHAZINE HCL	ORAL	12.5 mg	Q0169
PRONESTYL	IM, IV	1 g	J2690
PROPLEX T	IV	1 IU	J7194
PROPRANOLOL HCL	IV	1 mg	J1800
PROREX-25	IM	25 mg	J2950
PROREX-50	IM, IV	50 mg	J2550
PROSTAGLANDIN E1	IV	1.25 mcg	J0270
PROSTAPHLIN	IM, IV	1 g	J2690
PROSTIGMIN	IM, IV, SC	0.5 mg	J2710
PROSTIN VR PEDIATRIC	IV	1.25 mcg	J0270
PROTAMINE SULFATE	IV	10 mg	J2720
PROTIRELIN	IV	250 mcg	J2725
PROTOPAM CHLORIDE	IV, IM, SC	1 g	J2730
PROTROPIN	IM, SC	1 mg	J2940
PROVENTIL, CONCENTRATED FORM	INH	1 mg	J7618
PROVERA	IM	50 mg	J1051
PROVISC	OTH	20 to 25 mg	J7317
PULMICORT RESPULES, THROUGH DME, CONCENTRATED DOSE	INH	0.25 mg	J7633
PULMICORT,UNIT DOSE	INH	0.25-0.50 mg	J7626
PULMOZYME	INH	1 mg	J7639
PURINETHOL	ORAL	50 mg	S0108
PYRIDOXINE HCL	INJ	100 mg	J3415
QUELICIN	IV, IM	20 mg	J0330
QUINUPRISTIN/DALFOPRISTIN	IV	500 mg 150/350	J2770
RANTIDINE HCL	INJ	25 mg	J2780
RAPAMUNE	ORAL	1 mg/ml	J7520
RASBURICASE	IV	0.5 mg	J2783
RECOMBINATE	I V	1 IU	J7192
RECOMBINATE	IV	1 IU	J7190
REFLUDAN	IV	50 mg	Q2021
REGITINE	IM, IV	5 mg	J2760
REGLAN	IV	10 mg	J2765
REGRANEX GEL	OTH	0.5 g	S0157
REGULAR INSULIN	SC	5 units	J1815
RENACIDIN	OTH	50 ml	Q2004
RESPIGAM	IV	50 mg	J1565
RESPIRATORY SYNCYTIAL VIRUS IMMUNE GLOBULIN	IV	50 mg	J1565
RETAVASE	IV	18.8 mg	J2993
RETEPLASE	IV	18.8 mg	J2993
RETROVIR	IV	10 mg	J3485, S0104
RHEOMACRODEX	IV	500 ml	J7100
RHEUMATREX DOSE PACK	IV, IM, IT, IA	50 mg	J9260
RHEUMATREX DOSE PACK	ORAL	2.5 mg	J8610
RHO(D) IMMUNE GLOBULIN	IV	100 IU	J2792

Drug Name	Route	Unit	Code
RHO(D) IMMUNE GLOBULIN, HUMAN, FULL DOSE	IM	300 mcg	J2790
RHO D IMMUNE GLOBULIN, HUMAN, MINIDOSE	IM	50 mcg	
RHOGAM RHO(D) IMMUNE GLOBULIN, HUMAN	IM	300 MCG, full dose	
RINGER'S LACTATE	IV	1,000 cc	J7120
RITUXAN	IV	100 mg	J9310
RITUXIMAB	IV	100 mg	J9310
ROBAXIN	IV, IM	10 ml	J2800
ROCEPHIN	IV, IM	250 mg	J0696
ROFERON-A	SC, IM	3 million units	J9213
ROPLIVACAINE HYDROCHLORIDE	OTH	1 mg	J2795
RUBEX	IV	10 mg	J9000
SALINE HYPERTONIC SOLUTION	IV, IM	50, 100 meq, 20 cc vial	J7130
SALINE SOLUTION	IV, OTH	5 CC	
SALINE SOLUTION	IV, OTH	500 ML	
SALINE SOLUTION	IV	1,000 cc	J7030
SALINE SOLUTION	IV	250 cc	J7050
SALINE SOLUTION 5% DEXTROSE	IV	500 ml	J7042
SANDIMMUNE	IV	250 mg	J7516
SANDIMMUNE	ORAL	25 mg	J7515
SANDOGLOBULIN	IV	10 mg	J1564
SANDOSTATIN LAR	IM	1 mg	J2353
SARGRAMOSTIM	IV	50 mcg	
SELESTOJECT	IM, IV	4 mg	J0704
SENSORCAINE	OTH	30 mg	S0020
SEPTRA IV	IV	10 ml	S0039
SERMORELIN ACETATE	INJ	0.5 mg	Q2014
SILDENAFIL CITRATE	ORAL	25 mg	S0090
SIMULECT	IV	20 mg	Q2019
SIROLIMUS	ORAL	1 mg/ml	J7520
SMOKING CESSATION GUM			S4995
SMZ-TMP	IV	10 ml	S0039
SODIUM CHLORIDE, 0.9%	IV	2 ml	J2912
SODIUM FERRIC GLUCONATE COMPLEX IN SUCROSE	IV	12.5 mg	J2916
SODIUM HYALURONATE	INJ	20-25 mg	J7317
SOLGANAL	IM	50 mg	J2910
SOLU-CORTEF	IV, IM, SC	100 mg	J1720
SOLU-CORTEF	IV, IM, SC	50 mg	J1710
SOLU-CORTEF	IV, IM, SC	50 mg	J1710
SOLU-MEDROL	IM, IV	125 mg	J2930
SOLU-MEDROL	IM, IV	125 mg	J2930
SOLU-MEDROL	IM, IV	40 mg	J2920
SOLUREX	IM, IV	1 mg	J1100
SOLUREX LA	IM, IV	1 mg	J1094
SOMATREM	IM, SC	1 mg	J2940
SOMATROPIN	IM, SC	1 mg	J2941
SPARINE	IM	25 mg	J2950

Drug Name	Route	Unit	Code
SPECTINOMYCIN HCL	IM	2 g	J3320
SPORONOX	IV	50 mg	J1835
STADOL	INJ	1 mg	J0595
STADOL NS	NASAL SPRAY	25 mg	S0012
STILPHOSTROL	IV	250 mg	J9165
STREPTASE	IV	250,000 IU	J2995
STREPTOKINASE	IV	250,000 IU	J2995
STREPTOMYCIN	IM	1 g	J3000
STREPTOMYCIN SULFATE	IM	1 g	J3000
STREPTOZOCIN	IV	1 g	J9320
SUBLIMAZE	IM, IV	0.1 mg	J3010
SUCCINYLCHOLINE CHLORIDE	IV, IM	20 mg	J0330
SUCOSTRIN	IV, IM	20 mg	J0330
SULFAMETHOXAZOLE AND TRIMETHOPRIM	INJ	10 ml	S0039
SULFAMETHOXAZOLE AND TRIMETHOPRIM	IV	10 ml	S0039
SULFATRIM	IV	10 ml	S0039
SUMATRIPTAN SUCCINATE	SC	6 mg	J3030
SUPPRELIN	SC	10 mg	Q2020
SUS-PHRINE	SC IM	1 ml amp	J0170
SYNAGIS	IM	50 mg	C9003
SYNERCID	IV	500 mg 150/350	J2770
SYNTOCIONON	IV, IM	10 units	J2590
SYNVISC	OTH	16 mg	J7320
TACROLIMUS	IV	5 mg (1 amp)	J7525
TACROLIMUS	ORAL	1 mg	J7507
TAGAMET HCL	IV, IM	300 mg	S0023
TALWIN	IM, SC, IV	30 mg	J3070
TAXOL	IV	30 mg	J9265
TAXOTERE	IV	20 mg	J9170
TEEV	IM	1 cc	J0900
TEMODAR	ORAL	5 mg	J8700
TEMOZOLOMIDE	ORAL	5 mg	J8700
TENECTEPLASE	IV	50 mg	J3100
TENIPOSIDE	IV	50 mg	Q2017
TEQUIN	IV	10 mg	J1590
TERBUTALINE SULFATE	SC	1 mg	J3105
TERBUTALINE SULFATE, CONCENTRATED	INH	1 mg	J7680
TERBUTALINE SULFATE, UNIT DOSE	INH	1 mg	J7681
TERRAMYCIN IM	IM	50 mg	J2460
TEST-ESTRO CYPIONATES	IM	1 ml	J1060
TEST-ESTRO-C	IM	1 ml	J1060
TESTADIATE	IM	1 cc	J0900
TESTAJECT-LA	IM	1 cc, 200 mg	J1080
TESTAQUA	IM	50 mg	J3140
TESTONE LA 100	IM	100 mg	J3120
TESTONE LA 200	IM	200 mg	J3130
TESTOSTERONE CYPIONATE	IM	1 cc, 200 mg	J1080
TESTOSTERONE CYPIONATE	IM	100 mg	J1070

Drug Name	Route	Unit	Code
TESTOSTERONE CYPIONATE AND ESTRADIOL CYPIONATE	IM	1 ml	J1060
TESTOSTERONE CYPIONATE AND ESTRADIOL CYPIONATE	IM	1 ml	J1060
TESTOSTERONE ENANTHATE	IM	100 mg	J3120
TESTOSTERONE ENANTHATE	IM	200 mg	J3130
TESTOSTERONE ENANTHATE AND ESTRADIOL VALERATE	IM	1 CC	
TESTOSTERONE PROPIONATE	IM	100 mg	J3150
TESTOSTERONE SUSPENSION	IM	50 mg	J3140
TESTRIN PA	IM	100 mg	J3120
TETANUS IMMUNE GLOBULIN, HUMAN (SEE ALSO CPT CODE)	IM	250 units	J1670
TETRACYCLINE	IM, IV	250 mg	J0120
THEELIN	IM	1 mg	J1435
THEOPHYLLINE	IV	40 mg	J2810
THEOPHYLLINE ETHYLENADIAMINE	IV	250 mg	J0280
THERACYS	IV	per vial	J9031
THIAMINE HCL	INJ	100 mg	J3411
THIETHYLPERAZINE MALEATE	IM	10 mg	J3280
THIETHYLPERAZINE MALEATE	ORAL	10 mg	Q0174
THIOPLEX	IV, OTH	15 mg	J9340
THIOTEPA	IV, OTH	15 mg	J9340
THORAZINE	INJ	50 mg	J3230
THORAZINE	ORAL	10 mg	Q0171
THYMOGLOBULIN	IV	25 mg	J7511
THYPINONE	IV	250 mcg	J2725
THYROGEN	IM, SC	1.1 mg vial	J3240
THYROTROPIN ALPHA	IM, SC	1.1 mg vial	J3240
THYTROPAR	IM, SC	0.9 mg prov in 1.1 mg vial	J3240
TICARCILLIN DISODIUM AND CLAVULANATE POTASSIUM	IV, IM	3.1 g	S0040
TICE BCG	IV	1 vial	J9031
TIGAN	ORAL	250 mg	Q0173
TIMENTIN	IV, IM	3.1 g	S0040
TINZARPARIN	SC	1000 IU	J1655
TIROFIBAN HCL	INJ	12.5 mg	J3245
TNKASE	IV	50 mg	J3100
TOBI	INH	300 mg	J7682
TOBRAMYCIN	INH	300 mg	J7682
TOBRAMYCIN SULFATE	IM, IV	80 mg	J3260
TOLAZOLINE HCL	IV	25 mg	J2670
TOPOSAR	IV	10 mg	J9181
TOPOSAR	IV	100 mg	J9182
TOPOTECAN HYDROCHLORIDE		4 mg	J9350
TORADOL	IM, IV	per 15 mg	J1885
TORECAN	IM	10 mg	J3280
TORECAN	ORAL	10 mg	Q0174
TORNALATE	INH	1 mg	J7628
TORNALATE	INH	1 mg	J7629
TORSEMIDE	IV	10 mg/ml	J3265

Drug Name	Route	Unit	Code
TOTACILLIN-N	IM, IV	500 mg	J0290
TRASTUZUMAB	IV	10 mg	J9355
TRASYLOL	IV	10,000 kiu	Q2003
TRELSTAR DEPOT	IM	3.75 mg	J3315
TRI-KORT	IM	10 mg	J3301
TRIAM-A	IM	10 mg	J3301
TRIAMCINOLONE ACETONIDE	IM	10 mg	J3301
TRIAMCINOLONE, CONCENTRATED	INH	1 mg	J7683
TRIAMCINOLONE DIACETATE	IM	5 mg	J3302
TRIAMCINOLONE HEXACETONIDE	VAR	5 mg	J3303
TRIAMCINOLONE, THROUGH DME, UNIT DOSE FORM	INH	1 mg	J7684
TRIFLUPROMAZINE HCL	IM, IV	20 mg	J3400
TRILAFON	IM, IV	5 mg	J3310
TRILOG	IM	10 mg	J3301
TRILONE	IM	5 mg	J3302
TRIMETHOBENZAMIDE HCL	IM	200 mg	J3250
TRIMETHOBENZAMIDE HCL	ORAL	250 mg	Q0173
TRIMETREXATE GLUCURONATE	IV	25 mg	J3305
TRIPTORELIN PAMOATE	IM	3.75 mg	J3315
TRISENOX	IV	1 mg	J9017
TROBICIN	IM	2 g	J3320
TROVAN	IV	100 mg	J0200
UNASYN	IM, IV	1.5 gm	J0295
UNCLASSIFIED BIOLOGICS			J3590
UNCLASSIFIED DRUGS (SEE ALSO NOT ELSEWHERE CLASSIFIED)	-	-	J3490
UREA	IV	40 g	J3350
UREAPHIL	IV	40 g	J3350
URECHOLINE	SC	5 mg	J0520
UROFOLLITROPIN	SC	75 IU	Q2018
UROKINASE	IV	250,000 IU vial	J3365
UROKINASE	IV	5,000 IU vial	J3364
UROKINASE	IV	5,000 IU vial	J3364
UROKINASE, OPEN CATH	IV	250,000 IU vial	J3365
V-GAN 50	IM, IV	50 mg	J2550
VAGINAL RING	OTH		J7303
VALERGEN 20	IM	20 mg	J1390
VALERGEN 40	IM	40 mg	J0970
VALERGEN-10	IM	10 mg	J1380
VALERTEST NO. 1	IM	1 cc	J0900
VALERTEST NO. 2	IM	1 cc	J0900
VALIUM	IM, IV	5 MG	
VALRUBICIN	IV	200 mg	J9357
VALSTAR	IV	200 mg	J9357
VANCOCIN	IV, IM	500 mg	J3370
VANCOLED	IV, IM	500 mg	J3370
VANCOMYCIN HCL	IV, IM	500 mg	J3370
VELBAN	IV	1 mg	J9360
VELSAR	IV	1 mg	J9360

Drug Name	Route	Unit	Code
VENOFER	IM	1 mg	J1756
VENOGLUBULIN-S	IV	10 mg	J1564
VENTOLIN, CONCENTRATED	INH	1 mg	J7618
VEPESID	IV	10 mg	J9181
VEPESID	IV	100 mg	J9182
VEPESID	ORAL	50 mg	J8560
VERSED	IM, IV	1 mg	J2250
VERTEPORFIN	IV	15 mg	J3395
VESPRIN	IM, IV	20 mg	J3400
VFEND IV	INJ	10 mg	J3465
VIAGRA	ORAL	25 mg	S0090
VINBLASTINE SULFATE	IV	1 mg	J9360
VINCASAR PFS, ONCOVIN	IV	1 mg	J9370
VINCRISTINE SULFATE	IV	1 mg	J9370
VINCRISTINE SULFATE	IV	2 mg	J9375
VINCRISTINE SULFATE	IV	5 mg	J9380
VINORELBINE TARTRATE	IV	10 mg	J9390
VIRILON	IM	1 cc, 200 mg	J1080
VISTARIL	IM	25 mg	J3410
VISTARIL	ORAL	50 mg	Q0178
VISTIDE	IV	375 mg	J0740
VISUDYNE	IV	15 mg	J3395
VITAMIN B-12 CYANOCOBALAMIN	IM, SC	1,000 mcg	J3420
VITAMIN K	IM, SC, IV	1 mg	J3430
VITRASERT	OTH	4.5 mg	J7310
VITRAVENE	OTH	1.65 mg	J1452
VON WILLEBRAND FACTOR COMPLEX, HUMAN	IV	1 IU	Q2022
VORICONAZOLE	INJ	10 mg	J3465
VUMON	IV	50 mg	Q2017
WELLBRUTRIN SR	ORAL	60 150 mg tabs	S0106
WELLCOVORIN	IM, IV	50 mg	J0640
WYCILLIN	IM	600,000 units	J2510
WYDASE	SC, IV	150 units	J3470
XELODA	ORAL	500 mg	J8521
ZANOSAR	IV	1 gm	J9320
ZANTAC	INJ	25 mg	J2780
ZEMPLAR	IM, IV	1 mcg	J2501
ZEMPLAR	IV	1 mcg	J2501
ZENAPAX	OTH	25 mg	J7513
ZIDOVUDINE	IV	10 mg	J3485, S0104
ZINACEF	IM, IV	750 mg	J0697
ZINECARD	IV	250 mg	J1190
ZIPRASIDONE MESYLATE	IV	10 mg	J3486
ZITHROMAX	IV	500 mg	J0456
ZITHROMAX	ORAL	1 g	Q0144
ZOFRAN	ORAL	8 mg	Q0179
ZOLADEX	SC	3.6 mg	J9202
ZOLEDRONIC ACID	IV	1 mg	J3487

Drug Name	Route	Unit	Code
ZOLICEF	IV, IM	500 mg	J0690
ZOMETA	IV	1 mg	J3487
ZOSYN	IV	500 mg	S0081
ZOVIRAX	IV	50 mg	S0071
ZOVIRAX	ORAL, IV	50 mg	S0071

APPENDIX 4 — MEDICARE REFERENCES

REVISIONS TO THE CMS MANUAL SYSTEM

The Centers for Medicare and Medicaid Services (CMS) initiated its long awaited transition from a paper-based manual system to a Web-based system on October 1, 2003, which updates and restructures all manual instructions. The new system, called the online CMS Manual system, combines all of the various program instructions into an electronic manual, which can be found at http://www.cms.hhs.gov/manuals.

Effective September 30, 2003, the former method of publishing program memoranda (PMs) to communicate program instructions was replaced by the following four templates:

- One-time notification
- Manual revisions
- Business requirement
- Confidential requirements

The Office of Strategic Operations and Regulatory Affairs (OSORA), Division of Issuances, will continue to communicate advanced program instructions to the regions and contractor community every Friday as it currently does. These instructions will also contain a transmittal sheet to identify changes pertaining to a specific manual, requirement, or notification.

The Web-based system has been organized by functional area (e.g., eligibility, entitlement, claims processing, benefit policy, program integrity) in an effort to eliminate redundancy within the manuals, simplify the updating process, and make CMS program instructions available in a more timely manner. The initial release will include Pub. 100, Pub. 100-02, Pub. 100-03, Pub. 100-04, Pub. 100-05, Pub. 100-09, Pub. 100-15, and Pub. 100-20.

The Web-based system contains the functional areas included in the table below:

Publication #	Title
Pub. 100	Introduction
Pub. 100-1	Medicare General Information, Eligibility, and Entitlement
Pub. 100-2	Medicare Benefit Policy (basic coverage rules)
Pub. 100-3	Medicare National Coverage Determinations (national coverage decisions)
Pub. 100-4	Medicare Claims Processing (includes appeals, contractor interface with CWF, and MSN)
Pub. 100-5	Medicare Secondary Payer
Pub. 100-6	Medicare Financial Management (includes Intermediary Desk Review and Audit)
Pub. 100-7	Medicare State Operations
	(The new manual is under development. Please continue to use the paper-based manual.)
Pub. 100-8	Medicare Program Integrity
Pub. 100-9	Medicare Contractor Beneficiary and Provider Communications
Pub. 100-10	Medicare Quality Improvement Organization
Pub. 100-11	Reserved
Pub. 100-12	State Medicaid
	(The new manual is under development. Please continue to use the paper-based manual.)
Pub. 100-13	Medicaid State Children's Health Insurance Program
	(Under development)
Pub. 100-14	Medicare End Stage Renal Disease Network
Pub. 100-15	Medicare State Buy-In
Pub. 100-16	Medicare Managed Care
Pub. 100-17	Medicare Business Partners Systems Security
Pub. 100-18	Medicare Business Partners Security Oversight
Pub. 100-19	Demonstrations
Pub. 100-20	One-Time Notification

National Coverage Determinations Manual

The National Coverage Determinations Manual (NCD), which is the electronic replacement for the Coverage Issues Manual (CIM), is organized according to categories such as diagnostic services, supplies, and medical procedures. The table of contents lists each category and subject within that category. A revision transmittal sheet will identify any new material and recap the changes as well as provide an effective date for the change and any background information. At any time, one can refer to a transmittal indicated on the page of the manual to view this information.

By the time it is complete, the book will contain two chapters. Chapter 1 includes a description of national coverage determinations that have been made by CMS. When available, chapter 2 will contain a list of HCPCS codes related to each coverage determination. To make the manual easier to use, it is organized in accordance with CPT category sequences. Where there is no national coverage determination that affects a particular CPT category, the category is listed as reserved in the table of contents.

The following table is the crosswalk of the NCD to the CIM, and the Pubs 100 to MCM. However, at this time, many of the NCD and Pubs 100 policies are not yet available. The CMS Web site also contains a crosswalk of the CIM to the NCD, and pubs 100 to the MCM.

Medicare Benefit Policy Manual

The Medicare Benefit Policy Manual replaces current Medicare general coverage instructions that are not national coverage determinations. As a general rule, in the past these instructions have been found in chapter II of the Medicare Carriers Manual, the Medicare Intermediary Manual, other provider manuals, and program memoranda. New instructions will be published in this manual. As new transmittals are included they will be identified.

On the CMS Web site, a crosswalk from the new manual to the source manual is provided with each chapter and may be accessed from the chapter table of contents. In addition, the crosswalk for each section is shown immediately under the section heading.

The list below is the table of contents for the Medicare Benefit Policy Manual:

CHAPTER	TITLE
1	Inpatient Hospital Services
2	Inpatient Psychiatric Hospital Services
3	Duration of Covered Inpatient Services
4	Inpatient Psychiatric Benefit Days Reduction and Lifetime Limitation

MCM/CIM CROSSWALK TO PUBS 100 REFERENCE, AND NCD MANUAL

CIM	NCD PUB 100-3 REF
CIM 25-101	250.4
CIM 30-1	310.1
CIM 35-1	100.7
CIM 35-10	20.29
CIM 35-100	80.2
CIM 35-11	230.3
CIM 35-12	140.4
CIM 35-13	150.7
CIM 35-14	70.1
CIM 35-15	240.7
CIM 35-16	80.11
CIM 35-17	160.1
CIM 35-18	30.4
CIM 35-19	30.6
CIM 35-2	150.1
CIM 35-20	160.2
CIM 35-21	10.3
CIM 35-21.1	10.4
CIM 35-22	130.1
CIM 35-22.1	130.2
CIM 35-22.2	130.6
CIM 35-22.3	130.5
CIM 35-23	130.3
CIM 35-23.1	130.4
CIM 35-24	230.4
CIM 35-25	20.10
CIM 35-26	40.5
CIM 35-26.1	40.5
CIM 35-27	30.1
CIM 35-27.1	30.1.1
CIM 35-29	50.5
CIM 35-3	240.3
CIM 35-30	110.8
CIM 35-30.1	110.8.1
CIM 35-31	270.4
CIM 35-32	20.01
CIM 35-33	100.8, 230.2
CIM 35-34	20.23
CIM 35-35	20.28
CIM 35-37	20.1, 20.2
CIM 35-38	110.15
CIM 35-39	80.6
CIM 35-4	50.8
CIM 35-40	100.1

CIM 35-41	150.5		CIM 35-85	20.4
CIM 35-42	130.7		CIM 35-86	100.11
CIM 35-44	10.1		CIM 35-87	260.9
CIM 35-45	20.25		CIM 35-88	110.4
CIM 35-46	160.3, 160.7.1		CIM 35-89	170.3
CIM 35-47	140.2		CIM 35-9	80.10
CIM 35-48	150.2, 160.11		CIM 35-90	20.5
CIM 35-49	110.1		CIM 35-91	100.13
CIM 35-5	30.8		CIM 35-92	30.5
CIM 35-50	50.7		CIM 35-93	240.1
CIM 35-51	130.8		CIM 35-94	20.6
CIM 35-52	140.5		CIM 35-95	20.26
CIM 35-53	260.1		CIM 35-96	230.9
CIM 35-53.1	260.2		CIM 35-97	160.16
CIM 35-54	80.7		CIM 35-98	270.1
CIM 35-55	240.6		CIM 35-99	140.1
CIM 35-56	150.8		CIM 35-100	80.2
CIM 35-57	160.8		CIM 35-103	160.25
CIM 35-57.1	160.9		CIM 35-104	260.5
CIM 35-58	20.3		CIM 45-1	160.17
CIM 35-59	100.2		CIM 45-10	30.7
CIM 35-6	30.2		CIM 45-11	10.5
CIM 35-60	110.14		CIM 45-12	270.5
CIM 35-61	140.3		CIM 45-15	70.3
CIM 35-62	160.14		CIM 45-16	110.2
CIM 35-63	50.6		CIM 45-17	160.20
CIM 35-64	20.21		CIM 45-18	110.5
CIM 35-65	100.6		CIM 45-19	10.2
CIM 35-66	250.1		CIM 45-20	20.22
CIM 35-67	170.2		CIM 45-21	110.6
CIM 35-69	100.9		CIM 45-22	260.7
CIM 35-7	20.18		CIM 45-23	230.12
CIM 35-70	40.3		CIM 45-24	110.3
CIM 35-71	110.16		CIM 45-25	160.13
CIM 35-72	160.15		CIM 45-26	270.3
CIM 35-73	100.10		CIM 45-27	110.7
CIM 35-74	20.20		CIM 45-28	110.9
CIM 35-75	20.11		CIM 45-29	110.10
CIM 35-77	150.4, 160.12		CIM 45-3	40.4
CIM 35-78	20.12		CIM 45-30	80.3
CIM 35-79	10.6, 20.8.3		CIM 45-31	250.3
CIM 35-8	30.3		CIM 45-32	230.19
CIM 35-81	230.1		CIM 45-4	150.6
CIM 35-82	260.3		CIM 45-7	80.1
CIM 35-83	100.3		CIM 50-1	20.8.1, 20.8.1.1
CIM 35-84	160.4		CIM 50-10	230.6

CIM 50-12	220.1	CIM 50-52	190.9
CIM 50-13	220.2	CIM 50-53	110.11
CIM 50-14	220.3	CIM 50-54	20.16
CIM 50-15	20.15	CIM 50-55	210.1
CIM 50-16	250.2	CIM 50-56	190.11
CIM 50-17	190.10	CIM 50-57.1	160.23
CIM 50-19	70.4	CIM 50-58	220.12
CIM 50-18	190.4	CIM 50-59	220.13
CIM 50-2	110.13	CIM 50-6	20.14
CIM 50-20	190.2, 230.11	CIM 50-7	220.5
CIM 50-20.1	210.2	CIM 50-8	70.2
CIM 50-21	220.4	CIM 50-8.1	70.2.1
CIM 50-22	110.12	CIM 50-9	100.12
CIM 50-23	190.1	CIM 55-1	230.7
CIM 50-24	190.6	CIM 55-2	230.13
CIM 50-25	100.4	CIM 55-3	230.14
CIM 50-26	260.6	CIM 60-11	40.2
CIM 50-27	220.7	CIM 60-14	40.2, 280.14
CIM 50-28	70.5	CIM 60-15	280.5
CIM 50-29	190.3	CIM 60-16	280.6
CIM 50-3	20.13	CIM 60-17	240.4
CIM 50-30	220.8	CIM 60-18	280.7
CIM 50-31	160.10	CIM 60-19	280.8
CIM 50-32	20.7	CIM 60-20	280.13
CIM 50-33	230.2	CIM 60-21	240.5
CIM 50-34	300.1	CIM 60-22	160.18
CIM 50-35	190.5	CIM 60-23	50.1
CIM 50-36	220.6	CIM 60-24	230.8
CIM 50-37	20.17	CIM 60-25	270.2
CIM 50-38	80.8	CIM 60-3	280.2
CIM 50-39	160.21	CIM 60-4	240.2
CIM 50-39.1	160.22	CIM 60-5	280.9
CIM 50-4	230.5	CIM 60-6	280.3
CIM 50-41	190.7	CIM 60-7	20.8.2
CIM 50-40	160.5	CIM 60-8	280.4
CIM 50-42	20.19	CIM 60-9	280.1
CIM 50-43	220.9	CIM 65-1	80.4
CIM 50-44	150.3	CIM 65-10	180.2
CIM 50-45	190.8	CIM 65-11	230.16
CIM 50-46	30.9	CIM 65-13	160.19
CIM 50-47	20.27	CIM 65-14	50.3
CIM 50-48	220.10	CIM 65-15	20.9
CIM 50-49	80.9	CIM 65-16	20.9, 50.4
CIM 50-5	220.11	CIM 65-17	230.17
CIM 50-50	20.24	CIM 65-18	230.18
CIM 50-51	100.5	CIM 65-19	160.24

CIM 65-2	230.15	MCM 15505	Pub. 100-4, Chapter 12, Section 30.6.9, 30.6.9.1, 30.6.9.2,
CIM 65-3	80.5	MCM 15505.1	Pub. 100-4, chapter 12, Section 30.6.2
CIM 65-4	160.6	MCM 15505.2	Pub. 100-4, Chapter 12, Section 30.6.9.2
CIM 65-5	50.2	MCM 15506	Pub. 100-4, Chapter 12, Section 30.6.10
CIM 65-6	20.8	MCM 15507	Pub. 100-4, Chapter 12, Section 30.6.11
CIM 65-7	80.12	MCM 15508	Pub. 100-4, Chapter 12, Section 30.6.12
CIM 65-8	160.7	MCM 15509	Pub. 100-4, Chapter 12, Section 30.6.13
CIM 65-9	230.10	MCM 15509.1	Pub. 100-4, Chapter 12, Section 30.6.13
CIM 65-165	50.4	MCM 15510	Pub. 100-4, Chapter 12, Section 30.6.14
CIM 70-1	280.11	MCM 15511.1	Pub. 100-4, Chapter 12, Section 30.6.15.1
CIM 70-2	280.12	MCM 15511.2	Pub. 100-4, Chapter 12, Section 30.15.2
CIM 70-3	280.10	MCM 15511.3	Pub. 100-4, Chapter 12, Section 30.6.15.3
CIM 80-1	170.1	MCM 15512	Pub. 100-4, Chapter 12, Section 30.6.16
CIM 80-2	40.1	MCM 15513	Pub. 100-2, Chapter 15, Section 30 Pub. 100-4 Chapter 11, Section 40, 40.1, 40.1.3.1, Chapter 12, Section 180
CIM 80-3	180.1		
CIM 90-1	290.1		
CIM 90-2	290.2	MCM 15514	Pub. 100-4, Chapter 12, Section 30.6.2
MCM	Pub 100 Ref	MCM 15515	Pub. 100-4, Chapter 30, Section 30.6.14.1
MCM 15002	Pub. 100-4, Chapter 23, Section 30	MCM 2005.1	Pub. 100-2, Chapter 15, section 20.1
MCM 15004	Pub. 100-4, Chapter 12, Section 110; Chapter 23, Section 30	MCM 2005.2	Pub. 100-2, Chapter 15, Section 20.2
		MCM 2005.3	Pub. 100-2, Chapter 15, Section 20.3
MCM 15016	Pub. 100-2, Chapter 15, Section 30.2, Chapter 12, Section 100, 100.1.7, 100.1.8,	MCM 2020	Pub. 100-1, Chapter 5, Section 70 Pub. 100-2, Chapter 12, Section 10, 10.1.3 Chapter 15, Section 30 Pub. 100-4, Chapter 11, Section 40, 40.1, 40.1.3.1, Chapter 12, Section 100
MCM 15018	Pub. 100-4, Chapter 12, Section 50, 140.3.2		
MCM 15020	Pub. 100-4, Chapter 12, Section 60		
MCM 15021.1	Pub. 100-4, Chapter 13, Section 10 Chapter 23, Section 10, 10.1, 10.1.1, 10.1.2, 10.1.3, 10.1.4, 10.1.5, 10.1.6, 10.1.7	MCM 2020.26	Pub. 100-1, Chapter 5, Section 70.6 Pub. 100-2, Chapter 15, Section 30.5
		MCM 2049	Pub. 100-2, Chapter 15, Section 50, 50.1, 50.4, 50.4.1, 50.4.2, 50.4.3, 50.4.4, 50.4.4.1, 50.4.4.2, 50.4.5, 50.4.6, 50.4.7, 50.5, 50.5.1., 50.5.2.1, Pub. 100-4, Chapter 8 Section 60.4
MCM 15022	Pub. 100-4, Chapter 12, Section 70 Chapter 13, Section 20, 90		
MCM 15023	Pub. 100-4, Chapter 13, Section 100		
MCM 15026	Pub. 100-4, Chapter 12, Section 80.3	MCM 2049.2	Pub. 100-2, Chapter 15, Section 50
MCM 15030	Pub. 100-4, Chapter 12, Section 20.4.4	MCM 2049.3	Pub. 100-2, Chapter 15, Section 50.3, 50.4.2
MCM 15038	Pub. 100-4, Chapter 12, Section 40.6	MCM 2050	Pub. 100-2, Chapter 15, Section 60,
MCM 15049	NCD Manual Section 80.2	MCM 2050.1	Pub. 100-2, Chapter 15, Section 60.1
MCM 15050.	Pub. 100-4, Chapter 12, Section 200	MCM 2050.2	Pub. 100-2, Chapter 15, Section 60.2
MCM 15070	Pub. 100-4, Chapter 12, Section 30	MCM 2050.3	Pub. 100-2, Chapter 15, Section 60.3
MCM 15100	Pub. 100-4, Chapter 12, Section 30.1	MCM 2070	Pub. 100-2, Chapter 15, Section 80 Pub. 100-4, Chapter 13, Section 90
MCM 15200	Pub. 100-4, Chapter 12, Section 30.2		
MCM 15302	Pub. 100-4, Chapter 5, Section 100.10	MCM 2070.1	Pub. 100-1, Chapter 5, Section 90.2 Pub. 100-2, Chapter 15, Section 80.1, 80.1.1, 80.1.2, 80.1.3
MCM 15304	Pub. 100-4, Chapter 5, Section 100.10.1		
MCM 15350	Pub. 100-4 Chapter 8 Section 140	MCM 2070.2	Pub. 100-2, Chapter 15, Section 80.2 Pub. 100-4, Chapter 12, Section 160
MCM 15360	Pub. 100-4, Chapter 12, Section 30.4		
MCM 15400	Pub. 100-4, Chapter 12, Section 30.5	MCM 2070.3	Pub. 100-2, Chapter 15, Section 80.3, 80.3.1
MCM 15501	Pub. 100-4, Chapter 12, Section 30.6	MCM 2070.4	Pub. 100-2, Chapter 15, Section 80.4.1, 80.4.2, 80.4.3, 80.4.4, 80.4.5
MCM 15502	Pub. 100-4, Chapter 12, Section 30.6.7		
		MCM 2079	Pub. 100-2, Chapter 15, Section 100
MCM 15504	Pub. 100-4, Chapter 12, Section 30.6.8	MCM 2100	Pub. 100-2, Chapter 15, Section 110
		MCM 2100.1	Pub. 100-2, Chapter 15, Section 110.1

MCM 2100.2	Pub. 100-2, Chapter 15, Section 110.1
MCM 2100.3	Pub. 100-2, Chapter 15, Section 110.1
MCM 2100.4	Pub. 100-2, Chapter 15, Section 110.2
MCM 2100.5	Pub. 100-2, Chapter 15, Section 110.3
MCM 2120.1	Pub. 100-2, Chapter 10, Section 10.1, 10.1.1, 10.1.2, 10.1.3, 10.1.4, 10.1.5
MCM 2125	Pub. 100-2 Chapter 10, Section 20
MCM 2130	Pub. 100-2, Chapter 15, Section 120
MCM 2133	Pub. 100-2, Chapter 15, Section 130
MCM 2134	Pub. 100-2, Chapter 15, Section 140
MCM 2136	Pub. 100-2, Chapter 15, Section 150
MCM 2150	Pub. 100-2, Chapter 15, Section 160 Pub. 100-4, Chapter 12, Section 160, 170, 170.1
MCM 2152	Pub. 100-2, Chapter 15, Section 170 Pub. 100-4, Chapter 12, Section 150
MCM 2154	Pub. 100-2, Chapter 15, Section 180
MCM 2156	Pub. 100-2, Chapter 15, Section 190 Pub. 100-4, Chapter 12, Section 110, 110.3
MCM 2158	Pub. 100-2, Chapter 15, Section 200 Pub. 100-4, Chapter 12, Section 120, 120.1
MCM 2210	Pub. 100-2, Chapter 15, Section 230
MCM 2210.1	Pub. 100-2, Chapter 15, Section 230
MCM 2210.2	Pub. 100-2, Chapter 15, Section 230
MCM 2210.3	Pub. 100-2, Chapter 15, Section 230
MCM 2215	Pub. 100-2, Chapter 15, Section 230.1, Pub. 100-4, Chapter 5, Section 10
MCM 2216	Pub. 100-2, Chapter 15, Section 230.3
MCM 2217	Pub. 100-2, Chapter 15, Section 230.4
MCM 2218	Pub. 100-2, Chapter 15, Section 220.2
MCM 2250	Pub. 100-2, Chapter 15, Section 240
MCM 2251	Pub. 100-2, Chapter 15, Section 240.1, 240.1.1, 240.1.2, 240.1.3, 240.1.4, 240.1.5
MCM 2265	Pub. 100-2, , Chapter 15, Section 260, 260.1, 260.2, 260.3, 260.4 Pub. 100-4, Chapter 12, Section 90.3
MCM 2300	Pub. 100-2 Chapter 16, section 10
MCM 2300.1	Chapter 1, Section 120 Chapter 16, Section 180
MCM 2303	Pub. 100-2, Chapter 16, Section 10
MCM 2318	Pub. 100-2, Chapter 16, Section 80
MCM 2320	Pub. 100-2, Chapter 16, Section 90
MCM 2323	Pub. 100-2, Chapter 15, Section 290, Chapter 16, section 30
MCM 2329	Pub. 100-2, Chapter 16, section 120
MCM 2336	Pub. 100-2, Chapter 16, section 140
MCM 2455	Pub. 100, Chapter 3, Section 20.5
MCM 2470.	Pub. 100-1, Chapter 3, Section 30-30.3 Pub. 100-4, Chapter 12, Section 210
MCM 2472	Pub. 100-4, Chapter 12, Section 110.2, 120, 210.1
MCM 3045.4	Pub. 100-4, Chapter 1, Section 30.3.5
MCM 3312	Pub. 100-4, Chapter 20, Section 100.2, 100.2.2
MCM 3324	Pub. 100-4, Chapter 20, Section 50.3
MCM 4107	Pub. 100-4, Chapter 20, Section 30.1.2, Chapter 20, Section 100, 130, 130.2, 130.3, 130.4, 130.5, 130.6,
MCM 4118	Pub. 100-2, Chapter 15, Section 30.5
MCM 4120	Pub. 100-2, Chapter 15, Section 290
MCM 4141	Pub. 100-2, Chapter 15, Section 30
MCM 4142	Pub. 100-2, Chapter 15, Section 30
MCM 4146.	Pub. 100-4, Chapter 12, Section 110.2, 120, 210.1
MCM 4161	Pub. 100-2, Chapter 8, Section 70
MCM 4162.	Pub. 100-4, Chapter 12, Section 150
MCM 4172	Pub. 100-4, Chapter 12, Section 140, 140.1, 140.1.1, 140.1.2, 140.3.4, 140.4.2,
MCM 4173	Pub. 100-4, Chapter 13, Section 60
MCM 4175	Pub. 100-4, Chapter 11, Section 10, 40, 40.1, 40.1.3, 40.2, 40.2.2., 50, 120
MCM 4180	Pub. 100-2, Chapter 15, Section 280.2, 280.2.1, 280.2.2, 280.2.3, 280.2.4, 280.2.5 Pub. 100-4, Chapter 18, Section 60, 60.1, 60.2, 60.2.1, 60.2.2, 60.3, 60.4, 60.5, 60.6, 60.7, 60.8
MCM 4182	Pub. 100-4, Chapter 18, Section 50.2, 50.3, 50.3.1, 50.4, 50.5, 50.6, 50.7, 50.8
MCM 4270	Pub. 100-4, Chapter 8, Section 80, 90, 90.3.2, 130
MCM 4270.1	Pub. 100-4m Chapter 8, Sections 60.4.4, 60.4.4.1, 70, 90, 90.1, 90.2, 90.2.1, 90.2.2,
MCM 4270.2	Pub. 100-4, Chapter 8, Section 60.1, 90
MCM 4273.1	Pub. 100-2, Chapter 11, Section 90; Pub. 100-4, Chapter 8, , Section 60.4.2, 60.4.2.1
MCM 4277	NCD Manual Section 20.20
MCM 4281	NCD Manual, Section 70.2.1
MCM 4450	Pub. 100-4, Chapter 20, Section 100.2.2, 100.2.2.3
MCM 4471.2	Pub. 100-4 Chapter 8, Section 120.1
MCM 4480	Pub. 100-4, Chapter 18, Section 10, 10.1, 10.1.1, 10.1.2, 10.1.3, 10.2, 10.2.1, 10.2.5.2, 10.3
MCM 4601	Pub. 100-2, Chapter 15, Section 280.3 Pub. 100-4, Chapter 18, Section 20, 20.1, 20.2, 20.2.1, 20.3, 20.3.1, 20.3.2, 20.3.2.1, 20.3.2.2.
MCM 4602	Pub. 100-4, Chapter 13, Section 40.1
MCM 4603	Pub. 100-2, Chapter 15, Section 280.4 Pub. 100-4, Chapter 18, Section 30, 30.1, 30.2, 30.3, 30.4, 30.5, 30.6, 30.7, 30.8, 30.9, 40, 40.1, 40.2, 40.3, 40.4, 40.5, 40.6, 40.7
MCM 4826	Pub. 100-4, Chapter 12, Section 40.6
MCM 4827	Pub. 100-4, Chapter 12, Section 40.7

APPENDIX 4 — MEDICARE REFERENCES

MCM 4830	Pub. 100-4, Chapter 12, Section 50, 140.2
MCM 4900	Pub. 100-2, Chapter
MCM 5112.	Pub. 100-4, Chapter 12, Section 160, 160.1, 170, 170.1
MCM 5112.1	Pub. 100-4, Chapter 12, Section 160, 160.1, 170, 170.1
MCM 5113.	Pub. 100-4, Chapter 12, Section 150
MCM 5249	Pub. 100-2, Chapter 15, Section 50.5.1
MCM 8310	Pub. 100-4, Chapter 12, Section 50
MCM 8312	Pub. 100-4, Chapter 12, Section 50

COVERAGE ISSUES MANUAL

CIM 35-10   HYPERBARIC OXYGEN THERAPY

For purposes of coverage under Medicare, hyperbaric oxygen (HBO) therapy is a modality in which the entire body is exposed to oxygen under increased atmospheric pressure.

A. Covered Conditions. – Program reimbursement for HBO therapy will be limited to that which is administered in a chamber (including the one man unit) and is limited to the following conditions:

1. Acute carbon monoxide intoxication, (ICD-9 -CM diagnosis 986).

2. Decompression illness, (ICD-9-CM diagnosis 993.2, 993.3).

3. Gas embolism, (ICD-9-CM diagnosis 958.0, 999.1).

4. Gas gangrene, (ICD-9-CM diagnosis 400).

5. Acute traumatic peripheral ischemia. HBO therapy is an adjunctive treatment to be used in combination with accepted standard therapeutic measures when loss of function, limb, or life is threatened. (ICD-9-CM diagnosis 902.53, 903.01, 903.1, 904.0, 904.41.)

6. Crush injuries and suturing of severed limbs. As in the previous conditions, HBO therapy would be an adjunctive treatment when loss of function, limb, or life is threatened. (ICD-9-CM diagnosis 927.00-927.03, 927.09-927.11, 927.20-927.21, 927.8-927.9, 928.00-928.01, 928.10-928.11, 928.20-928.21, 928.3, 928.8-928.9, 929.0, 929.9, 996.90-996.99.)

7. Progressive necrotizing infections (necrotizing fasciitis), (ICD-9-CM diagnosis 728.86).

8. Acute peripheral arterial insufficiency, (ICD-9-CM diagnosis 444.21, 444.22, 444.81).

9. Preparation and preservation of compromised skin grafts (not for primary management of wounds), (ICD-9CM diagnosis 996.52; excludes artificial skin graft).

10. Chronic refractory osteomyelitis, unresponsive to conventional medical and surgical management, (ICD-9-CM diagnosis 730.10-730.19).

11. Osteoradionecrosis as an adjunct to conventional treatment, (ICD-9-CM diagnosis 526.89).

12. Soft tissue radionecrosis as an adjunct to conventional treatment, (ICD-9-CM diagnosis 990).

13. Cyanide poisoning, (ICD-9-CM diagnosis 987.7, 989.0).

14. Actinomycosis, only as an adjunct to conventional therapy when the disease process is refractory to antibiotics and surgical treatment, (ICD-9-CM diagnosis 039.0-039.4, 039.8, 039.9).

15. Diabetic wounds of the lower extremities in patients who meet the following three criteria:

a. Patient has type I or type II diabetes and has a lower extremity wound that is due to diabetes;

b. Patient has a wound classified as Wagner grade III or higher; and

c. Patient has failed an adequate course of standard wound therapy.

The use of HBO therapy is covered as adjunctive therapy only after there are no measurable signs of healing for at least 30-days of treatment with standard wound therapy and must be used in addition to standard wound care. Standard wound care in patients with diabetic wounds includes: assessment of a patient's vascular status and correction of any vascular problems in the affected limb if possible, optimization of nutritional status, optimization of glucose control, debridement by any means to remove devitalized tissue, maintenance of a clean, moist bed of granulation tissue with appropriate moist dressings, appropriate off-loading, and necessary treatment to resolve any infection that might be present. Failure to respond to standard wound care occurs when there are no measurable signs of healing for at least 30 consecutive days. Wounds must be evaluated at least every 30 days during administration of HBO therapy. Continued treatment with HBO therapy is not covered if measurable signs of healing have not been demonstrated within any 30-day period of treatment.

B. Noncovered Conditions. – All other indications not specified under §35-10 (A) are not covered under the Medicare program. No program payment may be made for any conditions other than those listed in §35-10(A).

No program payment may be made for HBO in the treatment of the following conditions:

1. Cutaneous, decubitus, and stasis ulcers.

2. Chronic peripheral vascular insufficiency.

3. Anaerobic septicemia and infection other than clostridial.

4. Skin burns (thermal).

5. Senility.

6. Myocardial infarction.

7. Cardiogenic shock.

8. Sickle cell anemia.

9. Acute thermal and chemical pulmonary damage, i.e., smoke inhalation with pulmonary insufficiency.

10. Acute or chronic cerebral vascular insufficiency.

11. Hepatic necrosis.

12. Aerobic septicemia.

13. Nonvascular causes of chronic brain syndrome (Pick's disease, Alzheimer's disease, Korsakoff's disease).

14. Tetanus.

15. Systemic aerobic infection.

16. Organ transplantation.

17. Organ storage.

18. Pulmonary emphysema.

19. Exceptional blood loss anemia.

20. Multiple Sclerosis.

21. Arthritic Diseases.

22. Acute cerebral edema.

C. Topical Application of Oxygen. – This method of administering oxygen does not meet the definition of HBO therapy as stated above. Also, its clinical efficacy has not been established. Therefore, no Medicare reimbursement may be made for the topical application of oxygen. (Cross refer: §35-31.)

CIM 35-100 PHOTODYNAMIC THERAPY

Photodynamic therapy is a medical procedure which involves the infusion of a photosensitive (light-activated) drug with a very specific absorption peak. This drug is chemically designed to have a unique affinity for the diseased tissue intended for treatment. Once introduced to the body, the drug accumulates and is retained in diseased tissue to a greater degree than in normal tissue. Infusion is followed by the targeted irradiation of this tissue with a non-thermal laser, calibrated to emit light at a wavelength that corresponds to the drug's absorption peak. The drug then becomes active and locally treats the diseased tissue.

Ocular photodynamic therapy (OPT)

OPT is used in the treatment of ophthalmologic diseases. OPT is only covered when used in conjunction with verteporfin (see §45-30 PHOTOSENSITIVE DRUGS).

Classic Subfoveal Choroidal Neovascular (CNV) Lesions. – OPT is covered with a diagnosis of neovascular age-related macular degeneration (AMD) with predominantly classic subfoveal choroidal neovascular (CNV) lesions (where the area of classic CNV occupies = 50% of the area of the entire lesion) at the initial visit as determined by a fluorescein angiogram. Subsequent follow-up visits will require a fluorescein angiogram prior to treatment. There are no requirements regarding visual acuity, lesion size, and number of re-treatments.

Occult Subfoveal Choroidal Neovascular (CNV) Lesions. – OPT is noncovered for patients with a diagnosis of age-related macular degeneration (AMD) with occult and no classic CNV lesions.

Other Conditions. – Use of OPT with verteporfin for other types of AMD (e.g., patients with minimally classic CNV lesions, atrophic, or dry AMD) is noncovered. OPT with verteporfin for other ocular indications such as pathologic myopia or presumed ocular histoplasmosis syndrome, is eligible for coverage through individual contractor discretion.

CIM 35-13 Prolotherapy, Joint Sclerotherapy, and Ligamentous Injections with Sclerosing Agents – Not Covered

The medical effectiveness of the above therapies has not been verified by scientifically controlled studies and coverage is denied on the ground that they are not reasonable and necessary.

CIM 35-20 Treatment of Motor Function Disorders with Electric Nerve Stimulation – Not Covered

No reimbursement may be made for electric nerve stimulation or for the services related to its implantation since this treatment cannot be considered reasonable and necessary. However, Medicare covers deep brain stimulation by implanting a stimulator device at the carrier's discretion.

TREATMENT OF MOTOR FUNCTION DISORDERS WITH ELECTRIC NERVE STIMULATION- NOT COVERED

While electric nerve stimulation has been employed to control chronic intractable pain for some time, its use in the treatment of motor function disorders, such as multiple sclerosis, is a recent innovation, and the medical effectiveness of such therapy has not been verified by scientifically controlled studies. Therefore, where electric nerve stimulation is employed to treat motor function disorders, no reimbursement may be made for the stimulator or for the services related to its implantation since this treatment cannot be considered reasonable and necessary.

See §§35-27 and 65-8.

NOTE: For Medicare coverage of deep brain stimulation for essential tremor and Parkinson's disease, see §65-19.

CIM 35-30 Blood Platelet Transfusions

Blood platelet transplants, which been shown as safe and effective in correcting thrombocytopenia and other blood defects, is covered under Medicare.

CIM 35-34 Fabric Wrapping Of Abdominal Aneurysms – Not Covered

Fabric wrapping of abdominal aneurysms is not a covered Medicare procedure. This is a treatment for abdominal aneurysms which involves wrapping aneurysms with cellophane or fascia lata. This procedure has not been shown to prevent eventual rupture. In extremely rare instances, external wall reinforcement may be indicated when the current accepted treatment (excision of the aneurysm and reconstruction with synthetic materials) is not a viable alternative, but external wall reinforcement is not fabric wrapping. Accordingly, fabric wrapping of abdominal aneurysms is not considered reasonable and necessary within the meaning of §1862(a)(1) of the Act.

CIM 35-45 Cardiac Catheterization Performed In Other Than A Hospital

Cardiac catheterization performed in a hospital setting for either inpatients or outpatients is a covered service. The procedure may also be covered when performed in a freestanding clinic when the carrier, in consult with the appropriate Peer Review Organization (PRO), determines that the procedure can be performed safely in the particular facility. Request PRO preauthorization.

CIM 35-46 Assessing Patient's Suitability For Electrical Nerve Stimulation Therapy

Electrical nerve stimulation assesses a patient's suitability for ongoing treatment with a transcutaneous or an implanted nerve stimulator. Accordingly, program payment may be made for the following techniques when used to determine the potential therapeutic usefulness of an electrical nerve stimulator:

• Transcutaneous Electrical Nerve Stimulation (TENS) – technique involves attaching a transcutaneous nerve stimulator to the surface of the skin over the peripheral nerve to be stimulated. If TENS significantly alleviates pain, it may be considered as primary treatment. If it produces no relief or greater discomfort than the original pain electrical nerve stimulation therapy is ruled out. However, where TENS produces incomplete relief, further evaluation with percutaneous electrical nerve stimulation may be considered to determine whether an implanted peripheral nerve stimulator would provide significant relief from pain.

• Percutaneous Electrical Nerve Stimulation (PENS) – diagnostic procedure involves stimulating peripheral nerves by a needle electrode inserted through the skin and is performed only in a physician's office, clinic, or hospital outpatient department. If pain is controlled by percutaneous stimulation, implantation of electrodes is warranted. The medical necessity for such diagnostic services furnished beyond the first month must be documented.

CIM 35-47 Breast Reconstruction Following Mastectomy

(Cosmetic surgery is excluded from coverage under §l862(a)(l0) of the Social Security Act.)

Reconstruction of the affected and the contralateral unaffected breast following a medically necessary mastectomy is considered a relatively safe and effective noncosmetic procedure. Accordingly, program payment may be made for breast reconstruction surgery following removal of a breast for any medical reason. Program payment may not be made for breast reconstruction for cosmetic reasons.

CIM 35-48 Osteogenic Stimulation

Electrical stimulation to augment bone repair can be either invasive or noninvasive. Invasive devices provide electrical stimulation directly at the fracture site either through percutaneously placed cathodes or by implanting a coiled cathode wire into the fracture site.

The noninvasive stimulator device is covered only for the following indications:

• Nonunion of long bone fractures

• Failed fusion, where a minimum of nine months has elapsed since the last surgery

• Congenital pseudarthroses

APPENDIX 4 — MEDICARE REFERENCES

• As an adjunct to spinal fusion surgery for patients at high risk of pseudarthrosis due to previously failed spinal fusion at the same site or for those undergoing multiple level fusion. A multiple level fusion involves 3 or more vertebrae (e.g., L3-L5, L4-S1, etc)

The invasive stimulator device is covered only for the following indications:

• Nonunion of long bone fractures

• As an adjunct to spinal fusion surgery for patients at high risk of pseudarthrosis due to previously failed spinal fusion at the same site or for those undergoing multiple level fusion

Effective for services performed on or after April 1, 2000, nonunion of long bone fractures, for both noninvasive and invasive devices, is considered to exist only when serial radiographs have confirmed that fracture healing has ceased for three or more months prior to starting treatment with the electrical osteogenic stimulator. Serial radiographs must include a minimum of two sets of radiographs, each including multiple views of the fracture site, separated by a minimum of 90 days.

Medicare does not cover ultrasonic osteogenic stimulators.

CIM 35-5   Cellular Therapy – Not Covered
Cellular therapy involves the practice of injecting humans with foreign proteins like the placenta or lungs of unborn lambs. Cellular therapy is without scientific or statistical evidence to document its therapeutic efficacy and, in fact, is considered a potentially dangerous practice. Accordingly, cellular therapy is not considered reasonable and necessary within the meaning of section 1862(a)(1) of the law.

CIM 35-64   Chelation Therapy For Treatment Of Atherosclerosis
Chelation therapy is the application of chelation techniques for the therapeutic or preventive effects of removing unwanted metal ions from the body. The application of chelation therapy using ethylenediamine-tetra-acetic acid (EDTA) for the treatment and prevention of atherosclerosis is controversial. There is no widely accepted rationale to explain the beneficial effects attributed to this therapy. Its safety is questioned and its clinical effectiveness has never been established by well designed, controlled clinical trials. It is not widely accepted and practiced by American physicians. EDTA chelation therapy for atherosclerosis is considered experimental. For these reasons, EDTA chelation therapy for the treatment or prevention of atherosclerosis is not covered.

Some practitioners refer to this therapy as chemoendarterectomy and may also show a diagnosis other than atherosclerosis, such as arteriosclerosis or calcinosis. Claims employing such variant terms should also be denied under this section.

Cross-refer: §45-20

CIM 35-65   Gastric Freezing
Gastric freezing for chronic peptic ulcer disease is a non-surgical treatment which was popular about 20 years ago but now is seldom done. It has been abandoned due to a high complication rate, only temporary improvement experienced by patients, and lack of effectiveness when tested by double- blind, controlled clinical trials. Since the procedure is now considered obsolete, it is not covered.

CIM 35-74   Cardiac Rehabilitation Programs
Cardiac rehabilitation programs are conducted in specialized, free-standing, cardiac rehabilitation clinics as well as in outpatient hospital departments. Exercise programs include specific types of exercise, individually prescribed for each patient.

Medicare covers cardiac rehabilitation programs for patients with a clear medical need, who are referred by their attending physician and (1) have a documented diagnosis of acute myocardial infarction within the preceding 12 months; or (2) have had coronary bypass surgery; and/or (3) have stable angina pectoris. The programs may be provided either by the outpatient department of a hospital or in a physician-directed clinic. Coverage for either program is subject to the following conditions:

1. The facility meets the definition of a hospital outpatient department or a physician- directed clinic.

2. The facility has available for immediate use all the necessary cardio-pulmonary emergency diagnostic and therapeutic life saving equipment accepted by the medical community as medically necessary.

3. The program is conducted in an area set aside for the exclusive use of the program while it is in session.

4. The program is staffed by personnel necessary to conduct the program safely and effectively, who are trained in both basic and advanced life support techniques and in exercise therapy for coronary disease.

Services of nonphysician personnel must be furnished under the direct supervision of a physician. Direct supervision means that a physician must be in the exercise program area and immediately available and accessible for an emergency at all times the exercise program is conducted. It does not require that a physician be physically present in the exercise room.

Stress testing performed to evaluate a prospective candidate may be covered for one or more of the following:

• Evaluation of chest pain, especially atypical chest pain

• Development of exercise prescriptions for patients with known cardiac disease

• Pre and postoperative evaluation of patients undergoing coronary artery by-pass procedures

A freestanding or hospital based cardiac rehabilitation clinic may provide diagnostic and therapeutic services other than stress testing and ECG monitoring, including diagnostic testing for a mental problem if the patient shows symptoms such as excessive anxiety or fear associated with the cardiac disease.

Services in connection with a cardiac rehabilitation exercise program may be provided for up to 36 sessions, usually three sessions a week in a single 12-week period. Coverage for continued participation is allowed only on a case-by-case basis with exit criteria taken into consideration. The following exit criteria guidelines apply:

• The patient has achieved a stable level of exercise tolerance without ischemia or dysrhythmia

• Symptoms of angina or dyspnea are stable at the patient's maximum exercise level

• Patient's resting blood pressure and heart rate are within normal limits

• The stress test is not positive during exercise

When claims are accompanied by acceptable documentation that the patient has not reached an exit level, coverage may be extended, but should not exceed 24 weeks

EXTERNAL COUNTERPULSATION (ECP) FOR SEVERE ANGINA – COVERED

External counterpulsation (ECP), commonly referred to as enhanced external counterpulsation, is a non-invasive outpatient treatment for coronary artery disease refractory to medical and/or surgical therapy. Although ECP devices are cleared by the Food and Drug Administration (FDA) for use in treating a variety of cardiac conditions, including stable or unstable angina pectoris, acute myocardial infarction and cardiogenic shock, the use of this device to treat cardiac conditions other than stable angina pectoris is not covered, since only that use has developed sufficient evidence to demonstrate its medical effectiveness. Non-coverage of hydraulic versions of these types of devices remains in force.

Coverage is provided for the use of ECP for patients who have been diagnosed with disabling angina (Class III or Class IV, Canadian Cardiovascular Society Classification or equivalent classification) who, in the opinion of a cardiologist or cardiothoracic surgeon, are not readily amenable to surgical intervention, such as PTCA or cardiac bypass because: (1) their condition is inoperable, or at high risk of operative complications or post-operative failure; (2) their coronary anatomy is not readily amenable to such procedures; or (3) they have co-morbid states which create excessive risk.

A full course of therapy usually consists of 35 one-hour treatments, which may be offered once or twice daily, usually 5 days per week. The patient is placed on a treatment table where their lower trunk and lower extremities are wrapped in a series of three compressive air cuffs which inflate and deflate in synchronization with the patient's cardiac cycle.

During diastole the three sets of air cuffs are inflated sequentially (distal to proximal) compressing the vascular beds within the muscles of the calves, lower thighs and upper thighs. This action results in an increase in diastolic pressure, generation of retrograde arterial blood flow and an increase in venous return. The cuffs are deflated simultaneously just prior to systole, which produces a rapid drop in vascular impedance, a decrease in ventricular workload and an increase in cardiac output.

The augmented diastolic pressure and retrograde aortic flow appear to improve myocardial perfusion, while systolic unloading appears to reduce cardiac workload and oxygen requirements. The increased venous return coupled with enhanced systolic flow appears to increase cardiac output. As a result of this treatment, most patients experience increased time until onset of ischemia, increased exercise tolerance, and a reduction in the number and severity of anginal episodes. Evidence was presented that this effect lasted well beyond the immediate post-treatment phase, with patients symptom-free for several months to two years.

This procedure must be done under direct supervision of a physician.

CIM 35-77   Treatment of Motor Function Disorders with Electric Nerve Stimulation – Not Covered
No reimbursement may be made for electric nerve stimulation or for the services related to its implantation since this treatment cannot be considered reasonable and necessary. However, Medicare covers deep brain stimulation by implanting a stimulator device at the carrier's discretion.

NEUROMUSCULAR ELECTRICAL STIMULATION (NMES)

Neuromuscular electrical stimulation (NMES) involves the use of a device that transmits an electrical impulse to activate muscle groups by way of electrodes. There are two broad categories of NMES. One type of device stimulates the muscle when the patient is in a resting state to treat muscle atrophy. The second type is used to enhance functional activity of neurologically impaired patients.

Treatment of Muscle Atrophy

Coverage of NMES to treat muscle atrophy is limited to the treatment of patients with disuse atrophy where the nerve supply to the muscle is intact, including brain, spinal cord and peripheral nerves and other non-neurological reasons for disuse atrophy. Examples include casting or splinting of a limb, contracture due to scarring of soft tissue as in burn lesions, and hip replacement surgery (until orthotic training begins). (See CIM 45-25 for an explanation of coverage of medically necessary supplies for the effective use of NMES).

Use for Walking in Patients with Spinal Cord Injury (SCI)

The type of NMES that is used to enhance the ability to walk of SCI patients is commonly referred to as functional electrical stimulation (FES). These devices are surface units that use electrical impulses to activate paralyzed or weak muscles in precise sequence. Coverage for the use of NMES/FES is limited to SCI patients, for walking, who have completed a training program, which consists of at least 32 physical therapy sessions with the device over a period of 3 months. The trial period of physical therapy will enable the physician treating the patient for his or her spinal cord injury to properly evaluate the person's ability to use these devices frequently and for the long term. Physical therapy sessions are only covered in the inpatient hospital, outpatient hospital, comprehensive outpatient rehabilitation facilities, and outpatient rehabilitation facilities. The physical therapy necessary to perform this training must be directly performed by the physical therapist as part of a one-on-one training program; this service cannot be done unattended.

The goal of physical therapy must be to train SCI patients on the use of NMES/FES devices to achieve walking, not to reverse or retard muscle atrophy.

Coverage for NMES/FES for walking will be limited to SCI patients with all of the following characteristics:

1) persons with intact lower motor units (L1 and below) (both muscle and peripheral nerve);

2) persons with muscle and joint stability for weight bearing at upper and lower extremities that can demonstrate balance and control to maintain an upright support posture independently;

3) persons that demonstrate brisk muscle contraction to NMES and have sensory perception of electrical stimulation sufficient for muscle contraction;

4) persons that possess high motivation, commitment and cognitive ability to use such devices for walking

5) persons that can transfer independently and can demonstrate independent standing tolerance for at least 3 minutes;

6) persons that can demonstrate hand and finger function to manipulate controls;

7) persons with at least 6-month post recovery spinal cord injury and restorative surgery;

8) persons without hip and knee degenerative disease and no history of long bone fracture secondary to osteoporosis; and

9) persons who have demonstrated a willingness to use the device long-term.

NMES/FES for walking will not be covered in SCI patients with any of the following:

1) persons with cardiac pacemakers;

2) severe scoliosis or severe osteoporosis;

3) skin disease or cancer at area of stimulation;

4) irreversible contracture; or

5) autonomic dysreflexia.

The only settings where therapists with the sufficient skills to provide these services are employed, are inpatient hospitals, outpatient hospitals, comprehensive outpatient rehabilitation facilities and outpatient rehabilitation facilities. The physical therapy necessary to perform this training must be part of a one-on-one training program.

Additional therapy after the purchase of the DME would be limited by our general policies on coverage of skilled physical therapy.

All other uses of NMES remain non-covered.

(Also reference Medicare Carriers' Manual, Part 3, Claims-§2210 and Medicare Intermediary Manual, Part 3, Claims-§3653 – See – Maintenance Program 271.1)

CIM 45-10   Laetrile and Related Substances – Not Covered
Laetrile (and the other drugs called by the various terms mentioned below) have been used primarily in the treatment or control of cancer. Although the terms "Laetrile," "laetrile," "amygdalin," "Sarcarcinase," "vitamin B-17," and "nitriloside" have been used interchangeably, the chemical identity of the substances to which these terms refer has varied.

The FDA has determined that neither Laetrile nor any other drug called by the various terms mentioned above, nor any other product which might be characterized as a "nitriloside" is generally recognized (by experts qualified by scientific training and experience to evaluate the safety and effectiveness of drugs) to be safe and effective for any therapeutic use. Therefore, use of this drug cannot be considered to be reasonable and necessary within the meaning of §1862(a)(1) of the Act and program payment may not be made for its use or any services furnished in connection with its administration.

A hospital stay only for the purpose of having laetrile (or any other drug called by the terms mentioned above) administered is not covered. Also, program payment may not be made for laetrile (or other drug noted above) when it is used during the course of an otherwise covered hospital stay, since the FDA has found such drugs to not be safe and effective for any therapeutic purpose.

Rev. 73

CIM 45-16   Certain Drugs Distributed By The National Cancer Institute (Effective for services furnished on or after October 1, 1980.)
Under its Cancer Therapy Evaluation, the Division of Cancer Treatment of the National Cancer Institute (NCI), in cooperation with the Food and Drug Administration, approves and distributes certain drugs for use in treating terminally ill cancer patients. One group of these drugs, designated as Group C drugs, unlike other drugs distributed by the NCI, are not limited to use in clinical trials for the purpose of testing their efficacy. Drugs are classified as Group C drugs only if there is sufficient evidence demonstrating their efficacy within a tumor type and that they can be safely administered.

A physician is eligible to receive Group C drugs from the Divison of Cancer Treatment only if the following requirements are met:

• A physician must be registered with the NCI as an investigator by having completed an FD-Form 1573;

• A written request for the drug, indicating the disease to be treated, must be submitted to the NCI;

• The use of the drug must be limited to indications outlined in the NCI's guidelines; and

• All adverse reactions must be reported to the Investigational Drug Branch of the Division of Cancer Treatment.

In view of these NCI controls on distribution and use of Group C drugs, intermediaries may assume, in the absence of evidence to the contrary, that a Group C drug and the related hospital stay are covered if all other applicable coverage requirements are satisfied.

If there is reason to question coverage in a particular case, the matter should be resolved with the assistance of the local PSRO, or if there is none, the assistance of your medical consultants.

Information regarding those drugs which are classified as Group C drugs may be obtained from:

Office of the Chief, Investigational Drug Branch

Division of Cancer Treatment, CTEP, Landow Building

Room 4C09, National Cancer Institute

Bethesda, Maryland 2020

CIM 45-20   Ethylenediamine-Tetra-Acetic (EDTA) Chelation Therapy For Treatment Of Atherosclerosis
The use of EDTA as a chelating agent to treat atherosclerosis, arteriosclerosis, calcinosis, or similar generalized condition not listed by the FDA as an approved use is not covered. Any such use of EDTA is considered experimental.

See §35-64 for an explanation of this conclusion.

CIM 45-22   Lymphocyte Immune Globulin, Anti-Thymocyte Globulin (Equine)
The Food and Drug Administration (FDA) has approved one lymphocyte immune globulin preparation, anti-thymocyte globulin (equine). Medicare covers equine when used for managing allograft rejection episodes in renal transplantation.

CIM 45-23   Dimethyl Sulfoxide (DMSO)
Medicare covers dimethyl sulfoxide (DMSO) when reasonable and necessary for a patient in the treatment of interstitial cystitis.

APPENDIX 4 — MEDICARE REFERENCES

CIM 45-24   Anti-Inhibitor Coagulant Complex (AICC)
Medicare covers anti-inhibitor coagulant complex (AICC) when furnished to patients with hemophilia A and inhibitor antibodies to factor VIII who have major bleeding episodes and fail to respond to other, less expensive therapies.

CIM 45-25   Treatment of Motor Function Disorders with Electric Nerve Stimulation – Not Covered
No reimbursement may be made for electric nerve stimulation or for the services related to its implantation since this treatment cannot be considered reasonable and necessary. However, Medicare covers deep brain stimulation by implanting a stimulator device at the carrier's discretion.

SUPPLIES USED IN THE DELIVERY OF TRANSCUTANEOUS ELECTRICAL NERVE STIMULATION (TENS) AND NEUROMUSCULAR ELECTRICAL STIMULATION (NMES) – (Effective for services rendered (i.e., items rented or purchased) on or after July 14, 1988.)

Transcutaneous Electrical Nerve Stimulation (TENS) and/or Neuromuscular Electrical Stimulation (NMES) can ordinarily be delivered to patients through the use of conventional electrodes, adhesive tapes and lead wires. There may be times, however, where it might be medically necessary for certain patients receiving TENS or NMES treatment to use, as an alternative to conventional electrodes, adhesive tapes and lead wires, a form-fitting conductive garment (i.e., a garment with conductive fibers which are separated from the patients' skin by layers of fabric).

A form-fitting conductive garment (and medically necessary related supplies) may be covered under the program only when:

1. It has received permission or approval for marketing by the Food and Drug Administration;

2. It has been prescribed by a physician for use in delivering covered TENS or NMES treatment; and

3. One of the medical indications outlined below is met:

The patient cannot manage without the conductive garment because there is such a large area or so many sites to be stimulated and the stimulation would have to be delivered so frequently that it is not feasible to use conventional electrodes, adhesive tapes and lead wires;

The patient cannot manage without the conductive garment for the treatment of chronic intractable pain because the areas or sites to be stimulated are inaccessible with the use of conventional electrodes, adhesive tapes and lead wires;

The patient has a documented medical condition such as skin problems that preclude the application of conventional electrodes, adhesive tapes and lead wires;

The patient requires electrical stimulation beneath a cast either to treat disuse atrophy, where the nerve supply to the muscle is intact, or to treat chronic intractable pain; or

The patient has a medical need for rehabilitation strengthening (pursuant to a written plan of rehabilitation) following an injury where the nerve supply to the muscle is intact.

A conductive garment is not covered for use with a TENS device during the trial period specified in §35-46 unless:

4. The patient has a documented skin problem prior to the start of the trial period; and

5. The carrier's medical consultants are satisfied that use of such an item is medically necessary for the patient.

(See conditions for coverage of the use of TENS in the diagnosis and treatment of chronic intractable pain in §§35-46 and 60-20 and the use of NMES in the treatment of disuse atrophy in §35-77.)

CIM 45-30   Photosensitive Drugs
Photosensitive drugs are the light-sensitive agents used in photodynamic therapy. Once introduced into the body, these drugs selectively identify and adhere to diseased tissue. The drugs remain inactive until they are exposed to a specific wavelength of light, by means of a laser, that corresponds to their absorption peak. The activation of a photosensitive drug results in a photochemical reaction which treats the diseased tissue without affecting surrounding normal tissue.

Verteporfin

Verteporfin, a benzoporphyrin derivative, is an intravenous lipophilic photosensitive drug with an absorption peak of 690 nm. This drug was first approved by the Food and Drug Administration (FDA) on April 12, 2000, and subsequently, approved for inclusion in the United States Pharmacopoeia on July 18, 2000, meeting Medicare's definition of a drug as defined under §1861(t)(1) of the Social Security Act. Effective July 1, 2001, Verteporfin is only covered when used in conjunction with ocular photodynamic therapy (see §35-

100 PHOTODYNAMIC THERAPY) when furnished intravenously incident to a physician's service. For patients with age-related macular degeneration, Verteporfin is only covered with a diagnosis of neovascular age-related macular degeneration (ICD-9-CM 362.52) with predominately classic subfoveal choroidal neovascular (CNV) lesions (where the area of classic CNV occupies = 50% of the area of the entire lesion) at the initial visit as determined by a fluorescein angiogram (CPT code 92235). Subsequent follow-up visits will require a fluorescein angiogram prior to treatment. OPT with verteporfin is covered for the above indication and will remain noncovered for all other indications related to AMD (see CIM § CIM § 35-100). OPT with Verteporfin for use in non-AMD conditions is eligible for coverage through individual contractor discretion.

CIM 45-4   Prolotherapy, Joint Sclerotherapy, and Ligamentous Injections with Sclerosing Agents – Not Covered
The medical effectiveness of the above therapies has not been verified by scientifically controlled studies and coverage is denied on the ground that they are not reasonable and necessary.

VITAMIN B12 INJECTIONS TO STRENGTHEN TENDONS, LIGAMENTS, ETC., OF THE FOOT – NOT COVERED

Vitamin B12 injections to strengthen tendons, ligaments, etc., of the foot are not covered under Medicare because (1) there is no evidence that vitamin B12 injections are effective for the purpose of strengthening weakened tendons and ligaments, and (2) this is nonsurgical treatment under the subluxation exclusion. Accordingly, vitamin B12 injections are not considered reasonable and necessary within the meaning of §1862(a)(1) of the Act.

See Intermediary Manual, §§3101.3 and 3158 and Carriers Manual, §§2050.5 and 2323.

CIM 45-7   Hydrophilic Contact Lens For Corneal Bandage
Medicare covers a hydrophilic contact lens approved by the Food and Drug Administration (FDA) and used as a supply incident to a physician's service.

CIM 50-1   Cardiac Pacemaker Evaluation Services
Medicare covers a variety of services for the post-implant follow-up and evaluation of implanted cardiac pacemakers (limited to lithium battery-powered pacemakers). There are two general types of pacemakers in current use:

1. Single-chamber pacemakers sense and pace the ventricles of the heart

2. Dual-chamber pacemakers sense and pace both the atria and the ventricles

These differences require different monitoring patterns over the expected life of the units involved, which is the patient's physician responsibility. A physician's prescription is required when the monitoring is done by some entity. Where a patient is monitored both clinically and transtelephonically include frequency data on both types of monitoring.

In order for transtelephonic monitoring services to be covered, the services must consist of the following elements:

• A minimum 30-second readable strip of the pacemaker in the free-running mode

• Unless contraindicated, a minimum 30-second readable strip of the pacemaker in the magnetic mode

• A minimum 30 seconds of readable ECG strip

The following guidelines are designed to assist in claims (apply 1980 guidelines to claims for the obsolete mercury-zinc battery-powered pacemakers). The guidelines are divided into categories:

1. Guideline I applies to the majority of pacemakers in use

2. Guideline II applies only to pacemaker systems (pacemaker and leads) that meet the standards of the Inter-Society Commission for Heart Disease Resources (ICHD) for longevity and end-of-life decay

Guideline I: Single-chamber pacemaker

First month – every two weeks

Second month through 36th month – every eight weeks

37th month to failure – every four weeks

Guideline I: Dual-chamber pacemaker

First month – every two weeks

Second month through 36th month – every four weeks

37th month to failure – every four weeks

Guideline II: Single-chamber pacemaker

First month – every two weeks

Second month through 48th month – every 12 weeks

49th through 72nd month – every eight weeks

Thereafter – every four weeks

Guideline II: Dual-chamber pacemaker

First month – every two weeks

Second month through 30th month – every 12 weeks.

31st month through 48th month every eight weeks

Thereafter – every 4 weeks.

Pacemaker monitoring is also covered when done by pacemaker clinics. Clinic visits may be done in conjunction with transtelephonic monitoring; however, the services rendered by a pacemaker clinic are more extensive than those currently possible by telephone. They include, for example, physical examination of patients and reprogramming of pacemakers.

Frequency of clinic visits is the decision of the patient's physician, taking into account, among other things, the medical condition of the patient. The following are recommendations for monitoring guidelines on lithium-battery pacemakers:

- Single-chamber pacemakers – twice in the first six months following implant, then once every 12 months

- Dual-chamber pacemakers – twice in the first six months, then once every six months

CIM 50-10   VABRA Aspirator

The VABRA aspirator collects uterine tissue for study to detect endometrial carcinoma and its is indicated where the patient exhibits clinical symptoms or signs suggestive of endometrial disease, such as irregular or heavy vaginal bleeding. Medicare does not for the aspirator or the related diagnostic services when furnished in connection with the exam of an asymptomatic patient. Payment for routine physical checkups is precluded, also.

CIM 50-15   Electrocardiographic Services

Medicare Part B covers electrocardiographic (EKG) services rendered by a physician, incident to services, or by an approved laboratory or supplier of portable X-ray services (the claim must identify the physician ordering the service and the physician making the interpretation). Practices may charge separately for an EKG interpretation by an attending or consulting physician.

In addition, Medicare covers an emergency as a laboratory service or a diagnostic service by a portable X-ray supplier only when evidence shows that a physician was in attendance at the time the service was performed or immediately thereafter. EKG services provided in the patient's home, payment is based on the reasonable charge of services supplied in the laboratory (or in the supplier's office), in the absence of documentation.

Medicare coverage of Long Term EKG Monitoring, referred to as long-term EKG recording, Holter recording, or dynamic electrocardiography depends on a complete patient evaluation prior to performance of this diagnostic study. Generally, a statement of the diagnostic impression of the referring physician with an indication of the patient's relevant signs and symptoms should be sufficient for determining medical necessity. Intermediaries or carriers may require whatever additional documentation.

Medicare covers patient-activated EKG recorders when used as an alternative to the long-term EKG for similar indications (e.g., detecting and characterizing symptomatic arrhythmias, regulation of anti-arrhythmic drug therapy). Medicare does not cover outpatient monitoring of recently discharged post-infarct patients.

Medicare covers computer interpretation of an EKG when furnished under the circumstances required for coverage of other electrocardiographic services. The certifying physician must be identified on the HCFA-1490. Where the laboratory's (or portable x-ray supplier's) reviewing physician is not identified, no professional component is involved and reimbursement is determined accordingly. If the supplying laboratory does not include professional review and certification of the hard copy, the patient's physician is reimbursed.

Medicare covers Transtelephonic Electrocardiographic Transmissions eEffective as a diagnostic service for the indications described below:

- To detect, characterize, and document symptomatic transient arrhythmias

- To overcome problems in regulating antiarrhythmic drug dosage

- To carry out early post-hospital monitoring of patients discharged after myocardial infarction

The transmitting devices must meet at least the following criteria:

1. Capable of transmitting EKG Leads, I, II, or III

2. Lead transmissions must be comparable to by a conventional EKG to permit interpretation of abnormal cardiac rhythms

CIM 50-20   Diagnostic Pap Smears

A diagnostic pap smear and related medically necessary services are covered under Medicare Part B when ordered by a physician under one of the following conditions:

- Previous cancer of the cervix, uterus, or vagina that has been or is being treated

- Previous abnormal pap smear

- Any abnormal findings of the vagina, cervix, uterus, ovaries, or adnexa

- Any significant complaint by the patient referable to the female reproductive system

- Any signs or symptoms that might in the physician's judgment reasonably be related to a gynecologic disorder.

In respect to the last bullet, the contractor's medical staff must determine whether in a particular case a previous malignancy at another site is an indication for a diagnostic pap smear or whether the test must be considered a screening pap smear as described in §50-20.1.

Use the following CPT codes for indicating diagnostic pap smears:

- 88150 Cytopathology, smears, cervical or vaginal (e.g., Papanicolaou), up to three smears; screening by technician under physician supervision

- 88151 Cytopathology, smears, cervical or vaginal (e.g., Papanicolaou), up to three smears; requiring interpretation by physician

CIM 50-24   Hair Analysis – Not Covered

Hair analysis to detect mineral traces as an aid in diagnosing human disease is not a covered service under Medicare.

CIM 50-26   DENTAL EXAMINATION PRIOR TO KIDNEY TRANSPLANTATION

Despite the "dental services exclusion" in §1862(a)(12) of the Act (see Intermediary Manual,§3162; Carriers Manual, §2336), an oral or dental examination performed on an inpatient basis as part of a comprehensive workup prior to renal transplant surgery is a covered service. This is because the purpose of the examination is not for the care of the teeth or structures directly supporting the teeth. Rather, the examination is for the identification, prior to a complex surgical procedure, of existing medical problems where the increased possibility of infection would not only reduce the chances for successful surgery but would also expose the patient to additional risks in undergoing such surgery.

Such a dental or oral examination would be covered under Part A of the program if performed by a dentist on the hospital's staff, or under Part B if performed by a physician. (When performing a dental or oral examination, a dentist is not recognized as a physician under §1861(r) of the law.)(See Carriers Manual §2020.3.)

CIM 50-34   Obsolete Or Unreliable Diagnostic Tests

A. Diagnostic Tests (Effective for services performed on or after May 15, 1980). – Do not routinely pay for the following diagnostic tests because they are obsolete and have been replaced by more advanced procedures. The listed tests may be paid for only if the medical need for the procedure is satisfactorily justified by the physician who performs it. When the services are subject to PRO review, the PRO is responsible for determining that satisfactory medical justification exists. When the services are not subject to PRO review, the intermediary or carrier is responsible for determining that satisfactory medical justification exists. This includes:

- Amylase, blood isoenzymes, electrophoretic,
- Chromium, blood,
- Guanase, blood,
- Zinc sulphate turbidity, blood,
- Skin test, cat scratch fever,
- Skin test, lymphopathia venereum,
- Circulation time, one test,
- Cephalin flocculation,
- Congo red, blood,
- Hormones, adrenocorticotropin quantitative animal tests,
- Hormones, adrenocorticotropin quantitative bioassay,
- Thymol turbidity, blood,
- Skin test, actinomycosis,
- Skin test, brucellosis,
- Skin test, psittacosis,
- Skin test, trichinosis,
- Calcium, feces, 24-hour quantitative,

- Starch, feces, screening,

- Chymotrypsin, duodenal contents,

- Gastric analysis, pepsin,

- Gastric analysis, tubeless,

- Calcium saturation clotting time,

- Capillary fragility test (Rumpel-Leede),

- Colloidal gold,

- Bendien's test for cancer and tuberculosis,

- Bolen's test for cancer,

- Rehfuss test for gastric acidity, and

- Serum seromucoid assay for cancer and other diseases.

B. Cardiovascular Tests (Effective for services performed on or after January 1, 1997). – Do not pay for the following phonocardiography and vectorcardiography diagnostic tests because they have been determined to be outmoded and of little clinical value. They include:

- CPT code 93201, Phonocardiogram with or without ECG lead; with supervision during recording with interpretation and report (when equipment is supplied by the physician),

- CPT code 93202, Phonocardiogram; tracing only, without interpretation and report (e.g., when equipment is supplied by the hospital, clinic),

- CPT code 93204, Phonocardiogram; interpretation and report,

- CPT code 93205, Phonocardiogram with ECG lead, with indirect carotid artery and/or jugular vein tracing, and/or apex cardiogram; with interpretation and report,

- CPT code 93208, Phonocardiogram; without interpretation and report

- CPT code 93209, Phonocardiogram; interpretation and report only,

- CPT code 93210, Intracardiac,

- CPT code 93220, Vectorcardiogram (VCG), with or without ECG; with interpretation and report,

- CPT code 93221, Vectorcardiogram; tracing only, without interpretation and report, and

- CPT code 93222, Vectorcardiogram; interpretation and report only.

CIM 50-36   POSITRON EMISSION TOMOGRAPHY (PET) SCANS

I. General Description

Positron emission tomography (PET) is a noninvasive diagnostic imaging procedure that assesses the level of metabolic activity and perfusion in various organ systems of the [human] body. A positron camera (tomograph) is used to produce cross-sectional tomographic images, which are obtained from positron emitting radioactive tracer substances (radiopharmaceuticals) such as 2-[F-18] Fluoro-D-Glucose (FDG), that are administered intravenously to the patient. The following indications may be covered for PET under certain circumstances. Details of Medicare PET coverage are discussed later in this section. Unless otherwise indicated, the clinical conditions below are covered when PET utilizes FDG as a tracer.

> NOTE: This manual section lists all Medicare-covered uses of PET scans. A particular use of PET scans is not covered unless this manual specifically provides that such use is covered. Although this section lists some non-covered uses of PET scans, it does not constitute an exhaustive list of all noncovered uses.

Covered Clinical Condition	Prior to July 1, 2001	July 1, 2001 through December 31, 2001	On or after January 1, 2002
Characterization of single pulmonary nodules	Effective 1/1/1998, any FDA approved	Any FDA approved FDA approved:	Full ring; Partial ring Certain coincidence systems
Initial staging of lung cancer (non small cell)	Effective 1/1/1998, any FDA approved	Any FDA approved; FDA approved:	Full ring; Partial ring; Certain coincidence systems
Determining location of colorectal tumors if rising CEA level suggests recurrence	Effective 7/1/1999, any FDA approved	Any FDA approved; FDA approved:	Full ring; Partial ring; Certain coincidence systems
Staging or restaging of lymphoma only when used as an alternative to a gallium scan	Effective 7/1/1999, any FDA approved	Any FDA approved; FDA approved:	Full ring; Partial ring; Certain coincidence systems
Evaluating recurrence of melanoma prior to surgery as an alternative to a gallium scan	Effective 7/1/1999, any FDA approved.	Any FDA approved; FDA approved:	Full ring; Partial ring; Certain coincidence systems
Diagnosis, staging, and restaging of colorectal cancer	Not covered by Medicare	Full ring	FDA approved:; Full ring; Partial ring
Diagnosis, staging, and restaging of esophageal cancer	Not covered by Medicare	Full ring Full and partial ring	FDA approved:; Full ring; Partial ring
Diagnosis, staging, and restaging of head and neck cancers (excluding CNS and thyroid)	Not covered by Medicare	Full ring	FDA approved:; Full ring; Partial ring
Diagnosis, staging, and restaging of lung cancer (non small cell)	Not covered by Medicare	Full ring	FDA approved:; Full ring; Partial ring
Diagnosis, staging, and restaging of lymphoma	Not covered by Medicare	Full ring	FDA approved:; Full ring; Partial ring
Diagnosis, staging, and restaging of melanoma (noncovered for evaluating regional nodes)	Not covered by Medicare	Full ring	FDA approved:; Full ring; Partial ring
Determination of myocardial viability only following an inconclusive SPECT	Not covered by Medicare	Full ring	FDA approved:; Full ring; Partial ring
Presurgical evaluation of refractory seizures	Not covered by Medicare	Full ring	FDA approved:; Full ring; Partial ring
Breast Cancer	Not covered	Not covered	Effective October 1, 2002, full and partial ring
Thyroid Cancer	Not covered	Not covered	Effective October 1, 2003, full and partial ring
Myocardial Viability Primary or initial diagnosis prior to revascularization	Not covered	Not covered	Effective October 1, 2002,

II. General Conditions of Coverage for FDG PET

A. Allowable FDG PET Systems

1. Definitions: For purposes of this section:

> a. "Any FDA approved" means all systems approved or cleared for marketing by the FDA to image radionuclides in the body.

> b. "FDA approved" means that the system indicated has been approved or cleared for marketing by the FDA to image radionuclides in the body.

> c. "Certain coincidence systems" refers to the systems that have all the following features:

> - Crystal at least 5/8-inch thick;

> - Techniques to minimize or correct for scatter and/or randoms; and

> - Digital detectors and iterative reconstruction.

Scans performed with gamma camera PET systems with crystals thinner than 5/8-inch will not be

covered by Medicare. In addition, scans performed with systems with crystals greater than or equal

to 5/8-inch in thickness, but that do not meet the other listed design characteristics are not covered

by Medicare.

2. Allowable PET systems by covered clinical indication:

Covered Clinical Condition	Prior to July 1, 2001	July 1, 2001 through December 31, 2001	On or after January 1, 2002
Characterization of single pulmonary nodules	Effective 1/1/1998, any FDA approved	Any FDA approved	FDA approved: Full ring Partial ring Certain coincidence systems
Initial staging of lung cancer (non small cell)	Effective 1/1/1998, any FDA approved	Any FDA approved	FDA approved: Full ring Partial ring Certain coincidence systems
Evaluating recurrence of melanoma prior to surgery as an alternative to a gallium scan	Effective 7/1/1999, any FDA approved.	Any FDA approved	FDA approved: Full ring Partial ring Certain coincidence systems
Diagnosis, staging, and restaging of colorectal cancer	Not covered by Medicare	Full ring	FDA approved: Full ring Partial ring
Diagnosis, staging, and restaging of esophageal cancer	Not covered by Medicare	Full ring	FDA approved: Full ring Partial ring
Diagnosis, staging, and restaging of head and neck cancers (excluding CNS and thyroid)	Not covered by Medicare Full and partial ring	Full ring	FDA approved: Full ring Partial ring
Diagnosis, staging, and restaging of lung cancer (non small cell)	Not covered by Medicare	Full ring	FDA approved: Full ring Partial ring
Diagnosis, staging, and restaging of lymphoma	Not covered by Medicare	Full ring	FDA approved: Full ring Partial ring
Diagnosis, staging, and restaging of melanoma (noncovered for evaluating regional nodes)	Not covered by Medicare	Full ring	FDA approved: Full ring Partial ring
Determination of myocardial viability only following an inconclusive SPECT	Not covered by Medicare	Full ring	FDA approved: Full ring Partial ring
Presurgical evaluation of refractory seizures	Not covered by Medicare	Full ring	FDA approved: Full ring Partial ring
Breast Cancer	Not covered	Not covered	Effective October 1, 2002, Full and partial
Myocardial Viability Primary or initial diagnosis prior to revascularization	Not covered	Not covered	Effective October 1, 2002

B. Regardless of any other terms or conditions, all uses of FDG PET scans, in order to be covered by the Medicare program, must meet the following general conditions prior to June 30, 2001:

1. Submission of claims for payment must include any information Medicare requires to assure that the PET scans performed were: (a) medically necessary, (b) did not unnecessarily duplicate other covered diagnostic tests, and (c) did not involve investigational drugs or procedures using investigational drugs, as determined by the Food and Drug Administration (FDA).

2. The PET scan entity submitting claims for payment must keep such patient records as Medicare requires on file for each patient for whom a PET scan claim is made.

C. Regardless of any other terms or conditions, all uses of FDG PET scans, in order to be covered by the Medicare program, must meet the following general conditions as of July 1,2001:

1. The provider of the PET scan should maintain on file the doctor's referral and documentation that the procedure involved only FDA approved drugs and devices, as is normal business practice.

2. The ordering physician is responsible for documenting the medical necessity of the study and that it meets the conditions specified in the instructions. The physician should have documentation in the beneficiary's medical record to support the referral to the PET scan provider.

III. Covered Indications for PET Scans and Limitations/Requirements for Usage

For all uses of PET relating to malignancies the following conditions apply:

1. Diagnosis: PET is covered only in clinical situations in which the PET results may assist in avoiding an invasive diagnostic procedure, or in which the PET results may assist in determining the optimal anatomical location to perform an invasive diagnostic procedure. In general, for most solid tumors, a tissue diagnosis is made prior to the performance of PET scanning. PET scans following a tissue diagnosis are performed for the purpose of staging, not diagnosis. Therefore, the use of PET in the diagnosis of lymphoma, esophageal, and colorectal cancers as well as in melanoma should be rare. PET is not covered for other diagnostic uses, and is not covered for screening (testing of patients without specific signs and symptoms of disease).

2. Staging and or Restaging: PET is covered in clinical situations in which 1) (a) the stage of the cancer remains in doubt after completion of a standard diagnostic workup, including conventional imaging (computed tomography, magnetic resonance imaging, or ultrasound) or (b) the use of PET would also be considered reasonable and necessary if it could potentially replace one or more conventional imaging studies when it is expected that conventional study information is insufficient for the clinical management of the patient and 2) clinical management of the patient would differ depending on the stage of the cancer identified. PET will be covered for restaging after the completion of treatment for the purpose of detecting residual disease, for detecting suspected recurrence or to determine the extent of a known recurrence. Use of PET would also be considered reasonable and necessary if it could potentially replace one or more conventional imaging studies when it is expected that conventional study information is insufficient for the clinical management of the patient.

3. Monitoring: Use of PET to monitor tumor response during the planned course of therapy (i.e., when no change in therapy is being contemplated) is not covered except for breast cancer. Restaging only occurs after a course of treatment is completed, and this is covered, subject to the conditions above. NOTE: In the absence of national frequency limitations, contractors, should, if necessary, develop frequency requirements on any or all of the indications covered on and after July 1, 2001.

IV. Coverage of PET for Perfusion of the Heart

A. Rubidium 82

Effective for services performed on or after March 14, 1995, PET scans performed at rest or with pharmacological stress used for noninvasive imaging of the perfusion of the heart for the diagnosis and management of patients with known or suspected coronary artery disease using the FDAapproved radiopharmaceutical Rubidium 82 (Rb 82) are covered, provided the requirements below are met.

Requirements:

The PET scan, whether at rest alone, or rest with stress, is performed in place of, but not in addition to, a single photon emission computed tomography (SPECT); or The PET scan, whether at rest alone or rest with stress, is used following a SPECT that was found to be inconclusive. In these cases, the PET scan must have been considered necessary in order to determine what medical or surgical intervention is required to treat the patient. (For purposes of this requirement, an inconclusive test is a test(s) whose results are equivocal, technically uninterpretable, or discordant with a patient's other clinical data and must be documented in the beneficiary's file.)

• For any PET scan for which Medicare payment is claimed for dates of services prior to July 1, 2001, the claimant must submit additional specified information on the claim form (including proper codes and/or modifiers), to indicate the results of the PET scan. The claimant must also include information on whether the PET scan was done after an inconclusive noninvasive cardiac test. The information submitted with respect to the previous noninvasive cardiac test must specify the type of test done prior to the PET scan and whether it was inconclusive or unsatisfactory. These explanations are in the form of special G codes used for billing PET scans using Rb 82. Beginning July 1, 2001, claims should be submitted with the appropriate codes.

B. Ammonia N-13

Effective for services performed on or after October 1, 2003, PET scans performed at rest or with pharmacological stress used for noninvasive imaging of the perfusion of the heart for the diagnosis and management of patients with known or suspected coronary artery disease using the FDAapproved radiopharmaceutical ammonia N-13 are covered, provided the requirements below are met.

Requirements:

The PET scan, whether at rest alone, or rest with stress, is performed in place of, but not in addition to, a single photon emission computed tomography (SPECT); or The PET scan, whether at rest alone or rest with stress, is used following a SPECT that was found to be inconclusive. In these cases, the PET scan must have been considered necessary in order to determine what medical or surgical intervention is required to treat the patient. (For purposes of this requirement, an inconclusive test is a test whose results are equivocal, technically uninterpretable, or discordant with a patient's other clinical data and must be documented in the beneficiary's file.) (This NCD last reviewed April 2003.)

V. Coverage of FDG PET for Lung Cancer

The coverage for FDG PET for lung cancer, effective January 1, 1998, has been expanded.

Beginning July 1, 2001, usage of FDG PET for lung cancer has been expanded to include diagnosis, staging, and restaging (see section III) of the disease.

A. Effective for services performed on or after January 1, 1998, Medicare covers regional FDG PET chest scans, on any FDA approved scanner, for the characterization of single pulmonary nodules (SPNs). The primary purpose of such characterization should be to determine the likelihood of malignancy in order to plan future management and treatment for the patient. Beginning July 1, 2001, documentation should be maintained in the beneficiary's medical file at the referring physician's office to support the medical necessity of the procedure, as is normal business practice.

Requirements:

• There must be evidence of primary tumor. Claims for regional PET chest scans for characterizing SPNs should include evidence of the initial detection of a primary lung tumor, usually by computed tomography (CT). This should include, but is not restricted to, a report on the results of such CT or other detection method, indicating an indeterminate or possibly malignant lesion, not exceeding four centimeters (cm) in diameter.above), which is necessary for anatomic information, in order to ensure that the PET scan is properly coordinated with other diagnostic modalities.

In cases of serial evaluation of SPNs using both CT and regional PET chest scanning, such PET scans will not be covered if repeated within 90 days following a negative PET scan. NOTE: A tissue sampling procedure (TSP) is not routinely covered in the case of a negative PET scan for characterization of SPNs, since the patient is presumed not to have a malignant lesion, based upon the PET scan results. When there has been a negative PET, the provider must submit additional information with the claim to support the necessity of a TSP, for review by the Medicare contractor.

B. Effective for services performed from January 1, 1998 through June 30, 2001, Medicare approved coverage of FDG PET for initial staging of non-small-cell lung carcinoma (NSCLC). Limitations: This service is covered only when the primary cancerous lung tumor has been pathologically confirmed; claims for PET must include a statement or other evidence of the detection of such primary lung tumor. The evidence should include, but is not restricted to, a surgical pathology report, which documents the presence of an NSCLC. Whole body PET scan results and results of concurrent computed tomography (CT) and follow-up lymph node biopsy must be properly coordinated with other diagnostic modalities. Claims must include both:

The results of concurrent thoracic CT, necessary for anatomic information, and

The results of any lymph node biopsy performed to finalize whether the patient will be a surgical candidate. The ordering physician is responsible for providing this biopsy result to the PET facility.

> NOTE: Where the patient is considered a surgical candidate, (given the presumed absence of metastatic NSCLC unless medical review supports a determination of medical necessity of a biopsy) a lymph node biopsy will not be covered in the case of a negative CT and negative PET. A lymph node biopsy will be covered in all other cases, i.e., positive CT + positive PET; negative CT + positive PET; positive CT + negative PET.

C. Beginning July 1, 2001, Medicare covers FDG PET for diagnosis, staging, and restaging of NSCLC. Documentation should be maintained in the beneficiary's medical file to support the medical necessity of the procedure, as is normal business practice. Requirements: PET is covered in either/or both of the following circumstances:

• Diagnosis – PET is covered only in clinical situations in which the PET results may assist in avoiding an invasive diagnostic procedure, or in which the PET results may assist in determining the optimal anatomical location to perform an invasive diagnostic procedure. In general, for most solid tumors, a tissue diagnosis is made prior to the performance of PET scanning.

PET scans following a tissue diagnosis are performed for the purpose of staging, not diagnosis. Therefore, the use of PET in the diagnosis of lymphoma, esophageal, and colorectal cancers as well as in melanoma should be rare. Staging and/or Restaging – PET is covered in clinical situations in which 1) (a) the stage of the cancer remains in doubt after completion of a standard diagnostic workup, including conventional imaging (computed tomography, magnetic resonance imaging, or ultrasound) or (b) the use of PET would also be considered reasonable and necessary if it could potentially replace one or more conventional imaging studies when it is expected that conventional study information is insufficient for the clinical management of the patient and 2) clinical management of the patient would differ depending on the stage of the cancer identified. PET will be covered for restaging after the completion of treatment for the purpose of detecting residual disease, for detecting suspected recurrence or to determine the extent of a known recurrence. Use of PET would also be considered reasonable and necessary if it could potentially replace one or more conventional imaging studies when it is expected that conventional study information is insufficient for the clinical management of the patient.

Documentation should be maintained in the beneficiary's medical record at the referring physician's office to support the medical necessity of the procedure, as is normal business practice.

VI. Coverage of FDG PET for Esophageal Cancer

A. Beginning July 1, 2001, Medicare covers FDG PET for the diagnosis, staging, and restaging of esophageal cancer. Medical evidence is present to support the use of FDG PET in pre-surgical staging of esophageal cancer.

Requirements: PET is covered in either/or both of the following circumstances:

• Diagnosis – PET is covered only in clinical situations in which the PET results may assist in avoiding an invasive diagnostic procedure, or in which the PET results may assist in determining the optimal anatomical location to perform an invasive diagnostic procedure. In general, for most solid tumors, a tissue diagnosis is made prior to the performance of PET scanning.

• PET scans following a tissue diagnosis are performed for the purpose of staging, not diagnosis. Therefore, the use of PET in the diagnosis of lymphoma, esophageal and colorectal cancers as well as in melanoma should be rare.

• Staging and/or Restaging – PET is covered in clinical situations in which 1) (a) the stage of the cancer remains in doubt after completion of a standard diagnostic workup, including conventional imaging (computed tomography, magnetic resonance imaging, or ultrasound) or (b) the use of PET would also be considered reasonable and necessary if it could potentially replace one or more conventional imaging studies when it is expected that conventional study information is insufficient for the clinical management of the patient, and 2) clinical management of the patient would differ depending on the stage of the cancer identified. PET will be covered for restaging after the completion of treatment for the purpose of detecting residual disease, for detecting suspected recurrence, or to determine the extent of a known recurrence. Use of PET would also be considered reasonable and necessary if it could potentially replace one or more conventional imaging studies when it is expected that conventional study information is insufficient for the clinical management of the patient.

Documentation should be maintained in the beneficiary's medical record at the referring physician's office to support the medical necessity of the procedure, as is normal business practice.

VII. Coverage of FDG PET for Colorectal Cancer

Medicare coverage of FDG PET for colorectal cancer where there is a rising level of carcinoembryonic antigen (CEA) was effective July 1, 1999 through June 30, 2001. Beginning July 1, 2001, usage of FDG PET for colorectal cancer has been expanded to include diagnosis, staging, and restaging of the disease (see part III).

A. Effective July 1, 1999, Medicare covers FDG PET for patients with recurrent colorectal carcinomas, which are suggested by rising levels of the biochemical tumor marker CEA.

> 1. Frequency Limitations: Whole body PET scans for assessment of recurrence of colorectal cancer cannot be ordered more frequently than once every 12 months unless medical necessity documentation supports a separate re-elevation of CEA within this period.

> 2. Limitations: Because this service is covered only in those cases in which there has been a recurrence of colorectal tumor, claims for PET should include a statement or other evidence of previous colorectal tumor, through June 30, 2001.

B. Beginning July 1, 2001, Medicare coverage has been expanded for colorectal carcinomas for diagnosis, staging and re-staging. New medical evidence supports the use of FDG PET as a useful tool in determining the presence of hepatic/extrahepatic metastases in the primary staging of colorectal carcinoma, prior to selecting a treatment regimen. Use of FDG PET is also supported in evaluating recurrent colorectal cancer beyond the limited presentation of a rising CEA level where the patient presents clinical signs or symptoms of recurrence.

Requirements: PET is covered in either/both of the following circumstances:

Diagnosis – PET is covered only in clinical situations in which the PET results may assist in avoiding an invasive diagnostic procedure, or in which the PET results may assist in determining the optimal anatomical location to perform an invasive diagnostic procedure. In general, for most solid tumors, a tissue diagnosis is made prior to the performance of PET scanning. PET scans following a tissue diagnosis are performed for the purpose of staging, not diagnosis. Therefore, the use of PET in the diagnosis of lymphoma, esophageal, and colorectal cancers as well as in melanoma should be rare.

• Staging and/or Restaging – PET is covered in clinical situations in which 1) (a) the stage of the cancer remains in doubt after completion of a standard diagnostic workup, including conventional imaging (computed tomography, magnetic resonance imaging, or ultrasound) or (b) the use of PET would also be considered reasonable and necessary if it could potentially replace one or more conventional imaging studies when it is expected that conventional study information is insufficient for the clinical management of the patient and 2) clinical management of the patient would differ depending on the stage of the cancer identified. PET will be covered for restaging after the completion of treatment for the purpose of detecting residual disease, for detecting suspected recurrence, or to determine the extent of a known recurrence. Use of PET would also be considered reasonable and necessary if it could potentially replace one or more conventional imaging studies when it is expected that conventional study information is insufficient for the clinical management of the patient.

Documentation that these conditions are met should be maintained by the referring physician in the beneficiary's medical record, as is normal business practice.

VIII. Coverage of FDG PET for Lymphoma

Medicare coverage of FDG PET to stage and re-stage lymphoma as alternative to a Gallium scan, was effective July 1, 1999. Beginning July 1, 2001, usage of FDG PET for lymphoma has been expanded to include diagnosis, staging and restaging (see section III) of the disease.

A. Effective July 1, 1999, FDG PET is covered for the staging and restaging of lymphoma.

Requirements:

• FDG PET is covered only for staging or follow-up restaging of lymphoma. Claims must include a statement or other evidence of previous diagnosis of lymphoma when used as an alternative to a Gallium scan

• To ensure that the PET scan is properly coordinated with other diagnostic modalities, claims must include the results of concurrent computed tomography (CT) and/or other diagnostic modalities when they are necessary for additional anatomic information.

• In order to ensure that the PET scan is covered only as an alternative to a Gallium scan, no PET scan may be covered in cases where it is done within 50 days of a Gallium scan done by the same facility where the patient has remained during the 50-day period. Gallium scans done by another facility less than 50 days prior to the PET scan will not be counted against this screen. The purpose of this screen is to assure that PET scans are covered only when done as an alternative to a Gallium scan within the same facility. We are aware that, in order to assure proper patient care, the treating physician may conclude that previously performed Gallium scans are either inconclusive or not sufficiently reliable.

Frequency Limitation for Restaging: PET scans will be allowed for restaging no sooner than 50 days following the last staging PET scan or Gallium scan, unless sufficient evidence is presented to convince the Medicare contractor that the restaging at an earlier date is medically necessary. Since PET scans for restaging are generally done following cycles of chemotherapy, and since such cycles usually take at least 8 weeks, we believe this screen will adequately prevent medically unnecessary scans while allowing some adjustments for unusual cases. In all cases, the determination of the medical necessity for a PET scan for re-staging lymphoma is the responsibility of the local Medicare contractor.

Beginning July 1, 2001, documentation should be maintained in the beneficiary's medical record at the referring physician's office to support the medical necessity of the procedure, as is normal business practice.

B. Effective for services performed on or after July 1, 2001, the Medicare program has broadened coverage of FDG PET for the diagnosis, staging and restaging of lymphoma.

Requirements: PET is covered in either/both of the following circumstances:

• Diagnosis – PET is covered only in clinical situations in which the PET results may assist in avoiding an invasive diagnostic procedure, or in which the PET results may assist in determining the optimal anatomical location to perform an invasive diagnostic procedure. In general, for most solid tumors, a tissue diagnosis is made prior to the performance of PET scanning. PET scans following a tissue diagnosis are performed for the purpose of staging, not diagnosis. Therefore, the use of PET in the diagnosis of lymphoma, esophageal, and colorectal cancers as well as in melanoma should be rare.

• Staging and/or Restaging – PET is covered in clinical situations in which 1) (a) the stage of the cancer remains in doubt after completion of a standard diagnostic workup, including conventional imaging (computed tomography, magnetic resonance imaging, or ultrasound) or (b) the use of PET would also be considered reasonable and necessary if it could potentially replace one or more conventional imaging studies when it is expected that conventional study information is insufficient for the clinical management of the patient, and 2) clinical management of the patient would differ depending on the stage of the cancer identified. PET will be covered for restaging after the completion of treatment for the purpose of detecting residual disease, for detecting suspected recurrence, or to determine the extent of a known recurrence. Use of PET would also be considered reasonable and necessary if it could potentially replace one or more conventional imaging studies when it is expected that conventional study information is insufficient for the clinical management of the patient.

Documentation that these conditions are met should be maintained by the referring physician in the beneficiary's medical record, as is normal business practice.

IX. Coverage of FDG PET for Melanoma

Medicare covered the evaluation of recurrent melanoma prior to surgery when used as an alternative to a Gallium scan, effective July 1, 1999. For services furnished on or after July 1, 2001 FDG PET is covered for the diagnosis, staging, and restaging of malignant melanoma (see part III). FDG PET is not covered for the use of evaluating regional nodes in melanoma patients.

A. Effective for services furnished July 1, 1999 through June 30, 2001, in the case of patients with recurrent melanoma prior to surgery, FDG PET (when used as an alternative to a Gallium scan) is covered for tumor evaluation.

Frequency Limitations: Whole body PET scans cannot be ordered more frequently than once every 12 months, unless medical necessity documentation, maintained in the beneficiaries medical record, supports the specific need for anatomic localization of possible recurrent tumor within this period. Limitations: The FDG PET scan is covered only as an alternative to a Gallium scan. PET scans can not be covered in cases where it is done within 50 days of a Gallium scan done by the same PET facility where the patient has remained under the care of the same facility during the 50-day period. Gallium scans done by another facility less than 50 days prior to the PET scan will not be counted against this screen. The purpose of this screen is to assure that PET scans are covered only when done as an alternative to a Gallium scan within the same facility. We are aware that, in order to assure proper patient care, the treating physician may conclude that previously performed Gallium scans are either inconclusive or not sufficiently reliable to make the determination covered by this provision. Therefore, we will apply this 50-day rule only to PET scans done by the same facility that performed the Gallium scan.

Beginning July 1, 2001, documentation should be maintained in the beneficiary's medical file at the referring physician's office to support the medical necessity of the procedure, as is normal business practice.

B. Effective for services performed on or after July 1, 2001 FDG PET scan coverage for thediagnosis, staging and restaging of melanoma (not the evaluation regional nodes) has been broadened.

Limitations: PET scans are not covered for the evaluation of regional nodes.

Requirements: PET is covered in either/both of the following circumstances:

• Diagnosis – PET is covered only in clinical situations in which the PET results may assist in avoiding an invasive diagnostic procedure, or in which the PET results may assist in determining the optimal anatomical location to perform an invasive diagnostic procedure. In general, for most solid tumors, a tissue diagnosis is made prior to the performance of PET scanning. PET scans following a tissue diagnosis are performed for the purpose of staging, not diagnosis. Therefore, the use of PET in the diagnosis of lymphoma, esophageal, and colorectal cancers as well as in melanoma should be rare.

• Staging and/or Restaging – PET is covered in clinical situations in which 1) (a) the stage of the cancer remains in doubt after completion of a standard diagnostic workup, including conventional imaging (computed tomography, magnetic resonance imaging, or ultrasound) or (b) the use of PET would also be considered reasonable and necessary if it could potentially replace one or more conventional imaging studies when it is expected that conventional study information is insufficient for the clinical management of the patient, and 2) clinical management of the patient would differ depending on the stage of the cancer identified. PET will be covered for restaging after the completion of treatment for the purpose of detecting residual disease, for detecting suspected recurrence, or to determine the extent of a known recurrence. Use of PET would also be considered reasonable and necessary if it could potentially replace one or more conventional imaging studies when it is expected that conventional study information is insufficient for the clinical management of the patient.

Documentation that these conditions are met should be maintained by the referring physician in the beneficiary's medical file, as is normal business practice.

X. Coverage of FDG PET for Head and Neck Cancers

Effective for services performed on or after July 1, 2001, Medicare will provide coverage for cancer of the head and neck, excluding the central nervous system (CNS) and thyroid. The head and neck cancers encompass a diverse set of malignancies of which the majority is squamous cell carcinomas.

Patients may present with metastases to cervical lymph nodes but conventional forms of diagnostic imaging fail to identify the primary tumor. Patients that present with cancer of the head and neck are left with two options either to have a neck dissection or to have radiation of both sides of the neck with random biopsies. PET scanning attempts to reveal the site of primary tumor to prevent the adverse effects of random biopsies or unneeded radiation.

Limitations: PET scans for head and neck cancers are not covered for CNS or thyroid cancers (prior to October 1, 2003). Refer to section XIV for coverage for thyroid cancer effective October 1, 2003.

Requirements: PET is covered in either/or both of the following circumstances

• Diagnosis – PET is covered only in clinical situations in which the PET results may assist in avoiding an invasive diagnostic procedure, or in which the PET results may assist in determining the optimal anatomical location to perform an invasive diagnostic procedure. In general, for most solid tumors, a tissue diagnosis is made prior to the performance of PET scanning. PET scans following a tissue diagnosis are performed for the purpose of staging, not diagnosis. Therefore, the use of PET in the diagnosis of lymphoma, esophageal, and colorectal cancers as well as in melanoma should be rare.

• Staging and/or Restaging – PET is covered in clinical situations in which 1) (a) the stage of the cancer remains in doubt after completion of a standard diagnostic workup, including conventional imaging (computed tomography, magnetic resonance imaging, or ultrasound) or (b) the use of PET would also be considered reasonable and necessary if it could potentially replace one or more conventional imaging studies when it is expected that conventional study information is insufficient for the clinical management of the patient, and 2) clinical management of the patient would differ depending on the stage of the cancer identified. PET will be covered for restaging after the completion of treatment for the purpose of detecting residual disease, for detecting suspected recurrence, or to determine the extent of a known recurrence. Use of PET would also be considered reasonable and necessary if it could potentially replace one or more conventional imaging studies when it is expected that conventional study information is insufficient for the clinical management of the patient.

Documentation that these conditions are met should be maintained by the referring physician in the beneficiary's medical record, as is normal business practice.

XI. Coverage of FDG PET for Myocardial Viability

The identification of patients with partial loss of heart muscle movement or hibernating myocardium is important in selecting candidates with compromised ventricular function to determine appropriateness for revascularization. Diagnostic tests such as FDG PET distinguish between dysfunctional but viable myocardial tissue and scar tissue in order to affect management decisions in patients with ischemic cardiomyopathy and left ventricular dysfunction.

FDG PET is covered for the determination of myocardial viability following an inconclusive SPECT from July 1, 2001 through September 30, 2002. Only full ring PET scanners are covered from July 1, 2001 through December 31, 2001. However, as of January 1, 2002, full and partial ring scanners are covered.

Rev. 171

06-03 COVERAGE ISSUES – DIAGNOSTIC SERVICES 50-36 (Cont.)

Beginning October 1, 2002, Medicare covers FDG PET for the determination of myocardial viability as a primary or initial diagnostic study prior to revascularization, or following an inconclusive

SPECT. Studies performed by full and partial ring scanners are covered.

Limitations: In the event that a patient has received a single photon computed tomography test (SPECT) with inconclusive results, a PET scan may be covered. However, if a patient received a FDG PET study with inconclusive results, a follow up SPECT is not covered.

Documentation that these conditions are met should be maintained by the referring physician in the beneficiary's medical record, as is normal business practice.

(See §50-58 of the CIM for SPECT coverage.)

XII. Coverage of FDG PET for Refractory Seizures

Beginning July 1, 2001, Medicare will cover FDG-PET for pre-surgical evaluation for the purpose of localization of a focus of refractory seizure activity.

Limitations: Covered only for pre-surgical evaluation.

Documentation that these conditions are met should be maintained by the referring physician in the beneficiary's medical record, as is normal business practice.

XIII. Breast Cancer

Beginning October 1, 2002, Medicare covers FDG PET as an adjunct to other imaging modalities for staging patients with distant metastasis, or restaging patients with locoregional recurrence or metastasis. Monitoring treatment of a breast cancer tumor when a change in therapy is contemplated is also covered as an adjunct to other imaging modalities.

Limitations: Effective October 1, 2002, Medicare continues to have a national non-coverage determination for initial diagnosis of breast cancer and staging of axillary lymph nodes. Medicare coverage for staging patients with distant metastasis or restaging patients with locoregional recurrence or metastasis; and for monitoring tumor response to treatment for women with locally advanced and metastatic breast cancer when a change in therapy is anticipated, .is only covered as an adjunct to other imaging modalities.

Documentation that these conditions are met should be maintained by the referring physician in the beneficiary's medical record, as is normal business practice.

XIV. Thyroid Cancer

1. Effective for services furnished on or after October 1, 2003, Medicare covers the use of FDG PET for thyroid cancer only for restaging of recurrent or residual thyroid cancers of follicular cell origin that have been previously treated by thyroidectomy and radioiodine ablation and have a serum thyroglobulin >10ng/ml and negative I-131 whole body scan performed.

2. All other uses of FDG PET in the diagnosis and treatment of thyroid cancer remain noncovered.

(This NCD last reviewed April 2003.)

Rev. 171

50-36 (Cont.) COVERAGE ISSUES – DIAGNOSTIC SERVICES 06-03

XV. Soft Tissue Sarcoma – NOT COVERED

Following a thorough review of the scientific literature, including a technology assessment on the topic, Medicare maintains its national noncoverage determination for all uses of FDG PET for soft tissue sarcoma.

(This NCD last reviewed April 2003.)

XVI. Dementia and Neurogenerative Diseases – NOT COVERED

Following a thorough review of the scientific literature, including a technology assessment on the topic and consideration by the Medicare Coverage Advisory Committee, Medicare maintains its national noncoverage determination for all uses of FDG-PET for the diagnosis and management of dementia or other neurogenerative diseases

(This NCD last reviewed April 2003.)

Rev. 171

General Description

Positron emission tomography (PET) is a noninvasive diagnostic imaging procedure that assesses the level of metabolic activity and perfusion in various organ systems of the [human] body. A positron camera (tomograph) is used to produce cross-sectional tomographic images, which are obtained from positron emitting radioactive tracer substances (radiopharmaceuticals) such as 2-[F-18] Fluoro-D-Glucose (FDG), that are administered intravenously to the patient.

The following indications may be covered for PET under certain circumstances. Details of Medicare PET coverage are discussed later in this section. Unless otherwise indicated, the clinical conditions below are covered when PET utilizes FDG as a tracer.

NOTE: All other uses of PET scans not listed in this manual are NOT covered.

Clinical Condition	Effective Date	Coverage
Solitary Pulmonary Nodules (SPNs)	January 1, 1998	Characterization
Lung Cancer (Non Small Cell)	January 1, 1998	Initial staging
Lung Cancer (Non Small Cell)	July 1, 2001	Diagnosis, staging and restaging
Esophageal Cancer	July 1, 2001	Diagnosis, staging and restaging
Colorectal Cancer	July 1, 1999	Determining location of tumors if rising CEA level suggests recurrence
Colorectal Cancer	July 1, 2001	Diagnosis, staging and restaging
Lymphoma	July 1, 1999	Staging and restaging only when used as an alternative to Gallium scan
Lymphoma	July 1, 2001	Diagnosis, staging and restaging
Melanoma	July 1, 1999	Evaluating recurrence prior to surgery as an alternative to a Gallium scan
Melanoma	July 1, 2001	Diagnosis, staging and restaging; Non-covered for evaluating regional nodes
Breast Cancer	October 1, 2002	As an adjunct to standard imaging modalities for staging patients with distant metastasis or restaging patients with locoregional recurrence or metastasis; as an adjunct to standard imaging modalities for monitoring tumor response to treatment for women with locally advanced and

		metastatic breast cancer when a change in therapy is anticipated.
Head and Neck Cancers (excluding CNS and thyroid)	July 1, 2001	Diagnosis, staging and restaging
Myocardial Viability	July 1, 2001 to Sept 30, 2002	Covered only following inconclusive SPECT
Myocardial Viability	October 1, 2001	Primary or initial diagnosis, or following an inconclusive SPECT prior to revascularization. SPECT may not be used following an inconclusive PET scan
Refractory Seizures	July 1, 2001	Covered for pre-surgical evaluation only
Perfusion of the heart using Rubidium 82* tracer	March 14, 1995	Covered for noninvasive imaging of the perfusion of the heart

Regardless of any other terms or conditions, all uses of FDG PET scans, in order to be covered by the Medicare program, must meet the following general conditions prior to June 30, 2001:

Submission of claims for payment must include any information Medicare requires to assure that the PET scans performed were: (a) medically necessary, (b) did not unnecessarily duplicate other covered diagnostic tests, and (c) did not involve investigational drugs or procedures using investigational drugs, as determined by the Food and Drug Administration (FDA).

The PET scan entity submitting claims for payment must keep such patient records as Medicare requires on file for each patient for whom a PET scan claim is made.

Regardless of any other terms or conditions, all uses of FDG PET scans, in order to be covered by the Medicare program, must meet the following general conditions as of July 1, 2001:

The provider of the PET scan should maintain on file the doctor's referral and documentation that the procedure involved only FDA approved drugs and devices, as is normal business practice.

The ordering physician is responsible for documenting the medical necessity of the study and that it meets the conditions specified in the instructions. The physician should have documentation in the beneficiary's medical record to support the referral to the PET scan provider.

Covered Indications for PET Scans and Limitations/Requirements for Usage

For all uses of PET relating to malignancies the following conditions apply:

Diagnosis: PET is covered only in clinical situations in which the PET results may assist in avoiding an invasive diagnostic procedure, or in which the PET results may assist in determining the optimal anatomical location to perform an invasive diagnostic procedure. In general, for most solid tumors, a tissue diagnosis is made prior to the performance of PET scanning. PET scans following a tissue diagnosis are performed for the purpose of staging, not diagnosis. Therefore, the use of PET in the diagnosis of lymphoma, esophageal, and colorectal cancers as well as in melanoma should be rare.

PET is not covered for other diagnostic uses, and is not covered for screening (testing of patients without specific signs and symptoms of disease).

Rev. 156

Staging and or Restaging: PET is covered in clinical situations in which 1) (a) the stage of the cancer remains in doubt after completion of a standard diagnostic workup, including conventional imaging (computed tomography, magnetic resonance imaging, or ultrasound) or (b) the use of PET would also be considered reasonable and necessary if it could potentially replace one or more conventional imaging studies when it is expected that conventional study information is insufficient for the clinical management of the patient and 2) clinical management of the patient would differ depending on the stage of the cancer identified. PET will be covered for restaging after the completion of treatment for the purpose of detecting residual disease, for detecting suspected recurrence or to determine the extent of a known recurrence. Use of PET would also be considered reasonable and necessary if it could potentially replace one or more conventional imaging studies when it is expected that conventional study information is insufficient for the clinical management of the patient.

Monitoring: Use of PET to monitor tumor response during the planned course of therapy (i.e. when no change in therapy is being contemplated) is not covered except for breast cancer. Restaging only occurs after a course of treatment is completed, and this is covered, subject to the conditions above.

NOTE: In the absence of national frequency limitations, contractors may, if necessary, develop frequency requirements on any or all of the indications covered on and after July 1, 2001.

Coverage of PET for Perfusion of the Heart Using Rubidium 82

Effective for services performed on or after March 14, 1995, PET scans performed at rest or with pharmacological stress used for noninvasive imaging of the perfusion of the heart for the diagnosis and management of patients with known or suspected coronary artery disease using the FDA-approved radiopharmaceutical Rubidium 82 (Rb 82) are covered, provided the requirements below are met.

Requirements:

The PET scan, whether at rest alone, or rest with stress, is performed in place of, but not in addition to, a single photon emission computed tomography (SPECT); or

The PET scan, whether at rest alone or rest with stress, is used following a SPECT that was found to be inconclusive. In these cases, the PET scan must have been considered necessary in order to determine what medical or surgical intervention is required to treat the patient. (For purposes of this requirement, an inconclusive test is a test(s) whose results are equivocal, technically uninterpretable, or discordant with a patient's other clinical data and must be documented in the beneficiary's file.)

For any PET scan for which Medicare payment is claimed for dates of services prior to July 1, 2001, the claimant must submit additional specified information on the claim form (including proper codes and/or modifiers), to indicate the results of the PET scan. The claimant must also include information on whether the PET scan was done after an inconclusive noninvasive cardiac test. The information submitted with respect to the previous noninvasive cardiac test must specify the type of test done prior to the PET scan and whether it was inconclusive or unsatisfactory. These explanations are in the form of special G codes used for billing PET scans using Rb 82. Beginning July 1, 2001 claims should be submitted with the appropriate codes.

Rev. 156

Coverage of FDG PET for Lung Cancer

The coverage for FDG PET for lung cancer, effective January 1, 1998, has been expanded. Beginning July 1, 2001 usage of FDG PET for lung cancer has been expanded to include diagnosis, staging, and restaging (see section III) of the disease.

Effective for services performed on or after January 1, 1998, Medicare covers regional FDG PET chest scans, on any FDA approved scanner, for the characterization of single pulmonary nodules (SPNs). The primary purpose of such characterization should be to determine the likelihood of malignancy in order to plan future management and treatment for the patient.

Beginning July 1, 2001, documentation should be maintained in the beneficiary's medical file at the referring physician's office to support the medical necessity of the procedure, as is normal business practice.

Requirements:

There must be evidence of primary tumor. Claims for regional PET chest scans for characterizing SPNs should include evidence of the initial detection of a primary lung tumor, usually by computed tomography (CT). This should include, but is not restricted to, a report on the results of such CT or other detection method, indicating an indeterminate or possibly malignant lesion, not exceeding four centimeters (cm) in diameter.

PET scan claims must include the results of concurrent thoracic CT (as noted above), which is necessary for anatomic information, in order to ensure that the PET scan is properly coordinated with other diagnostic modalities.

In cases of serial evaluation of SPNs using both CT and regional PET chest scanning, such PET scans will not be covered if repeated within 90 days following a negative PET scan.

NOTE: A tissue sampling procedure (TSP) is not routinely covered in the case of a negative PET scan for characterization of SPNs, since the patient is presumed not to have a malignant lesion, based upon the PET scan results. When there has been a negative PET, the provider must submit additional information with the claim to support the necessity of a TSP, for review by the Medicare contractor.

Effective for services performed from January 1, 1998 through June 30, 2001, Medicare approved coverage of FDG PET for initial staging of non-small-cell lung carcinoma (NSCLC).

Limitations: This service is covered only when the primary cancerous lung tumor has been pathologically confirmed; claims for PET must include a statement or other evidence of the detection of such primary lung tumor. The evidence should include, but is not restricted to, a surgical pathology report, which documents the presence of an NSCLC. Whole body PET scan results and results of concurrent computed tomography (CT) and follow-up lymph node biopsy must be properly coordinated with other diagnostic modalities. Claims must include both:

The results of concurrent thoracic CT, necessary for anatomic information, and

The results of any lymph node biopsy performed to finalize whether the patient will be a surgical candidate. The ordering physician is responsible for providing this biopsy result to the PET facility.

Rev. 156

NOTE: Where the patient is considered a surgical candidate, (given the presumed absence of metastatic NSCLC unless medical review supports a determination of medical necessity of a biopsy) a lymph node biopsy will not be covered in the case of a negative CT and negative PET. A lymph node biopsy will be covered in all other cases, i.e., positive CT + positive PET; negative CT + positive PET; positive CT + negative PET.

Beginning July 1, 2001, Medicare covers FDG PET for diagnosis, staging, and restaging of NSCLC. Documentation should be maintained in the beneficiary's medical file to support the medical necessity of the procedure, as is normal business practice.

Requirements: PET is covered in either/or both of the following circumstances:

Diagnosis – PET is covered only in clinical situations in which the PET results may assist in avoiding an invasive diagnostic procedure, or in which the PET results may assist in determining the optimal anatomical location to perform an invasive diagnostic procedure. In general, for most solid tumors, a tissue diagnosis is made prior to the performance of PET scanning. PET scans following a tissue diagnosis are performed for the purpose of staging, not diagnosis. Therefore, the use of PET in the diagnosis of lymphoma, esophageal, and colorectal cancers as well as melanoma should be rare.

Staging and/or Restaging – PET is covered in clinical situations in which 1)(a) the stage of the cancer remains in doubt after completion of a standard diagnostic workup, including conventional imaging (computed tomography, magnetic resonance imaging, or ultrasound) or (b) the use of PET would also be considered reasonable and necessary if it could potentially replace one or more conventional imaging studies when it is expected that conventional study information is insufficient for the clinical management of the patient and 2) clinical management of the patient would differ depending on the stage of the cancer identified. PET will be covered for restaging after the completion of treatment for the purpose of detecting residual disease, for detecting suspected recurrence or to determine the extent of a known recurrence. Use of PET would also be considered reasonable and necessary if it could potentially replace one or more conventional imaging studies when it is expected that conventional study information is insufficient for the clinical management of the patient.

Documentation should be maintained in the beneficiary's medical record at the referring physician's office to support the medical necessity of the procedure, as is normal business practice.

Coverage of FDG PET for Esophageal Cancer

Beginning July 1, 2001, Medicare covers FDG PET for the diagnosis, staging, and restaging of esophageal cancer. Medical evidence is present to support the use of FDG PET in presurgical staging of esophageal cancer.

Requirements: PET is covered in either/or both of the following circumstances:

Diagnosis – PET is covered only in clinical situations in which the PET results may assist in avoiding an invasive diagnostic procedure, or in which the PET results may assist in determining the optimal anatomical location to perform an invasive diagnostic procedure. In general, for most solid tumors, a tissue diagnosis is made prior to the performance of PET scanning. PET scans following a tissue diagnosis are performed for the purpose of staging, not diagnosis. Therefore, the use of PET in the diagnosis of lymphoma, esophageal and colorectal cancers as well as in melanoma should be rare.

Staging and/or Restaging – PET is covered in clinical situations in which 1)(a) the stage of the cancer remains in doubt after completion of a standard diagnostic workup, including conventional imaging (computed tomography, magnetic resonance imaging, or ultrasound)

Rev. 156

or (b) the use of PET would also be considered reasonable and necessary if it could potentially replace one or more conventional imaging studies when it is expected that conventional study information is insufficient for the clinical management of the patient, and 2) clinical management of the patient would differ depending on the stage of the cancer identified. PET will be covered for restaging after the completion of treatment for the purpose of detecting residual disease, for detecting suspected recurrence, or to determine the extent of a known recurrence. Use of PET would also be considered reasonable and necessary if it could potentially replace one or more conventional imaging studies when it is expected that conventional study information is insufficient for the clinical management of the patient.

Documentation should be maintained in the beneficiary's medical record at the referring physician's office to support the medical necessity of the procedure, as is normal business practice.

Coverage of FDG PET for Colorectal Cancer

Medicare coverage of FDG PET for colorectal cancer where there is a rising level of carcinoembryonic antigen (CEA) was effective July 1, 1999 through June 30, 2001. Beginning July 1, 2001 usage of FDG PET for colorectal cancer has been expanded to include diagnosis, staging, and restaging of the disease(see part III).

Effective July 1, 1999, Medicare covers FDG PET for patients with recurrent colorectal carcinomas, which are suggested by rising levels of the biochemical tumor marker CEA.

Frequency Limitations: Whole body PET scans for assessment of recurrence of colorectal cancer cannot be ordered more frequently than once every 12 months unless medical necessity documentation supports a separate re-elevation of CEA within this period.

Limitations: Because this service is covered only in those cases in which there has been a recurrence of colorectal tumor, claims for PET should include a statement or other evidence of previous colorectal tumor, through June 30, 2001.

Beginning July 1, 2001, Medicare coverage has been expanded for colorectal carcinomas for diagnosis, staging and re-staging. New medical evidence supports the use of FDG PET as a useful tool in determining the presence of hepatic/extrahepatic metastases in the primary staging of colorectal carcinoma, prior to selecting a treatment regimen. Use of FDG PET is also supported in evaluating recurrent colorectal cancer beyond the limited presentation of a rising CEA level where the patient presents clinical signs or symptoms of recurrence.

Requirements: PET is covered in either/both of the following circumstances:

Diagnosis – PET is covered only in clinical situations in which the PET results may assist in avoiding an invasive diagnostic procedure, or in which the PET results may assist in determining the optimal anatomical location to perform an invasive diagnostic procedure. In general, for most solid tumors, a tissue diagnosis is made prior to the performance of PET scanning. PET scans following a tissue diagnosis are performe

CIM 50-4   Gravlee Jet Washer

The Gravlee Jet Washer is a sterile, disposable, diagnostic device for detecting endometrial cancer. The use of this device is indicated where the patient exhibits clinical symptoms or signs suggestive of endometrial disease, such as irregular or heavy vaginal bleeding.

Program payment cannot be made for the washer or the related diagnostic services when furnished in connection with the examination of an asymptomatic patient. Payment for routine physical checkups is precluded under the statute. (See §1862(a)(7) of the Act.)

(See Intermediary Manual, §3157 and Carriers Manual, §2320.)

CIM 50-42   Ambulatory Blood Pressure Monitoring With Fully And Semi-Automatic (Patient-Activated) Portable Monitors – Not Covered

The clinical usefulness of the data obtained from these devices is not clearly established, and, accordingly, program payment may not be made for the use of such devices at this time.

Ambulatory blood pressure monitoring (ABPM) involves the use of a non-invasive device which is used to measure blood pressure in 24-hour cycles. These 24-hour measurements are stored in the device and are later interpreted by the physician. ABPM must be performed for at least 24 hours to meet coverage criteria.

ABPM is only covered for those patients with suspected white coat hypertension. Suspected white coat hypertension is defined as 1) office blood pressure >140/90 mm Hg on at least three separate clinic/office visits with two separate measurements made at each visit; 2) at least two documented blood pressure measurements taken outside the office which are <140/90 mm Hg; and 3) no evidence of end-organ damage. The information obtained by ABPM is necessary in order to determine the appropriate management of the patient. ABPM is not covered for any other uses. In the rare circumstance that ABPM needs to be performed more than once in a patient, the qualifying criteria described above must be met for each subsequent ABPM test.

For those patients that undergo ABPM and have an ambulatory blood pressure of <135/85 with no evidence of end-organ damage, it is likely that their cardiovascular risk is similar to that of normotensives. They should be followed over time. Patients for which ABPM demonstrates a blood pressure of >135/85 may be at increased cardiovascular risk, and a physician may wish to consider antihypertensive therapy.

(This NCD last reviewed January 16, 2003)

CIM 50-44   Bone (Mineral) Density Studies

Medicare covers the following bone (mineral) density studies

    1. Single Photon Absorptiometry – A non-invasive radiological technique that provides a quantitative measurement of the bone mineral of cortical and trabecular bone, and is used in assessing an individual's treatment response at appropriate intervals. Medicare covers when used in assessing changes in bone density of patients with osteodystrophy or osteoporosis performed on the same individual at intervals of 6 to 12 months.

    2. Bone Biopsy – A physiologic test used in ascertaining a differential diagnosis of bone disorders and is used primarily to differentiate osteomalacia from osteoporosis. Bone biopsy is covered under Medicare when used for the qualitative evaluation of bone no more than four times per patient, unless there is special justification given.

3. Photodensitometry (radiographic absorptiometry) – A noninvasive radiological procedure that provides a quantitative measurement of the bone mineral of cortical bone, and is used for monitoring gross bone change.

CIM 50-50   Displacement Cardiography

Displacement cardiography, including cardiokymography and photokymography, is a noninvasive diagnostic test used in evaluating coronary artery disease.

A. Cardiokymography. – (Effective For Services Rendered On Or After October 12, 1988).

Cardiokymography is a covered service only when it is used as an adjunct to electrocardiographic stress testing in evaluating coronary artery disease and only when the following clinical indications are present:

- For male patients, atypical angina pectoris or nonischemic chest pain; or

- For female patients, angina, either typical or atypical.

B. Photokymography. – NOT COVERED

Photokymography remains excluded from coverage.

CIM 50-55   Prostate Cancer Screening Tests – Covered (Effective for services furnished on or after January 1, 2000)

A. General. – Section 4103 of the Balanced Budget Act of 1997 provides for coverage of certain prostate cancer screening tests subject to certain coverage, frequency, and payment limitations. Effective for services furnished on or after January 1, 2000. Medicare will cover prostate cancer screening tests/procedures for the early detection of prostate cancer. Coverage of prostate cancer screening tests includes the following procedures furnished to an individual for the early detection of prostate cancer:

- Screening digital rectal examination; and

- Screening prostate specific antigen blood test.

B. Screening Digital Rectal Examinations. – Screening digital rectal examinations (HCPCS code G0102) are covered at a frequency of once every 12 months for men who have attained age 50 (at least 11 months have passed following the month in which the last Medicare-covered screening digital rectal examination was performed). Screening digital rectal examination means a clinical examination of an individual's prostate for nodules or other abnormalities of the prostate. This screening must be performed by a doctor of medicine or osteopathy (as defined in §1861(r)(1) of the Act), or by a physician assistant, nurse practitioner, clinical nurse specialist, or certified nurse midwife (as defined in §1861(aa) and §1861(gg) of the Act) who is authorized under State law to perform the examination, fully knowledgeable about the beneficiary's medical condition, and would be responsible for using the results of any examination performed in the overall management of the beneficiary's specific medical problem.

C. Screening Prostate Specific Antigen Tests. – Screening prostate specific antigen tests (code G0103) are covered at a frequency of once every 12 months for men who have attained age 50 (at least 11 months have passed following the month in which the last Medicare-covered screening prostate specific antigen test was performed). Screening prostate specific antigen tests (PSA) means a test to detect the marker for adenocarcinoma of prostate. PSA is a reliable immunocytochemical marker for primary and metastatic adenocarcinoma of prostate. This screening must be ordered by the beneficiary's physician or by the beneficiary's physician assistant, nurse practitioner, clinical nurse specialist, or certified nurse midwife (the term "attending physician" is defined in §1861(r)(1) of the Act to mean a doctor of medicine or osteopathy and the terms "physician assistant, nurse practitioner, clinical nurse specialist, or certified nurse midwife" are defined in §1861(aa) and §1861(gg) of the Act) who is fully knowledgeable about the beneficiary's medical condition, and who would be responsible for using the results of any examination (test) performed in the overall management of the beneficiary's specific medical problem.

CIM 50-57   Current Perception Threshold/Sensory Nerve Conduction Threshold Test (SNCT) Noncovered

The Current Perception Threshold/Sensory Nerve Conduction Threshold (SsNCT) test is a diagnostic test used to diagnose sensory neuropathies. The device is a noninvasive test that uses transcutaneous electrical stimuli to evoke a sensation. There is insufficient scientific or clinical evidence to consider this device reasonable and necessary within the meaning of Section 1862(a)(1)(A) of the law and will not be covered by Medicare.

CIM 55-1   Water Purification And Softening Systems Used In Conjunction With Home Dialysis

A. Water Purification Systems. – Water used for home dialysis should be chemically free of heavy trace metals and/or organic contaminants which could be hazardous to the patient. It should also be as free of bacteria as possible but need not be biologically sterile. Since the characteristics of natural water supplies in most areas of the country are such that some type of water purification system is needed, such a system used in conjunction with a home dialysis (either peritoneal or hemodialysis) unit is covered under Medicare.

There are two types of water purification systems which will satisfy these requirements:

Deionization – The removal of organic substances, mineral salts of magnesium and calcium (causing hardness), compounds of fluoride and chloride from tap water using the process of filtration and ion exchange; or

Reverse Osmosis – The process used to remove impurities from tap water utilizing pressure to force water through a porous membrane.

Use of both a deionization unit and reverse osmosis unit in series, theoretically to provide the advantages of both systems, has been determined medically unnecessary since either system can provide water which is both chemically and bacteriologically pure enough for acceptable use in home dialysis. In addition, spare deionization tanks are not covered since they are essentially a precautionary supply rather than a current requirement for treatment of the patient.

Activated carbon filters used as a component of water purification systems to remove unsafe concentrations of chlorine and chloramines are covered when prescribed by a physician.

B. Water Softening System. – Except as indicated below, a water softening system used in conjunction with home dialysis is excluded from coverage under Medicare as not being reasonable and necessary within the meaning of §1862(a)(1) of the law. Such a system, in conjunction with a home dialysis unit, does not adequately remove the hazardous heavy metal contaminants (such as arsenic) which may be present in trace amounts.

A water softening system may be covered when used to pretreat water to be purified by a reverse osmosis (RO) unit for home dialysis where:

- The manufacturer of the RO unit has set standards for the quality of water entering the RO (e.g., the water to be purified by the RO must be of a certain quality if the unit is to perform as intended);

- The patient's water is demonstrated to be of a lesser quality than required; and

- The softener is used only to soften water entering the RO unit, and thus, used only for dialysis. (The softener need not actually be built into the RO unit, but must be an integral part of the dialysis system.)

C. Developing Need When a Water Softening System is Replaced with a Water Purification Unit in an Existing Home Dialysis System. – The medical necessity of water purification units must be carefully developed when they replace water softening systems in existing home dialysis systems. A purification system may be ordered under these circumstances for a number of reasons. For example, changes in the medical community's opinions regarding the quality of water necessary for safe dialysis may lead the physician to decide the quality of water previously used should be improved, or the water quality itself may have deteriorated. Patients may have dialyzed using only an existing water softener previous to Medicare ESRD coverage because of inability to pay for a purification system. On the other hand, in some cases, the installation of a purification system is not medically necessary. Thus, when such a case comes to your attention, ask the physician to furnish the reason for the changes. Supporting documentation, such as the supplier's recommendations or water analysis, may be required. All such cases should be reviewed by your medical consultants.

Cross-refer: Intermediary Manual, §§3113, 3643 (item 1c); Carriers Manual, §§2100, 2100.2 2130, 2105 (item 1c); Hospital Manual, §235.

CIM 55-1A   Water Purification And Softening Systems Used In Conjunction With Home Dialysis

A. Water Purification Systems. – Water used for home dialysis should be chemically free of heavy trace metals and/or organic contaminants which could be hazardous to the patient. It should also be as free of bacteria as possible but need not be biologically sterile. Since the characteristics of natural water supplies in most areas of the country are such that some type of water purification system is needed, such a system used in conjunction with a home dialysis (either peritoneal or hemodialysis) unit is covered under Medicare.

There are two types of water purification systems which will satisfy these requirements:

Deionization – The removal of organic substances, mineral salts of magnesium and calcium (causing hardness), compounds of fluoride and chloride from tap water using the process of filtration and ion exchange; or

Reverse Osmosis – The process used to remove impurities from tap water utilizing pressure to force water through a porous membrane.

Use of both a deionization unit and reverse osmosis unit in series, theoretically to provide the advantages of both systems, has been determined medically unnecessary since either system can provide water which is both chemically and bacteriologically pure enough for acceptable use in home dialysis. In addition, spare deionization tanks are not covered since they are essentially a precautionary supply rather than a current requirement for treatment of the patient.

Activated carbon filters used as a component of water purification systems to remove unsafe concentrations of chlorine and chloramines are covered when prescribed by a physician.

B. Water Softening System. – Except as indicated below, a water softening system used in conjunction with home dialysis is excluded from coverage under Medicare as not being reasonable and necessary within the meaning of §l862(a)(1) of the law. Such a system, in conjunction with a home dialysis unit, does not adequately remove the hazardous heavy metal contaminants (such as arsenic) which may be present in trace amounts.

A water softening system may be covered when used to pretreat water to be purified by a reverse osmosis (RO) unit for home dialysis where:

- The manufacturer of the RO unit has set standards for the quality of water entering the RO (e.g., the water to be purified by the RO must be of a certain quality if the unit is to perform as intended);

- The patient's water is demonstrated to be of a lesser quality than required; and

- The softener is used only to soften water entering the RO unit, and thus, used only for dialysis. (The softener need not actually be built into the RO unit, but must be an integral part of the dialysis system.)

C. Developing Need When a Water Softening System is Replaced with a Water Purification Unit in an Existing Home Dialysis System. – The medical necessity of water purification units must be carefully developed when they replace water softening systems in existing home dialysis systems. A purification system may be ordered under these circumstances for a number of reasons. For example, changes in the medical community's opinions regarding the quality of water necessary for safe dialysis may lead the physician to decide the quality of water previously used should be improved, or the water quality itself may have deteriorated. Patients may have dialyzed using only an existing water softener previous to Medicare ESRD coverage because of inability to pay for a purification system. On the other hand, in some cases, the installation of a purification system is not medically necessary. Thus, when such a case comes to your attention, ask the physician to furnish the reason for the changes. Supporting documentation, such as the supplier's recommendations or water analysis, may be required. All such cases should be reviewed by your medical consultants.

Cross-refer: Intermediary Manual, §§3113, 3643 (item 1c); Carriers Manual, §§2100, 2100.2 2130, 2105 (item 1c); Hospital Manual, §235.

CIM 55-1B Water Purification And Softening Systems Used In Conjunction With Home Dialysis

A. Water Purification Systems. – Water used for home dialysis should be chemically free of heavy trace metals and/or organic contaminants which could be hazardous to the patient. It should also be as free of bacteria as possible but need not be biologically sterile. Since the characteristics of natural water supplies in most areas of the country are such that some type of water purification system is needed, such a system in conjunction with a home dialysis (either peritoneal or hemodialysis) unit is covered under Medicare.

There are two types of water purification systems which will satisfy these requirements:

Deionization – The removal of organic substances, mineral salts of magnesium and calcium (causing hardness), compounds of fluoride and chloride from tap water using the process of filtration and ion exchange; or

Reverse Osmosis – The process used to remove impurities from tap water utilizing pressure to force water through a porous membrane.

Use of both a deionization unit and reverse osmosis unit in series, theoretically to provide the advantages of both systems, has been determined medically unnecessary since either system can provide water which is both chemically and bacteriologically pure enough for acceptable use in home dialysis. In addition, spare deionization tanks are not covered since they are essentially a precautionary supply rather than a current requirement for treatment of the patient.

Activated carbon filters used as a component of water purification systems to remove unsafe concentrations of chlorine and chloramines are covered when prescribed by a physician.

B. Water Softening System. – Except as indicated below, a water softening system used in conjunction with home dialysis is excluded from coverage under Medicare as not being reasonable and necessary within the meaning of §l862(a)(1) of the law. Such a system, in conjunction with a home dialysis unit, does not adequately remove the hazardous heavy metal contaminants (such as arsenic) which may be present in trace amounts.

A water softening system may be covered when used to pretreat water to be purified by a reverse osmosis (RO) unit for home dialysis where:

- The manufacturer of the RO unit has set standards for the quality of water entering the RO (e.g., the water to be purified by the RO must be of a certain quality if the unit is to perform as intended);

- The patient's water is demonstrated to be of a lesser quality than required; and

- The softener is used only to soften water entering the RO unit, and thus, used only for dialysis. (The softener need not actually be built into the RO unit, but must be an integral part of the dialysis system.)

C. Developing Need When a Water Softening System is Replaced with a Water Purification Unit in an Existing Home Dialysis System. – The medical necessity of water purification units must be carefully developed when they replace water softening systems in existing home dialysis systems. A purification system may be ordered under these circumstances for a number of reasons. For example, changes in the medical community's opinions regarding the quality of water necessary for safe dialysis may lead the physician to decide the quality of water previously used should be improved, or the water quality itself may have deteriorated. Patients may have dialyzed using only an existing water softener previous to Medicare ESRD coverage because of inability to pay for a purification system. On the other hand, in some cases, the installation of a purification system is not medically necessary. Thus, when such a case comes to your attention, ask the physician to furnish the reason for the changes. Supporting documentation, such as the supplier's recommendations or water analysis, may be required. All such cases should be reviewed by your medical consultants.

Cross-refer: Intermediary Manual, §§3113, 3643 (item 1c); Carriers Manual, §§2100, 2100.2 2130, 2105 (item 1c); Hospital Manual, §235.

CIM 60-11 Home Blood Glucose Monitors

There are several different types of blood glucose monitors which use reflectance meters to determine blood glucose levels. Medicare coverage of these devices varies, both with respect to the type of device and the medical condition of the patient for whom the device is prescribed.

Reflectance colorimeter devices used for measuring blood glucose levels in clinical settings are not covered as durable medical equipment for use in the home because their need for frequent professional recalibration makes them unsuitable for home use. However, some types of blood glucose monitors which use a reflectance meter specifically designed for home use by diabetic patients may be covered as durable medical equipment, subject to the conditions and limitations described below.

Blood glucose monitors are meter devices which read color changes produced on specially treated reagent strips by glucose concentrations in the patient's blood. The patient, using a disposable sterile lancet, draws a drop of blood, places it on a reagent strip and, following instructions which may vary with the device used, inserts it into the device to obtain a reading. Lancets, reagent strips, and other supplies necessary for the proper functioning of the device are also covered for patients for whom the device is indicated. Home blood glucose monitors enable certain patients to better control their blood glucose levels by frequently checking and appropriately contacting their attending physician for advice and treatment. Studies indicate that the patient's ability to carefully follow proper procedures is critical to obtaining satisfactory results with these devices. In addition, the cost of the devices, with their supplies, limits economical use to patients who must make frequent checks of their blood glucose levels. Accordingly, coverage of home blood glucose monitors is limited to patients meeting the following conditions:

- The patient must be an insulin-treated diabetic;

- The patient's physician states that the patient is capable of being trained to use the particular device prescribed in an appropriate manner. In some cases, the patient may not be able to perform this function, but a responsible individual can be trained to use the equipment and monitor the patient to assure that the intended effect is achieved. This is permissible if the record is properly documented by the patient's physician; and

- The device is designed for home rather than clinical use.

There is also a blood glucose monitoring system designed especially for use by those with visual impairments. The monitors used in such systems are identical in terms of reliability and sensitivity to the standard blood glucose monitors described above. They differ by having such features as voice synthesizers, automatic timers, and specially designed arrangements of supplies and materials to enable the visually impaired to use the equipment without assistance.

These special blood glucose monitoring systems are covered under Medicare if the following conditions are met:

- The patient and device meet the four conditions listed above for coverage of standard home blood glucose monitors; and

• The patient's physician certifies that he or she has a visual impairment severe enough to require use of this special monitoring system.

The additional features and equipment of these special systems justify a higher reimbursement amount than allowed for standard blood glucose monitors. Separately identify claims for such devices and establish a separate reimbursement amount for them. For those carriers using HCPCS, the procedure code and definition is: E0609 – Blood Glucose Monitor – with special features (e.g., voice synthesizers, automatic timer).

CIM 60-14   Infusion Pumps

The Following Indications For Treatment Using Infusion Pumps Are Covered Under Medicare:

A.   External Infusion Pumps. -

1.   Iron Poisoning (Effective for Services Performed On or After 9/26/84). – When used in the administration of deferoxamine for the treatment of acute iron poisoning and iron overload, only external infusion pumps are covered.

2.   Thromboembolic Disease (Effective for Services Performed On or After 9/26/84). – When used in the administration of heparin for the treatment of thromboembolic disease and/or pulmonary embolism, only external infusion pumps used in an institutional setting are covered.

3.   Chemotherapy for Liver Cancer (Effective for Services Performed On or After 1/29/85). – The external chemotherapy infusion pump is covered when used in the treatment of primary hepatocellular carcinoma or colorectal cancer where this disease is unresectable or where the patient refuses surgical excision of the tumor.

4.   Morphine for Intractable Cancer Pain (Effective for Services Performed On or After 4/22/85). – Morphine infusion via an external infusion pump is covered when used in the treatment of intractable pain caused by cancer (in either an inpatient or outpatient setting, including a hospice).

5.   Continuous subcutaneous insulin infusion pumps (CSII) (Effective for Services Performed On or After 4/1/2000).

An external infusion pump and related drugs/supplies are covered as medically necessary in the home setting in the following situation: Treatment of diabetes

In order to be covered, patients must meet criterion A or B:

(A)   The patient has completed a comprehensive diabetes education program, and has been on a program of multiple daily injections of insulin (i.e. at least 3 injections per day), with frequent self-adjustments of insulin dose for at least 6 months prior to initiation of the insulin pump, and has documented frequency of glucose self-testing an average of at least 4 times per day during the 2 months prior to initiation of the insulin pump, and meets one or more of the following criteria while on the multiple daily injection regimen:

(1) Glycosylated hemoglobin level (HbAlc) > 7.0 percent

(2) History of recurring hypoglycemia

(3) Wide fluctuations in blood glucose before mealtime

(4) Dawn phenomenon with fasting blood sugars frequently exceeding 200 mg/dl

(5) History of severe glycemic excursions

(B) The patient with diabetes has been on a pump prior to enrollment in Medicare and has documented frequency of glucose self-testing an average of at least 4 times per day during the month prior to Medicare enrollment.

Diabetes needs to be documented by a fasting C-peptide level that is less than or equal to 110 percent of the lower limit of normal of the laboratory's measurement method. (Effective for Services Performed on or after January 1, 2002.)

Continued coverage of the insulin pump would require that the patient has been seen and evaluated the treating physician at least every 3 months.

The pump must be ordered by and follow-up care of the patient must be managed by a physician who manages multiple patients with CSII and who works closely with a team including nurses, diabetes educators, and dietitians who are knowledgeable in the use of CSII.

6. Other uses of external infusion pumps are covered if the contractor's medical staff verifies the appropriateness of the therapy and of the prescribed pump for the individual patient.

NOTE: Payment may also be made for drugs necessary for the effective use of an external infusion pump as long as the drug being used with the pump is itself reasonable and necessary for the patient's treatment.

B. Implantable Infusion Pumps. -

1. Chemotherapy for Liver Cancer (Effective for Services Performed On or After 9/26/84). – The implantable infusion pump is covered for intra-arterial infusion of 5-FUdR for the treatment of liver cancer for patients with primary hepatocellular carcinoma or Duke's Class D colorectal cancer, in whom the metastases are limited to the liver, and where (1) the disease is unresectable or (2) where the patient refuses surgical excision of the tumor.

2. Anti-Spasmodic Drugs for Severe Spasticity. – An implantable infusion pump is covered when used to administer anti-spasmodic drugs intrathecally (e.g., baclofen) to treat chronic intractable spasticity in patients who have proven unresponsive to less invasive medical therapy as determined by the following criteria:

• As indicated by at least a 6-week trial, the patient cannot be maintained on noninvasive methods of spasm control, such as oral anti-spasmodic drugs, either because these methods fail to control adequately the spasticity or produce intolerable side effects, and

• Prior to pump implantation, the patient must have responded favorably to a trial intrathecal dose of the anti-spasmodic drug.

3. Opioid Drugs for Treatment of Chronic Intractable Pain. – An implantable infusion pump is covered when used to administer opioid drugs (e.g., morphine) intrathecally or epidurally for treatment of severe chronic intractable pain of malignant or nonmalignant origin in patients who have a life expectancy of at least 3 months and who have proven unresponsive to less invasive medical therapy as determined by the following criteria:

• The patient's history must indicate that he/she would not respond adequately to non-invasive methods of pain control, such as systemic opioids (including attempts to eliminate physical and behavioral abnormalities which may cause an exaggerated reaction to pain); and

• A preliminary trial of intraspinal opioid drug administration must be undertaken with a temporary intrathecal/epidural catheter to substantiate adequately acceptable pain relief and degree of side effects (including effects on the activities of daily living) and patient acceptance.

4. Coverage of Other Uses of Implanted Infusion Pumps . – Determinations may be made on coverage of other uses of implanted infusion pumps if the contractor's medical staff verifies that:

• The drug is reasonable and necessary for the treatment of the individual patient;

• It is medically necessary that the drug be administered by an implanted infusion pump; and

• The FDA approved labelling for the pump must specify that the drug being administered and the purpose for which it is administered is an indicated use for the pump.

5. Implantation of Infusion Pump Is Contraindicated. – The implantation of an infusion pump is contraindicated in the following patients:

• Patients with a known allergy or hypersensitivity to the drug being used (e.g., oral baclofen, morphine, etc.);

• Patients who have an infection;

• Patients whose body size is insufficient to support the weight and bulk of the device; and

• Patients with other implanted programmable devices since crosstalk between devices may inadvertently change the prescription.

NOTE: Payment may also be made for drugs necessary for the effective use of an implantable infusion pump as long as the drug being used with the pump is itself reasonable and necessary for the patient's treatment.

THE FOLLOWING INDICATIONS FOR TREATMENT USING INFUSION PUMPS ARE NOT COVERED UNDER MEDICARE:

A. External Infusion Pumps. -

1. Vancomycin (Effective for Services Beginning On or After September 1, 1996). – Medicare coverage of vancomycin as a durable medical equipment infusion pump benefit is not covered. There is insufficient evidence to support the necessity of using an external infusion pump, instead of a disposable elastomeric pump or the gravity drip method, to administer vancomycin in a safe and appropriate manner.

B. Implantable Infusion Pump. -

1. Thromboembolic Disease (Effective for Services Performed On or After 9/26/84). – According to the Public Health Service, there is insufficient published clinical data to support the safety and effectiveness of the heparin implantable pump. Therefore, the use of an implantable infusion pump for

infusion of heparin in the treatment of recurrent thromboembolic disease is not covered.

2. Diabetes – Implanted infusion pumps for the infusion of insulin to treat diabetes is not covered. The data do not demonstrate that the pump provides effective administration of insulin.

CIM 60-14a   Infusion Pumps

The Following Indications For Treatment Using Infusion Pumps Are Covered Under Medicare:

A. External Infusion Pumps. -

1. Iron Poisoning (Effective for Services Performed On or After 9/26/84). – When used in the administration of deferoxamine for the treatment of acute iron poisoning and iron overload, only external infusion pumps are covered.

2. Thromboembolic Disease (Effective for Services Performed On or After 9/26/84). – When used in the administration of heparin for the treatment of thromboembolic disease and/or pulmonary embolism, only external infusion pumps used in an institutional setting are covered.

3. Chemotherapy for Liver Cancer (Effective for Services Performed On or After 1/29/85). – The external chemotherapy infusion pump is covered when used in the treatment of primary hepatocellular carcinoma or colorectal cancer where this disease is unresectable or where the patient refuses surgical excision of the tumor.

4. Morphine for Intractable Cancer Pain (Effective for Services Performed On or After 4/22/85). – Morphine infusion via an external infusion pump is covered when used in the treatment of intractable pain caused by cancer (in either an inpatient or outpatient setting, including a hospice).

5. Continuous subcutaneous insulin infusion pumps (CSII) (Effective for Services Performed On or After 4/1/2000). -

An external infusion pump and related drugs/supplies are covered as medically necessary in the home setting in the following situation: Treatment of diabetes

In order to be covered, patients must meet criterion A or B:

(A) The patient has completed a comprehensive diabetes education program, and has been on a program of multiple daily injections of insulin (i.e. at least 3 injections per day), with frequent self-adjustments of insulin dose for at least 6 months prior to initiation of the insulin pump, and has documented frequency of glucose self-testing an average of at least 4 times per day during the 2 months prior to initiation of the insulin pump, and meets one or more of the following criteria while on the multiple daily injection regimen:

(1) Glycosylated hemoglobin level (HbAlc) > 7.0 percent

(2) History of recurring hypoglycemia

(3) Wide fluctuations in blood glucose before mealtime

(4) Dawn phenomenon with fasting blood sugars frequently exceeding 200 mg/dl

(5) History of severe glycemic excursions

(B) The patient with diabetes has been on a pump prior to enrollment in Medicare and has documented frequency of glucose self-testing an average of at least 4 times per day during the month prior to Medicare enrollment.

Diabetes needs to be documented by a fasting C-peptide level that is less than or equal to 110 percent of the lower limit of normal of the laboratory's measurement method. (Effective for Services Performed on or after January 1, 2002.)

Continued coverage of the insulin pump would require that the patient has been seen and evaluated the treating physician at least every 3 months.

The pump must be ordered by and follow-up care of the patient must be managed by a physician who manages multiple patients with CSII and who works closely with a team including nurses, diabetes educators, and dietitians who are knowledgeable in the use of CSII.

6. Other uses of external infusion pumps are covered if the contractor's medical staff verifies the appropriateness of the therapy and of the prescribed pump for the individual patient.

NOTE: Payment may also be made for drugs necessary for the effective use of an external infusion pump as long as the drug being used with the pump is itself reasonable and necessary for the patient's treatment.

B. Implantable Infusion Pumps. -

1. Chemotherapy for Liver Cancer (Effective for Services Performed On or After 9/26/84). – The implantable infusion pump is covered for intra-arterial infusion of 5-FUdR for the treatment of liver cancer for patients with primary hepatocellular carcinoma or Duke's Class D colorectal cancer, in whom the metastases are limited to the liver, and where (1) the disease is unresectable or (2) where the patient refuses surgical excision of the tumor.

2. Anti-Spasmodic Drugs for Severe Spasticity. – An implantable infusion pump is covered when used to administer anti-spasmodic drugs intrathecally (e.g., baclofen) to treat chronic intractable spasticity in patients who have proven unresponsive to less invasive medical therapy as determined by the following criteria:

- As indicated by at least a 6-week trial, the patient cannot be maintained on noninvasive methods of spasm control, such as oral anti-spasmodic drugs, either because these methods fail to control adequately the spasticity or produce intolerable side effects, and

- Prior to pump implantation, the patient must have responded favorably to a trial intrathecal dose of the anti-spasmodic drug.

3. Opioid Drugs for Treatment of Chronic Intractable Pain. – An implantable infusion pump is covered when used to administer opioid drugs (e.g., morphine) intrathecally or epidurally for treatment of severe chronic intractable pain of malignant or nonmalignant origin in patients who have a life expectancy of at least 3 months and who have proven unresponsive to less invasive medical therapy as determined by the following criteria:

- The patient's history must indicate that he/she would not respond adequately to non-invasive methods of pain control, such as systemic opioids (including attempts to eliminate physical and behavioral abnormalities which may cause an exaggerated reaction to pain); and

- A preliminary trial of intraspinal opioid drug administration must be undertaken with a temporary intrathecal/epidural catheter to substantiate adequately acceptable pain relief and degree of side effects (including effects on the activities of daily living) and patient acceptance.

4. Coverage of Other Uses of Implanted Infusion Pumps . – Determinations may be made on coverage of other uses of implanted infusion pumps if the contractor's medical staff verifies that:

- The drug is reasonable and necessary for the treatment of the individual patient;

- It is medically necessary that the drug be administered by an implanted infusion pump; and

- The FDA approved labelling for the pump must specify that the drug being administered and the purpose for which it is administered is an indicated use for the pump.

5. Implantation of Infusion Pump Is Contraindicated. – The implantation of an infusion pump is contraindicated in the following patients:

- Patients with a known allergy or hypersensitivity to the drug being used (e.g., oral baclofen, morphine, etc.);

- Patients who have an infection;

- Patients whose body size is insufficient to support the weight and bulk of the device; and

- Patients with other implanted programmable devices since crosstalk between devices may inadvertently change the prescription.

NOTE: Payment may also be made for drugs necessary for the effective use of an implantable infusion pump as long as the drug being used with the pump is itself reasonable and necessary for the patient's treatment.

THE FOLLOWING INDICATIONS FOR TREATMENT USING INFUSION PUMPS ARE NOT COVERED UNDER MEDICARE:

A. External Infusion Pumps. -

1. Vancomycin (Effective for Services Beginning On or After September 1, 1996). – Medicare coverage of vancomycin as a durable medical equipment infusion pump benefit is not covered. There is insufficient evidence to support the necessity of using an external infusion pump, instead of a disposable elastomeric pump or the gravity drip method, to administer vancomycin in a safe and appropriate manner.

B. Implantable Infusion Pump. -

1. Thromboembolic Disease (Effective for Services Performed On or After 9/26/84). – According to the Public Health Service, there is insufficient published clinical data to support the safety and effectiveness of the heparin implantable pump. Therefore, the use of an implantable infusion pump for infusion of heparin in the treatment of recurrent thromboembolic disease is not covered.

2. Diabetes – Implanted infusion pumps for the infusion of insulin to treat diabetes is not covered. The data do not demonstrate that the pump provides effective administration of insulin.

CIM 60-14b   Infusion Pumps

The Following Indications For Treatment Using Infusion Pumps Are Covered Under Medicare:

A. External Infusion Pumps. -

1. Iron Poisoning (Effective for Services Performed On or After 9/26/84). – When used in the administration of deferoxamine for the treatment of acute iron poisoning and iron overload, only external infusion pumps are covered.

2. Thromboembolic Disease (Effective for Services Performed On or After 9/26/84). – When used in the administration of heparin for the treatment of thromboembolic disease and/or pulmonary embolism, only external infusion pumps used in an institutional setting are covered.

3. Chemotherapy for Liver Cancer (Effective for Services Performed On or After 1/29/85). – The external chemotherapy infusion pump is covered when used in the treatment of primary hepatocellular carcinoma or colorectal cancer where this disease is unresectable or where the patient refuses surgical excision of the tumor.

4. Morphine for Intractable Cancer Pain (Effective for Services Performed On or After 4/22/85). – Morphine infusion via an external infusion pump is covered when used in the treatment of intractable pain caused by cancer (in either an inpatient or outpatient setting, including a hospice).

5. Continuous subcutaneous insulin infusion pumps (CSII) (Effective for Services Performed On or After 4/1/2000).

An external infusion pump and related drugs/supplies are covered as medically necessary in the home setting in the following situation: Treatment of diabetes

In order to be covered, patients must meet criterion A or B:

(A) The patient has completed a comprehensive diabetes education program, and has been on a program of multiple daily injections of insulin (i.e. at least 3 injections per day), with frequent self-adjustments of insulin dose for at least 6 months prior to initiation of the insulin pump, and has documented frequency of glucose self-testing an average of at least 4 times per day during the 2 months prior to initiation of the insulin pump, and meets one or more of the following criteria while on the multiple daily injection regimen:

(1) Glycosylated hemoglobin level (HbAlc) > 7.0 percent

(2) History of recurring hypoglycemia

(3) Wide fluctuations in blood glucose before mealtime

(4) Dawn phenomenon with fasting blood sugars frequently exceeding 200 mg/dl

(5) History of severe glycemic excursions

(B) The patient with diabetes has been on a pump prior to enrollment in Medicare and has documented frequency of glucose self-testing an average of at least 4 times per day during the month prior to Medicare enrollment.

Diabetes needs to be documented by a fasting C-peptide level that is less than or equal to 110 percent of the lower limit of normal of the laboratory's measurement method. (Effective for Services Performed on or after January 1, 2002.)

Continued coverage of the insulin pump would require that the patient has been seen and evaluated the treating physician at least every 3 months.

The pump must be ordered by and follow-up care of the patient must be managed by a physician who manages multiple patients with CSII and who works closely with a team including nurses, diabetes educators, and dietitians who are knowledgeable in the use of CSII.

6. Other uses of external infusion pumps are covered if the contractor's medical staff verifies the appropriateness of the therapy and of the prescribed pump for the individual patient.

NOTE: Payment may also be made for drugs necessary for the effective use of an external infusion pump as long as the drug being used with the pump is itself reasonable and necessary for the patient's treatment.

B. Implantable Infusion Pumps. -

1. Chemotherapy for Liver Cancer (Effective for Services Performed On or After 9/26/84). – The implantable infusion pump is covered for intra-arterial infusion of 5-FUdR for the treatment of liver cancer for patients with primary hepatocellular carcinoma or Duke's Class D colorectal cancer, in whom the metastases are limited to the liver, and where (1) the disease is unresectable or (2) where the patient refuses surgical excision of the tumor.

2. Anti-Spasmodic Drugs for Severe Spasticity. – An implantable infusion pump is covered when used to administer anti-spasmodic drugs intrathecally (e.g., baclofen) to treat chronic intractable spasticity in patients who have proven unresponsive to less invasive medical therapy as determined by the following criteria:

• As indicated by at least a 6-week trial, the patient cannot be maintained on noninvasive methods of spasm control, such as oral anti-spasmodic drugs, either because these methods fail to control adequately the spasticity or produce intolerable side effects, and

• Prior to pump implantation, the patient must have responded favorably to a trial intrathecal dose of the anti-spasmodic drug.

3. Opioid Drugs for Treatment of Chronic Intractable Pain. – An implantable infusion pump is covered when used to administer opioid drugs (e.g., morphine) intrathecally or epidurally for treatment of severe chronic intractable pain of malignant or nonmalignant origin in patients who have a life expectancy of at least 3 months and who have proven unresponsive to less invasive medical therapy as determined by the following criteria:

• The patient's history must indicate that he/she would not respond adequately to non-invasive methods of pain control, such as systemic opioids (including attempts to eliminate physical and behavioral abnormalities which may cause an exaggerated reaction to pain); and

• A preliminary trial of intraspinal opioid drug administration must be undertaken with a temporary intrathecal/epidural catheter to substantiate adequately acceptable pain relief and degree of side effects (including effects on the activities of daily living) and patient acceptance.

4. Coverage of Other Uses of Implanted Infusion Pumps . – Determinations may be made on coverage of other uses of implanted infusion pumps if the contractor's medical staff verifies that:

• The drug is reasonable and necessary for the treatment of the individual patient;

• It is medically necessary that the drug be administered by an implanted infusion pump; and

• The FDA approved labelling for the pump must specify that the drug being administered and the purpose for which it is administered is an indicated use for the pump.

5. Implantation of Infusion Pump Is Contraindicated. – The implantation of an infusion pump is contraindicated in the following patients:

• Patients with a known allergy or hypersensitivity to the drug being used (e.g., oral baclofen, morphine, etc.);

• Patients who have an infection;

• Patients whose body size is insufficient to support the weight and bulk of the device; and

• Patients with other implanted programmable devices since crosstalk between devices may inadvertently change the prescription.

NOTE: Payment may also be made for drugs necessary for the effective use of an implantable infusion pump as long as the drug being used with the pump is itself reasonable and necessary for the patient's treatment.

THE FOLLOWING INDICATIONS FOR TREATMENT USING INFUSION PUMPS ARE NOT COVERED UNDER MEDICARE:

A. External Infusion Pumps. -

1. Vancomycin (Effective for Services Beginning On or After September 1, 1996). – Medicare coverage of vancomycin as a durable medical equipment infusion pump benefit is not covered. There is insufficient evidence to support the necessity of using an external infusion pump, instead of a disposable elastomeric pump or the gravity drip method, to administer vancomycin in a safe and appropriate manner.

B. Implantable Infusion Pump. -

1. Thromboembolic Disease (Effective for Services Performed On or After 9/26/84). – According to the Public Health Service, there is insufficient published clinical data to support the safety and effectiveness of the heparin implantable pump. Therefore, the use of an implantable infusion pump for infusion of heparin in the treatment of recurrent thromboembolic disease is not covered.

2. Diabetes – Implanted infusion pumps for the infusion of insulin to treat diabetes is not covered. The data do not demonstrate that the pump provides effective administration of insulin.

CIM 60-15   Safety Roller (Effective for Claims Adjudicated On or After 6/3/85)

"Safety roller" is the generic name applied to devices for patients who cannot use standard wheeled walkers. They may be appropriate, and therefore covered, for some patients who are obese, have severe neurological disorders, or restricted use of one hand, which makes it impossible to use a wheeled walker that does not have the sophisticated braking system found on safety rollers.

In order to assure that payment is not made for a safety roller when a less expensive standard wheeled walker would satisfy the patient's medical needs, carriers refer safety roller claims to their medical consultants. The medical consultant determines whether some or all of the features provided in a safety roller are necessary, and therefore covered and reimbursable. If it is determined that the patient could use a standard wheeled walker, the charge for the safety roller is reduced to the charge of a standard wheeled walker.

Some obese patients who could use a standard wheeled walker if their weight did not exceed the walker's strength and stability limits can have it reinforced and its wheel base expanded. Such modifications are routine mechanical adjustments and justify a moderate surcharge. In these cases

SAFETY ROLLER (Effective for Claims Adjudicated On or After 6/3/85)

"Safety roller" is the generic name applied to devices for patients who cannot use standard wheeled walkers. They may be appropriate, and therefore covered, for some patients who are obese, have severe neurological disorders, or restricted use of one hand, which makes it impossible to use a wheeled walker that does not have the sophisticated braking system found on safety rollers.

In order to assure that payment is not made for a safety roller when a less expensive standard wheeled walker would satisfy the patient's medical needs, carriers refer safety roller claims to their medical consultants. The medical consultant determines whether some or all of the features provided in a safety roller are necessary, and therefore covered and reimbursable. If it is determined that the patient could use a standard wheeled walker, the charge for the safety roller is reduced to the charge of a standard wheeled walker.

Some obese patients who could use a standard wheeled walker if their weight did not exceed the walker's strength and stability limits can have it reinforced and its wheel base expanded. Such modifications are routine mechanical adjustments and justify a moderate surcharge. In these cases the carrier reduces the charge for the safety roller to the charge for the standard wheeled walker plus the surcharge for modifications.

In the case of patients with medical documentation showing severe neurological disorders or restricted use of one hand which makes it impossible for them to use a wheeled walker that does not have a sophisticated braking system, a reasonable charge for the safety roller may be determined without relating it to the reasonable charge for a standard wheeled walker. (Such reasonable charge should be developed in accordance with the instructions in Medicare Carriers Manual §§5010 and 5205.)

Cross Refer: Carriers Manual §§2100ff., §60-9.

CIM 60-16   Pneumatic Compression Devices

Pneumatic compression devices consist of an inflatable garment for the arm or leg and an electrical pneumatic pump that fills the garment with compressed air. The garment is intermittently inflated and deflated with cycle times and pressures that vary between devices. Pneumatic devices are covered for the treatment of lymphedema or for the treatment of chronic venous insufficiency with venous stasis ulcers.

Lymphedema

Lymphedema is the swelling of subcutaneous tissues due to the accumulation of excessive lymph fluid. The accumulation of lymph fluid results from impairment to the normal clearing function of the lymphatic system and/or from an excessive production of lymph. Lymphedema is divided into two broad classes according to etiology. Primary lymphedema is a relatively uncommon, chronic condition which may be due to such causes as Milroy's Disease or congenital anomalies. Secondary lymphedema, which is much more common, results from the destruction of or damage to formerly functioning lymphatic channels, such as surgical removal of lymph nodes or post radiation fibrosis, among other causes.

Pneumatic compression devices are covered in the home setting for the treatment of lymphedema if the patient has undergone a four-week trial of conservative therapy and the treating physician determines that there has been no significant improvement or if significant symptoms remain after the trial. The trial of conservative therapy must include use of an appropriate compression bandage system or compression garment, exercise, and elevation of the limb. The garment may be prefabricated or custom-fabricated but must provide adequate graduated compression.

Chronic Venous Insufficiency With Venous Stasis Ulcers

Chronic venous insufficiency (CVI) of the lower extremities is a condition caused by abnormalities of the venous wall and valves, leading to obstruction or reflux of blood flow in the veins. Signs of CVI include hyperpigmentation, stasis dermatitis, chronic edema, and venous ulcers.

Pneumatic compression devices are covered in the home setting for the treatment of CVI of the lower extremities only if the patient has one or more venous stasis ulcer(s) which have failed to heal after a 6 month trial of conservative therapy directed by the treating physician. The trial of conservative therapy must include a compression bandage system or compression garment, appropriate dressings for the wound, exercise, and elevation of the limb.

General Coverage Criteria

Pneumatic compression devices are covered only when prescribed by a physician and when they are used with appropriate physician oversight, i.e., physician evaluation of the patient's condition to determine medical necessity of the device, assuring suitable instruction in the operation of the machine, a treatment plan defining the pressure to be used and the frequency and duration of use, and ongoing monitoring of use and response to treatment.

The determination by the physician of the medical necessity of a pneumatic compression device must include (1) the patient's diagnosis and prognosis; (2) symptoms and objective findings, including measurements which establish the severity of the condition; (3) the reason the device is required, including the treatments which have been tried and failed; and (4) the clinical response to an initial treatment with the device. The clinical response includes the change in pre-treatment measurements, ability to tolerate the treatment session and parameters, and ability of the patient (or caregiver) to apply the device for continued use in the home.

The only time that a segmented, calibrated gradient pneumatic compression device (HCPCs code E0652) would be covered is when the individual has unique characteristics that prevent them from receiving satisfactory pneumatic compression treatment using a nonsegmented device in conjunction with a segmented appliance or a segmented compression device without manual control of pressure in each chamber.

Cross Refer: §60-9.

CIM 60-17   Continuous Positive Airway Pressure (CPAP)

CPAP is a non-invasive technique for providing single levels of air pressure from a flow generator, via a nose mask, through the nares. The purpose is to prevent the collapse of the oropharyngeal walls and the obstruction of airflow during sleep, which occurs in obstructive sleep apnea (OSA).

Effective for services furnished between and including January 12, 1987 and March 31, 2002:

The diagnosis of OSA requires documentation of at least 30 episodes of apnea, each lasting a minimum of 10 seconds, during 6-7 hours of recorded sleep. The use of CPAP is covered under Medicare when used in adult patients with moderate or severe OSA for whom surgery is a likely alternative to CPAP.

Initial claims must be supported by medical documentation (separate documentation where electronic billing is used), such as a prescription written by the patient's attending physician, that specifies:

  • a diagnosis of moderate or severe obstructive sleep apnea, and

  • surgery is a likely alternative.

The claim must also certify that the documentation supporting a diagnosis of OSA (described above) is available.

Effective for services furnished on or after April 1, 2002:

The use of CPAP devices are covered under Medicare when ordered and prescribed by the licensed treating physician to be used in adult patients with OSA if either of the following criteria using the Apnea-Hyopopnea Index (AHI) are met:

  • AHI = 15 events per hour, or

  • AHI = 5 and = 14 events per hour with documented symptoms of excessive daytime sleepiness, impaired cognition, mood disorders or insomnia, or documented hypertension, ischemic heart disease or history of stroke.

The AHI is equal to the average number of episodes of apnea and hyponea per hour and must be based on a mimimum of 2 hours of sleep recorded by polysomnography using actual recorded hours of sleep (i.e., the AHI may not be extrapolated or projected).

Apnea is defined as a cessation of airflow for at least 10 seconds. Hypopnea is defined as an abnormal respiratory event lasting at least 10 seconds with at least a 30% reduction in thoracoabdominal movement or airflow as compared to baseline, and with at least a 4% oxygen desaturation.

The polysomnography must be performed in a facility – based sleep study laboratory, and not in the home or in a mobile facility.

Initial claims for CPAP devices must be supported by information contained in the medical record indicating that the patient meets Medicare's stated coverage criteria.

Cross Refer: §60-9.

CIM 60-18   Hospital Beds

A. General Requirements for Coverage of Hospital Beds. – A physician's prescription, and such additional documentation as the contractors' medical staffs may consider necessary, including medical records and physicians' reports, must establish the medical necessity for a hospital bed due to one of the following reasons:

• The patient's condition requires positioning of the body; e.g., to alleviate pain, promote good body alignment, prevent contractures, avoid respiratory infections, in ways not feasible in an ordinary bed; or

• The patient's condition requires special attachments that cannot be fixed and used on an ordinary bed.

B. Physician's Prescription. – The physician's prescription, which must accompany the initial claim, and supplementing documentation when required, must establish that a hospital bed is medically necessary. If the stated reason for the need for a hospital bed is the patient's condition requires positioning, the prescription or other documentation must describe the medical condition, e.g., cardiac disease, chronic obstructive pulmonary disease, quadriplegia or paraplegia, and also the severity and frequency of the symptoms of the condition, that necessitates a hospital bed for positioning.

If the stated reason for requiring a hospital bed is the patient's condition requires special attachments, the prescription must describe the patient's condition and specify the attachments that require a hospital bed.

C. Variable Height Feature. – In well documented cases, the contractors' medical staffs may determine that a variable height feature of a hospital bed, approved for coverage under subsection A above, is medically necessary and, therefore, covered, for one of the following conditions:

• Severe arthritis and other injuries to lower extremities; e.g., fractured hip. The condition requires the variable height feature to assist the patient to ambulate by enabling the patient to place his or her feet on the floor while sitting on the edge of the bed;

• Severe cardiac conditions. For those cardiac patients who are able to leave bed, but who must avoid the strain of "jumping" up or down;

• Spinal cord injuries, including quadriplegic and paraplegic patients, multiple limb amputee and stroke patients. For those patients who are able to transfer from bed to a wheelchair, with or without help; or

• Other severely debilitating diseases and conditions, if the variable height feature is required to assist the patient to ambulate.

D. Electric Powered Hospital Bed Adjustments. – Electric powered adjustments to lower and raise head and foot may be covered when the contractor's medical staff determines that the patient's condition requires frequent change in body position and/or there may be an immediate need for a change in body position (i.e., no delay can be tolerated) and the patient can operate the controls and cause the adjustments. Exceptions may be made to this last requirement in cases of spinal cord injury and brain damaged patients.

E. Side Rails. – If the patient's condition requires bed side rails, they can be covered when an integral part of, or an accessory to, a hospital bed.

Cross refer: Carriers Manual, §5015.4

CIM 60-19   Air-Fluidized Bed (Effective for services rendered on or after: 07/30/90)

An air-fluidized bed uses warm air under pressure to set small ceramic beads in motion which simulate the movement of fluid. When the patient is placed in the bed, his body weight is evenly distributed over a large surface area which creates a sensation of "floating." Medicare payment for home use of the air-fluidized bed for treatment of pressure sores can be made if such use is reasonable and necessary for the individual patient.

A decision that use of an air-fluidized bed is reasonable and necessary requires that:

• The patient has a stage 3 (full thickness tissue loss) or stage 4 (deep tissue destruction) pressure sore;

• The patient is bedridden or chair bound as a result of severely limited mobility;

• In the absence of an air-fluidized bed, the patient would require institutionalization;

• The air-fluidized bed is ordered in writing by the patient's attending physician based upon a comprehensive assessment and evaluation of the patient after completion of a course of conservative treatment designed to optimize conditions that promote wound healing. This course of treatment must have been at least one month in duration without progression toward wound healing. This month of prerequisite conservative treatment may include some period in an institution as

long as there is documentation available to verify that the necessary conservative treatment has been rendered.

• Use of wet-to-dry dressings for wound debridement, begun during the period of conservative treatment and which continue beyond 30 days, will not preclude coverage of air-fluidized bed. Should additional debridement again become necessary, while a patient is using an air-fluidized bed (after the first 30-day course of conservative treatment) that will not cause the air-fluidized bed to become non-covered. In all instances documentation verifying the continued need for the bed must be available.

• Conservative treatment must include:

– Frequent repositioning of the patient with particular attention to relief of pressure over bony prominences (usually every 2 hours);

– Use of a specialized support surface (Group II) designed to reduce pressure and shear forces on healing ulcers and to prevent new ulcer formation;

– Necessary treatment to resolve any wound infection;

– Optimization of nutrition status to promote wound healing;

– Debridement by any means (including wet to dry dressings-which does not require an occlusive covering) to remove devitalized tissue from the wound bed;

– Maintenance of a clean, moist bed of granulation tissue with appropriate moist dressings protected by an occlusive covering, while the wound heals.

• A trained adult caregiver is available to assist the patient with activities of daily living, fluid balance, dry skin care, repositioning, recognition and management of altered mental status, dietary needs, prescribed treatments, and management and support of the air-fluidized bed system and its problems such as leakage;

• A physician directs the home treatment regimen, and reevaluates and recertifies the need for the air-fluidized bed on a monthly basis; and

• All other alternative equipment has been considered and ruled out.

Home use of the air-fluidized bed is not covered under any of the following circumstances:

• The patient has coexisting pulmonary disease (the lack of firm back support makes coughing ineffective and dry air inhalation thickens pulmonary secretions);

• The patient requires treatment with wet soaks or moist wound dressings that are not protected with an impervious covering such as plastic wrap or other occlusive material; an air-fluidized bed;

• The caregiver is unwilling or unable to provide the type of care required by the patient on an air-fluidized bed;

• Structural support is inadequate to support the weight of the air-fluidized bed system (it generally weighs 1600 pounds or more);

• Electrical system is insufficient for the anticipated increase in energy consumption; or

• Other known contraindications exist.

Coverage of an air-fluidized bed is limited to the equipment itself. Payment for this covered item may only be made if the written order from the attending physician is furnished to the supplier prior to the delivery of the equipment. Payment is not included for the caregiver or for architectural adjustments such as electrical or structural improvement.

Cross refer: Carriers Manual, §5102.2.

CIM 60-21   Intrapulmonary Percussive Ventilator (LPV) – Not Covered

IPV is a mechanized form of chest physical therapy. Instead of a therapist clapping or slapping the patient's chest wall, the IPV delivers mini-bursts (more than 200 per minute) of respiratory gasses to the lungs via a mouthpiece. Its intended purpose is to mobilize endobronchial secretions and diffuse patchy atelectasis. The patient controls variables such as inspiratory time, peak pressure and delivery rates.

Studies do not demonstrate any advantage of IPV over that achieved with good pulmonary care in the hospital environment and there are no studies in the home setting. There are no data to support the effectiveness of the device. Therefore, IPV in the home setting is not covered.

CIM 60-23   Speech Generating Devices

Effective January 1, 2001, augmentative and alternative communication devices or communicators, which are hereafter referred to as "speech generating devices" are now considered to fall within the DME benefit category established by §1861(n) of the Social Security Act. They may be covered if the contractor's medical staff determines that the patient suffers from a severe speech impairment and that the medical condition warrants the use of a device based on the following definitions.

Definition of Speech Generating Devices

Speech generating devices are defined as speech aids that provide an individual who has a severe speech impairment with the ability to meet his functional speaking needs. Speech generating are characterized by:

• Being a dedicated speech device, used solely by the individual who has a severe speech impairment;

• May have digitized speech output, using pre-recorded messages, less than or equal to 8 minutes recording time;

• May have digitized speech output, using pre-recorded messages, greater than 8 minutes recording time;

• May have synthesized speech output, which requires message formulation by spelling and device access by physical contact with the device-direct selection techniques;

• May have synthesized speech output, which permits multiple methods of message formulation and multiple methods of device access; or

• May be software that allows a laptop computer, desktop computer or personal digital assistant (PDA) to function as a speech generating device.

Devices that would not meet the definition of speech generating devices and therefore, do not fall within the scope of §1861(n) are characterized by:

• Devices that are not dedicated speech devices, but are devices that are capable of running software for purposes other than for speech generation, e.g., devices that can also run a word processing package, an accounting program, or perform other non-medical function.

• Laptop computers, desktop computers, or PDAs, which may be programmed to perform the same function as a speech generating device, are non-covered since they are not primarily medical in nature and do not meet the definition of DME. For this reason, they cannot be considered speech generating devices for Amedicare coverage purposes.

• A device that is useful to someone without severe speech impairment is not considered a speech generating device for Medicare coverage purposes.

CIM 60-3   White Cane For Use By A Blind Person – Not Covered
A white cane for use by a blind person is more an identifying and self-help device rather than an item which makes a meaningful contribution in the treatment of an illness or injury.

CIM 60-4   Home Use Of Oxygen
A. General. – Medicare coverage of home oxygen and oxygen equipment under the durable medical equipment (DME) benefit (see §1861(s)(6)of the Act) is considered reasonable and necessary only for patients with significant hypoxemia who meet the medical documentation, laboratory evidence, and health conditions specified in subsections B, C, and D. This section also includes special coverage criteria for portable oxygen systems. Finally, a statement on the absence of coverage of the professional services of a respiratory therapist under the DME benefit is included in subsection F.

B. Medical documentation. – Initial claims for oxygen services must include a completed Form HCFA-484 (Certificate of Medical Necessity: Oxygen) to establish whether coverage criteria are met and to ensure that the oxygen services provided are consistent with the physician's prescription or other medical documentation. The treating physician's prescription or other medical documentation must indicate that other forms of treatment (e.g., medical and physical therapy directed at secretions, bronchospasm and infection) have been tried, have not been sufficiently successful, and oxygen therapy is still required. While there is no substitute for oxygen therapy, each patient must receive optimum therapy before long-term home oxygen therapy is ordered. Use Form HCFA-484 for recertifications. (See Medicare Carriers Manual §3312 for completion of Form HCFA-484.)

The medical and prescription information in section B of Form HCFA-484 can be completed only by the treating physician, the physician's employee, or another clinician (e.g., nurse, respiratory therapist, etc.) as long as that person is not the DME supplier. Although hospital discharge coordinators and medical social workers may assist in arranging for physician-prescribed home oxygen, they do not have the authority to prescribe the services. Suppliers may not enter this information. While this section may be completed by nonphysician clinician or a physician employee, it must be reviewed and the form HCFA-484 signed by the attending physician.

A physician's certification of medical necessity for oxygen equipment must include the results of specific testing before coverage can be determined.

Claims for oxygen must also be supported by medical documentation in the patient's record. Separate documentation is used with electronic billing. (See Medicare Carriers Manual, Part 3,§4105.5.) This documentation may be in the form of a prescription written by the patient's attending physician who has recently examined the patient (normally within a month of the start of therapy) and must specify:

• A diagnosis of the disease requiring home use of oxygen;

The oxygen flow rate; and

Rev. 116/04-99

• An estimate of the frequency, duration of use (e.g., 2 liters per minute, 10 minutes per hour, 12 hours per day), and duration of need (e.g., 6 months or lifetime).

NOTE: A prescription for "Oxygen PRN" or "Oxygen as needed" does not meet this last requirement. Neither provides any basis for determining if the amount of oxygen is reasonable and necessary for the patient.

A member of the carrier's medical staff should review all claims with oxygen flow rates of more than 4 liters per minute before payment can be made.

The attending physician specifies the type of oxygen delivery system to be used (i.e., gas, liquid, or concentrator) by signing the completed form HCFA-484. In addition the supplier or physician may use the space in section C for written confirmation of additional details of the physician's order. The additional order information contained in section C may include the means of oxygen delivery (mask, nasal, cannula, etc.), the specifics of varying flow rates, and/or the noncontinuous use of oxygen as appropriate. The physician confirms this order information with their signature in section D.

New medical documentation written by the patient's attending physician must be submitted to the carrier in support of revised oxygen requirements when there has been a change in the patient's condition and need for oxygen therapy.

Carriers are required to conduct periodic, continuing medical necessity reviews on patients whose conditions warrant these reviews and on patients with indefinite or extended periods of necessity as described in Medicare Carriers Manual, Part 3, §4105.5. When indicated, carriers may also request documentation of the results of a repeat arterial blood gas or oximetry study.

NOTE: Section 4152 of OBRA 1990 requires earlier recertification and retesting of oxygen patients who begin coverage with an arterial blood gas result at or above a partial pressure of 55 or an arterial oxygen saturation percentage at or above 89. (See Medicare Carriers Manual §4105.5 for certification and retesting schedules.)

C. Laboratory Evidence. – Initial claims for oxygen therapy must also include the results of a blood gas study that has been ordered and evaluated by the attending physician. This is usually in the form of a measurement of the partial pressure of oxygen (PO2) in arterial blood. (See Medicare Carriers Manual, Part 3, §2070.1 for instructions on clinical laboratory tests.) A measurement of arterial oxygen saturation obtained by ear or pulse oximetry, however, is also acceptable when ordered and evaluated by the attending physician and performed under his or her supervision or when performed by a qualified provider or supplier of laboratory services. When the arterial blood gas and the oximetry studies are both used to document the need for home oxygen therapy and the results are conflicting, the arterial blood gas study is the preferred source of documenting medical need. A DME supplier is not considered a qualified provider or supplier of laboratory services for purposes of these guidelines. This prohibition does not extend to the results of blood gas test conducted by a hospital certified to do such tests. The conditions under which the laboratory tests are performed must be specified in writing and submitted with the initial claim, i.e., at rest, during exercise, or during sleep.

The preferred sources of laboratory evidence are existing physician and/or hospital records that reflect the patient's medical condition. Since it is expected that virtually all patients who qualify for home oxygen coverage for the first time under these guidelines have recently been discharged from a hospital where they submitted to arterial blood gas tests, the carrier needs to request that such test results be submitted in support of their initial claims for home oxygen. If more than one arterial blood gas test is performed during the patient's hospital stay, the test result obtained closest to, but no earlier than 2 days prior to the hospital discharge date is required as evidence of the need for home oxygen therapy.

Rev. 116/ 04-99

For those patients whose initial oxygen prescription did not originate during a hospital stay, blood gas studies should be done while the patient is in the chronic stable state, i.e., not during a period of an acute illness or an exacerbation of their underlying disease."

Carriers may accept a attending physician's statement of recent hospital test results for a particular patient, when appropriate, in lieu of copies of actual hospital records.

A repeat arterial blood gas study is appropriate when evidence indicates that an oxygen recipient has undergone a major change in their condition relevant to home use of oxygen. If the carrier has reason to believe that there has been a major change in the patient's physical condition, it may ask for documentation of the results of another blood gas or oximetry study.

D. Health Conditions. – Coverage is available for patients with significant hypoxemia in the chronic stable state if: (1) the attending physician has determined that the patient has a health condition outlined in subsection D.1, (2) the patient meets the blood gas evidence requirements specified in subsection D.3, and (3) the patient has appropriately tried other alternative treatment measures without complete success. (See subsection B.)

1. Conditions for Which Oxygen Therapy May Be Covered. -

• A severe lung disease, such as chronic obstructive pulmonary disease, diffuse interstitial lung disease, whether of known or unknown etiology; cystic fibrosis bronchiectasis; widespread pulmonary neoplasm; or

• Hypoxia-related symptoms or findings that might be expected to improve with oxygen therapy. Examples of these symptoms and findings are pulmonary hypertension, recurring congestive heart failure due to chronic cor pulmonale, erythrocytosis, impairment of the cognitive process, nocturnal restlessness, and morning headache.

2. Conditions for Which Oxygen Therapy Is Not Covered. -

• Angina pectoris in the absence of hypoxemia. This condition is generally not the result of a low oxygen level in the blood, and there are other preferred treatments;

• Breathlessness without cor pulmonale or evidence of hypoxemia. Although intermittent oxygen use is sometimes prescribed to relieve this condition, it is potentially harmful and psychologically addicting;

• Severe peripheral vascular disease resulting in clinically evident desaturation in one or more extremities. There is no evidence that increased PO2 improves the oxygenation of tissues with impaired circulation; or

• Terminal illnesses that do not affect the lungs.

Rev 116/04-99

3. Covered Blood Gas Values. – If the patient has a condition specified in subsection D.1, the carrier must review the medical documentation and laboratory evidence that has been submitted for a particular patient (see subsections B and C) and determine if coverage is available under one of the three group categories outlined below.

a. Group I. – Except as modified in subsection d, coverage is provided for patients with significant hypoxemia evidenced by any of the following:

(1) An arterial PO2 at or below 55 mm Hg, or an arterial oxygen saturation at or below 88 percent, taken at rest, breathing room air.

(2) An arterial PO2 at or below 55 mm Hg, or an arterial oxygen saturation at or below 88 percent, taken during sleep for a patient who demonstrates an arterial PO2 at or above 56 mm Hg, or an arterial oxygen saturation at or above 89 percent, while awake; or a greater than normal fall in oxygen level during sleep (a decrease in arterial PO2 more than 10 mm Hg, or decrease in arterial oxygen saturation more than 5 percent) associated with symptoms or signs reasonably attributable to hypoxemia (e.g., impairment of cognitive processes and nocturnal restlessness or insomnia). In either of these cases, coverage is provided only for use of oxygen during sleep, and then only one type of unit will be covered. Portable oxygen, therefore, would not be covered in this situation.

(3) An arterial PO2 at or below 55 mm Hg or an arterial oxygen saturation at or below 88 percent, taken during exercise for a patient who demonstrates an arterial PO2 at or above 56 mm Hg, or an arterial oxygen saturation at or above 89 percent, during the day while at rest. In this case, supplemental oxygen is provided for during exercise if there is evidence the use of oxygen improves the hypoxemia that was demonstrated during exercise when the patient was breathing room air.

b. Group II. – Except as modified in subsection d, coverage is available for patients whose arterial PO2 is 56-59 mm Hg or whose arterial blood oxygen saturation is 89 percent, if there is evidence of:

(1) Dependent edema suggesting congestive heart failure;

(2) Pulmonary hypertension or cor pulmonale, determined by measurement of pulmonary artery pressure, gated blood pool scan, echocardiogram, or "P" pulmonale on EKG (P wave greater than 3 mm in standard leads II, III, or AVFL; or

(3) Erythrocythemia with a hematocrit greater than 56 percent.

c. Group III. – Except as modified in subsection d, carriers must apply a rebuttable presumption that a home program of oxygen use is not medically necessary for patients with arterial PO2 levels at or above 60 mm Hg, or arterial blood oxygen saturation at or above 90 percent. In order for claims in this category to be reimbursed, the carrier's reviewing physician needs to review any documentation submitted in rebuttal of this presumption and grant specific approval of the claims. HCFA expects few claims to be approved for coverage in this category.

d. Variable Factors That May Affect Blood Gas Values. – In reviewing the arterial PO2 levels and the arterial oxygen saturation percentages specified in subsections D. 3. a, b and c, the carrier's medical staff must take into account variations in oxygen measurements that may result from such factors as the patient's age, the altitude level, or the patient's decreased oxygen carrying capacity.

Rev 116/04-99

E. Portable Oxygen Systems. – A patient meeting the requirements specified below may qualify for coverage of a portable oxygen system either (1) by itself or (2) to use in addition to a stationary oxygen system. A portable oxygen system is covered for a particular patient if:

• The claim meets the requirements specified in subsections A-D, as appropriate; and

• The medical documentation indicates that the patient is mobile in the home and would benefit from the use of a portable oxygen system in the home. Portable oxygen systems are not covered for patients who qualify for oxygen solely based on blood gas studies obtained during sleep.

F. Respiratory Therapists. – Respiratory therapists' services are not covered under the provisions for coverage of oxygen services under the Part B durable medical equipment benefit as outlined above. This benefit provides for coveravge of home use of oxygen and oxygen equipment, but does not include a professional component in the delivery of such services.

(See §60-9; Intermediary Manual, Part 3, §3113ff; and Medicare Carriers Manual, Part 3, §2100ff.)

CIM 60-5   Power-Operated Vehicles That May Be Used As Wheelchairs

Power-operated vehicles that may be appropriately used as wheelchairs are covered under the durable medical equipment provision.

These vehicles have been appropriately used in the home setting for vocational rehabilitation and to improve the ability of chronically disabled persons to cope with normal domestic, vocational and social activities. They may be covered if a wheelchair is medically necessary and the patient is unable to operate a wheelchair manually.

A specialist in physical medicine, orthopedic surgery, neurology, or rheumatology must provide an evaluation of the patient's medical and physical condition and a prescription for the vehicle to assure that the patient requires the vehicle and is capable of using it safely. When an intermediary determines that such a specialist is not reasonably accessible, e.g., more than 1 day's round trip from the beneficiary's home, or the patient's condition precludes such travel, a prescription from the beneficiary's physician is acceptable.

The intermediary's medical staff reviews all claims for a power-operated vehicle, including the specialists' or other physicians' prescriptions and evaluations of the patient's medical and physical conditions, to insure that all coverage requirements are met. (See §60-9 and Intermediary Manual, Part 3, §3629.)

CIM 60-6   Specially Sized Wheelchairs

Payment may be made for a specially sized wheelchair even though it is more expensive than a standard wheelchair. For example, a narrow wheelchair may be required because of the narrow doorways of a patient's home or because of a patient's slender build. Such difference in the size of the wheelchair from the standard model is not considered a deluxe feature.

A physician's certification or prescription that a special size is needed is not required where you can determine from the information in file or other sources that a specially sized wheelchair (rather than a standard one) is needed to accommodate the wheelchair to the place of use or the physical size of the patient.

To determine the reasonable charge in these cases, use the criteria set out in Carriers Manual, §§5022, 5022.1, 5200, and 5205, as necessary.

Cross-refer: Intermediary Manual, §§3113.2C, 3642.1, 3643 (item 3); Carriers Manual, §§2100.2c, 2105, 4105.2, 5107; Hospital Manual, §§235.2c, 420.1 (item 13).

APPENDIX 4 — MEDICARE REFERENCES

CIM 60-7   Cardiac Pacemaker Evaluation Services

Medicare covers a variety of services for the post-implant follow-up and evaluation of implanted cardiac pacemakers (limited to lithium battery-powered pacemakers). There are two general types of pacemakers in current use:

1. Single-chamber pacemakers sense and pace the ventricles of the heart

2. Dual-chamber pacemakers sense and pace both the atria and the ventricles

These differences require different monitoring patterns over the expected life of the units involved, which is the patient's physician responsibility. A physician's prescription is required when the monitoring is done by some entity. Where a patient is monitored both clinically and transtelephonically include frequency data on both types of monitoring.

In order for transtelephonic monitoring services to be covered, the services must consist of the following elements:

• A minimum 30-second readable strip of the pacemaker in the free-running mode

• Unless contraindicated, a minimum 30-second readable strip of the pacemaker in the magnetic mode

• A minimum 30 seconds of readable ECG strip

The following guidelines are designed to assist in claims (apply 1980 guidelines to claims for the obsolete mercury-zinc battery-powered pacemakers). The guidelines are divided into categories:

1. Guideline I applies to the majority of pacemakers in use

2. Guideline II applies only to pacemaker systems (pacemaker and leads) that meet the standards of the Inter-Society Commission for Heart Disease Resources (ICHD) for longevity and end-of-life decay

Guideline I: Single-chamber pacemaker

First month – every two weeks

Second month through 36th month – every eight weeks

37th month to failure – every four weeks

Guideline I: Dual-chamber pacemaker

First month – every two weeks

Second month through 36th month – every four weeks

37th month to failure – every four weeks

Guideline II: Single-chamber pacemaker

First month – every two weeks

Second month through 48th month – every 12 weeks

49th through 72nd month – every eight weeks

Thereafter – every four weeks

Guideline II: Dual-chamber pacemaker

First month – every two weeks

Second month through 30th month – every 12 weeks.

31st month through 48th month every eight weeks

Thereafter – every 4 weeks.

Pacemaker monitoring is also covered when done by pacemaker clinics. Clinic visits may be done in conjunction with transtelephonic monitoring; however, the services rendered by a pacemaker clinic are more extensive than those currently possible by telephone. They include, for example, physical examination of patients and reprogramming of pacemakers.

Frequency of clinic visits is the decision of the patient's physician, taking into account, among other things, the medical condition of the patient. The following are recommendations for monitoring guidelines on lithium-battery pacemakers:

• Single-chamber pacemakers – twice in the first six months following implant, then once every 12 months

• Dual-chamber pacemakers – twice in the first six months, then once every six months

CIM 60-8   Seat Lift

Reimbursement may be made for the rental or purchase of a medically necessary seat lift when prescribed by a physician for a patient with severe arthritis of the hip or knee and patients with muscular dystrophy or other neuromuscular diseases when it has been determined the patient can benefit therapeutically from use of the device. In establishing medical necessity for the seat lift, the evidence must show that the item is included in the physician's course of treatment, that it is likely to effect improvement, or arrest or retard deterioration in the patient's condition, and that the severity of the condition is such that the alternative would be chair or bed confinement.

Coverage of seat lifts is limited to those types which operate smoothly, can be controlled by the patient, and effectively assist a patient in standing up and sitting down without other assistance. Excluded from coverage is the type of lift which operates by a spring release mechanism with a sudden, catapult-like motion and jolts the patient from a seated to a standing position. Limit the payment for units which incorporate a recliner feature along with the seat lift to the amount payable for a seat lift without this feature. Cross Refer: Carriers Manual, § 5107

CIM 60-9   Durable Medical Equipment Reference List.

The durable medical equipment (DME) list which follows is designed to facilitate your processing of DME claims. This section is designed to be used as a quick reference tool for determining the coverage status of certain pieces of DME and especially for those items which are commonly referred to by both brand and generic names. The information contained herein is applicable (where appropriate) to all DME coverage determinations discussed in the DME portion of this manual. The list is organized into two columns. The first column lists alphabetically various generic categories of equipment on which national coverage decisions have been made by HCFA; and the second column notes the coverage status of each equipment category.

In the case of equipment categories that have been determined by HCFA to be covered under the DME benefit, the list outlines the conditions of coverage that must be met if payment is to be allowed for the rental or purchase of the DME by a particular patient, or cross-refers to another section of the manual where the applicable coverage criteria are described in more detail. With respect to equipment categories that cannot be covered as DME, the list includes a brief explanation of why the equipment is not covered. This DME list will be updated periodically to reflect any additional national coverage decisions that HCFA may make with regard to other categories of equipment.

When you receive a claim for an item of equipment which does not appear to fall logically into any of the generic categories listed, you have the authority and responsibility for deciding whether those items are covered under the DME benefit. These decisions must be made by each contractor based on the advice of its medical consultants, taking into account:

• The general DME coverage instructions in the Carriers Manual, §2100ff and Intermediary Manual, §3113ff (see below for brief summary);

• Whether the item has been approved for marketing by the Food and Drug Administration (FDA) (see Carriers Manual, §2303.1 and Intermediary Manual, §3151.1) and is otherwise generally considered to be safe and effective for the purpose intended; and

• Whether the item is reasonable and necessary for the individual patient.

As provided in the Carriers Manual, § 2100.1, and Intermediary Manual, §3113.1, the term DME is defined as equipment which can withstand repeated use; i.e., could normally be rented, and used by successive patients;

• Is primarily and customarily used to serve a medical purpose;

• Generally is not useful to a person in the absence of illness or injury; and

• Is appropriate for use in a patient's home.

Durable Medical Equipment Reference List:

Item	Coverage Status
Air Cleaners	deny – environmental control equipment; not primarily medical in nature (§l86l(n) of the Act)
Air Conditioners	deny – environmental control equipment; not primarily medical in nature (§l861(n) of the Act)
Air-Fluidized Bed	(See §60-19.)
Alternating Pressure Pads, and Matresses and Lambs Wool Pads	covered if patient has, or is highly susceptible to, decubitus ulcers and patient's physician has specified that he will be supervising its use in connection with his course of treatment.
Audible/Visible Signal Pacemaker Monitor	(See Self-Contained Pacemaker Monitor.)
Augmentative Communication Device	(See Speech Generating Devices, §60-23.)
Bathtub Lifts	deny – convenience item; not primarily medical in nature (§l861(n) of the Act)
Bathtub Seats	deny – comfort or convenience item; hygienic equipment; not primarily medical in nature (§l861(n) of the Act)
Bead Bed	(See §60-19.)

Bed Baths (home type)	deny – hygienic equipment; not primarily medical in nature (§1861(n) of the Act)
Bed Lifter (bed elevator)	deny – not primarily medical in nature (§1861(n) of the Act.
Bedboards	deny – not primarily medical in nature (§1861(n) of the Act)
Bed Pans (autoclavable hospital type)	covered if patient is bed confined
Bed Side Rails	(See Hospital Beds, §60-I8.)
Beds-Lounge (power or manual)	deny – not a hospital bed; comfort or convenience item; not primarily medical in nature (§186l(n) of the Act)
Beds – Oscillating	deny – institutional equipment; inappropriate for home use
Bidet Toilet Seat	(See Toilet Seats.)
Blood Glucose Analyzer Reflectance Colorimeter	deny – unsuitable for home use (See §60-11.)
Blood Glucose Monitor	covered if patient meets certain conditions (See §60-11.)
Braille Teaching Texts	deny – educational equipment; not primarily medical in nature (§1861(n) of the Act)
Canes	covered if patient's condition impairs ambulation (See §60-3.)
Carafes	deny – convenience item; not primarily medical in nature (§186l(n) of the Act)
Catheters	deny – nonreusable disposable supply (§1861(n) of the Act)
Commodes	covered if patient is confined to bed or room NOTE: The term "room confined" means that the patient's condition is such that leaving the room is medically contraindicated. The accessibility of bathroom facilities generally would not be a factor in this determination. However, confinement of a patient to his home in a case where there are no toilet facilities in the home may be equated to room confinement. Moreover, payment may also be made if a patient's medical condition confines him to a floor of his home and there is no bathroom located on that floor (See hospital beds in §60-18 for definition of "bed confinement".)
Communicator	(See §60-23, Speech Generating Devices)
Continuous Passive Motion	Continuous passive motion devices are devices covered for patients who have received a total knee replacement. To qualify for coverage, use of the device must commence within 2 days following surgery. In addition, coverage is limited to that portion of the three week period following surgery during which the device is used in the patient's home. There is insufficient evidence to justify coverage of these devices for longer periods of time or for other applications.
Continuous Positive Airway Pressure (CPAP)	(See §60-17.)
Crutches	covered if patient's condition impairs Ambulation
Cushion Lift Power Seat	(See Seat Lifts.)
Dehumidifiers (room or central heating system type)	deny – environmental control equipment; not primarily medical in nature (§1861(n) of the Act
Diathermy Machines (standard pulses wave types)	deny – inappropriate for home use (See and §35-41.)
Digital Electronic Pacemaker Monitor	(See Self-Contained Pacemaker Monitor.)
Disposable Sheets and Bags	deny – nonreusable disposable supplies (§1861(n) of the Act)
Elastic Stockings	deny – nonreusable supply; not rental-type items (§l861(n) of the Act)
Electric Air Cleaners	deny – (See Air Cleaners.) (§1861(n) of the Act)
Electric Hospital Beds	(See Hospital Beds §60-18.)
Electrostatic Machines	deny – (See Air Cleaners and Air Conditioners.) (§1861(n) of the Act)
Elevators	deny – convenience item; not primarily medical in nature (§1861(n) of the Act)
Emesis Basins	deny – convenience item; not primarily medical in nature (§1861(n) of the Act)
Esophageal Dilator	deny – physician instrument; inappropriate for patient use
Exercise Equipment	deny – not primarily medical in nature (§1861(n) of the Act)
Fabric Supports	deny – nonreusable supplies; not rental-type it (§1861(n) of the Act)
Face Masks (oxygen)	covered if oxygen is covered (See § 60-4.)
Face Masks (surgical)	deny – nonreusable disposable items (§1861(n) of the Act)
Flowmeter	(See Medical Oxygen Regulators)
Fluidic Breathing Assister	(See IPPB Machines.)
Fomentation Device	(See Heating Pads.)
Gel Flotation Pads and Mattresses	(See Alternating Pressure Pads and Mattresses.)
Grab Bars	deny – self-help device; not primarily medical in nature (§1861(n) of the Act)
Heat and Massage Foam Cushion Pad	deny – not primarily medical in nature; personal comfort item (§§ 1861(n) and 1862(a)(6) of the Act)
Heating and Cooling Plants	deny – environmental control equipment; not primarily medical in nature(§1861(n) of the Act)
Heating Pads	covered if the contractor's medical staff determines patient's medical condition is one for which the application of heat in the form of a heating pad is therapeutically effective.
Heat Lamps	covered if the contractor's medical staff determines patient's medical condition is one for which the application of heat in the form of a heat lamp is therapeutically effective.
Hospital Beds	(See § 60-18.)
Hot Packs	(See Heating Pads.)
Humidifiers (oxygen)	(See Oxygen Humidifiers.)
Humidifiers (room or central heating system types)	deny – environmental control equipment; not medical in nature (§1861(n) of the Act)
Hydraulic Lift	(See Patient Lifts.)
Incontinent Pads	deny – nonreusable supply; hygienic item (§ l861(n) of the Act.)
Infusion Pumps	For external and implantable pumps, see §60-14. If the pump is used with an enteral or parenteral ralnutritional therapy system, see §§65-10 – 65.10.2 0.2 for special coverage rules.
Injectors (hypodermic jet devices for injection of insulin	deny – noncovered self-administered drug supply, § 1861(s)(2)(A) of the Act)
IPPB Machines	covered if patient's ability to breathe is severely impaired
Iron Lungs	(See Ventilators.)
Irrigating Kit	deny – nonreusable supply; hygienic equipment (§1861(n) of the Act)
Lambs Wool Pads	covered under same conditions as alternating pressure pads and mattresses
Leotards	deny – (See Pressure Leotards.) (§1861(n)of the Act)
Lymphedema Pumps	covered (See §60-16.)(segmental and non-segmental therapy types)

Massage Devices	deny – personal comfort items; not primarily medical in nature (§§I861(n) and I862(a)(6) of the Act)
Mattress	covered only where hospital bed is medically necessary (Separate Charge for replacement mattresss should not be allowed where hospital bed with mattress is rented.) (See §60-18.)
Medical Oxygen Regulators	covered if patient's ability to breathe is severely impaired (See §60-4.)
Mobile Geriatric Chair	(See Rolling Chairs.)
Motorized Wheelchairs	(See Wheelchairs (power operated).)
Muscle Stimulators	Covered for certain conditions (See §35-77.)
Nebulizers	covered if patient's ability to breathe is severely impaired
Oscillating Beds	deny – institutional equipment – inappropriate for home use
Overbed Tables	deny – convenience item; not primarily medical in nature (§I861(n) of the Act)
Oxygen	covered if the oxygen has been prescribed for use in connection with medically necessary durable medical equipment (See §60-4.)
Oxygen Humidifiers	covered if a medical humidifier has been prescribed for use in connection with medically necessary durable medical equipment for purposes of moisturizing oxygen (See §60-4.)
Oxygen Regulators (Medical)	(See Medical Oxygen Regulators.)
Oxygen Tents	(See § 60-4.)
Paraffin Bath Units (Portable)	(See Portable Paraffin Bath Units.)
Paraffin Bath Units (Standard)	deny – institutional equipment; inappropriate for home use
Parallel Bars	deny – support exercise equipment; primarily for institutional use; in the home setting other devices (e.g., a walker) satisfy the patient's need
Patient Lifts	covered if contractor's medical staff determines patient's condition is such that periodic movement is necessary to effect improvement or to arrest or retard deterioration in his condition.
Percussors	covered for mobilizing respiratory tract secretions in patients with chronic obstructive lung disease, chronic bronchitis, or emphysema, when patient or operator of powered percussor has received appropriate training by a physician or therapist, and no one competent to administer manual therapy is available.
Portable Oxygen Systems:	1. Regulated (adjustable – covered under conditions specified in flow rate)§60-4. Refer all claims to medical staff for this determination. 2. Preset (flow rate – deny – emergency, first-aid, or not adjustable) precautionary equipment; essentially not therapeutic in nature
Portable Paraffin Bath Units	covered when the patient has undergone a successful trial period of paraffin therapy ordered by a physician and the patient's condition is expected to be relieved by long term use of this modality.
Portable Room Heaters	deny – environmental control equipment; not primarily medical in nature (§I861(n) of the Act)
Portable Whirlpool Pumps	deny – not primarily medical in nature; personal comfort items (§§I861(n) and I862(a)(6) of the Act)
Postural Drainage Boards	covered if patient has a chronic pulmonary condition
Preset Portable Oxygen Units	deny – emergency, first-aid, or precautionary equipment; essentially not therapeutic in nature
Pressure Leotards	deny – nonreusable supply, not rental-type item (§I861(n) of the Act)
Pulse Tachometer	deny – not reasonable or necessary for monitoring pulse of homebound patient with or without a cardiac pacemaker
Quad-Canes	(See Walkers.)
Raised Toilet Seats	deny – convenience item; hygienic equipment; not primarily medical in nature (§I861(n) of the Act)
Reflectance Colorimeters	(See Blood Glucose Analyzers.)
Respirators	(See Ventilators.)
Rolling Chairs	covered if the contractor's medical staff determines that the patient's condition is such that there is a medical need for this item and it has been prescribed by the patient's physician in lieu of a wheelchair. Coverage is limited to those rollabout chairs having casters of at least 5 inches in diameter and specifically designed to meet the needs of ill, injured, or otherwise impaired individuals. Coverage is denied for the wide range of chairs with smaller casters as are found in general use in homes, offices, and institutions for many purposes not related to the care or treatment of ill or injured persons. This type is not primarily medical in nature. (§I861(n) of the Act)
Safety Roller	(See §60-15.)
Sauna Baths	deny – not primarily medical in nature; personal comfort items (§§I861(n) and I862(a)(6) of the Act)
Seat Lift	covered under the conditions specified in §60-8. Refer all to medical staff for this determination.
Self-Contained Pacemaker Monitor	covered when prescribed by a physician for a patient with a cardiac pacemaker (See §§50-1C and 60-7.)
Sitz Bath	covered if the contractor's medical staff determines patient has an infection or injury of the perineal area and the item has been prescribed by the patient's physician as a part of his planned regimen of treatment in the patient's home.
Spare Tanks of Oxygen	deny – convenience or precautionary supply
Speech Teaching Machine	deny – education equipment; not primarily medical in nature (§I861(n) of the Act)
Stairway Elevators	deny – (See Elevators.) (§I861(n) of the Act)
Standing Table	deny – convenience item; not primarily medical in nature (§I861(n) of the Act)
Steam Packs	these packs are covered under the same condition as a heating pad (See Heating Pads.)
Suction Machine	covered if the contractor's medical staff determines that the machine specified in the claim is medically required and appropriate for home use without technical or professional supervision.
Support Hose	deny (See Fabric Supports.) (§I861(n) of the Act)
Surgical Leggings	deny – nonreusable supply; not rental-type item (§I861(n) of the Act)
Telephone Alert Systems	deny – these are emergency communications systems and do not serve a diagnostic or therapeutic purpose
Telephone Arms	deny – convenience item; not medical in nature (§I861(n) of the Act)
Toilet Seats	deny – not medical equipment (§I861(n) of the Act)
Traction Equipment	covered if patient has orthopedic impairment requiring traction equipment which prevents ambulation during the period of use (Consider covering devices usable during ambulation; e.g., cervical traction collar, under the brace provision)

Trapeze Bars	covered if patient is bed confined and the patient needs a trapeze bar to sit up because of respiratory condition, to change body position for other medical reasons, or to get in and out of bed.
Treadmill Exerciser	deny – exercise equipment;not primarily medical in nature(§l861(n) of the Act)
Ultraviolet Cabinet	covered for selected patients with generalized intractable psoriasis. Using appropriate consultation, the contractor should determine whether medical and other factors justify treatment at home rather than at alternative sites, e.g., outpatient department of a hospital.
Urinals (autoclavable hospital type)	covered if patient is bed confined
Vaporizers	covered if patient has a respiratory illness
Ventilators	covered for treatment of neuromuscular diseases, thoracic restrictive diseases, and chronic respiratory failure consequent to chronic obstructive pulmonary disease. Includes both positive and negative pressure types.
Walkers	covered if patient's condition impairs ambulation (See also §60-15.)
Water and Pressure Pads and Mattresses	(See Alternating Pressure Pads and Mattresses.)
Wheelchairs	covered if patient's condition is such that without the use of a wheelchair he would otherwise be bed or chair confined. An individual may qualify for a wheelchair and still be considered bed confined.
Wheelchairs (power operated) and wheelchairs with other special features	covered if patient's condition is such and that a wheelchair is medically necessary and the patient is unable to operate the wheelchair manually. Any claim involving a power wheelchair or a wheelchair with other special features should be referred for medical consultation since payment for the special features is limited to those which are medically required because of the patient's condition. (See §60-5 for power operated and §60-6 for specially sized wheelchairs.) NOTE: A power-operated vehicle that may appropriately be used as a wheelchair can be covered. (See §60-5 for coverage details.)
Whirlpool Bath Equipment	covered if patient is homebound and has a (standard) condition for which the whirlpool bath can be expected to provide substantial therapeutic benefit justifying its cost. Where patient is not homebound but has such a condition, payment is restricted to the cost of providing the services elsewhere; e.g., an outpatient department of a participating hospital, if that alternative is less costly. In all cases, refer claim to medical staff for a determination.
Whirlpool Pumps	deny – (See Portable Whirlpool Pumps.) (§l861(n) of the Act)
White Cane	deny – (See §60-3.)

CIM 65-1   Hydrophilic Contact Lens For Corneal Bandage
Medicare covers a hydrophilic contact lens approved by the Food and Drug Administration (FDA) and used as a supply incident to a physician's service.

CIM 65-10   Enteral And Parenteral Nutritional Therapy Covered As Prosthetic Device (Effective for items and services furnished on or after 07-11-84.)
There are patients who, because of chronic illness or trauma, cannot be sustained through oral feeding. These people must rely on either enteral or parenteral nutritional therapy, depending upon the particular nature of their medical condition.

Coverage of nutritional therapy as a Part B benefit is provided under the prosthetic device benefit provision, which requires that the patient must have a permanently inoperative internal body organ or function thereof. (See Intermediary Manual, §3110.4.) Therefore, enteral and parenteral nutritional therapy are not covered under Part B in situations involving temporary impairments. Coverage of such therapy, however, does not require a medical judgment that the impairment giving rise to the therapy will persist throughout the patient's remaining years. If the medical record, including the judgment of the attending physician, indicates that the impairment will be of long and indefinite duration, the test of permanence is considered met.

If the coverage requirements for enteral or parenteral nutritional therapy are met under the prosthetic device benefit provision, related supplies, equipment and nutrients are also covered under the conditions in the following paragraphs and the Intermediary Manual, §3110.4.

CIM 65-14   Cochlear Implantation
Medicare coverage is provided only for those patients who meet all of the following guidelines:

- Diagnosis of bilateral severe-to-profound sensorineural hearing impairment with limited benefit from appropriate hearing (or vibrotactile) aids
- Cognitive ability to use auditory clues and a willingness to undergo an extended program of rehabilitation
- Freedom from middle ear infection, an accessible cochlear lumen that is structurally suited to implantation, and freedom from lesions in the auditory nerve and acoustic areas of the central nervous system
- No contraindications to surgery
- The device must be used in accordance withe the FDA-approved labeling

Cochlear implants may be covered for adults (over age 18) for prelinguistically, perilinguistically, and postlinguistically deafened adults. Postlinguistically deafened adults must demonstrate test scores of 30 percent or less on sentence recognition scores from tape-recorded tests in the patient's best listening condition.

Cochlear implants may be covered for prelinguistically and postlinguistically

deafened children aged 2 through 17. Bilateral profound sensorineural deafness must be demonstrated by the inability to improve on age appropriate closed-set word identification tasks with amplification.

CIM 65-16   Tracheostomy Speaking Valve
A trachea tube has been determined to satisfy the definition of a prosthetic device, and the tracheostomy speaking valve is an add on to the trachea tube which may be considered a medically necessary accessory that enhances the function of the tube. In other words, it makes the system a better prosthesis. As such, a tracheostomy speaking valve is covered as an element of the trachea tube which makes the tube more effective.

CIM 65-3   Scleral Shell
Scleral shell (or shield) is a catchall term for different types of hard scleral contact lenses.

A scleral shell fits over the entire exposed surface of the eye as opposed to a corneal contact lens which covers only the central non-white area encompassing the pupil and iris. Where an eye has been rendered sightless and shrunken by inflammatory disease, a scleral shell may, among other things, obviate the need for surgical enucleation and prosthetic implant and act to support the surrounding orbital tissue.

In such a case, the device serves essentially as an artificial eye. In this situation, payment may be made for a scleral shell under §1861(s)(8) of the law.

Scleral shells are occasionally used in combination with artificial tears in the treatment of "dry eye" of diverse etiology. Tears ordinarily dry at a rapid rate, and are continually replaced by the lacrimal gland. When the lacrimal gland fails, the half-life of artificial tears may be greatly prolonged by the use of the scleral contact lens as a protective barrier against the drying action of the atmosphere. Thus, the difficult and sometimes hazardous process of frequent installation of artificial tears may be avoided. The lens acts in this instance to substitute, in part, for the functioning of the diseased lacrimal gland and would be covered as a prosthetic device in the rare case when it is used in the treatment of "dry eye."

Cross-refer: HCFA-Pub. 13-3, §§3110.4, 3110.5; HCFA-Pub. 14-3, §§2130, 2133; HCFA- Pub. 10, §§210.4, 211

CIM 65-5   Electronic Speech Aids
Electronic speech aids are covered under Part B as prosthetic devices when the patient has had a laryngectomy or his larynx is permanently inoperative. There are two types of speech aids. One operates by placing a vibrating head against the throat; the other amplifies sound waves through a tube which is inserted into the user's mouth. A patient who has had radical neck surgery and/or extensive radiation to the anterior part of the neck would generally be able to use only the "oral tube" model or one of the more sensitive and more expensive "throat contact" devices.

Cross-refer: HCFA-Pub. 13-3, §3110.4; HCFA-Pub. 14-3, §2130; HCFA-Pub. 10, §228.4

CIM 65-8   Treatment of Motor Function Disorders with Electric Nerve Stimulation – Not Covered

No reimbursement may be made for electric nerve stimulation or for the services related to its implantation since this treatment cannot be considered reasonable and necessary. However, Medicare covers deep brain stimulation by implanting a stimulator device at the carrier's discretion.

CIM 65-9   Incontinence Control Devices

Prior to collagen implant therapy, a skin test for collagen sensitivity must be administered and evaluated over a four week period. In male patients, the evaluation must include a complete history and physical examination and a simple cystometrogram to determine that the bladder fills and stores properly. The patient then is asked to stand upright with a full bladder and to cough or otherwise exert abdominal pressure on his bladder. If the patient leaks, the diagnosis of ISD is established. In female patients, the evaluation must include a complete history and physical examination (including a pelvic exam) and a simple cystometrogram to rule out abnormalities of bladder compliance and abnormalities of urethral support. Following that determination, an abdominal leak point pressure (ALLP) test is performed. If the patient has an ALLP of less than 100 cm H2O, the diagnosis of ISD is established.

To use a collagen implant, physicians must have urology training in the use of a cystoscope and must complete a collagen implant training program. Coverage of a collagen implant, and the procedure to inject it, is limited to the following types of patients with stress urinary incontinence due to ISD:

    a. Male or female patients with congenital sphincter weakness secondary to conditions such as myelomeningocele

    b. Male or female patients with acquired sphincter weakness secondary to spinal cord lesions

    c. Male patients following trauma, including prostatectomy and/or radiation

    d. Female patients without urethral hypermobility and with abdominal leak point pressures of 100 centimeters H2O or less

Patients whose incontinence does not improve with 5 injection procedures are considered treatment failures, and no further treatment of urinary incontinence by collagen implant is covered. Patients who have a reoccurrence of incontinence following successful treatment with collagen implants in the past may benefit from additional treatment sessions. Coverage of additional sessions must be supported by medical justification.

CIM 70-1   Corset Used as Hernia Support

A hernia support (whether in the form of a corset or truss) which meets the definition of a brace is covered under Part B under §1861(s)(9) of the Act.

See Intermediary Manual, §3110.5; Medicare Carriers Manual, §2133; and Hospital Manual, §228.5.

CIM 70-2   Sykes Hernia Control

Based on professional advice, it has been determined that the sykes hernia control (a spring-type, U-shaped, strapless truss) is not functionally more beneficial than a conventional truss. Make program reimbursement for this device only when an ordinary truss would be covered. (Like all trusses, it is only of benefit when dealing with a reducible hernia). Thus, when a charge for this item is substantially in excess of that which would be reasonable for a conventional truss used for the same condition, base reimbursement on the reasonable charges for the conventional truss.

See Intermediary Manual, §3110.5; Medicare Carriers Manual, §2133; and Hospital Manual, §228.5.

MEDICARE CARRIERS MANUAL

MCM 15022   Payment Conditions For Radiology Services

    A. Professional Component (PC). – Pay for the PC of radiology services furnished by a physician to an individual patient in all settings under the fee schedule for physician services regardless of the specialty of the physician who performs the service. For services furnished to hospital patients, pay only if the services meet the conditions for fee schedule payment in §15014.C.1 and are identifiable, direct, and discrete diagnostic or therapeutic services to an individual patient, such as an interpretation of diagnostic procedures and the PC of therapeutic procedures. The interpretation of a diagnostic procedure includes a written report.

    B. Technical Component TC). -

        1. Hospital Patients. – Do not pay for the TC of radiology services furnished to Hospital patients. Payments for physicians' radiological services to the hospital, e.g., administrative or supervisory services, and for provider services needed to produce the radiology service is made by the intermediary as provider services through various payment mechanisms.

        2. Services Not Furnished in Hospitals. – Pay under the fee schedule for the TC of radiology services furnished to beneficiaries who are not patients of any

hospital in a physician's office, a freestanding imaging or radiation oncology center, or other setting that is not part of a hospital.

        3. Services Furnished in Leased Departments. – In the case of procedures furnished in a leased hospital radiology department to a beneficiary who is neither an inpatient nor an outpatient of any hospital, e.g., the patient is referred by an outside physician and is not registered as a hospital outpatient, both the PC and the TC of the services are payable under the fee schedule.

        4. Purchased TC Services. – Apply the purchased services limitation as set forth in §15048 to the TC of radiologic services other than screening mammography procedures.

        5. Computerized Axial Tomography (CT) Procedures. – Do not reduce or deny payment for medically necessary multiple CT scans of different areas of the body that are performed on the same day.

The TC RVUs for CT procedures that specify "with contrast" include payment for high osmolar contrast media. When separate payment is made for low osmolar contrast media under the conditions set forth in subsection F.1, reduce payment for the contrast media as set forth in subsection F.2.

        6. Magnetic Resonance Imaging (MRI) Procedures. – Do not make additional payments for 3 or more MRI sequences. The RVUs reflect payment levels for 2 sequences.

The TC RVUs for MRI procedures that specify "with contrast" include payment for paramagnetic contrast media. Do not make separate payment under code A4647.

A diagnostic technique has been developed under which an MRI of the brain or spine is first performed without contrast material, then another MRI is performed with a standard (0.1mmol/kg) dose of contrast material and, based on the need to achieve a better image, a third MRI is performed with an additional double dosage (0.2mmol/kg) of contrast material. When the high-dose contrast technique is utilized

Do not pay separately for the contrast material used in the second MRI procedure;

*Pay for the contrast material given for the third MRI procedure through supply code A4643 when billed with CPT codes 70553, 72156, 72157, and 72158;

* Do not pay for the third MRI procedure. For example, in the case of an MRI of the brain, if CPT code 70553 (without contrast material, followed by contrast material(s) and further sequences) is billed, make no payment for CPT code 70551 (without contrast material(s)), the additional procedure given for the purpose of administering the double dosage, furnished during the same session. Medicare does not pay for the third procedure (as distinguished from the contrast material) because the CPT definition of code 70553 includes all further sequences; and

* Do not apply the payment criteria for low osmolar contrast media in subsection F to billings for code A4643.

        7. Stressing Agent. – Make separate payment under code J1245 for pharmacologic stressing agents used in connection with nuclear medicine and cardiovascular stress testing procedures furnished to beneficiaries in settings in which TCs are payable. Such an agent is classified as a supply and covered as an integral part of the diagnostic test. However, pay for code J1245 under the policy for determining payments for "incident to" drugs.

    H. Nuclear Medicine (CPT 78000 Through 79999). -

        1. Payments for Radionuclides. – The TC RVUs for nuclear medicine procedures (CPT codes 78XXX for diagnostic nuclear medicine, and codes 79XXX for therapeutic nuclear medicine) do not include the radionuclide used in connection with the procedure. These substances are separately billed under codes A4641 and A4642 for diagnostic procedures and code 79900 for therapeutic procedures and are paid on a "By Report" basis depending on the substance used. In addition, CPT code 79000 is separately payable in connection with certain clinical brachytherapy procedures. (See subsection D.3.)

        2. Application of Multiple Procedure Policy (CPT Modifier 51). – Apply the multiple procedure reduction as set forth in §15038 to the following nuclear medicine diagnostic procedures: codes 78306, 78320, 78803, 78806, and 78807.

        3. Generation and Interpeteration of Automated Data. – Payment for CPT codes 78890 and 78891 is bundled into payments for the primary procedure.

        4. Positron Emission Tomography (PET) Scans (HCPCS Codes G0030 -G0047). – For procedures furnished on or after March 14, 1995, pay for PET procedure of the heart under the limited coverage policy set forth in §50-36 of the Coverage Issues Manual (HCFA Pub. 6) using the billing instructions in §4173 of the Medicare Carriers Manual.

    D. Radiation Oncology (Therapeutic Radiology) (CPT 77261-77799). -

        1. Weekly Radiation Therapy Management (CPT 77419-77430). – Pay for a physician's weekly treatment management services under codes 77419, 77420,

77425, and 77430. Instruct billing entities to indicate on each claim the number of fractions for which payment is sought.

A weekly unit of treatment management is equal to five fractions or treatment sessions. A week for the purpose of making payments under these codes is comprised of five fractions regardless of the actual time period in which the services are furnished. It is not necessary that the radiation therapist personally examine the patient during each fraction for the weekly treatment management code to be payable. Multiple fractions representing two or more treatment sessions furnished on the same day may be counted as long as there has been a distinct break in therapy sessions, and the fractions are of the character usually furnished on different days. If, at the final billing of the treatment course, there are three or four fractions beyond a multiple of five, those three or four fractions are paid for as a week. If there are one or two fractions beyond a multiple of five, consider payment for these services as having been made through prior payments.

EXAMPLE: 18 fractions = 4 weekly services

62 fractions = 12 weekly services

8 fractions = 2 weekly services

6 fractions = 1 weekly service

If billings have occurred which indicate that the treatment course has ended (and, therefore, the number of residual fractions has been determined), but treatments resume, adjust your payments for the additional services consistent with the above policy.

EXAMPLE: 8 fractions = payment for 2 weeks

2 additional fractions are furnished by the same physician. No additional Medicare payment is made for the 2 additional fractions.

There are situations in which beneficiaries receive a mixture of simple (code 77420), intermediate (code 77425), and complex (code 77430) treatment management services during a course of treatment. In such cases, pay under the weekly treatment management code that represents the more frequent of the fractions furnished during the five-fraction week. For example, an intermediate weekly treatment management service is payable when, in a grouping of five fractions, a beneficiary receives three intermediate and two simple fractions.

2. Services Bundled Into Treatment Management Codes. – Make no separate payment for any of the following services rendered by the radiation oncologists or in conjunction with radiation therapy:

Code	Description
11920	Tattooing, intradermal introduction of insoluble opaque pigments to correct color defects of skin; 6.0 sq. cm or less
11921	6.1 to 20.0 sq. cm
11922	each additional 20.0 sq. cm
16000	Initial treatment, first degree burn, when no more than local treatment is required
16010	Dressings and/or debridement, initial or subsequent; under anesthesia, small
16015	under anesthesia, medium or large, or with major debridement
16020	without anesthesia, office or hospital, small
16025	without anesthesia, medium (e.g., whole face or whole extremity)
16030	without anesthesia, large (e.g., more than one extremity)
36425	Venipuncture, cut down age 1 or over
53670	Catheterization, urethra; simple
53675	complicated (may include difficult removal of balloon catheter)
99211	Office or other outpatient visit, established patient; Level I
99212	Level II
99213	Level III
99214	Level IV
99215	Level V
99238	Hospital discharge day management
99281	Emergency department visit, new or established patient; Level I
99282	Level II
99283	Level III
99284	Level IV
99285	Level V

Code	Description
90780	IV infusion therapy, administered by physician or under direct supervision of physician; up to one hour 90781each additional hour, up to eight (8) hours 90841Individual medical psychotherapy by a physician, with continuing medical diagnostic evaluation, and drug management when indicated, including psychoanalysis, insight oriented, behavior modifying or supportive psychotherapy; time unspecified
90843	approximately 20 to 30 minutes
90844	approximately 45 to 50 minutes
90847	Family medical psychotherapy (conjoint psychotherapy) by a physician, with continuing medical diagnostic evaluation, and drug management when indicated
99050	Services requested after office hours in addition to basic service
99052	Services requested between 10:00 PM and 8:00 AM in addition to basic service
99054	Services requested on Sundays and holidays in addition to basic service
99058	Office services provided on an emergency basis
99071	Educational supplies, such as books, tapes, and pamphlets, provided by the physician for the patient's education at cost to physician
99090	Analysis of information data stored in computers (e.g., ECG, blood pressures, hematologic data)
99150	Prolonged physician attendance requiring physician detention beyond usual service (e.g., operative standby, monitoring ECG, EEG, intrathoracic pressures, intravascular pressures, blood gases during surgery, standby for newborn care following caesarean section); 30 minutes to one hour
99151	more than one hour
99180	Hyperbaric oxygen therapy initial
99182	Subsequent
99185	Hypothermia; regional
99371	Telephone call by a physician to patient or for consultation or medical management or for coordinating medical management with other health care professionals; simple or brief (e.g., to report on tests and/or laboratory results, to clarify or alter previous instructions, to integrate new information from other health professionals into the medical treatment plan, or to adjust therapy)
99372	intermediate (e.g., to provide advice to an established patient on a new problem, to initiate therapy that can be handled by telephone, to discuss test results in detail, to coordinate medical management of a new problem in an established patient, to discuss and evaluate new information and details, or to initiate a new plan of care)
99373	complex or lengthy (e.g., lengthy counseling session with anxious or distraught patient, detailed or prolonged discussion with family members regarding seriously ill patient, lengthy communication necessary to coordinate complex services or several different health professionals working on different aspects of the total patient care plan)

* Anesthesia (whatever code billed)

* Care of Infected Skin (whatever code billed)

* Checking of Treatment Charts

* Verification of Dosage, As Needed (whatever code billed)

* Continued Patient

* Evaluation, Examination,Written Progress Notes, As Needed (whatever code billed)

* Final Physical

* Examination (whatever code billed)

* Medical Prescription Writing (whatever code billed

* Nutritional

* Pain Management (whatever code billed)

* Review & Revision of Treatment Plan (whatever code billed)

* Routine Medical Management of Unrelated Problem (whatever code billed)

* Special Care of Ostomy (whatever code billed)

* Written Reports, Progress Note (whatever code billed)

* Follow-up Examination and Care for 90 Days After Last Treatment (whatever code billed)

3.Radiation Treatment Delivery (CPT 77401-77417). – Pay for these TC services on a daily basis under CPT codes 77401-77416 for radiation treatment delivery. Do not use local codes and RVUs in paying for the TC of radiation oncology services. Multiple treatment sessions on the same day are payable as long as there has been a distinct break in therapy services, and the individual sessions are of the character usually furnished on different days. Pay for CPT code 77417 (Therapeutic radiology port film(s)) on a weekly (5 fractions) basis.

4. Clinical Brachytherapy (CPT Codes 77750-77799). – Apply the bundled services policy in §15022.D.2. to procedures in this family of codes other than CPT code 77776. For procedures furnished in settings in which you make TC payments, pay separately for the expendable source associated with these procedures under CPT code 79900 except in the case of remote afterloading high intensity brachytherapy procedures (CPT codes 77781-77784). In the 4 codes cited, the expendable source is included in the RVUs for the TC of the procedures.

5. Radiation Physics Services (CPT Codes 77300-77399). – Until further notice, pay for the PC and TC of CPT codes 77300-77334 and 77739 on the same basis as you pay for radiologic services generally. For PC billings in all settings, presume that the radiologist participated in the provision of the service, e.g., reviewed/validated the physicist's calculation. CPT codes 77336 and 77370 are technical services only codes that are payable by carriers only in settings in which TCs are payable.

E. Supervision and Interpretation (S&I) Codes and Interventional Radiology. -

1. Physician Presence. – Radiologic S&I codes are used to describe the personal supervision of the performance of the radiologic portion of a procedure by one or more physicians and the interpretation of the findings. In order to bill for the supervision aspect of the procedure, the physician must be present during its performance. This kind of personal supervision of the performance of the procedure is a service to an individual beneficiary and differs from the type of general supervision of the radiologic procedures performed in a hospital for which intermediaries pay the costs as physician services to the hospital. The interpretation of the procedure may be performed later by another physician. In situations in which a cardiologist, for example, bills for the supervision (the "S") of the S&I code, and a radiologist bills for the interpretation (the "I") of the code, both physicians should use a -52 modifier indicating a reduced service, e.g., the interpretation only. Pay no more for the fragmented S&I code than you would if a single physician furnished both aspects of the procedure.

2. Multiple Procedure Reduction. – Make no multiple procedure reductions in the S&I or primary nonradiologic codes in these types of procedures, or in any procedure codes for which the descriptor and RVUs reflect a multiple service reduction. For additional procedure codes that do not reflect such a reduction, apply the multiple procedure reductions set forth in §15038.

F. Low Osmolar Contrast Media (LOCM) (HCPCS Codes A4644-A4646). -

1. Payment Criteria. – Make separate payments for LOCM (HCPCS codes A4644, A4645, and A4646) in the case of all medically necessary intrathecal radiologic procedures furnished to nonhospital patients. In the case of intraarterial and intravenous radiologic procedures, pay separately for LOCM only when it is used for nonhospital patients with one or more of the following characteristics:

*A history of previous adverse reaction to contrast material, with the exception of a sensation of heat, flushing, or a single episode of nausea or vomiting;

*A history of asthma or allergy;

*   Significant cardiac dysfunction including recent or imminent cardiac decompensation, severe arrhythmia, unstable angina pectoris, recent myocardial infarction, and pulmonary hypertension;

*Generalized severe debilitation; or

*Sickle cell disease.

If the beneficiary does not meet any of these criteria, the payment for contrast media is considered to be bundled into the TC of the procedure, and the beneficiary may not be billed for LOCM.

2. Payment Level. – A LOCM pharmaceutical is considered to be a supply which is an integral part of the diagnostic test. However, determine payment in the same manner as for a drug furnished incident to a physician's service with the following additional requirement. Reduce the lower of the estimated actual acquisition cost or the national average wholesale price by 8 percent to take into account the fact that the TC RVUs of the procedure codes reflect less expensive contrast media.

G. Services of Portable X-Ray Suppliers. – Services furnished by portable X-ray suppliers (see §2070.4) may have as many as four components.

1. Professional Component. – Pay the PC of radiologic services furnished by portable X-ray suppliers on the same basis as other physician fee schedule services.

2. Technical Component. – Pay the TC of radiology services furnished by portable X-ray suppliers under the fee schedule on the same basis as TC services generally.

3. Transportation Component (HCPCS Codes R0070-R0076). – This component represents the transportation of the equipment to the patient. Establish local RVUs for the transportation R codes based on your knowledge of the nature of the service furnished. Allow only a single transportation payment for each trip the portable X-ray supplier makes to a particular location. When more than one Medicare patient is X-rayed at the same location, e.g., a nursing home, prorate the single fee schedule transportation payment among all patients receiving the services. For example, if two patients at the same location receive X-rays, make one-half of the transportation payment for each.

Use any information regarding the number of patients X-rayed in each location that the supplier visits during each trip that the supplier of the X-ray may volunteer on the bill or claim for payment. If such information is not indicated, assume that at least four patients were X-rayed at the same location, and pay only one-fourth of the fee schedule payment amount for any one patient. Advise the suppliers in your area regarding the way in which you use this information.

NOTE: No transportation charge is payable unless the portable X-ray equipment used was actually transported to the location where the X-ray was taken. For example, do not allow a transportation charge when the X-ray equipment is stored in a nursing home for use as needed. However, a set-up payment (see subsection G.4) is payable in such situations. Further, for services furnished on or after January 1, 1997, make no separate payment under HCPCS code R0076 for the transportation of EKG equipment by portable X-ray suppliers or any other entity.

4. Set-Up Component (HCPCS Code Q0092). – Pay a set-up component for each radiologic procedure (other than retakes of the same procedure) during both single patient and multiple patient trips under Level II HCPCS code Q0092. Do not make the set-up payment for EKG services furnished by the portable X-ray supplier.

MCM 15030   Supplies

Make a separate payment for supplies furnished in connection with a procedure only when one of the two following conditions exists:

A. HCPCS codes A4550, A4200, and A4263 are billed in conjunction with the appropriate procedure in the Medicare Physician Fee Schedule Data Base (place of service is physician's office); or

B. The supply is a pharmaceutical or radiopharmaceutical diagnostic imaging agent (including codes A4641 through A4647); pharmacologic stressing agent (code J1245); or therapeutic radionuclide (CPT code 79900). The procedures performed are:

– Diagnostic radiologic procedures (including diagnostic nuclear medicine) requiring pharmaceutical or radiopharmaceutical contrast media and/or pharmocological stressing agent,

– Other diagnostic tests requiring a pharmacological stressing agent,

– Clinical brachytherapy procedures (other than remote afterloading high intensity brachytherapy procedures (CPT codes 77781 through 77784) for which the expendable source is included in the TC RVUs), or

– Therapeutic nuclear medicine procedures.

MCM 15360   Echocardiography Services

Q0188 is the new HCPCS Level II Code for contrast agents used in echocardiography (Codes 93303 – 93350). The code is carrier-priced.

MCM 2020.1 Definition of Physician

Physician means a doctor of medicine, doctor of osteopathy (including osteopathic practitioner), doctor of dental surgery or dental medicine (within the limitations in §2020.3), a chiropractor (within the limitations in §2020.26), or doctor of podiatry or surgical chiropody (within the limitations in §2020.4), or doctor of optometry (within the limitations in §2020.25) legally authorized to practice by a State in which he/she performs this function. The services performed by a physician within these definitions are subject to any limitations imposed by the State on the scope of practice.

The issuance by a State of a license to practice medicine constitutes legal authorization. Temporary State licenses also constitute legal authorization to practice medicine. If State law authorizes local political subdivisions to establish higher standards for medical practitioners than those set by the State licensing board, the local standards are used in determining whether a particular physician has legal authorization. If State licensing law limits the scope of practice of a particular type of medical practitioner, only the services within these limitations are covered.

NOTE: The term physician does not include such practitioners as a Christian Science practitioner or naturopath.

MCM 2020.2   Doctors of Medicine and Osteopathy

The requirement that a doctor of medicine be legally authorized to practice medicine and surgery by the State in which he/she performs his/her services means a physician is licensed to practice medicine and surgery.

A doctor of osteopathy who is legally authorized to practice medicine and surgery by the State in which he/she performs his/her services qualifies as a physician. In addition, a licensed osteopath or osteopathic practitioner qualifies as a physician to the extent that he/she performs services within the scope of his/her practice as defined by State law.

MCM 2020.3   Dentists

A dentist qualifies as a physician if he/she is a doctor of dental surgery or dental medicine who is legally authorized to practice dentistry by the State in which he/she performs such functions and who is acting within the scope of his/her license when he/she performs such functions. Such services include any otherwise covered service that may legally and alternatively be performed by doctors of medicine, osteopathy, and dentistry; e.g., dental examinations to detect infections prior to certain surgical procedures, treatment of oral infections, and interpretations of diagnostic x-ray examinations in connection with covered services. Because the general exclusion of payment for dental services has not been withdrawn, payment for the services of dentists is also limited to those procedures which are not primarily provided for the care, treatment, removal, or replacement of teeth or structures directly supporting teeth. (Sections 2136, 2336, and Coverage Issues Manual, §50-26 also concern this exclusion.) The coverage or exclusion of any given dental service is not affected by the professional designation of the physician rendering the services; i.e., an excluded dental service remains excluded and a covered dental service is still covered whether furnished by a dentist or a doctor of medicine or osteopathy.

MCM 2049   Drugs And Biologicals

The Medicare program provides limited benefits for outpatient drugs. The program covers drugs that are furnished "incident to" a physician's service provided that the drugs are not usually selfadministered by the patients who take them.

Generally, drugs and biologicals are covered only if all of the following requirements are met:

- They meet the definition of drugs or biologicals (see §2049.1);

- They are of the type that are not usually self-administered by the patients who take them. (See §2049.2);

- They meet all the general requirements for coverage of items as incident to a physician's services (see §§2050.1 and 2050.3);

- They are reasonable and necessary for the diagnosis or treatment of the illness or injury for which they are administered according to accepted standards of medical practice (see §2049.4);

- They are not excluded as immunizations (see §2049.4.B); and

- They have not been determined by the FDA to be less than effective. (See §2049.4 D.)

Drugs that are usually self-administered by the patient, such as those in pill form, or are used for self-injection, are generally not covered by Part B. However, there are a limited number of selfadministered drugs that are covered because the Medicare statute explicitly provides coverage.

Examples of self-administered drugs that are covered include blood clotting factors, drugs used in immunosuppressive therapy, erythropoietin for dialysis patients, osteoporosis drugs for certain homebound patients, and certain oral cancer drugs. (See §§2100.5 and 2130.D for coverage of drugs which are necessary to the effective use of DME or prosthetic devices.)

2049.1 Definition of Drug or Biological. – Drugs and biologicals must be determined to meet the statutory definition. Section 1861(t)(1) provides that the terms "drugs" and "biologicals" "include only such drugs (including contrast agents) and biologicals, respectively, as are included (or approved for inclusion) in one of several pharmacopoeias (except for any drugs and biologicals unfavorably evaluated therein), or as are approved by the pharmacy and drug therapeutics committee (or equivalent committee) of the medical staff of the hospital furnishing such drugs and biologicals for use in such hospital." One such pharmacopeia is the United States Pharmacopeia, Drug Indications (USP DI). The inclusion of an item in the USP DI does not necessarily mean that the item is a drug or biological. The USP DI is a database of drug information developed by the U.S. Pharmacopeia but maintained by Micromedex, which contains medically accepted uses for generic and brand name drug products. Inclusion in such reference (or approval by a hospital committee) is a necessary condition for a product to be considered a drug or biological under the Medicare program, however, it is not enough. Rather, the product must also meet all other program requirements to be determined to be a drug or biological.

Determining Self-Administration of Drug or Biological. – Whether a drug or biological is of a type which cannot be self-administered is based on the usual method of administration of the form of that drug or biological as furnished by the physician. Whole blood is a biological which cannot be self-administered and is covered when furnished incident to a physician's services. Payment may also be made for blood fractions if all coverage requirements are satisfied. (See §2455 on Part B blood deductible.)

Medicare carriers have discretion in applying the criteria in this instruction in determining whether drugs are subject to this exclusion in their local areas. Carriers are to follow the instructions below when applying the exclusion for drugs that are usually self-administered by the patient. Each individual contractor must make its own individual determination on each drug. Contractors must continue to apply the policy that not only the drug is medically reasonable and necessary for any individual claim, but also that the route of administration is medically reasonable and necessary. That is, if a drug is available in both oral and injectable forms, the injectable form of the drug must be medically reasonable and necessary as compared to using the oral form. (See §2049.4.2) For certain injectable drugs, it will be apparent due to the nature of the condition(s) for which they are administered or the usual course of treatment for those conditions, they are, or are not, usually self-administered. For example, an injectable drug used to treat migraine headaches is usually selfadministered. On the other hand, an injectable drug, administered at the same time as chemotherapy, used to treat anemia secondary to chemotherapy is not usually self-administered. Administered – The term "administered" refers only to the physical process by which the drug enters the patient's body. It does not refer to whether the process is supervised by a medical professional (for example, to observe proper technique or side-effects of the drug). Only injectable (including intravenous) drugs are eligible for inclusion under the "incident to" benefit. Other routes of administration including, but not limited to, oral drugs, suppositories, topical medications are all considered to be usually self-administered by the patient. Usually – In arriving at a single determination as to whether a drug is usually self-administered, contractors should make a separate determination for each indication for a drug as to whether that drug is usually self-administered. After determining whether a drug is usually self-administered for each indication, contractors should determine the relative contribution of each indication to total use of the drug (i.e., weighted average) in order to make an overall determination as to whether the drug is usually self-administered. For example, if a drug has three indications, is not self-administered for the first indication, but is selfadministered for the second and third indications, and the first indication makes up 40% of total usage, the second indication makes up 30% of total usage, and the third indication makes up 30% of total usage, then the drug would be considered usually self-administered. Reliable statistical information on the extent of self-administration by the patient may not always be available. Consequently, we offer the following guidance for each contractor's consideration in making this determination in the absence of such data:

1. Absent evidence to the contrary, drugs delivered intravenously should be presumed to be not usually self-administered by the patient. 2. Absent evidence to the contrary, drugs delivered by intramuscular injection should be presumed to be not usually self-administered by the patient. (For example, interferon beta-1a, tradename Avonex, when delivered by intramuscular injection is not usually self administered by the patient.) The contractor may consider the depth and nature of the particular intramuscular injection in applying this presumption.

3. Absent evidence to the contrary, drugs delivered by subcutaneous injection should be presumed to be self-administered by the patient. In applying these presumptions, contractors should examine the use of the particular drug and consider the following factors:

A. Acute condition. – For the purposes of determining whether a drug is usually selfadministered, an acute condition means a condition that begins over a short time period, is likely to be of short duration and/or the expected course of treatment is for a short, finite interval. A course of treatment consisting of scheduled injections lasting less than two weeks, regardless of frequency or route of administration, is considered acute. Evidence to support this may include Food and Drug administration (FDA) approval language, package inserts, drug compendia, and other information.

Frequency of administration. – How often is the injection given? For example, if the drug is administered once per month, it is less likely to be self-administered by the patient. However, if it is administered once or more per week, it is likely that the drug is self-administered by the patient. By the patient – The term "by the patient" means Medicare beneficiaries as a collective whole. Include only the patients themselves and not other individuals (that is, do not include spouses, friends, or other care-givers). Base your determination on whether the drug is self-administered by the patient a majority of the time that the drug is used on an outpatient basis by Medicare beneficiaries for medically necessary indications. Ignore all instances when the drug is administered on an inpatient basis. Make this determination on a drug-by-drug basis, not on a beneficiary-bybeneficiary basis. In evaluating whether beneficiaries as a collective whole self-administer, do not consider individual beneficiaries who do not have the capacity to self-administer any drug due to a condition other than the condition for which they are taking the drug in question. For example, an individual afflicted with paraplegia or advanced dementia would not have the capacity to selfadminister any injectable drug, so such individuals would not be included in the population upon which the determination for self-administration by the patient was based. Note that some individuals afflicted with a less severe stage of an otherwise debilitating condition would be included in the population upon which the determination for "self-administered by the patient" was based; for example, an early onset of dementia. Evidentiary Criteria – In making a self-administration determination, contractors are only required to consider the following types of evidence: peer reviewed medical literature, standards of medical practice, evidence-based practice guidelines, FDA approved label, and package inserts. Contractors may also consider other evidence submitted by interested individuals or groups subject to their judgment. Contractors should also use these evidentiary criteria when reviewing requests for making a determination as to whether a drug is usually self-administered, and requests for reconsideration of a pending or published determination. Please note that prior to August 1, 2002, one of the principal factors used to determine whether a drug was subject to the self-administered exclusion was whether the FDA label contained instructions for self-administration. However, we note that under the standard in effect after August 1, 2002, the fact that the FDA label includes instructions for self-administration is not, by itself, a determining factor that a drug is subject to this exclusion.

Provider Notice of Non-Covered Drugs – Contractors must describe the process they will use to determine whether a drug is usually self-administered and thus does not meet the "incident to" benefit category. Contractors must place a description of the process on their Web site. Contractors must publish a list of the injectable drugs that are subject to the self-administered exclusion on their Web site, including the data and rationale that led to the determination. Contractors will report the workload associated with developing new coverage statements in CAFM 21208. Contractors must provide notice 45 days prior to the date that these drugs will not be covered. During the 45-day time period, contractors will maintain existing medical review and payment procedures. After the 45-day notice, contractors may deny payment for the drugs subject to the notice.

Contractors must not develop local medical review policies (LMRPs) for this purpose because further elaboration to describe drugs that do not meet the 'incident to' and the 'not usually selfadministered' provisions of the statute are unnecessary. Current LMRPs based solely on these provisions must be withdrawn. LMRPs that address the self-administered exclusion and other information may be reissued absent the self-administered drug exclusion material. Contractors will report this workload in CAFM 21206. However, contractors may continue to use and write LMRPs to describe reasonable and necessary uses of drugs that are not usually self-administered.

Conferences Between Contractors – Contractors' Medical Directors may meet and discuss whether a drug is usually self-administered without reaching a formal consensus. Each contractor uses its discretion as to whether or not it will participate in such discussions. Each contractor must make its own individual determinations, except that fiscal intermediaries may, at their discretion, follow the determinations of the local carrier with respect to the self-administered exclusion.

Beneficiary Appeals – If a beneficiary's claim for a particular drug is denied because the drug is subject to the "self-administered drug" exclusion, the beneficiary may appeal the denial. Because it is a "benefit category" denial and not a denial based on medical necessity, an Advance Beneficiary Notice (ABN) is not applicable. A "benefit category" denial (i.e., a denial based on the fact that there is no benefit category under which the drug may be covered) does not trigger the financial liability protection provisions of Limitation On Liability [under §1879 of the Act]. Therefore, physicians or providers may charge the beneficiary for an excluded drug. See Chapter XV of the Medicare Carrier Manual for more detail on the appeals process.

Provider and Physician Appeals – A physician accepting assignment may appeal a denial under the provisions found in §12000 of the Medicare Carriers Manual. See Chapter XV of the Medicare Carrier Manual for more detail on the appeals process.

Reporting Requirements – Each carrier must report to CMS, every September 1 and March 1, its complete list of injectable drugs that the contractor has determined are excluded when furnished incident to a physician's service on the basis that the drug is usually self-administered. We anticipate that contractors will review injectable drugs on a rolling basis and publish their list of excluded drugs as it is developed. For example, contractors should not wait to publish this list until every drug has been reviewed. Contractors must send their exclusion list to the following e-mail address: drugdata@cms.hhs.gov.
Below is an example of the Microsoft Excel template that should be submitted to CMS.

Carrier Name
State
Carrier
ID #
HCPCS Descriptor
Effective date of exclusion
End date of exclusion
Comments

2049.3 Incident-to Requirements. – In order for Medicare payment to be made for a drug, the "incident to" requirements are met. "Incident to" a physician's professional service means that the services are furnished as an integral, although incidental, part of the physician's personal professional services in the course of diagnosis or treatment of an illness or injury. See §2050.1 for more detail on incident-to requirements. In order to meet all the general requirements for coverage under the incident-to provision, an FDA approved drug or biological must be furnished by a physician and administered by him/her or by auxiliary personnel employed by him/her under his/her personal supervision. The charge, if any, for the drug or biological must be included in the physician's bill, and the cost of the drug or biological must represent an expense to the physician. Drugs and biologicals furnished by other health professionals may also meet these requirements. (See §§2154, 2156, 2158 and 2160 for specific instructions.)

2049.4 Reasonableness and Necessity. – Use of the drug or biological must be safe and effective and otherwise reasonable and necessary. (See §2303.) Drugs or biologicals approved for marketing by the Food and Drug Administration (FDA) are considered safe and effective for purposes of this requirement when used for indications specified on the labeling. Therefore, you may pay for the use of an FDA approved drug or biological, if:

- It was injected on or after the date of the FDA's approval;
- It is reasonable and necessary for the individual patient; and
- All other applicable coverage requirements are met.

Deny coverage for drugs and biologicals which have not received final marketing approval by the FDA unless you receive instructions from HCFA to the contrary. For specific guidelines on coverage of Group C cancer drugs, see the Coverage Issues Manual.

If there is reason to question whether the FDA has approved a drug or biological for marketing, obtain satisfactory evidence of FDA's approval. Acceptable evidence includes a copy of the FDA's letter to the drug's manufacturer approving the New Drug Application (NDA); or listing of the drug or biological in the FDA's Approved Drug Products or FDA Drug and Device Product Approvals; or a copy of the manufacturer's package insert, approved by the FDA as part of the labeling of the drug, containing its recommended uses and dosage, as well as possible adverse reactions and recommended precautions in using it. When necessary, the RO may be able to help in obtaining information.

An unlabeled use of a drug is a use that is not included as an indication on the drug's label as approved by the FDA. FDA approved drugs used for indications other than what is indicated on the official label may be covered under Medicare if the carrier determines the use to be medically accepted, taking into consideration the major drug compendia, authoritive medical literature and/or accepted standards of medical practice. In the case of drugs used in an anti-cancer chemotherapeutic regimen, unlabeled uses are covered for a medically accepted indication as defined in §2049.4.C.

Determinations as to whether medication is reasonable and necessary for an individual patient should be made on the same basis as all other such determinations (i.e., with the advice of medical consultants and with reference to accepted standards of medical practice and the medical circumstances of the individual case). The following guidelines identify three categories with specific examples of situations in which medications would not be reasonable and necessary according to accepted standards of medical practice.

1. Not for Particular Illness. – Medications given for a purpose other than the treatment of a particular condition, illness, or injury are not covered (except for certain immunizations). Exclude the charge for medications, e.g., vitamins, given simply for the general good and welfare of the patient and not as accepted therapy for a particular illness.

2. Injection Method Not Indicated. – Medication given by injection (parenterally) is not covered if standard medical practice indicates that the administration of the medication by mouth (orally) is effective and is an accepted or preferred method of administration. For example, the accepted standards of medical practice for the treatment of certain diseases is to initiate therapy with parenteral penicillin and to complete therapy with oral penicillin. Exclude the entire charge for penicillin injections given after the initiation of therapy if oral penicillin is indicated unless there are special medical circumstances which justify additional injections.

3. Excessive Medications. – Medications administered for treatment of a disease which exceed the frequency or duration of injections indicated by accepted standards of medical practice are not covered. For example, the accepted standard of medical practice in the maintenance treatment of pernicious anemia is one vitamin B-12 injection per month. Exclude the entire charge for injections given in excess of this frequency unless there are special medical circumstances which justify additional injections.

Supplement the guidelines as necessary with guidelines concerning appropriate use of specific injections in other situations. Use the guidelines to screen out questionable cases for special review, further development or denial when the injection billed for would not be reasonable and necessary. Coordinate any type of drug treatment review with the PRO.

If a medication is determined not to be reasonable and necessary for diagnosis or treatment of an illness or injury according to these guidelines, exclude the entire charge (i.e., for both the drug and its administration). Also exclude from payment any charges for other services (such as office visits) which were primarily for the purpose of administering a noncovered injection (i.e., an injection that is not reasonable and necessary for the diagnosis or treatment of an illness or injury).

A. Antigens. – Payment may be made for a reasonable supply of antigens that have been prepared for a particular patient if: (1) the antigens are prepared by a physician who is a doctor of medicine or osteopathy, and (2) the physician who prepared the antigens has examined the patient and has determined a plan of treatment and a dosage regimen. Antigens must be administered in accordance with the plan of treatment and by a doctor of medicine or osteopathy or by a properly instructed person (who could be the patient) under the supervision of the doctor. The associations of allergists that HCFA consulted advised that a reasonable supply of antigens is considered to be not more than a 12-week supply of antigens that has been prepared for a particular patient at any one time. The purpose of the reasonable supply limitation is to assure that the antigens retain their potency and effectiveness over the period in which they are to be administered to the patient. (See §§2005.2 and 2050.2.)

B. Immunizations. – Vaccinations or inoculations are excluded as immunizations unless they are directly related to the treatment of an injury or direct exposure to a disease or condition, such as anti-rabies treatment, tetanus antitoxin or booster vaccine, botulin antitoxin, antivenin sera, or immune globulin. In the absence of injury or direct exposure, preventive immunization (vaccination or inoculation) against such diseases as smallpox, polio, diphtheria, etc., is not covered. However, pneumococcal, hepatitis B, and influenza virus vaccines are exceptions to this rule. (See items 1, 2, and 3.) In cases where a vaccination or inoculation is excluded from coverage, deny the entire charge.

1. Pneumococcal Pneumonia Vaccinations. – Effective for services furnished on or after May 1, 1981, the Medicare Part B program covers pneumococcal pneumonia vaccine and its administration when furnished in compliance with any applicable State law by any provider of services or any entity or individual with a supplier number. This includes revaccination of patients at highest risk of pneumococcal infection. Typically, these vaccines are administered once in a lifetime except for persons at highest risk. Effective July 1, 2000, Medicare does not require for coverage purposes that the vaccine must be ordered by a doctor of medicine or osteopathy. Therefore, the beneficiary may receive the vaccine upon request without a physician's order and without physician supervision.

An initial vaccine may be administered only to persons at high risk (see below) of pneumococcal disease. Revaccination may be administered only to persons at highest risk of serious pneumococcal infection and those likely to have a rapid decline in pneumococcal antibody levels, provided that at least 5 years have passed since receipt of a previous dose of pneumococcal vaccine.

Persons at high risk for whom an initial vaccine may be administered include all people age 65 and older; immunocompetent adults who are at increased risk of pneumococcal disease or its complications because of chronic illness (e.g., cardiovascular disease, pulmonary disease, diabetes mellitus, alcoholism, cirrhosis, or cerebrospinal fluid leaks); and individuals with compromised immune systems (e.g., splenic dysfunction or anatomic asplenia, Hodgkin's disease, lymphoma, multiple myeloma, chronic renal failure, HIV infection, nephrotic syndrome, sickle cell disease, or organ transplantation).

Persons at highest risk and those most likely to have rapid declines in antibody levels are those for whom revaccination may be appropriate. This group includes persons with functional or anatomic asplenia (e.g., sickle cell disease, splenectomy), HIV infection, leukemia, lymphoma, Hodgkin's disease, multiple myeloma, generalized malignancy, chronic renal failure, nephrotic syndrome, or other conditions associated with immunosuppression such as organ or bone marrow transplantation, and those receiving immunosuppressive chemotherapy. Routine revaccination of people age 65 or older who are not at highest risk is not appropriate.

Those administering the vaccine should not require the patient to present an immunization record prior to administering the pneumococcal vaccine, nor should they feel compelled to review the patient's complete medical record if it is not available. Instead, provided that the patient is competent, it is acceptable for them to rely on the patient's verbal history to determine prior vaccination status. If the patient is uncertain about their vaccination history in the past 5 years, the vaccine should be given. However, if the patient is certain he/she was vaccinated in the last 5 years, the vaccine should not be given. If the patient is certain that the vaccine was given and that more than 5 years have passed since receipt of the previous dose, revaccination is not appropriate unless the patient is at highest risk.

2. Hepatitis B Vaccine. – With the enactment of P.L. 98-369, coverage under Part B was extended to hepatitis B vaccine and its administration, furnished to a Medicare beneficiary who is at high or intermediate risk of contracting hepatitis B. This coverage is effective for services furnished on or after September 1, 1984.

High-risk groups currently identified include (see exception below):

- End stage renal disease (ESRD) patients;
- Hemophiliacs who receive Factor VIII or IX concentrates;
- Clients of institutions for the mentally retarded;
- Persons who live in the same household as an Hepatitis B Virus (HBV) carrier;
- Homosexual men; and
- Illicit injectable drug abusers.

Intermediate risk groups currently identified include:

- Staff in institutions for the mentally retarded; and
- Workers in health care professions who have frequent contact with blood or blood-derived body fluids during routine work.

EXCEPTION: Persons in the above-listed groups would not be considered at high or intermediate risk of contracting hepatitis B, however, if there is laboratory evidence positive for antibodies to hepatitis B. (ESRD patients are routinely tested for hepatitis B antibodies as part of their continuing monitoring and therapy.)

For Medicare program purposes, the vaccine may be administered upon the order of a doctor of medicine or osteopathy by home health agencies, skilled nursing facilities, ESRD facilities, hospital outpatient departments, persons recognized under the incident to physicians' services provision of law, and doctors of medicine and osteopathy.

A charge separate from the ESRD composite rate will be recognized and paid for administration of the vaccine to ESRD patients.

For ESRD laboratory tests, see Coverage Issues Manual, §50-17.

3. Influenza Virus Vaccine. – Effective for services furnished on or after May 1, 1993, the Medicare Part B program covers influenza virus vaccine and its administration when furnished in compliance with any applicable State law by any provider of services or any entity or individual with a supplier number. Typically, these vaccines are administered once a year in the fall or winter. Medicare does not require for coverage purposes that the vaccine must be ordered by a doctor of medicine or osteopathy. Therefore, the beneficiary may receive the vaccine upon request without a physician's order and without physician supervision.

C. Unlabeled Use For Anti-Cancer Drugs. – Effective January 1, 1994, unlabeled uses of FDA approved drugs and biologicals used in an anti-cancer chemotherapeutic regimen for a medically accepted indication are evaluated under the conditions described in this paragraph. A regimen is a combination of anti-cancer agents which has been clinically recognized for the treatment of a specific type of cancer. An example of a drug regimen is: Cyclophosphamide + vincristine + prednisone (CVP) for non-Hodgkin's lymphoma.

In addition to listing the combination of drugs for a type of cancer, there may be a different regimen or combinations which are used at different times in the history of the cancer (induction, prophylaxis of CNS involvement, post remission, and relapsed or refractory disease). A protocol may specify the combination of drugs, doses, and schedules for administration of the drugs. For purposes of this provision, a cancer treatment regimen includes drugs used to treat toxicities or side effects of the cancer treatment regimen when the drug is administered incident to a chemotherapy treatment. Contractors must not deny coverage based solely on the absence of FDA approved labeling for the use, if the use is supported by one of the following and the use is not listed as "not indicated"# in any of the three compendia. (See note at the end of this subsection.)

4. American Hospital Formulary Service Drug Information. – Drug monographs are arranged in alphabetical order within therapeutic classifications. Within the text of the monograph, information concerning indications is provided, including both labeled and unlabeled uses. Unlabeled uses are identified with daggers. The text must be analyzed to make a determination whether a particular use is supported.

5. American Medical Association Drug Evaluations. – Drug evaluations are organized into sections and chapters that are based on therapeutic classifications. The evaluation of a drug provides information concerning indications, including both labeled and unlabeled uses. Unlabeled uses are not specifically identified as such. The text must be analyzed to make a determination whether a particular use is supported. In making these

determinations, also refer to the AMA Drug Evaluations Subscription, Volume III, section 17 (Oncolytic Drugs), chapter 1 (Principles of Cancer Chemotherapy), tables 1 and 2.

Table 1, Specific Agents Used In Cancer Chemotherapy, lists the anti-neoplastic agents which are currently available for use in various cancers. The indications presented in this table for a particular anti- cancer drug include labeled and unlabeled uses (although they are not identified as such). Any indication appearing in this table is considered to be a medically accepted use.

Table 2, Clinical Responses To Chemotherapy, lists some of the currently preferred regimens for various cancers. The table headings include (1) type of cancer, (2) drugs or regimens currently preferred, (3) alternative or secondary drugs or regimens, and (4) other drugs or regimens with reported activity.

A regimen appearing under the preferred or alternative/secondary headings is considered to be a medically accepted use.

A regimen appearing under the heading "Other Drugs or Regimens With Reported Activity" is considered to be for a medically accepted use provided:

- The preferred and alternative/secondary drugs or regimens are contraindicated; or

- A preferred and/or alternative/secondary drug or regimen was used but was not tolerated or was ineffective; or

- There was tumor progression or recurrence after an initial response.

6. United States Pharmacopoeia Drug Information (USPDI). – Monographs are arranged in alphabetic order by generic or family name. Indications for use appear as accepted, unaccepted, or insufficient data. An indication is considered to be a medically accepted use only if the indication is listed as accepted. Unlabeled uses are identified with brackets. A separate indications index lists all indications included in USPDI along with the medically accepted drugs used in treatment or diagnosis.

7. A Use Supported by Clinical Research That Appears in Peer Reviewed Medical Literature. – This applies only when an unlabeled use does not appear in any of the compendia or is listed as insufficient data or investigational. If an unlabeled use of a drug meets these criteria, contact the compendia to see if a report regarding this use is forthcoming. If a report is forthcoming, use this information as a basis for your decision making. The compendium process for making decisions concerning unlabeled uses is very thorough and continuously updated. Peer reviewed medical literature includes scientific, medical, and pharmaceutical publications in which original manuscripts are published, only after having been critically reviewed for scientific accuracy, validity, and reliability by unbiased independent experts. This does not include in-house publications of pharmaceutical manufacturing companies or abstracts (including meeting abstracts).

In determining whether there is supportive clinical evidence for a particular use of a drug, your medical staff (in consultation with local medical specialty groups) must evaluate the quality of the evidence in published peer reviewed medical literature. When evaluating this literature, consider (among other things) the following:

- The prevalence and life history of the disease when evaluating the adequacy of the number of subjects and the response rate. While a 20 percent response rate may be adequate for highly prevalent disease states, a lower rate may be adequate for rare diseases or highly unresponsive conditions.

- The effect on the patient's well-being and other responses to therapy that indicate effectiveness, e.g., a significant increase in survival rate or life expectancy or an objective and significant decrease in the size of the tumor or a reduction in symptoms related to the tumor. Stabilization is not considered a response to therapy.

- The appropriateness of the study design. Consider:

  1. Whether the experimental design in light of the drugs and conditions under investigation is appropriate to address the investigative question. (For example, in some clinical studies, it may be unnecessary or not feasible to use randomization, double blind trials, placebos, or crossover.);

  2. That nonrandomized clinical trials with a significant number of subjects may be a basis for supportive clinical evidence for determining accepted uses of drugs; and

  3. That case reports are generally considered uncontrolled and anecdotal information and do not provide adequate supportive clinical evidence for determining accepted uses of drugs.

Use peer reviewed medical literature appearing in the following publications:

- American Journal of Medicine;

- Annals of Internal Medicine;

- The Journal of the American Medical Association;

- Journal of Clinical Oncology;

- Blood;

- Journal of the National Cancer Institute;

- The New England Journal of Medicine;

- British Journal of Cancer;

- British Journal of Hematology;

- British Medical Journal;

- Cancer;

- Drugs;

- European Journal of Cancer (formerly the European Journal of Cancer and Clinical Oncology);

- Lancet; or

- Leukemia.

You are not required to maintain copies of these publications. If a claim raises a question about the use of a drug for a purpose not included in the FDA approved labeling or the compendia, ask the physician to submit copies of relevant supporting literature.

4. Unlabeled uses may also be considered medically accepted if determined by you to be medically accepted generally as safe and effective for the particular use. NOTE: If a use is identified as not indicated by HCFA or the FDA or if a use is specifically identified as not indicated in one or more of the three compendia mentioned or if you determine based on peer reviewed medical literature that a particular use of a drug is not safe and effective, the off- label usage is not supported and, therefore, the drug is not covered.

5. Less Than Effective Drug. – This is a drug that has been determined by the Food and Drug Administration (FDA) to lack substantial evidence of effectiveness for all labeled indications. Also, a drug that has been the subject of a Notice of an Opportunity for a Hearing (NOOH) published in the Federal Register before being withdrawn from the market, and for which the Secretary has not determined there is a compelling justification for its medical need, is considered less than effective. This includes any other drug product that is identical, similar, or related. Payment may not be made for a less than effective drug.

Because the FDA has not yet completed its identification of drug products that are still on the market, existing FDA efficacy decisions must be applied to all similar products once they are identified.

6. Denial of Medicare Payment for Compounded Drugs Produced in Violation of Federal Food, Drug, and Cosmetic Act. – The Food and Drug Administration (FDA) has found that, from time to time, firms established as retail pharmacies engage in mass production of compounded drugs, beyond the normal scope of pharmaceutical practice, in violation of the Federal Food, Drug, and Cosmetic Act (FFDCA). By compounding drugs on a large scale, a company may be operating as a drug manufacturer within the meaning of the FFDCA, without complying with requirements of that law. Such companies may be manufacturing drugs which are subject to the new drug application (NDA) requirements of the FFDCA, but for which FDA has not approved an NDA or which are misbranded or adulterated. If the manufacturing and processing procedures used by these facilities have not been approved by the FDA, the FDA has no assurance that the drugs these companies are producing are safe and effective. The safety and effectiveness issues pertain to such factors as chemical stability, purity, strength, bioequivalency, and bioavailability.

Section 1862(a)(1)(A) of the Act requires that drugs must be reasonable and necessary in order to by covered under Medicare. This means, in the case of drugs, they must have been approved for marketing by the FDA. Section 2049.4 instructs carriers to deny coverage for drugs that have not received final marketing approval by the FDA, unless instructed otherwise by HCFA. Section 2300.1 instructs carriers to deny coverage of services related to the use of noncovered drugs as well. Hence, if DME or a prosthetic device is used to administer a noncovered drug, coverage is denied for both the nonapproved drug and the DME or prosthetic device.

In those cases in which the FDA has determined that a company is producing compounded drugs in violation of the FFDCA, Medicare does not pay for the drugs because they do not meet the FDA approval requirements of the Medicare program. In addition, Medicare does not pay for the DME or prosthetic device used to administer such a drug if FDA determines that a required NDA has not been approved or that the drug is misbranded or adulterated.

HCFA will notify you when the FDA has determined that compounded drugs are being produced in violation of the FFDCA. Do not stop Medicare payment for such a drug unless you are notified that it is appropriate to do so through a subsequent instruction. In addition, if you or ROs become aware that other companies are possibly operating in violation of the FFDCA, notify:

Health Care Financing Administration

Bureau of Policy Development

Office of Physician and Ambulatory Care Policy

Baltimore, MD 21244-1850

2049.5 Self-Administered Drugs and Biologicals. – Drugs that are self-administered are not covered by Medicare Part B unless the statute provides for such coverage. This includes blood clotting factors, drugs used in immunosuppressive therapy, erythropoietin for dialysis patients, certain oral anti-cancer drugs, and oral anti-nausea drugs when used in certain situations.

A. Immunosuppressive Drugs. – Until January 1, 1995, immunosuppressive drugs are covered under Part B for a period of one year following discharge from a hospital for a Medicare covered organ transplant. HCFA interprets the 1-year period after the date of the transplant procedure to mean 365 days from the day on which an inpatient is discharged from the hospital. Beneficiaries are eligible to receive additional Part B coverage within 18 months after the discharge date for drugs furnished in 1995; within 24 months for drugs furnished in 1996; within 30 months for drugs furnished in 1997; and within 36 months for drugs furnished after 1997.

Covered drugs include those immunosuppressive drugs that have been specifically labeled as such and approved for marketing by the FDA, as well as those prescription drugs, such as prednisone, that are used in conjunction with immunosuppressive drugs as part of a therapeutic regimen reflected in FDA approved labeling for immunosuppressive drugs. Therefore, antibiotics, hypertensives, and other drugs that are not directly related to rejection are not covered. The FDA had identified and approved for marketing five specifically labeled immunosuppressive drugs. They are Sandimmune (cyclosporine), Sandoz Pharmaceutical; Imuran (azathioprine), Burroughs Wellcome; Atgam (antithymocyte globulin), Upjohn; and Orthoclone OKT3 (Muromonab-CD3), Ortho Pharmaceutical and, Prograf (tacrolimus), Fujisawa USA, Inc. You are expected to keep informed of FDA additions to the list of the immunosuppressive drugs.

B. Erythropoietin (EPO). – The statute provides that EPO is covered for the treatment of anemia for patients with chronic renal failure who are on dialysis. Coverage is available regardless of whether the drug is administered by the patient or the patient's caregiver. EPO is a biologically engineered protein which stimulates the bone marrow to make new red blood cells.

NOTE: Non-ESRD patients who are receiving EPO to treat anemia induced by other conditions such as chemotherapy or the drug zidovudine (commonly called AZT) must meet the coverage requirements in §2049.

EPO is covered for the treatment of anemia for patients with chronic renal failure who are on dialysis when:

- It is administered in the renal dialysis facility; or

- It is self-administered in the home by any dialysis patient (or patient caregiver) who is determined competent to use the drug and meets the other conditions detailed below.

NOTE: Payment may not be made for EPO under the incident to provision when EPO is administered in the renal dialysis facility. (See §5202.4.)

Medicare covers EPO and items related to its administration for dialysis patients who use EPO in the home when the following conditions are met.

1. Patient Care Plan. – A dialysis patient who uses EPO in the home must have a current care plan (a copy of which must be maintained by the designated back-up facility for Method II patients) for monitoring home use of EPO which includes the following:

a. Review of diet and fluid intake for aberrations as indicated by hyperkalemia and elevated blood pressure secondary to volume overload;

b. Review of medications to ensure adequate provision of supplemental iron;

c. Ongoing evaluations of hematocrit and iron stores;

d. Reevaluation of the dialysis prescription taking into account the patient's increased appetite and red blood cell volume;

e. Method for physician and facility (including back-up facility for Method II patients) follow-up on blood tests and a mechanism (such as a patient log) for keeping the physician informed of the results;

f. Training of the patient to identify the signs and symptoms of hypotension and hypertension; and

g. The decrease or discontinuance of EPO if hypertension is uncontrollable.

2. Patient Selection. – The dialysis facility, or the physician responsible for all dialysis-related services furnished to the patient, must make a comprehensive assessment that includes the following:

a. Pre-selection monitoring. The patient's hematocrit (or hemoglobin), serum iron, transferrin saturation, serum ferritin, and blood pressure must be measured.

b. Conditions the patient must meet. The assessment must find that the patient meets the following conditions: (1) Is a dialysis patient; (2) Has a hematocrit (or comparable hemoglobin level) that is as follows:

(a) For a patient who is initiating EPO treatment, no higher than 30 percent unless there is medical documentation showing the need for EPO despite a hematocrit (or comparable hemoglobin level) higher than 30 percent. Patients with severe angina, severe pulmonary distress, or severe hypotension may require EPO to prevent adverse symptoms even if they have higher hematocrit or hemoglobin levels.

(b) For a patient who has been receiving EPO from the facility or the physician, between 30 and 36 percent; and (3) Is under the care of:

(a) A physician who is responsible for all dialysis-related services and who prescribes the EPO and follows the drug labeling instructions when monitoring the EPO home therapy; and

(b) A renal dialysis facility that establishes the plan of care and monitors the progress of the home EPO therapy.

c. The assessment must find that the patient or a caregiver meets the following conditions:

1. Is trained by the facility to inject EPO and is capable of carrying out the procedure;

2. Is capable of reading and understanding the drug labeling; and

3. Is trained in, and capable of observing, aseptic techniques.

a. Care and storage of drug. The assessment must find that EPO can be stored in the patient's residence under refrigeration and that the patient is aware of the potential hazard of a child's having access to the drug and syringes.

4. Responsibilities of Physician or Dialysis Facility. – The patient's physician or dialysis facility must:

a. Develop a protocol that follows the drug label instructions;

b. Make the protocol available to the patient to ensure safe and effective home use of EPO;

c. Through the amounts prescribed, ensure that the drug on hand at any time does not exceed a 2-month supply; and

d. Maintain adequate records to allow quality assurance for review by the network and State survey agencies. For Method II patients, current records must be provided to and maintained by the designated back-up facility.

See §5202.4 for information on EPO payment.

Submit claims for EPO in accordance with §§4273.1 and 4273.2.

C. Oral Anti-Cancer Drugs. – Effective January 1, 1994, Medicare Part B coverage is extended to include oral anti-cancer drugs that are prescribed as anti-cancer chemotherapeutic agents providing they have the same active ingredients and are used for the same indications as anti-cancer chemotherapeutic agents which would be covered if they were not self administered and they were furnished incident to a physician's service as drugs and biologicals.

This provision applies only to the coverage of anti-neoplastic chemotherapeutic agents. It does not apply to oral drugs and/or biologicals used to treat toxicity or side effects such as nausea or bone marrow depression. Medicare will cover anti-neoplastic chemotherapeutic agents, the primary drugs which directly fight the cancer, and self-administered antiemetics which are necessary for the administration and absorption of the anti-neoplastic chemotherapeutic agents when a high likelihood of vomiting exists. The substitution of an oral form of an anti-neoplastic drug requires that the drug be retained for absorption. The antiemetics drug is covered as a necessary means for administration of the oral drug (similar to a syringe and needle necessary for injectable administration). Oral drugs prescribed for use with the primary drug which enhance the anti-neoplastic effect of the primary drug or permit the patient to tolerate the primary anti-neoplastic drug in higher doses for longer periods are not covered. Self-administered antiemetics to reduce the side effects of nausea and vomiting brought on by the primary drug are not included beyond the administration necessary to achieve drug absorption.

In order to assure uniform coverage policy, regional carriers and FIs must be apprised of local carriers' anti-cancer drug medical review policies which may impact on future medical review policy development. Local carrier's current and proposed anti-cancer drug medical review polices should be provided by local carrier medical directors to regional carrier or FI medical directors, upon request.

For an oral anti-cancer drug to be covered under Part B, it must:

- Be prescribed by a physician or other practitioner licensed under State law to prescribe such drugs as anti-cancer chemotherapeutic agents;

- Be a drug or biological that has been approved by the Food and Drug Administration (FDA);

- Have the same active ingredients as a non-self-administrable anti-cancer chemotherapeutic drug or biological that is covered when furnished incident to a physician's service. The oral anti-cancer drug and the non-self-administrable drug must have the same chemical/generic name as indicated by the FDA's Approved Drug Products (Orange Book), Physician's Desk Reference (PDR), or an authoritative drug compendium; – or, effective January 1, 1999, be a prodrug – an oral drug ingested into the body that metabolizes into the same active ingredient that is found in the non-self-administrable form of the drug;

- Be used for the same indications, including unlabeled uses, as the non-self-administrable version of the drug; and

- Be reasonable and necessary for the individual patient.

D. Oral Anti-Nausea Drugs – Section 4557 of the Balanced Budget Act of 1997 amends §1861(s)(2) by extending the coverage of oral anti-emetic drugs under the following conditions:

- Coverage is provided only for oral drugs approved by FDA for use as anti-emetics;

- The oral anti-emetic(s) must either be administered by the treating physician or in accordance with a written order from the physician as part of a cancer chemotherapy regimen;

- Oral anti-emetic drug(s) administered with a particular chemotherapy treatment must be initiated within 2 hours of the administration of the chemotherapeutic agent and may be continued for a period not to exceed 48 hours from that time.

- The oral anti-emetic drug(s) provided must be used as a full therapeutic replacement for the intravenous anti-emetic drugs that would have otherwise been administered at the time of the chemotherapy treatment.

Only drugs pursuant to a physician's order at the time of the chemotherapy treatment qualify for this benefit. The dispensed number of dosage units may not exceed a loading dose administered within 2 hours of that treatment, plus a supply of additional dosage units not to exceed 48 hours of therapy. However, more than one oral anti-emetic drug may be prescribed and will be covered for concurrent usage within these parameters if more than one oral drug is needed to fully replace the intravenous drugs that would otherwise have been given.

Oral drugs that are not approved by the FDA for use as anti-emetics and which are used by treating physicians adjunctively in a manner incidental to cancer chemotherapy are not covered by this benefit and are not reimbursable within the scope of this benefit.

It is recognized that a limited number of patients will fail on oral anti-emetic drugs. Intravenous anti-emetics may be covered (subject to the rules of medical necessity) when furnished to patients who fail on oral anti-emetic therapy.

This coverage, effective for services on or after January 1, 1998, is subject to regular Medicare Part B coinsurance and deductible provisions.

NOTE: Existing coverage policies authorizing the administration of suppositories to prevent vomiting when oral cancer drugs are used are unchanged by this new coverage.

E. Hemophilia Clotting Factors. – Section 1861(s)(2)(I) of the Act provides Medicare coverage of blood clotting factors for hemophilia patients competent to use such factors to control bleeding without medical supervision, and items related to the administration of such factors. Hemophilia, a blood disorder characterized by prolonged coagulation time, is caused by deficiency of a factor in plasma necessary for blood to clot. (The discovery in 1964 of a cryoprecipitate rich in antihemophilic factor activity facilitated management of acute bleeding episodes.) For purposes of Medicare Part B coverage, hemophilia encompasses the following conditions:

- Factor VIII deficiency (classic hemophilia);

- Factor IX deficiency (also termed plasma thromboplastin component (PTC) or Christmas factor deficiency); and

- Von Willebrand's disease.

Claims for blood clotting factors for hemophilia patients with these diagnoses may be covered if the patient is competent to use such factors without medical supervision.

The amount of clotting factors determined to be necessary to have on hand and thus covered under this provision is based on the historical utilization pattern or profile developed by the carrier for each patient. It is expected that the treating source; e.g., a family physician or comprehensive hemophilia diagnostic and treatment center, has such information. From this data, the contractor is able to make reasonable projections concerning the quantity of clotting factors anticipated to be needed by the patient over a specific period of time. Unanticipated occurrences involving extraordinary events, such as automobile accidents of inpatient hospital stays, will change this base line data and should be appropriately considered. In addition, changes in a patient's medical needs over a period of time require adjustments in the profile. (See §5245 for payment policies.)

MCM 2049.2

Determining Self-Administration of Drug or Biological. – Whether a drug or biological is of a type which cannot be self-administered is based on the usual method of administration of the form of that drug or biological as furnished by the physician. Whole blood is a biological which cannot be self-administered and is covered when furnished incident to a physician's services. Payment may also be made for blood fractions if all coverage requirements are satisfied. (See §2455 on Part B blood deductible.)

Medicare carriers have discretion in applying the criteria in this instruction in determining whether drugs are subject to this exclusion in their local areas. Carriers are to follow the instructions below when applying the exclusion for drugs that are usually self-administered by the patient. Each individual contractor must make its own individual determination on each drug. Contractors must continue to apply the policy that not only the drug is medically reasonable and necessary for any individual claim, but also that the route of administration is medically reasonable and necessary. That is, if a drug is available in both oral and injectable forms, the injectable form of the drug must be medically reasonable and necessary as compared to using the oral form. (See §2049.4.2) For certain injectable drugs, it will be apparent due to the nature of the condition(s) for which they are administered or the usual course of treatment for those conditions, they are, or are not, usually self-administered. For example, an injectable drug used to treat migraine headaches is usually selfadministered. On the other hand, an injectable drug, administered at the same time as chemotherapy, used to treat anemia secondary to chemotherapy is not usually self-administered. Administered – The term "administered" refers only to the physical process by which the drug enters the patient's body. It does not refer to whether the process is supervised by a medical professional (for example, to observe proper technique or side-effects of the drug). Only injectable (including intravenous) drugs are eligible for inclusion under the "incident to" benefit. Other routes of administration including, but not limited to, oral drugs, suppositories, topical medications are all considered to be usually self-administered by the patient. Usually – In arriving at a single determination as to whether a drug is usually self-administered, contractors should make a separate determination for each indication for a drug as to whether that drug is usually self-administered. After determining whether a drug is usually self-administered for each indication, contractors should determine the relative contribution of each indication to total use of the drug (i.e., weighted average) in order to make an overall determination as to whether the drug is usually self-administered. For example, if a drug has three indications, is not self-administered for the first indication, but is selfadministered for the second and third indications, and the first indication makes up 40% of total usage, the second indication makes up 30% of total usage, and the third indication makes up 30% of total usage, then the drug would be considered usually self-administered. Reliable statistical information on the extent of self-administration by the patient may not always be available.

Consequently, we offer the following guidance for each contractor's consideration in making this determination in the absence of such data:

1. Absent evidence to the contrary, drugs delivered intravenously should be presumed to be not usually self-administered by the patient.

2. Absent evidence to the contrary, drugs delivered by intramuscular injection should be presumed to be not usually self-administered by the patient. (For example, interferon beta-1a, tradename Avonex, when delivered by intramuscular injection is not usually self administered by the patient.) The contractor may consider the depth and nature of the particular intramuscular injection in applying this presumption.

3. Absent evidence to the contrary, drugs delivered by subcutaneous injection should be presumed to be self-administered by the patient. In applying these presumptions, contractors should examine the use of the particular drug and consider the following factors:

A. Acute condition. – For the purposes of determining whether a drug is usually selfadministered, an acute condition means a condition that begins over a short time period, is likely to be of short duration and/or the expected course of treatment is for a short, finite interval. A course of treatment consisting of scheduled injections lasting less than two weeks, regardless of frequency or route of administration, is considered acute. Evidence to support this may include Food and Drug administration (FDA) approval language, package inserts, drug compendia, and other information.

Frequency of administration. – How often is the injection given? For example, if the drug is administered once per month, it is less likely to be self-administered by the patient. However, if it is administered once or more per week, it is likely that the drug is self-administered by the patient. By the patient – The term "by the patient" means Medicare beneficiaries as a collective whole. Include only the patients themselves and not other individuals (that is, do not include spouses, friends, or other care-givers). Base your determination on whether the drug is self-administered by the patient a majority of the time that the drug is used on an outpatient basis by Medicare beneficiaries for medically necessary indications. Ignore all instances when the drug is administered on an inpatient basis. Make this determination on a drug-by-drug basis, not on a beneficiary-bybeneficiary basis. In evaluating whether beneficiaries as a collective whole self-administer, do not consider individual beneficiaries who do not have the capacity to self-administer any drug due to a condition other than the condition for which they are taking the drug in question. For example, an individual afflicted with paraplegia or advanced dementia would not have the capacity to selfadminister any injectable drug, so such individuals would not be included in the population upon which the determination for self-administration by the patient was based. Note that some individuals afflicted with a less severe stage of an otherwise debilitating condition would be included in the population upon which the determination for "self-administered by the patient" was based; for example, an early onset of dementia. Evidentiary Criteria – In making a self-administration determination, contractors are only required to consider the following types of evidence: peer reviewed medical literature, standards of medical practice, evidence-based practice guidelines, FDA approved label, and package inserts. Contractors may also consider other evidence submitted by interested individuals or groups subject to their judgment. Contractors should also use these evidentiary criteria when reviewing requests for making a determination as to whether a drug is usually self-administered, and requests for reconsideration of a pending or published determination. Please note that prior to August 1, 2002, one of the principal factors used to determine whether a drug was subject to the self-administered exclusion was whether the FDA label contained instructions for self-administration. However, we note that under the standard in effect after August 1, 2002, the fact that the FDA label includes instructions for self-administration is not, by itself, a determining factor that a drug is subject to this exclusion.

Provider Notice of Non-Covered Drugs – Contractors must describe the process they will use to determine whether a drug is usually self-administered and thus does not meet the "incident to" benefit category. Contractors must place a description of the process on their Web site. Contractors must publish a list of the injectable drugs that are subject to the self-administered exclusion on their Web site, including the data and rationale that led to the determination. Contractors will report the workload associated with developing new coverage statements in CAFM 21208. Contractors must provide notice 45 days prior to the date that these drugs will not be covered. During the 45-day time period, contractors will maintain existing medical review and payment procedures. After the 45-day notice, contractors may deny payment for the drugs subject to the notice.

Contractors must not develop local medical review policies (LMRPs) for this purpose because further elaboration to describe drugs that do not meet the 'incident to' and the 'not usually selfadministered' provisions of the statute are unnecessary. Current LMRPs based solely on these provisions must be withdrawn. LMRPs that address the self-administered exclusion and other information may be reissued absent the self-administered drug exclusion material. Contractors will report this workload in CAFM

21206. However, contractors may continue to use and write LMRPs to describe reasonable and necessary uses of drugs that are not usually self-administered.

Conferences Between Contractors – Contractors' Medical Directors may meet and discuss whether a drug is usually self-administered without reaching a formal consensus. Each contractor uses its discretion as to whether or not it will participate in such discussions. Each contractor must make its own individual determinations, except that fiscal intermediaries may, at their discretion, follow the determinations of the local carrier with respect to the self-administered exclusion.

Beneficiary Appeals – If a beneficiary's claim for a particular drug is denied because the drug is subject to the "self-administered drug" exclusion, the beneficiary may appeal the denial. Because it is a "benefit category" denial and not a denial based on medical necessity, an Advance Beneficiary Notice (ABN) is not applicable. A "benefit category" denial (i.e., a denial based on the fact that there is no benefit category under which the drug may be covered) does not trigger the financial liability protection provisions of Limitation On Liability [under §1879 of the Act]. Therefore, physicians or providers may charge the beneficiary for an excluded drug. See Chapter XV of the Medicare Carrier Manual for more detail on the appeals process.

Provider and Physician Appeals – A physician accepting assignment may appeal a denial under the provisions found in §12000 of the Medicare Carriers Manual. See Chapter XV of the Medicare Carrier Manual for more detail on the appeals process.

Reporting Requirements – Each carrier must report to CMS, every September 1 and March 1, its complete list of injectable drugs that the contractor has determined are excluded when furnished incident to a physician's service on the basis that the drug is usually self-administered. We anticipate that contractors will review injectable drugs on a rolling basis and publish their list of excluded drugs as it is developed. For example, contractors should not wait to publish this list until every drug has been reviewed. Contractors must send their exclusion list to the following e-mail address: drugdata@cms.hhs.gov. Below is an example of the Microsoft Excel template that should be submitted to CMS.

Carrier Name
State
Carrier
ID #
HCPCS Descriptor
Effective date of exclusion
End date of exclusion
Comments

MCM 2049.3   Incident-to Requirements.
In order for Medicare payment to be made for a drug, the "incident to" requirements are met. "Incident to" a physician's professional service means that the services are furnished as an integral, although incidental, part of the physician's personal professional services in the course of diagnosis or treatment of an illness or injury. See §2050.1 for more detail on incident-to requirements. In order to meet all the general requirements for coverage under the incident-to provision, an FDA approved drug or biological must be furnished by a physician and administered by him/her or by auxiliary personnel employed by him/her under his/her personal supervision. The charge, if any, for the drug or biological must be included in the physician's bill, and the cost of the drug or biological must represent an expense to the physician. Drugs and biologicals furnished by other health professionals may also meet these requirements. (See §§2154, 2156, 2158 and 2160 for specific instructions.)

MCM 2070.1   Independent Laboratories. – Diagnostic laboratory services furnished by an independent laboratory are covered under medical insurance if the laboratory is an approved Independent Clinical Laboratory. (However, as is the case of all diagnostic services, in order to be covered these services must be related to a patient's illness or injury (or symptom or complaint) and ordered by a physician. See §2020.I for the definition of a "physician".)

A. Definition of Independent. – An independent laboratory is one which is independent both of an attending or consulting physician's office and of a hospital which meets at least the requirements to qualify as an emergency hospital as defined in section l86l(e) of the Act. (A consulting physician is one whose services include history taking, examination of the patient, and, in each case, furnishing to the attending physician an opinion regarding diagnosis or treatment. A physician providing clinical laboratory services for patients of other physicians is not considered to be a consulting physician.)

A laboratory which is operated by or under the supervision of a hospital (or the organized medical staff of the hospital) which does not meet at least the definition of an emergency hospital is considered to be an independent laboratory. However, a laboratory serving hospital patients and operated on the premises of a hospital which meets the definition of an emergency hospital is presumed to be subject to the supervision of the hospital or its organized medical staff and is not an independent laboratory. A laboratory which a physician or group of physicians maintains for performing diagnostic tests in connection with his own or the group practice is also not considered to be an independent laboratory.

An out-of-hospital laboratory is ordinarily presumed to be independent unless there is written evidence establishing that it is operated by or under the supervision of a hospital which meets at least the definition of an emergency hospital or of the organized medical staff of such a hospital.

Where a laboratory operated on hospital premises is claimed to be independent or where an out-of-hospital facility is designated as a hospital laboratory, the RO makes the determination concerning the laboratory's status.

B. Clinical Defined. – A clinical laboratory is a laboratory where microbiological, serological, chemical, hematological, radioassay, cytological, immunohematological, or pathological examinations are performed on materials derived from the human body, to provide information for the diagnosis, prevention, or treatment of a disease or assessment of a medical condition.

C. Approval of Laboratories. – An approved independent clinical laboratory is one which is approved by the Secretary of Health, Education, and Welfare as meeting the specific conditions for coverage under the program. These require that: (I) where State or applicable local law provides for licensing of independent clinical laboratories, the laboratory is either licensed under such law or it is approved as meeting the requirements for licensing laboratories; and (2) such laboratories also meet the health and safety requirements prescribed by the Secretary of Health, Education, and Welfare. See "Conditions for Coverage of Services of Independent Laboratories. (HIRM I Subpart M)

Diagnostic laboratory tests performed by a laboratory of a nonparticipating hospital which meet the statutory definition of an emergency hospital are covered only if the laboratory meets the requirements set forth in the regulations for hospital laboratories.

Services rendered by an independent clinical laboratory are covered under medical insurance only if the laboratory has been approved under the program. Carriers are furnished lists of approved laboratories and their approved specialties by HCFA. If you have any reason to question the lists concerning additions or deletions of particular laboratories or specialties, clarifying information should be requested from the RO.

Laboratory Certification and Decertification

You must notify your physicians of the initial certification of the laboratories in your service areas and also furnished certification information about laboratories outside your service area upon request from individual physicians or clinics. This information is available from the RO (see § 2070.ID below). Where there are any changes in the certification of a laboratory, i.e., addition or deletion of tests for which the laboratory is certified, notify the physicians in your service areas of these changes.

When some or all of the services of an independent laboratory no longer meet the conditions for coverage, inform all physicians having an interest in the laboratory's certification status of the effective date of decertification, reasons for the decertification, and the applicability of the determination to the various categories of diagnostic tests performed by the independent laboratory. Notification to the physicians must be made prior to the termination date since you cannot honor any bill for services performed after the termination date.

If you issue a monthly bulletin or newsletter to physicians in your service area you may wish to use this vehicle to inform the physicians involved. If, in a particular instance, timely notification cannot be made by use of the regular monthly bulletin or newsletter, a special bulletin will be necessary. In cases where there are a limited number of physicians in a remote area, a notification to all physicians in your service area may not be necessary. In these situations, you may wish to limit the scope of the notification and use means other than the monthly newsletter. You must secure the prior approval of the regional office for limited notification.

For notices of decertification, you will receive a copy of the decertification letter to the laboratory from the RO. Language suitable for use in the carrier notices to physicians concerning the reasons for the decertification will also be supplied. The following information will be included in the notification:

1. Name and address of laboratory;
2. Effective date of decertification;
3. Which services are not covered (all or particular specialty(ies); and
4. Reason for decertification.

Your notification to the physicians should contain a statement that no payment can be made under title XVIII on behalf of Medicare patients receiving these services from the laboratory on or after the effective decertification dates.

A copy of all notifications to physicians concerning laboratory decertifications, whether by regular monthly newsletter or by a special bulletin, should be sent to the RO Contractor Operations Staff on the date of issuance.

NOTE: The notification to physicians also applies to services performed by suppliers of portable X-ray services (see §2070.4B).

D. The Specialty Provision. – One of the conditions for coverage of services of independent laboratories is that the laboratory agrees to perform tests for Medicare beneficiaries only in the specialties for which it is certified. Clinical laboratory services rendered in a specialty for which an independent laboratory is not certified are not covered and claims for payment of benefits for these services must be denied.

HCFA furnishes lists to the carriers showing specialties and subspecialties in which each laboratory has been certified. The lists are updated quarterly. Each carrier receives two lists showing the independent laboratories located in its service area: one list by provider number and the other list alphabetical. For information on laboratories not located within a carrier's service area, the RO's maintain national lists showing all approved laboratories. A key is furnished for interpreting the codes on the lists. See §§ 4110ff. for additional information.

Following is a list of covered clinical laboratory test procedures and calculations by specialty and subspecialty that may be performed by independent laboratories participating in the Medicare program (hospital laboratories are not currently approved by specialty/subspecialty). The list contains most of the common test procedures but is not considered all inclusive. Test procedures and calculations that may be performed in more than one specialty/subspecialty are asterisked and cross-referred.

This list is also used by State agencies of certification of the laboratories in the various specialty and subspecialty categories.

GLOSSARY OF LABORATORY TESTS AND CALCULATIONS LISTED BY CATEGORY

010 Historcompatibility Testing (Tissue Typing)

Antiglobulin Crossmatch for Transplantation Antiglobulin microcytotoxicity Technique Capillary Agglutination Cell-mediated lympholysis Test HLA Typing – Platelet Complement Fixation (FLCF) HLA Typing – Lymphocyte Complement Fixation HLA Typing – B27, specific B lymphocyte antigen HLA Typing – Total Leukocyte Aggregation Test (LAT) Leukoagglutination or Phytohemagglutination Lymphocyte Antibody Lymphocytolytic Interaction (LALI) Lymphocyte – dependent antibody-mediated lysis (LDA) Mixed Leukocyte Culture Mixed Lymphocyte Reaction (Mixed Lymphocyte Culture)-MLR, MLC Screening Sera for HLA antibodies Detection of Leukocyte antibodies by the Complement Consumption Test Separation of multiple HLA antibody specificities by platelet absorption and acid elution Other techniques: Target Cells (terminology used) Killer Cells

100 MICROBIOLOGY

110 Bacteriology (with antimicrobial susceptibility

Acid-fast culture, primary isolation

Acid-fast culture, identification

Acid-fast smear

Antimicrobial susceptibility test (mycobacteriology)

Antimicrobial susceptibility test (general bacteriology)

Antogenous vaccine

Culture, primary isolation

Culture, identification

Culture, for Mycoplasma pneumoniae

Gram Smear

Leptospirosis (Blood, Urine and CSF)

*Mycoplasma pneumoniae CF test-220

*More than one specialty category

PKU (Guthrie only)

Pyrogen test

Pyrogen test (Samples containing protein)

*Streptococcus MG agglutination-220

*Tularemia agglutination-220

120 Mycology

*Coccidiomycosis, Precipitin-220

Culture for Fungi Identification

Abscess

Blood

Bone Marrow

CSF (cerebrospinal fluid)

Eye

Skin, Hair, Nail

Sputum

Tissue Section

Vaginal

Culture, Primary isolation

*Histoplasma agglutionation-220

Mycelia Direct Examination – fungal smear

130 Parasitology

Blood Specimen for Filariasis

*Blood Specimen for Malaria-400

Purged Stool for Amebiasis

Routine Stool for Ova and Parasite

Scotch Tape Test for Enterobius Vermicularis

Stool, urine for Schistosomiasis toxoplasmosis

*Toxoplasmosis agglutionation-220

*Trichina agglutionation-l30

Vaginal Swab for Trichomonas vaginalis

140 Virology (including Rickettsiae and chlamydiae) (isolation and identification)

150 Other

*Febrile Group-220

Fluorescent stains for bacterial identification

*Immunoflourescence Methods – 220

Phage typing for staphylococci/other bacterial organisms

200 SEROLOGY

*More than one specialty category

210 Syphilis

Automated reagin test (ART)

Dark field Examination

Flourescent treponemal antibodies (FTA)

Kolmer, qual.

Kolmer, quant.

Rapid Plasma Reagin test (RPR Card Test)

Reagin Screen Test (RST)

Spinal Fluid, VDRL

VDRL (Venereal Disease Research Laboratory), qualitative slide

220 Serology-Other

Non-syphilis serology

(Diagnostic Immunology)

Alpha – l – antitrypsin

Alpha – l – fetoprotein (AFP) – 330

Anti-deoxuribonuclease (ADNase)

Anti-mitrochonorial antibody

Anti-nuclear antibodies (ANA)

Anti-parietal cell antibody

Anti-skeltal muscle antibody

Anti-smooth muscle antibody

Anti-streptococcalhyaluronidase (ASH)

Anti-streptolysin O (ASO) Test

Anti-thyroglobulin antibodies

Anti-toxoplasmosis antibody

Beta-lc/Beta la globulin

Brucella Agglutination

*Carcinoembryonic Antigen Assay (CEA) – 330

*Coccidiomycosis, Precipitin-l20

Cold Agglutinin

Complement, (Total Serum (C') & C'3 and components

C-reactive protein (CRP)

Free DNA Antibody

Free DNA Antigen

*Febrile group (Brucella, typhoid O & H, OX-I9, OX-K and OX-2)-l50

Gamma globulin, by salt pptn.

*Glucose-6 Phosphate Dehydrogenase (G-6-PD) – l30, 400

*Hepatitis B Antigen (HBsAg) – 330, 540

*Hepatitis B Antibody (Anti-HBs-330, 540

Heterophile antibodies (Presumptive)

Heterophile with absorptions (Differential)

*Histoplasma aggluatination – l20

I – Immunoglobulin Quantitation – See serum specific proteins

*Immunofluorescence Methods (Flourescent Antibody Techniques-Identification of Group A streptococci;

Neisseria gonorrhoeae, etc) – l50

*More than one specialty category

Infectious Mononucleosis

Leptospira agglutination

Lupus erythematosus – latex agglultination (LE)

*Mycoplasma pneumoniae CF test – ll0

Ox cell hemolysin test

Q-Fever, Agglutination Titre

Q-Fever, Complement Fixation

Radioallergo Sorbent Test (RAST Test)

Rheumatoid Arthritis-latex fixation (RA)

Rose test

Rubella CF antibody

Bubella HI antibody

Serum Specific Proteins – Immunoglobulin quantitation (IgG; IgA; IgM; IgD; IgE)

Sheep Cell Agglutination test for RA

*Streptococcus MG agglutination – ll0

Thyroid auto-antibodies

*Trichina agglutination – l30

*Toxoplasmosis Agglutination – l30

*Tularemia agglutination – ll0

300 CLINICAL CHEMISTRY – ROUTINE

310 Clinical Chemistry – Routine

Blood Urine, Stool, Cerebro-Spinal Fluid Chemistry (includes electrophoresis and enzymes

Acetone-acetoacetic acid-serum

Acid mucopolysaccharides, qualitative

Acid phosphatase

Acidity, titration

Albumin

Albumin-globulin (A/G) ratio (calculation)

Aldolase

Alkaline phospahtase, serum

Alpha-hydroxybutyric dehydrogenase (HED)

Alpha-amino acid nitrogen

Delta-aminolevulinic acid (ALA)

Amino acids, fractionated quant.

p-aminohippuric acid (PAH)

Aminophylline

Ammonia, Blood Urine

Amylase, Serum, Urine

Arterial Blood pH

Ascorbic Acid (Vitamin C)

Atyherogenic Index (AI)

Bicarbonate

Bile Acids, fractionated

Bilirubin, total

Bilirubin, Total and Direct

Blood gas and pH (calculation) (Pco2; po2; % 02 saturation; base-total)

*More than one specialty category

Boric Acid

Bromide

Bromsulfalcin, dye analysis only (BSP) – Sulfobromphthalein

Excretion – Liver

BUN (Blood Urea Nitrogen)

Calcium, Serum, Urine, Feces

Carbon Dioxide Content

Carotene

Cephalin Flocculation

Ceruloplasmin

Chloride

Cholesterol, total

Cholesterol, total and esters

Cholinesterase, serum, plasma, RBC

Chondroitin sulfate, qual.

Citric acid, serum, urine

C02-combining power

Creatine phosphokinase (CPK) – also known as creatine kinase

Creatine, urine, serum

Creatinine, urine, serum

Creatinine Clearance

Cryoglobulins

Cystine

Diastase

Electrolytes (Na, K, Cl) – sodium, potassium, chloride

FATS, serum or stool

Fatty acids, unesterified

Folate, RBC, serum

Free Fatty acids

Galactose, by chromatography

Gamma glutamyl transpetidase (Gamma-GTP)

Globulins, total

Glucose

Glucose tolerance

*Glucose-6-Phosphate Dehydrogenase-220,400

Glutathione Reductase

Glycoprotein

Guanase

Haptoglobin

*Hemoglobin electrophoresis – 400

Hexosamine

Hippuric acid quant.

Histamine

Homogentisic acid quant.

Icterus index (calculation)

Indocyanine green excretion-liver dye test

Iron, total, serum, urine

*More than one specialty category

Iron-binding capacity and total iron

Unsaturated iron binding capacity-UIBEL

Isocitric dehydrogenase (ICD)

Kynurenic and Xanthurenic acids

Lactic acid

Lactose tolerance test

LDH (lactic dehydrogenase), serum, CSF

LDH (fractionated)

LDH Isoenzymes by electrophoresis

Leucine aminopeptidase (LAP), serum, urine

Lipase

Lipid Profile-Phospholipids, cholesterol, triglycerides

Lipids, total and fractionated, serum

Lipids, total, feces

Lipids, total and split fat, feces

Lipids per dry weight, feces

B-Liporpotein screening

Lipoproteins by electrophoresis

Lipoproteins, phenotyping

Lipoproteins by ultracentrigufation

Lithium

Macroglobulin by ultracentrifugation

Magnesium, serum

Magnesium, urine

Manganese

Melanin, qualitative

Methylmalonic acid

Mucopolysaccharides, acid, qual.

Mucoprotein

Nitrogen, total, Urine, Feces

Non-esterified fatty acids (NEFA)

Non-protein nitrogen (NPN)

5'-Nucleotidase

Orinase Tolerance Test (Tolbutamide)

Ornithine carbamyl transferase (OCT)

Osmolatity by freezing point depression

Oxalate

Paraldehyde (as acetaldehyde)

PCO2

Pepsinogen

pH

Phenylpyruvic acid, qual.

Phosphoethanolamine by column chromatography

Phosphogalactose transferase

Phospholipids

Phospholipids, cholesterol, triglycerides

Phosphorus, Serum & Urine

PKU (exluding Guthrie method)

P02

Potassium, Serum, Urine, Feces

Protein, total

Protein, quant., urine, CSF

Protein fractionation by electrophoresis

Protoporphyrin, REC

Pyruvic acid

Reducing sugars by chromatography, qual., blood

Salicylates, serum, urine – 330

SGOT (Serum glutamic – oxalacetic transaminase) – also known as aspartate amino transferase

SGPT (Serum glutamic – pyruvic transaminase) – also know as alanine amino transferase

Silica, in lung tissue

Sodium, Serum, Urine, Feces

Spinal Fluid, Chlorides

Spinal Fluid, Sugar

Spinal Fluid, Total Protein

Split fat and total lipids, feces

Stercobilinogen

Sugars, qual., by paper chromatography

Sulfa level

Sulfate

Sweat Chlorides

Thiocyanate

Thymol Turbidity

Trichloracetic acid (TCA)

Trichlorethanol

Triglycerides

Triglycerides, phospholipids, cholesterol, total lipids

Tryspin

Tryptamine

Tryrosine

Urea clearance

Uric acid (phosphotungstate method)

Uropepsin

Vitamin A

Vitamin B2

*Vitamin BI2-400

Xanthurenic and kynurenic acids

Xylose (for tolerance test)

320 Urinalysis (Routine and Calculi)-Clinical Microscopy

Acetone-acetoacetic acid (urine)

Addis Count

*More than one specialty category

Basic chemical profile

Qualitative glucose

Qualitative bile

Qualitative Ketone bodies

Qualitative blood

Qualitative nitrate

Qualitative protein (predominantly albumin)

pH

Specific gravity

Color and appearance

Bile, urine

Calculi, qualitative

Coproporphyrin

Diagnex Blue (Tubeless gastric)

Galactose (for tolerance test)

Hippuric acid

Homogentisic acid, qualitative

Microscopic examination of urine sediment (cells, casts)

Myoglobin, semi-quantitive

Para-aminohippuric acid (PAH)

Pentose Sugar in urine (qual) screening

Phenosulfonphthalein excretion test-renal function test (P.S.P.)

Porphobilinogen, quant.

Porphyrins, urine

Porphyrins, feces

Protein, Bence-Jones

Protoporphyrin

Reducing sugars by chromatography, qual., urine

*Serotonin, urine – 5HIAA – 330

Urinalysis (including Microscopic)

Urobilinogen, urine, feces

Uroporphyrin

320 Chemistry – Other (including Toxiocology)

Alkaloids and other organic bases

*Alpha-I-fetoprotein – 220

Amphetamine

Anti-convulsant group

Antimony

Arsenic, quantitative

Barbiturates

Barbiturates, tissue, quant.

Beryllium

Bismuth

*More than one specialty category

Blood Alcohol ethyl)

Bromides, serum

Bromides, urine

Cadmium

Carbon Monoxide (Carboxyhemoglobin)

*Carcinoembryonic Antigen Assay (CEA) – 220

Chloramphenicol (Chloromycetin)

Chromium

Codeine, urine

Copper, Serum, Urine

Cyanide

Darvon

Dicumarol

Digitalis

Digitoxin

Digoxin

Dilantin

Doriden (glutethimide)

Elavil

Ethyl Alcohol (ethanol)

Fluoride

Gentamicin (by RIA)

Gold

Heavy metals (arsenic, lead, mercury) – Reinsch Test

*Hepatitis B Antigen (HBsAg) – 220, 540

*Hepatitis B Antibody (Anti-HBs) – 220, 540

Hypnotic and Tranquilizer Screen

Lead

Librium

Meprobamate (Miltown, Equanil)

Mercury

Methaqualone

Minerals

Nickel

Nicotine

Phenacetin

Phenols

Phenothiazines

Quinidine

Reinsch Test

*Salicylates, serum, urine – 3l0

Selenium

Strychnine

Thallium

Theophylline

Trace Elements

Trofranil – Imipramine)

*More than one specialty category

Valium

Volatiles by gas chromatography

(Acetaldehyde, acetone, ethanol, diethyl ether, isopropanol, methanol; other may be detected)

Zinc

330 Chemistry – Other (Endocrinology)

Adrenocorticotrophic hormone

Anti-diuretic hormone

Andrenaline-noradrenaline, total

Adrenaline-noradrenaline fractionation

A/E/DHA, by chromatography

Aldosterone

Calcitonin

Catecholamines, total

Chorionic gonadotropin, quant. BIOASSAY

Chorionic gonadodotropin, quant., IMMUNOASSAY

Cortiosol, plasma

11-Deoxy: 11-oxy ratio of 17-KGS

Dehydroepiandrosterone (DHA)

Estradiol receptor assay

Estriol, placental

Estrogens, total

Estrogens, fractionated (Brown method)

Estrogen receptor assay

Etiocholanolone, dehydroepiandrosterone, androsterone and total 17-Ketosteriods (A/E/DHA)

Ferminiminoglutamic acid (FIGLU)

Free thyroxine (Includes T4-by-column)

FSH (Follicle stimulating Hormone)

Gastrin

Growth hormone (GH OR HGH) 5-HIAA (5 OH-indoleacetic acid, serotonin metabolite)

Homovanillic Acid (HVA)

Human growth hormone (HGH)

Hydroxbutyric dehydrogenase (HBD)

17-Hydroxycorticosteroids, plasma (cortisol by fluorescence method)

17-Hydroxycorticosteroids, urine

11-R-Hydroxylase inhibition test

Hydroxyproline, free

Hydroxyproline, total

5-Hydroxytryptamine

Indole-3-Acetic Acid

Insulin

Insulin (for clearance test)

Inulin

Iodine, T4-by-column chromatography

Iodine, total, fluids, feces

Iodine, total inorganic and PBI

17-Ketosteroids, total, plasma, urine

17-Ketosteroids, beta: alpha ratio

17-Ketosteroids, separated by chromatography (7 compounds)

17-Ketogenic steroids (l7KGS)

Long-acting thyroid stimulator and Thyroid stimulating hormone (LATS and TSH)

Luteinizing hormone (LH)

Metanephrines (total)

11-Oxysteroids

Parathyroid hormone

PBI

PBI, total and inorganic iodine

Phenylalanine

Phenylketonuria (PKU) screening

Pituitary gonadotropins (FSH)

Placental estroil

Placidyl

Plasma cortisol

Pregnanediol

Pragnanetriol

Progesterone

Prolactin

Renin activity

Serotonin, Blood – 5HIAA, 5-hydroxyindoleacetic acid

*Serotonin metabolite, urine – 320

Testosterone

Tetrahydro compound S (THS)

Thyroid stimulating hormone

Thyroxine by column chromatography (T4)

Thyroxine, Free (T4)

Thyroxine by Murphy-Pattee method (T4)

Thyroxine-binding globulin (TBG)

Thyroxine-binding globulin (TBG) without T4 test)

Triiodothyronine (T3)

Vanillyl mandelic acid (VMA)

400 HEMATOLOGY

A2 hemoglobin

A2 and fetal hemoglobin

Basophillic stippling

*Blood specimen for malaria – 130

Cell count – spinal fluid

Complete Blood Count with Differential

Differential

Eosinophile Count

Erythrocyte Sedimentation Rate, Sed Rate

*Folate, R.B.C., Serum – 310

Fragility Test, erythrocytes

*More than one specialty category

*G-6-PD (Glucose-6-Phosphate dehydrogenase) – 220, 310

Hemoglobin A2

Hemoglobin, Fetal

Hemoglobin, Fetal and A2

Hemoglobin-binding protein

*Hemoglobin electrophoresis – 310

Hematocrit

Hemoglobin (cyanmethemoglobin method)

Hemoglobin (iron assay)

Hemoglobin, plasma, urine

Indices, Wintrobe (calculation)

Methemalbumin (Schumm Test)

Platelet Count

Red Blood Count (Erythrocyte Count, RBC)

Reticulocyte Count

Screening test for DIC – Disseminated Intravascular Coagulation

Sickle Cell Preparation

Sulfhemoglobin, methemoglobin, and total Hgb

*Vitamin B-l2 – 310

White Blood Count (Leukocyte Count, WBC)

Coagulation Studies Hematology

Bleeding time (Duke) or Ivy and Clotting time (Lee and White)

Complete Coagulation Study

Factor Assays (Factor VIII, IX, VII, XI)

Fibrin-Fibrinogen I egradation Products

Fibrinogen

Partial Thromboplastin Time (APTT, PTT)

Prothrombin Time (Pro time, PT)

Prothrombin Consumption

Prothrombin Utilization

Tests for Circulating Anticoagulants

Cellular Study Hematology

Bone Marrow Aspirate

Eosinophile Smear

Leukocyte Alkaline Phosphatase

Lupus crythematosus Preparation (L.E. Pre)

*Blood Specimen for malaria – See 130 and for other parasites

Molecular abnormality studies

Hemoglobinopathy

Synovial Fluid – Cell Count or Differential

500 IMMUNOHEMATOLOGY

510 A Subgrouping

Blood Grouping, A., B, O, and AB

Rh factor Including Du

Rh Cenotype (C, D, E, c, e)

*M+N Type – 540

*Husband's red cell genotype – 540

*More than one specialty category

520 Antibody Indentification

*Antibody screening test – Indirect Coombs – 540

Antibody titration

Rh antibody titer and blocking antibodies

530 Compatibility Testing – Crossmatch

540 Blood Typing for paternity tests

Direct Coomb's Test

*Hepatitis B Antigen (HBsAg) – 220, 330

*Hepatitis B Antibody (Anti-HBs) – 220, 330

*Husband's Red Cell Genotype – 510

*Indirect Coombs – Antibody screening test – 520

*M + N typing – 510

Rho Gam Workup

600 PATHOLOGY

601 Histopathology

Tissue Decalcification

Bone Marrow Biopsy

Tissue Pathology

Surgical pathology

Frozen sections

Autopsy and sections

620 Oral Pathology

630 Exfoliative Cytology

Cytology – Female Genital Tract

Cytology – nongynecological fluid cytologies

700 PHYSIOLOGICAL TESTING

710 EKG Services

800 RADIOBIOASSAY and NUCLIDES RADIOBIOASSAY

Blood volume – RBC Mass (Cr 51)

I131 Therapy

Polonium

Schilling test (Cobalt 60 – labelled B-12)

Thyroid function studies (1131 Uptake) (IST-3)

Tritium

900 ALL SPECIALTIES AND SUBSPECIALTIES

*More than one specialty category

E. Certification Changes. – Each page of the lists of approved specialties also includes a column "Certification Changed" in which the following codes are used:

"C" indicates a change in the laboratory's approved certification since the preceding listing.

"A" discloses an accretion.

"TERM" – Laboratory not approved for payment after the indicated date which follows the code. The reason for termination also is given in the following codes:

1. Involuntary termination – no longer meets requirements

2. Voluntary withdrawal

3. Laboratory closed, merged with other interests, or organizational change

4. Ownership change with new ownership participating under different name

5. Ownership change with new owner not participating

6. Change in ownership – new provider number assigned

7. Involuntary termination – failure to abide by agreement

8. Former "emergency" hospital now fully participating

F. Carrier Contacts With Independent Clinical Laboratories. – An important role of the carrier is as a communicant of necessary information to independent clinical laboratories. Experience has shown that the failure to inform laboratories of Medicare regulations and claims processing procedures may have an adverse effect on prosecution of laboratories suspected of fraudulent activities with respect to tests performed by, or billed on behalf of, independent laboratories. United Stated Attorneys often have to prosecute under a handicap or may simply refuse to prosecute cases where there is no evidence that a laboratory has been specifically informed of Medicare regulations and claims processing procedures.

To assure that laboratories are aware of Medicare regulations and carrier's policy, carrier newsletters should be sent to independent laboratories when any changes are made in coverage policy or claims processing procedures. Additionally, to completely document efforts to fully inform independent laboratories of Medicare policy and their responsibilities, previously issued newsletters should be periodically re-issued to remind laboratories of existing requirements. Some items which should be discussed are the requirements to have the same fee schedule for Medicare and private patients, to specify whether the tests are manual or automated, to indicate the numeric designation 6 or 12 when billing for SMA tests, to document fully the medical necessity for pick-up of specimens from a skilled nursing facility or a beneficiary's home, and, in cases when a laboratory service is referred from one independent laboratory to another independent laboratory, to identify the laboratory actually performing the test.

Additionally, when carrier professional relations representatives make personal contacts with particular laboratories, they should prepare and retain reports of contact indicating dates, persons present, and issues discussed.

G. Independent Laboratory Service to a Patient in His Home or an Institution. – Where it is medically necessary for an independent laboratory to visit a patient to obtain a specimen or to perform EKGs, the service would be covered in the following circumstances:

1. Patient Confined to His Home. – If a patient is confined to his home or other place of residence used as his home, (see §2051.1 for the definition of a "homebound patient"), medical necessity would exist, for example, where a laboratory technician draws a blood specimen or takes an EKG tracing. However, where the specimen is a type which would require only the services of a messenger and would not require the skills of a laboratory technician, e.g., urine or sputum, a specimen pickup service would not be considered medically necessary.

2. Place of Residence is an Institution. – Medical necessity could also exist where the patient's place of residence is an institution including a skilled nursing facility, that does not perform venipunctures. This would apply even though the institution meets the basic definition of a skilled nursing facility and would not ordinarily be considered a beneficiary's home under the rules in § 2100.3. (This policy is intended for independent laboratories only and does not expand the range of coverage of services to homebound patients under the incident to provision.) A trip by an independent laboratory technician to a facility (other than a hospital) for the purpose of performing a venipuncture or taking an EKG tracing is considered medically necessary only if (a) the patient was confined to the facility, and (b) the facility did not have on duty personnel qualified to perform this service. When facility personnel actually obtained and prepared the specimens for the independent laboratory to pick them up, the laboratory provides this pickup service as a service to the facility in the same manner as it does for physicians.

MCM 2070.4 Coverage of Portable X-ray Services Not Under the Direct Supervision of a Physician

A. Diagnostic X-ray Tests. – Diagnostic x-ray services furnished by a portable x-ray supplier are covered under Part B when furnished in a place or residence used as the patient's home and in nonparticipating institutions. These services must be performed under the general supervision of a physician and certain conditions relating to health and safety (as prescribed by the Secretary) must be met.

Diagnostic portable x-ray services are also covered under Part B when provided in participating SNFs and hospitals, under circumstances in which they cannot be covered under hospital insurance, i.e., the services are not furnished by the participating institution either directly or under arrangements that provide for the institution to bill for the services. (See §2255 for reimbursement for Part B services furnished to inpatients of participating and nonparticipating institutions.)

B. Applicability of Health and Safety Standards. – The health and safety standards apply to all suppliers of portable x-ray services, except physicians who provide immediate personal supervision during the administration of diagnostic x-ray services. Payment is made only for services of approved suppliers who have been found to meet the standards. Notice of the coverage dates for services of approved suppliers are given to carriers by the RO.

When the services of a supplier of portable x-ray services no longer meet the conditions of coverage, physicians having an interest in the supplier's certification status must be notified. The notification action regarding suppliers of portable x-

ray equipment is the same as required for decertification of independent laboratories, and the procedures explained in §2070.IC should be followed.

C. Scope of Portable X-Ray Benefit. – In order to avoid payment for services which are inadequate or hazardous to the patient, the scope of the covered portable x-ray benefit is defined as:

- Skeletal films involving arms and legs, pelvis, vertebral column, and skull;

- Chest films which do not involve the use of contrast media (except routine screening procedures and tests in connection with routine physical examinations); and

- Abdominal films which do not involve the use of contrast media.

D. Exclusions From Coverage as Portable X-Ray Services. – Procedures and examinations which are not covered under the portable x-ray provision include the following:

- Procedures involving fluoroscopy;

- Procedures involving the use of contrast media; procedures requiring the administration of a substance to the patient or injection of a substance into the patient and/or special manipulation of the patient;

- Procedures which require special medical skill or knowledge possessed by a doctor of medicine or doctor of osteopathy or which require that medical judgment be exercised;

- Procedures requiring special technical competency and/or special equipment or materials;

- Routine screening procedures; and

- Procedures which are not of a diagnostic nature.

E. Reimbursement Procedure. -

1. Name of Ordering Physician. – Assure that portable x-ray tests have been provided on the written order of a physician. Accordingly, if a bill does not include the name of the physician who ordered the service, that information must be obtained before payment may be made.

2. Reason Chest X-Ray Ordered. – Because all routine screening procedures and tests in connection with routine physical examinations are excluded from coverage under Medicare, all bills for portable x-ray services involving the chest contain, in addition to the name of the physician who ordered the service, the reason an x-ray test was required. If this information is not shown, it is obtained from either the supplier or the physician. If the test was for an excluded routine service, no payment may be made.

See also §§4110 ff. for additional instructions on reviewing bills involving portable -ray.

Electrocardiograms. – The taking of an electrocardiogram tracing by an approved supplier of portable x-ray services may be covered as an "other diagnostic test." The health and safety standards referred to in §2070.4B are thus also applicable to such diagnostic EKG services, e.g., the technician must meet the personnel qualification requirements in the Conditions for Coverage of Portable x-ray Services. (See §50-15 (Electrocardiographic Services) in the Coverage Issues Manual.)

MCM 2079 Surgical Dressings, and Splints, Casts, and Other Devices Used For Reductions of Fractures and Dislocations

Surgical dressings are limited to primary and secondary dressings required for the treatment of a wound caused by, or treated by, a surgical procedure that has been performed by a physician or other health care professional to the extent permissible under State law. In addition, surgical dressings required after debridement of a wound are also covered, irrespective of the type of debridement, as long as the debridement was reasonable and necessary and was performed by a health care professional who was acting within the scope of his or her legal authority when performing this function. Surgical dressings are covered for as long as they are medically necessary.

Primary dressings are therapeutic or protective coverings applied directly to wounds or lesions either on the skin or caused by an opening to the skin. Secondary dressing materials that serve a therapeutic or protective function and that are needed to secure a primary dressing are also covered. Items such as adhesive tape, roll gauze, bandages, and disposable compression material are examples of secondary dressings. Elastic stockings, support hose, foot coverings, leotards, knee supports, surgical leggings, gauntlets, and pressure garments for the arms and hands are examples of items that are not ordinarily covered as surgical dressings. Some items, such as transparent film, may be used as a primary or secondary dressing.

If a physician, certified nurse midwife, physician assistant, nurse practitioner, or clinical nurse specialist applies surgical dressings as part of a professional service that is billed to Medicare, the surgical dressings are considered incident to the professional services of the health care practitioner. (See §§2050.1, 2154, 2156, 2158, and 2160.) When surgical dressings are not covered incident to the services of a health care practitioner and are obtained by the patient from a supplier (e.g., a drug store,physician, or other health care practitioner that qualifies as a supplier) on an order from a physician or other health care professional authorized under State law or regulation to make such an order, the surgical dressings are covered separately under Part B.

Splints and casts, etc., include dental splints.

MCM 2100   Durable Medical Equipment – General

Expenses incurred by a beneficiary for the rental or purchase of durable medical equipment (DME) are reimbursable if the following three requirements are met. The decision whether to rent or purchase an item of equipment resides with the beneficiary.

A. The equipment meets the definition of DME (§2100.1); and

B. The equipment is necessary and reasonable for the treatment of the patient's illness or injury or to improve the functioning of his malformed body member (§2100.2); and

C. The equipment is used in the patient's home (§2100.3).

Payment may also be made under this provision for repairs, maintenance, and delivery of equipment as well as for expendable and nonreusable items essential to the effective use of the equipment subject to the conditions in §2100.4.

See §2105 and its appendix for coverage guidelines and screening list of DME. See §4105.3 for models of payment: decisions as to rental or purchase, lump sum and periodic payments, etc. Where covered DME is furnished to a beneficiary by a supplier of services other than a provider of services, reimbursement is made by the carrier on the basis of the reasonable charge. If the equipment is furnished by a provider of services, reimbursement is made to the provider by the intermediary on a reasonable cost basis; see Coverage Issues Appendix 25-1 for hemodialysis equipment and supplies.

MCM 2100.1   Definition of Durable Medical Equipment. – Durable medical equipment is equipment which (a) can withstand repeated use, and (b) is primarily and customarily used to serve a medical purpose, and (c) generally is not useful to a person in the absence of an illness or injury; and (d) is appropriate for use in the home.

All requirements of the definition must be met before an item can be considered to be durable medical equipment.

A. Durability. – An item is considered durable if it can withstand repeated use, i.e., the type of item which could normally be rented. Medical supplies of an expendable nature such as, incontinent pads, lambs wool pads, catheters, ace bandages, elastic stockings, surgical face masks, irrigating kits, sheets and bags are not considered "durable" within the meaning of the definition. There are other items which, although durable in nature, may fall into other coverage categories such as braces, prosthetic devices, artificial arms, legs, and eyes.

B. Medical Equipment. – Medical equipment is equipment which is primarily and customarily used for medical purposes and is not generally useful in the absence of illness or injury. In most instances, no development will be needed to determine whether a specific item of equipment is medical in nature. However, some cases will require development to determine whether the item constitutes medical equipment. This development would include the advice of local medical organizations (hospitals, medical schools, medical societies) and specialists in the field of physical medicine and rehabilitation. If the equipment is new on the market, it may be necessary, prior to seeking professional advice, to obtain information from the supplier or manufacturer explaining the design, purpose, effectiveness and method of using the equipment in the home as well as the results of any tests or clinical studies that have been conducted.

Equipment Presumptively Medical. – Items such as hospital beds, wheelchairs, hemodialysis equipment, iron lungs, respirators, intermittent positive pressure breathing machines, medical regulators, oxygen tents, crutches, canes, trapeze bars, walkers, inhalators, nebulizers, commodes, suction machines and traction equipment presumptively constitute medical equipment. (Although hemodialysis equipment is a prosthetic device (§ 2l30), it also meets the definition of DME, and reimbursement for the rental or purchase of such equipment for use in the beneficiary's home will be made only under the provisions for payment applicable to DME. See 25-l and 25-2 of the Coverage Issues Appendix for coverage of home use of hemodialysis.)

NOTE: There is a wide variety in type of respirators and suction machines. The carrier's medical staff should determine whether the apparatus specified in the claim is appropriate for home use.

Equipment Presumptively Nonmedical. – Equipment which is primarily and customarily used for a nonmedical purpose may not be considered "medical" equipment for which payment can be made under the medical insurance program. This is true even though the item has some remote medically related use. For example, in the case of a cardiac patient, an air conditioner might possibly be used to lower room temperature to reduce fluid loss in the patient and to restore an environment conducive to maintenance of the proper fluid balance. Nevertheless, because the primary and customary use of an air

conditioner is a nonmedical one, the air conditioner cannot be deemed to be medical equipment for which payment can be made.

Other devices and equipment used for environmental control or to enhance the environmental setting in which the beneficiary is placed are not considered covered DME. These include, for example, room heaters, humidifiers, dehumidifiers, and electric air cleaners. Equipment which basically serves comfort or convenience functions or is primarily for the convenience of a person caring for the patient, such as elevators, stairway elevators, and posture chairs do not constitute medical equipment.

Similarly,physical fitness equipment, e.g., an exercycle; first-aid or precautionary-type equipment, e.g., present portable oxygen units; self-help devices, e.g., safety grab bars; and training equipment, e.g., speech teaching machines and braille training texts, are considered nonmedical in nature.

_ Special Exception Items. – Specified items of equipment may be covered under certain conditions even though they do not meet the definition of DME because they are not primarily and customarily used to serve a medical purpose and/or are generally useful in the absence of illness or injury. These items would be covered when it is clearly established that they serve a therapeutic purpose in an individual case and would include:

Gel pads and pressure and water mattresses (which generally serve a preventive purpose) when prescribed for a patient who had bed sores or there is medical evidence indicating that he is highly susceptible to such ulceration; and

Heat lamps for a medical rather than a soothing or cosmetic purpose, e.g., where the need for heat therapy has been established.

In establishing medical necessity (§2100.2) for the above items, the evidence must show that the item is included in the physician's course of treatment and a physician is supervising its use. (See also Appendix to § 2105.)

NOTE: The above items represent special exceptions and no extension of coverage to other items should be inferred.

MCM 2100.4   Repairs, Maintenance, Replacement, and Delivery

Under the circumstances specified below, payment may be made for repair, maintenance, and replacement of medically required DME which the beneficiary owns or is purchasing, including equipment which had been in use before the user enrolled in Part B of the program. Since renters of equipment usually recover from the rental charge the expenses they incur in maintaining in working order the equipment they rent out, separately itemized charges for repair, maintenance and replacement of rented equipment are not covered, except in the case setout in subsection E.

However, payment generally is not made for repair, maintenance, and replacement of purchased equipment that requires frequent and substantial servicing, capped rental equipment, or oxygen equipment. See §5102.3 for exceptions.

A. Repairs. – Repairs to equipment which a beneficiary is purchasing or already owns are covered when necessary to make the equipment serviceable. If the expense for repairs exceeds the estimated expense of purchasing or renting another item of equipment for the remaining period of medical need, no payment can be made for the amount of the excess. (See subsection C where claims for repairs suggest malicious damage or culpable neglect.)

B. Maintenance. – Routine periodic servicing, such as testing, cleaning, regulating and checking of the beneficiary's equipment is not covered. Such routine maintenance is generally expected to be done by the owner rather than by a retailer or some other person who charges the beneficiary. Normally, purchasers of DME are given operating manuals which describe the type of servicing an owner may perform to properly maintain the equipment. Thus, hiring a third party to do such work is for the convenience of the beneficiary and is not covered.

However, more extensive maintenance which, based on the manufacturers' recommendations, is to be performed by authorized technicians, is covered as repairs. This might include, for example, breaking down sealed components and performing tests which require specialized testing equipment not available to the beneficiary.

C. Replacement. – Replacement of equipment which the beneficiary owns or is purchasing is covered in cases of loss or irreparable damage or wear and when required because of a change in the patient's condition. Expenses for replacement required because of loss or irreparable damage may be reimbursed without a physician's order when in the judgment of the carrier the equipment as originally ordered, considering the age of the order, still fills the patient's medical needs. However, claims involving replacement equipment necessitated because of wear or a change in the patient's condition must be supported by a current physician's order. (See §2306D in regard to payment for equipment replaced under a warranty.)

Cases suggesting malicious damage, culpable neglect or wrongful disposition of equipment as discussed in §2100.6 should be investigated and denied where the carrier determines that it is unreasonable to make program payment under the circumstances. Refer such cases to the program integrity specialist in the RO.

D. Delivery. – Reasonable charges for delivery of DME whether rented or purchased are covered if the supplier customarily makes separate charges for delivery and this is a common practice among the other local suppliers. See §5105 for the rules that apply for making reimbursement for such charges.

E. Leased Renal Dialysis Equipment. – Generally, where renal dialysis equipment is leased directly from the manufacturer, the rental charge is closely related to the manufacturer's cost of the equipment which means it does not include a margin for recovering the cost of repairs beyond the initial warranty period. In view of physical distance and other factors which may make it impractical for the manufacturer to perform repairs, it is not feasible to make the manufacturer responsible for all repairs and include a margin for the additional costs. Therefore, reimbursement may be made for the repair and maintenance of home dialysis equipment leased directly from the manufacturer (or other party acting essentially as an intermediary between the patient and the manufacturer for the purpose of assuming the financial risk) if the rental charge does not include a margin to recover these costs, and then only when the patient is free to secure repairs locally in the most economical manner.

Where, on the other hand, a third party is in the business of medical equipment retail supply and rental, the presumption that there is a margin in the rental charge for dialysis equipment to cover the costs of repair services will, therefore, continue to be applied in these situations, and the patient must look to the supplier to perform (or cover the cost of) necessary repairs, maintenance, and replacement of the home dialysis equipment.

In all cases, whether the dialysis equipment is being purchased, is owned outright, or is being leased, Medicare payment is to be made only after the initial warranty period has expired. Generally, reimbursement for repairs, maintenance, and replacement parts for medically necessary home dialysis equipment may be made in a lump sum payment. However, where extensive repairs are required and the charge for repairing the item represents a substantial proportion of the purchase price of a replacement system, exercise judgment with respect to a possible need to make periodic payments, instead of a lump- sum payment, for repair of such equipment.

As in the case of the maintenance of purchased DME, routine periodic servicing of leased dialysis equipment, including most testing and cleaning, is not covered. While reimbursement will be made for more extensive maintenance and necessary repairs of leased dialysis equipment, the patient or family member is expected to perform those services for which the training for home or self-dialysis would have qualified them, e.g., replacement of a light bulb.

Reasonable charges for travel expenses related to the repair of leased dialysis equipment are covered if the repairman customarily charges for travel and this is a common practice among other repairman in the area. When a repair charge includes an element for travel, however, the location of other suitably qualified repairmen will be considered in determining the allowance for travel.

NOTE: The above cover age instructions pertain to a special case and no extension of such cover age with respect to other items should be inferred.

MCM 2100.5   Coverage of Supplies and Accessories.

Reimbursement may be made for supplies, e.g., oxygen (see §60-4 in the Coverage Issues Manual for the coverage of oxygen in the home), that are necessary for the effective use of durable medical equipment. Such supplies include those drugs and biologicals which must be put directly into the equipment in order to achieve the therapeutic benefit of the durable medical equipment or to assure the proper functioning of the equipment, e.g., tumor chemotherapy agents used with an infusion pump or heparin used with a home dialysis system. However, the coverage of such drugs or biologicals does not preclude the need for a determination that the drug or biological itself is reasonable and necessary for treatment of the illness or injury or to improve the functioning of a malformed body member.

In the case of prescription drugs, other than oxygen, used in conjunction with durable medical equipment, prosthetic, orthotics, and supplies (DMEPOS) or prosthetic devices, the entity that dispenses the drug must furnish it directly to the patient for whom a prescription is written. The entity that dispenses the drugs must have a Medicare supplier number, must possess a current license to dispense prescription drugs in the State in which the drug is dispensed, and must bill and receive payment in its own name. A supplier that is not the entity that dispenses the drugs cannot purchase the drugs used in conjunction with DME for resale to the beneficiary. Payments made for drugs provided on or after December 1, 1996 to suppliers not having a valid pharmacy license to dispense prescription drugs must be recouped.

Reimbursement may be made for replacement of essential accessories such as hoses, tubes, mouth pieces, etc., for necessary DME, only if the beneficiary owns or is purchasing the equipment.

MCM 2120.1   Vehicle and Crew Requirement

A. The Vehicle. – The vehicle must be a specially designed and equipped automobile or other vehicle (in some areas of the United States this might be a boat or plane) for transporting the sick or injured. It must have customary patient care equipment including a stretcher, clean linens, first aid supplies, oxygen equipment, and it must also have such other safety and lifesaving equipment as is required by State or local authorities.

B. The Crew. – The ambulance crew must consist of at least two members. Those crew members charged with the care or handling of the patient must include one individual with adequate first aid training, i.e., training at least equivalent to that provided by the standard and advanced Red Cross first aid courses. Training "equivalent" to the standard and advanced Red Cross first aid training courses included ambulance service training and experience acquired in military service, successful completion by the individual of a comparable first aid course furnished by or under the sponsorship of State or local authorities, an educational institution, a fire department, a hospital, a professional organization, or other such qualified organization. On-the-job training involving the administration of first aid under the supervision of or in conjunction with trained first aid personnel for a period of time sufficient to assure the trainee's proficiency in handling the wide range of patient care services that may have to be performed by a qualified attendant can also be considered as "equivalent training."

C. Verification of Compliance. – In determining whether the vehicles and personnel of each supplier meet all of the above requirements, carriers may accept the supplier's statement (absent information to the contrary) that its vehicles and personnel meet all of the requirements if (l) the statement describes the first aid, safety, and other patient care items with which the vehicles are equipped, (2) the statement shows the extent of first aid training acquired by the personnel assigned to those vehicles, (3) the statement contains the supplier's agreement to notify the carrier of any change in operation which could affect the coverage of his ambulance services, and (4) the information provided indicates that the requirements are met. The statement must be accompanied by documentary evidence that the ambulance has the equipment required by State and local authorities. Documentary evidence could include a letter from such authorities, a copy of a license, permit certificate, etc., issued by the authorities. The statement and supporting documentation would be kept on file by the carrier.

When a supplier does not submit such a statement or whenever there is a question about a supplier's compliance with any of the above requirements for vehicle and crew (including suppliers who have completed the statement), carriers should take appropriate action including, where necessary, on-site inspection of the vehicles and verification of the qualifications of personnel to determine whether the ambulance service qualifies for reimbursement under Medicare. Since the requirements described above for coverage of ambulance services are applicable to the overall operation of the ambulance supplier's service, it is not required that information regarding personnel and vehicles be obtained on an individual trip basis.

D. Ambulance of Providers of Services. – The Part A intermediary is responsible for the processing of claims for ambulance service furnished by participating hospitals, skilled nursing facilities and home health agencies and has the responsibility to determine the compliance of provider's ambulance and crew. Since provider ambulance services furnished "under arrangements" with suppliers can be covered only if the supplier meets the above requirements, the Part A intermediary may ask the carrier to identify those suppliers who meet the requirements.

E. Equipment and Supplies. – As mentioned above, the ambulance must have customary patient care equipment and first aid supplies. Reusable devices and equipment such as backboards, neckboards and inflatable leg and arm splints are considered part of the general ambulance service and would be included in the charge for the trip. On the other hand, separate reasonable charge based on actual quantities used may be recognized for nonreusable items and disposable supplies such as oxygen, gauze and dressings required in the care of the patient during his trip.

MCM 2125   Coverage Guidelines For Ambulance Service Claims

Reimbursement may be made for expenses incurred by a patient for ambulance service provided conditions l, 2, and 3 in the left-hand column have been met. The right-hand column indicates the documentation needed to establish that the condition has been met.

Conditions   Review Action

1.   Patient was transported by an approved supplier of ambulance services.

Ambulance supplier is listed in the carriers table of approved ambulance companies. (§2120.1C)

2. The patient was suffering from an illness or injury which contraindicated transportation by other means. (§2120.2A)

2. (a) Presume the requirement was met if file shows the patient:

(i) Was transported in an emergency situation, e.g., as a result of an accident, injury, or acute illness, or

(ii) Needed to be restrained, or

(iii) Was unconscious or in shock, or

(iv) Required oxygen or other emergency treatment on the way to his destination, or

(v) Had to remain immobile because of a fracture that had not been set or the possibility of a fracture, or

(vi) Sustained an acute stroke or myocardial infarction,

(vii) Was experiencing severe hemorrhage, or

(viii) Was bed confined before and after the ambulance trip, or

(ix) Could be moved only by stretcher.

(b) In the absence of any of the conditions listed in (a)above additional documentation should be obtained to establish medical need where the evidence indicates the existence of the circumstances listed below:

(i) Patient's condition would not ordinarily require movement by stretcher, or

(ii) The individual was not admitted as a hospital inpatient (except in accident cases), or

(iii) The ambulance was used solely because other means of transportation were unavailable, or

(iv) The individual merely needed assistance in getting from his room or home to a vehicle.

(c) Where the information indicates a situation not listed in 2(a) or 2(b) above, refer the case to your supervisor.

3 The patient was transported from and to points listed below.(§2120.3)
3. Claims should show points of pickup and destination.

(a) From patient's residence (or other place where need arose) to hospital or skilled nursing home.

(a) (i) Condition met if trip began within the institution's service area as shown in the carrier's locality guide.

(ii) Condition met where the trip began outside the institution's service area if the institution was the nearest one with appropriate facilities. Refer to supervisor for determination.

NOTE: A patient's residence is the place where he makes his home and dwells permanently, or for an extended period of time. A skilled nursing home is one which is listed in the Directory of Medical Facilities as a participating SNF or as an institution which meets section 1861(j)(1) of the law.

NOTE: A claim for ambulance service to a participating hospital or skilled nursing facility should not be denied on the grounds that there is a nearer nonparticipating institution having appropriate facilities.

(b) Skilled nursing home to a hospital or hospital to a skilled nursing home.

(b) (i) Condition met if pickup point is within the service area of the destination as shown in the carrier's locality guide.

(ii) Condition met where the pickup point is outside the service area of the destination if the destination institution was the nearest one with appropriate facilities. Refer to supervisor for determination.

(c) Hospital to hospital or skilled nursing home to skilled nursing home.

(c) Condition met if the discharging institution was not an appropriate facility and the admitting institution was the nearest one with appropriate facilities.

(d) From a hospital or skilled nursing home to patient's residence.

(d) (i) Condition met if patient's residence is within the institution's service area as shown in the carrier's locality guide.

(ii) Condition met where the patient's residence is outside the institution's service area if the institution was the nearest one with appropriate facilities. Refer to supervisor for determination.

(e) Round trip for hospital or participating skilled nursing facility inpatients to the nearest hospital or nonhospital treatment facility

(e) Condition met if the medically necessary diagnostic or therapeutic service required by the patient's condition is not available at the institution where the beneficiary is an inpatient.

NOTE: Ambulance service to a physician's office or a physician-directed clinic is not covered. (See §2120.3G where a stop is made at a physician's office enroute to a hospital and 2120.3C for additional exceptions.)

4. Ambulance services involving hospital admissions in Canada or Mexico are covered (§§2312ff.) if following conditions are met:

(a) The foreign hospitalization has been determined to be covered; and

(b) The ambulance service meets the coverage requirements set forth in §§ 2120-2120.3.

If the foreign hospitalization has been determined to be covered on the basis of emergency services (§ 2312.2A) the necessity requirement (§ 2120.2) and the destination requirement (§ 2120.3) are considered met.

5. Make partial payment for otherwise covered ambulance service which exceeded limits defined in item 3. (Claims supervisors are to make all partial payment determinations.) Base the payment on the amount payable had the patient been transported: (1) from the pickup point to the nearest appropriate facility, or (2) from the nearest appropriate facility to his/her residence where he/she is being returned home from a distant institution. (See §5215.2.)

MCM 2130 Prosthetic Devices.

A. General. – Prosthetic devices (other than dental) which replace all or part of an internal body organ (including contiguous tissue), or replace all or part of the function of a permanently inoperative or malfunctioning internal body organ are covered when furnished on a physician's order. This does not require a determination that there is no possibility that the patient's condition may improve sometime in the future. If the medical record, including the judgment of the attending physician, indicates the condition is of long and indefinite duration, the test of permanence is considered met. (Such a device may also be covered under §2050.I as a supply when furnished incident to a physician's service.)

Examples of prosthetic devices include cardiac pacemakers, prosthetic lenses (see subsection B), breast prostheses (including a surgical brassiere) for postmastectomy patients, maxillofacial devices and devices which replace all or part of the ear or nose. A urinary collection and retention system with or without a tube is a prosthetic device replacing bladder function in case of permanent urinary incontinence. The Foley catheter is also considered a prosthetic device when ordered for a patient with permanent urinary incontinence. However, chucks, diapers, rubber sheets, etc., are supplies that are not covered under this provision. (Although hemodialysis equipment is a prosthetic device, payment for the rental or purchase of such equipment for use in the home is made only under the provisions for payment applicable to durable medical equipment (see §4105ff) or the special rules that apply to the ESRD program.)

NOTE: Medicare does not cover a prosthetic device dispensed to a patient prior to the time at which the patient undergoes the procedure that makes necessary the use of the device. For example, do not make a separate Part B payment for an intraocular lens (IOL) or pacemaker that a physician, during an office visit prior to the actual surgery, dispenses to the patient for his/her use. Dispensing a prosthetic device in this manner raises health and safety issues. Moreover, the need for the device cannot be clearly established until the procedure that makes its use possible is successfully performed. Therefore, dispensing a prosthetic device in this manner is not considered reasonable and necessary for the treatment of the patient's condition.

Colostomy (and other ostomy) bags and necessary accouterments required for attachment are covered as prosthetic devices. This coverage also includes irrigation and flushing equipment and other items and supplies directly related to ostomy care, whether the attachment of a bag is required.

Accessories and/or supplies which are used directly with an enteral or parenteral device to achieve the therapeutic benefit of the prosthesis or to assure the proper functioning of the device are covered under the prosthetic device benefit subject to the additional guidelines in the Coverage Issues Manual §§65-10 – 65-10.3.

Covered items include catheters, filters, extension tubing, infusion bottles, pumps (either food or infusion), intravenous (I.V.) pole, needles, syringes, dressings, tape, Heparin Sodium (parenteral only), volumetric monitors (parenteral only), and parenteral and enteral nutrient solutions. Baby food and other regular grocery products that can be blenderized and used with the enteral system are not covered. Note that some of these items, e.g., a food pump and an I.V. pole, qualify as DME. Although coverage of the enteral and parenteral nutritional therapy systems is provided on the basis of the prosthetic device benefit, the payment rules relating to rental or purchase of DME apply to such items. (See §4105.3.) Code claims in accordance with the Healthcare Common Procedure Coding System (HCPCS).

APPENDIX 4 — MEDICARE REFERENCES

The coverage of prosthetic devices includes replacement of and repairs to such devices as explained in subsection D.

B. Prosthetic Lenses. – The term "internal body organ" includes the lens of an eye. Prostheses replacing the lens of an eye include post-surgical lenses customarily used during convalescence from eye surgery in which the lens of the eye was removed. In addition, permanent lenses are also covered when required by an individual lacking the organic lens of the eye because of surgical removal or congenital absence. Prosthetic lenses obtained on or after the beneficiary's date of entitlement to supplementary medical insurance benefits may be covered even though the surgical removal of the crystalline lens occurred before entitlement.

1. Prosthetic Cataract Lenses. – Make payment for one of the following prosthetic lenses or combinations of prosthetic lenses when determined to be medically necessary by a physician (see §2020.25 for coverage of prosthetic lenses prescribed by a doctor of optometry) to restore essentially the vision provided by the crystalline lens of the eye: prosthetic bifocal lenses in frames; prosthetic lenses in frames for far vision, and prosthetic lenses in frames for near vision; or when a prosthetic contact lens(es) for far vision is prescribed (including cases of binocular and monocular aphakia), make payment for the contact lens(es) and prosthetic lenses in frames for near vision to be worn at the same time as the contact lens(es), and prosthetic lenses in frames to be worn when the contacts have been removed.

Make payment for lenses which have ultraviolet absorbing or reflecting properties, in lieu of payment for regular (untinted) lenses, if it has been determined that such lenses are medically reasonable and necessary for the individual patient.

Do not make payment for cataract sunglasses obtained in addition to the regular (untinted) prosthetic lenses since the sunglasses duplicate the restoration of vision function performed by the regular prosthetic lenses.

2. Payment for IOLs Furnished in Ambulatory Surgical Centers (ASCs). Effective for services furnished on or after March 12, 1990, payment for IOLs inserted during or subsequent to cataract surgery in a Medicare certified ASC is included in the payment for facility services that are furnished in connection with the covered surgery. Section 5243.3 explains payment procedures for ASC facility services and the IOL allowance.

3. Limitation on Coverage of Conventional Lenses. – Make payment for no more than one pair of conventional eyeglasses or conventional contact lenses furnished after each cataract surgery with insertion of an IOL.

C. Dentures. – Dentures are excluded from coverage. However, when a denture or a portion thereof is an integral part (built-in) of a covered prosthesis (e.g., an obturator to fill an opening in the palate), it is covered as part of that prosthesis.

D. Supplies, Repairs, Adjustments, and Replacement. – Make payment for supplies that are necessary for the effective use of a prosthetic device (e.g., the batteries needed to operate an artificial larynx). Adjustment of prosthetic devices required by wear or by a change in the patient's condition is covered when ordered by a physician. To the extent applicable, follow the provisions relating to the repair and replacement of durable medical equipment in §2100.4 for the repair and replacement of prosthetic devices. (See §2306.D in regard to payment for devices replaced under a warranty.) Regardless of the date that the original eyewear was furnished (i.e., whether before, on, or after January 1, 1991), do not pay for replacement of conventional eyeglasses or contact lenses covered under subsection B.3.

Necessary supplies, adjustments, repairs, and replacements are covered even when the device had been in use before the user enrolled in Part B of the program, so long as the device continues to be medically required.

MCM 2133   Leg, Arm, Back, and Neck Braces, Trusses, and Artificial Legs, Arms, and Eyes

These appliances are covered when furnished incident to physicians' services or on a physician's order. A brace includes rigid and semi-rigid devices, which are used for the purpose of supporting a weak or deformed body member or restricting or eliminating motion in a diseased or injured part of the body. Elastic stockings, garter belts, and similar devices do not come within the scope of the definition of a brace. Back braces include, but are not limited to, special corsets, e.g., sacroiliac, sacrolumbar, dorsolumbar corsets and belts. A terminal device (e.g., hand or hook) is covered under this provision whether an artificial limb is required by the patient. (See §2323.) Stump stockings and harnesses (including replacements) are also covered when these appliances are essential to the effective use of the artificial limb.

Adjustments to an artificial limb or other appliance required by wear or by a change in the patient's condition are covered when ordered by a physician. To the extent applicable, follow the provisions in §2100.4 relating to the repair and replacement of durable medical equipment for the repair and replacement of artificial limbs, braces, etc. Adjustments, repairs and replacements are covered even when the item had been in use before the user enrolled in Part B of the program so long as the device continues to be medically required.

MCM 2134   Therapeutic Shoes for Individuals with Diabetes

Coverage of therapeutic shoes (depth or custom-molded) along with inserts for individuals with diabetes is available as of May 1, 1993. These diabetic shoes are covered if the requirements as specified in this section concerning certification and prescription are fulfilled. In addition, this benefit provides for a pair of diabetic shoes even if only one foot suffers from diabetic foot disease. Each shoe is equally equipped so that the affected limb, as well as the remaining limb, is protected.

Claims for therapeutic shoes for diabetics are processed by the Durable Medical Equipment Regional Carriers (DMERCs.)

A. Definitions. – The following items may be covered under the diabetic shoe benefit:

1. Custom-Molded Shoes. – Custom-molded shoes are shoes that are:

– Constructed over a positive model of the patient's foot;

– Made from leather or other suitable material of equal quality;

– Have removable inserts that can be altered or replaced as the patient's condition warrants; and

– Have some form of shoe closure.

2. Depth Shoes. – Depth shoes are shoes that:

– Have a full length, heel-to-toe filler that, when removed, provides a minimum of 3/16 inch of additional depth used to accommodate custom-molded or customized inserts;

– Are made from leather or other suitable material of equal quality;

– Have some form of shoe closure; and

– Are available in full and half sizes with a minimum of 3 widths so that the sole is graded to the size and width of the upper portions of the shoes according to the American standard last sizing schedule or its equivalent. (The American standard last sizing schedule is the numerical shoe sizing system used for shoes sold in the United States.)

3. Inserts. – Inserts are total contact, multiple density, removable inlays that are directly molded to the patient's foot or a model of the patient's foot and that are made of a suitable material with regard to the patient's condition.

B.Coverage. -

1. Limitations. – For each individual, coverage of the footwear and inserts is limited to one of the following within one calendar year:

– No more than one pair of custom-molded shoes (including inserts provided with such shoes) and two additional pairs of inserts; or

– No more than one pair of depth shoes and three pairs of inserts (not including the non-customized removable inserts provided with such shoes).

2. Coverage of Diabetic Shoes and Brace. – Orthopedic shoes, as stated in §2323.D, generally are not covered. This exclusion does not apply to orthopedic shoes that are an integral part of a leg brace. In situations in which an individual qualifies for both diabetic shoes and a leg brace, these items are covered separately. Thus, the diabetic shoes may be covered if the requirements for this section are met, while the brace may be covered if the requirements of §2133 are met.

3. Substitution of Modifications for Inserts. – An individual may substitute modification(s) of custom-molded or depth shoes instead of obtaining a pair(s) of inserts in any combination. Payment for the modification(s) may not exceed the limit set for the inserts for which the individual is entitled. The following is a list of the most common shoe modifications available, but it is not meant as an exhaustive list of the modifications available for diabetic shoes:

– Rigid Rocker Bottoms. – These are exterior elevations with apex positions for 51 percent to 75 percent distance measured from the back end of the heel. The apex is a narrowed or pointed end of an anatomical structure. The apex must be positioned behind the metatarsal heads and tapering off sharply to the front tip of the sole. Apex height helps to eliminate pressure at the metatarsal heads. Rigidity is ensured by the steel in the shoe. The heel of the shoe tapers off in the back in order to cause the heel to strike in the middle of the heel.

– Roller Bottoms (Sole or Bar). – These are the same as rocker bottoms, but the heel is tapered from the apex to the front tip of the sole.

– Metatarsal Bars. – An exterior bar is placed behind the metatarsal heads in order to remove pressure from the metatarsal heads. The bars are of various shapes, heights, and construction depending on the exact purpose.

– Wedges (Posting). – Wedges are either of hind foot, fore foot, or both and may be in the middle or to the side. The function is to shift or transfer weight bearing upon standing or during ambulation to the opposite side for added support, stabilization, equalized weight distribution, or balance.

– Offset Heels. – This is a heel flanged at its base either in the middle, to the side, or a combination, that is then extended upward to the shoe in order to stabilize extreme positions of the hind foot.

– Other modifications to diabetic shoes include, but are not limited to:

Flared heels;

Velcro closures; and

Inserts for missing toes.

4. Separate Inserts. – Inserts may be covered and dispensed independently of diabetic shoes if the supplier of the shoes verifies in writing that the patient has appropriate footwear into which the insert can be placed. This footwear must meet the definitions found above for depth shoes and custom-molded shoes.

C. Certification. – The need for diabetic shoes must be certified by a physician who is a doctor of medicine or a doctor of osteopathy and who is responsible for diagnosing and treating the patient's diabetic systemic condition through a comprehensive plan of care. This managing physician must:

Document in the patient's medical record that the patient has diabetes;

Certify that the patient is being treated under a comprehensive plan of care for his or her diabetes, and that he or she needs diabetic shoes; and

Document in the patient's record that the patient has one or more of the following conditions:

– Peripheral neuropathy with evidence of callus formation;

– History of pre-ulcerative calluses;

– History of previous ulceration;

– Foot deformity;

– Previous amputation of the foot or part of the foot; or

– Poor circulation.

D. Prescription. – Following certification by the physician managing the patient's systemic diabetic condition, a podiatrist or other qualified physician who is knowledgeable in the fitting of diabetic shoes and inserts may prescribe the particular type of footwear necessary.

E. Furnishing Footwear. – The footwear must be fitted and furnished by a podiatrist or other qualified individual such as a pedorthist, an orthotist, or a prosthetist. The certifying physician may not furnish the diabetic shoes unless he or she is the only qualified individual in the area. It is left to the discretion of each carrier to determine the meaning of "in the area."

F. Payment. – For 1994, payment for diabetic shoes and inserts is limited to 80 percent of the reasonable charge, up to a limit of $348 for one pair of custom-molded shoes including any initial inserts, $59 for each additional pair of custom-molded shoe inserts, $116 for one pair of depth shoes, and $59 for each pair of depth shoe inserts. These limits are based on 1988 amounts that were set forth in §1833(o) of the Act and then adjusted by the same percentage increases allowed for DME for fee screen limits by applying the same update factor that is applied to DME fees, except that if the updated limit is not a multiple of $1, it is rounded to the nearest multiple of $1. Although percentage increase in payment for diabetic shoes are the same percentage increases that are used for payment of DME through the DME fee schedule, the shoes are not subject to DME coverage rules or the DME fee schedule. In addition, diabetic shoes are neither considered DME nor orthotics, but a separate category of coverage under Medicare Part B. (See §1861(s)(12) and §1833(o) of the Act.)

Payment for the certification of diabetic shoes and for the prescription of the shoes is considered to be included in the payment for the visit or consultation during which these services are provided. If the sole purpose of an encounter with the beneficiary is to dispense or fit the shoes, then no payment may be made for a visit or consultation provided on the same day by the same physician. Thus, a separate payment is not made for certification of the need for diabetic shoes, the prescribing of diabetic shoes, or the fitting of diabetic shoes unless the physician documents that these services were not the sole purpose of the visit or consultation.

MCM 2136   Dental Services
As indicated under the general exclusions from coverage, items, and services in connection with the care, treatment, filling, removal, or replacement of teeth or structures directly supporting the teeth are not covered. Structures directly supporting the teeth means the periodontium, which includes the gingivae, dentogingival junction, periodontal membrane, cementum of the teeth, and alveolar process.

In addition to the following, see §2020.3 and Coverage Issues Manual, §50-26 for specific services which may be covered when furnished by a dentist. If an otherwise noncovered procedure or service is performed by a dentist as incident to and as an integral part of a covered procedure or service performed by him/her, the total service performed by the dentist on such an occasion is covered.

EXAMPLE 1: The reconstruction of a ridge performed primarily to prepare the mouth for dentures is a noncovered procedure. However, when the reconstruction of a ridge is performed as a result of and at the same time as the surgical removal of a tumor (for other than dental purposes), the totality of surgical procedures is a covered service.

EXAMPLE 2: Make payment for the wiring of teeth when this is done in connection with the reduction of a jaw fracture.

The extraction of teeth to prepare the jaw for radiation treatment of neoplastic disease is also covered. This is an exception to the requirement that to be covered, a noncovered procedure or service performed by a dentist must be an incident to and an integral part of a covered procedure or service performed by him/her. Ordinarily, the dentist extracts the patient's teeth, but another physician, e.g., a radiologist, administers the radiation treatments.

When an excluded service is the primary procedure involved, it is not covered, regardless of its complexity or difficulty. For example, the extraction of an impacted tooth is not covered. Similarly, an alveoplasty (the surgical improvement of the shape and condition of the alveolar process) and a frenectomy are excluded from coverage when either of these procedures is performed in connection with an excluded service, e.g., the preparation of the mouth for dentures. In a like manner, the removal of a torus palatinus (a bony protuberance of the hard palate) may be a covered service. However, with rare exception, this surgery is performed in connection with an excluded service, i.e., the preparation of the mouth for dentures. Under such circumstances, do not pay for this procedure.

Whether such services as the administration of anesthesia, diagnostic X-rays, and other related procedures are covered depends upon whether the primary procedure being performed by the dentist is itself covered. Thus, an X-ray taken in connection with the reduction of a fracture of the jaw or facial bone is covered. However, a single X-ray or X-ray survey taken in connection with the care or treatment of teeth or the periodontium is not covered.

Make payment for a covered dental procedure no matter where the service is performed. The hospitalization or nonhospitalization of a patient has no direct bearing on the coverage or exclusion of a given dental procedure.

Payment may also be made for services and supplies furnished incident to covered dental services. For example, the services of a dental technician or nurse who is under the direct supervision of the dentist or physician are covered if the services are included in the dentist's or physician's bill.

MCM 2210.3   Durable Medical Equipment Reference List.
The durable medical equipment (DME) list which follows is designed to facilitate your processing of DME claims. This section is designed to be used as a quick reference tool for determining the coverage status of certain pieces of DME and especially for those items which are commonly referred to by both brand and generic names. The information contained herein is applicable (where appropriate) to all DME coverage determinations discussed in the DME portion of this manual. The list is organized into two columns. The first column lists alphabetically various generic categories of equipment on which national coverage decisions have been made by HCFA; and the second column notes the coverage status of each equipment category.

In the case of equipment categories that have been determined by HCFA to be covered under the DME benefit, the list outlines the conditions of coverage that must be met if payment is to be allowed for the rental or purchase of the DME by a particular patient, or cross-refers to another section of the manual where the applicable coverage criteria are described in more detail. With respect to equipment categories that cannot be covered as DME, the list includes a brief explanation of why the equipment is not covered. This DME list will be updated periodically to reflect any additional national coverage decisions that HCFA may make with regard to other categories of equipment.

When you receive a claim for an item of equipment which does not appear to fall logically into any of the generic categories listed, you have the authority and responsibility for deciding whether those items are covered under the DME benefit. These decisions must be made by each contractor based on the advice of its medical consultants, taking into account:

• The general DME coverage instructions in the Carriers Manual, §2100ff and Intermediary Manual, §3113ff (see below for brief summary);

• Whether the item has been approved for marketing by the Food and Drug Administration (FDA) (see Carriers Manual, §2303.1 and Intermediary Manual, §3151.1) and is otherwise generally considered to be safe and effective for the purpose intended; and

• Whether the item is reasonable and necessary for the individual patient.

As provided in the Carriers Manual, § 2100.1, and Intermediary Manual, §3113.1, the term DME is defined as equipment which can withstand repeated use; i.e., could normally be rented, and used by successive patients;

• Is primarily and customarily used to serve a medical purpose;

• Generally is not useful to a person in the absence of illness or injury; and

• Is appropriate for use in a patient's home.

Durable Medical Equipment Reference List:

Item Coverage Status

Item	Coverage Status
Air Cleaners	deny – environmental control equipment; not primarily medical in nature (§186l(n) of the Act)
Air Conditioners	deny – environmental control equipment; not primarily medical in nature (§1861(n) of the Act)
Air-Fluidized Bed	(See §60-19.)
Alternating Pressure Pads, and Matresses and Lambs Wool Pads	covered if patient has, or is highly susceptible to, decubitus ulcers and patient's physician has specified that he will be supervising its use in connection with his course of treatment.
Audible/Visible Signal Pacemaker Monitor	(See Self-Contained Pacemaker Monitor.)
Augmentative Communication Device	(See Speech Generating Devices, §60-23.)
Bathtub Lifts	deny – convenience item; not primarily medical in nature (§1861(n) of the Act)
Bathtub Seats	deny – comfort or convenience item; hygienic equipment; not primarily medical in nature (§1861(n) of the Act)
Bead Bed	(See §60-19.)
Bed Baths (home type)	deny – hygienic equipment; not primarily medical in nature (§1861(n) of the Act)
Bed Lifter (bed elevator)	deny – not primarily medical in nature (§1861(n) of the Act.
Bedboards	deny – not primarily medical in nature (§1861(n) of the Act)
Bed Pans (autoclavable hospital type)	covered if patient is bed confined
Bed Side Rails	(See Hospital Beds, 60-l8.)
Beds-Lounge (power or manual)	deny – not a hospital bed; comfort or convenience item; not primarily medical in nature (§186l(n) of the Act)
Beds – Oscillating	deny – institutional equipment; inappropriate for home use
Bidet Toilet Seat	(See Toilet Seats.)
Blood Glucose Analyzer Reflectance Colorimeter	deny – unsuitable for home use (See §60-11.)
Blood Glucose Monitor	covered if patient meets certain conditions (See §60-11.)
Braille Teaching Texts	deny – educational equipment; not primarily medical in nature (§1861(n) of the Act)
Canes	covered if patient's condition impairs ambulation (See §60-3.)
Carafes	deny – convenience item; not primarily medical in nature (§1861(n) of the Act)
Catheters	deny – nonreusable disposable supply (§1861(n) of the Act)
Commodes	covered if patient is confined to bed or room NOTE: The term "room confined" means that the patient's condition is such that leaving the room is medically contraindicated. The accessibility of bathroom facilities generally would not be a factor in this determination. However, confinement of a patient to his home in a case where there are no toilet facilities in the home may be equated to room confinement. Moreover,

payment may also be made if a patient's medical condition confines him to a floor of his home and there is no bathroom located on that floor (See hospital beds in §60-18 for definition of "bed confinement".)

Item	Coverage Status
Communicator	(See §60-23, Speech Generating Devices)
Continuous Passive Motion	Continuous passive motion devices are devices covered for patients who have received a total knee replacement. To qualify for coverage, use of the device must commence within 2 days following surgery. In addition, coverage is limited to that portion of the three week period following surgery during which the device is used in the patient's home. There is insufficient evidence to justify coverage of these devices for longer periods of time or for other applications.
Continuous Positive Airway Pressure (CPAP)	(See §60-17.)
Crutches	covered if patient's condition impairs Ambulation
Cushion Lift Power Seat	(See Seat Lifts.)
Dehumidifiers (room or central heating system type)	deny – environmental control equipment; not primarily medical in nature (§1861(n) of the Act
Diathermy Machines (standard pulses wave types)	deny – inappropriate for home use (See and §35-41.)
Digital Electronic Pacemaker Monitor	(See Self-Contained Pacemaker Monitor.)
Disposable Sheets and Bags	deny – nonreusable disposable supplies (§1861(n) of the Act)
Elastic Stockings	deny – nonreusable supply; not rental-type items (§1861(n) of the Act)
Electric Air Cleaners	deny – (See Air Cleaners.) (§1861(n) of the Act)
Electric Hospital Beds	(See Hospital Beds §60-18.)
Electrostatic Machines	deny – (See Air Cleaners and Air Conditioners.) (§1861(n) of the Act)
Elevators	deny – convenience item; not primarily medical in nature (§1861(n) of the Act)
Emesis Basins	deny – convenience item; not primarily medical in nature (§1861(n) of the Act)
Esophageal Dilator	deny – physician instrument; inappropriate for patient use
Exercise Equipment	deny – not primarily medical in nature (§1861(n) of the Act)
Fabric Supports	deny – nonreusable supplies; not rental-type it (§1861(n) of the Act)
Face Masks (oxygen)	covered if oxygen is covered (See § 60-4.)
Face Masks (surgical)	deny – nonreusable disposable items (§1861(n) of the Act)
Flowmeter	(See Medical Oxygen Regulators)
Fluidic Breathing Assister	(See IPPB Machines.)
Fomentation Device	(See Heating Pads.)
Gel Flotation Pads and Mattresses	(See Alternating Pressure Pads and Mattresses.)
Grab Bars	deny – self-help device; not primarily medical in nature (§1861(n) of the Act)
Heat and Massage Foam Cushion Pad	deny – not primarily medical in nature; personal comfort item (§§ 1861(n) and 1862(a)(6) of the Act)
Heating and Cooling Plants	deny – environmental control equipment; not primarily medical in nature(§1861(n) of the Act)
Heating Pads	covered if the contractor's medical staff determines patient's medical condition is one for which the application of heat in the form of a heating pad is therapeutically effective.
Heat Lamps	covered if the contractor's medical staff determines patient's medical condition is one for

	which the application of heat in the form of a heat lamp is therapeutically effective.		movement is necessary to effect improvement or to arrest or retard deterioration in his condition.
Hospital Beds	(See § 60-18.)	Percussors	covered for mobilizing respiratory tract secretions in patients with chronic obstructive lung disease, chronic bronchitis, or emphysema, when patient or operator of powered percussor has received appropriate training by a physician or therapist, and no one competent to administer manual therapy is available.
Hot Packs	(See Heating Pads.)		
Humidifiers (oxygen)	(See Oxygen Humidifiers.)		
Humidifiers (room or central heating system types)	deny – environmental control equipment; not medical in nature (§I861(n) of the Act)		
Hydraulic Lift	(See Patient Lifts.)	Portable Oxygen Systems:	1. Regulated (adjustable – covered under conditions specified in flow rate)§60-4. Refer all claims to medical staff for this determination. 2. Preset (flow rate – deny – emergency, first-aid, or not adjustable) precautionary equipment; essentially not therapeutic in nature
Incontinent Pads	deny – nonreusable supply; hygienic item (§ I861(n) of the Act.)		
Infusion Pumps	For external and implantable pumps, see §60-14. If the pump is used with an enteral or parenteral ralnutritional therapy system, see §§65-10 – 65.10.2 0.2 for special coverage rules.		
		Portable Paraffin Bath Units	covered when the patient has undergone a successful trial period of paraffin therapy ordered by a physician and the patient's condition is expected to be relieved by long term use of this modality.
Injectors (hypodermic jet devices for injection of insulin	deny – noncovered self-administered drug supply, § 1861(s)(2)(A) of the Act		
IPPB Machines	covered if patient's ability to breathe is severely impaired	Portable Room Heaters	deny – environmental control equipment; not primarily medical in nature (§I861(n) of the Act)
Iron Lungs	(See Ventilators.)	Portable Whirlpool Pumps	deny – not primarily medical in nature; personal comfort items (§§I861(n) and I862(a)(6) of the Act)
Irrigating Kit	deny – nonreusable supply; hygienic equipment (§I861(n) of the Act)		
Lambs Wool Pads	covered under same conditions as alternating pressure pads and mattresses	Postural Drainage Boards	covered if patient has a chronic pulmonary condition
Leotards	deny – (See Pressure Leotards.) (§I861(n)of the Act)	Preset Portable Oxygen Units	deny – emergency, first-aid, or precautionary equipment; essentially not therapeutic in nature
Lymphedema Pumps	covered (See §60-16.)(segmental and non-segmental therapy types)	Pressure Leotards	deny – nonreusable supply, not rental-type item (§I861(n) of the Act)
Massage Devices	deny – personal comfort items; not primarily medical in nature (§§I861(n) and I862(a)(6) of the Act)	Pulse Tachometer	deny – not reasonable or necessary for monitoring pulse of homebound patient with or without a cardiac pacemaker
		Quad-Canes	(See Walkers.)
Mattress	covered only where hospital bed is medically necessary (Separate Charge for replacement mattresss should not be allowed where hospital bed with mattress is rented.) (See §60-18.)	Raised Toilet Seats	deny – convenience item; hygienic equipment; not primarily medical in nature (§I861(n) of the Act)
		Reflectance Colorimeters	(See Blood Glucose Analyzers.)
Medical Oxygen Regulators	covered if patient's ability to breathe is severely impaired (See §60-4.)	Respirators	(See Ventilators.)
Mobile Geriatric Chair	(See Rolling Chairs.)	Rolling Chairs	covered if the contractor's medical staff determines that the patient's condition is such that there is a medical need for this item and it has been prescribed by the patient's physician in lieu of a wheelchair. Coverage is limited to those rollabout chairs having casters of at least 5 inches in diameter and specifically designed to meet the needs of ill, injured, or otherwise impaired individuals. Coverage is denied for the wide range of chairs with smaller casters as are found in general use in homes, offices, and institutions for many purposes not related to the care or treatment of ill or injured persons. This type is not primarily medical in nature. (§I861(n) of the Act)
Motorized Wheelchairs	(See Wheelchairs (power operated).)		
Muscle Stimulators	Covered for certain conditions (See §35-77.)		
Nebulizers	covered if patient's ability to breathe is severely impaired		
Oscillating Beds	deny – institutional equipment – inappropriate for home use		
Overbed Tables	deny – convenience item; not primarily medical in nature (§I861(n) of the Act)		
Oxygen	covered if the oxygen has been prescribed for use in connection with medically necessary durable medical equipment (See §60-4.)		
Oxygen Humidifiers	covered if a medical humidifier has been prescribed for use in connection with medically necessary durable medical equipment for purposes of moisturizing oxygen (See §60-4.)	Safety Roller	(See §60-15.)
		Sauna Baths	deny – not primarily medical in nature; personal comfort items (§§I861(n) and (I862(a)(6) of the Act)
Oxygen Regulators (Medical)	(See Medical Oxygen Regulators.)	Seat Lift	covered under the conditions specified in §60-8. Refer all to medical staff for this determination.
Oxygen Tents	(See § 60-4.)		
Paraffin Bath Units (Portable)	(See Portable Paraffin Bath Units.)	Self-Contained Pacemaker Monitor	covered when prescribed by a physician for a patient with a cardiac pacemaker (See §§50-1C and 60-7.)
Paraffin Bath Units (Standard)	deny – institutional equipment; inappropriate for home use		
Parallel Bars	deny – support exercise equipment; primarily for institutional use; in the home setting other devices (e.g., a walker) satisfy the patient's need	Sitz Bath	covered if the contractor's medical staff determines patient has an infection or injury of the perineal area and the item has been prescribed by the patient's physician as a part of his planned regimen of treatment in the patient's home.
Patient Lifts	covered if contractor's medical staff determines patient's condition is such that periodic		

Spare Tanks of Oxygen	deny – convenience or precautionary supply
Speech Teaching Machine	deny – education equipment; not primarily medical in nature (§1861(n) of the Act)
Stairway Elevators	deny – (See Elevators.) (§1861(n) of the Act)
Standing Table	deny – convenience item; not primarily medical in nature (§1861(n) of the Act)
Steam Packs	these packs are covered under the same condition as a heating pad (See Heating Pads.)
Suction Machine	covered if the contractor's medical staff determines that the machine specified in the claim is medically required and appropriate for home use without technical or professional supervision.
Support Hose	deny (See Fabric Supports.) (§1861(n) of the Act)
Surgical Leggings	deny – nonreusable supply; not rental-type item (§1861(n) of the Act)
Telephone Alert Systems	deny – these are emergency communications systems and do not serve a diagnostic or therapeutic purpose
Telephone Arms	deny – convenience item; not medical in nature (§1861(n) of the Act)
Toilet Seats	deny – not medical equipment (§1861(n)of the Act)
Traction Equipment	covered if patient has orthopedic impairment requiring traction equipment which prevents ambulation during the period of use (Consider covering devices usable during ambulation; e.g., cervical traction collar, under the brace provision)
Trapeze Bars	covered if patient is bed confined and the patient needs a trapeze bar to sit up because of respiratory condition, to change body position for other medical reasons, or to get in and out of bed.
Treadmill Exerciser	deny – exercise equipment;not primarily medical in nature(§1861(n) of the Act)
Ultraviolet Cabinet	covered for selected patients with generalized intractable psoriasis. Using appropriate consultation, the contractor should determine whether medical and other factors justify treatment at home rather than at alternative sites, e.g., outpatient department of a hospital.
Urinals (autoclavable hospital type)	covered if patient is bed confined
Vaporizers	covered if patient has a respiratory illness
Ventilators	covered for treatment of neuromuscular diseases, thoracic restrictive diseases, and chronic respiratory failure consequent to chronic obstructive pulmonary disease. Includes both positive and negative pressure types.
Walkers	covered if patient's condition impairs ambulation (See also §60-15.)
Water and Pressure Pads and Mattresses	(See Alternating Pressure Pads and Mattresses.)
Wheelchairs	covered if patient's condition is such that without the use of a wheelchair he would otherwise be bed or chair confined. An individual may qualify for a wheelchair and still be considered bed confined.
Wheelchairs (power operated) and wheelchairs with other special features	covered if patient's condition is such and that a wheelchair is medically necessary and the patient is unable to operate the wheelchair manually. Any claim involving a power wheelchair or a wheelchair with other special features should be referred for medical consultation since payment for the special features is limited to those which are medically required because of the patient's condition. (See §60-5 for power operated and §60-6 for specially sized

	wheelchairs.) NOTE: A power-operated vehicle that may appropriately be used as a wheelchair can be covered. (See §60-5 for coverage details.)
Whirlpool Bath Equipment	covered if patient is homebound and has a standard) condition for which the whirlpool bath can be expected to provide substantial therapeutic benefit justifying its cost. Where patient is not homebound but has such a condition, payment is restricted to the cost of providing the services elsewhere; e.g., an outpatient department of a participating hospital, if that alternative is less costly. In all cases, refer claim to medical staff for a determination.
Whirlpool Pumps	deny – (See Portable Whirlpool Pumps.) (§1861(n) of the Act)
White Cane	deny – (See §60-3.)

MCM 2300 **General Exclusions From Coverage, No payment can be made under either the hospital insurance or supplementary medical insurance programs for certain items and services.,**

A. Not reasonable and necessary (§2303)

B. No legal obligation to pay for or provide services (§2306)

C. Furnished or paid for by government instrumentalities (§2309)

D. Not provided within United States (§2312)

E. Resulting from war (§2315)

F. Personal comfort (§2318)

G. Routine services and appliances (§2320)

H. Supportive devices for feet (§2323)

I. Custodial care (§2326)

J. Cosmetic surgery (§2329)

K. Charges by immediate relatives or members of household (§2332)

L. Dental services (§2336)

M. Paid or expected to be paid under worker's compensation (§2370)

N. Nonphysician services provided to a hospital inpatient which were not provided directly or arranged for by the hospital (§2390).2300.1 Services Related to and Required as a Result of Services Which Are Not Covered Under Medicare

A. Medical and hospital services are sometimes required to treat a condition that arises as a result of services which are not covered because they are determined to be not reasonable and necessary or because they are excluded from coverage for other reasons. Services "related to" noncovered services (e.g., cosmetic surgery, noncovered organ transplants, noncovered artificial organ implants, etc.), including services related to followup care and complications of noncovered services which require treatment during a hospital stay in which the noncovered service was performed, are not covered services under Medicare. Services "not related to" noncovered services are covered under Medicare

B. Identify which services are related to noncovered services and which are not. Following are some examples of services "related to" and "not related to" noncovered services while the beneficiary is an inpatient:,

1. A beneficiary was hospitalized for a noncovered service and broke a leg while in the hospital. Services related to care of the broken leg during this stay is a clear cut example of "not related to" services and are covered under Medicare

2. A beneficiary was admitted to the hospital for covered services, but during the course of hospitalization became a candidate for a noncovered transplant or implant and actually received the transplant or implant during that hospital stay. When the original admission was entirely unrelated to the diagnosis that led to a recommendation for a noncovered transplant or implant, the services related to the admitting condition would be covered

3. A beneficiary was admitted to the hospital for covered services related to a condition which ultimately led to identification of a need for transplant and receipt of a transplant during the same hospital stay. If, on the basis of the nature of the services and a comparison of the date they are received with the date on which the beneficiary is identified as a transplant candidate, the services could reasonably be attributed to preparation for the noncovered transplant, the services would be "related to" noncovered services and would also be noncovered

C. After a beneficiary has been discharged from the hospital stay in which he received noncovered services, medical and hospital services required to treat a condition or complication that arises as a result of the prior noncovered services may be covered when they are reasonable and necessary in all other respects. Thus, coverage could be provided for subsequent inpatient stays or outpatient treatment ordinarily covered by Medicare, even if the need for treatment arose because of a previous noncovered procedure. Some examples of services that may be found to be covered under this policy are the reversal of intestinal bypass surgery for obesity, repair of complications from transsexual surgery or from cosmetic surgery, removal of a noncovered bladder stimulator, or treatment of any infection at the surgical site of a noncovered transplant that occurred following discharge from the hospital., However, any subsequent services that could be expected to have been incorporated into a global fee should be denied. Thus, where a patient undergoes cosmetic surgery and the treatment regimen calls for a series of postoperative visits to the surgeon for evaluating the patient's progress, these visits should be denied. (See Intermediary Manual, §3637.15 and Hospital Manual, §415.18 for billing procedures.)

MCM 2303   Services Not Reasonable and Necessary,

Items and services which are not reasonable and necessary for the diagnosis or treatment of illness or injury, or to improve the functioning of a malformed body member; e.g., payment cannot be made for the rental of a special hospital bed to be used by the patient in his home unless it was a reasonable and necessary part of the patient's treatment. See also §2318.

MCM 2320   Routine Services and Appliances,

Routine physical checkups; eyeglasses, contact lenses, and eye examinations for the purpose of prescribing, fitting or changing eyeglasses; eye refractions; hearing aids and examinations for hearing aids; and immunizations are not covered., The routine physical checkup exclusion applies to (a) examinations performed without relationship to treatment or diagnosis for a specific illness, symptom, complaint, or injury, and (b) examinations required by third parties such as insurance companies, business establishments, or Government agencies. (If the claim is for a diagnostic test or examination performed solely for the purpose of establishing a claim under title IV of Public Law 91-173 (Black Lung Benefits), advise the claimant to contact his/her Social Security office regarding the filing of a claim for reimbursement under that program.), The exclusions apply to eyeglasses or contact lenses and eye examinations for the purpose of prescribing, fitting, or changing eyeglasses or contact lenses for refractive errors. The exclusions do not apply to physician services (and services incident to a physician's service) performed in conjunction with an eye disease (e.g., glaucoma or cataracts) or to postsurgical prosthetic lenses which are customarily used during convalescence from eye surgery in which the lens of the eye was removed or to permanent prosthetic lenses required by an individual lacking the organic lens of the eye, whether by surgical removal or congenital disease. Such prosthetic lens is a replacement for an internal body organ (the lens of the eye). (See §2130.), The coverage of services rendered by an ophthalmologist is dependent on the purpose of the examination rather than on the ultimate diagnosis of the patient's condition. When a beneficiary goes to an ophthalmologist with a complaint or symptoms of an eye disease or injury, the ophthalmologist's services (except for eye refractions) are covered regardless of the fact that only eyeglasses were prescribed. However, when a beneficiary goes to his/her ophthalmologist for an eye examination with no specific complaint, the expenses for the examination are not covered even though as a result of such examination the doctor discovered a pathologic condition., In the absence of evidence to the contrary, you may carrier may assume that an eye examination performed by an ophthalmologist on the basis of a complaint by the beneficiary or symptoms of an eye disease was not for the purpose of prescribing, fitting, or changing eyeglasses., Expenses for all refractive procedures, whether performed by an ophthalmologist (or any other physician) or an optometrist and without regard to the reason for performance of the refraction, are excluded from coverage. (See §§4125 and 5217 for claims review and reimbursement instructions concerning refractive services.), With the exception of vaccinations for pneumococcal pneumonia, hepatitis B, and influenza, which are specifically covered under the law, vaccinations or inoculations are generally excluded as immunizations unless they are directly related to the treatment of an injury or direct exposure such as antirabies treatment, tetanus antitoxin or booster vaccine, botulin antitoxin, antivenin, or immune globulin.

MCM 2323   Foot Care And Supportive Devices For Feet

NOTE: See §4281 for the relationship between foot care and the coverage and billing of the diagnosis and treatment of peripheral neuropathy with loss of protective sensation (LOPS) in people with diabetes.

A. Exclusion of Coverage. – The following foot care services are generally excluded from coverage under both Part A and Part B. Exceptions to this general exclusion for limited treatment of routine foot care services are described in subsections A.2 and B. (See §4120 for procedural instructions in applying foot care exclusions.)

1. Treatment of Flat Foot. – The term "flat foot" is defined as a condition in which one or more arches of the foot have flattened out. Services or devices directed toward the care or correction of such conditions, including the prescription of supportive devices, are not covered.

2. Treatment of Subluxation of Foot. – Subluxations of the foot are defined as partial dislocations or displacements of joint surfaces, tendons ligaments, or muscles of the foot. Surgical or nonsurgical treatments undertaken for the sole purpose of correcting a subluxated structure in the foot as an isolated entity are not covered. This exclusion does not apply to medical or surgical treatment of subluxation of the ankle joint (talocrural joint). In addition, reasonable and necessary medical or surgical services, diagnosis, or treatment for medical conditions that have resulted from or are associated with partial displacement of structures is covered. For example, if a patient has osteoarthritis that has resulted in a partial displacement of joints in the foot, and the primary treatment is for the osteoarthritis, coverage is provided.

3. Routine Foot Care. – Except as provided in subsection B, routine foot care is excluded from coverage. Services that normally are considered routine and not covered by Medicare include the following:

    o The cutting or removal of corns and calluses;

    o The trimming, cutting, clipping, or debriding of nails; and

    o Other hygienic and preventive maintenance care, such as cleaning and soaking the feet, the use of skin creams to maintain skin tone of either ambulatory or bedfast patients, and any other service performed in the absence of localized illness, injury, or symptoms involving the foot.

B. Exceptions to Routine Foot Care Exclusion. –

1. Necessary and Integral Part of Otherwise Covered Services. – In certain circumstances, services ordinarily considered to be routine may be covered if they are performed as a necessary and integral part of otherwise covered services, such as diagnosis and treatment of ulcers, wounds, or infections.

2. Treatment of Warts on Foot. – The treatment of warts (including plantar warts) on the foot is covered to the same extent as services provided for the treatment of warts located elsewhere on the body.

3. Presence of Systemic Condition. – The presence of a systemic condition such as metabolic, neurologic, or peripheral vascular disease may require scrupulous foot care by a professional that in the absence of such condition(s) would be considered routine (and, therefore, excluded from coverage). Accordingly, foot care that would otherwise be considered routine may be covered when systemic condition(s) result in severe circulatory embarrassment or areas of diminished sensation in the individual's legs or feet. (See subsection C.)

In these instances, certain foot care procedures that otherwise are considered routine (e.g., cutting or removing corns and calluses, or trimming, cutting, clipping, or debriding nails) may pose a hazard when performed by a nonprofessional person on patients with such systemic conditions. (See §4120 for procedural instructions.)

4. Mycotic Nails. – In the absence of a systemic condition, treatment of mycotic nails may be covered.

MCM 2336   Dental Services and Exclusion.,

Items and services in connection with the care, treatment, filling, removal, or replacement of teeth, or structures directly supporting the teeth are not covered. "Structures directly supporting the teeth" means the periodontium, which includes the gingivae, dentogingival junction, periodontal membrane, cementum, and alveolar process. However, payment may be made for other services of a dentist. (See §§2020.3, 2136 and Coverage Issues Manual §50-26.), The hospitalization or nonhospitalization of a patient has no direct bearing on the coverage or exclusion of a given dental procedure. (See also §§2020.3 and 2136 for additional information on dental services.)

MCM 2455   Medical Insurance Blood Deductible,

A. General. – Program payment under Part B may not be made for the first three units of whole blood, or packed red cells, received by a beneficiary in a calendar year. For purpose of the blood deductible, a unit of whole blood means a pint of whole blood. The term whole blood means human blood from which none of the liquid or cellular components has been removed. Where packed red cells are furnished, a unit of packed red cells is considered equivalent to a pint of whole blood. After the three unit deductible has been satisfied, payment may be made for all blood charges, subject to the normal coverage and reasonable charge criteria.,

NOTE: Blood is a biological and can be covered under Part B only when furnished incident to a physician's services. (See §§2050.1ff. for a more complete explanation of services rendered "incident to a physician's services."),

B. Application of the Blood Deductible. – The blood deductible applies only to whole blood or packed red cells. Other components of blood such as platelets, fibrinogen, plasma, gamma globulin, and serum albumin are not subject to the blood deductible. These components of blood are covered biologicals., The blood deductible involves only the charges for the blood (or packed red cells). Charges for the administration of blood or packed cells are not subject to the blood deductible. Accordingly, although payment may not be made for the first three pints of blood and/or units of packed red cells furnished to a beneficiary in a calendar year, payment may be made (subject to the cash deductible) for the administration charges for all covered pints or units including the first three furnished in a calendar year., The blood deductible applies only to the first three pints and/or units furnished in a calendar year, even though more than one physician or clinic furnished blood. Furthermore, to count toward the deductible, the blood must be covered with respect to all applicable criteria (i.e., it must be medically necessary, it must be furnished incident to a physician's services, etc.). (See §2050.5.),

C. Physician or Supplier Right to Charge for Deductible Blood. — A physician or other supplier who accepts assignment may bill a beneficiary the reasonable charge for unreplaced deductible blood (i.e., any of the first three units in a calendar year) but may not charge for blood, which has been replaced., Once a physician or supplier accepts a replacement unit of whole blood or packed red cells from a beneficiary or another individual acting on his behalf, the beneficiary may not be charged for the blood., When a supplier accepts blood donated in advance, in anticipation of need by a specific beneficiary, whether the beneficiary's own blood, that is, an autologous donation, or blood furnished by another individual or blood assurance group, such donations are considered replacement for units subsequently furnished the beneficiary.,

D. Distinction Between Blood Charges and Blood Administration Charges. — Since the blood deductible applies only to charges for blood and does not apply to charges for blood administration, these two charges must be considered separately. Where a bill for unreplaced blood shows only a single blood charge, break down the charge between blood and blood administration in accordance with the supplier's customary charges for these items. If the supplier does not customarily bill separately for blood and for blood administration, the portion of the single charge that is considered to be a charge for blood is determined by reference to the established reasonable charge in the locality as it applies to blood. The remainder of the charge is considered a blood administration charge.,

E. Relationship to Other Deductibles. — Part B payment for all blood administration charges and for blood charges after the beneficiary has received three pints and/or units in a calendar year is subject to the annual cash deductible and coinsurance provisions. Expenses incurred in meeting the Part B blood deductible do not count as incurred expenses under Part B for purposes of meeting the cash deductible or for purposes of payment., There is also a Part A blood deductible applicable to the first three pints of whole blood or equivalent units of packed red cells received by a beneficiary in a benefit period. The Part A and Part B blood deductibles are applied separately.,

F. Example of Application of the Part B Blood Deductible. — In 1991, a beneficiary received three pints of blood from a physician for which the total charge is $100 per pint. (The physician does not specify how much of the charge is for blood, and how much is for blood administration.) The physician accepted assignment and submitted a claim for Part B payment., Determine that the beneficiary has not met any part of the Part B blood deductible and has met only $40 of the cash deductible. You determine that the physician's customary charge for blood administration is $50 per unit and that it is reasonable. Consequently, charges for blood administration are $50 per unit or a total of $150 for the three units furnished and charges for blood are $50 per unit or a total of $150 for the three units furnished. The beneficiary replaces one pint of blood. Since the beneficiary had not met any of the Part B blood deductible, none of the $150 in blood charges are payable nor may any of such charges be applied to satisfy the annual cash deductible ($100). Of the $150 in blood administration charges, $60 is applied to satisfy the beneficiary's unmet cash deductible and a payment of $72 is made on the remaining $90 in charges ($90 x 80%). Since the physician accepted assignment and since the beneficiary replaced one pint of blood, the physician may charge the beneficiary the reasonable charge only for the two remaining deductible pints

MCM 4107   Durable Medical Equipment

Billing And Payment Considerations Under The Fee Schedule, The Omnibus Budget Reconciliation Act of 1987 requires that payment for DME, prosthetics and orthotics be made under fee schedules effective January 1, 1989. The allowable charge is limited to the lower of the actual charge for the equipment, or the fee schedule amount. The equipment is categorized into one of six classes:, Inexpensive or other routinely purchased DME;, Items requiring frequent and substantial servicing;, Customized items;, Prosthetic and orthotic devices;, Capped rental items; or, Oxygen and oxygen equipment., The fee schedule allowances for each class are determined in accord with §§5102ff.,

4107.1   General Billing and Claims Processing — Subject to some of the specific billing and processing requirements, bills are to be submitted, processed and paid in accordance with §§4105ff. and 5102ff., You are responsible for processing outpatient and non-institutional claims for DME and oxygen previously paid by fiscal intermediaries to hospitals, CORFs, SNFs, and OPT providers. Prosthetic, orthotic, and inpatient DME and oxygen claims, however, continue to be billed by these providers to their FIs. You will not receive any claims from HHAs which have transferred to regional home health intermediaries (RHHIs). Issue billing numbers as necessary and pay the appropriate fee schedule amounts. If the item billed is in the capped rental category, develop with the beneficiary or assignee, as appropriate, to determine the length of time the beneficiary has continuously rented the item. Process in accordance with §4107.4., Payable bills or claims must specify whether equipment is rented or purchased. For purchased equipment, the itemized bill or claim must also indicate whether equipment is new or used. If the supplier fails to indicate on an assigned claim whether equipment was new or used, assume purchased equipment is used and process the claim accordingly, i.e., pay on the basis of the used purchase fee. If an unassigned purchase claim does not specify whether the item was new or used, develop the claim in accordance with §3311., 4107.2 Rent/Purchase Decisions. — For services provided on or after October 1, 1988, discontinue making rent/purchase decisions on rental claims. (See §5101.2.) For purchase claims with dates of service before January 1, 1989, continue to make rent/purchase decisions. Discontinue making rent/purchase decisions for purchase claims with dates of service on or after January 1, 1989. Do not pay for oxygen delivery systems, items requiring frequent and substantial servicing or capped rental items that were purchased on or after June 1, 1989., 4107.3 Comparability and Inherent Reasonableness Limitations. — For services provided on or after January 1, 1989, do not apply the comparable circumstances provision in §5026. Also, for services provided between January 1, 1989 and December 31, 1990, do not apply the special payment limitation provisions in §5246 to DME and orthotics/prosthetics subject to the fee schedules in §§5102ff., 4107.4 15 Month Ceiling on Capped Rental Items. — Ensure that your system accurately computes the 15 month period for capped rental items. (See §§5102.1.E.3 and 5102.3.C.1 and 2.), 4107.5 Transcutaneous Electrical

Nerve Stimulator (TENS). — To permit an attending physician time to determine whether purchase of a TENS unit is medically appropriate, ensure that your system allows no more than 10 percent of the fee schedule purchase amount for up to two months of rental prior to purchase. Do not apply the rentals toward the purchase allowance., 4107.6 Written Order Prior to DeliveryEnsure that your system will pay for the equipment listed below only when the supplier has a written order in hand prior to delivery. Otherwise, do not pay for that item even if a written order is subsequently furnished. However, you can pay for a similar item if it is subsequently provided by an unrelated supplier which has a written order in hand prior to delivery. The HCPCS codes for the equipment requiring a written order are:, ? E0180, ? E0190, ? E0181, ? E0192, ? E0182, ? E0195, ? E0183, ? E0620, ? E0184, ? E0720, ? E0185, ? E0730, ? E0188, ? E1230, ? E0189, 4107.7 Special Requirements for Oxygen Claims. — There are a number of billing considerations for oxygen claims. The chart in §4107.9 indicates what is payable under which situation.,

A. Monthly Billing. — Fee schedule payments for stationary oxygen system rentals are all inclusive and represent a monthly allowance per beneficiary. Accordingly, a supplier must bill on a monthly basis for stationary oxygen equipment and contents furnished during a rental month., A portable equipment add-on is also payable when portable oxygen is prescribed and you determine it to be medically necessary in accordance with Medicare coverage requirements. The portable add-on must be claimed in order to be paid. (See §4107.10.), Claims may be submitted when expenses are incurred for initial rentals of oxygen systems or, no sooner than the monthly anniversary date in the case of an established oxygen patient. In the latter situation, suppliers must indicate the monthly volume of oxygen contents delivered, rounded in accordance with subsection D.3,, Where the beneficiary has purchased a stationary system (other than a concentrator and/or a portable delivery system), oxygen contents must be billed and paid on a monthly basis, except for unassigned oxygen contents claims submitted by a beneficiary. For beneficiary filed claims, allow, on a claim- by-claim basis, the submitted charge until the applicable monthly fee for oxygen contents has been met.,

B. Reduced Number of HCPCS Codes. — The number of HCPCS codes for billing of oxygen claims have been reduced. See §4107.9 for the codes and their definitions.,

C. Use of Payment Modifiers. — The monthly payment amount for stationary oxygen is subject to adjustment depending on the amount of oxygen prescribed (liters per minute (LPM)), and whether or not portable oxygen is also prescribed. (See §5102.1.) To make proper payment adjustments, supplier claims must indicate the appropriate HCPCS modifier described below, if applicable. On unassigned claims, suppliers should indicate this information on the itemized bill., If the prescribed amount of oxygen is less than 1 LPM, the modifier is "QE". Reduce the monthly payment amount for stationary oxygen by 50 percent., If the prescribed amount of oxygen is greater than 4 LPM, the modifier is "QG". Increase the monthly payment amount for stationary oxygen by 50 percent. Conduct prepayment medical review of these claims., If the prescribed amount of oxygen exceeds 4 LPM and portable

oxygen is prescribed, the modifier is "QF". Increase the monthly payment for stationary oxygen by the higher of 50 percent of the monthly stationary oxygen payment amount, or the fee schedule amount for the portable oxygen add-on. (See §5102.1.F.2.j.) Conduct a prepayment medical review of these claims.,
09-91 CLAIMS REVIEW AND ADJUDICATION PROCEDURES 4107.8,

D. Units Required. – Excluding concentrators, suppliers must furnish units of oxygen contents in Item 24.F. of their HCFA-1500 claims, or the itemized bill furnished to the beneficiary for unassigned claims.,

    1. Initial Oxygen Claims. – When submitting an initial claim for rental of a gaseous or liquid oxygen delivery system, units of oxygen contents furnished for the first month need not be indicated. Base your payment upon the lower of the actual charge for the initial rental month or the monthly payment amount.,

    2. Subsequent Oxygen Claims. – For dates of service subsequent to the initial rental month, suppliers should indicate actual content usage for the month billed or, if billed prospectively, the actual content usage during the previous rental month, rounded in accordance with subsection D. Base your payment determination on the lower of the actual charge submitted or the monthly payment amount., For applying these instructions, treat claims submitted under recertifications of continuing and uninterrupted need for oxygen therapy as subsequent claims if a change in suppliers is not involved., If a change in suppliers has occurred, apply the initial rule in subsection D.1 above for specifying oxygen contents delivered for the initial rental month by the new supplier., Develop subsequent rental claims for gaseous or liquid oxygen delivery systems that do not include "unit" information. (See §3311.),

    3. Rounding of Oxygen Contents. – For stationary gas system rentals, suppliers should indicate, in item 24.F. of the HCFA-1500, oxygen contents in unit multiples of 50 cubic feet, rounded to the nearest increment of 50. For example, if 73 cubic feet of oxygen was delivered during the rental month, the item 24.F. unit entry "01" indicates the nearest 50 cubic foot increment. For stationary liquid systems, units of contents should be specified in multiples of 10 pounds of liquid contents delivered, rounded to the nearest 10 pound increment. For example, if 63 pounds of liquid oxygen were delivered during the applicable rental month billed, the unit entry "06" is made in Item 24.F. For units of portable contents only (i.e., no stationary gas or liquid system used), round to the nearest five cubic feet or one liquid pound, respectively., Periodically audit supplier records to verify that gaseous and liquid content usage is reported correctly.,

E. Conserving Device Modifier. – Suppliers must indicate if an oxygen conserving device is being used with an oxygen delivery system by using HCPCS modifier "QH".

4107.8 EOMB Messages. – The following EOMB messages are suggested: (See §§7012ff. for other applicable messages.),

    A. General. -, "This is the maximum approved amount for this item." (Use when payment is reduced for a line item.),

    B. Inexpensive/Frequently Purchased Equipment. - "The total approved amount for this item is _____ whether this item is purchased or rented." (Use in first month.), "This is your next to last rental payment.", "This is your last rental payment.", "This item has been rented up to the Medicare payment limit.", "The approved amount has been reduced by the previously approved rental amounts.",

    C. Items Requiring Frequent and Substantial Servicing. – Use the general rental messages in §4107.8A, if applicable. If the beneficiary has purchased the item prior to June 1, 1989, follow §7014.6. If the beneficiary purchase an item in this category on or after June 1, 1989, use the following message:, "This equipment can only be paid for on a rental basis.",

    D. Customized Items and Other Prosthetic and Orthotic Devices. - "The total approved amount for this item is _____.",

    E. Capped Rental Items. - "Under a provision of Medicare law, monthly rental payments for this item can continue for up to 15 months from the first rental month or until the equipment is no longer needed, whichever comes first.", "If you no longer are using this equipment or have recently moved and will rent this item from a different supplier, please contact our office." (Use on beneficiary's EOMB.), "This is your next to last rental payment.", "This is your last rental payment.", "This item has been rented up to the 15 month Medicare payment limit.", "Your equipment supplier must supply and service this item for as long as you continue to need it.", "Medicare cannot pay for maintenance and/or servicing of this item until 6 months have elapsed since the end of the 15th paid rental month.", If the beneficiary purchased a capped rental item prior to June 1, 1989, follow §7014.6. If the beneficiary purchased a capped rental item on or after June 1, 1989, use the following denial message:, "This equipment can only be paid for on a rental basis.",

F. Oxygen and Oxygen Equipment. - "The monthly allowance includes payment for all covered oxygen contents and supplies.", "Payment for the amount of oxygen supplied has been reduced or denied based on the patient's medical condition." (To supplier after medical review.), "The approved amount has been reduced to the amount allowable for medically necessary oxygen therapy." (To beneficiary.), "Payment denied because the allowance for this item is included in the monthly payment amount.", "Payment denied because Medicare oxygen coverage requirements are not met.", If the beneficiary purchased an oxygen system prior to June 1, 1989, follow §7014.6. If the beneficiary purchased an oxygen system on or after June 1, 1989, use the following denial message:, "This item can only be paid for on a rental basis.",

G. Items Requiring a Written Order Prior to Delivery. - "Payment is denied because the supplier did not obtain a written order from your doctor prior to the delivery of this item.", 4107.9 Oxygen HCPCS Codes Effective 1/1/89. -, NEW, OLD, DEFINITION, Q0036 notes (1), and (8), E1377-E1385, E1397, Oxygen concentrator, See High humidity Q0038 See note (2), E0400, E0405, Oxygen contents, gaseous, per unit (for use with owned gaseous stationary systems or when both a stationary and portable gaseous system are owned; 1 unit = 50 cubic ft.), Q0039 See note (2), E0410, E0415O, Oxygen contents, liquid, per unit, (for use with owned stationary liquid systems or when both a stationary and portable liquid system are owned; 1 unit = 10 lbs.), Rev. 1400/Page 4-28.5, Q0040, See note (2), E0416, Portable oxygen contents, per unit (for use only with portable gaseous systems when no stationary gas system is used; 1 unit = 5 cubic ft.), Q0041, See note (2), None, Portable oxygen contents, liquid, per unit (for use only with portable liquid systems when no stationary liquid system is used; 1 unit = 1 lb.), Q0042, E0425, Stationary compressed See note (3)gas system rental, includes contents (per unit), regulator with flow gauge, humidifier, nebulizer, cannula or mask & tubing; 1 unit = 50 cubic ft., E0425, See notes (4), and (8), Same, No change, E0430, See notes (8), and (9), Same, No change, E0435, See notes (7), and 8, Same, No change in terminology, but and (8)see note (7)., Q0043, E0440, Stationary liquid (see note (3) oxygen system rental), includes contents (per unit), use of reservoir, contents indicator, flowmeter, humidifier, nebulizer, cannula or mask and tubing; 1 unit of contents = 10 lbs., 0440, See note (4), Same, No change, E0455, Same, No change See note (6), E0555, See note (6), Same, No change, Page 4-28.6/Rev. 1400, E0580, Same, No change, See note (6), E1351, Same, No change, See note (6), E1352, See note (6), Same, No change, E1353, Same, See notes (6), and (8), No change, E1354, See note (6), Same, No change, E1371, Same, See note (6), No change, E1374, See note (6), Same, No change, E1400, See note (1), and (8), E1388-E1396, Same as Q0014, E1401, See notes (1), and (8), E1388-E1396, Same as Q0015, E1402, Same, No change, E1403, Same, No change, E1404, Same, No change, E1405, Q0037, Combine the fee See note (10)schedule amounts for the stationary oxygen system and the nebulizer with a compressor and heater (code E0585) to determine the fee schedule amount to apply to oxygen enrichers with a heater (code E1405), E1406, Q0037, Combine the fee schedule amounts for the stationary oxygen system and the nebulizer with only a compressor (i.e., without a heater, code E0570) to determine the fee schedule amount to apply to oxygen enrichers without a heater (code E1406),

MCM 4107.6   Written Order Prior to Delivery

Ensure that your system will pay for the equipment listed below only when the supplier has a written order in hand prior to delivery. Otherwise, do not pay for that item even if a written order is subsequently furnished. However, you can pay for a similar item if it is subsequently provided by an unrelated supplier which has a written order in hand prior to delivery. The HCPCS codes for the equipment requiring a written order are:

- E0180
- E0181
- E0182
- E0183
- E0184
- E0185
- E0188
- E0189
- E0190
- E0192
- E0195
- E0620
- E0720
- E0730
- E1230

MCM 4107.8   EOMB Messages, – The following EOMB messages are suggested: (See §§7012ff, for other applicable messages),

A. General,

    • This is the maximum approved amount for this item, (Use when payment is reduced for a line item),

B Inexpensive/Frequently Purchased Equipment,

• The total approved amount for this item is _____ whether this item is purchased or rented, (Use in first month),

• This is your next to last rental payment,

• This is your last rental payment,

• This item has been rented up to the Medicare payment limit,

• The approved amount has been reduced by the previously approved rental amounts,

C Items Requiring Frequent and Substantial Servicing, – Use the general rental messages in §4107, 8A, if applicable, If the beneficiary has purchased the item prior to June 1, 1989, follow §7014, 6, If the beneficiary purchase an item in this category on or after June 1, 1989, use the following message:,

• This equipment can only be paid for on a rental basis,

D. Customized Items and Other Prosthetic and Orthotic Devices,

• The total approved amount for this item is _____,

E. Capped Rental Items,

• Under a provision of Medicare law, monthly rental payments for this item can continue for up to 15 months from the first rental month or until the equipment is no longer needed, whichever comes first,

• If you no longer are using this equipment or have recently moved and will rent this item from a different supplier, please contact our office, (Use on beneficiary's EOMB),

• This is your next to last rental payment,

• This is your last rental payment,

• This item has been rented up to the 15 month Medicare payment limit,

• Your equipment supplier must supply and service this item for as long as you continue to need it,

• Medicare cannot pay for maintenance and/or servicing of this item until 6 months have elapsed since the end of the 15th paid rental month, If the beneficiary purchased a capped rental item prior to June 1, 1989, follow §7014 6, If the beneficiary purchased a capped rental item on or after June 1, 1989, use the following denial message:,

• This equipment can only be paid for on a rental basis,

F Oxygen and Oxygen Equipment,

• The monthly allowance includes payment for all covered oxygen contents and supplies,

• Payment for the amount of oxygen supplied has been reduced or denied based on the patient's medical condition (To supplier after medical review),

• The approved amount has been reduced to the amount allowable for medically necessary oxygen therapy (To beneficiary),

• Payment denied because the allowance for this item is included in the monthly payment amount,

• Payment denied because Medicare oxygen coverage requirements are not met, If the beneficiary purchased an oxygen system prior to June 1, 1989, follow §7014, 6, If the beneficiary purchased an oxygen system on or after June 1, 1989, use the following denial message:,

• This item can only be paid for on a rental basis,

G Items Requiring a Written Order Prior to Delivery,

• Payment is denied because the supplier did not obtain a written order from your doctor prior to the delivery of this item

MCM 4107.9   Home Use Of Oxygen,

A. General. – Medicare coverage of home oxygen and oxygen equipment under the durable medical equipment (DME) benefit (see §1861(s)(6) of the Act) is considered reasonable and necessary only for patients with significant hypoxemia who meet the medical documentation, laboratory evidence, and health conditions specified in subsections B, C, and D. This section also includes special coverage criteria for portable oxygen systems. Finally, a statement on the absence of coverage of the professional services of a respiratory therapist under the DME benefit is included in subsection F.,

B. Medical documentation. – Initial claims for oxygen services must include a completed Form HCFA-484 (Certificate of Medical Necessity: Oxygen) to establish whether coverage criteria are met and to ensure that the oxygen services provided are consistent with the physician's prescription or other medical documentation. The treating physician's prescription or other medical documentation must indicate that other forms of treatment (e.g., medical and physical therapy directed at secretions, bronchospasm and infection) have been tried, have not been

sufficiently successful, and oxygen therapy is still required. While there is no substitute for oxygen therapy, each patient must receive optimum therapy before long-term home oxygen therapy is ordered. Use Form HCFA-484 for recertifications. (See Medicare Carriers Manual §3312 for completion of Form HCFA-484.), The medical and prescription information in section B of Form HCFA-484 can be completed only by the treating physician, the physician's employee, or another clinician (e.g., nurse, respiratory therapist, etc.) as long as that person is not the DME supplier. Although hospital discharge coordinators and medical social workers may assist in arranging for physician-prescribed home oxygen, they do not have the authority to prescribe the services. Suppliers may not enter this information. While this section may be completed by nonphysician clinician or a physician employee, it must be reviewed and the form HCFA-484 signed by the attending physician., A physician's certification of medical necessity for oxygen equipment must include the results of specific testing before coverage can be determined., Claims for oxygen must also be supported by medical documentation in the patient's record. Separate documentation is used with electronic billing. (See Medicare Carriers Manual, Part 3,§4105.5.) This documentation may be in the form of a prescription written by the patient's attending physician who has recently examined the patient (normally within a month of the start of therapy) and must specify:,

• A diagnosis of the disease requiring home use of oxygen;,

• The oxygen flow rate; and,

• An estimate of the frequency, duration of use (e.g., 2 liters per minute, 10 minutes per hour, 12 hours per day), and duration of need (e.g., 6 months or lifetime)., NOTE: A prescription for "Oxygen PRN" or "Oxygen as needed" does not meet this last requirement. Neither provides any basis for determining if the amount of oxygen is reasonable and necessary for the patient., A member of the carrier's medical staff should review all claims with oxygen flow rates of more than 4 liters per minute before payment can be made., The attending physician specifies the type of oxygen delivery system to be used (i.e., gas, liquid, or concentrator) by signing the completed form HCFA-484. In addition the supplier or physician may use the space in section C for written confirmation of additional details of the physician's order. The additional order information contained in section C may include the means of oxygen delivery (mask, nasal, cannula, etc.), the specifics of varying flow rates, and/or the noncontinuous use of oxygen as appropriate. The physician confirms this order information with their signature in section D., New medical documentation written by the patient's attending physician must be submitted to the carrier in support of revised oxygen requirements when there has been a change in the patient's condition and need for oxygen therapy., Carriers are required to conduct periodic, continuing medical necessity reviews on patients whose conditions warrant these reviews and on patients with indefinite or extended periods of necessity as described in Medicare Carriers Manual, Part 3, §4105.5. When indicated, carriers may also request documentation of the results of a repeat arterial blood gas or oximetry study., NOTE: Section 4152 of OBRA 1990 requires earlier recertification and retesting of oxygen patients who begin coverage with an arterial blood gas result at or above a partial pressure of 55 or an arterial oxygen saturation percentage at or above 89. (See Medicare Carriers Manual §4105.5 for certification and retesting schedules.),

C. Laboratory Evidence. – Initial claims for oxygen therapy must also include the results of a blood gas study that has been ordered and evaluated by the attending physician. This is usually in the form of a measurement of the partial pressure of oxygen (PO2) in arterial blood. (See Medicare Carriers Manual, Part 3, §2070.1 for instructions on clinical laboratory tests.) A measurement of arterial oxygen saturation obtained by ear or pulse oximetry, however, is also acceptable when ordered and evaluated by the attending physician and performed under his or her supervision or when performed by a qualified provider or supplier of laboratory services. When the arterial blood gas and the oximetry studies are both used to document the need for home oxygen therapy and the results are conflicting, the arterial blood gas study is the preferred source of documenting medical need. A DME supplier is not considered a qualified provider or supplier of laboratory services for purposes of these guidelines. This prohibition does not extend to the results of blood gas test conducted by a hospital certified to do such tests. The conditions under which the laboratory tests are performed must be specified in writing and submitted with the initial claim, i.e., at rest, during exercise, or during sleep., The preferred sources of laboratory evidence are existing physician and/or hospital records that reflect the patient's medical condition. Since it is expected that virtually all patients who qualify for home oxygen coverage for the first time under these guidelines have recently been discharged from a hospital where they submitted to arterial blood gas tests, the carrier needs to request that such test results be submitted in support of their initial claims for home oxygen. If more than one arterial blood gas test is performed during the patient's hospital stay, the test result obtained closest to, but no earlier than 2 days prior to the hospital discharge date is required as evidence of the need for home oxygen therapy., For those patients whose initial oxygen prescription did not originate during a hospital stay, blood gas studies should be done while the patient is in the chronic stable state, i.e., not during a period of an acute illness or an exacerbation of their underlying disease.", Carriers may accept a attending physician's statement of recent hospital test results for a particular patient, when appropriate, in lieu of copies of actual hospital records., A repeat arterial blood gas study is appropriate when evidence indicates that an oxygen recipient has undergone a major change in their condition relevant to home use of oxygen. If the carrier has reason to believe that there has been a major change in the patient's physical condition, it may ask for documentation of the results of another blood gas or oximetry study.,

D. Health Conditions. – Coverage is available for patients with significant hypoxemia in the chronic stable state if: (1) the attending physician has determined that the patient has a health condition outlined in subsection D.1, (2) the patient meets the blood gas evidence requirements specified in subsection D.3, and (3) the patient has appropriately tried other alternative treatment measures without complete success. (See subsection B.),

1. Conditions for Which Oxygen Therapy May Be Covered. -,

• A severe lung disease, such as chronic obstructive pulmonary disease, diffuse interstitial lung disease, whether of known or unknown etiology; cystic fibrosis bronchiectasis; widespread pulmonary neoplasm; or,

• Hypoxia-related symptoms or findings that might be expected to improve with oxygen therapy. Examples of these symptoms and findings are pulmonary hypertension, recurring congestive heart failure due to chronic cor pulmonale, erythrocytosis, impairment of the cognitive process, nocturnal restlessness, and morning headache.,

2. Conditions for Which Oxygen Therapy Is Not Covered. -,

• Angina pectoris in the absence of hypoxemia. This condition is generally not the result of a low oxygen level in the blood, and there are other preferred treatments;, • Breathlessness without cor pulmonale or evidence of hypoxemia. Although intermittent oxygen use is sometimes prescribed to relieve this condition, it is potentially harmful and psychologically addicting;,

• Severe peripheral vascular disease resulting in clinically evident desaturation in one or more extremities. There is no evidence that increased PO2 improves the oxygenation of tissues with impaired circulation; or,

• Terminal illnesses that do not affect the lungs.,

3. Covered Blood Gas Values. – If the patient has a condition specified in subsection D.1, the carrier must review the medical documentation and laboratory evidence that has been submitted for a particular patient (see subsections B and C) and determine if coverage is available under one of the three group categories outlined below.,

a. Group I. – Except as modified in subsection d, coverage is provided for patients with significant hypoxemia evidenced by any of the following:,

(1) An arterial PO2 at or below 55 mm Hg, or an arterial oxygen saturation at or below 88 percent, taken at rest, breathing room air.,

(2) An arterial PO2 at or below 55 mm Hg, or an arterial oxygen saturation at or below 88 percent, taken during sleep for a patient who demonstrates an arterial PO2 at or above 56 mm Hg, or an arterial oxygen saturation at or above 89 percent, while awake; or a greater than normal fall in oxygen level during sleep (a decrease in arterial PO2 more than 10 mm Hg, or decrease in arterial oxygen saturation more than 5 percent) associated with symptoms or signs reasonably attributable to hypoxemia (e.g., impairment of cognitive processes and nocturnal restlessness or insomnia). In either of these cases, coverage is provided only for use of oxygen during sleep, and then only one type of unit will be covered. Portable oxygen, therefore, would not be covered in this situation.,

(3) An arterial PO2 at or below 55 mm Hg or an arterial oxygen saturation at or below 88 percent, taken during exercise for a patient who demonstrates an arterial PO2 at or above 56 mm Hg, or an arterial oxygen saturation at or above 89 percent, during the day while at rest. In this case, supplemental oxygen is provided for during exercise if there is evidence the use of oxygen improves the hypoxemia that was demonstrated during exercise when the patient was breathing room air.,

b. Group II. – Except as modified in subsection d, coverage is available for patients whose arterial PO2 is 56-59 mm Hg or whose arterial blood oxygen saturation is 89 percent, if there is evidence of:,

(1) Dependent edema suggesting congestive heart failure;,

(2) Pulmonary hypertension or cor pulmonale, determined by measurement of pulmonary artery pressure, gated blood pool scan, echocardiogram, or "P" pulmonale on EKG (P wave greater than 3 mm in standard leads II, III, or AVFL; or,

(3) Erythrocythemia with a hematocrit greater than 56 percent.,

c. Group III. – Except as modified in subsection d, carriers must apply a rebuttable presumption that a home program of oxygen use is not medically necessary for patients with arterial PO2 levels at or above 60 mm Hg, or arterial blood oxygen saturation at or above 90 percent. In order for claims in this category to be reimbursed, the carrier's reviewing physician needs to review any documentation submitted in rebuttal of this presumption and grant specific approval of the claims. HCFA expects few claims to be approved for coverage in this category.,

d. Variable Factors That May Affect Blood Gas Values. – In reviewing the arterial PO2 levels and the arterial oxygen saturation percentages specified in subsections D. 3. a, b and c, the carrier's medical staff must take into account variations in oxygen measurements that may result from such factors as the patient's age, the altitude level, or the patient's decreased oxygen carrying capacity.,

E. Portable Oxygen Systems. – A patient meeting the requirements specified below may qualify for coverage of a portable oxygen system either (1) by itself or (2) to use in addition to a stationary oxygen system. A portable oxygen system is covered for a particular patient if:,

• The claim meets the requirements specified in subsections A-D, as appropriate; and,

• The medical documentation indicates that the patient is mobile in the home and would benefit from the use of a portable oxygen system in the home. Portable oxygen systems are not covered for patients who qualify for oxygen solely based on blood gas studies obtained during sleep.,

F. Respiratory Therapists. – Respiratory therapists' services are not covered under the provisions for coverage of oxygen services under the Part B durable medical equipment benefit as outlined above. This benefit provides for coveravge of home use of oxygen and oxygen equipment, but does not include a professional component in the delivery of such services., (See §60-9; Intermediary Manual, Part 3, §3113ff; and Medicare Carriers Manual, Part 3, §2100ff.)

MCM 4120   Foot Care And Supportive Devices For Feet
NOTE: See §4281 for the relationship between foot care and the coverage and billing of the diagnosis and treatment of peripheral neuropathy with loss of protective sensation (LOPS) in people with diabetes.

4120.1 Application of Foot Care Exclusions to Physicians' Services. – The exclusion of foot care is determined by the nature of the service (§2323). Thus, reimbursement for an excluded service should be denied whether performed by a podiatrist, osteopath, or a doctor of medicine, and without regard to the difficulty or complexity of the procedure. When an itemized bill shows both covered services and noncovered services not integrally related to the covered service, the portion of charges attributable to the noncovered services should be denied. (For example, if an itemized bill shows surgery for an ingrown toenail and also removal of calluses not necessary for the performance of toe surgery, any additional charge attributable to removal of the calluses should be denied.)

In reviewing claims involving foot care, the carrier should be alert to the following exceptional situations:

1. Payment may be made for incidental noncovered services performed as a necessary and integral part of, and secondary to, a covered procedure. For example, if trimming of toenails is required for application of a cast to a fractured foot, the carrier need not allocate and deny a portion of the charge for the trimming of the nails. However, a separately itemized charge for such excluded service should be disallowed. When the primary procedure is covered the administration of anesthesia necessary for the performance of such procedure is also covered.

2. Payment may be made for initial diagnostic services performed in connection with a specific symptom or complaint if it seems likely that its treatment would be covered even though the resulting diagnosis may be one requiring only noncovered care.

MCM 4173   Positron Emission Tomography (PET) Scans
BACKGROUND:

For dates of service on or after March 14, 1995, Medicare covers one use of PET scans, imaging of the perfusion of the heart using Rubidium 82 (Rb 82).

For dates of service on or after January 1, 1998, Medicare expanded coverage of PET scans for the characterization of solitary pulmonary nodules and for the initial staging of lung cancer, conditioned upon its ability to effect the management and treatment of patients with either suspected or demonstrated lung cancer. All other uses of PET scans remain not covered by Medicare.

Beginning for dates of service on or after July 1, 1999, Medicare will cover PET scans for evaluation of recurrent colorectal cancer in patients with levels of carinoembryonic antigen (CEA), staging lymphoma (both Hodgkins and non-Hodgkins) in place of a Gallium study or lymphangiogram, and for the staging of recurrent melanoma prior to surgery.

See Coverage Issues Manual §50-36 for specific coverage criteria for PET scans.

Regardless of any other terms or conditions, all uses of PET scans, in order to be covered by Medicare program, must meet the following conditions:

Scans must be performed using PET scanners that have either been approved or cleared for marketing by the FDA as PET scanners;

Submission of claims for payment must include any information Medicare requires to assure that the PET scans performed were: (a) reasonable and necessary; (b) did not unnecessarily duplicate other covered diagnostic tests, and (c) did not involve investigational drugs or procedures using investigational drugs, as determined by the Food and Drug Administration (FDA); and

The PET scan entity submitting claims for payment must keep such patient records as Medicare requires on file for each patient for whom a PET scan claim is made.

4173.1 Conditions for Medicare Coverage of PET Scans for Noninvasive Imaging of the Perfusion of the Heart. – Pet scans done at rest or with pharmacological stress used for noninvasive imaging of the perfusion of the heart for the diagnosis management of patients with known or suspected coronary artery disease using the FDA-approved radiopharmaceutical Rubidium 82 (Rb 82) are covered for services performed on or after March 15, 1995, provided such scans meet either of the two following conditions:

The PET scan, whether rest alone or rest with stress, is used in place of, but not in addition to, a single photon emission computed tomography (SPECT); or

The PET scan, whether rest alone or rest with stress, is used following a SPECT that was found inconclusive. In these cases, the PET scan must have been considered necessary in order to determine what medical or surgical intervention is required to treat the patient. (For purposes of this requirement, an inconclusive test is a test whose results are equivocal, technically uninterpretable, or discordant with a patient's other clinical data.)

NOTE: PET scans using Rubidium 82, whether rest or stress are not covered by Medicare for routine screening of asymptomatic patients, regardless of the level of risk factors applicable to such patients.

4173.2 Conditions of Coverage of PET Scans for Characterization of Solitary Pulmonary Nodules (SPNs) and PET Scans Using FDG to Initially Stage Lung Cancer. – PET scans using the glucose analog 2-[fluorine-18]-fluoro-2-deoxy-D-glucose(FDG) are covered for services on or after January 1, 1998, subject to the condition and limitations described in CIM 50-36.

NOTE: A Tissue Sampling Procedure (TSP) should not be routinely covered in the case of a negative PET scan for characterization of SPNs, since the patient is presumed not to have a malignant lesion, based upon the PET scan results. Claims for a TSP after a negative PET must be submitted with documentation in order to determine if the TSP is reasonable and necessary in spite of a negative PET. Claims submitted for a TSP after a negative PET without documentation should be denied. Physicians should discuss with their patients the implications of this decision, both with respect to the patient's responsibility for payment for such a biopsy if desired, as well as the confidence the physician has in the results of such PET scans, prior to ordering such scans for this purpose. This physician-patient decision should occur with a clear discussion and understanding of the sensitivity and specificity trade-offs between a computerized tomography (CT) and PET scans. In cases where a TSP is performed, it is the responsibility of the physician ordering the TSP to provide sufficient documentation of the reasonableness and necessity for such procedure or procedures. Such documentation should include, but is not necessarily limited to, a description of the features of the PET scan that call into question whether it is an accurate representation of the patient's condition, the existence of other factors in the patient's condition that call into question the accuracy of the PET scan, and such other information as the contractor deems necessary to determine whether the claim for the TSP should be covered and paid.

In cases of serial evaluation of SPNs using both CT and regional PET chest scanning, such PET scans will not be covered if repeated within 90 days following a negative PET scan.

4173.3 Conditions of Coverage of PET Scans for Recurrence of Colorectal Cancer, Staging and Characterization of Lymphoma, and Recurrence of Melanoma. – Medicare adds coverage for these three new indications for PET, one for evaluation of recurrent colorectal cancer in patients with rising levels of carcinoembryonic antigen (CEA), one for staging of lymphoma (both Hodgkins and non-Hodgkins) when the PET scan substitutes for a Gallium scan, and one for the detection of recurrent melanoma, provided certain conditions are met. All three indications are covered only when using

the radiopharmaceutical FDA (2-[fluorine-18]-fluoro-2-deoxy-D-glucose), and are further predicated on the legal availability of FDG for use in such scans.

4173.4 Billing Requirements for PET Scans. –

Effective for Services on or After January 1, 1998, Claims for Characterizing SPNs Should Include. –

NOTE: PET scans are not covered by Medicare for routine screening of asymptomatic patients, regardless of the level of risk factors applicable to such patients.

B. Effective for services on or after January 1, 1998, claims for staging metastatic non-small-cell lung carcinoma (NSCLC) must include:

Since this service is covered only in those cases in which a primary cancerous lung tumor has been confirmed, claims for PET must show evidence of the detection of such primary lung tumor. For example, a diagnosis code indicating the existence of a primary tumor or any other evidence you deem appropriate. A surgical pathology report which documents the presence of an NSCLC must be kept on file with the provider. If you deem it necessary, contact the provider for a copy of this documentation.

Whole body PET scan results and results of concurrent CT and follow-up lymph node biopsy. In order to ensure that the PET scan is properly coordinated with other diagnostic modalities, claims must include both (1) the results of concurrent thoracic CT, which is necessary for anatomic information, and (2) the results of any lymph node biopsy performed to finalize whether the patient will be a surgical candidate.

NOTE: A lymph node biopsy is not covered in the case of a negative CT and negative PET where the patient is considered a surgical candidate, given the presumed absence of metastatic NSCLC.

C. Effective for Dates of Service on or After July 1, 1999 PET Claims For the Following Conditions Must Include:

Recurring colorectal cancer with rising CEA:

– A statement or other evidence of previous colorectal tumor;

– The results of the concurrent CT, which is necessary for anatomic information; and

– The necessary procedure codes and/or modifiers.

Staging or restaging of lymphoma in place of a Gallium study or lymphangiogram:

– A statement or other evidence of previously-made diagnosis of lymphoma;

– The results of the concurrent CT, which is necessary for anatomic information; and – The date of the last Gallium scan or lymphangiogram when done in the same facility as the PET scan.

Recurrent Melanoma prior to surgery:

– A statement or other evidence of previous melanoma;

– The results of the concurrent CT, which is necessary for anatomic information; and – The date of the last Gallium scan when done in the same facility as the PET scan.

As with any claim but particularly in view of the limitations on this coverage, you may decide to conduct post-payment reviews to determine that the use of PET scans is consistent with this instruction. PET scan facilities must keep patient record information on file for each Medicare patient for whom a PET scan claim is made. These medical records will be used in any post- payment reviews and must include the information necessary to substantial the need for the PET scan.

4173.5 HCPCS and Modifiers for PET Scans. – Providers should use HCPCS codes G0030 through G0047 to indicate the conditions under which a PET scan was done for imaging of the perfusion of the heart. These codes represent the global service, so providers performing just the technical or professional component of the test should use modifier TC or 26, respectively. The following codes should be reported for PET scans used for the imaging of the lungs:

G0125 – PET lung imaging of solitary pulmonary nodules using 2-[fluorine-18]-fluoro-2-deoxy-D-glucose (FDG), following CT (71250/71260 or 71270); or

G0126 – PET lung imaging of solitary pulmonary nodules using 2-[fluorine-18]-fluoro-2-deoxy-D-glucose (FDG), following CT (71250/71260 or 71270); for initial staging of pathologically diagnosed NSCLC, or

G0163 – Positron Emission Tomography (PET), whole body, for recurrence of colorectal or colorectal metastatic cancer; or

G0164 – Positron Emission Tomography (PET), whole body, for staging and characterization of lymphoma; or

G0165 – Positron Emission Tomography (PET), whole body, for recurrence of melanoma or melanoma metastic cancer

NOTE: The payment for the radio tracer, or radio pharmaceutical is included in the relative value units of the technical components of the above procedure codes. Do not make any separate payments for these agents for PET scans.

In addition, providers must indicate the results of the PET scan and the previous test using a two digit modifier. (The modifier is not required for technical component-only billings or billings to the intermediary.) The first character should indicate the result of the PET scan; the second character should indicate the results of the prior test. Depending on the procedure codes with which the modifiers are used, the meaning of the modifier will be apparent. The test result modifiers and their descriptions are as follows:

Modifier	Description
N	Negative;
E	Equivocal;
P	Positive, but not suggestive of, extensive ischemia or not suggestive of malignant single pulmonary nodule; and
S	Positive and suggestive of; extensive ischemia (greater than 20 percent of the left ventricle) or malignant single pulmonary nodule.

These modifiers may be used in any combination.

4173.6 Claims Processing Instructions for PET Scan Claims. –

FDA Approval. – PET scans are covered only when performed at a PET imaging center with a PET scanner that has been approved or cleared by the FDA. When submitting the claim, the provider is certifying this and must be able to produce a copy of this approval upon request. An official approval letter need not be submitted with the claim.

You may consider conducting a review on a post-payment basis to verify, based on a sample of PET scan claims, that the PET scan was performed at a center with a PET scanner which was approved or cleared for marketing.

EOMB and Remittance Messages. – Providers must indicate the results of the PET scan and the previous test using a two-digit modifier as specified in §4173.4. Deny assigned claims received prior to April 1, 1996 without such modifier, using the following EOMB message:

"Your service was denied because information required to make payment was missing. We have asked your provider to resubmit a claim with the missing information so that it may be reprocessed." (Message 9.33)

Deny unassigned claims received prior to April 1, 1996, without the two-digit modifier using the following EOMB message:

"Medicare cannot pay for this service because the claim is missing information/documentation. Please ask your provider to submit a new, complete claim to us." (Messages 9.8 and 9.15)

Claims received on or after April 1, 1996, without the two-digit modifier must be returned as unprocessable. (See §3005.)

Use the following remittance message for assigned claims:

"The procedure code is inconsistent with the modifier used, or a required modifier is missing." (Reason Code 4)

Assigned claims for dates of service on or after January 1, 1998, without the proper documentation must be denied using the following EOMB message:

"Your service was denied because information required to make payment was missing. We have asked your provider to resubmit a claim with the missing information so that it may be reprocessed." (Message 9.33)

Type of Service. – The type of service for the PET scan codes in the "G" range is 4, Diagnostic Radiology.

MCM 4182   Prostate Cancer Screening Tests – Covered (Effective for services furnished on or after January 1, 2000),

A. General. – Section 4103 of the Balanced Budget Act of 1997 provides for coverage of certain prostate cancer screening tests subject to certain coverage, frequency, and payment limitations. Effective for services furnished on or after January 1, 2000. Medicare will cover prostate cancer screening tests/procedures for the early detection of prostate cancer. Coverage of prostate cancer screening tests includes the following procedures furnished to an individual for the early detection of prostate cancer:,

• Screening digital rectal examination; and,

• Screening prostate specific antigen blood test.,

B. Screening Digital Rectal Examinations. – Screening digital rectal examinations (HCPCS code G0102) are covered at a frequency of once every 12 months for men who have attained age 50 (at least 11 months have passed following the month in which the last Medicare-covered screening digital rectal examination was performed). Screening digital rectal examination means a clinical examination of

an individual's prostate for nodules or other abnormalities of the prostate. This screening must be performed by a doctor of medicine or osteopathy (as defined in §1861(r)(1) of the Act), or by a physician assistant, nurse practitioner, clinical nurse specialist, or certified nurse midwife (as defined in §1861(aa) and §1861(gg) of the Act) who is authorized under State law to perform the examination, fully knowledgeable about the beneficiary's medical condition, and would be responsible for using the results of any examination performed in the overall management of the beneficiary's specific medical problem.,

C. Screening Prostate Specific Antigen Tests. – Screening prostate specific antigen tests (code G0103) are covered at a frequency of once every 12 months for men who have attained age 50 (at least 11 months have passed following the month in which the last Medicare-covered screening prostate specific antigen test was performed). Screening prostate specific antigen tests (PSA) means a test to detect the marker for adenocarcinoma of prostate. PSA is a reliable immunocytochemical marker for primary and metastatic adenocarcinoma of prostate. This screening must be ordered by the beneficiary's physician or by the beneficiary's physician assistant, nurse practitioner, clinical nurse specialist, or certified nurse midwife (the term "attending physician" is defined in §1861(r)(1) of the Act to mean a doctor of medicine or osteopathy and the terms "physician assistant, nurse practitioner, clinical nurse specialist, or certified nurse midwife" are defined in §1861(aa) and §1861(gg) of the Act) who is fully knowledgeable about the beneficiary's medical condition, and who would be responsible for using the results of any examination (test) performed in the overall management of the beneficiary's specific medical problem.

MCM 4270   ESRD Bill Processing Procedures

Physicians, independent laboratories, and beneficiaries must submit claims (Form CMS-1500, Form CMS-1490S or electronic equivalent) to their local carrier for services furnished to end stage renal disease (ESRD) beneficiaries. Suppliers of Method II dialysis equipment and supplies will submit their claims (Form CMS-1500 or electronic equivalent) to the appropriate Durable Medical Equipment Regional Carriers (DMERCs). All ESRD facilities must submit their claims to their appropriate fiscal intermediary (FI).

MCM 4273.1   Completion of Initial Claim for EPO

The following information is required. Due to space limitations, some items must be documented on a separate form. Therefore, initial claims are generally submitted on paper unless your electronic billers are able to submit supplemental documentation with EMC claims. Return incomplete assigned claims in accordance with §3311. Develop incomplete unassigned claims.,

A. Diagnoses. – The diagnoses must be submitted according to ICD-9-CM and correlated to the procedure. This information is in Items 23A and 24D, of the Form HCFA-1500.,

B. Hematocrit (HCT)/Hemoglobin (Hgb). – There are special HCPCS codes for reporting the injection of EPO. These allow the simultaneous reporting of the patient's latest HCT or Hgb reading before administration of EPO., Instruct the physician and/or staff to enter a separate line item for injections of EPO at different HCT/Hgb levels. The Q code for each line items is entered in Item 24C.,

1. Code Q9920 – Injection of EPO, per l,000 units, at patient HCT of 20 or less/Hgb of 6.8 or less.,

2. Codes Q9921 through Q9939 – Injection of EPO, per 1,000 units, at patient HCT of 2l to 39/Hgb of 6.9 to 13.1. For HCT levels of 2l or more, up to a HCT of 39/Hgb of 6.9 to 13.1, a Q code that includes the actual HCT levels is used. To convert actual Hgb to corresponding HCT values for Q code reporting, multiply the Hgb value by 3 and round to the nearest whole number. Use the whole number to determine the appropriate Q code.,

EXAMPLES: If the patient's HCT is 25/Hgb is 8.2-8.4, Q9925 must be entered on the claim. If the patient's HCT is 39/Hgb is 12.9-13.1, Q9939 is entered.,

3. Code Q9940 – Injection of EPO, per l,000 units at patient HCT of 40 or above., A single line item may include multiple doses of EPO administered while the patient's HCT level remained the same.,

C. Units Administered. – The standard unit of EPO is 1,000. The number of 1,000 units administered per line item is included on the claim. The physician's office enters 1 in the units field for each multiple of 1,000 units. For example, if 12,000 units are administered, 12 is entered. This information is shown in Item 24F (Days/Units) on Form , HCFA-1500., In some cases, the dosage for a single line item does not total an even multiple of 1,000. If this occurs, the physician's office rounds down supplemental dosages of 0 to 499 units to the prior 1,000 units. Supplemental dosages of 500 to 999 are rounded up to the next 1,000 units.,

EXAMPLES:

A patient's HCT reading on August 6 was 22/Hgb was 7.3. The patient received 5,000 units of EPO on August 7, August 9 and August 11, for a total of 15,000 units. The first line of Item 24 of Form HCFA-1500 shows:,

Dates of, Service Procedure, Code
Days or, Units, 8/7-8/11
Q9922   15, On September 13, the patient's HCT reading increased to 27/Hgb increased to 9. The patient received 5,100 units of EPO on September 13, September 15, and September 17, for a total of 15,300 units. Since less than 15,500 units were given, the figure is rounded down to 15,000. This line on the claim form shows:, Dates of , Service Procedure, Code Days or, Units, 9/13-9/17
Q9927   15, On October 16, the HCT level increased to 33/Hgb increased to 11. The patient received doses of 4,850 units on October 16, October 18, and October 20 for a total of 14,550 units. Since more than 14,500 units were administered, the figure is rounded up to 15,000. Form HCFA-1500 shows:, Dates of, Service Procedure, Code Days or, Units, 10/16-10/20
Q9933   15,

D. Date of the patient's most recent HCT or Hgb.,

E. Most recent HCT or Hgb level prior to initiation of EPO therapy.,

F. Date of most recent HCT or Hgb level prior to initiation of EPO therapy.,

G. Patient's most recent serum creatinine, within the last month, prior to initiation of EPO therapy.,

H. Date of most recent serum creatinine prior to initiation of EPO therapy.,

I. Patient's weight in kilograms.,

J. Patient's starting dose per kilogram. (The usual starting dose is 50-100 units per kilogram.), When a claim is submitted on Form HCFA-1500, these items are submitted on a separate document. It is not necessary to enter them into your claims processing system. This information is used in utilization review.

MCM 4450   Parenteral And Enteral Nutrition (PEN),

PEN coverage is determined by information provided by the attending physician and the PEN supplier. A certification of medical necessity (CMN) contains pertinent information needed to ensure consistent coverage and payment determinations nationally. A completed CMN must accompany and support the claims for PEN to establish whether coverage criteria are met and to ensure that the PEN provided is consistent with the attending physician's prescription., The medical and prescription information on a PEN CMN can be completed most appropriately by the attending physician, or from information in the patient's records by an employee of the physician for the physician's review and signature. Although PEN suppliers may assist in providing PEN items they cannot complete the CMN since they do not have the same access to patient information needed to properly enter medical or prescription information.,

A. Scheduling and Documenting Certifications and Recertifications of Medical Necessity for PEN. – A PEN CMN must accompany the initial claim submitted. The initial certification is valid for three months. Establish the schedule on a case-by-case basis for recertifying the need for PEN therapy. A change in prescription for a beneficiary past the initial certification period does not restart the certification process. A period of medical necessity ends when PEN is not medically required for two consecutive months. The entire certification process, if required, begins after the period of two consecutive months have elapsed.,

B. Initial Certifications. – In reviewing the claim and the supporting data on the CMN, compare certain items, especially pertinent dates of treatment. For example, the start date of PEN coverage cannot precede the date of physician certification. The estimated duration of therapy must be contained on the CMN. Use this information to verify that the test of permanence is met. Once coverage is established, the estimated length of need at the start of PEN services will determine the recertification schedule. (See §4450 A.), Verify that the information shown on the certification supports the need for PEN supplies as billed. A diagnosis must show a functional impairment that precludes the enteral patient from swallowing and the parenteral patient from absorbing nutrients., The attending physician and/or his/her designated employee are in a position to accurately complete the patient's medical information including:,

• The patient's general condition, estimated duration of therapy, and other treatments or therapies (see §3329 B.2.);,

• The patient's clinical assessment relating to the need for PEN therapy (see §3329 B.3.); and,

• The nutritional support therapy (i.e., the enteral or parenteral formulation). (See §3329 B.4.), Initial assigned claims with the following conditions can be denied without development:,

• Inappropriate or missing diagnosis or functional impairment;,

• Estimated duration of therapy is less than 90 consecutive days;,

• Duration of therapy is not listed;,

• Supplies have not been provided;,

• Supplies were provided prior to onset date of therapy; and,

• Stamped physician's signature., Develop unassigned claims for missing or incomplete information. (See §3329 C.), Review all claims with initial certifications and recertifications before payment is authorized.,

C. Revised Certifications/Change in Prescription. – Remind suppliers to submit revised certifications if the attending physician changes the PEN prescription. A revised certification is appropriate when:,

• There is a change in the attending physician's orders in the category of nutrients and/or calories prescribed;,

• There is a change by more than one liter in the daily volume of parenteral solutions;,

• There is a change from home-mix to pre-mix or pre-mix to home-mix parenteral solutions;,

• There is a change from enteral to parenteral or parenteral to enteral therapy; or,

• There is a change in the method of infusion (e.g., from gravity-fed to pump-fed)., Do not adjust payments on PEN claims unless a revised or renewed certification documents the necessity for the change. Adjust payments timely, if necessary, for supplies since the PEN prescription was changed., Do not exceed payment levels for the most current certification or recertification if a prescription change is not documented by a new recertification., Adjust your diary for scheduled recertifications. When the revised certification has been considered, reschedule the next recertification according to the recertification schedule. (See § 4450 A.),

D. Items Requiring Special Attention. -,

1. Nutrients. – Category IB of enteral nutrients contains products that are natural intact protein/protein isolates commonly known as blenderized nutrients. Additional documentation is required to justify the necessity of Category IB nutrients. The attending physician must provide sufficient information to indicate that the patient:,

• Has an intolerance to nutritionally equivalent (semi-synthetic) products;,

• Had a severe allergic reaction to a nutritionally equivalent (semi-synthetic) product; or,

• Was changed to a blenderized nutrient to alleviate adverse symptoms expected to be of permanent duration with continued use of semi-synthetic products., Also, enteral nutrient categories III through VI require additional medical justification for coverage., Parenteral nutrition may be either "self-mixed" (i.e., the patient is taught to prepare the nutrient solution aseptically) or "pre-mixed" (i.e., the nutrient solution is prepared by trained professionals employed or contracted by the PEN supplier). The attending physician must provide information to justify the reason for "pre-mixed" parenteral nutrient solutions.,

2. Prospective Billing. – Pay for no more than a one-month supply of parenteral or enteral nutrients for any one prospective billing period. Claims submitted retroactively may include multiple months.,

3. Pumps. – Enteral nutrition may be administered by syringe, gravity, or pump. The attending physician must specify the reason that necessitates the use of an enteral feeding pump. Ensure that the equipment for which payment is claimed is consistent with that prescribed (e.g., expect a claim for an I.V. pole, if a pump is used)., Effective April 1, 1990, claims for parenteral and enteral pumps are limited to rental payments for a total of 15 months during a period of medical need. A period of medical need ends when enteral or parenteral nutrients are not medically necessary for two consecutive months., Do not allow additional rental payments once the 15-month limit is reached, unless the attending physician changes the prescription between parenteral and enteral nutrients., Do not continue rental payments after a pump is purchased unless the attending physician changes the prescription between parenteral and enteral nutrients., Do not begin a new 15-month rental period when a patient changes suppliers. The new supplier is entitled to the balance remaining on the 15-month rental period., Effective October 1, 1990, necessary maintenance and servicing of pumps after the 15-month rental limit is reached, includes repairs and extensive maintenance that involves the breaking down of sealed components or performing tests that require specialized testing equipment not available to the beneficiary or nursing home.,

4. Supplies. – Enteral care kits contain all the necessary supplies for the enteral patient using the syringe, gravity, or pump method of nutrient administration. Parenteral nutrition care kits and their components are considered all inclusive items necessary to administer therapy during a monthly period., Compare the enteral feeding care kits on the claim with the method of administration indicated on the CMN.,

• Reduce the allowance to the amount paid for a gravity-fed care kit when billed for a pump feeding kit in the absence of documentation or unacceptable documentation for a pump.,

• Limit payment to a one-month supply.,

• Deny payment for additional components included as part of the PEN supply kit.,

5. Attending Physician Identification. – A CMN must contain the attending physician's Unique Physician Identification Number (UPIN) and be signed and dated by the attending physician. A stamped signature is unacceptable., Deny certifications and recertifications altered by "whiting out" or "pasting over" and entering new data. Consider suppliers that show a pattern of altering CMNs for educational contact and/or audit., Be alert to certifications from suppliers who have questionable utilization or billing practices or who are under sanction. Consider an audit of any such situations.

APPENDIX 5 — COMPANIES ACCEPTING HCPCS LEVEL II CODES

ACS
34 N LAST CHANCE GULCH STE 200
HELENA, MT 59601-4163
PO BOX 4936
HELENA, MT 59604-4936
PHONE: (406) 449-7693
FAX: (406) 442-4402
IN-STATE: (800) 624-3958

ACTIVA BENEFITS SERVICES
2905 LUCERNE STE 110
GRAND RAPIDS, MI 49546
PHONE: (616) 787-7616
FAX: (616) 787-4590
NATIONAL: (800) 269-7196

ADMINISTRATION SYSTEMS RESEARCH CORP
3033 ORCHARD VISTA DR SE
GRAND RAPIDS, MI 49546-7000
PO BOX 6392
GRAND RAPIDS, MI 49516-6392
PHONE: (616) 957-1751
FAX: (616) 957-8986
NATIONAL: (800) 968-2449
IN-STATE: (800) 968-2449

ADMINISTRATIVE PROCEDURES
2111 W LINCOLN HWY
MERRILLVILLE, IN 46410-5253
PHONE: (219) 769-6944
FAX: (219) 769-4834
NATIONAL: (800) 759-6944
IN-STATE: (800) 759-6944

ADMINISTRATIVE SERVICES, INC
7990 SW 117TH AVE
MIAMI, FL 33183-3815
PO BOX 839000
MIAMI, FL 33283-9000
PHONE: (305) 595-4040
FAX: (305) 596-6820
NATIONAL: (800) 749-1858

ADMIRAL INSURANCE CO
1255 CALDWELL RD
CHERRY HILL, NJ 08034-3220
PO BOX 5725
CHERRY HILL, NJ 08034-0524
PHONE: (856) 429-9200
FAX: (856) 429-8611

ADVANCED BENEFIT ADMINISTRATORS
6420 SW MACADAM AVE STE 380
PORTLAND, OR 97239-3519
PHONE: (503) 245-3770
FAX: (503) 245-4122
NATIONAL: (800) 443-6531

AETNA / U.S. HEALTHCARE
1385 E SHAW AVE
FRESNO, CA 93710-7901
PHONE: (559) 241-1000
FAX: (559) 241-1226
NATIONAL: (800) 756-7039

2201 RENAISSANCE BLVD
KING OF PRUSSIA, PA 19406-2766
PO BOX 1125
BLUE BELL, PA 19422-0770
PHONE: (484) 322-2000
NATIONAL: (800) 872-3862

ONE PRUDENTIAL CIR
SUGARLAND, TX 77479-3833
PO BOX 851
HOUSTON, TX 77001-0851
PHONE: (281) 637-3241
FAX: (281) 637-3556
NATIONAL: (800) 876-7778

AFLAC
1932 WYNNTON RD
COLUMBUS, GA 31999-7251
PHONE: (706) 323-3431
FAX: (877) 442-3522
NATIONAL: (800) 992-3522
IN-STATE: (800) 992-3522

ALLEGIANCE BENEFIT PLAN MANAGEMENT, INC.
2806 S GARFIELD ST
MISSOULA, MT 59801-7733
PO BOX 3018
MISSOULA, MT 59806-3018
PHONE: (406) 721-2222
FAX: (406) 721-2252
NATIONAL: (800) 877-1122

ALLIED ADMINISTRATORS, INC
777 DAVIS ST
SAN FRANCISCO, CA 94111-1405
PO BOX 2500
SAN FRANCISCO, CA 94126-2500
PHONE: (415) 986-6276
FAX: (415) 439-5857
NATIONAL: (888) 877-8363

2831 CAMINO DEL RIO S STE 311
SAN DIEGO, CA 92108-3829
PHONE: (619) 297-8235
FAX: (619) 574-0645

ALPHA DATA SYSTEMS, INC
1545 W MOCKINGBIRD LN STE 6000
DALLAS, TX 75235-5099
PHONE: (214) 638-1488
FAX: (214) 688-7718
NATIONAL: (800) 441-2448

ALTERNATIVE RISK MANAGEMENT LIMITED
111 W CAMPBELL STE 400
ARLINGTON HEIGHTS, IL 60005-1406
PHONE: (847) 394-1700
FAX: (847) 394-6328
NATIONAL: (800) 392-1770

ALTICOR
7575 E FULTON ST
ADA, MI 49355-0001
PHONE: (616) 787-1000
FAX: (616) 787-4590
NATIONAL: (800) 269-7196

ALTIUS HEALTH PLANS
10421 S JORDAN GTWY STE 400
SOUTH JORDAN, UT 84095-3918
PO BOX 95950
SOUTH JORDAN, UT 84095-0950
PHONE: (801) 355-1234
FAX: (801) 323-6400
NATIONAL: (800) 365-1334

AMALGAMATED LIFE & HEALTH INSURANCE CO
730 BROADWAY
NEW YORK, NY 10030-9502
PO BOX 1442
NEW YORK, NY 10116-1442
PHONE: (212) 539-5111
FAX: (212) 674-6679

AMERICAN BENEFIT PLAN ADMINISTRATORS
625 E 70TH AVE STE 1
DENVER, CO 80229-6726
PHONE: (303) 227-0107
FAX: (303) 227-0155
NATIONAL: (800) 247-7876
IN-STATE: (800) 247-7876

AMERICAN COMMERCIAL LINES
1701 E MARKET ST
JEFFERSONVILLE, IN 47130-4717
PO BOX 610
JEFFERSONVILLE, IN 47131-0610
PHONE: (812) 288-0100
FAX: (812) 288-1720
NATIONAL: (800) 548-7689

AMERICAN COMMUNITY MUTUAL INSURANCE CO
39201 SEVEN MILE RD
LIVONIA, MI 48152-1056
PHONE: (734) 591-9000
FAX: (734) 591-4628
NATIONAL: (800) 991-2642

AMERICAN HEALTH GROUP
100 PLUMLEY DR
PARIS, TN 38242
PO BOX 1500
MAUMEE, OH 43537
PHONE: (731) 642-5582
FAX: (731) 642-6872
NATIONAL: (800) 305-0406

AMERICAN MEDICAL & LIFE INSURANCE CO
35 N BROADWAY
HICKSVILLE, NY 11801-4236
PHONE: (516) 822-8700
FAX: (516) 931-1010
NATIONAL: (800) 822-0004

AMERICAN NATIONAL INSURANCE CO
ONE MOODY PLZ FL 18
GALVESTON, TX 77550-7960
PO BOX 1520
GALVESTON, TX 77553-1520
PHONE: (800) 899-6503
FAX: (409) 766-6694
NATIONAL: (800) 899-6806

AMERICAN POSTAL WORKERS UNION HEALTH PLAN
12345 NEW COLUMBIA PIKE
SILVER SPRING, MD 20904-0000

PO BOX 967-0967
SILVER SPRING, MD 20910
PHONE: (301) 622-1700
FAX: (301) 622-6074
NATIONAL: (800) 222-2798

AMERICAN REPUBLIC INSURANCE CO
601 6TH AVE
DES MOINES, IA 50309-1605
PO BOX 1
DES MOINES, IA 50301
PHONE: (515) 245-2000
FAX: (515) 245-4282
NATIONAL: (800) 247-2190
IN-STATE: (515) 247-2435

AMERICAN TRUST ADMINISTRATORS, INC
7101 COLLEGE BLVD STE 1200
OVERLAND PARK, KS 66210
PO BOX 87
SHAWNEE MISSION, KS 66201-0087
PHONE: (913) 451-4900
FAX: (913) 451-0598
NATIONAL: (800) 843-4121

ANTHEM BLUE CROSS
6900 WESTCLIFF DR STE 600
LAS VEGAS, NV 89145-0199
PO BOX 17549
DENVER, CO 80217-0549
PHONE: (702) 228-2583
FAX: (702) 228-1259

ANTHEM BLUE CROSS / BLUE SHIELD
TWO GANNETT DR
SOUTH PORTLAND, ME 04106-6913
PHONE: (207) 822-8282
FAX: (207) 822-7014
NATIONAL: (800) 482-0966
IN-STATE: (800) 822-6011

2015 STAPLES MAIL RD
RICHMOND, VA 23230-2521
PO BOX 27401
RICHMOND, VA 23279-7401
PHONE: (804) 354-7000
FAX: (804) 354-7600
NATIONAL: (800) 451-1527

ANTHEM BLUE CROSS / BLUE SHIELD OF COLORADO
700 BROADWAY
DENVER, CO 80273
PO BOX 17549
DENVER, CO 80217-0549
PHONE: (303) 831-2131
NATIONAL: (800) 332-3842

ANTHEM BLUE CROSS / BLUE SHIELD OF NEW HAMPSHIRE
3000 GOFFS FALLS RD
MANCHESTER, NH 03111-0001
PHONE: (603) 695-7000
FAX: (603) 695-7067
NATIONAL: (800) 225-2666

ANTHEM, INC
120 MONUMENT CIR STE 200
INDIANAPOLIS, IN 46204-4902
PHONE: (317) 488-6000
NATIONAL: (800) 331-1476

ARIZONA HEALTH CARE COST CONTAINMENT SYSTEM
801 E JEFFERSON
PHOENIX, AZ 85034-2217
PO BOX 25520
PHOENIX, AZ 85002-5520
PHONE: (602) 417-4000
FAX: (602) 252-6536
NATIONAL: (800) 523-0231
IN-STATE: (800) 654-8713

ARIZONA PHYSICIANS, IPA, INC
3141 N 3RD AVE
PHOENIX, AZ 85013-4345
PO BOX 36740
PHOENIX, AZ 85067
PHONE: (602) 274-6102
FAX: (602) 664-5466
NATIONAL: (800) 348-4058

ARKANSAS BEST CORP
3801 OLD GREENWOOD RD
FT SMITH, AR 72903-5937
PO BOX 10048
FT SMITH, AR 72917-0048
PHONE: (479) 785-6178
FAX: (479) 785-6011

ARKANSAS BLUE CROSS / BLUE SHIELD
SOUTHEAST REGION 1800 W 73RD ST
PINE BLUFF, AR 71603-8328
PO BOX 1245
PINE BLUFF, AR 71613
PHONE: (870) 536-1223
FAX: (870) 543-2915

707 E MATTHEWS AVE
JONESBORO, AR 72401-3127
PO BOX 1475
JONESBORO, AR 72403
PHONE: (870) 935-4871
FAX: (870) 974-5713
NATIONAL: (800) 299-4124

601 S GAINES ST
LITTLE ROCK, AR 72201-0000
PO BOX 2181
LITTLE ROCK, AR 72203
PHONE: (501) 378-2000
FAX: (501) 378-3732
NATIONAL: (800) 238-8379

ARTHUR J. GALLAGAR & CO
2345 GRAND BLVD STE 800
KANSAS CITY, MO 64108-2671
PO BOX 419115
KANSAS CITY, MO 64141-6115
PHONE: (816) 421-7788
FAX: (816) 472-5517
NATIONAL: (800) 934-4624
IN-STATE: (800) 934-4624

ASSOCIATED ADMINISTRATORS, INC
2929 NW 31ST AVE
PORTLAND, OR 97210-1799
PO BOX 5096
PORTLAND, OR 97208-5096
PHONE: (503) 223-3185
FAX: (503) 727-7444
NATIONAL: (800) 888-9603

ASSUMPTION MUTUAL LIFE INSURANCE CO
770 MAIN ST
MONCTON, NB E1C-8L1
PO BOX 160
MONCTON, NB E1C-8L1
PHONE: (506) 853-6040
FAX: (506) 853-5459
NATIONAL: (800) 455-7337

ASSURE CARE
PO BOX 1570
EAST LANSING, MI 48826
PHONE: (517) 351-6616
FAX: (517) 351-6633
NATIONAL: (800) 968-6616

ATLANTIC MUTUAL / CENTENNIAL INSURANCE CO
180 GLASTONBURY BLVD
GLASTONBURY, CT 06033-6510
PO BOX 6510
GLASTONBURY, CT 06033-6510
PHONE: (860) 657-9966
FAX: (860) 657-7962
NATIONAL: (800) 289-2299

ATRIUM HEALTH PLAN
400 SECOND ST S STE 270
HUDSON, WI 54016-5802
PHONE: (715) 386-6886
FAX: (715) 386-8326
NATIONAL: (800) 535-4041
IN-STATE: (800) 535-4041

AUTO OWNERS INSURANCE CO
6101 ANACAPRI BLVD
LANSING, MI 48917-3994
PO BOX 30660
LANSING, MI 48909-8160
PHONE: (517) 323-1200
FAX: (517) 323-8796
NATIONAL: (800) 346-0346

AUTOMOBILE MECHANICS LOCAL NO 701
500 W PLAINFIELD RD STE 100
COUNTRYSIDE, IL 60525-3582
PHONE: (708) 482-0110
FAX: (708) 482-9140
NATIONAL: (800) 704-6270

BABB INC
850 RIDGE AVE
PITTSBURGH, PA 15212-6095
PHONE: (412) 237-2020
FAX: (412) 322-1756
NATIONAL: (800) 245-6102
IN-STATE: (800) 892-1015

BASHAS' SUPERMARKETS
22402 S BASHA RD
CHANDLER, AZ 85248-4908
PO BOX 488
CHANDLER, AZ 85244-0488
PHONE: (480) 895-9350
FAX: (602) 914-9239
NATIONAL: (800) 755-7292
IN-STATE: (800) 879-6400

BEHAVIORAL HEALTHCARE OPTIONS
900 S RANCHO DR 1ST FLOOR
LAS VEGAS, NV 89106-3804
PO BOX 15645
LAS VEGAS, NV 89114-5645
PHONE: (702) 877-5000
FAX: (702) 877-1834
NATIONAL: (877) 393-6094

BENEFIT CLAIMS PAYORS, INC
1717 W NORTHERN AVE STE 200
PHOENIX, AZ 85021-5478
PO BOX 37400
PHOENIX, AZ 85069-7400
PHONE: (602) 861-6868
FAX: (602) 861-6878
NATIONAL: (800) 266-6868

BENEFIT COORDINATORS CORP
111 RYAN CT STE 300
PITTSBURGH, PA 15205-1310
PHONE: (412) 276-1111
FAX: (412) 276-6650
NATIONAL: (800) 685-6100

BENEFIT PLAN ADMINISTRATORS, INC
101 S JEFFERSON ST
ROANOKE, VA 24011-1322
PO BOX 11746
ROANOKE, VA 24022-1746
PHONE: (540) 345-2721
FAX: (540) 342-0282
NATIONAL: (800) 277-8973

BENEFIT PLANNERS, INC
12668 SILICON DR
SAN ANTONIO, TX 78249-3411
PO BOX 690450
SAN ANTONIO, TX 78269-0450
PHONE: (210) 699-1872
FAX: (210) 697-3108
NATIONAL: (800) 292-5386

BENEFIT RESOURCE, INC
3246 HWY 69 N
BEAUMONT, TX 77705
PO DRAWER C
BEAUMONT, TX 77627
PHONE: (409) 727-2343
FAX: (409) 727-0247

BENEFIT & RISK MANAGEMENT SERVICES
10860 GOLD CTR DR STE 100
RANCHO CORDOVA, CA 95670-6068
PO BOX 2650
RANCHO CORDOVA, CA 95741-2650
PHONE: (916) 858-2950
FAX: (916) 858-2970
NATIONAL: (800) 959-4767

BENEFIT SUPPORT, INC
305 GREEN ST NW
GAINESVILLE, GA 30501-3384
PO BOX 2977
GAINESVILLE, GA 30503-2977
PHONE: (770) 532-2690
FAX: (770) 532-2318
NATIONAL: (800) 777-4782
IN-STATE: (800) 777-4782

BENEFIT SYSTEMS & SERVICES, INC
760 PASQUINELLI DR STE 320
WESTMONT, IL 60559-5555
PHONE: (630) 789-2082
FAX: (630) 789-2093
NATIONAL: (800) 423-1841

BENESIGHT
317 N MAIN ST
PUEBLO, CO 81003
PO BOX 320
PUEBLO, CO 81002
PHONE: (719) 595-2000
FAX: (719) 595-3189
NATIONAL: (888) 891-2390

PO BOX 360
PUEBLO, CO 81002
PHONE: (800) 551-9988
FAX: (407) 708-5044
NATIONAL: (800) 562-7079

1250 E COPELAND RD STE 500
ARLINGTON, TX 76011-4911
PO BOX 380
PUEBLO, CO 81002
PHONE: (817) 436-5400
FAX: (817) 436-5458
NATIONAL: (800) 432-5925

600 COLONIAL CENTER PKWY
LAKE MARY, FL 32746
PHONE: (407) 660-0202
FAX: (407) 708-1379
NATIONAL: (800) 551-9988

7878 N 16TH ST STE 140
PHOENIX, AZ 85020-4463
PO BOX 375
PUEBLO, CO 81002
PHONE: (602) 906-5000
FAX: (602) 906-5070
NATIONAL: (800) 223-5228

973 FEATHER STONE RD STE 200
ROCKFORD, IL 61107
PO BOX 350
PUEBLO, CO 81002
PHONE: (815) 395-0080
FAX: (815) 395-0139
NATIONAL: (800) 648-4480

BENICORP INSURANCE CO
7702 WOODLAND DR STE 200
INDIANAPOLIS, IN 46278-1717
PO BOX 68917
INDIANAPOLIS, IN 46268-0917
PHONE: (317) 290-1205
FAX: (317) 216-7877
NATIONAL: (800) 837-1205

APPENDIX 5 — COMPANIES ACCEPTING HCPCS LEVEL II CODES

BEST LIFE AND HEALTH INSURANCE CO
2505 MCCABE WY
IRVINE, CA 92614-6243
PO BOX 19721
IRVINE, CA 92623-9721
PHONE: (949) 253-4080
FAX: (949) 222-1005
NATIONAL: (800) 433-0088

BLUE CROSS / BLUE SHIELD
3350 PEACHTREE RD NE
ATLANTA, GA 30326-1048
PO BOX 4445
ATLANTA, GA 30302-4445
PHONE: (404) 842-8000
FAX: (404) 842-8010
NATIONAL: (800) 441-2273

818 KEEAUMOKU ST
HONOLULU, HI 96814-2365
PO BOX 860
HONOLULU, HI 96808-0860
PHONE: (808) 948-5110
FAX: (808) 948-6555
NATIONAL: (800) 648-3190
IN-STATE: (800) 790-4672

4366 KUKUI GROVE ST STE 103
LIHUE, HI 96766-2006
PHONE: (808) 245-3393
FAX: (808) 245-3596

75-166 KALANI ST STE 202
KAILUA-KONA, HI 96740-1857
PHONE: (808) 329-5291
FAX: (808) 329-5293

33 LONO AVE STE 350
KAHULUI, HI 96732-1608
PHONE: (808) 871-6295
FAX: (808) 871-7429

670 PONAHAWAI ST STE 121
HILO, HI 96720-2660
PHONE: (808) 935-5441
FAX: (808) 935-5444

1133 SW TOPEKA AVE
TOPEKA, KS 66629-0001
PHONE: (785) 291-4010
FAX: (785) 291-8848
NATIONAL: (800) 291-7000

611 CASCADE W PKY SE
GRAND RAPIDS, MI 49546-2143
PO BOX 68710
GRAND RAPIDS, MI 49516
PHONE: (616) 957-5057
FAX: (616) 957-3476
NATIONAL: (800) 968-2583

25925 TELEGRAPH RD
SOUTHFIELD, MI 48086
PO BOX 5043
SOUTHFIELD, MI 48086-5043
PHONE: (248) 354-7450
FAX: (248) 799-6969

NATIONAL: (800) 662-6667
IN-STATE: (800) 662-6667
600 E LAFAYETTE BLVD
DETROIT, MI 48207
PO BOX 2888
DETROIT, MI 48231-2888
PHONE: (313) 225-9000
FAX: (313) 225-6239
NATIONAL: (800) 637-2227

3545 LAKELAND DR
JACKSON, MS 39232-9799
PO BOX 1043
JACKSON, MS 39215-1043
PHONE: (601) 932-3704
FAX: (601) 939-7035
NATIONAL: (800) 222-8046
IN-STATE: (800) 222-8046

12800 INDIAN SCHOOL NE
ALBUQUERQUE, NM 87112-4722
PO BOX 27630
ALBUQUERQUE, NM 87125-7630
PHONE: (505) 291-3500
FAX: (505) 291-3541
NATIONAL: (800) 835-8699

1215 S BOULDER AVE RM 205
TULSA, OK 74102
PO BOX 3283
TULSA, OK 74102
PHONE: (918) 560-3500
FAX: (918) 560-7891
NATIONAL: (800) 942-5837

I-20 E AT ALPINE RD
COLUMBIA, SC 29219-0001
PO BOX 100300
COLUMBIA, SC 29202
PHONE: (803) 788-3860
NATIONAL: (800) 868-2500
IN-STATE: (800) 288-2227

500 HWY 151 E
PLATTEVILLE, WI 53818
PO BOX 262
PLATTEVILLE, WI 53818
PHONE: (608) 342-3189
FAX: (608) 348-5168

145 S PIONEER RD
FOND DU LAC, WI 54935-3871
PO BOX 110
FOND DU LAC, WI 54936-0110
PHONE: (920) 923-7575
FAX: (920) 923-7572
NATIONAL: (800) 822-7442

4000 HOUSE AVE
CHEYENNE, WY 82001-5460
PO BOX 2266
CHEYENNE, WY 82003-2266
PHONE: (307) 634-1393
FAX: (307) 778-8582
NATIONAL: (800) 442-2376
IN-STATE: (800) 442-2376

BLUE CROSS / BLUE SHIELD HMO NEW MEXICO
12800 INDIAN SCHOOL RD NE
ALBUQUERQUE, NM 87112-4722
PO BOX 27630
ALBUQUERQUE, NM 87125
PHONE: (505) 291-3500
FAX: (505) 237-5310
NATIONAL: (800) 423-1630
IN-STATE: (800) 423-1630

BLUE CROSS / BLUE SHIELD OF ALABAMA
450 RIVERCHASE PKY E
BIRMINGHAM, AL 35298-0001
PO BOX 995
BIRMINGHAM, AL 35244
PHONE: (205) 988-2100
FAX: (205) 981-4965
NATIONAL: (800) 292-8855

BLUE CROSS / BLUE SHIELD OF ARIZONA
2444 W LAS PALMARITAS DR
PHOENIX, AZ 85021-4883
PO BOX 2924
PHOENIX, AZ 85002-3466
PHONE: (602) 864-4400
FAX: (602) 864-4242
NATIONAL: (800) 232-2345

BLUE CROSS / BLUE SHIELD OF DELAWARE
ONE BRANDYWINE GTWY
WILMINGTON, DE 19801-1173
PO BOX 1991
WILMINGTON, DE 19899-1991
PHONE: (302) 421-3000
FAX: (302) 421-3110
NATIONAL: (800) 633-2563
IN-STATE: (800) 292-7865

BLUE CROSS / BLUE SHIELD OF FLORIDA
4800 DEERWOOD CAMPUS PKY
JACKSONVILLE, FL 32246
PO BOX 1798
JACKSONVILLE, FL 32231-1798
PHONE: (904) 791-6111
FAX: (904) 791-8738
NATIONAL: (800) 322-2808

BLUE CROSS / BLUE SHIELD OF GEORGIA
2357 WARM SPRINGS RD
COLUMBUS, GA 31909
PO BOX 9907
COLUMBUS, GA 31908-9907
PHONE: (706) 571-5371
FAX: (706) 571-5487
NATIONAL: (800) 241-7475

BLUE CROSS / BLUE SHIELD OF ILLINOIS
75 EXECUTIVE DR STE 300
AURORA, IL 60504-7947
PO BOX 2037
AURORA, IL 60507-2037
PHONE: (630) 978-7878
FAX: (630) 978-8460
NATIONAL: (800) 538-8833

BLUE CROSS / BLUE SHIELD OF MINNESOTA
3535 BLUE CROSS RD
EAGON, MN 55122-1154
PO BOX 64560
ST PAUL, MN 55164-0560
PHONE: (651) 662-8000
FAX: (651) 662-2777
NATIONAL: (800) 382-2000

IN-STATE: (800) 382-2000

BLUE CROSS / BLUE SHIELD OF MISSOURI
1831 CHESTNUT ST
ST LOUIS, MO 63103-2275
PO BOX 66834
ST LOUIS, MO 63166-6834
PHONE: (314) 923-4444
FAX: (314) 923-6618
NATIONAL: (800) 634-4395
IN-STATE: (800) 392-8740

BLUE CROSS / BLUE SHIELD OF MONTANA
404 FULLER AVE
HELENA, MT 59601-5092
PO BOX 4309
HELENA, MT 59604-4309
PHONE: (406) 444-8200
FAX: (406) 442-6941
NATIONAL: (800) 447-7828

560 N PARK AVE
HELENA, MT 59601-2702
PO BOX 4309
HELENA, MT 59604-4309
PHONE: (406) 444-8200
FAX: (406) 791-4119
NATIONAL: (800) 447-7828
IN-STATE: (800) 447-7828

BLUE CROSS / BLUE SHIELD OF NEBRASKA
7261 MERCY RD
OMAHA, NE 68124
PO BOX 3248
OMAHA, NE 68180-3248
PHONE: (402) 390-1800
FAX: (402) 392-2141
NATIONAL: (800) 642-8980

1233 LINCOLN MALL
LINCOLN, NE 68508-2847
PO BOX 3248
OMAHA, NE 68180-3248
PHONE: (402) 458-4800
FAX: (402) 477-2952
NATIONAL: (800) 562-6394

BLUE CROSS / BLUE SHIELD OF NORTH CAROLINA
5901 CHAPEL HILL BLVD
DURHAM, NC 27702
PO BOX 2291
DURHAM, NC 27702-2291
PHONE: (919) 489-7431
FAX: (919) 765-2433
NATIONAL: (800) 446-8053
IN-STATE: (800) 222-5028

BLUE CROSS / BLUE SHIELD OF PUERTO RICO
1441 ROOSEVELT AVE
SAN JUAN, PR 00936-0000
PO BOX 363628
SAN JUAN, PR 00936-3628
PHONE: (787) 749-4949
FAX: (787) 749-4190

BLUE CROSS / BLUE SHIELD OF RHOAD ISLAND
444 WESTMINSTER ST
PROVIDENCE, RI 02903-3279
PHONE: (401) 459-1000
FAX: (401) 351-2050

NATIONAL: (800) 637-3718

BLUE CROSS / BLUE SHIELD OF TEXAS
4242 SUNSET DR
SANTA ANGELO, TX 76904-5652
PO BOX 660044
DALLAS, TX 75266-0044
PHONE: (915) 224-2000
FAX: (915) 224-2030
NATIONAL: (877) 299-2377

BLUE CROSS / BLUE SHIELD OF VERMONT
445 INDUSTRIAL LN
MONTPELIER, VT 05602-0000
PO BOX 186
MONTPELIER, VT 05601-0186
PHONE: (802) 223-6131
FAX: (802) 223-1077
NATIONAL: (800) 457-6648
IN-STATE: (800) 247-2583

BLUE CROSS / BLUE SHIELD OF WISCONSIN
2270 EASTRIDGE CTR
EAU CLAIRE, WI 54701-3409
PO BOX 3157
EAU CLAIRE, WI 54702
PHONE: (715) 836-1200
FAX: (715) 836-1299
NATIONAL: (800) 848-3308

BLUE CROSS / BLUE SHIELD UNITED OF WISCONSIN
401 W MICHIGAN ST
MILWAUKEE, WI 53203
PO BOX 2025
MILWAUKEE, WI 53201-2025
PHONE: (414) 226-5000
FAX: (414) 226-5226
NATIONAL: (800) 558-1584

BLUE CROSS OF CALIFORNIA
21555 OXNARD ST
WOODLAND HILLS, CA 91367-4943
PO BOX 4239
WOODLAND HILLS, CA 91365-4239
PHONE: (818) 703-2345
FAX: (818) 703-2848
NATIONAL: (800) 999-3643

BLUE CROSS OF IDAHO HEALTH SERVICE, INC
3000 E PINE AVE
MERIDIAN, ID 83642-5995
PO BOX 7408
BOISE, ID 83707-1408
PHONE: (208) 345-4550
FAX: (208) 331-7311
NATIONAL: (800) 627-6655

BLUE CROSS OF NORTHEASTERN PENNSYLVANIA
19 N MAIN ST
WILKES-BARRE, PA 18711-0302
PO BOX 69699
HARRISBURG, PA 17106-9699
PHONE: (570) 200-4300
FAX: (570) 200-6840
NATIONAL: (800) 829-8599

BLUE SHIELD OF CALIFORNIA
6300 CANOGA AVE
WOODLAND HILLS, CA 91367-2580
PHONE: (818) 598-8000
FAX: (818) 228-5104
NATIONAL: (800) 804-7420

PO BOX 272510
CHICO, CA 95927-2510
NATIONAL: (800) 824-8839

BLUE SHIELD OF CALIFORNIA SERVICE CTR
CHICO, CA 95240-0843
PO BOX 272530
CHICO, CA 95927-2530
PHONE: (209) 367-2800
NATIONAL: (800) 535-8000
IN-STATE: (800) 633-0337

BLUE SHIELD OF NORTHEASTERN NEW YORK
30 CENTURY HILL
LATHAM, NY 12110
PO BOX 80
BUFFALO, NY 14240
PHONE: (518) 220-5700
FAX: (518) 220-5305
NATIONAL: (800) 888-1238
IN-STATE: (800) 888-1238

BMI HEALTH PLANS
628 W BROADWAY ST STE 200
NORTH LITTLE ROCK, AR 72114-5545
PO BOX 9416
NORTH LITTLE ROCK, AR 72119-5989
PHONE: (501) 375-5500
FAX: (501) 375-4718
NATIONAL: (800) 883-3895

BOON-CHAPMAN
7600 CHEVY CHASE DR STE 300
AUSTIN, TX 78752-1566
PO BOX 9201
AUSTIN, TX 78766-9201
PHONE: (512) 454-2681
FAX: (512) 459-1552
NATIONAL: (800) 252-9653

BRIDGE BENEFITS INC
1720 INDIAN WOOD CIR STE E
MAUMEE, OH 43537
PHONE: (419) 897-1400
FAX: (419) 897-9648
NATIONAL: (800) 428-8194

BSI
11200 LOMAS BLVD NE
ALBUQUERQUE, NM 87112-5580
PO BOX 11020
ALBUQUERQUE, NM 87192-0020
PHONE: (505) 292-5533
FAX: (505) 998-1470
NATIONAL: (800) 274-5533

BUFFALO ROCK CO, INC
103 OXMOOR RD
BIRMINGHAM, AL 35209-5915
PO BOX 10048
BIRMINGHAM, AL 35202-0048
PHONE: (205) 942-3435
FAX: (205) 940-7768

BUNZL DISTRIBUTION USA, INC
701 EMERSON RD STE 500
ST LOUIS, MO 63141-6754
PO BOX 419111
ST LOUIS, MO 63141-9111
PHONE: (314) 997-5959
FAX: (314) 997-0247
NATIONAL: (888) 997-4515

C AND O EMPLOYEES' HOSPITAL ASSOCIATION
511 MAIN ST 2ND FL
CLIFTON FORGE, VA 24422-1166
PHONE: (540) 862-5728
FAX: (540) 862-3552
NATIONAL: (800) 679-9135

CAHABA GBA
400 E COURT AVE
DES MOINES, IA 50309-2017
PO BOX 9169
DES MOINES, IA 50306
PHONE: (515) 471-7275
FAX: (515) 471-7222

CAM ADMINISTRATIVE SERVICES, INC
25800 NORTHWESTERN HWY STE 700
SOUTHFIELD, MI 48075-8410
PO BOX 5131
SOUTHFIELD, MI 48086-5131
PHONE: (248) 827-1080
FAX: (248) 827-2112
NATIONAL: (800) 732-8906

CANADA LIFE ASSURANCE CO
630 RENE LEVESQUE BLVD W STE 2890
MONTREAL, PQ H3B-4V5
PHONE: (514) 874-1838
FAX: (514) 874-1607
NATIONAL: (800) 363-3520

CAPITAL BLUE CROSS
2500 ELMERTON AVE
HARRISBURG, PA 17177
PO BOX 779503
HARRISBURG, PA 17177-9503
PHONE: (717) 541-7000
FAX: (717) 541-3702
NATIONAL: (866) 682-2242

CAPITAL DISTRICT PHYSICIANS' HEALTH PLAN, INC
1223 WASHINGTON AVE
ALBANY, NY 12206-1055
PHONE: (518) 641-3000
FAX: (518) 452-0003
NATIONAL: (888) 258-0477

CAPITAL HEALTH PLAN
2140 CENTERVILLE PL
TALLAHASSEE, FL 32308-4418
PO BOX 15349
TALLAHASSEE, FL 32317-5349
PHONE: (850) 383-3300
FAX: (850) 383-1031
NATIONAL: (800) 390-1434
IN-STATE: (800) 390-1434

CARE CHOICES HMO
34605 12 MILE RD
FARMINGTON HILLS, MI 48331
PHONE: (248) 489-6000
FAX: (248) 489-6109
NATIONAL: (800) 852-9780

CARE FIRST BLUE CROSS / BLUE SHIELD
1099 WINTERSON RD
LINTHICUM HEIGHTS, MD 21090-2216
PHONE: (410) 850-7461
FAX: (410) 855-8840
NATIONAL: (800) 422-1996

SEVEN COMMERCE DR
CUMBERLAND, MD 21502
PO BOX 1725
CUMBERLAND, MD 21501-1725
PHONE: (301) 724-8001
FAX: (301) 724-8008

CARITEN HEALTHCARE
1420 CENTERPOINT BLVD
KNOXVILLE, TN 37932
PO BOX 22987
KNOXVILLE, TN 37933-2987
PHONE: (865) 470-7470
FAX: (865) 470-7421
NATIONAL: (800) 793-1495

1021 W OAKLAND AVE STE 300
JOHNSON CITY, TN 37604-2192
PHONE: (423) 952-3180
FAX: (423) 952-3188
NATIONAL: (888) 224-5775

CAROLINA BENEFIT ADMINISTRATORS LLC
333 S PINE ST
SPARTANBURG, SC 29302-2626
PO BOX 3257
SPARTANBURG, SC 29304-3257
PHONE: (864) 573-6937
FAX: (864) 582-2265
NATIONAL: (800) 476-2295

CBCA, INC
10900 HAMPSHIRE AVE S
MINNEAPOLIS, MN 55438-2306
PHONE: (952) 829-3500
FAX: (952) 946-7694
NATIONAL: (800) 824-3882
IN-STATE: (800) 824-3882

ONE HUNTINGTON QUANDRANGLE STE 4N
MELVILLE, NY 11747-4414
PO BOX 9021
MELVILLE, NY 11747
PHONE: (631) 694-4900
FAX: (631) 694-5650

CENTRAL DATA SERVICES, INC
60 BLVD OF THE ALLIES/ 5 GATEWAY CTR STE 620
PITTSBURGH, PA 15222-1219
PHONE: (412) 201-2242
FAX: (412) 201-2250

CENTRAL PENNSYLVANIA TEAMSTERS HEALTH & WELFARE FUND
1055 SPRING ST
WYOMISSING, PA 19610-1747
PO BOX 15224
READING, PA 19612-5224
PHONE: (610) 320-5500
FAX: (610) 320-9209
NATIONAL: (800) 331-0420
IN-STATE: (800) 422-8330

CHER BUMPS & ASSOCIATES, INC
6100 N ROBINSON STE 204
OKLAHOMA CITY, OK 73118-7494
PO BOX 548805
OKLAHOMA CITY, OK 73154-8805
PHONE: (405) 840-3033
FAX: (405) 858-7361
NATIONAL: (888) 840-8924

CHUBB GROUP OF INSURANCE COMPANIES
120 5TH AVE
PITTSBURGH, PA 15222-3008
PHONE: (412) 391-6585
FAX: (412) 456-8979
NATIONAL: (800) 252-4670
IN-STATE: (800) 248-5254

4999 VALISE DR
MECHANICSBURG, PA 17055-0000
PO BOX 2063
MECHANICSBURG, PA 17055-0797
PHONE: (717) 791-6000
FAX: (717) 791-6040
NATIONAL: (800) 577-9992
IN-STATE: (800) 909-0900

fCORVCHURCHILL ADMINISTRATIVE PLANS, INC
270 SYLVAN AVE
ENGLEWOOD CLIFFS, NJ 07632-2521
PHONE: (201) 871-8400
FAX: (201) 871-2460

CIGNA CORPORATION
1601 CHESTNUT ST TWO LIBERTY PL
PHILADELPHIA, PA 19192-1550
PHONE: (215) 761-1000
FAX: (215) 761-7105
NATIONAL: (800) 832-3211
IN-STATE: (800) 832-3211

WILDE BLDG 900 COTTAGE GROVE RD STE A118
HARTFORD, CT 06152-1315
PHONE: (860) 226-6000
NATIONAL: (800) 832-3211

590 NAAMANS RD
CLAYMONT, DE 19703
PO BOX 15050
WILMINGTON, DE 19850-5050
NATIONAL: (800) 441-2668

3200 PARKLANE DR
PITTSBURGH, PA 15275
PO BOX 2300
PITTSBURGH, PA 15230-2300
PHONE: (412) 747-7477
NATIONAL: (800) 793-9338
IN-STATE: (800) 238-2125

1000 POLARIS PKY
COLUMBUS, OH 43240-2008
PO BOX 182331
COLUMBUS, OH 43218-2331
PHONE: (614) 785-1310
FAX: (614) 786-7777
NATIONAL: (800) 832-3211
IN-STATE: (800) 832-3211

600 E TAYLOR
SHERMAN, TX 75090-2881
PO BOX 9025
SHERMAN, TX 75091-9321
PHONE: (903) 892-8167
FAX: (903) 893-5778
NATIONAL: (800) 525-5803
IN-STATE: (800) 238-8801

CIGNA HEALTHCARE MEDICARE ADMINISTRATION
TWO VANTAGE WY
NASHVILLE, TN 37228-1504
PO BOX 1465
NASHVILLE, TN 37202-1465
PHONE: (615) 244-5680
FAX: (615) 782-4651
NATIONAL: (800) 342-8900
IN-STATE: (800) 627-2782

CIGNA HEALTHCARE OF NEW HAMPSHIRE, INC
TWO COLLEGE PARK DR
HOOKSETT, NH 03106-1636
PO BOX 2041
CONCORD, NH 03302
PHONE: (603) 225-5077
FAX: (603) 268-7981
NATIONAL: (800) 531-3121
IN-STATE: (800) 531-3121

CIGNA HEALTHCARE OF NORTH CAROLINA
701 CORPORATE CTR DR
RALEIGH, NC 27610
PO BOX 28087
RALEIGH, NC 27607
PHONE: (919) 854-7000
FAX: (919) 854-7118
NATIONAL: (800) 849-9300

CITY OF MESA EMPLOYEE BENEFITS
200 S CENTER ST BLDG 1
MESA, AZ 85210-1502
PO BOX 1466
MESA, AZ 85211-1466
PHONE: (480) 644-2299
FAX: (480) 644-3013

CLAIMSWARE, INC
704 CONGAREE RD
GREENVILLE, SC 29607
PO BOX 6125
GREENVILLE, SC 29606-6125
PHONE: (864) 234-8200
FAX: (864) 234-8202
NATIONAL: (800) 992-8088

CNA
333 S WABASH AVE
CHICAGO, IL 60685-1040
PHONE: (312) 822-5000
FAX: (312) 822-6419

COAST BENEFITS
3850 S VALLEY VIEW BLVD
LAS VEGAS, NV 89103-2904
PO BOX 80040
LAS VEGAS, NV 89180-0040
PHONE: (702) 889-1155
FAX: (702) 889-1284

COMBINED BENEFITS ADMINISTRATORS
4704 W JENNIFER AVE STE 104
FRESNO, CA 93722-6419
PHONE: (559) 275-3984
FAX: (559) 271-0419
NATIONAL: (800) 709-4734

COMBINED INSURANCE
5050 N BROADWAY ST
CHICAGO, IL 60640-3007
PHONE: (773) 275-8000
FAX: (776) 765-1849
NATIONAL: (800) 225-4500

IN-STATE: (800) 225-4500

COMPANION HEALTH CARE CORP
4101 PERCIVAL RD
COLUMBIA, SC 29229
PO BOX 6170
COLUMBIA, SC 29260-6170
PHONE: (803) 786-8466
FAX: (803) 714-6443
NATIONAL: (800) 327-3183

COMPBENEFITS
100 MANSELL CT E STE 400
ROSWELL, GA 30076-4859
PHONE: (770) 552-7101
FAX: (770) 998-6871
NATIONAL: (800) 295-6279

COMPUSYS, INC
1200 SAN PEDRO NE
ALBUQUERQUE, NM 87192-0000
PO BOX 11399
ALBUQUERQUE, NM 87192-0399
PHONE: (505) 262-1921
FAX: (505) 266-0922
NATIONAL: (800) 926-5581

COMPUSYS OF COLORADO, INC
10620 E BETHANY DR BLDG 7
AURORA, CO 80014-2602
PHONE: (303) 745-0147
FAX: (303) 745-7010

COMPUSYS OF UTAH
2156 W 2200 S
SALT LAKE CITY, UT 84119-1376
PHONE: (801) 973-1001
FAX: (801) 973-1007

COMPUTER SCIENCE CORP
800 N PEARL ST
ALBANY, NY 12204-1898
PO BOX 4444
ALBANY, NY 12204-0444
PHONE: (518) 447-9200
FAX: (518) 447-9240
IN-STATE: (800) 522-5518

CONNECTICARE INC & AFFILIATES
30 BATTERSON PARK RD
FARMINGTON, CT 06032-2574
PO BOX 546
FARMINGTON, CT 06034-0546
PHONE: (860) 674-5700
FAX: (860) 674-5728
NATIONAL: (800) 251-7722

CONSTRUCTION INDUSTRY WELFARE FUND
34 E SPRINGFIELD AVE
CHAMPAIGN, IL 61820-5367
PHONE: (217) 352-5269
FAX: (217) 352-5297

CONTINENTAL AMERICA
2801 DEVINE ST
COLUMBIA, SC 29205-2556
PO BOX 1807
COLUMBIA, SC 29202-1807
PHONE: (803) 256-6265
FAX: (803) 779-4406
NATIONAL: (800) 433-3036

CONTINENTAL GENERAL INSURANCE
6201 JOHNSON DR
SHAWNEE MISSION, KS 66202
PO BOX 772
SHAWNEE MISSION, KS 66201-0772
PHONE: (913) 722-1110
FAX: (913) 384-3258
NATIONAL: (800) 444-0321

CONTINENTAL GENERAL INSURANCE CO
8901 INDIAN HILLS DR
OMAHA, NE 68134-4071
PO BOX 247007
OMAHA, NE 68124-7007
PHONE: (402) 397-3200
FAX: (402) 952-4771
NATIONAL: (800) 545-8905
IN-STATE: (800) 397-3200

CONTRA COSTA HEALTH PLAN
595 CENTER AVE STE 100
MARTINEZ, CA 94553-4629
PHONE: (925) 313-6000
FAX: (925) 313-6002
IN-STATE: (877) 661-6230

COOPERATIVE BENEFIT ADMINISTRATORS
7101 A ST
LINCOLN, NE 68510
PO BOX 6249
LINCOLN, NE 68506-0249
PHONE: (402) 483-9200
FAX: (402) 483-9201

CORESOURCE, INC
6100 FAIRVIEW RD STE 1000
CHARLOTTE, NC 28210-9916
PHONE: (704) 552-0900
FAX: (704) 552-8635
NATIONAL: (800) 327-5462
IN-STATE: (800) 821-0345

CORESTAR JACKSON CLAIM CENTER
146 INDUSTRIAL PARK
JACKSON, MN 56143-9511
PHONE: (507) 847-5740
FAX: (507) 847-2358
NATIONAL: (800) 274-6965

CORPORATE DIVERSIFIED SERVICES
2401 S 73RD ST STE 1
OMAHA, NE 68124-2307
PO BOX 2835
OMAHA, NE 68103-2835
PHONE: (402) 393-3133
FAX: (402) 398-3773
NATIONAL: (800) 642-4089

CORVEL CORP
4860 COX RD STE 210
GLEN ALLEN, VA 23060-9248
PO BOX 2910
GLEN ALLEN, VA 23058
PHONE: (804) 273-1999
FAX: (804) 273-9817
NATIONAL: (800) 275-8130

1701 48TH ST STE 275
WEST DES MOINES, IA 50266-6703
PHONE: (515) 225-9668
FAX: (515) 225-9772
NATIONAL: (800) 929-1160

999 OAKMENT PLZ STE 360
WESTMONT, IL 60559
PHONE: (630) 789-1177
FAX: (630) 789-1276

3125 POPLARWOOD CT STE 202
RALEIGH, NC 27604-1020
PHONE: (919) 790-2260
FAX: (919) 790-1522

3550 N CENTRAL AVE STE 915
PHOENIX, AZ 85012-2117
PHONE: (602) 287-8722
FAX: (602) 287-8714
NATIONAL: (800) 230-8288

15303 DALLAS PKWY STE LB30
ADDISON, TX 75001-0000
PHONE: (972) 239-1391
FAX: (972) 386-5133
NATIONAL: (800) 239-1391

11200 WESTHEIMER STE 410
HOUSTON, TX 77042-3229
PHONE: (713) 977-8880
FAX: (713) 977-0229
NATIONAL: (800) 298-6993

3001 NE BROADWAY ST STE 600
MINNEAPOLIS, MN 55413
PHONE: (612) 436-2400
FAX: (612) 436-2499
NATIONAL: (800) 275-8893

6902 PEARL RD STE 200
CLEVELAND, OH 44130-3621
PHONE: (440) 885-7377
FAX: (440) 886-5344
NATIONAL: (800) 275-6463

11350 RANDOM HILLS RD STE 420
FAIRFAX, VA 22030
PHONE: (703) 385-5646
FAX: (703) 385-0180
NATIONAL: (800) 496-3385

1600 A ST STE 307
ANCHORAGE, AK 99501-5148
PHONE: (907) 274-2785
FAX: (907) 274-7583
NATIONAL: (800) 478-6824

ONE CALLERIA BLVD STE 1775
METAIRIE, LA 70001
PHONE: (504) 835-5515
FAX: (504) 835-4357
NATIONAL: (800) 503-6881

30 RIVER PARK PL W ST 280
FRESNO, CA 93720-1547
PHONE: (559) 447-0100
FAX: (559) 447-0197
NATIONAL: (800) 483-4177

725 PRIMERA BLVD STE 210
LAKE MARY, FL 32746-2125
PHONE: (407) 805-0060
FAX: (407) 805-0092
NATIONAL: (800) 229-4637

600 COMMERICAL CT STE B
SAVANNAH, GA 31406
PHONE: (912) 355-8841
FAX: (912) 355-8061
NATIONAL: (888) 495-0440

450 E 96TH ST STE 340
INDIANAPOLIS, IN 46240-3797
PHONE: (317) 816-6996
FAX: (317) 816-6990
NATIONAL: (800) 559-7958

345 RIVERVIEW STE 500
WICHITA, KS 67203
PHONE: (316) 264-2900
FAX: (316) 264-2977
NATIONAL: (800) 626-0149

12910 SHELBYVILLE RD STE 236
LOUISVILLE, KY 40243-1595
PHONE: (502) 244-5300
FAX: (502) 244-8855
NATIONAL: (800) 834-0937

289 GREAT RD STE 304
ACTON, MA 01720-4770
PHONE: (978) 266-9136
FAX: (978) 266-9167

38705 SEVEN MILE RD STE 230
LIVONIA, MI 48152-2632
PHONE: (734) 432-1500
FAX: (734) 432-1510

3668 S GEYER RD STE 360
ST LOUIS, MO 63127
PHONE: (314) 835-1100
FAX: (314) 835-1001
NATIONAL: (888) 249-3465

443 1/2 MAIN ST
KALISPELL, MT 59901-4872
PHONE: (406) 755-7901
FAX: (406) 755-7979
NATIONAL: (800) 935-0660

440 REGENCY PKWY DR STE 147
OMAHA, NE 68114-3790
PHONE: (402) 393-0400
FAX: (402) 393-0500
NATIONAL: (800) 711-4478

51 HADDENFIELD RD STE 200
CHERRY HILL, NJ 08002
PHONE: (856) 661-9670
FAX: (856) 661-9671
NATIONAL: (800) 491-8350

TWO WILLIAM ST STE 305
WHITE PLAINS, NY 10601-1910
PHONE: (914) 285-1201
FAX: (877) 531-3187
NATIONAL: (877) 909-3926

100 ELWOOD DAVIS RD
N SYRACUSE, NY 13212
PHONE: (315) 451-8670
FAX: (315) 451-8675
NATIONAL: (800) 267-8351

150 MOTOR PKY STE 104
HAUPPAUGE, NY 11788-5167
PHONE: (631) 231-0013
FAX: (631) 952-2255

1000 MADISON AVE
NORRISTOWN, PA 19403-2426
PHONE: (610) 676-0200
FAX: (610) 676-0202

416 PONCE DE LEON AVE STE 200
HATO REY, PR 00918-3418
PHONE: (787) 474-2187
FAX: (787) 753-3587
IN-STATE: (877) 974-2187

3150 LENOX PARK BLVD STE 117
MEMPHIS, TN 38115
PHONE: (901) 818-0451
FAX: (901) 818-0429
NATIONAL: (877) 731-4003

901 NE LOOP 410 STE 500
SAN ANTONIO, TX 78209
PHONE: (210) 824-5052
FAX: (210) 824-8972
NATIONAL: (800) 215-9383
IN-STATE: (800) 215-9383

1100 E 6600 S STE 420
MURRAY, UT 84121-7415
PHONE: (801) 269-8723
FAX: (801) 269-0096
NATIONAL: (800) 275-9868

1320 CENTRAL PARK BLVD STE 410
FREDRICKSBURG, VA 22401
PHONE: (540) 786-1500
FAX: (540) 548-4428

2101 4TH AVE STE 1800
SEATTLE, WA 98121-2345
PHONE: (206) 256-6331
FAX: (206) 441-5730

COTTAGE HEALTH SYSTEM
PUEBLO AT BATH ST
SANTA BARBARA, CA 93105-4351
PO BOX 689
SANTA BARBARA, CA 93102-0689
PHONE: (805) 569-8220
FAX: (805) 569-8218

COUNTY OF LOS ANGELES
333 WILSHIRE BLVD STE 1000
COMMERCE, CA 90022-5111
PHONE: (213) 738-2279
FAX: (213) 637-0820

COVENANT ADMINISTRATORS, INC
11330 LAKEFIELD DR BLDG 2
DULUTH, GA 30097
PO BOX 740042
ATLANTA, GA 30374-0042
PHONE: (678) 258-8000
FAX: (678) 258-8297
NATIONAL: (800) 374-6101
IN-STATE: (888) 239-3909

COVENTRY HEALTH CARE OF KANSAS
8320 WARD PKY
KANSAS CITY, MO 64114
PHONE: (816) 221-8400
FAX: (816) 221-7709
NATIONAL: (800) 468-1442

CPIC LIFE
PO BOX 3007
LODI, CA 95241-1911
PHONE: (209) 367-3415
FAX: (209) 367-3450
NATIONAL: (800) 642-5599
IN-STATE: (800) 537-0666

CRAWFORD & CO
4341 B ST STE 301
ANCHORAGE, AK 99503-5927
PHONE: (907) 561-5222
FAX: (907) 561-7383
IN-STATE: (888) 549-5222

**CT PIPE TRADES BENEFIT FUNDS
ADMINISTRATORS INC**
1155 FILAFDEANE HWY
WEATHERSFIELD, CT 06109-0000
PHONE: (860) 571-9191
FAX: (860) 571-9217
NATIONAL: (800) 848-2129

CTI ADMINISTRATORS, INC
100 COURT AVE STE 306
DES MOINES, IA 50309-2295
PHONE: (515) 244-7322
FAX: (515) 244-8650
NATIONAL: (800) 245-8813

DAKOTACARE
1323 S MINNESOTA AVE
SIOUX FALLS, SD 57105-0624
PHONE: (605) 334-4000
FAX: (605) 336-0270
NATIONAL: (800) 628-3778
IN-STATE: (800) 325-5598

DALLAS GENERAL LIFE INSURANCE CO
14160 DALLAS PKWY STE 500
DALLAS, TX 75254-4319
PO BOX 749008
DALLAS, TX 75374-9008
PHONE: (972) 404-0295
FAX: (972) 503-9388
NATIONAL: (800) 840-8137
IN-STATE: (800) 840-8137

DC CHARTERED HEALTH PLAN, INC
820 FIRST ST NE LOWR LL100
WASHINGTON, DC 20002-8036
PO BOX 75366
WASHINGTON, DC 20013-5366
PHONE: (202) 408-4710
FAX: (202) 408-4730
NATIONAL: (800) 799-4710

DELMARVA HEALTH PLAN, INC
301 BAY ST STE 401
EASTON, MD 21601-2797
PO BOX 2410
EASTON, MD 21601-2410
PHONE: (410) 822-7223
FAX: (410) 822-8152
NATIONAL: (800) 334-3427
IN-STATE: (800) 334-3427

DETROIT & VICINITY TROWEL TRADES
2075 W BIG BEAVER RD STE 750
TROY, MI 48084-3446
PHONE: (248) 822-0100
FAX: (248) 822-0126
NATIONAL: (800) 435-4080

DIRECT RESPONSE, INC
7930 CENTURY BLVD
CHANHASSEN, MN 55317
PO BOX 96
MINNEAPOLIS, MN 55440
PHONE: (952) 556-5600
FAX: (952) 556-8200
IN-STATE: (800) 328-3323

**DIRECT RESPONSE INSURANCE
ADMINISTRATIVE SERVICES, INC**
7930 CENTURY BLVD
CHANHASSEN, MN 55317-8001
PO BOX 96
MINNEAPOLIS, MN 55440-0096
PHONE: (952) 556-5600
FAX: (952) 556-8145
NATIONAL: (800) 328-2791

DISTRICT 6 HEALTH FUND
254 W 31ST ST 8TH FL
NEW YORK, NY 10016-1001
PHONE: (212) 696-5545
FAX: (212) 696-5556
NATIONAL: (800) 331-1070

DIVERSIFIED GROUP ADMINISTRATORS
201 S JOHNSON RD BLVD 1 STE 301
HOUSTON, PA 15342-1300
PO BOX 330
CANONSBURG, PA 15317-0330
PHONE: (724) 746-8700
FAX: (724) 746-8628
NATIONAL: (800) 221-8490

DIVISION 1181 ATU NEW YORK WELFARE
101-49 WOODHAVEN BLVD
OZONE PARK, NY 11416-2300
PHONE: (718) 845-5800
FAX: (718) 641-0122

EASTERN BENEFIT SYSTEMS
200 FREEWAY DR E
EAST ORANGE, NJ 07018
PHONE: (973) 676-6100
FAX: (973) 676-6794
NATIONAL: (800) 524-0227
IN-STATE: (800) 772-3610

EASTERN SHORE TEAMSTERS
1323 N SALISBURY BLVD
SALISBURY, MD 21801-3674
PHONE: (410) 742-1031
FAX: (410) 742-1059

EDUCATORS MUTUAL INSURANCE
852 E ARROWHEAD LN
MURRAY, UT 84107-5298
PHONE: (801) 262-7476
FAX: (801) 269-9734
NATIONAL: (800) 548-5264
IN-STATE: (800) 662-5850

ELECTRIC INSURANCE CO
152 CONANT ST
BEVERLY, MA 01915-1692
PO BOX 1030
BEVERLY, MA 01915-1030
PHONE: (978) 921-0660
FAX: (978) 524-5512
NATIONAL: (800) 227-2757

ELECTRONIC DATA SYSTEMS
3215 PROSPECT PARK DR
RANCHO CORDOVA, CA 95670-6017
PO BOX 15508
SACRAMENTO, CA 65852
PHONE: (916) 636-1100
IN-STATE: (800) 541-5555

EMC NATIONAL LIFE
4095 NW URBANDALE DR
URBANDALE, IA 50322
PO BOX 9197
WEST DES MOINES, IA 50266-9197
PHONE: (515) 645-4000
FAX: (515) 645-4215
NATIONAL: (800) 232-5818

EMERALD HEALTH NETWORK, INC
1100 SUPERIOR AVE 16TH FL
CLEVELAND, OH 44114
PO BOX 94808
CLEVELAND, OH 44101-4808
PHONE: (216) 479-2030
FAX: (216) 479-2039
NATIONAL: (800) 683-6830

EMI
700 CENTRAL PKY
STUART, FL 34994-3985
PHONE: (772) 287-7650
FAX: (772) 287-1387
NATIONAL: (800) 431-2221

EMPIRE BLUE CROSS / BLUE SHIELD
11 W 42ND ST
NEW YORK, NY 10036-8002
PHONE: (212) 476-1000
FAX: (212) 476-1281
NATIONAL: (800) 261-5962

11 CORPORATE WOODS BLVD
ALBANY, NY 12211-2345
PO BOX 11800
ALBANY, NY 12211-0800
PHONE: (518) 367-4737
FAX: (518) 367-5373

EMPLOYEE BENEFIT CONSULTANTS
9275 N 49TH ST STE 300
MILWAUKEE, WI 53223-1499
PHONE: (414) 365-4600

FAX: (414) 365-4611
NATIONAL: (800) 558-7798

EMPLOYEE BENEFIT SERVICES
1312 N HEARNE AVE STE 100
SHREVEPORT, LA 71107
PO BOX 70100
SHREVEPORT, LA 71137-0100
PHONE: (318) 424-1987
FAX: (318) 424-9702
NATIONAL: (800) 488-6360

EMPLOYEE BENEFIT SYSTEMS CORP
214 N MAIN ST
BURLINGTON, IA 52601
PO BOX 1053
BURLINGTON, IA 52601-1053
PHONE: (319) 752-3200
FAX: (319) 753-6114
NATIONAL: (800) 373-1327

EMPLOYER PLAN SERVICES, INC
2180 N LOOP W STE 400
HOUSTON, TX 77018-8010
PHONE: (713) 932-8917
FAX: (713) 932-1162
NATIONAL: (800) 447-6588

EMPLOYERS INSURANCE CO OF NEVADA
9790 GATEWAY DR
RENO, NV 89511-5942
PHONE: (775) 327-2700
NATIONAL: (888) 682-6671

EMS ADMINISTRATIVE SERVICE CORP
3800 SAND SHELL
FT WORTH, TX 76137-2429
PO BOX 161125
FORT WORTH, TX 76161
PHONE: (817) 335-2582
FAX: (817) 335-9734

ENTERPRISE GROUP PLANNING
5910 HARPER RD
CLEVELAND, OH 44139-1835
PHONE: (440) 349-2210
FAX: (440) 349-4268
IN-STATE: (800) 229-2210

EQUITABLE PLAN SERVICES, INC
PO BOX 720460
OKLAHOMA CITY, OK 73172-0460

PO BOX 770466
OKLAHOMA CITY, OK 73177-0466
PHONE: (405) 755-2929
FAX: (405) 755-1185
NATIONAL: (800) 749-2631

ERIN GROUP ADMINISTRATORS, INC
1871 SANTA BARBARA DR
LANCASTER, PA 17601
PO BOX 7777
LANCASTER, PA 17604-7777
PHONE: (717) 581-1300
FAX: (717) 581-6529
NATIONAL: (800) 433-3746

ERISA ADMINISTRATIVE SERVICES, INC
PO BOX 10187
PHOENIX, AZ 85064-0187
PHONE: (602) 234-0593
FAX: (602) 234-9718

1429 SECOND ST
SANTA FE, NM 87505-3486
PO BOX 9054
SANTA FE, NM 87504
PHONE: (505) 988-4974
FAX: (505) 988-8943
NATIONAL: (800) 233-3164

12325 HYMEADOW DR BLDG 4 STE 100
AUSTIN, TX 78750-0001
PHONE: (512) 250-9397
FAX: (512) 335-7298
NATIONAL: (800) 933-7472

ESIS
39300 CIVIC CTR DR STE 300
FREMONT, CA 94538-2337
PO BOX 5025
FREMONT, CA 94537-5025
PHONE: (510) 790-4600
FAX: (510) 790-4631
NATIONAL: (800) 525-0615

EXCELLUS BLUE CROSS / BLUE SHIELD
8278 WILLETT PKY
BALDWINSVILLE, NY 13027-1302
PHONE: (800) 337-3338
FAX: (315) 448-6959
NATIONAL: (800) 223-4780

**EXCELLUS BLUE CROSS / BLUE SHIELD OF
ROCHESTER**
165 COURT ST
ROCHESTER, NY 14647-0001
PO BOX 41965
ROCHESTER, NY 14604
PHONE: (585) 454-1700
FAX: (585) 238-3620
NATIONAL: (800) 847-1200
IN-STATE: (800) 847-1200

FALLON COMMUNITY HEALTH PLAN, INC
10 CHESTNUT ST
WORCESTER, MA 01608-2898
PO BOX 15121
WORCESTER, MA 01615-0121
PHONE: (508) 799-2100
FAX: (508) 797-4292
NATIONAL: (800) 333-2535

FARMLAND MUTUAL
1100 BELL ST
DES MOINES, IA 50309
PHONE: (515) 508-3300
FAX: (800) 842-1482
NATIONAL: (800) 247-2484

FEDERAL EXPRESS FREIGHT EAST
2200 FORWARD DR
HARRISON, AR 72601-2004
PO BOX 0840
HARRISON, AR 72602-0840
PHONE: (870) 741-9000
FAX: (870) 365-4116
NATIONAL: (800) 874-4723

FEDERATED MUTUAL INSURANCE CO
4301 ANCHOR PLZ PKY STE 425
TAMPA, FL 33634
PO BOX 31716
TAMPA, FL 33631-3716
PHONE: (813) 496-8100
FAX: (813) 496-8101

8100 THREE CHOPT RD STE 240
RICHMOND, VA 23229-4833
PO BOX K178
RICHMOND, VA 23288
PHONE: (804) 282-4263
FAX: (804) 282-5742
NATIONAL: (800) 446-3039

302 PERIMETER CTR N STE 200
ATLANTA, GA 30346-2405
PO BOX 467500
ATLANTA, GA 31146
PHONE: (770) 390-3900
FAX: (800) 416-0027

5701 W TAVALI BLVD STE 2000
GLENDALE, AZ 85306-0000
PO BOX 35910
PHOENIX, AZ 85069
PHONE: (602) 944-5566
FAX: (602) 375-7062

2910 W TOWN PKY STE 300A
WEST DES MOINES, IA 50266
PO BOX 65509
WEST DES MOINES, IA 50265
PHONE: (515) 225-6661
FAX: (515) 327-1429

FIDELITY SECURITY LIFE INSURANCE CO
3130 BROADWAY
KANSAS CITY, MO 64111
PO BOX 418131
KANSAS CITY, MO 64141-9131
PHONE: (816) 756-1060
FAX: (816) 968-0600
NATIONAL: (800) 821-7303

FIFERV HEALTH
1415 MURFREESBORO RD
NASHVILLE, TN 37217
PO BOX 305154
NASHVILLE, TN 37230-5154
PHONE: (615) 360-4560
FAX: (615) 360-2861
NATIONAL: (800) 255-8109

FINANCIAL BENEFIT, INC
104 W 9TH ST STE 200
KANSAS CITY, MO 64105
PO BOX 13163
KANSAS CITY, MO 64199-3163
PHONE: (816) 842-2080
FAX: (816) 842-2081
NATIONAL: (800) 981-8238

FIRST ADMINISTRATORS, INC
604 LOCUST ST STE 1700
DES MOINES, IA 50309
PO BOX 9120
DES MOINES, IA 50306-9120
PHONE: (515) 243-3210
FAX: (515) 282-0719
NATIONAL: (800) 622-3339

FIRST HEALTH SERVICES CORP
4411 BUSINESS PARK BLVD STE 16
ANCHORAGE, AK 99503-7117
PHONE: (907) 561-5650
FAX: (907) 561-7195
IN-STATE: (800) 770-5650

FISERV HEALTH-KANSAS
300 W DOUGLAS STE 800
WICHITA, KS 67201-2697
PO BOX 2697
WICHITA, KS 67201-2697
PHONE: (316) 264-5311
FAX: (316) 264-8077
NATIONAL: (800) 235-7160

FLORIDA 1ST SERVICE ADMINISTRATORS, INC
3425 LAKE ALFRED RD STE 2
WINTER HAVEN, FL 33881-1492
PO BOX 9126
WINTER HAVEN, FL 33883-9126
PHONE: (863) 293-0785
FAX: (863) 297-9095
NATIONAL: (800) 226-3155
IN-STATE: (800) 226-3155

FLORIDA HEALTH CARE PLAN, INC
1340 RIDGEWOOD AVE
HOLLY HILL, FL 32117
PO BOX 9910
DAYTONA BEACH, FL 32120-9910
PHONE: (386) 676-7100
FAX: (386) 676-7148
NATIONAL: (800) 352-9824

FOX-EVERETT, INC
3780 I-55 N FRONTAGE RD STE 200
JACKSON, MS 39211
PO BOX 23096
JACKSON, MS 39225-3096
PHONE: (601) 981-6000
FAX: (601) 718-5399
NATIONAL: (877) 476-6327

FRANK M. VACCARO & ASSOCIATES, INC
27 ROLAND AVE
MALAREL, NJ 08054
PHONE: (215) 638-3682
FAX: (215) 638-1294
NATIONAL: (800) 883-3682

FRINGE BENEFIT COORDINATORS
1239 NW 10TH AVE
GAINESVILLE, FL 32601-4154
PHONE: (352) 372-2028
FAX: (352) 372-9805
IN-STATE: (800) 654-1452

GALLAGHER BENEFIT ADMINISTRATORS, INC
750 WARRENVILLE RD STE 200
LISLE, IL 60532-1297
PHONE: (630) 493-9570
FAX: (630) 493-3800
NATIONAL: (800) 323-1726

GARDNER & WHITE
8902 N MERIDIAN ST STE 202
INDIANAPOLIS, IN 46260-5307
PO BOX 40619
INDIANAPOLIS, IN 46240-0619
PHONE: (317) 581-1580
FAX: (317) 587-0780
NATIONAL: (800) 347-5737

GATES MCDONALD HEALTH PLUS
3455 MILL RUN DR
HILLIARD, OH 43026
PO BOX 182720
COLUMBUS, OH 43218-2720
PHONE: (614) 777-3000
FAX: (614) 777-3352
NATIONAL: (800) 336-4733

GERBER LIFE INSURANCE CO
1311 MALMARONECK AVE
WHITE PLAINS, NY 10605
PHONE: (914) 272-4000
FAX: (914) 272-4099
NATIONAL: (800) 253-3074

GILSBAR, INC
2100 COVINGTON CTR
COVINGTON, LA 70433
PO BOX 998
COVINGTON, LA 70434-0998
PHONE: (985) 892-3520
FAX: (985) 898-1666

GOLDEN RULE LIFE INSURANCE CO
712 11TH ST
LAWRENCEVILLE, IL 62439-2395
PHONE: (618) 943-8000
FAX: (618) 943-8031

7440 WOODLAND DR
INDIANAPOLIS, IN 46278-1719
PHONE: (317) 297-4123
FAX: (317) 290-8927
IN-STATE: (800) 265-7791

GRAND VALLEY HEALTH PLAN
829 FOREST HILLS AVE SE
GRAND RAPIDS, MI 49546-2325
PHONE: (616) 949-2410
FAX: (616) 949-4978

GREAT-WEST LIFE & ANNUITY
8350 N CENTRAL EXPY STE M1000
DALLAS, TX 75206-1607
PHONE: (972) 813-7000
NATIONAL: (800) 685-3020

6101 YELLOWSTONE
CHEYENNE, WY 82009
PO BOX 12018
CHEYENNE, WY 82003
PHONE: (800) 685-1060
NATIONAL: (800) 685-1060

3131 E CAMELBACK RD STE 240
PHOENIX, AZ 85016-4535
PHONE: (602) 667-9537
FAX: (602) 508-8972
NATIONAL: (800) 233-5402
IN-STATE: (800) 233-5402

GROCER'S INSURANCE GROUP
6605 SE LAKE RD
PORTLAND, OR 97222-2161
PO BOX 22146
PORTLAND, OR 97269
PHONE: (503) 833-1600
FAX: (503) 833-1699
NATIONAL: (800) 777-3602

GROUP BENEFIT SERVICES, INC
SIX N PARK DR STE 310
HUNT VALLEY, MD 21030
PHONE: (410) 832-1300
FAX: (410) 832-1315
NATIONAL: (800) 638-6085

GROUP HEALTH MANAGERS
26205 FIVE MILE RD
REDFORD, MI 48239-3154
PHONE: (313) 535-7100
FAX: (313) 535-7434
NATIONAL: (800) 992-2508

GROUP HEALTH PLAN OF SAINT LOUIS
111 CORPORATE OFFICE DR STE 400
EARTH CITY, MO 63045-1528
PHONE: (314) 453-1700
FAX: (314) 506-1959
NATIONAL: (800) 743-3901

GROUP SERVICES & ADMINISTRATION, INC
3113 CLASSEN BLVD
OKLAHOMA CITY, OK 73118-3818
PHONE: (405) 528-4400
FAX: (405) 528-5558
NATIONAL: (800) 475-4445

GUARANTEE RESERVE LIFE INSURANCE CO
530 RIVER OAKS W
CALUMET CITY, IL 60409-5460
PHONE: (708) 868-4232
FAX: (708) 891-8886
NATIONAL: (800) 323-8764
IN-STATE: (811) 472-5246

GULF GUARANTY EMPLOYEE BENEFIT SERVICES, INC
4785 I-55 N STE 210
JACKSON, MS 39206
PO BOX 14977
JACKSON, MS 39236-4977
PHONE: (601) 981-9505
FAX: (601) 981-6805
NATIONAL: (800) 890-7337

HARRINGTON BENEFIT SERVICES, INC
675 BROOKSEDGE BLVD
WESTERVILLE, OH 43081
PO BOX 16789
COLUMBUS, OH 43216
PHONE: (614) 212-7000
FAX: (614) 212-7080
NATIONAL: (800) 848-4623

HARRINGTON BENEFITS ADMINISTRATION
PO BOX 750
PUEBLO, CO 81002
PHONE: (888) 715-5609

HEALTH ALLIANCE MEDICAL PLANS
102 E MAIN ST
URBANA, IL 61801
PHONE: (217) 337-8100
FAX: (217) 337-8008
NATIONAL: (800) 851-3379

HEALTH ALLIANCE PLAN OF MICHIGAN
2850 W GRAND BLVD
DETROIT, MI 48202-2692
PHONE: (313) 872-8100
NATIONAL: (800) 422-4641
IN-STATE: (800) 367-3292

HEALTH AMERICA
3721 TECHPORT DR
HARRISBURG, PA 17111
PO BOX 67103
HARRISBURG, PA 17106-7103
PHONE: (717) 540-4260
FAX: (717) 541-5921
NATIONAL: (800) 788-6445

HEALTH CARE ADMINISTRATORS, INC
415 N 26TH ST STE 101
LAFAYETTE, IN 47904-6108
PO BOX 6108
LAFAYETTE, IN 47903-6108
PHONE: (765) 448-7400
FAX: (765) 448-7700
NATIONAL: (888) 448-7447

HEALTH CARE SERVICE CORP
300 E RANDOLPH ST
CHICAGO, IL 60601-5099
PO BOX 1364
CHICAGO, IL 60690
PHONE: (312) 653-6000
NATIONAL: (800) 892-2803

HEALTH CARE SOLUTIONS GROUP
2401 CHANDLER RD STE 300
MUSKOGEE, OK 74403
PO BOX 1309
MUSKOGEE, OK 74402
PHONE: (918) 687-1261
FAX: (918) 781-4976
NATIONAL: (800) 749-1422

HEALTH GUARD
280 GRANITE RUN DR STE 105
LANCASTER, PA 17601-6810
PHONE: (717) 581-4580
FAX: (717) 560-9413
NATIONAL: (800) 781-3646

HEALTH INSURANCE PLAN OF GREATER NEW YORK
SEVEN W 34TH ST
NEW YORK, NY 10001-8190
PHONE: (212) 630-5000
FAX: (212) 630-5062
NATIONAL: (800) 447-8255

HEALTH NET HMO, INC
44 VANTAGE WY STE 300
NASHVILLE, TN 37228
PHONE: (615) 291-7000
FAX: (615) 401-4647
NATIONAL: (800) 881-9466

HEALTH NET OF CALIFORNIA
21281 BURBANK BLVD
WOODLAND HILLS, CA 91367-6607
PO BOX 9103
VAN NUYS, CA 91409-9103
PHONE: (818) 676-5000
NATIONAL: (800) 641-7761
IN-STATE: (800) 929-9224

HEALTH NET OF OREGON
13221 SW 68TH PWY
TIGARD, OR 97223
PHONE: (888) 802-7001
NATIONAL: (888) 802-7001

HEALTH PARTNERS
8100 34TH AVE S
BLOOMINGTON, MN 55425
PO BOX 1309
MINNEAPOLIS, MN 55440-1309
PHONE: (952) 883-6000
FAX: (952) 883-6100
NATIONAL: (800) 883-2177

HEALTH PLAN OF NEVADA, INC
2724 TENAYA WAY
LAS VEGAS, NV 89128-0424
PO BOX 15645
LAS VEGAS, NV 89114-5645
PHONE: (702) 242-7444
FAX: (702) 242-9038

HEALTH PLAN, THE
52160 NATIONAL RD E
ST CLAIRSVILLE, OH 43950
PHONE: (740) 695-3585
FAX: (740) 695-5297
NATIONAL: (800) 624-6961

HEALTH SERVICES BENEFITS ADMINISTRATORS
160 AIRWAY BLVD
LIVERMORE, CA 94551-7600
PHONE: (925) 449-7070
FAX: (925) 443-2035
IN-STATE: (800) 528-4357

HEALTHCARE PARTNERS MEDICAL GROUP, INC
1149 W 190TH ST STE 101
TORRANCE, CA 90248-4333
PO BOX 6099
TORRANCE, CA 90504
PHONE: (310) 214-0811
FAX: (310) 352-6219
NATIONAL: (800) 403-4160

HERITAGE INSURANCE MANAGERS, INC
919 ISOM RD STE A
SAN ANTONIO, TX 78216-4136
PO BOX 659570
SAN ANTONIO, TX 78265-9570
PHONE: (210) 829-7467
FAX: (210) 822-4113
NATIONAL: (800) 456-7480

HIGHMARK BLUE CROSS / BLUE SHIELD
120 FIFTH AVE PL
PITTSBURGH, PA 15222-3099
PHONE: (412) 544-7000
NATIONAL: (800) 547-3627

HMA, INC
1600 W BROADWAY RD STE 300
TEMPE, AZ 85282-1137
PO BOX 2069
TEMPE, AZ 86326
PHONE: (480) 921-8944
FAX: (480) 894-5230
NATIONAL: (800) 448-3585

HOMETOWN HEALTH PLAN
240 S ROCK BLVD STE 123
RENO, NV 89502-1823
PHONE: (775) 982-3000
FAX: (775) 982-3160
NATIONAL: (800) 336-0123

HOMETOWN HEALTH PLAN (NETWORK)
100 LILLIAN GISH BLVD
MASSILLON, OH 44647
PHONE: (330) 834-2200
FAX: (330) 837-6869
IN-STATE: (877) 236-2289

HORIZON BLUE CROSS / BLUE SHIELD OF NEW JERSEY
THREE PENN PLZ E
NEWARK, NJ 07105-2200

PHONE: (973) 466-4000
NATIONAL: (800) 355-2583

HORTICA
ONE HORTICULTURE LANE
EDWARDSVILLE, IL 62025
PO BOX 428
EDWARDSVILLE, IL 62025
PHONE: (618) 656-4240
FAX: (618) 656-7581
NATIONAL: (800) 851-7740

HOTEL EMPLOYEES & RESTAURANT EMPLOYEES INT'L UNION WELFARE FUNDS
711 N COMMONS DR
AURORA, IL 60504
PO BOX 6020
AURORA, IL 60598
PHONE: (630) 236-5100
FAX: (630) 236-4394

HUMAN RESOURCE BENEFIT ADMINISTRATORS
16 INVERNESS PL EAST
ENGLEWOOD, CO 80112-5656
PHONE: (303) 792-3311
FAX: (303) 790-0599
NATIONAL: (800) 742-4722

HUMANA HEALTHPLAN OF OHIO
655 EDEN PARK DR STE 100
CINCINNATI, OH 45202-6056
PO BOX 14600
LEXINGTON, KY 40512
PHONE: (513) 784-5200
FAX: (513) 784-5310
NATIONAL: (800) 543-7158

HUMANA INSURANCE COMPANY

PO BOX 14603
LEXINGTON, KY 40512-4603
NATIONAL: (800) 457-4708
IN-STATE: (800) 448-6262

IDAHO FARM BUREAU MUTUAL INSURANCE CO
325 E MAIN
ST ANTHONY, ID 83445-1546
PO BOX 528
ST ANTHONY, ID 83445-0528
PHONE: (208) 624-3171
FAX: (208) 624-3173

711 N MAIN
BELLEVUE, ID 83313-5081
PHONE: (208) 788-3529
FAX: (208) 788-3619

118 W IDAHO AVE
HOMEDALE, ID 83628-0000
PO BOX 1197
HOMEDALE, ID 83628-1197
PHONE: (208) 337-4041
FAX: (208) 337-4042

IHC HEALTH PLANS
4646 W LAKE PARK BLVD
SALT LAKE CITY, UT 84120-8212
PHONE: (801) 442-5000
FAX: (801) 442-5003
NATIONAL: (800) 538-5038
IN-STATE: (800) 442-5038

IMA OF KANSAS
250 N WATER ST STE 600
WICHITA, KS 67202
PO BOX 2992
WICHITA, KS 67201
PHONE: (316) 267-9221
FAX: (316) 266-6385
NATIONAL: (800) 288-6732
IN-STATE: (800) 288-6732

IMCENTUS BENEFITS
3450 N ROCK RD STE 605
WICHITA, KS 67226-1356
PO BOX 8902
WICHITA, KS 67208-0902
PHONE: (316) 631-3939
FAX: (316) 631-3788
NATIONAL: (800) 285-1551

INSURANCE CO OF THE WEST
11455 EL CAMINO REAL
SAN DIEGO, CA 92130-2045
PO BOX 85563
SAN DIEGO, CA 92186-5563
PHONE: (858) 350-2400
FAX: (858) 350-2543
NATIONAL: (800) 877-1111

INSURANCE MANAGEMENT ADMINISTRATORS OF LOUISIANA
1325 BARKSDALE BLVD STE 300
BOSSIER CITY, LA 71111-1120
PO BOX 71120
BOSSIER CITY, LA 71171
PHONE: (318) 747-0577
FAX: (318) 747-5074

INSURERS ADMINISTRATIVE CORP / IAC
2101 W PEORIA AVE STE 100
PHOENIX, AZ 85029-4925
PO BOX 39119
PHOENIX, AZ 85069-9119
PHONE: (602) 870-1400
FAX: (602) 395-0496
NATIONAL: (800) 843-3106

INSUREX BENEFITS ADMINISTRATORS
1835 UNION AVE STE 400
MEMPHIS, TN 38104
PO BOX 41779
MEMPHIS, TN 38174-1779
PHONE: (901) 725-6435
FAX: (901) 725-6437

INTEGRATED HEALTH SERVICES
235 ELM ST NE
ALBUQUERQUE, NM 87102-3672
FAX: (505) 242-7114
NATIONAL: (800) 454-5909

INTERACTIVE MEDICAL SYSTEMS, INC
5621 DEPARTURE DR STE 117
RALEIGH, NC 27616
PO BOX 19108
RALEIGH, NC 27619
PHONE: (919) 877-9933
FAX: (919) 877-0615
NATIONAL: (800) 426-8739

INTERCONTINENTAL CORP
135 N PENNSYLVANIA ST STE 770
INDIANAPOLIS, IN 46204-2445
PHONE: (317) 238-5700
FAX: (317) 637-6634
NATIONAL: (800) 962-6831

J.P. FARLEY CORP
29055 CLEMENS RD
WESTLAKE, OH 44145-1135
PO BOX 458022
WESTLAKE, OH 44145-8022
PHONE: (440) 250-4300
FAX: (440) 250-4301
NATIONAL: (800) 634-0173

JAS INC
4885 S 900 E STE 202
SALT LAKE CITY, UT 84117-5725
PHONE: (801) 266-3256
FAX: (801) 266-4383
NATIONAL: (800) 345-3248

JFP BENEFIT MANAGEMENT
100 S JACKSON ST STE 200
JACKSON, MI 49201
PO BOX 189
JACKSON, MI 49204-0189
PHONE: (517) 784-0535
FAX: (517) 784-0821
IN-STATE: (800) 589-7660

JLT SERVICES CORP
13 CORNELL RD
LATHAM, NY 12110
PHONE: (518) 782-3000
FAX: (518) 782-3157
NATIONAL: (800) 366-5273

JM FAMILY ENTERPRISES
8019 BAYBERRY RD
JACKSONVILLE, FL 32256-7411
PHONE: (904) 443-6650
FAX: (904) 443-6670
NATIONAL: (800) 736-3936

JOHN ALDEN LIFE INSURANCE CO
1005 MAIN ST
BOISE, ID 83702-5751
PO BOX 1599
BOISE, ID 83701-1599
PHONE: (208) 368-7770
FAX: (208) 336-1050
NATIONAL: (800) 328-4316

KAISER PERMANENTE
711 KAPIOLANI BLVD
HONOLULU, HI 96813-5237
PO BOX 31000
HONOLULU, HI 96849-5086
PHONE: (808) 432-5340
FAX: (808) 597-5349
NATIONAL: (800) 596-5955
IN-STATE: (800) 596-5955

500 NE MULTNOMAH STE 100
PORTLAND, OR 97232-2031
PHONE: (503) 813-2700
FAX: (503) 813-2710
NATIONAL: (800) 813-2000

KEYSTONE MERCY HEALTH PLAN
200 STEVENS DR STE 350
PHILADELPHIA, PA 19113
PHONE: (800) 521-6007
FAX: (215) 937-5300
NATIONAL: (800) 521-6007
IN-STATE: (800) 521-6007

KITSAP PHYSICIANS SERVICE
400 WARREN AVE
BREMERTON, WA 98337-1487
PO BOX 339
BREMERTON, WA 98337
PHONE: (360) 377-5576
FAX: (360) 415-6514
NATIONAL: (800) 552-7114

KLAIS & CO
1867 W MARKET ST
AKRON, OH 44313-6977
PHONE: (330) 867-8443
FAX: (330) 867-0827
NATIONAL: (800) 331-1096

LANCER CLAIM SERVICE CORP
333 CITY BLVD W
ORANGE, CA 92868-2903
PO BOX 7048
ORANGE, CA 92863
PHONE: (714) 939-0700
FAX: (714) 978-8023
NATIONAL: (800) 821-0540
IN-STATE: (800) 645-5324

LANDMARK HEALTH CARE
1750 HOWE AVE STE 300
SACRAMENTO, CA 95825-3369
PHONE: (916) 929-7806
FAX: (916) 929-8350
NATIONAL: (800) 638-4557

LEWER AGENCY, INC
4534 WORNALL RD
KANSAS CITY, MO 64111
PHONE: (816) 753-4390
FAX: (816) 561-6840
NATIONAL: (800) 821-7715

LIFE INSURANCE CO OF GEORGIA
PO BOX 8119
FT WASHINGTON, PA 19034-8119
NATIONAL: (800) 877-7756

**LOMA LINDA UNIVERSITY ADVENTIST
HEALTH SCIENCES CENTER**
11161 ANDERSON ST STE 200
LOMA LINDA, CA 92354-2825
PO BOX 1770
LOMA LINDA, CA 92354-0570
PHONE: (909) 558-4386
FAX: (909) 558-4775

LOOMIS BENEFITS WEST
111 SW COLUMBIA STE 1230
PORTLAND, OR 97201-5814
PO BOX 1020
PORTLAND, OR 97207-1020
PHONE: (503) 221-9410
FAX: (503) 228-1433
NATIONAL: (800) 367-3721

M-PLAN
8802 N MERIDIAN ST STE 100
INDIANAPOLIS, IN 46260-5371
PHONE: (317) 571-5300
FAX: (317) 571-5306
NATIONAL: (800) 878-8802

**MANAGED BENEFITS ADMINISTRATOR &
INSURANCE CONSULTANTS, INC**
3625 S WEST TEMPLE STE 200
SALT LAKE CITY, UT 84115-4539
PO BOX 651109
SALT LAKE CITY, UT 84165-1109
PHONE: (801) 268-3334
FAX: (801) 268-3335
NATIONAL: (800) 877-3727
IN-STATE: (800) 877-3727

MANAGED HEALTH, INC
25 BROADWAY STE 900
NEW YORK, NY 10004-1010
PHONE: (212) 801-1626
FAX: (212) 801-1799
NATIONAL: (888) 260-1010

**MARICOPA INTEGRATED SYSTEM
HEALTHCARE**
2502 E UNIVERSITY DR
PHOENIX, AZ 85034-6913
PHONE: (602) 344-8700

MARSH ADVANTAGE AMERICA
145 N CHURCH ST STE 300 BTC-80
SPARTANBURG, SC 29306-5163
PO BOX 1227
SPARTANBURG, SC 29304-1227
PHONE: (864) 585-4338
FAX: (864) 573-7709
NATIONAL: (800) 868-7526

MED-PAY, INC
1650 E BATTLEFIELD STE 300
SPRINGFIELD, MO 65804
PO BOX 10909
SPRINGFIELD, MO 65808
PHONE: (417) 886-6886
FAX: (417) 886-2276
NATIONAL: (800) 777-9087

MEDICAID FISCAL AGENT - ALABAMA
301 TECHNACENTER DR
MONTGOMERY, AL 36117-6008
PHONE: (334) 215-0111
FAX: (334) 215-4298

MEDICAID FISCAL AGENT - ALASKA
PO BOX 240808
ANCHORAGE, AK 99524-0808
PHONE: (907) 561-5650
NATIONAL: (800) 770-5650

MEDICAID FISCAL AGENT - ARIZONA
801 E JEFFERSON
PHOENIX, AZ 85034
PHONE: (602) 417-4000

MEDICAID FISCAL AGENT - ARKANSAS
500 PRESIDENT CLINTON AVE STE 400
LITTLE ROCK, AR 72201-1745
PO BOX 8036
LITTLE ROCK, AR 72203-2501
PHONE: (501) 374-6608
FAX: (501) 374-0549
IN-STATE: (800) 457-4454

MEDICAID FISCAL AGENT - CALIFORNIA
714 P ST STE 1253
SACRAMENTO, CA 95814
PHONE: (916) 445-4171

MEDICAID FISCAL AGENT - COLORADO
1575 SHERMAN ST
DENVER, CO 80203-1714
PHONE: (303) 866-2993
FAX: (303) 866-4411

MEDICAID FISCAL AGENT - CONNECTICUT
PO BOX 2941
HARTFORD, CT 06104
PHONE: (860) 832-9259
FAX: (860) 832-5921
NATIONAL: (800) 842-8440
IN-STATE: (800) 842-8440

MEDICAID FISCAL AGENT - DELAWARE
PO BOX 907
NEW CASTLE, DE 19720
PHONE: (302) 454-7154
NATIONAL: (800) 390-6093

**MEDICAID FISCAL AGENT - DISTRICT OF
COLUMBIA**
825 N CAPITAL ST NE 5FL
WASHINGTON DC, DC 20002
PHONE: (202) 442-5988

MEDICAID FISCAL AGENT - FLORIDA
2727 MAHAN DR MAIL STOP 8
TALLAHASSEE, FL 32308
PHONE: (850) 488-3560
FAX: (850) 488-2520

MEDICAID FISCAL AGENT - GEORGIA
736 PARK N BLVD
CLARKSTON, GA 30021
PHONE: (404) 298-1228
NATIONAL: (800) 766-4456
IN-STATE: (800) 766-4456

MEDICAID FISCAL AGENT - ILLINOIS
201 S GRAND AVE E
SPRINGFIELD, IL 62794
PO BOX 19105
SPRINGFIELD, IL 62793
PHONE: (217) 782-2570
FAX: (217) 782-5672
NATIONAL: (800) 252-8942

MEDICAID FISCAL AGENT - INDIANA
402 W WASHINGTON ST
INDIANAPOLIS, IN 46207-7083
PO BOX 7083
INDIANAPOLIS, IN 56207-7083
PHONE: (317) 533-4454
FAX: (317) 233-4693

MEDICAID FISCAL AGENT - KANSAS
3600 SW TOPEKA BLVD
TOPEKA, KS 66604
PO BOX 3571
TOPEKA, KS 66601
PHONE: (785) 267-5339
FAX: (785) 267-1437
NATIONAL: (800) 933-6593

MEDICAID FISCAL AGENT - KENTUCKY
275 E MAIN ST 6WA
FRANKFORT, KY 40621-0001
PHONE: (502) 564-4321
FAX: (502) 564-0509

MEDICAID FISCAL AGENT - MAINE
442 CIVIC CTR DR
AUGUSTA, ME 04333-0001
PO BOX M500
AUGUSTA, ME 04333
PHONE: (207) 287-2674
FAX: (207) 287-2675
IN-STATE: (800) 321-5557

MEDICAID FISCAL AGENT - MARYLAND
201 W PRESTON ST
BALTIMORE, MD 21201
PO BOX 1935
BALTIMORE, MD 21203
PHONE: (410) 767-5503
FAX: (410) 333-7118
NATIONAL: (800) 445-1159

MEDICAID FISCAL AGENT - MICHIGAN
3200 S WALNUT ST
LANSING, MI 48913
PHONE: (517) 373-3500

MEDICAID FISCAL AGENT - MISSISSIPPI
385 B HIGHLAND COLONY PKY
RIDGELAND, MS 39157
PO BOX 23076
JACKSON, MS 38225-3076
PHONE: (800) 884-3222
FAX: (601) 206-3059
NATIONAL: (800) 884-3222

MEDICAID FISCAL AGENT - MISSOURI
905 WEATHERED ROCK RD
JEFFERSON CITY, MO 65101
PO BOX 5600
JEFFERSON CITY, MO 65102
PHONE: (573) 635-2434

MEDICAID FISCAL AGENT - NEBRASKA
PO BOX 95044
LINCOLN, NE 68509-5044
PHONE: (402) 471-2306

MEDICAID FISCAL AGENT - NEW HAMPSHIRE
SEVEN EAGLE SQ
CONCORD, NH 03301-4955
PO BOX 2001
CONCORD, NH 03302
PHONE: (603) 225-4899
FAX: (603) 225-7964
IN-STATE: (800) 423-8303

MEDICAID FISCAL AGENT - NEW JERSEY
3705 QUAKERBRIDGE RD STE 101
TRENTON, NJ 08619-1209
PO BOX 4808
TRENTON, NJ 08650
PHONE: (609) 588-6000
FAX: (609) 584-8270
NATIONAL: (800) 776-6334
IN-STATE: (800) 676-6562

MEDICAID FISCAL AGENT - NEW MEXICO
1720 RANDOLPH RD STE A
ALBUQUERQUE, NM 87106-4256
PO BOX 25700
ALBUQUERQUE, NM 87125
PHONE: (505) 246-9988
FAX: (505) 246-8485
IN-STATE: (800) 282-4477

MEDICAID FISCAL AGENT - NORTH CAROLINA
4905 WATERS EDGE DR
RALEIGH, NC 27606
PHONE: (919) 851-8888
FAX: (919) 859-6964
NATIONAL: (800) 688-6696

MEDICAID FISCAL AGENT - NORTH DAKOTA
600 E BLVD AVE STE 325
BISMARCK, ND 58505-0261
PHONE: (701) 328-2321
FAX: (701) 328-1544
NATIONAL: (800) 755-2604

MEDICAID FISCAL AGENT - OKLAHOMA
201 NW 63RD STE 100
OKLAHOMA CITY, OK 73116-8210
PHONE: (405) 841-3400
FAX: (405) 841-3510
IN-STATE: (800) 522-0114

MEDICAID FISCAL AGENT - PENNSYLVANIA
7TH AND FORSTER ST
HARRISBURG, PA 17120
PO BOX 2675
HARRISBURG, PA 17105-2675
PHONE: (717) 787-1870
FAX: (717) 787-4639
NATIONAL: (800) 537-8862

MEDICAID FISCAL AGENT - RHODE ISLAND
600 NEW LONDON AVE
CRANSTON, RI 02920-3037
PHONE: (401) 462-2121
FAX: (401) 462-6338

MEDICAID FISCAL AGENT - SOUTH CAROLINA
PO BOX 8206
COLUMBIA, SC 29202-8206
NATIONAL: (888) 549-0820

MEDICAID FISCAL AGENT - SOUTH DAKOTA
700 GOVERNERS DR
PIERRE, SD 57501
PHONE: (605) 773-3165

MEDICAID FISCAL AGENT - TENNESSEE
729 CHURCH ST
NASHVILLE, TN 37247
NATIONAL: (800) 669-1851

MEDICAID FISCAL AGENT - TEXAS
701 W 51 ST
AUSTIN, TX 78751
PO BOX 149030
AUSTIN, TX 78714-9030
NATIONAL: (888) 834-7406

MEDICAID FISCAL AGENT - UTAH
PO BOX 143106
SALT LAKE CITY, UT 84114-3106
PHONE: (801) 538-6155
FAX: (801) 538-6805
NATIONAL: (800) 662-9651

MEDICAID FISCAL AGENT - VERMONT
312 HURRICANE LN STE 101
WILLISTON, VT 05495-2087
PO BOX 888
WILLISTON, VT 05495-0888
PHONE: (802) 879-4450
FAX: (802) 878-3440
IN-STATE: (800) 925-1706

MEDICAID FISCAL AGENT - VIRGINIA
600 E BROAD ST STE 1300
RICHMOND, VA 23219
PHONE: (804) 786-7933

MEDICAID FISCAL AGENT - WASHINGTON
PO BOX 45562
OLYMPIA, WA 98504-5562
NATIONAL: (800) 562-6188

MEDICAID FISCAL AGENT - WISCONSIN
6406 BRIDGE RD
MADISON, WI 53784-1846
PO BOX 6190
MADISON, WI 53716-6190
PHONE: (608) 221-4746
FAX: (608) 221-9280
NATIONAL: (800) 947-9627

MEDICAID FISCAL AGENT - WYOMING
PO BOX 547
CHEYENNE, WY 82003-0547
PHONE: (307) 772-8401
FAX: (307) 772-8405
NATIONAL: (800) 251-1268

MEDICAL NETWORK OF COLORADO SPRINGS
555 E PIKES PEAK AVE STE 108
COLORADO SPRINGS, CO 80903-3612
PO BOX 828
COLORADO SPRINGS, CO 80901
PHONE: (719) 365-5025
FAX: (719) 365-5004
NATIONAL: (800) 207-1018

MEDICARE - PART A INTERMEDIARIES
730 CHESTNUT ST
CHATTANOOGA, TN 37402-1790
PHONE: (866) 641-2007
FAX: (423) 752-6518

2357 WARM SPRINGS RD
COLUMBUS, GA 31904
PO BOX 9048
COLUMBUS, GA 31908-9048
PHONE: (800) 322-3380
FAX: (706) 571-5431
NATIONAL: (800) 241-7475

3301 DODGE ST
OMAHA, NE 68175
PO BOX 1602
OMAHA, NE 68101-1602
PHONE: (877) 647-6528
FAX: (402) 351-8047
NATIONAL: (866) 580-5987

2444 W LAS PALMARITAS DR
PHOENIX, AZ 85021-4860
PHONE: (602) 864-4100
FAX: (602) 864-4653
NATIONAL: (877) 567-3128

601 N GAINES ST
LITTLE ROCK, AR 72203-0000
PO BOX 1418
LITTLE ROCK, AR 72203-2181
FAX: (501) 378-2576
NATIONAL: (866) 548-0527

120 5TH AVE PL
PITTSBURGH, PA 15230-3099
PO BOX 1089
PITTSBURGH, PA 15230-1089
PHONE: (800) 560-6170

8115 KNUE RD
INDIANAPOLIS, IN 46250-1936
PO BOX 37630
INDIANAPOLIS, IN 46250-7630
PHONE: (317) 841-4400
NATIONAL: (800) 999-7608

1133 SW TOPEKA BLVD
TOPEKA, KS 66629-0001
PO BOX 3543
TOPEKA, KS 66601-3543
PHONE: (785) 291-7000

3360 10TH AVE S
GREAT FALLS, MT 59405-3451
PO BOX 5017
GREAT FALLS, MT 59403-5017
PHONE: (877) 567-7202
FAX: (406) 791-4113
NATIONAL: (866) 737-8928
IN-STATE: (877) 602-7762

7261 MERCY RD
OMAHA, NE 68124-2349
PO BOX 24563
OMAHA, NE 68124-0563
PHONE: (877) 869-6503
FAX: (402) 398-3640

3000 GOFFS FALLS RD
MANCHESTER, NH 03111-0001
FAX: (603) 695-7741
NATIONAL: (866) 680-0749

33 LOUIS RD
BINGHAMTON, NY 13905
PO BOX 5200
BINGHAMTON, NY 13902
PHONE: (877) 567-7205
FAX: (607) 766-6542
NATIONAL: (800) 252-6550

444 WESTMINSTER ST
PROVIDENCE, RI 02903-3206
PHONE: (866) 339-3714
FAX: (404) 459-1777
NATIONAL: (800) 662-5170

4000 HOUSE AVE
CHEYENNE, WY 82001-1446
PO BOX 908
CHEYENNE, WY 82003-0908
PHONE: (307) 432-2860
FAX: (307) 432-2901
NATIONAL: (877) 567-3093

MEDICARE - PART B CARRIERS
1701 NW 63RD ST
OKLAHOMA CITY, OK 73116
PHONE: (405) 843-9379
NATIONAL: (877) 567-9230

4305 13TH AVE SW
FARGO, ND 58103-3309
PO BOX 6708
FARGO, ND 58108-6708
PHONE: (701) 277-6500
FAX: (701) 282-1188
NATIONAL: (877) 908-8431
IN-STATE: (877) 908-8431

402 OTTERSON DR
CHICO, CA 95928-8206
PHONE: (530) 634-7000
FAX: (530) 896-7182
NATIONAL: (877) 591-1587
IN-STATE: (866) 502-9054

8115 KNUE RD
INDIANAPOLIS, IN 46250-1936
PO BOX 6160
INDIANAPOLIS, IN 46204-6160
PHONE: (317) 841-4400
FAX: (317) 841-4691

1133 SW TOPEKA BLVD
TOPEKA, KS 66629
PO BOX 239
TOPEKA, KS 66601
PHONE: (785) 291-7000
FAX: (785) 291-7098
NATIONAL: (877) 567-7270

1601 ENGEL ST
MADISON, WI 53713
PO BOX 1787
MADISON, WI 53701-1787
PHONE: (877) 567-7176
NATIONAL: (877) 908-8475

33 LEWIS RD
BINGHAMTON, NY 13905
PO BOX 5236
BINGHAMTON, NY 13902-5236
PHONE: (607) 887-6900
FAX: (716) 887-8548
NATIONAL: (877) 567-7173

3400 S PARK PL STE F
GROVE CITY, OH 43123
PO BOX 16786
COLUMBUS, OH 43216-6786
PHONE: (614) 277-7004
NATIONAL: (800) 282-0530

PO BOX 890157
CAMP HILL, PA 17089-0157
PHONE: (866) 488-0548
FAX: (717) 730-5810
NATIONAL: (800) 382-1274
IN-STATE: (800) 633-4227

1441 F.D. ROOSEVELT AVE
CAPARRA, PR 00920-2717
PO BOX 71391
SAN JUAN, PR 00936-1391
PHONE: (787) 749-4080
FAX: (787) 749-4900
NATIONAL: (877) 715-1921

PO BOX 100190 GM 220
COLUMBIA, SC 29202-3190
PHONE: (866) 238-9654
FAX: (803) 935-0595

1707 W BROADWAY
MADISON, WI 53713
PO BOX 1787
MADISON, WI 53701-1787
PHONE: (608) 221-4711
FAX: (608) 301-2625
NATIONAL: (877) 567-7176

MENNONITE MUTUAL AID ASSOCIATION
1110 N MAIN ST
GOSHEN, IN 46528
PO BOX 483
GOSHEN, IN 46527
PHONE: (574) 533-9511
FAX: (574) 533-5264
NATIONAL: (800) 348-7468

MERCHANTS INSURANCE GROUP
250 MAIN ST
BUFFALO, NY 14202
PO BOX 903
BUFFALO, NY 14240
PHONE: (716) 849-3333
FAX: (716) 849-3105
NATIONAL: (800) 462-1077

MERCYCARE INSURANCE CO
3430 PALMER DR
JANESVILLE, WI 53546
PO BOX 2770
JANESVILLE, WI 53547
PHONE: (608) 752-3431
FAX: (608) 752-3751
NATIONAL: (800) 752-3431

MHF INSURANCE ADMINISTRATORS, INC.
3563 PHILLIPS HWY STE 108
JACKSONVILLE, FL 32207
PO BOX 48098
JACKSONVILLE, FL 32247-8098
PHONE: (904) 727-5088
FAX: (904) 727-9545
NATIONAL: (800) 830-3856

MIDWEST SECURITY ADMINISTRATORS
1150 SPRINGHURST DR STE 140
GREEN BAY, WI 54304
PO BOX 19035
GREEN BAY, WI 54307-9035
PHONE: (920) 496-2500
FAX: (920) 496-2515
NATIONAL: (800) 236-2515

MIDWEST SECURITY INSURANCE CO
2700 MIDWEST DR
ONALASKA, WI 54650
PHONE: (608) 783-7130
FAX: (608) 783-8581
NATIONAL: (800) 542-6642

MOLINA HEALTHCARE OF UTAH
7050 UNION PARK CENTER STE 200
SALT LAKE CITY, UT 84147
PO BOX 22630
LONG BEACH, FL 90801
PHONE: (801) 858-0400

MOLINA HEALTHCARE OF WASHINGTON, INC
21540 30TH DR SE STE 400
BOTHELL, WA 98021-7015
PO BOX 1469
BOTHELL, WA 98041-1469
PHONE: (425) 424-1100
FAX: (425) 487-8987
NATIONAL: (800) 869-7175

508 6TH AVE STE 900
SPOKANE, WA 99204-2730
PO BOX 2470
SPOKANE, WA 99210
PHONE: (509) 459-6690
FAX: (800) 816-3778
NATIONAL: (800) 869-7175

MOUNTAIN STATE BLUE CROSS / BLUE SHIELD
700 MARKET SQ
PARKERSBURG, WV 26101-4629
PO BOX 1948
PARKERSBURG, WV 26102
PHONE: (304) 424-7700
FAX: (304) 424-0326
NATIONAL: (800) 344-5514

NALC HEALTH BENEFIT PLAN
20547 WAVERLY CT
ASHBURN, VA 20149-0001
PHONE: (703) 729-4677
FAX: (703) 729-0076
NATIONAL: (888) 636-6252

NATIONAL CLAIMS ADMINISTRATIVE SOURCES
10715 RED RUN BLVD STE 125
OWINGS MILLS, MD 21117
PO BOX 1196
OWINGS MILLS, MD 21117-1196
PHONE: (443) 471-4000
FAX: (443) 471-1924
NATIONAL: (800) 423-9791

NATIONAL HEALTH INSURANCE CO
1901 N HWY 360
GRAND PRAIRIE, TX 75050-1412
PO BOX 619999
DALLAS, TX 75261-6199
PHONE: (817) 640-1900
FAX: (817) 640-3437
NATIONAL: (800) 237-1900

NATIONAL HERITAGE INSURANCE COMPANY
PO BOX 1465
NASHVILLE, TN 37202
PHONE: (866) 502-9056
NATIONAL: (866) 502-9054

NATIONWIDE HEALTH PLAN
5525 PARK CTR CIR
DUBLIN, OH 43017
PO BOX 182690
DUBLIN, OH 43218
PHONE: (614) 854-2184
FAX: (614) 858-3401
NATIONAL: (800) 626-2904

NEBRASKA HEALTH & HUMAN SERVICES
301 CENTENNIAL MALL S
LINCOLN, NE 68509
PO BOX 95026
LINCOLN, NE 68509-5026
PHONE: (402) 471-9147
FAX: (402) 471-9092
NATIONAL: (800) 430-3244

NORTH AMERICA ADMINISTRATORS, LP
1212 8TH AVE SOUTH
NASHVILLE, TN 37203
PO BOX 1984
NASHVILLE, TN 37202-1984
PHONE: (615) 256-3561
FAX: (615) 255-6654
NATIONAL: (800) 411-3650

OCHSNER HEALTH PLAN
ONE GALLERIA BLVD STE 850
METAIRIE, LA 7001-7542
PHONE: (504) 209-6600
FAX: (504) 836-6566
NATIONAL: (800) 999-5979

ODS HEALTH PLAN
601 SW 2ND AVE
PORTLAND, OR 97204-3156
PO BOX 40384
PORTLAND, OR 97240
PHONE: (503) 228-6554
FAX: (503) 948-5577
NATIONAL: (800) 852-5195

OLYMPIC HEALTH MANAGEMENT
2219 RIMLAND DR
BELLINGHAM, WA 98226-8660
PO BOX 5348
BELLINGHAM, WA 98227
PHONE: (360) 647-9080
FAX: (360) 392-9100
NATIONAL: (888) 858-8544

OSF HEALTH PLANS
7915 N HALE AVE STE D
PEORIA, IL 61615
PO BOX 5128
PEORIA, IL 61601-5128
PHONE: (309) 677-8200
FAX: (309) 677-8330
NATIONAL: (800) 673-4699

PACIFIC LIFE AND ANNUITY CO
4000 NORTH CENTRAL AVE STE 2000
PHOENIX, AZ 85012-3513
PO BOX 33699
PHOENIX, AZ 85067-3699
PHONE: (602) 230-0680
FAX: (602) 263-0545
NATIONAL: (800) 733-3227

PAN AMERICAN LIFE INSURANCE CO
601 POYDRAS ST
NEW ORLEANS, LA 70130
PO BOX 60219
NEW ORLEANS, LA 70160-0219
PHONE: (504) 566-1300
FAX: (504) 566-3109
NATIONAL: (877) 939-4500

PARTNERS NATIONAL HEALTH PLANS
5635 HAYNES MILL RD
WINSTON-SALEM, NC 27105-1322
PO BOX 24907
WINSTON-SALEM, NC 27114-4907
PHONE: (336) 760-4822
FAX: (336) 760-3198
NATIONAL: (800) 942-5695
IN-STATE: (800) 942-5695

PEER REVIEW ORGANIZATIONS
40600 ANN ARBOR RD STE 200
PLYMOUTH, MI 48170-4495
PHONE: (734) 459-0900
FAX: (734) 454-7295

PENN WESTERN BENEFITS, INC
7701 THORNDIKE RD
GREENSBORO, NC 27409
PO BOX 7834
GREENSBORO, NC 27417-0834
PHONE: (336) 665-9400
FAX: (336) 664-1300
NATIONAL: (888) 792-7828

PERSONAL INSURANCE ADMINISTRATORS
3719 E THOUSAND OAKS BLVD
THOUSAND OAKS, CA 91362-3607
PO BOX 5004
THOUSAND OAKS, CA 91359-5004
PHONE: (805) 777-0032
FAX: (805) 777-0033
NATIONAL: (800) 468-4343

PERSONALCARE HEALTH MANAGEMENT
2110 FOX DR
CHAMPAIGN, IL 61820-7399
PHONE: (217) 366-1226
FAX: (217) 366-5410
NATIONAL: (888) 366-6730

PHYSICIANS BENEFITS TRUST
1440 N RENAISSANCE DR
PARK RIDGE, IL 60068-1400
PHONE: (847) 803-3100
FAX: (847) 493-4600
NATIONAL: (800) 621-0748

PHYSICIANS HEALTH PLAN OF NORTHERN INDIANA, INC
8101 W JEFFERSON BLVD
FT WAYNE, IN 46804
PO BOX 2359
FT WAYNE, IN 46801-2359
PHONE: (260) 432-6690
FAX: (260) 432-0493
NATIONAL: (800) 982-6257

PHYSICIANS HEALTH PLAN OF SOUTHWEST MICHIGAN
106 FARMER'S ALLEY STE 300
KALAMAZOO, MI 49005
PO BOX 51100
KALAMAZOO, MI 49005-1100
PHONE: (616) 341-8000
FAX: (616) 341-6832
NATIONAL: (800) 548-6574
IN-STATE: (800) 722-3644

PIMA HEALTH SYSTEM
5055 E BROADWAY A200
TUCSON, AZ 85711-3644
PHONE: (520) 512-5500
FAX: (520) 745-6386
NATIONAL: (800) 423-3801

PINNACLE WEST CORP
400 N 5TH
PHOENIX, AZ 85004-3902
PO BOX 53970
PHOENIX, AZ 85072-3970
PHONE: (602) 250-2601
FAX: (602) 250-2453

PREFERRED HEALTH SYSTEMS INSURANCE CO
8535 E 21ST ST N
WICHITA, KS 67206
PO BOX 49288
WICHITA, KS 67201-9288
PHONE: (316) 609-2345
FAX: (316) 609-2347
NATIONAL: (800) 990-0345

PREMERA BLUE CROSS
7001 220TH ST SW
MOUNT LAKE TERRACE, WA 98043-2124
PO BOX 327
SEATTLE, WA 98111
PHONE: (425) 918-4000
FAX: (425) 918-4900
NATIONAL: (800) 527-6675

PRIME HEALTH OF ALABAMA
1400 UNIVERSITY BLVD S
MOBILE, AL 36609-2947
PO BOX 851239
MOBILE, AL 36685-1239
PHONE: (251) 342-0022
FAX: (251) 380-3236
NATIONAL: (800) 544-9449

PROFESSIONAL ADMINISTRATION GROUP
8310 W 120TH TERR
OVERLAND PARK, KS 66213-1236
PO BOX 13391
OVERLAND PARK, KS 66282-3391
PHONE: (913) 327-7108
FAX: (913) 451-4762

PROFESSIONAL ADMINISTRATORS, INC
3751 MAGUIRE BLVD STE 100
ORLANDO, FL 32803
PO BOX 140415
ORLANDO, FL 32814-0415
PHONE: (407) 896-0521
FAX: (407) 897-6976
NATIONAL: (800) 741-0521
IN-STATE: (800) 432-2686

PROFESSIONAL BENEFIT ADMINISTRATORS, INC
15 SPINNING WHEEL RD STE 210
HINSDALE, IL 60521
PO BOX 4687
OAK BROOK, IL 60522-4687
PHONE: (630) 655-3755
FAX: (630) 655-3781

PROTECTED HOME MUTUAL LIFE INSURANCE CO
30 E STATE ST
SHARON, PA 16146-1705
PHONE: (724) 981-1520
FAX: (724) 981-2682
NATIONAL: (800) 223-8821
IN-STATE: (800) 222-8894

PUBLIC EMPLOYEES HEALTH PROGRAM
560 E 200 S
SALT LAKE CITY, UT 84102-2004
PHONE: (801) 366-7555
FAX: (801) 366-7596
NATIONAL: (800) 765-7347
IN-STATE: (800) 765-7347

REGENCE BLUE CROSS / BLUE SHIELD OF OREGON
100 SW MARKET ST
PORTLAND, OR 97207-5766
PO BOX 900 & 1271
PORTLAND, OR 97207-0900
PHONE: (503) 225-5221
NATIONAL: (800) 452-7390

201 HIGH ST S
SALEM, OR 97308-3674
PO BOX 12625
SALEM, OR 97309-0625
PHONE: (503) 585-9211
FAX: (503) 588-4350
NATIONAL: (800) 228-0978
IN-STATE: (800) 228-0978

100 SW MARKET ST
PORTLAND, OR 97207-5766
PO BOX 900 & 1271
PORTLAND, OR 97207-0900
PHONE: (503) 225-5221
NATIONAL: (800) 452-7390

REGENCE BLUE CROSS / BLUE SHIELD OF UTAH
2890 E COTTONWOOD PKY
SALT LAKE CITY, UT 84121-7035
PO BOX 30270
SALT LAKE CITY, UT 84130-0270
PHONE: (801) 333-2000
FAX: (801) 333-6523
NATIONAL: (800) 624-6519

4723 HARRISON BLVD STE 101
OGDEN, UT 84403-4399
PHONE: (801) 476-9140
FAX: (801) 476-9138
NATIONAL: (800) 638-0050

REGENCE BLUE SHIELD
333 GILKEY RD
BURLINGTON, WA 98233-2823
PHONE: (360) 755-4000
FAX: (360) 755-4567
NATIONAL: (800) 659-7229
IN-STATE: (800) 659-7229

REGENCE BLUE SHIELD OF IDAHO
1602 21ST AVE
LEWISTON, ID 83501-4061
PO BOX 1106
LEWISTON, ID 83501-1106
PHONE: (208) 746-2671
FAX: (208) 798-2090
NATIONAL: (800) 632-2022

REGENCE BLUE SHIELD OF WASHINGTON
1800 NINTH AVE
SEATTLE, WA 98101-1322
PO BOX 21267
SEATTLE, WA 98111-3267
PHONE: (206) 464-3600
FAX: (206) 389-5669
NATIONAL: (800) 544-4246
IN-STATE: (800) 458-3523

REGIONAL MEDICAL ADMINISTRATORS, INC
1831 N PARK AVE
GLEN RAVEN, NC 27217
PO BOX 4128
GLEN RAVEN, NC 27215-0901
PHONE: (336) 226-7950
FAX: (336) 570-0599
NATIONAL: (800) 711-1507

RIVERBEND GOVERNMENT BENEFITS ADMINISTRATOR
730 CHESTNUT ST
CHATTANOOGA, TN 37402
FAX: (423) 752-6518
NATIONAL: (877) 296-6189
IN-STATE: (877) 296-6189

RMSCO, INC
115 CONTINUUM
LIVERPOOL, NY 13088
PO BOX 6309
SYRACUSE, NY 13217
PHONE: (315) 474-8200
FAX: (315) 476-8440

ROBERT, BOUCK & ASSOCIATES
126 N 30TH ST STE 205
QUINCY, IL 62301
PHONE: (217) 223-8354
FAX: (217) 223-8621

ROCKFORD HEALTH PLANS
3401 N PERRYVILLE RD
ROCKFORD, IL 61114
PHONE: (815) 971-1000
FAX: (815) 282-0634

ROCKY MOUNTAIN HEALTH PLANS
2775 CROSSROADS BLVD
GRAND JUNCTION, CO 81506
PO BOX 10600
GRAND JUNCTION, CO 81502
PHONE: (970) 244-7760
FAX: (970) 244-7880
NATIONAL: (800) 843-0719
IN-STATE: (800) 843-0719

ROYAL STATE GROUP
819 S BERETANIA ST STE 100
HONOLULU, HI 96813-2501
PHONE: (808) 539-1600
FAX: (808) 538-1458

ROYAL & SUNALLIANCE
25 NEW CHARDON ST
BOSTON, MA 02114-4774
PHONE: (617) 742-7750
FAX: (617) 557-4252
NATIONAL: (800) 367-7036
IN-STATE: (800) 367-7036

SAN DIEGO ELECTRICAL HEALTH & WELFARE TRUST
4675 VIEWRIDGE AVE STE B
SAN DIEGO, CA 92123-1644
PO BOX 231219
SAN DIEGO, CA 92194-1219
PHONE: (858) 569-6322
FAX: (858) 573-0830
NATIONAL: (800) 632-2569

SEABURY & SMITH, INC
2610 NORTHGATE DR
IOWA CITY, IA 52244
PO BOX 1520
IOWA CITY, IA 52244-1520
PHONE: (319) 887-4000
FAX: (319) 351-0603

SECURITY HEALTH PLAN OF WISCONSIN, INC
1515 SAINT JOSEPH AVE
MARSHFIELD, WI 54449
PO BOX 8000
MARSHFIELD, WI 54449-8000
PHONE: (715) 221-9555
FAX: (715) 221-9500
NATIONAL: (800) 472-2363

SELF INSURED SERVICES CO
300 SECURITY BLDG
DUBUQUE, IA 52001
PO BOX 389
DUBUQUE, IA 52004-0389
PHONE: (563) 583-7344
FAX: (563) 587-5500
NATIONAL: (800) 793-5235

SELMAN & CO
6110 PARKLAND BLVD
CLEVELAND, OH 44124-4187
PO BOX 248108
CLEVELAND, OH 44124-4187
PHONE: (440) 646-9336
FAX: (440) 646-9339
NATIONAL: (800) 735-6262

SENTRY INSURANCE MUTUAL CO
1800 N POINT DR
STEVENS POINT, WI 54481
PO BOX 8026
STEVENS POINT, WI 54481-8026
PHONE: (715) 346-6000
FAX: (715) 346-6161
NATIONAL: (800) 638-8763

SHELTER INSURANCE COMPANIES
1817 W BROADWAY
COLUMBIA, MO 65218-0001
PO BOX 6006
COLUMBIA, MO 65205-6006
PHONE: (573) 445-8441
FAX: (573) 445-3199
NATIONAL: (800) 743-5837

SIERRA HEALTH & LIFE INSURANCE CO, INC
2720 N TENAYA WY
LAS VEGAS, NV 89128-0424
PO BOX 15645
LAS VEGAS, NV 89114
PHONE: (702) 242-7000
FAX: (702) 242-9038
NATIONAL: (800) 888-2264
IN-STATE: (800) 888-2264

SOUTHEASTERN INDIANA HEALTH ORGANIZATION
417 WASHINGTON ST
COLUMBUS, IN 47201
PO BOX 1787
COLUMBUS, IN 47202-1787
PHONE: (812) 378-7000
FAX: (812) 378-7048
NATIONAL: (800) 443-2980

SOUTHERN BENEFIT ADMINISTRATORS, INC
2001 CALDWELL DR
GOODLETTSVILLE, TN 37072
PO BOX 1449
GOODLETTSVILLE, TN 37070-1449
PHONE: (615) 859-0131
FAX: (615) 859-0818
NATIONAL: (800) 831-4914

SOUTHERN CALIFORNIA PIPE TRADES TRUST FUND
501 SHATTO PL 5TH FL
LOS ANGELES, CA 90020-1713
PHONE: (213) 385-6161
FAX: (213) 487-3640
IN-STATE: (800) 595-7473

SOUTHERN GROUP ADMINISTRATORS, INC
200 S MARSHALL ST
WINSTON-SALEM, NC 27101-5251
PHONE: (336) 723-7111
FAX: (336) 722-4748
NATIONAL: (800) 334-8159

SOUTHWEST ADMINISTRATORS
1000 S FREEMONT AVE BLDG A9 WEST
ALHAMBRA, CA 91803-8800
PO BOX 1121
ALHAMBRA, CA 91802-1121
PHONE: (626) 284-4792
NATIONAL: (877) 350-4792

SPECIAL AGENTS MUTUAL BENEFIT ASSOCIATION
11301 OLD GEORGETOWN RD
ROCKVILLE, MD 20852-2800
PO BOX 23819
TUCSON, AZ 85734
PHONE: (301) 984-1440
FAX: (301) 984-6224
NATIONAL: (800) 638-6589

STANDARD LIFE & ACCIDENT INSURANCE CO
ONE MOODY PLZ
GALVESTON, TX 77550-7947
PO BOX 1800
GALVESTON, TX 77553-1800
PHONE: (888) 350-1488
FAX: (409) 621-3094

STATE OF NEW YORK INSURANCE DEPT LIQUIDATION BUREAU
123 WILLIAM ST
NEW YORK, NY 10038-3804
PHONE: (212) 341-6400
FAX: (212) 341-6104

STATES GENERAL INSURANCE CO
115 W 7TH ST STE 1205
FT WORTH, TX 76102
PHONE: (817) 338-4395
FAX: (817) 820-6824
NATIONAL: (800) 782-8375

SUN LIFE FINANCIAL
ONE SUN LIFE EXECUTIVE PARK
WELLESLEY HILLS, MA 02481-0000
PHONE: (781) 237-6030
FAX: (781) 431-7472
NATIONAL: (800) 786-5433

TEACHERS PROTECTIVE MUTUAL LIFE INSURANCE CO
116-118 N PRINCE ST
LANCASTER, PA 17608
PO BOX 597
LANCASTER, PA 17608-0597
PHONE: (717) 394-7156
FAX: (717) 394-7024
NATIONAL: (800) 555-3122

THREE RIVERS BENEFIT CORP
518 8TH ST
SIOUX CITY, IA 51104
PO BOX 3440
SIOUX CITY, IA 51102-3440
PHONE: (712) 258-1525
FAX: (712) 255-3521
NATIONAL: (800) 798-8115

TOTAL HEALTH CARE, INC
3011 W GRAND BLVD STE 1600
DETROIT, MI 48202
PHONE: (313) 871-2000
FAX: (313) 871-6400
IN-STATE: (800) 826-2862

TOTAL HEALTH CHOICE
8701 SW 137TH AVE STE 200
MIAMI, FL 33183
PO BOX 830010
MIAMI, FL 33283-0010
PHONE: (305) 408-5700
FAX: (305) 408-5710
NATIONAL: (800) 887-6888

TOUCHPOINT HEALTH PLAN
FIVE INNOVATION CT
APPLETON, WI 54914
PO BOX 507
APPLETON, WI 54912-0507
PHONE: (920) 735-6300
FAX: (920) 831-6886
NATIONAL: (800) 735-6305

TOWER LIFE INSURANCE CO
TOWER LIFE BLDG 310 S ST MARY ST STE 500
SAN ANTONIO, TX 78205-3164
PHONE: (210) 554-4400
FAX: (210) 554-4401
NATIONAL: (800) 880-4576

TR PAUL, INC
14 COMMERCE RD
NEWTOWN, CT 06470-1607
PO BOX 5508
NEWTOWN, CT 06470-5508
PHONE: (203) 426-8161
FAX: (203) 270-0927
NATIONAL: (800) 678-8161

TRICARE
REGIONS 3 & 4
PO BOX 7031
CAMDEN, SC 29020-7031
PHONE: (843) 665-7822
FAX: (843) 629-1420
NATIONAL: (888) 288-2227

PO BOX 870001
SURFSIDE BEACH, SC 29587-8706
PHONE: (843) 650-6100
NATIONAL: (800) 930-2929

1717 W BROADWAY
MADISON, WI 53713-1895
PO BOX 8999
MADISON, WI 53708-8999
PHONE: (608) 221-4711
NATIONAL: (800) 406-2832
IN-STATE: (800) 406-2833

REGION 1
PO BOX 7011
CAMDEN, SC 29020-7011
PHONE: (843) 665-7822
NATIONAL: (800) 578-1294

REGION 5
PO BOX 7021
CAMDEN, SC 29020-7021
PHONE: (843) 665-7822
NATIONAL: (800) 493-1613

REGION 8
PO BOX 870030
SURFSIDE BEACH, SC 29587-8730
PHONE: (843) 650-6100
NATIONAL: (800) 225-4816

REGION 1
PO BOX 7011
CAMDEN, SC 29020-7011
PHONE: (843) 665-7822
NATIONAL: (800) 578-1294

TRINITY UNIVERSAL INSURANCE CO
10000 N CENTRAL EXPY
DALLAS, TX 75231-4177
PO BOX 655028
DALLAS, TX 75265-5028
PHONE: (214) 360-8000
FAX: (214) 360-8076
NATIONAL: (800) 777-2249

TRIPLE-S INC, OF PUERTO RICO
1441 ROOSEVELT AVE
SAN JUAN, PR 00920-0000
PO BOX 363628
SAN JUAN, PR 00936-3628
PHONE: (787) 749-4949
FAX: (787) 749-4143

TRUSTEED PLANS SERVICE CORP
6901 6TH AVE
TACOMA, WA 98406-1705
PO BOX 1894
TACOMA, WA 98401-1894
PHONE: (253) 564-5850
FAX: (253) 564-5881
NATIONAL: (800) 426-9786

TRUSTMARK INSURANCE
400 FIELD DR
LAKE FOREST, IL 60045-2586
PHONE: (847) 615-1500
FAX: (847) 615-3910
NATIONAL: (800) 877-9077
IN-STATE: (800) 877-9077

8324 S AVE
BOARDMAN, OH 44512
PHONE: (330) 758-9526
FAX: (330) 758-3242
NATIONAL: (800) 544-7312

TUCKER ADMINISTRATORS, INC
3800 ARCO CORPORATED DR STE 480
CHARLOTTE, NC 28273-0001
PHONE: (704) 525-9666
FAX: (704) 525-9534

UCARE MINNESOTA
2000 SUMMER ST NE
MINNEAPOLIS, MN 55413
PO BOX 52
MINNEAPOLIS, MN 55440-0052
PHONE: (612) 676-6500
FAX: (612) 676-6501
NATIONAL: (800) 203-7225

UICI
9151 GRAPEVINE HWY
NORTH RICHLAND HILLS, TX 76180-5605
PO BOX 982009
NORTH RICHLAND HILLS, TX 76182-2009
PHONE: (817) 255-3100
FAX: (817) 255-8101
NATIONAL: (800) 527-5504
IN-STATE: (800) 733-1110

UNICARE HEALTH PLANS OF THE MIDWEST
220 REMINGTON BLVD
BOLINGBROOK, IL 60440
PO BOX 5033
BOLINGBROOK, IL 60440-5033
PHONE: (312) 297-6000
NATIONAL: (877) 864-2273

UNICARE LIFE AND HEALTH INSURANCE
3200 GREENFIELD RD
DEARBORN, MI 48120
PO BOX 4479
DEARBORN, MI 48126
PHONE: (313) 336-5550
FAX: (313) 594-5047
NATIONAL: (800) 843-8184

**UNICARE LIFE AND HEALTH INSURANCE
COMPANY**
233 S WACKER DR STE 3900
CHICAGO, IL 60606
PHONE: (312) 234-7000
FAX: (312) 234-8005
NATIONAL: (877) 864-2273

UNICARE LIFE & HEALTH INSURANCE CO
3820 AMERICAN DR
PLANO, TX 75070-6126
PO BOX 833933
RICHARDSON, TX 75083
PHONE: (972) 599-6000
FAX: (972) 599-3609
NATIONAL: (800) 333-3304
IN-STATE: (800) 333-3304

3179 TEMPLE AVE STE 200
POMONA, CA 91768-3249
PO BOX 6007
LOS ANGELES, CA 90067-0007
PHONE: (909) 444-6000
NATIONAL: (877) 864-2273

UNION LABOR LIFE INSURANCE CO
111 MASSACHUSETTS AVE NW
WASHINGTON, DC 20001-1461
PHONE: (202) 682-0900
FAX: (202) 962-8904
NATIONAL: (800) 431-5425

**UNITED COMMERCIAL TRAVELERS OF
AMERICA**
632 N PARK ST
COLUMBUS, OH 43215-8619
PO BOX 159019
COLUMBUS, OH 43215-8619
PHONE: (614) 228-3276
FAX: (614) 228-0365
NATIONAL: (800) 848-0123

**UNITED FOOD & COMMERCIAL WORKERS
TRUST FUND**
6425 KATELLA AVE
CYPRESS, CA 90630-5246
PO BOX 6010
CYPRESS, CA 90630-0010
PHONE: (714) 220-2297
FAX: (714) 828-6573

UNITED HEALTHCARE
PO BOX 659759
SAN ANTONIO, TX 78265-9759
PHONE: (218) 279-6500
FAX: (218) 279-6761
NATIONAL: (800) 318-7689

UNITED HERITAGE LIFE INSURANCE CO
707 E UNITED HERITAGE CT
MERIDIAN, ID 83642-3527
PO BOX 7777
MERIDIAN, ID 83680-7777
PHONE: (208) 493-6100
FAX: (800) 240-9734
NATIONAL: (800) 657-6351

UNITED MEDICAL RESOURCES, INC
5151 PFEIFFER RD ML 400
CINCINNATI, OH 45242
PO BOX 145804
CINCINNATI, OH 45250-5804
PHONE: (513) 619-3000
FAX: (513) 619-3010
NATIONAL: (800) 436-3100

UNITY HEALTH INSURANCE
840 CAROLINA ST
SAUK CITY, WI 53583
PO BOX 610
SAUK CITY, WI 53583
PHONE: (608) 643-2491
FAX: (608) 643-2564
NATIONAL: (800) 362-3308

USI ADMINISTRATORS
10 CHATHAM CTR SO
SAVANNAH, GA 31405
PO BOX 9888
SAVANNAH, GA 31412-0088
PHONE: (912) 691-1551
FAX: (912) 352-8935
NATIONAL: (800) 631-3441

VICARE NATIONAL BENEFIT PLANS
1000 COMMERCIAL LN
SUFFOLK, VA 23434
PHONE: (757) 923-3400
FAX: (757) 923-2607
NATIONAL: (800) 582-2001

VISION SERVICE PLAN
3333 QUALITY DR
RANCHO CORDOVA, CA 95670-7985
PO BOX 997100
SACRAMENTO, CA 95899-7100
PHONE: (916) 851-5000
FAX: (916) 851-5152
NATIONAL: (800) 852-7600

WAKELY & ASSOCIATES
33 N GARDEN AVE STE 1100
CLEARWATER, FL 33755-6606
PO BOX 10811
CLEARWATER, FL 33757-8811
PHONE: (727) 584-8128
FAX: (727) 581-0578
NATIONAL: (877) 872-5500

WALMART BENEFITS
922 W WALNUT STE A
ROGERS, AR 72756-3206
PHONE: (479) 621-2929
FAX: (479) 621-2654
NATIONAL: (800) 421-1362

WARD NORTH AMERICA, INC
3330 ARCTIC BLVD STE 206
ANCHORAGE, AK 99503-4580
PHONE: (907) 561-1725
FAX: (907) 562-6595

WEA TRUST
45 NOB HILL RD
MADISON, WI 53713
PO BOX 7338
MADISON, WI 53707-7338
PHONE: (608) 276-4000
FAX: (608) 276-9119
NATIONAL: (800) 279-4000

WELBORN HEALTH PLANS
421 CHESTNUT ST
EVANSVILLE, IN 47713
PHONE: (812) 426-6600
FAX: (812) 426-9476
NATIONAL: (800) 521-0265

WELFARE & PENSION ADMIN SERV
2815 SECOND AVE STE 300
SEATTLE, WA 98121-3209
PO BOX 34684
SEATTLE, WA 98124
PHONE: (206) 441-7574
FAX: (206) 441-9110
NATIONAL: (800) 331-6158
IN-STATE: (800) 732-1121

WELL CARE HMO, INC
6800 N DALE MABRY HWY STE 270-299
TAMPA, FL 33614
PHONE: (813) 290-6200
FAX: (813) 290-6260
NATIONAL: (800) 799-3081

**WELLMARK BLUE CROSS / BLUE SHIELD OF
IOWA**
HAMILTON BLVD I-29
SIOUX CITY, IA 51103-5216
PO BOX 1677
SIOUX CITY, IA 51102-1677
PHONE: (712) 279-8500
FAX: (712) 279-8450
NATIONAL: (800) 526-9048

**WELLMARK BLUE CROSS / BLUE SHIELD OF
SOUTH DAKOTA**
1601 W MADISON ST
SIOUX FALLS, SD 57104-5710
PHONE: (605) 373-7200
FAX: (605) 373-7497
NATIONAL: (800) 831-4818

WELLNESS PLAN, THE
2875 W GRAND BLVD
DETROIT, MI 48202-2623
PO BOX 02577
DETROIT, MI 48202-2577
PHONE: (313) 202-8500
FAX: (313) 202-8510
NATIONAL: (800) 875-9355
IN-STATE: (800) 323-3894

WESLEY MEDICAL CENTER
550 N HILLSIDE ST
WICHITA, KS 67214-4910
PO BOX 403101
ATLANTA, GA 30384-3101
PHONE: (316) 688-2000
FAX: (316) 688-7931
NATIONAL: (800) 444-6755

**WESTCHESTER TEAMSTERS HEALTH &
WELFARE**
160 S CENTRAL AVE
ELMSFORD, NY 10523
PHONE: (914) 592-9330
FAX: (914) 592-1519

WESTERN MUTUAL INSURANCE CO
4393 S RIVERBOAT RD
TAYLORSVILLE, UT 84123-2503
PO BOX 572450
MURRAY, UT 84157-2450
PHONE: (801) 263-8000
FAX: (801) 263-1189
NATIONAL: (800) 748-5340

WESTPORT BENEFITS
120 S CENTRAL AVE STE 160
ST LOUIS, MO 63105
PO BOX 66743
ST LOUIS, MO 63166-6743
PHONE: (314) 889-2100
FAX: (314) 889-2297
NATIONAL: (800) 548-2041

WEYCO, INC
2370 SCIENCE PKY
OKEMOS, MI 48864
PO BOX 30132
LANSING, MI 48909
PHONE: (517) 349-7010
FAX: (517) 349-8555
NATIONAL: (800) 748-0003

WHEELER COMPANIES, THE
TWO PERIMETER PARK STE 160 E
BIRMINGHAM, AL 35243-2329
PO BOX 43350
BIRMINGHAM, AL 35243-0350
PHONE: (205) 995-8688
FAX: (205) 980-9047
NATIONAL: (800) 741-8688

WISCONSIN PHYSICIANS SERVICE
1717 W BROADWAY
MADISON, WI 53713
PO BOX 8190
MADISON, WI 53708-8999
PHONE: (608) 221-4711
1717 W BROADWAY
MADISON, WI 53713
PO BOX 8190
MADISON, WI 53708
PHONE: (608) 221-4711
NATIONAL: (800) 765-4977

WORLD INSURANCE CO
11808 GRANT ST
OMAHA, NE 68164
PO BOX 3160
OMAHA, NE 68103-0160
PHONE: (402) 496-8000
FAX: (402) 496-8199
NATIONAL: (800) 786-7557

ZENITH ADMINISTRATORS, INC
221 MAIN ST 2ND FL
SAN FRANCISCO, CA 94105-1909
PHONE: (415) 546-7800
FAX: (415) 546-0600
NATIONAL: (800) 388-0508

5565 STERRETT PL STE 210
COLUMBIA, MD 21044
PO BOX 1100
COLUMBIA, MD 21044-0100
PHONE: (410) 884-1440
FAX: (410) 997-3657
NATIONAL: (800) 235-5805

8700 TURNPIKE DR STE 200
WESTMINSTER, CO 80031
PHONE: (303) 430-1118
FAX: (303) 430-0224

104 S FREYA STE 220
SPOKANE, WA 99202-4867
PHONE: (509) 534-5625
FAX: (509) 534-5910
NATIONAL: (800) 522-2403

2873 N DIRKSEN PKY STE 200
SPRINGFIELD, IL 62702
PHONE: (217) 753-4531
FAX: (217) 753-3953
NATIONAL: (800) 538-6466

8207 CALLAGHAN RD STE 300
SAN ANTONIO, TX 78230-4780
PHONE: (210) 349-7774
FAX: (210) 349-0315
NATIONAL: (800) 443-1606

3100 BROADWAY STE 400
KANSAS CITY, MO 64111
PHONE: (816) 756-0173
FAX: (816) 531-6518
NATIONAL: (866) 756-0414

2450 SEVERN AVE STE 517
METAIRIE, LA 70001-1237
PHONE: (504) 831-1544
FAX: (504) 831-1894

8207 CALLAGHAN RD STE 300
SAN ANTONIO, TX 78230-4780
PHONE: (210) 349-7774
FAX: (210) 349-0315
NATIONAL: (800) 443-1606

52 ACCORD PARK DR
NORWELL, MA 02061-1628
PHONE: (781) 871-3100
FAX: (781) 871-3163

33 EASTLAND ST
SPRINGFIELD, MA 01109-2348
PHONE: (413) 733-0177
FAX: (413) 733-3325
NATIONAL: (800) 634-2700

6011 W SAINT JOSEPH STE 401
LANSING, MI 48917
PHONE: (517) 323-9250
FAX: (517) 323-1093

2801 COHO ST STE 300
MADISON, WI 53713
PHONE: (608) 274-4773
FAX: (608) 277-1088
NATIONAL: (800) 397-3373

314 W SUPERIOR ST STE 750
DULUTH, MN 55802
PHONE: (218) 727-6668
FAX: (218) 727-5697

104 S FREYA STE 220
SPOKANE, WA 99202-4867
PHONE: (509) 534-5625
FAX: (509) 534-5910
NATIONAL: (800) 522-2403

9600 SW OAK STE 380
TIGARD, OR 97223-6586
PHONE: (503) 226-2741
FAX: (503) 226-7900
NATIONAL: (800) 547-5900

201 QUEEN ANNE AVE N STE 100
SEATTLE, WA 98109-4824
PHONE: (206) 282-4100
FAX: (206) 285-1701
NATIONAL: (800) 426-5980

APPENDIX 6 — HCPCS CODES FOR WHICH CPT CODES SHOULD BE REPORTED

HCPCS Level II	PM	Source
C1300 (report for hospital outpatient)	AB-702-183	
For other than OPPS use A4290, E0752, E0756	A-03-020 -- Report separately with 64561, 64575, 64581, 64585, 64590, 64595	
C8909-C8911		-Medicare Claims Processing Manual, Ch. 13, Sec. 40.1.2 (Rev. 10/1/03)
C8918-C8920	A-03-051	- Medicare Claims Processing Manual, Ch. 13, Sec. 40.1.2 (Rev. 10/1/03)
C8090-C8902		- Medicare Claims Processing Manual, Ch. 13, Sec. 40.1.2 (Rev. 10/1/03)
G0001	AB-02-163	
G0008, G0009, G0010	B-03-001	
G0008, G0009, G0010		
G0030		
G0031		
G0102		CCI 9.3
Comprehensive code G0103		CCC 9.3
Comprehensive code G0104		CCI 9.3
Comprehensive code G0105		CCI 9.3
Comprehensive code G0106		CCI 9.3
Comprehensive code G0107		CCI 9.3
G0144	AB-02-163	
G0145	AB-02-163	
G0202-G0205	Hospital Manual, Ch. 10, Sec. 458	-
G0206-G0207	Hospital Manual, Ch. 10, Sec. 458	-
Not allowed if a surgical procedure or any service that has a status indicator of "T" with the exception of Q0081)G0244	A-02-129	
G0248	AB-02-180	
G0256	A-02-129	
G0257	A-02-129	
G0259	A-02-129	
G0261	A-02-129	
G0265	AB-02-163	
G0266	AB-02-163	
G0268	A-02-129	
G0267	AB-02-163	
(OPPS only) G0292	A-02-129	
(OPPS only) G0293	A-02-129	
(OPPS only) G0294	A-02-129	
L8042		
L8045		
L8040		
L8041, L8042, L8044, L8046		
P9612	AB-02-163	
P9615	AB-02-163	
Comprehensive code P3000		Transmittal 800, CCI
Q code was deleted.		1788 (2-3-2003)
Q code was deleted.		1788 (2-3-2003)
Q code was deleted		1788 (2-3-2003)
Q code was deleted		1788 (2-3-2003
Q code was deleted		1788 (2-3-2003
Q code was deleted		1788 (2-3-2003
Q code was deleted		1788 (2-3-2003

APPENDIX 7 — NEW, CHANGED AND DELETED HCPCS CODES FOR 2004

NEW CODES AS OF NOVEMBER 7, 2003

A0800	A4216	A4217
A4248	A4366	A4416
A4417	A4418	A4419
A4420	A4423	A4424
A4425	A4426	A4427
A4428	A4429	A4430
A4431	A4432	A4433
A4434	A4638	A4671
A4672	A4673	A4674
A4728	A6407	A6441
A6442	A6443	A6444
A6445	A6446	A6447
A6448	A6449	A6450
A6451	A6452	A6453
A6454	A6455	A6456
A6550	A6551	A7046
A7520	A7521	A7522
A7523	A7524	A7525
A7526	A9280	A9525
A9526	A9528	A9529
A9530	A9531	A9532
A9533	A9534	A9999
C1080	C1081	C1082
C1083	C1814	C1818
C1819	C1884	C8918
C8919	C8920	C9123
C9202	C9203	C9207
C9208	C9209	C9210
C9211	C9212	E0118
E0140	E0190	E0240
E0247	E0248	E0300
E0301	E0302	E0303
E0304	E0470	E0471
E0472	E0561	E0562
E0637	E0638	E0675
E0955	E0956	E0957
E0960	E0981	E0982
E0983	E0984	E0985
E0986	E1002	E1003
E1004	E1005	E1006
E1007	E1008	E1009
E1010	E1019	E1021
E1028	E1029	E1030
E1391	E1634	E2120
E2201	E2202	E2203
E2204	E2300	E2301
E2310	E2311	E2320
E2321	E2322	E2323
E2324	E2325	E2326
E2327	E2328	E2329
E2330	E2331	E2340
E2341	E2342	E2343
E2351	E2360	E2361
E2362	E2363	E2364
E2365	E2366	E2367
E2399	E2402	E2500
E2502	E2504	E2506
E2508	E2510	E2511
E2512	E2599	G0296
G0297	G0298	G0299
G0300	G0302	G0303
G0304	G0305	G0306
G0307	G0308	G0309
G0310	G0311	G0312
G0313	G0314	G0315
G0316	G0317	G0318
G0319	G0320	G0321
G0322	G0323	G0324
G0325	G0326	G0327
G0328	G0338	G0339
G0340	G3001	H2010
H2011	H2012	H2013
H2014	H2015	H2016
H2017	H2018	H2019
H2020	H2021	H2022
H2023	H2024	H2025
H2026	H2027	H2028
H2029	H2030	H2031
H2032	H2033	H2034
H2035	H2036	H2037
J0152	J0215	J0583
J0595	J1335	J1595
J2001	J2185	J2280
J2353	J2354	J2505
J2783	J3411	J3415
J3465	J3486	J7303
J7621	J9098	J9178
J9263	J9395	K0552
K0600	K0601	K0602
K0603	K0604	K0605
K0606	K0607	K0608
K0609	K0618	K0619
K0620	L0112	L0861
L1831	L1907	L1951
L1971	L3031	L3917
L5673	L5679	L5681
L5683	L8511	L8512
L8513	L8514	L8631
L8659	P9051	P9052
P9053	P9054	P9055
P9056	P9057	P9058
P9059	P9060	Q0137
Q0182	Q3031	Q4054
Q4055	Q4075	Q4076
Q4077	S0107	S0115
S0136	S0137	S0138
S0139	S0140	S0141
S0317	S2070	S2085
S2090	S2091	S2095
S2113	S2135	S2213
S2225	S2230	S2235
S2362	S2363	S3000
S3625	S3820	S3822
S3823	S3828	S3829
S3833	S3834	S3840
S3841	S3842	S3843
S3844	S3845	S3846
S3847	S3848	S3849
S3850	S3851	S3852
S3853	S5108	S5109
S5550	S5551	S5552
S5553	S5560	S5561
S5565	S5566	S5570
S5571	S8075	S8120
S8121	S8460	S8948
S8990	S9335	S9434
S9476	T2010	T2011
T2012	T2013	T2014
T2015	T2016	T2017
T2018	T2019	T2020
T2021	T2022	T2023
T2024	T2025	T2026
T2027	T2028	T2029
T2030	T2031	T2032
T2033	T2034	T2035
T2036	T2037	T2038
T2039	T2040	T2041
T2042	T2043	T2044
T2045	T2046	T2048
T2101	T5001	T5999
V2121	V2221	V2321
V2745	V2756	V2761
V2762	V2782	V2783
V2784	V2786	V2797

CHANGED CODES AS OF NOVEMBER 7, 2003

A0225	A4326	A4538
A4623	A6025	C1716
C1718	C1719	C1720
C2616	C9009	E0141
E0143	E0144	E0147
E0149	E0203	E0950
E0951	E0952	E0958
E0959	E0961	E0966
E0967	E0972	E0973
E0974	E0978	E0990
E0992	E0995	E1225
E1226	E1390	G0122
G0247	G0275	G0278
J0880	J1650	J7308
K0455	L1843	L1844
L1950	L2405	L3902
L4350	L4360	L4386
L5646	L5648	L5848
L5984	L6620	L6675
L6676	L7900	L8658
M0100	M0301	P9017
S0316	S2150	S9123
S9326	S9327	S9330
S9331	S9338	S9364
S9365	S9366	S9367
S9368	S9494	S9537
S9542	S9558	S9559
S9900	V5274	V5362
V5363	V5364	

DELETED CODES AS OF NOVEMBER 7, 2003

A4214	A4319	A4323
A4621	A4622	A4631
A4644	A4645	A4646
A4712	A6421	A6422
A6424	A6426	A6428
A6430	A6432	A6434
A6436	A6438	A6440
A7019	A7020	A9518
C1010	C1011	C1015
C1016	C1017	C1018
C1020	C1021	C1022
C1166	C1167	C1207
C1774	C9010	C9111
C9116	C9119	C9120
C9204	C9205	C9503
E0142	E0145	E0146
E0165	E0943	E0975
E0976	E0979	E0991
E0993	E1066	E1069
G0025	G0110	G0111
G0112	G0113	G0114
G0115	G0116	G0167
G0236	G0262	G0272
G0273	G0274	J0151
J1910	J2000	J2352
J7508	J9180	K0016
K0022	K0025	K0026
K0027	K0028	K0029
K0030	K0031	K0032
K0033	K0035	K0036
K0048	K0049	K0054
K0055	K0057	K0058
K0062	K0063	K0079
K0080	K0082	K0083
K0084	K0085	K0086
K0087	K0088	K0089
K0100	K0103	K0107
K0112	K0113	K0268
K0460	K0461	K0531
K0532	K0533	K0534
K0538	K0539	K0540
K0541	K0542	K0543
K0544	K0545	K0546
K0547	K0549	K0550
K0556	K0557	K0558
K0559	K0560	K0581
K0582	K0583	K0584
K0585	K0586	K0587
K0588	K0589	K0590
K0591	K0592	K0593
K0594	K0595	K0596
K0597	K0610	K0611
K0612	K0613	K0614
K0615	K0616	K0617
K0621	K0622	K0623
K0624	K0625	K0626
L1885	L2102	L2104
L2122	L2124	Q0086
Q2010	Q4052	Q4054
Q4078	Q9920	Q9921
Q9922	Q9923	Q9924
Q9925	Q9926	Q9927
Q9928	Q9929	Q9930
Q9931	Q9932	Q9933
Q9934	Q9935	Q9936
Q9937	Q9938	Q9939
Q9940	S0009	S0079
S0124	S0130	S0135
S0193	S8180	S8181
S8470	S9546	S9802
S9803	S9806	T1008
T1011	V2116	V2117
V2216	V2217	V2316
V2317	V2740	V2741
V2742	V2743	

APPENDIX 8 — MEDICARE NATIONAL AVERAGE PAYMENT

The following table represents commercial and/or Medicare national average payment (NAP) for services, supplies (DME, orthotics, prosthetics, etc.), drugs and non—physician procedures reported using HCPCS Level II codes. Not all HCPCS Level II codes are included in this listing since data concerning the commercial and Medicare national average payments were not available. Please remember these are average payments and do not represent actual payment applicable to specific carriers, localities or third party payers. The NAP should be used as a broad benchmark tool only.

For the commercial NAP, the average 60th percentile value for the code was calculated by taking the summation of the fees for each code at the 60th percentile across all of geographical areas and dividing by the number of areas.

The Medicare data shown is the average of the floor and ceiling limits of those procedures fee amounts (Medicare Physician Fee Schedule Data Base FY2003 without the geographical practice cost index factor), or the national amount from the Clinical Lab Fee Schedule. The average 60th percentile value for the HCPCS code was calculated by taking the summation of the fees for each code at the 60th percentile across all geographical areas and dividing by the number of areas.

CODE	COMMERCIAL	MEDICARE	CODE	COMMERCIAL	MEDICARE	CODE	COMMERCIAL	MEDICARE
A0021	0.00	0.00	A4222	25.70	43.23	A4326	2.30	9.98
A0080	4.00	0.00	A4230	11.00	0.00	A4327	3.10	41.28
A0090	0.40	0.00	A4231	13.20	0.00	A4328	15.00	9.67
A0100	15.00	0.00	A4232	3.30	2.45	A4329	13.00	0.00
A0110	13.00	0.00	A4244	1.20	0.00	A4330	11.10	6.62
A0120	45.00	0.00	A4245	8.50	0.00	A4331	4.47	2.94
A0130	24.00	0.00	A4246	5.00	0.00	A4332	0.16	0.11
A0140	160.00	0.00	A4247	5.00	0.00	A4333	2.81	2.04
A0160	0.22	0.00	A4250	15.00	0.00	A4334	5.76	4.56
A0170	23.00	0.00	A4253	46.90	0.00	A4335	0.90	0.00
A0180	79.00	0.00	A4254	7.50	0.00	A4338	12.00	11.34
A0190	50.00	0.00	A4255	0.00	3.80	A4340	20.00	29.37
A0200	0.00	0.00	A4256	12.50	10.58	A4344	17.95	14.82
A0210	0.00	0.00	A4257	0.50	11.80	A4346	21.69	18.12
A0225	439.20	0.00	A4258	28.00	16.70	A4347	20.67	18.83
A0380	7.86	0.00	A4259	17.00	11.79	A4348	6.10	25.75
A0382	10.00	0.00	A4260	450.05	0.00	A4351	2.11	1.68
A0384	33.23	0.00	A4261	45.00	0.00	A4352	7.00	5.94
A0390	8.00	0.00	A4262	0.00	0.00	A4353	9.00	6.48
A0392	50.00	0.00	A4263	60.02	0.00	A4354	10.20	10.92
A0394	25.00	0.00	A4265	5.00	3.14	A4355	8.50	8.24
A0396	39.50	0.00	A4266	0.00	0.00	A4356	55.01	42.21
A0398	9.57	0.00	A4267	0.00	0.00	A4357	10.33	8.98
A0420	21.20	0.00	A4268	0.00	0.00	A4358	7.90	6.14
A0422	48.80	0.00	A4269	0.00	0.00	A4359	36.99	28.34
A0424	10.00	0.00	A4270	25.00	0.00	A4360	0.90	0.00
A0425	8.50	0.00	A4280	5.00	5.20	A4361	18.00	16.99
A0426	449.94	0.00	A4281	0.00	0.00	A4362	5.00	3.20
A0427	485.04	0.00	A4282	0.00	0.00	A4364	3.00	2.71
A0428	324.94	0.00	A4283	0.00	0.00	A4365	15.38	10.47
A0429	344.03	0.00	A4284	0.00	0.00	A4367	12.00	6.80
A0430	1200.00	0.00	A4285	0.00	0.00	A4368	0.83	0.24
A0431	3960.00	0.00	A4286	0.00	0.00	A4369	3.60	2.24
A0432	450.00	0.00	A4290	7.70	122.34	A4370	8.68	3.18
A0433	510.00	0.00	A4300	20.00	0.00	A4371	5.64	3.38
A0434	890.60	0.00	A4301	20.00	0.00	A4372	5.65	3.87
A0435	20.00	0.00	A4305	24.00	0.00	A4373	9.75	5.81
A0436	50.00	0.00	A4306	21.88	0.00	A4374	12.30	7.81
A0888	8.50	0.00	A4310	7.95	7.14	A4375	8.00	15.89
A0999	0.00	0.00	A4311	20.00	13.73	A4376	53.30	44.01
A4206	0.49	0.00	A4312	12.28	16.69	A4377	4.80	3.97
A4207	1.00	0.00	A4313	25.00	17.13	A4378	9.80	28.45
A4208	0.26	0.00	A4314	27.48	23.40	A4379	14.90	13.90
A4209	0.50	0.00	A4315	29.00	24.41	A4380	5.00	34.53
A4210	0.00	0.00	A4316	32.29	26.27	A4381	6.60	4.27
A4211	1.10	0.00	A4319	8.63	5.86	A4382	25.20	22.78
A4212	11.00	0.00	A4320	6.05	4.93	A4383	8.50	26.08
A4213	1.41	0.00	A4321	1.90	0.00	A4384	9.20	8.90
A4214	2.42	1.62	A4322	2.85	2.81	A4385	7.02	4.72
A4215	0.50	0.00	A4323	9.00	8.12	A4386	9.16	6.22
A4220	58.70	0.00	A4324	2.75	2.01	A4387	3.90	0.00
A4221	7.60	20.94	A4325	2.00	1.67	A4388	6.06	4.04

APPENDIX 8 — MEDICARE NATIONAL AVERAGE PAYMENT

CODE	COMMERCIAL	MEDICARE	CODE	COMMERCIAL	MEDICARE	CODE	COMMERCIAL	MEDICARE
A4389	8.90	5.76	A4562	49.00	49.53	A4709	10.30	0.00
A4390	12.70	8.89	A4565	14.00	0.00	A4712	1.48	0.00
A4391	9.80	0.00	A4570	25.01	0.00	A4714	0.00	0.00
A4392	10.80	0.00	A4572	18.00	0.00	A4719	10.60	0.00
A4393	12.80	0.00	A4575	550.00	0.00	A4720	0.00	0.00
A4394	3.21	2.39	A4580	40.00	0.00	A4721	27.40	0.00
A4395	0.09	0.05	A4590	44.98	0.00	A4722	29.90	0.00
A4396	7.47	37.45	A4595	19.95	26.65	A4723	32.70	0.00
A4397	6.05	4.43	A4606	1.60	0.00	A4724	3.60	0.00
A4398	5.89	12.78	A4608	0.00	53.79	A4725	29.30	0.00
A4399	17.95	11.34	A4609	0.00	0.00	A4726	35.20	0.00
A4400	42.85	45.21	A4610	0.00	0.00	A4730	2.00	0.00
A4402	0.53	1.48	A4611	0.00	0.00	A4735	2.10	0.00
A4404	2.51	1.57	A4612	0.00	0.00	A4736	0.00	0.00
A4405	0.00	3.15	A4613 UE	0.00	96.47	A4737	0.00	0.00
A4406	7.72	5.31	A4613 RR	0.00	13.35	A4740	0.00	0.00
A4407	10.63	8.11	A4613 NU	0.00	133.40	A4750	18.00	0.00
A4408	0.00	9.13	A4614	30.00	22.00	A4755	17.00	0.00
A4409	10.53	5.76	A4615	2.75	0.00	A4760	0.00	0.00
A4410	0.00	8.36	A4616	1.00	0.00	A4765	8.00	0.00
A4413	0.00	5.09	A4617	10.00	0.00	A4766	4.00	0.00
A4414	5.80	4.56	A4618	11.50	0.00	A4770	10.00	0.00
A4415	0.00	5.55	A4619	1.03	1.12	A4771	0.00	0.00
A4421	1.00	0.00	A4620	5.00	0.00	A4772	41.55	0.00
A4422	0.00	0.11	A4621	6.50	1.29	A4773	17.00	0.00
A4450	0.30	0.09	A4622	74.98	52.98	A4774	0.00	0.00
A4452	0.40	0.34	A4623	8.25	6.06	A4780	0.00	0.00
A4454	3.00	2.42	A4624	3.00	0.00	A4790	0.00	0.00
A4455	1.44	1.33	A4625	8.60	6.41	A4800	10.00	0.00
A4458	0.00	0.00	A4626	2.38	2.95	A4801	5.75	0.00
A4460	6.00	1.10	A4627	28.00	0.00	A4802	0.00	0.00
A4462	12.50	3.05	A4628	1.19	0.00	A4820	85.80	0.00
A4464	22.00	0.00	A4629	5.75	4.29	A4850	0.00	0.00
A4465	18.00	0.00	A4630	5.25	0.00	A4860	5.90	0.00
A4470	0.00	0.00	A4631	120.03	0.00	A4870	0.00	0.00
A4480	7.00	0.00	A4632	0.00	0.00	A4880	0.00	0.00
A4481	0.40	0.35	A4633	0.00	0.00	A4890	0.00	0.00
A4483 UE	0.00	0.00	A4634	0.00	0.00	A4900	1490.90	0.00
A4483 RR	0.00	0.00	A4635	8.48	0.00	A4901	275.00	0.00
A4483 NU	0.00	0.00	A4636	4.24	0.00	A4905	0.00	0.00
A4490	13.40	0.00	A4637	2.93	0.00	A4910	3.50	0.00
A4495	13.13	0.00	A4639	0.00	0.00	A4911	12.50	0.00
A4500	10.00	0.00	A4640	55.13	0.00	A4912	8.23	0.00
A4510	25.00	0.00	A4641	0.00	0.00	A4913	0.00	0.00
A4521	0.00	0.00	A4642	60.00	0.00	A4914	24.99	0.00
A4522	0.00	0.00	A4643	13.00	0.00	A4918	0.00	0.00
A4523	0.00	0.00	A4644	1.30	0.00	A4919	0.00	0.00
A4524	0.00	0.00	A4645	2.60	0.00	A4920	0.00	0.00
A4525	0.00	0.00	A4646	1.60	0.00	A4921	0.70	0.00
A4526	0.00	0.00	A4647	150.03	0.00	A4927	5.00	0.00
A4527	1.34	0.00	A4649	0.00	0.00	A4928	0.40	0.00
A4528	0.00	0.00	A4650	46.50	0.00	A4929	0.28	0.00
A4529	0.00	0.00	A4651	1.70	0.00	A4930	0.00	0.00
A4530	1.00	0.00	A4652	2.90	0.00	A4931	0.00	0.00
A4531	1.00	0.00	A4653	0.00	0.00	A4932	0.00	0.00
A4532	0.00	0.00	A4655	7.40	0.00	A5051	2.99	0.00
A4533	0.00	0.00	A4656	1.30	0.00	A5052	2.27	0.00
A4534	0.00	0.00	A4657	0.50	0.00	A5053	2.29	1.61
A4535	0.00	0.00	A4660	18.65	0.00	A5054	2.10	0.00
A4536	0.00	0.00	A4663	25.00	0.00	A5055	2.46	1.33
A4537	0.00	0.00	A4670	93.12	0.00	A5061	4.89	0.00
A4538	0.00	0.00	A4680	0.00	0.00	A5062	3.12	2.06
A4550	45.01	0.00	A4690	0.00	0.00	A5063	3.40	0.00
A4554	2.03	0.00	A4700	12.90	0.00	A5064	0.00	0.00
A4556	10.00	11.23	A4705	14.27	0.00	A5071	7.61	0.00
A4557	17.50	19.52	A4706	18.90	0.00	A5072	4.45	3.26
A4558	7.00	5.04	A4707	4.80	0.00	A5073	4.83	0.00
A4561	39.99	19.91	A4708	0.00	0.00	A5074	5.09	0.00

CODE	COMMERCIAL	MEDICARE	CODE	COMMERCIAL	MEDICARE	CODE	COMMERCIAL	MEDICARE
A5075	4.51	0.00	A6230	0.00	0.00	A7001	38.13	0.00
A5081	4.04	3.06	A6231	4.60	4.33	A7002	4.50	0.00
A5082	15.30	11.00	A6232	8.50	6.37	A7003	4.00	0.00
A5093	4.02	1.81	A6233	0.00	17.75	A7004	2.00	0.00
A5102	5.00	20.89	A6234	7.00	6.05	A7005	38.01	0.00
A5105	46.17	37.71	A6235	12.25	15.56	A7006	10.01	0.00
A5112	5.50	32.03	A6236	29.40	25.21	A7007	6.33	0.00
A5113	4.60	4.35	A6237	9.40	7.32	A7008	13.00	0.00
A5114	8.52	8.27	A6238	22.67	21.08	A7009	0.00	0.00
A5119	12.88	10.04	A6239	0.00	0.00	A7010	26.99	0.00
A5121	7.05	6.90	A6240	14.50	11.32	A7011	24.99	0.00
A5122	14.60	11.89	A6241	0.00	2.38	A7012	5.18	0.00
A5123	7.21	5.25	A6242	7.64	5.62	A7013	1.00	0.00
A5126	1.59	1.22	A6243	0.00	11.39	A7014	0.00	0.00
A5131	19.74	14.67	A6244	0.00	36.34	A7015	3.00	0.00
A5200	15.50	10.46	A6245	7.10	6.73	A7016	7.18	0.00
A5500	78.50	0.00	A6246	0.00	9.18	A7017	2.70	0.00
A5501	252.50	0.00	A6247	0.00	22.00	A7018	0.75	0.35
A5502	42.00	0.00	A6248	16.76	15.02	A7019	0.24	0.32
A5503	50.00	0.00	A6250	0.30	0.00	A7020	5.90	2.55
A5504	38.00	0.00	A6251	2.17	1.84	A7025	0.00	0.00
A5505	36.10	0.00	A6252	3.10	3.01	A7026	0.00	0.00
A5506	0.00	0.00	A6253	7.24	5.87	A7030	0.00	0.00
A5507	41.00	0.00	A6254	2.30	1.12	A7031	0.00	0.00
A5508	50.00	0.00	A6255	3.10	2.81	A7032	0.00	0.00
A5509	38.40	0.00	A6256	7.00	0.00	A7033	0.00	0.00
A5510	35.00	0.00	A6257	2.00	1.42	A7034	148.00	0.00
A5511	40.00	0.00	A6258	4.92	3.98	A7035	60.00	0.00
A6000	0.00	0.00	A6259	11.00	10.12	A7036	0.00	0.00
A6010	0.00	28.64	A6260	1.00	0.00	A7037	0.00	0.00
A6011	0.00	2.11	A6261	3.63	0.00	A7038	6.80	0.00
A6021	23.00	19.45	A6262	2.14	0.00	A7039	0.00	0.00
A6022	32.90	19.45	A6263	0.35	0.27	A7042	0.00	178.59
A6023	0.00	176.03	A6264	0.63	0.46	A7043	0.00	25.57
A6024	16.00	5.73	A6265	0.20	0.11	A7044	0.00	0.00
A6025	25.01	0.00	A6266	1.90	1.78	A7501	0.00	97.16
A6154	14.22	13.30	A6402	0.42	0.11	A7502	0.00	46.17
A6196	9.26	6.80	A6403	1.00	0.40	A7503	5.40	10.48
A6197	17.25	15.21	A6404	0.63	0.00	A7504	1.10	0.62
A6198	0.00	0.00	A6405	0.49	0.31	A7505	6.00	4.33
A6199	6.00	4.90	A6406	0.95	0.74	A7506	0.30	0.31
A6200	0.86	8.79	A6410	0.00	0.36	A7507	6.00	2.31
A6201	0.00	19.24	A6411	0.00	0.00	A7508	2.90	2.66
A6202	1.10	32.27	A6412	0.00	0.00	A7509	0.00	1.31
A6203	3.46	3.10	A6421	0.00	0.00	A9150	0.00	0.00
A6204	7.13	5.77	A6422	0.00	0.00	A9160	0.00	0.00
A6205	20.00	0.00	A6424	0.00	0.00	A9170	0.00	0.00
A6206	8.00	0.00	A6426	0.00	0.00	A9190	0.00	0.00
A6207	8.34	6.79	A6428	0.00	0.00	A9270	0.00	0.00
A6208	4.60	0.00	A6430	0.00	0.00	A9300	0.00	0.00
A6209	7.40	6.92	A6432	0.00	0.00	A9500	125.00	0.00
A6210	23.20	18.43	A6434	0.00	0.00	A9502	140.00	0.00
A6211	44.75	27.17	A6436	0.00	0.00	A9503	35.00	0.00
A6212	10.00	8.98	A6438	0.00	0.00	A9504	0.00	0.00
A6213	23.00	0.00	A6440	0.00	10.53	A9505	72.00	0.00
A6214	12.55	9.52	A6501	0.00	0.00	A9507	2175.00	0.00
A6215	0.00	0.00	A6502	0.00	0.00	A9508	23.00	0.00
A6216	0.25	0.05	A6503	0.00	0.00	A9510	100.00	0.00
A6217	0.50	0.00	A6504	0.00	0.00	A9511	0.00	0.00
A6218	0.76	0.00	A6505	0.00	0.00	A9512	0.00	0.00
A6219	0.94	0.88	A6506	0.00	0.00	A9513	0.00	0.00
A6220	3.04	2.39	A6507	0.00	0.00	A9514	0.00	0.00
A6221	0.70	0.00	A6508	0.00	0.00	A9515	0.00	0.00
A6222	1.06	1.97	A6509	0.00	0.00	A9516	0.00	0.00
A6223	2.85	2.24	A6510	0.00	0.00	A9517	0.00	0.00
A6224	3.69	3.34	A6511	0.00	0.00	A9518	0.00	0.00
A6228	0.00	0.00	A6512	0.00	0.00	A9519	0.00	0.00
A6229	2.00	3.34	A7000	11.90	0.00	A9520	0.00	0.00

CODE		COMMERCIAL	MEDICARE	CODE	COMMERCIAL	MEDICARE	CODE	COMMERCIAL	MEDICARE
A9521		0.00	0.00	C1010	0.00	0.00	C1096	0.00	0.00
A9522		0.00	0.00	C1011	0.00	0.00	C1097	104.00	0.00
A9523		0.00	0.00	C1012	0.00	0.00	C1098	86.00	0.00
A9524		0.00	0.00	C1013	0.00	0.00	C1099	70.00	0.00
A9600		0.00	0.00	C1014	0.00	0.00	C1100	0.00	0.00
A9603		0.00	0.00	C1015	0.00	0.00	C1101	0.00	0.00
A9605		0.00	0.00	C1016	0.00	0.00	C1102	0.00	0.00
A9699		0.00	0.00	C1017	0.00	0.00	C1103	0.00	0.00
A9700		186.60	0.00	C1018	0.00	0.00	C1104	0.00	0.00
A9900		0.00	0.00	C1019	0.00	0.00	C1105	0.00	0.00
A9901		20.00	0.00	C1020	0.00	0.00	C1106	0.00	0.00
B4034		7.00	0.00	C1021	0.00	0.00	C1107	0.00	0.00
B4035		13.30	0.00	C1022	0.00	0.00	C1109	0.00	0.00
B4036		11.00	0.00	C1024	0.00	0.00	C1110	0.00	0.00
B4081		36.39	0.00	C1025	0.00	0.00	C1111	0.00	0.00
B4082		19.16	0.00	C1026	0.00	0.00	C1112	0.00	0.00
B4083		5.81	0.00	C1027	0.00	0.00	C1113	0.00	0.00
B4084		20.99	0.00	C1028	0.00	0.00	C1114	0.00	0.00
B4085		24.90	0.00	C1029	0.00	0.00	C1115	0.00	0.00
B4086		28.70	0.00	C1030	0.00	0.00	C1116	0.00	0.00
B4100		0.00	0.00	C1033	0.00	0.00	C1117	0.00	0.00
B4150		2.06	0.00	C1034	0.00	0.00	C1118	0.00	0.00
B4151		1.84	0.00	C1035	0.00	0.00	C1119	0.00	0.00
B4152		1.52	0.00	C1036	0.00	0.00	C1120	0.00	0.00
B4153		7.31	0.00	C1037	0.00	0.00	C1121	0.00	0.00
B4154		8.76	0.00	C1038	0.00	0.00	C1122	0.00	0.00
B4155		18.25	0.00	C1039	0.00	0.00	C1123	0.00	0.00
B4156		8.15	0.00	C1040	0.00	0.00	C1124	0.00	0.00
B4164		30.53	0.00	C1042	0.00	0.00	C1125	0.00	0.00
B4168		57.86	0.00	C1043	0.00	0.00	C1126	0.00	0.00
B4172		0.00	0.00	C1047	0.00	0.00	C1127	0.00	0.00
B4176		0.00	0.00	C1048	0.00	0.00	C1128	0.00	0.00
B4178		182.10	0.00	C1050	0.00	0.00	C1129	0.00	0.00
B4180		47.65	0.00	C1051	0.00	0.00	C1130	0.00	0.00
B4184		118.97	0.00	C1053	0.00	0.00	C1131	0.00	0.00
B4186		125.85	0.00	C1054	0.00	0.00	C1132	0.00	0.00
B4189		180.04	0.00	C1055	0.00	0.00	C1133	0.00	0.00
B4193		203.72	0.00	C1056	0.00	0.00	C1134	0.00	0.00
B4197		248.01	0.00	C1057	0.00	0.00	C1135	0.00	0.00
B4199		292.99	0.00	C1058	47.50	0.00	C1136	0.00	0.00
B4216		20.90	0.00	C1059	0.00	0.00	C1137	0.00	0.00
B4220		10.50	0.00	C1060	0.00	0.00	C1143	0.00	0.00
B4222		10.10	0.00	C1061	0.00	0.00	C1144	0.00	0.00
B4224		33.51	0.00	C1063	0.00	0.00	C1145	0.00	0.00
B5000		120.02	0.00	C1064	89.90	0.00	C1147	0.00	0.00
B5100		182.73	0.00	C1065	0.00	0.00	C1148	0.00	0.00
B5200		430.00	0.00	C1066	0.00	0.00	C1149	0.00	0.00
B9000	UE	0.00	0.00	C1067	0.00	0.00	C1151	0.00	0.00
B9000	RR	102.98	0.00	C1068	0.00	0.00	C1152	0.00	0.00
B9000	NU	0.00	0.00	C1069	0.00	0.00	C1153	0.00	0.00
B9002	RR	135.81	0.00	C1071	0.00	0.00	C1154	0.00	0.00
B9002	NU	0.00	0.00	C1072	0.00	0.00	C1155	0.00	0.00
B9004	UE	60.00	0.00	C1073	0.00	0.00	C1156	0.00	0.00
B9004	RR	30.00	0.00	C1074	0.00	0.00	C1157	0.00	0.00
B9004	NU	0.00	0.00	C1075	0.00	0.00	C1158	0.00	0.00
B9006	UE	0.00	0.00	C1076	0.00	0.00	C1159	0.00	0.00
B9006	RR	21.80	0.00	C1077	0.00	0.00	C1160	0.00	0.00
B9006	NU	0.00	0.00	C1078	0.00	0.00	C1161	0.00	0.00
B9998		0.00	0.00	C1079	0.00	0.00	C1162	0.00	0.00
B9999		0.00	0.00	C1084	0.00	0.00	C1163	0.00	0.00
C1000		0.00	0.00	C1086	0.00	0.00	C1164	0.00	0.00
C1001		0.00	0.00	C1087	1.00	0.00	C1166	0.00	0.00
C1003		0.00	0.00	C1088	0.00	0.00	C1167	27.00	0.00
C1004		0.00	0.00	C1090	0.00	0.00	C1171	0.00	0.00
C1006		0.00	0.00	C1091	0.00	0.00	C1172	0.00	0.00
C1007		0.00	0.00	C1092	0.00	0.00	C1173	0.00	0.00
C1008		0.00	0.00	C1094	69.10	0.00	C1174	0.00	0.00
C1009		0.00	0.00	C1095	0.00	0.00	C1178	0.00	0.00

CODE	COMMERCIAL	MEDICARE	CODE	COMMERCIAL	MEDICARE	CODE	COMMERCIAL	MEDICARE
C1180	0.00	0.00	C1700	0.00	0.00	C1785	0.00	0.00
C1181	0.00	0.00	C1701	0.00	0.00	C1786	0.00	0.00
C1182	0.00	0.00	C1702	0.00	0.00	C1787	0.00	0.00
C1183	0.00	0.00	C1703	0.00	0.00	C1788	835.00	0.00
C1184	0.00	0.00	C1704	0.00	0.00	C1789	0.00	0.00
C1188	0.80	0.00	C1705	0.00	0.00	C1790	0.00	0.00
C1200	0.00	0.00	C1706	18.00	0.00	C1791	0.00	0.00
C1201	0.00	0.00	C1707	0.00	0.00	C1792	0.00	0.00
C1202	88.00	0.00	C1708	0.00	0.00	C1793	0.00	0.00
C1203	0.00	0.00	C1709	0.00	0.00	C1794	0.00	0.00
C1205	0.00	0.00	C1710	0.00	0.00	C1795	0.00	0.00
C1207	0.00	0.00	C1711	0.00	0.00	C1796	0.00	0.00
C1300	206.00	0.00	C1712	0.00	0.00	C1797	0.00	0.00
C1302	0.00	0.00	C1713	497.00	0.00	C1798	0.00	0.00
C1303	0.00	0.00	C1714	0.00	0.00	C1799	0.00	0.00
C1304	0.00	0.00	C1715	63.50	0.00	C1800	0.00	0.00
C1305	0.00	0.00	C1716	0.00	0.00	C1801	0.00	0.00
C1306	0.00	0.00	C1717	0.00	0.00	C1802	0.00	0.00
C1311	0.00	0.00	C1718	159.00	0.00	C1803	0.00	0.00
C1312	0.00	0.00	C1719	0.00	0.00	C1804	0.00	0.00
C1313	0.00	0.00	C1720	336.00	0.00	C1805	0.00	0.00
C1314	0.00	0.00	C1721	0.00	0.00	C1806	0.00	0.00
C1315	0.00	0.00	C1722	0.00	0.00	C1810	0.00	0.00
C1316	0.00	0.00	C1723	0.00	0.00	C1811	0.00	0.00
C1317	0.00	0.00	C1724	0.00	0.00	C1812	0.00	0.00
C1318	0.00	0.00	C1725	844.00	0.00	C1813	0.00	0.00
C1319	0.00	0.00	C1726	0.00	0.00	C1814	0.00	0.00
C1320	0.00	0.00	C1727	0.00	0.00	C1815	0.00	0.00
C1325	0.00	0.00	C1728	0.00	0.00	C1816	0.00	0.00
C1326	0.00	0.00	C1729	11.80	0.00	C1817	0.00	0.00
C1328	0.00	0.00	C1730	425.50	0.00	C1850	0.00	0.00
C1333	0.00	0.00	C1731	0.00	0.00	C1851	0.00	0.00
C1334	0.00	0.00	C1732	0.00	0.00	C1852	0.00	0.00
C1335	0.00	0.00	C1733	0.00	0.00	C1853	0.00	0.00
C1336	0.00	0.00	C1750	0.00	0.00	C1854	0.00	0.00
C1337	0.00	0.00	C1751	23.70	0.00	C1855	0.00	0.00
C1348	99.60	0.00	C1752	0.00	0.00	C1856	0.00	0.00
C1350	0.00	0.00	C1753	0.00	0.00	C1857	0.00	0.00
C1351	0.00	0.00	C1754	0.00	0.00	C1858	0.00	0.00
C1352	0.00	0.00	C1755	0.00	0.00	C1859	0.00	0.00
C1353	0.00	0.00	C1756	0.00	0.00	C1860	0.00	0.00
C1354	0.00	0.00	C1757	0.00	0.00	C1861	0.00	0.00
C1355	0.00	0.00	C1758	86.90	0.00	C1862	0.00	0.00
C1356	0.00	0.00	C1759	0.00	0.00	C1863	0.00	0.00
C1357	0.00	0.00	C1760	648.00	0.00	C1864	0.00	0.00
C1358	0.00	0.00	C1762	0.00	0.00	C1865	0.00	0.00
C1359	0.00	0.00	C1763	0.00	0.00	C1866	0.00	0.00
C1361	0.00	0.00	C1764	0.00	0.00	C1867	0.00	0.00
C1362	0.00	0.00	C1765	0.00	0.00	C1868	0.00	0.00
C1363	0.00	0.00	C1766	0.00	0.00	C1869	0.00	0.00
C1364	0.00	0.00	C1767	0.00	0.00	C1870	0.00	0.00
C1365	0.00	0.00	C1768	0.00	0.00	C1871	0.00	0.00
C1366	0.00	0.00	C1769	149.00	0.00	C1872	0.00	0.00
C1367	0.00	0.00	C1770	0.00	0.00	C1873	0.00	0.00
C1369	0.00	0.00	C1771	0.00	0.00	C1874	0.00	0.00
C1370	0.00	0.00	C1772	0.00	0.00	C1875	0.00	0.00
C1371	0.00	0.00	C1773	0.00	0.00	C1876	3337.10	0.00
C1372	0.00	0.00	C1774	16.00	0.00	C1877	0.00	0.00
C1375	0.00	0.00	C1775	0.00	0.00	C1878	0.00	0.00
C1376	0.00	0.00	C1776	0.00	0.00	C1879	0.00	0.00
C1377	0.00	0.00	C1777	0.00	0.00	C1880	0.00	0.00
C1378	0.00	0.00	C1778	0.00	0.00	C1881	0.00	0.00
C1379	0.00	0.00	C1779	0.00	0.00	C1882	0.00	0.00
C1420	0.00	0.00	C1780	0.00	0.00	C1883	0.00	0.00
C1421	0.00	0.00	C1781	408.80	0.00	C1884	0.00	0.00
C1450	0.00	0.00	C1782	0.00	0.00	C1885	0.00	0.00
C1451	0.00	0.00	C1783	0.00	0.00	C1887	145.50	0.00
C1500	0.00	0.00	C1784	0.00	0.00	C1888	0.00	0.00

CODE	COMMERCIAL	MEDICARE	CODE	COMMERCIAL	MEDICARE	CODE	COMMERCIAL	MEDICARE
C1891	0.00	0.00	C2597	0.00	0.00	C4004	0.00	0.00
C1892	0.00	0.00	C2598	0.00	0.00	C4005	0.00	0.00
C1893	0.00	0.00	C2599	0.00	0.00	C4006	0.00	0.00
C1894	53.30	0.00	C2601	0.00	0.00	C4007	0.00	0.00
C1895	0.00	0.00	C2602	0.00	0.00	C4008	0.00	0.00
C1896	0.00	0.00	C2603	0.00	0.00	C4009	0.00	0.00
C1897	0.00	0.00	C2604	0.00	0.00	C4300	0.00	0.00
C1898	0.00	0.00	C2605	0.00	0.00	C4301	0.00	0.00
C1899	0.00	0.00	C2606	0.00	0.00	C4302	0.00	0.00
C1900	0.00	0.00	C2607	0.00	0.00	C4303	0.00	0.00
C1929	0.00	0.00	C2608	0.00	0.00	C4304	0.00	0.00
C1930	0.00	0.00	C2609	0.00	0.00	C4305	0.00	0.00
C1931	0.00	0.00	C2610	0.00	0.00	C4306	0.00	0.00
C1932	0.00	0.00	C2611	0.00	0.00	C4307	0.00	0.00
C1933	0.00	0.00	C2612	0.00	0.00	C4308	0.00	0.00
C1934	0.00	0.00	C2614	0.00	0.00	C4309	0.00	0.00
C1935	0.00	0.00	C2615	0.00	0.00	C4310	0.00	0.00
C1936	0.00	0.00	C2616	0.00	0.00	C4311	0.00	0.00
C1937	0.00	0.00	C2617	406.10	0.00	C4312	0.00	0.00
C1938	0.00	0.00	C2618	0.00	0.00	C4313	0.00	0.00
C1939	0.00	0.00	C2619	0.00	0.00	C4314	0.00	0.00
C1940	0.00	0.00	C2620	0.00	0.00	C4315	0.00	0.00
C1941	0.00	0.00	C2621	0.00	0.00	C4316	0.00	0.00
C1942	0.00	0.00	C2622	0.00	0.00	C4317	0.00	0.00
C1943	0.00	0.00	C2625	0.00	0.00	C4600	0.00	0.00
C1944	0.00	0.00	C2626	0.00	0.00	C4601	0.00	0.00
C1945	0.00	0.00	C2627	0.00	0.00	C4602	0.00	0.00
C1946	0.00	0.00	C2628	0.00	0.00	C4603	0.00	0.00
C1947	0.00	0.00	C2629	0.00	0.00	C4604	0.00	0.00
C1948	0.00	0.00	C2630	0.00	0.00	C4605	0.00	0.00
C1949	0.00	0.00	C2631	0.00	0.00	C4606	0.00	0.00
C1979	0.00	0.00	C2632	0.00	0.00	C4607	0.00	0.00
C1980	0.00	0.00	C2676	0.00	0.00	C5000	0.00	0.00
C1981	0.00	0.00	C2700	0.00	0.00	C5001	0.00	0.00
C2000	0.00	0.00	C2701	0.00	0.00	C5002	0.00	0.00
C2001	0.00	0.00	C2702	0.00	0.00	C5003	0.00	0.00
C2002	0.00	0.00	C2703	0.00	0.00	C5004	0.00	0.00
C2003	0.00	0.00	C2704	0.00	0.00	C5005	0.00	0.00
C2004	0.00	0.00	C2801	0.00	0.00	C5006	0.00	0.00
C2005	0.00	0.00	C2802	0.00	0.00	C5007	0.00	0.00
C2006	0.00	0.00	C2803	0.00	0.00	C5008	0.00	0.00
C2007	0.00	0.00	C2804	0.00	0.00	C5009	0.00	0.00
C2008	0.00	0.00	C2805	0.00	0.00	C5010	0.00	0.00
C2009	0.00	0.00	C2806	0.00	0.00	C5011	0.00	0.00
C2010	0.00	0.00	C2807	0.00	0.00	C5012	0.00	0.00
C2011	0.00	0.00	C2808	0.00	0.00	C5013	0.00	0.00
C2012	0.00	0.00	C3001	0.00	0.00	C5014	0.00	0.00
C2013	0.00	0.00	C3002	0.00	0.00	C5015	0.00	0.00
C2014	0.00	0.00	C3003	0.00	0.00	C5016	0.00	0.00
C2015	0.00	0.00	C3004	0.00	0.00	C5017	0.00	0.00
C2016	0.00	0.00	C3400	0.00	0.00	C5018	0.00	0.00
C2017	0.00	0.00	C3401	0.00	0.00	C5019	0.00	0.00
C2018	0.00	0.00	C3500	0.00	0.00	C5020	0.00	0.00
C2019	0.00	0.00	C3510	0.00	0.00	C5021	0.00	0.00
C2020	0.00	0.00	C3551	0.00	0.00	C5022	0.00	0.00
C2021	0.00	0.00	C3552	0.00	0.00	C5023	0.00	0.00
C2022	0.00	0.00	C3553	0.00	0.00	C5024	0.00	0.00
C2023	0.00	0.00	C3554	0.00	0.00	C5025	0.00	0.00
C2100	0.00	0.00	C3555	0.00	0.00	C5026	0.00	0.00
C2101	0.00	0.00	C3556	0.00	0.00	C5027	0.00	0.00
C2102	0.00	0.00	C3557	0.00	0.00	C5028	0.00	0.00
C2103	0.00	0.00	C3800	0.00	0.00	C5029	0.00	0.00
C2104	0.00	0.00	C3801	0.00	0.00	C5030	0.00	0.00
C2151	0.00	0.00	C3851	0.00	0.00	C5031	0.00	0.00
C2152	0.00	0.00	C4000	0.00	0.00	C5032	0.00	0.00
C2153	0.00	0.00	C4001	0.00	0.00	C5033	0.00	0.00
C2200	0.00	0.00	C4002	0.00	0.00	C5034	0.00	0.00
C2300	0.00	0.00	C4003	0.00	0.00	C5035	0.00	0.00

CODE	COMMERCIAL	MEDICARE	CODE	COMMERCIAL	MEDICARE	CODE	COMMERCIAL	MEDICARE
C5036	0.00	0.00	C6056	0.00	0.00	C8551	0.00	0.00
C5037	0.00	0.00	C6057	0.00	0.00	C8552	0.00	0.00
C5038	0.00	0.00	C6058	0.00	0.00	C8597	0.00	0.00
C5039	0.00	0.00	C6080	0.00	0.00	C8598	0.00	0.00
C5040	0.00	0.00	C6200	0.00	0.00	C8599	0.00	0.00
C5041	0.00	0.00	C6201	0.00	0.00	C8600	0.00	0.00
C5042	0.00	0.00	C6202	0.00	0.00	C8650	0.00	0.00
C5043	0.00	0.00	C6203	0.00	0.00	C8724	0.00	0.00
C5044	0.00	0.00	C6204	0.00	0.00	C8725	0.00	0.00
C5045	0.00	0.00	C6205	0.00	0.00	C8748	0.00	0.00
C5046	0.00	0.00	C6206	0.00	0.00	C8749	0.00	0.00
C5047	0.00	0.00	C6207	0.00	0.00	C8750	0.00	0.00
C5048	0.00	0.00	C6208	0.00	0.00	C8775	0.00	0.00
C5130	0.00	0.00	C6209	0.00	0.00	C8776	0.00	0.00
C5131	0.00	0.00	C6210	0.00	0.00	C8777	0.00	0.00
C5132	0.00	0.00	C6300	0.00	0.00	C8800	0.00	0.00
C5133	0.00	0.00	C6500	0.00	0.00	C8801	0.00	0.00
C5134	0.00	0.00	C6501	0.00	0.00	C8802	0.00	0.00
C5279	0.00	0.00	C6502	0.00	0.00	C8830	0.00	0.00
C5280	0.00	0.00	C6525	0.00	0.00	C8890	0.00	0.00
C5281	0.00	0.00	C6600	0.00	0.00	C8891	0.00	0.00
C5282	0.00	0.00	C6650	0.00	0.00	C8900	0.00	0.00
C5283	0.00	0.00	C6651	0.00	0.00	C8901	0.00	0.00
C5284	0.00	0.00	C6652	0.00	0.00	C8902	0.00	0.00
C5600	0.00	0.00	C6700	0.00	0.00	C8903	0.00	0.00
C5601	0.00	0.00	C8099	0.00	0.00	C8904	0.00	0.00
C6001	0.00	0.00	C8100	0.00	0.00	C8905	0.00	0.00
C6002	0.00	0.00	C8102	0.00	0.00	C8906	0.00	0.00
C6003	0.00	0.00	C8500	0.00	0.00	C8907	0.00	0.00
C6004	66.90	0.00	C8501	0.00	0.00	C8908	0.00	0.00
C6005	23.90	0.00	C8502	0.00	0.00	C8909	0.00	0.00
C6006	0.00	0.00	C8503	0.00	0.00	C8910	0.00	0.00
C6012	0.00	0.00	C8504	0.00	0.00	C8911	0.00	0.00
C6013	0.00	0.00	C8505	0.00	0.00	C8912	0.00	0.00
C6014	0.00	0.00	C8506	0.00	0.00	C8913	0.00	0.00
C6015	0.00	0.00	C8507	0.00	0.00	C8914	0.00	0.00
C6016	0.00	0.00	C8508	0.00	0.00	C9000	0.00	0.00
C6017	0.00	0.00	C8509	0.00	0.00	C9001	0.00	0.00
C6018	0.00	0.00	C8510	0.00	0.00	C9002	0.00	0.00
C6019	0.00	0.00	C8511	0.00	0.00	C9003	856.00	0.00
C6020	0.00	0.00	C8512	0.00	0.00	C9004	0.00	0.00
C6021	0.00	0.00	C8513	0.00	0.00	C9005	0.00	0.00
C6022	0.00	0.00	C8514	0.00	0.00	C9006	0.00	0.00
C6023	0.00	0.00	C8516	0.00	0.00	C9007	0.00	0.00
C6024	0.00	0.00	C8518	0.00	0.00	C9008	0.00	0.00
C6025	0.00	0.00	C8519	0.00	0.00	C9009	0.00	0.00
C6026	0.00	0.00	C8520	0.00	0.00	C9010	90.70	0.00
C6027	0.00	0.00	C8521	0.00	0.00	C9011	0.00	0.00
C6028	0.00	0.00	C8522	0.00	0.00	C9012	0.00	0.00
C6029	0.00	0.00	C8523	0.00	0.00	C9013	0.00	0.00
C6030	0.00	0.00	C8524	0.00	0.00	C9017	0.00	0.00
C6031	0.00	0.00	C8525	0.00	0.00	C9018	9.20	0.00
C6032	0.00	0.00	C8526	0.00	0.00	C9019	619.50	0.00
C6033	0.00	0.00	C8528	0.00	0.00	C9020	7.60	0.00
C6034	0.00	0.00	C8529	0.00	0.00	C9100	0.00	0.00
C6035	0.00	0.00	C8530	0.00	0.00	C9102	0.00	0.00
C6036	0.00	0.00	C8531	0.00	0.00	C9103	0.00	0.00
C6037	0.00	0.00	C8532	0.00	0.00	C9104	0.00	0.00
C6038	0.00	0.00	C8533	0.00	0.00	C9105	550.00	0.00
C6039	0.00	0.00	C8534	0.00	0.00	C9106	0.00	0.00
C6040	0.00	0.00	C8535	0.00	0.00	C9107	0.00	0.00
C6041	0.00	0.00	C8536	0.00	0.00	C9108	0.00	0.00
C6050	0.00	0.00	C8539	0.00	0.00	C9109	0.00	0.00
C6051	0.00	0.00	C8540	0.00	0.00	C9110	0.00	0.00
C6052	0.00	0.00	C8541	0.00	0.00	C9111	0.00	0.00
C6053	0.00	0.00	C8542	0.00	0.00	C9112	0.00	0.00
C6054	0.00	0.00	C8543	0.00	0.00	C9113	0.00	0.00
C6055	0.00	0.00	C8550	0.00	0.00	C9114	0.00	0.00

CODE		COMMERCIAL	MEDICARE	CODE		COMMERCIAL	MEDICARE	CODE		COMMERCIAL	MEDICARE
C9115		1605.00	0.00	E0145	NU	0.00	0.00	E0177	UE	0.00	73.65
C9116		0.00	0.00	E0146	UE	0.00	0.00	E0177	RR	0.00	11.24
C9117		0.00	0.00	E0146	RR	0.00	17.61	E0177	NU	0.00	98.18
C9118		0.00	0.00	E0146	NU	0.00	0.00	E0178	UE	0.00	84.18
C9119		0.00	0.00	E0147	UE	0.00	398.80	E0178	RR	0.00	13.89
C9120		0.00	0.00	E0147	RR	0.00	53.17	E0178	NU	0.00	112.24
C9121		0.00	0.00	E0147	NU	321.48	531.70	E0179	UE	0.00	8.71
C9200		0.00	0.00	E0148	UE	0.00	88.14	E0179	RR	0.00	1.15
C9201		0.00	0.00	E0148	RR	0.00	11.77	E0179	NU	0.00	11.07
C9202		0.00	0.00	E0148	NU	149.97	117.52	E0180	UE	0.00	0.00
C9203		0.00	0.00	E0149	UE	0.00	154.84	E0180	RR	0.00	20.10
C9204		0.00	0.00	E0149	RR	39.01	20.65	E0180	NU	0.00	0.00
C9500		0.00	0.00	E0149	NU	230.05	206.46	E0181	UE	0.00	0.00
C9501		0.00	0.00	E0153	UE	0.00	48.13	E0181	RR	0.00	22.28
C9502		0.00	0.00	E0153	RR	0.00	7.25	E0181	NU	0.00	0.00
C9503		0.00	0.00	E0153	NU	88.99	64.18	E0182	UE	0.00	0.00
C9504		0.00	0.00	E0154	UE	0.00	49.55	E0182	RR	0.00	24.22
C9505		0.00	0.00	E0154	RR	12.00	7.92	E0182	NU	0.00	0.00
C9506		0.00	0.00	E0154	NU	93.99	65.22	E0184	UE	0.00	138.12
C9700		0.00	0.00	E0155	UE	0.00	22.25	E0184	RR	0.00	22.73
C9701		0.00	0.00	E0155	RR	0.00	3.56	E0184	NU	0.00	180.10
C9702		0.00	0.00	E0155	NU	39.00	29.20	E0185	UE	0.00	227.07
C9703		0.00	0.00	E0156	UE	0.00	18.36	E0185	RR	0.00	41.57
C9708		0.00	0.00	E0156	RR	0.00	3.13	E0185	NU	0.00	295.87
C9711		0.00	0.00	E0156	NU	30.00	24.45	E0186	UE	0.00	0.00
E0100	UE	0.00	15.54	E0157	UE	0.00	56.84	E0186	RR	0.00	18.78
E0100	RR	0.00	5.50	E0157	RR	0.00	8.32	E0186	NU	0.00	0.00
E0100	NU	24.67	19.49	E0157	NU	0.00	75.78	E0187	UE	0.00	0.00
E0105	UE	0.00	35.02	E0158	UE	0.00	22.47	E0187	RR	0.00	21.47
E0105	RR	0.00	8.20	E0158	RR	0.00	3.29	E0187	NU	0.00	0.00
E0105	NU	50.01	45.43	E0158	NU	37.99	29.77	E0188		64.99	0.00
E0110	UE	0.00	53.82	E0159		30.37	0.00	E0189		80.00	0.00
E0110	RR	22.50	14.79	E0160	UE	0.00	22.91	E0191	RR	0.00	0.95
E0110	NU	69.00	71.77	E0160	RR	0.00	4.01	E0191	NU	0.00	9.24
E0111	UE	0.00	38.02	E0160	NU	0.00	30.58	E0192	UE	0.00	268.49
E0111	RR	0.00	7.80	E0161	UE	0.00	18.17	E0192	RR	43.79	36.06
E0111	NU	60.00	49.27	E0161	RR	0.00	3.30	E0192	NU	0.00	357.99
E0112	UE	0.00	26.12	E0161	NU	0.00	24.27	E0193	RR	951.33	835.70
E0112	RR	0.00	9.19	E0162	UE	0.00	104.53	E0194	UE	0.00	0.00
E0112	NU	24.94	34.23	E0162	RR	0.00	14.15	E0194	RR	2700.00	3010.27
E0113	UE	0.00	14.67	E0162	NU	0.00	134.78	E0194	NU	0.00	0.00
E0113	RR	0.00	4.77	E0163	UE	0.00	78.67	E0196	UE	0.00	0.00
E0113	NU	26.01	19.55	E0163	RR	25.72	22.60	E0196	RR	48.00	30.06
E0114	UE	37.01	33.00	E0163	NU	122.65	102.02	E0196	NU	0.00	0.00
E0114	RR	15.90	7.93	E0164	UE	0.00	125.85	E0197	UE	0.00	180.04
E0114	NU	48.01	43.65	E0164	RR	0.00	24.45	E0197	RR	0.00	28.28
E0116	UE	0.00	19.32	E0164	NU	179.98	167.80	E0197	NU	0.00	204.96
E0116	RR	0.00	5.00	E0165	UE	0.00	0.00	E0198	UE	0.00	155.53
E0116	NU	31.74	25.66	E0165	RR	25.00	17.19	E0198	RR	0.00	21.23
E0117		0.00	0.00	E0165	NU	235.08	0.00	E0198	NU	0.00	204.96
E0130	UE	0.00	50.63	E0166	UE	0.00	0.00	E0199	UE	0.00	22.24
E0130	RR	0.00	15.56	E0166	RR	26.99	28.81	E0199	RR	0.00	2.95
E0130	NU	89.93	64.97	E0166	NU	0.00	0.00	E0199	NU	0.00	29.65
E0135	UE	0.00	59.50	E0167	UE	0.00	8.36	E0200	UE	0.00	55.03
E0135	RR	20.00	15.97	E0167	RR	0.00	1.17	E0200	RR	0.00	9.96
E0135	NU	89.98	77.55	E0167	NU	12.00	11.10	E0200	NU	0.00	73.34
E0141	UE	0.00	79.99	E0168	UE	0.00	104.69	E0202	RR	99.99	57.92
E0141	RR	0.00	20.69	E0168	RR	23.65	14.03	E0203		0.00	0.00
E0141	NU	0.00	106.65	E0168	NU	188.00	139.60	E0205	UE	0.00	134.63
E0142	UE	0.00	121.16	E0169	UE	0.00	0.00	E0205	RR	0.00	19.74
E0142	RR	0.00	24.45	E0169	RR	0.00	46.72	E0205	NU	0.00	179.51
E0142	NU	0.00	159.08	E0169	NU	0.00	0.00	E0210	UE	0.00	22.65
E0143	UE	0.00	83.23	E0175	UE	0.00	45.09	E0210	RR	0.00	2.84
E0143	RR	25.50	19.97	E0175	RR	0.00	6.13	E0210	NU	0.00	30.19
E0143	NU	134.98	111.22	E0175	NU	0.00	61.27	E0215	UE	0.00	49.16
E0144		101.70	0.00	E0176	UE	0.00	73.65	E0215	RR	0.00	6.86
E0145	UE	0.00	0.00	E0176	RR	0.00	13.09	E0215	NU	0.00	65.53
E0145	RR	0.00	19.20	E0176	NU	0.00	99.08	E0217	UE	0.00	344.40

CODE		COMMERCIAL	MEDICARE	CODE		COMMERCIAL	MEDICARE	CODE		COMMERCIAL	MEDICARE
E0217	RR	0.00	51.14	E0272	UE	0.00	139.72	E0372		21.70	0.00
E0217	NU	0.00	459.24	E0272	RR	0.00	19.55	E0373		0.00	0.00
E0218	UE	0.00	0.00	E0272	NU	0.00	187.19	E0424	RR	326.90	211.64
E0218	RR	0.00	0.00	E0273	UE	0.00	0.00	E0425	UE	0.00	0.00
E0218	NU	0.00	0.00	E0273	RR	0.00	0.00	E0425	NU	0.00	0.00
E0220	UE	0.00	5.86	E0273	NU	0.00	0.00	E0430	UE	0.00	0.00
E0220	RR	0.00	0.83	E0274	UE	0.00	0.00	E0430	NU	0.00	0.00
E0220	NU	0.00	7.84	E0274	RR	22.00	0.00	E0431	RR	63.99	33.27
E0221		8.30	0.00	E0274	NU	0.00	0.00	E0434	RR	0.00	33.27
E0225	UE	0.00	269.62	E0275	UE	0.00	10.62	E0435	UE	0.00	0.00
E0225	RR	0.00	35.44	E0275	RR	0.00	1.48	E0435	NU	0.00	0.00
E0225	NU	0.00	359.50	E0275	NU	0.00	14.16	E0439	RR	395.73	211.64
E0230	UE	0.00	5.87	E0276	UE	0.00	9.73	E0440	UE	0.00	0.00
E0230	RR	0.00	0.88	E0276	RR	0.00	1.45	E0440	NU	0.00	0.00
E0230	NU	0.00	7.85	E0276	NU	0.00	12.31	E0441		20.00	150.76
E0231		0.00	0.00	E0277	UE	0.00	0.00	E0442		2.00	150.76
E0232		0.00	0.00	E0277	RR	899.84	702.41	E0443		15.12	19.81
E0235	UE	0.00	0.00	E0277	NU	42.40	0.00	E0444		2.00	19.81
E0235	RR	24.99	15.97	E0280	UE	0.00	26.50	E0445		0.00	0.00
E0235	NU	0.00	0.00	E0280	RR	0.00	3.80	E0450	UE	0.00	0.00
E0236	UE	0.00	0.00	E0280	NU	0.00	35.34	E0450	RR	1183.00	882.93
E0236	RR	69.98	40.93	E0290	UE	0.00	0.00	E0450	NU	0.00	0.00
E0236	NU	0.00	0.00	E0290	RR	0.00	69.14	E0454		0.00	0.00
E0238	UE	0.00	18.39	E0290	NU	0.00	0.00	E0455	UE	0.00	0.00
E0238	RR	0.00	2.52	E0291	UE	0.00	0.00	E0455	RR	0.00	0.00
E0238	NU	0.00	25.01	E0291	RR	0.00	50.23	E0455	NU	0.00	0.00
E0239	UE	0.00	312.09	E0291	NU	0.00	0.00	E0457	UE	0.00	426.29
E0239	RR	0.00	41.62	E0292	UE	0.00	0.00	E0457	RR	0.00	56.84
E0239	NU	0.00	416.10	E0292	RR	0.00	77.74	E0457	NU	0.00	568.42
E0241		30.01	0.00	E0292	NU	0.00	0.00	E0459	UE	0.00	0.00
E0242		0.00	0.00	E0293	UE	0.00	0.00	E0459	RR	0.00	47.08
E0243		45.00	0.00	E0293	RR	0.00	66.15	E0459	NU	0.00	0.00
E0244		49.57	0.00	E0293	NU	0.00	0.00	E0460	UE	0.00	0.00
E0245		75.01	0.00	E0294	UE	0.00	0.00	E0460	RR	870.00	678.55
E0246		43.99	0.00	E0294	RR	177.00	120.85	E0460	NU	0.00	0.00
E0249	UE	0.00	69.10	E0294	NU	0.00	0.00	E0461		0.00	0.00
E0249	RR	0.00	10.13	E0295	UE	0.00	0.00	E0462	UE	0.00	0.00
E0249	NU	0.00	92.13	E0295	RR	176.06	117.80	E0462	RR	0.00	269.55
E0250	UE	0.00	0.00	E0295	NU	0.00	0.00	E0462	NU	0.00	0.00
E0250	RR	124.02	90.43	E0296	UE	0.00	0.00	E0480	UE	0.00	0.00
E0250	NU	0.00	0.00	E0296	RR	0.00	151.89	E0480	RR	56.16	40.65
E0251	UE	0.00	0.00	E0296	NU	0.00	0.00	E0480	NU	0.00	0.00
E0251	RR	0.00	68.53	E0297	UE	0.00	0.00	E0481		1255.00	0.00
E0251	NU	0.00	0.00	E0297	RR	0.00	130.12	E0482		425.00	0.00
E0255	UE	0.00	0.00	E0297	NU	0.00	0.00	E0483		0.00	0.00
E0255	RR	132.00	108.67	E0298	UE	0.00	0.00	E0484		0.00	0.00
E0255	NU	0.00	51.14	E0298	RR	0.00	0.00	E0500	UE	0.00	0.00
E0256	UE	0.00	0.00	E0298	NU	0.00	0.00	E0500	RR	125.00	101.54
E0256	RR	0.00	77.10	E0305	UE	0.00	0.00	E0500	NU	0.00	0.00
E0256	NU	0.00	0.00	E0305	RR	23.02	16.46	E0550	UE	0.00	0.00
E0260	UE	0.00	0.00	E0305	NU	0.00	0.00	E0550	RR	55.02	46.37
E0260	RR	189.92	155.34	E0310	UE	0.00	135.89	E0550	NU	449.96	0.00
E0260	NU	0.00	0.00	E0310	RR	27.01	21.06	E0555	UE	0.00	0.00
E0261	UE	0.00	0.00	E0310	NU	0.00	179.58	E0555	RR	0.00	0.00
E0261	RR	155.00	126.67	E0315		0.00	0.00	E0555	NU	7.00	0.00
E0261	NU	0.00	0.00	E0316		0.00	0.00	E0560	UE	0.00	118.99
E0265	UE	0.00	0.00	E0325	UE	0.00	6.19	E0560	RR	23.99	18.60
E0265	RR	225.06	184.89	E0325	RR	0.00	1.40	E0560	NU	0.00	158.66
E0265	NU	0.00	0.00	E0325	NU	0.00	9.35	E0565	UE	0.00	0.00
E0266	UE	0.00	0.00	E0326	UE	0.00	7.28	E0565	RR	94.99	56.44
E0266	RR	200.00	164.27	E0326	RR	0.00	1.10	E0565	NU	0.00	0.00
E0266	NU	0.00	0.00	E0326	NU	0.00	9.72	E0570	UE	60.00	0.00
E0270	UE	0.00	0.00	E0350	UE	0.00	0.00	E0570	RR	25.00	18.25
E0270	RR	0.00	0.00	E0350	RR	0.00	0.00	E0570	NU	224.98	0.00
E0270	NU	0.00	0.00	E0350	NU	0.00	0.00	E0571		50.00	0.00
E0271	UE	0.00	160.45	E0352		45.50	0.00	E0572		0.10	0.00
E0271	RR	40.01	21.33	E0370		0.00	0.00	E0574		53.30	0.00
E0271	NU	0.00	205.39	E0371		508.70	0.00	E0575	UE	0.00	0.00

CODE		COMMERCIAL	MEDICARE	CODE		COMMERCIAL	MEDICARE	CODE		COMMERCIAL	MEDICARE
E0575	RR	83.33	95.07	E0650	UE	0.00	499.65	E0753		2900.00	0.00
E0575	NU	530.19	0.00	E0650	RR	99.04	82.21	E0754		1450.00	1009.35
E0580	UE	0.00	92.98	E0650	NU	0.00	666.21	E0755		0.00	0.00
E0580	RR	0.00	12.40	E0651	UE	0.00	637.16	E0756		0.00	7095.86
E0580	NU	0.00	123.99	E0651	RR	111.96	86.79	E0757		0.00	5069.86
E0585	UE	0.00	0.00	E0651	NU	1234.13	849.54	E0758		0.00	4462.63
E0585	RR	0.00	32.44	E0652	UE	0.00	3674.59	E0759		0.00	637.11
E0585	NU	0.00	0.00	E0652	RR	570.00	484.66	E0760		29.70	0.00
E0590		6.30	0.00	E0652	NU	6002.54	4903.84	E0761		0.00	0.00
E0600	UE	0.00	0.00	E0655	UE	0.00	74.97	E0765		0.00	0.00
E0600	RR	65.02	42.36	E0655	RR	0.00	11.73	E0776	UE	0.00	97.43
E0600	NU	375.06	0.00	E0655	NU	0.00	99.83	E0776	RR	29.52	17.25
E0601	UE	0.00	0.00	E0660	UE	0.00	110.82	E0776	NU	73.26	132.43
E0601	RR	160.01	103.33	E0660	RR	0.00	15.39	E0779		120.00	0.00
E0601	NU	1299.94	0.00	E0660	NU	0.00	147.77	E0780		35.00	0.00
E0602		45.01	0.00	E0665	UE	0.00	95.17	E0781	RR	450.00	245.01
E0603	UE	0.00	0.00	E0665	RR	0.00	13.02	E0782		0.00	0.00
E0603	RR	40.00	0.00	E0665	NU	0.00	126.72	E0783		0.00	0.00
E0603	NU	0.00	0.00	E0666	UE	0.00	95.82	E0784		5496.40	0.00
E0604	UE	0.00	0.00	E0666	RR	0.00	13.17	E0785		0.00	393.66
E0604	RR	52.04	0.00	E0666	NU	0.00	127.73	E0786		0.00	0.00
E0604	NU	0.00	0.00	E0667	UE	0.00	224.62	E0791	UE	25.00	0.00
E0605	UE	0.00	20.14	E0667	RR	45.00	33.82	E0791	RR	28.00	292.49
E0605	RR	0.00	2.84	E0667	NU	499.97	299.49	E0791	NU	0.00	0.00
E0605	NU	0.00	24.45	E0668	UE	0.00	306.57	E0830		1750.00	0.00
E0606	UE	0.00	0.00	E0668	RR	45.02	40.34	E0840	UE	0.00	50.81
E0606	RR	0.00	21.22	E0668	NU	496.13	408.74	E0840	RR	0.00	15.10
E0606	NU	0.00	0.00	E0669	UE	0.00	127.20	E0840	NU	0.00	67.79
E0607	UE	0.00	0.00	E0669	RR	0.00	16.97	E0850	UE	0.00	72.89
E0607	RR	0.00	0.00	E0669	NU	0.00	169.56	E0850	RR	0.00	13.35
E0607	NU	79.20	0.00	E0671		450.00	0.00	E0850	NU	0.00	97.18
E0608	RR	357.90	259.33	E0672		0.00	0.00	E0855	UE	0.00	348.69
E0609	UE	0.00	0.00	E0673		0.00	0.00	E0855	RR	64.00	46.49
E0609	RR	0.00	0.00	E0690	UE	0.00	943.20	E0855	NU	0.00	464.94
E0609	NU	0.00	0.00	E0690	RR	0.00	130.19	E0860	UE	0.00	27.30
E0610	UE	0.00	165.04	E0690	NU	0.00	1260.56	E0860	RR	0.00	6.02
E0610	RR	0.00	23.21	E0691		0.00	0.00	E0860	NU	0.00	35.64
E0610	NU	0.00	220.02	E0692		0.00	0.00	E0870	UE	0.00	81.05
E0615	UE	0.00	332.19	E0693		0.00	0.00	E0870	RR	0.00	12.40
E0615	RR	0.00	54.12	E0694		0.00	0.00	E0870	NU	0.00	107.59
E0615	NU	0.00	442.91	E0700		48.00	0.00	E0880	UE	0.00	87.90
E0616		0.00	0.00	E0701		0.00	0.00	E0880	RR	0.00	18.23
E0617		0.00	0.00	E0710		29.00	0.00	E0880	NU	0.00	116.13
E0618		0.00	0.00	E0720	UE	0.00	0.00	E0890	UE	0.00	89.72
E0619		0.00	0.00	E0720	RR	74.99	0.00	E0890	RR	0.00	30.37
E0620		0.00	0.00	E0720	NU	365.81	340.01	E0890	NU	0.00	111.38
E0621	UE	0.00	66.94	E0730	UE	233.13	0.00	E0900	UE	0.00	88.91
E0621	RR	0.00	8.56	E0730	RR	99.96	0.00	E0900	RR	0.00	25.55
E0621	NU	126.98	88.79	E0730	NU	400.66	342.77	E0900	NU	0.00	118.51
E0625	UE	0.00	0.00	E0731	UE	0.00	0.00	E0910	UE	0.00	0.00
E0625	RR	0.00	0.00	E0731	RR	0.00	0.00	E0910	RR	31.36	18.50
E0625	NU	0.00	0.00	E0731	NU	400.00	329.94	E0910	NU	0.00	0.00
E0627	UE	0.00	234.03	E0740		75.00	0.00	E0920	UE	0.00	0.00
E0627	RR	50.00	31.21	E0744	UE	0.00	0.00	E0920	RR	71.02	42.68
E0627	NU	583.13	312.02	E0744	RR	0.00	84.70	E0920	NU	0.00	0.00
E0628	UE	0.00	234.03	E0744	NU	0.00	0.00	E0930	UE	0.00	0.00
E0628	RR	0.00	31.21	E0745	UE	0.00	0.00	E0930	RR	0.00	42.27
E0628	NU	0.00	312.02	E0745	RR	125.00	82.80	E0930	NU	0.00	0.00
E0629	UE	0.00	229.41	E0745	NU	950.00	0.00	E0935	RR	60.00	21.03
E0629	RR	0.00	30.60	E0746	UE	15.00	0.00	E0940	UE	0.00	0.00
E0629	NU	0.00	305.91	E0746	RR	0.00	0.00	E0940	RR	41.44	32.16
E0630	UE	0.00	0.00	E0746	NU	0.00	0.00	E0940	NU	0.00	0.00
E0630	RR	116.57	94.25	E0747	UE	0.00	2424.10	E0941	UE	0.00	0.00
E0630	NU	0.00	0.00	E0747	RR	0.00	324.22	E0941	RR	84.99	40.16
E0635	UE	0.00	0.00	E0747	NU	4470.79	3262.67	E0941	NU	0.00	0.00
E0635	RR	0.00	113.19	E0748		4995.00	0.00	E0942	UE	0.00	13.77
E0635	NU	0.00	0.00	E0749		0.00	0.00	E0942	RR	0.00	2.17
E0636		0.00	0.00	E0752		531.30	390.64	E0942	NU	25.00	18.36

CODE		COMMERCIAL	MEDICARE	CODE		COMMERCIAL	MEDICARE	CODE		COMMERCIAL	MEDICARE
E0943	UE	0.00	19.19	E0970	NU	0.00	0.00	E1012		0.00	0.00
E0943	RR	0.00	3.00	E0971	UE	0.00	45.61	E1013		0.00	0.00
E0943	NU	42.02	25.60	E0971	RR	10.35	6.90	E1014		0.00	0.00
E0944	UE	0.00	31.82	E0971	NU	62.97	60.82	E1015		0.00	0.00
E0944	RR	0.00	4.26	E0972	UE	0.00	0.00	E1016		0.00	0.00
E0944	NU	0.00	42.44	E0972	RR	0.00	0.00	E1017		0.00	0.00
E0945	UE	0.00	31.74	E0972	NU	75.98	0.00	E1018		0.00	0.00
E0945	RR	0.00	4.11	E0973	UE	0.00	0.00	E1020		0.00	0.00
E0945	NU	0.00	41.00	E0973	RR	0.00	0.00	E1025		0.00	0.00
E0946	UE	0.00	0.00	E0973	NU	87.48	0.00	E1026		0.00	0.00
E0946	RR	72.97	54.73	E0974	UE	0.00	0.00	E1027		0.00	0.00
E0946	NU	0.00	0.00	E0974	RR	0.00	0.00	E1031	UE	0.00	0.00
E0947	UE	0.00	420.73	E0974	NU	0.00	0.00	E1031	RR	55.01	46.72
E0947	RR	63.00	58.18	E0975	UE	0.00	0.00	E1031	NU	0.00	0.00
E0947	NU	0.00	560.98	E0975	RR	0.00	0.00	E1035		0.00	0.00
E0948	UE	0.00	382.68	E0975	NU	0.00	0.00	E1037		0.00	0.00
E0948	RR	95.02	54.24	E0976	UE	0.00	0.00	E1038		0.00	0.00
E0948	NU	0.00	542.60	E0976	RR	0.00	0.00	E1050	UE	0.00	0.00
E0950	UE	0.00	0.00	E0976	NU	0.00	0.00	E1050	RR	124.99	94.20
E0950	RR	0.00	0.00	E0977	UE	0.00	45.40	E1050	NU	0.00	0.00
E0950	NU	0.00	0.00	E0977	RR	0.00	5.83	E1060	UE	0.00	0.00
E0951	UE	0.00	13.07	E0977	NU	0.00	60.51	E1060	RR	160.97	116.62
E0951	RR	0.00	1.81	E0978	UE	0.00	0.00	E1060	NU	0.00	0.00
E0951	NU	0.00	17.42	E0978	RR	0.00	0.00	E1065	UE	0.00	2016.91
E0952	UE	0.00	0.00	E0978	NU	48.99	0.00	E1065	RR	0.00	244.49
E0952	RR	0.00	0.00	E0979	UE	0.00	0.00	E1065	NU	0.00	2689.21
E0952	NU	0.00	0.00	E0979	RR	0.00	0.00	E1066	UE	0.00	0.00
E0953	UE	0.00	0.00	E0979	NU	0.00	0.00	E1066	RR	0.00	0.00
E0953	RR	0.00	0.00	E0980	UE	0.00	22.81	E1066	NU	0.00	0.00
E0953	NU	0.00	0.00	E0980	RR	0.00	3.06	E1069	UE	0.00	0.00
E0954	UE	0.00	0.00	E0980	NU	0.00	30.58	E1069	RR	0.00	0.00
E0954	RR	0.00	0.00	E0990	UE	0.00	0.00	E1069	NU	140.05	0.00
E0954	NU	0.00	0.00	E0990	RR	14.50	0.00	E1070	UE	0.00	0.00
E0958	UE	0.00	0.00	E0990	NU	0.00	0.00	E1070	RR	154.99	101.32
E0958	RR	0.00	40.36	E0991	UE	0.00	0.00	E1070	NU	0.00	0.00
E0958	NU	0.00	0.00	E0991	RR	0.00	0.00	E1083	UE	0.00	0.00
E0959	UE	0.00	0.00	E0991	NU	0.00	0.00	E1083	RR	0.00	72.84
E0959	RR	0.00	0.00	E0992	UE	0.00	0.00	E1083	NU	0.00	0.00
E0959	NU	0.00	0.00	E0992	RR	0.00	0.00	E1084	UE	0.00	0.00
E0961	UE	0.00	0.00	E0992	NU	0.00	0.00	E1084	RR	130.03	90.75
E0961	RR	5.00	0.00	E0993	UE	0.00	0.00	E1084	NU	0.00	0.00
E0961	NU	42.52	0.00	E0993	RR	0.00	0.00	E1085	UE	0.00	0.00
E0962	UE	0.00	41.27	E0993	NU	0.00	0.00	E1085	RR	0.00	0.00
E0962	RR	0.00	5.50	E0994	UE	0.00	12.24	E1085	NU	0.00	0.00
E0962	NU	0.00	55.03	E0994	RR	0.00	1.65	E1086	UE	0.00	0.00
E0963	UE	0.00	49.42	E0994	NU	0.00	16.31	E1086	RR	108.04	0.00
E0963	RR	0.00	6.68	E0995	UE	0.00	0.00	E1086	NU	0.00	0.00
E0963	NU	75.66	65.73	E0995	RR	0.00	0.00	E1087	UE	0.00	0.00
E0964	UE	0.00	55.03	E0995	NU	0.00	0.00	E1087	RR	132.84	117.02
E0964	RR	0.00	7.39	E0996	UE	0.00	0.00	E1087	NU	0.00	0.00
E0964	NU	80.03	73.34	E0996	RR	0.00	0.00	E1088	UE	0.00	0.00
E0965	UE	0.00	58.81	E0996	NU	0.00	0.00	E1088	RR	170.02	139.46
E0965	RR	0.00	7.85	E0997	UE	0.00	46.15	E1088	NU	0.00	0.00
E0965	NU	0.00	78.40	E0997	RR	0.00	6.60	E1089	UE	0.00	0.00
E0966	UE	0.00	0.00	E0997	NU	0.00	61.52	E1089	RR	0.00	0.00
E0966	RR	0.00	0.00	E0998	UE	0.00	26.58	E1089	NU	0.00	0.00
E0966	NU	0.00	0.00	E0998	RR	0.00	3.67	E1090	UE	0.00	0.00
E0967	UE	0.00	91.70	E0998	NU	0.00	35.41	E1090	RR	174.01	0.00
E0967	RR	0.00	12.55	E0999	UE	0.00	79.77	E1090	NU	0.00	0.00
E0967	NU	0.00	122.22	E0999	RR	0.00	10.65	E1091		79.00	0.00
E0968	UE	0.00	0.00	E0999	NU	0.00	106.35	E1092	UE	0.00	0.00
E0968	RR	0.00	16.59	E1000	UE	0.00	0.00	E1092	RR	168.39	118.87
E0968	NU	0.00	0.00	E1000	RR	0.00	0.00	E1092	NU	0.00	0.00
E0969	UE	0.00	108.67	E1000	NU	0.00	0.00	E1093	UE	0.00	0.00
E0969	RR	0.00	14.35	E1001	UE	0.00	68.04	E1093	RR	163.02	102.23
E0969	NU	0.00	144.89	E1001	RR	0.00	9.52	E1093	NU	0.00	0.00
E0970	UE	0.00	0.00	E1001	NU	0.00	90.71	E1100	UE	0.00	0.00
E0970	RR	0.00	0.00	E1011		0.00	0.00	E1100	RR	0.00	96.03

CODE		COMMERCIAL	MEDICARE	CODE		COMMERCIAL	MEDICARE	CODE		COMMERCIAL	MEDICARE
E1100	NU	0.00	0.00	E1226	NU	0.00	0.00	E1390	NU	0.00	0.00
E1110	UE	0.00	0.00	E1227	UE	0.00	192.54	E1399		0.00	0.00
E1110	RR	142.96	94.04	E1227	RR	0.00	25.67	E1405	UE	0.00	0.00
E1110	NU	0.00	0.00	E1227	NU	0.00	256.69	E1405	RR	0.00	0.00
E1130	UE	0.00	0.00	E1228	UE	0.00	0.00	E1405	NU	0.00	0.00
E1130	RR	40.00	0.00	E1228	RR	0.00	25.92	E1406	UE	0.00	0.00
E1130	NU	0.00	0.00	E1228	NU	0.00	0.00	E1406	RR	0.00	0.00
E1140	UE	0.00	0.00	E1230	UE	0.00	1654.65	E1406	NU	0.00	0.00
E1140	RR	92.02	0.00	E1230	RR	199.93	205.77	E1500		0.00	0.00
E1140	NU	0.00	0.00	E1230	NU	2751.14	2092.16	E1510	UE	0.00	0.00
E1150	UE	0.00	0.00	E1231		0.00	0.00	E1510	RR	0.00	0.00
E1150	RR	104.97	75.46	E1232		0.00	0.00	E1510	NU	0.00	0.00
E1150	NU	0.00	0.00	E1233		0.00	0.00	E1520	UE	0.00	0.00
E1160	UE	0.00	0.00	E1234		0.00	0.00	E1520	RR	0.00	0.00
E1160	RR	59.97	57.82	E1235		0.00	0.00	E1520	NU	0.00	0.00
E1160	NU	0.00	0.00	E1236		0.00	0.00	E1530	UE	0.00	0.00
E1161		0.00	0.00	E1237		0.00	0.00	E1530	RR	0.00	0.00
E1170	UE	0.00	0.00	E1238		0.00	0.00	E1530	NU	0.00	0.00
E1170	RR	0.00	82.61	E1240	UE	0.00	0.00	E1540	UE	0.00	0.00
E1170	NU	0.00	0.00	E1240	RR	133.00	95.30	E1540	RR	0.00	0.00
E1171	UE	0.00	0.00	E1240	NU	754.30	0.00	E1540	NU	0.00	0.00
E1171	RR	0.00	74.14	E1250	UE	0.00	0.00	E1550	UE	0.00	0.00
E1171	NU	0.00	0.00	E1250	RR	105.00	0.00	E1550	RR	0.00	0.00
E1172	UE	0.00	0.00	E1250	NU	0.00	0.00	E1550	NU	0.00	0.00
E1172	RR	0.00	90.61	E1260	UE	0.00	0.00	E1560	UE	0.00	0.00
E1172	NU	0.00	0.00	E1260	RR	122.04	0.00	E1560	RR	0.00	0.00
E1180	UE	0.00	0.00	E1260	NU	0.00	0.00	E1560	NU	0.00	0.00
E1180	RR	0.00	93.74	E1270	UE	0.00	0.00	E1570	UE	0.00	0.00
E1180	NU	0.00	0.00	E1270	RR	120.00	73.02	E1570	RR	0.00	0.00
E1190	UE	0.00	0.00	E1270	NU	0.00	0.00	E1570	NU	0.00	0.00
E1190	RR	0.00	108.29	E1280	UE	0.00	0.00	E1575	UE	0.00	0.00
E1190	NU	0.00	0.00	E1280	RR	168.00	121.42	E1575	RR	0.00	0.00
E1195	UE	0.00	0.00	E1280	NU	0.00	0.00	E1575	NU	0.00	0.00
E1195	RR	178.01	116.21	E1285	UE	0.00	0.00	E1580	UE	0.00	0.00
E1195	NU	0.00	0.00	E1285	RR	0.00	0.00	E1580	RR	0.00	0.00
E1200	UE	0.00	0.00	E1285	NU	0.00	0.00	E1580	NU	0.00	0.00
E1200	RR	0.00	80.49	E1290	UE	0.00	0.00	E1590	UE	0.00	0.00
E1200	NU	0.00	0.00	E1290	RR	159.96	0.00	E1590	RR	0.00	0.00
E1210	UE	0.00	0.00	E1290	NU	0.00	0.00	E1590	NU	0.00	0.00
E1210	RR	356.01	380.05	E1295	UE	0.00	0.00	E1592	UE	0.00	0.00
E1210	NU	0.00	0.00	E1295	RR	129.05	112.36	E1592	RR	0.00	0.00
E1211	UE	0.00	0.00	E1295	NU	0.00	0.00	E1592	NU	0.00	0.00
E1211	RR	0.00	387.12	E1296	UE	0.00	341.10	E1594	UE	0.00	0.00
E1211	NU	0.00	0.00	E1296	RR	0.00	46.20	E1594	RR	545.00	0.00
E1212	UE	0.00	0.00	E1296	NU	0.00	454.80	E1594	NU	0.00	0.00
E1212	RR	0.00	0.00	E1297	UE	0.00	72.57	E1600	UE	0.00	0.00
E1212	NU	0.00	0.00	E1297	RR	0.00	10.75	E1600	RR	0.00	0.00
E1213	UE	0.00	0.00	E1297	NU	0.00	96.77	E1600	NU	0.00	0.00
E1213	RR	377.90	0.00	E1298	UE	0.00	293.90	E1610	UE	0.00	0.00
E1213	NU	0.00	0.00	E1298	RR	0.00	40.10	E1610	RR	0.00	0.00
E1220		4115.00	0.00	E1298	NU	0.00	391.88	E1610	NU	0.00	0.00
E1221	UE	0.00	0.00	E1300	UE	0.00	0.00	E1615	UE	0.00	0.00
E1221	RR	0.00	43.95	E1300	RR	0.00	0.00	E1615	RR	0.00	0.00
E1221	NU	0.00	0.00	E1300	NU	0.00	0.00	E1615	NU	0.00	0.00
E1222	UE	0.00	0.00	E1310	UE	0.00	1489.76	E1620	UE	0.00	0.00
E1222	RR	0.00	62.71	E1310	RR	0.00	169.90	E1620	RR	0.00	0.00
E1222	NU	0.00	0.00	E1310	NU	0.00	1986.35	E1620	NU	0.00	0.00
E1223	UE	0.00	0.00	E1340		17.00	0.00	E1625	UE	0.00	0.00
E1223	RR	0.00	68.47	E1353	UE	0.00	0.00	E1625	RR	0.00	0.00
E1223	NU	0.00	0.00	E1353	RR	2.13	0.00	E1625	NU	0.00	0.00
E1224	UE	0.00	0.00	E1353	NU	0.00	0.00	E1630	UE	0.00	0.00
E1224	RR	0.00	75.07	E1355	UE	0.00	0.00	E1630	RR	0.00	0.00
E1224	NU	0.00	0.00	E1355	RR	8.80	0.00	E1630	NU	0.00	0.00
E1225	UE	0.00	0.00	E1355	NU	0.00	0.00	E1632	UE	0.00	0.00
E1225	RR	0.00	41.81	E1372	UE	0.00	111.63	E1632	RR	0.00	0.00
E1225	NU	0.00	0.00	E1372	RR	30.00	21.92	E1632	NU	0.00	0.00
E1226	UE	0.00	0.00	E1372	NU	0.00	150.81	E1635	UE	0.00	0.00
E1226	RR	0.00	0.00	E1390	RR	409.95	211.64	E1635	RR	0.00	0.00

CODE		COMMERCIAL	MEDICARE	CODE	COMMERCIAL	MEDICARE	CODE	COMMERCIAL	MEDICARE
E1635	NU	0.00	0.00	G0050	100.00	0.00	G0193	0.00	0.00
E1636	UE	0.00	0.00	G0101	54.01	0.00	G0194	0.00	0.00
E1636	RR	0.00	0.00	G0102	25.00	0.00	G0195	176.00	0.00
E1636	NU	0.00	0.00	G0103	74.90	0.00	G0196	175.00	0.00
E1637		0.00	0.00	G0104	220.95	0.00	G0197	0.00	0.00
E1638		0.00	0.00	G0105	810.14	0.00	G0198	0.00	0.00
E1639		0.00	0.00	G0106	0.00	0.00	G0199	0.00	0.00
E1640	UE	0.00	0.00	G0107	15.00	0.00	G0200	0.00	0.00
E1640	RR	0.00	0.00	G0108	73.00	0.00	G0201	112.00	0.00
E1640	NU	0.00	0.00	G0109	40.00	0.00	G0202	197.00	0.00
E1699		0.00	0.00	G0110	0.00	0.00	G0203	0.00	0.00
E1700	UE	0.00	239.24	G0111	0.00	0.00	G0204	229.00	0.00
E1700	RR	0.00	31.29	G0112	0.00	0.00	G0205	0.00	0.00
E1700	NU	0.00	318.98	G0113	0.00	0.00	G0206	170.00	0.00
E1701		0.00	9.82	G0114	0.00	0.00	G0207	0.00	0.00
E1702		0.00	20.88	G0115	0.00	0.00	G0210	3000.00	0.00
E1800		195.00	0.00	G0116	0.00	0.00	G0211	3200.00	0.00
E1801		395.00	0.00	G0117	55.00	0.00	G0212	3100.00	0.00
E1802		0.00	0.00	G0118	0.00	0.00	G0213	0.00	0.00
E1805		11.20	0.00	G0120	0.00	0.00	G0214	3200.00	0.00
E1806		0.00	0.00	G0121	825.13	0.00	G0215	3250.00	0.00
E1810		134.00	0.00	G0122	0.00	0.00	G0216	0.00	0.00
E1811		395.00	0.00	G0123	43.20	0.00	G0217	0.00	0.00
E1815		335.00	0.00	G0124	15.00	0.00	G0218	3100.00	0.00
E1816		0.00	0.00	G0125	3200.00	0.00	G0219	0.00	0.00
E1818		0.00	0.00	G0126	0.00	0.00	G0220	3350.00	0.00
E1820		94.50	0.00	G0127	30.00	0.00	G0221	3025.00	0.00
E1821		0.00	0.00	G0128	40.00	0.00	G0222	3270.00	0.00
E1825		50.00	0.00	G0129	120.00	0.00	G0223	0.00	0.00
E1830		80.00	0.00	G0130	0.00	0.00	G0224	0.00	0.00
E1840		42.80	0.00	G0131	218.00	0.00	G0225	3100.00	0.00
E1900		0.00	0.00	G0132	120.00	0.00	G0226	0.00	0.00
E1902		0.00	0.00	G0141	35.00	0.00	G0227	0.00	0.00
E2000		0.00	0.00	G0143	50.00	0.00	G0228	0.00	0.00
E2100		0.00	0.00	G0144	0.00	0.00	G0229	0.00	0.00
E2101		300.00	0.00	G0145	0.00	0.00	G0230	0.00	0.00
G0001		11.20	0.00	G0147	0.00	0.00	G0231	0.00	0.00
G0002		78.60	0.00	G0148	30.00	0.00	G0232	0.00	0.00
G0004		474.98	0.00	G0151	130.00	0.00	G0233	0.00	0.00
G0005		79.99	0.00	G0152	100.00	0.00	G0234	0.00	0.00
G0006		64.20	0.00	G0153	110.60	0.00	G0236	27.00	0.00
G0007		99.98	0.00	G0154	112.00	0.00	G0237	40.00	0.00
G0008		10.00	0.00	G0155	32.50	0.00	G0238	50.00	0.00
G0009		10.00	0.00	G0156	3.60	0.00	G0239	32.00	0.00
G0010		10.00	0.00	G0163	0.00	0.00	G0240	0.00	0.00
G0015		193.01	0.00	G0164	0.00	0.00	G0241	0.00	0.00
G0016		110.02	0.00	G0165	0.00	0.00	G0242	0.00	0.00
G0025		53.99	0.00	G0166	335.00	0.00	G0243	0.00	0.00
G0026		20.00	0.00	G0167	0.00	0.00	G0244	31.90	0.00
G0027		0.00	0.00	G0168	96.00	0.00	G0245	92.00	0.00
G0030		0.00	0.00	G0173	0.00	0.00	G0246	0.00	0.00
G0031		0.00	0.00	G0174	0.00	0.00	G0247	45.00	0.00
G0032		0.00	0.00	G0175	0.00	0.00	G0248	0.00	0.00
G0033		0.00	0.00	G0176	100.00	0.00	G0249	0.00	0.00
G0034		0.00	0.00	G0177	100.00	0.00	G0250	0.00	0.00
G0035		0.00	0.00	G0178	0.00	0.00	G0251	0.00	0.00
G0036		0.00	0.00	G0179	75.00	0.00	G0252	0.00	0.00
G0037		0.00	0.00	G0180	91.10	0.00	G0253	0.00	0.00
G0038		0.00	0.00	G0181	141.00	0.00	G0254	0.00	0.00
G0039		0.00	0.00	G0182	150.00	0.00	G0255	0.00	0.00
G0040		0.00	0.00	G0184	0.00	0.00	G0256	0.00	0.00
G0041		0.00	0.00	G0185	725.00	0.00	G0257	0.00	0.00
G0042		0.00	0.00	G0186	0.00	0.00	G0258	0.00	0.00
G0043		0.00	0.00	G0187	0.00	0.00	G0259	0.00	0.00
G0044		0.00	0.00	G0188	0.00	0.00	G0260	0.00	0.00
G0045		0.00	0.00	G0190	14.80	0.00	G0261	0.00	0.00
G0046		0.00	0.00	G0191	0.00	0.00	G0262	0.00	0.00
G0047		0.00	0.00	G0192	0.00	0.00	G0263	0.00	0.00

CODE	COMMERCIAL	MEDICARE	CODE	COMMERCIAL	MEDICARE	CODE	COMMERCIAL	MEDICARE
G0264	0.00	0.00	H0030	0.00	0.00	J0270	5.00	0.00
G0265	0.00	0.00	H0031	0.00	0.00	J0275	32.00	0.00
G0266	0.00	0.00	H0032	0.00	0.00	J0280	5.00	0.00
G0267	0.00	0.00	H0033	0.00	0.00	J0282	80.02	0.00
G0268	0.00	0.00	H0034	0.00	0.00	J0285	24.00	0.00
G0269	0.00	0.00	H0035	0.00	0.00	J0286	196.22	0.00
G0270	0.00	0.00	H0036	0.00	0.00	J0287	0.00	0.00
G0271	0.00	0.00	H0037	0.00	0.00	J0288	0.00	0.00
G0272	0.00	0.00	H0038	0.00	0.00	J0289	0.00	0.00
G0273	0.00	0.00	H0039	0.00	0.00	J0290	2.18	0.00
G0274	0.00	0.00	H0040	0.00	0.00	J0295	20.80	0.00
G0275	0.00	0.00	H0041	0.00	0.00	J0300	6.75	0.00
G0278	0.00	0.00	H0042	0.00	0.00	J0330	1.05	0.00
G0279	0.00	0.00	H0043	0.00	0.00	J0340	4.60	0.00
G0280	0.00	0.00	H0044	0.00	0.00	J0350	0.00	0.00
G0281	0.00	0.00	H0045	0.00	0.00	J0360	52.45	0.00
G0282	0.00	0.00	H0046	0.00	0.00	J0380	0.00	0.00
G0283	0.00	0.00	H0047	0.00	0.00	J0390	0.00	0.00
G0288	0.00	0.00	H0048	0.00	0.00	J0395	7.70	0.00
G0289	0.00	0.00	H1000	0.00	0.00	J0400	0.00	0.00
G0290	0.00	0.00	H1001	105.90	0.00	J0456	37.85	0.00
G0291	0.00	0.00	H1002	45.00	0.00	J0460	6.00	0.00
G0292	0.00	0.00	H1003	102.00	0.00	J0470	74.00	0.00
G0293	0.00	0.00	H1004	7.00	0.00	J0475	400.20	0.00
G0294	0.00	0.00	H1005	0.00	0.00	J0476	0.00	0.00
G0295	0.00	0.00	H1010	0.00	0.00	J0500	5.70	0.00
G9001	0.00	0.00	H1011	0.00	0.00	J0510	0.00	0.00
G9002	0.00	0.00	H2000	0.00	0.00	J0515	0.00	0.00
G9003	0.00	0.00	H2001	0.00	0.00	J0520	6.00	0.00
G9004	0.00	0.00	H2010	0.00	0.00	J0530	20.00	0.00
G9005	0.00	0.00	H2011	0.00	0.00	J0540	29.99	0.00
G9006	0.00	0.00	H2012	0.00	0.00	J0550	51.49	0.00
G9007	0.00	0.00	H2013	0.00	0.00	J0560	20.00	0.00
G9008	0.00	0.00	H2014	0.00	0.00	J0570	30.00	0.00
G9009	0.00	0.00	H2015	0.00	0.00	J0580	50.01	0.00
G9010	0.00	0.00	H2016	0.00	0.00	J0585	6.00	0.00
G9011	0.00	0.00	H2017	0.00	0.00	J0587	12.49	0.00
G9012	30.60	0.00	H2018	0.00	0.00	J0590	5.30	0.00
G9016	0.00	0.00	H2019	0.00	0.00	J0592	0.00	0.00
H0001	0.00	0.00	H2020	0.00	0.00	J0600	40.00	0.00
H0002	0.00	0.00	H2021	0.00	0.00	J0610	2.00	0.00
H0003	0.00	0.00	H2022	0.00	0.00	J0620	10.00	0.00
H0004	80.00	0.00	H2023	0.00	0.00	J0630	48.74	0.00
H0005	65.00	0.00	H2024	0.00	0.00	J0635	15.31	0.00
H0006	0.00	0.00	H2025	0.00	0.00	J0636	57.00	0.00
H0007	0.00	0.00	H2026	0.00	0.00	J0637	0.00	0.00
H0008	0.00	0.00	H2027	0.00	0.00	J0640	35.48	0.00
H0009	0.00	0.00	H2028	0.00	0.00	J0670	7.50	0.00
H0010	0.00	0.00	H2029	0.00	0.00	J0690	5.94	0.00
H0011	0.00	0.00	H2030	0.00	0.00	J0692	22.60	0.00
H0012	0.00	0.00	H2031	0.00	0.00	J0694	23.00	0.00
H0013	0.00	0.00	H2032	0.00	0.00	J0695	37.50	0.00
H0014	0.00	0.00	H2033	0.00	0.00	J0696	26.00	0.00
H0015	180.00	0.00	H2034	0.00	0.00	J0697	20.00	0.00
H0016	0.00	0.00	H2035	0.00	0.00	J0698	30.00	0.00
H0017	0.00	0.00	H2036	0.00	0.00	J0702	10.00	0.00
H0018	0.00	0.00	H2037	0.00	0.00	J0704	15.00	0.00
H0019	0.00	0.00	J0120	171.00	0.00	J0706	0.00	0.00
H0020	11.00	0.00	J0130	990.85	0.00	J0710	20.00	0.00
H0021	0.00	0.00	J0150	45.00	0.00	J0713	14.21	0.00
H0022	0.00	0.00	J0151	318.95	0.00	J0715	13.77	0.00
H0023	0.00	0.00	J0170	3.50	0.00	J0720	22.00	0.00
H0024	0.00	0.00	J0190	0.00	0.00	J0725	6.00	0.00
H0025	0.00	0.00	J0200	0.00	0.00	J0730	0.00	0.00
H0026	0.00	0.00	J0205	39.52	0.00	J0735	74.99	0.00
H0027	0.00	0.00	J0207	660.40	0.00	J0740	1560.18	0.00
H0028	0.00	0.00	J0210	24.00	0.00	J0743	30.51	0.00
H0029	0.00	0.00	J0256	0.22	0.00	J0744	25.49	0.00

CODE	COMMERCIAL	MEDICARE	CODE	COMMERCIAL	MEDICARE	CODE	COMMERCIAL	MEDICARE
J0745	0.00	0.00	J1530	0.00	0.00	J2240	0.00	0.00
J0760	10.00	0.00	J1540	83.40	0.00	J2250	5.00	0.00
J0770	57.02	0.00	J1550	105.00	0.00	J2260	71.78	0.00
J0780	16.00	0.00	J1560	14.40	0.00	J2270	1.48	0.00
J0800	85.04	0.00	J1561	85.01	0.00	J2271	17.34	0.00
J0810	15.00	0.00	J1563	135.02	0.00	J2275	15.00	0.00
J0835	27.00	0.00	J1564	1.30	0.00	J2300	6.50	0.00
J0850	783.84	0.00	J1565	36.00	0.00	J2310	13.68	0.00
J0880	50.00	0.00	J1570	47.40	0.00	J2320	17.00	0.00
J0895	16.24	0.00	J1580	12.16	0.00	J2321	30.00	0.00
J0900	2.50	0.00	J1590	2.61	0.00	J2322	48.50	0.00
J0945	1.50	0.00	J1600	20.00	0.00	J2324	0.00	0.00
J0970	3.00	0.00	J1610	104.34	0.00	J2330	0.00	0.00
J1000	10.00	0.00	J1620	292.72	0.00	J2350	10.00	0.00
J1020	5.50	0.00	J1626	30.00	0.00	J2352	189.97	0.00
J1030	10.00	0.00	J1630	15.00	0.00	J2355	413.31	0.00
J1040	20.00	0.00	J1631	42.99	0.00	J2360	2.00	0.00
J1050	39.99	0.00	J1642	1.00	0.00	J2370	3.00	0.00
J1051	0.00	0.00	J1644	3.00	0.00	J2400	13.00	0.00
J1055	65.98	0.00	J1645	23.86	0.00	J2405	12.00	0.00
J1056	35.00	0.00	J1650	18.37	0.00	J2410	0.00	0.00
J1060	15.00	0.00	J1652	0.00	0.00	J2430	469.98	0.00
J1070	10.60	0.00	J1655	4.20	0.00	J2440	6.25	0.00
J1080	20.00	0.00	J1670	135.00	0.00	J2460	13.00	0.00
J1090	15.00	0.00	J1690	20.00	0.00	J2480	20.00	0.00
J1094	1.00	0.00	J1700	0.00	0.00	J2500	27.00	0.00
J1095	12.00	0.00	J1710	10.00	0.00	J2501	5.00	0.00
J1100	1.00	0.00	J1720	9.00	0.00	J2510	16.00	0.00
J1110	25.67	0.00	J1730	0.00	0.00	J2512	0.00	0.00
J1120	0.00	0.00	J1739	0.00	0.00	J2515	0.00	0.00
J1160	4.70	0.00	J1741	0.00	0.00	J2540	1.20	0.00
J1165	0.75	0.00	J1742	0.00	0.00	J2543	15.00	0.00
J1170	2.80	0.00	J1745	94.99	0.00	J2545	162.99	0.00
J1180	15.00	0.00	J1750	38.01	0.00	J2550	4.76	0.00
J1190	317.00	0.00	J1755	29.00	0.00	J2560	8.79	0.00
J1200	5.00	0.00	J1756	0.00	0.00	J2590	0.00	0.00
J1205	0.00	0.00	J1785	9.00	0.00	J2597	10.00	0.00
J1212	68.99	0.00	J1790	6.70	0.00	J2640	10.00	0.00
J1230	0.75	0.00	J1800	12.50	0.00	J2650	17.30	0.00
J1240	0.00	0.00	J1810	13.30	0.00	J2670	0.00	0.00
J1245	42.01	0.00	J1815	0.00	0.00	J2675	5.16	0.00
J1250	11.00	0.00	J1817	0.00	0.00	J2680	25.00	0.00
J1260	35.00	0.00	J1820	5.50	0.00	J2690	15.00	0.00
J1270	23.00	0.00	J1825	269.34	0.00	J2700	7.08	0.00
J1320	2.22	0.00	J1830	76.90	0.00	J2710	2.75	0.00
J1325	19.00	0.00	J1835	0.00	0.00	J2720	0.00	0.00
J1327	32.50	0.00	J1840	2.31	0.00	J2725	59.51	0.00
J1330	10.00	0.00	J1850	14.92	0.00	J2730	0.00	0.00
J1362	0.00	0.00	J1885	14.00	0.00	J2760	47.87	0.00
J1364	10.00	0.00	J1890	20.00	0.00	J2765	3.75	0.00
J1380	12.00	0.00	J1910	27.00	0.00	J2770	214.88	0.00
J1390	3.75	0.00	J1930	0.00	0.00	J2780	4.00	0.00
J1410	60.00	0.00	J1940	2.00	0.00	J2788	0.00	0.00
J1435	2.20	0.00	J1950	540.98	0.00	J2790	137.99	0.00
J1436	0.00	0.00	J1955	87.54	0.00	J2792	38.99	0.00
J1438	164.18	0.00	J1956	39.66	0.00	J2795	0.22	0.00
J1440	301.68	0.00	J1960	0.00	0.00	J2800	20.00	0.00
J1441	497.06	0.00	J1970	0.00	0.00	J2810	0.00	0.00
J1450	133.16	0.00	J1980	12.48	0.00	J2820	60.99	0.00
J1452	0.00	0.00	J1990	0.00	0.00	J2860	0.00	0.00
J1455	12.54	0.00	J2000	5.00	0.00	J2910	22.99	0.00
J1460	9.00	0.00	J2010	10.00	0.00	J2912	3.10	0.00
J1470	119.20	0.00	J2020	58.39	0.00	J2915	62.49	0.00
J1480	80.00	0.00	J2060	15.00	0.00	J2916	8.00	0.00
J1490	89.50	0.00	J2150	8.00	0.00	J2920	5.00	0.00
J1500	68.00	0.00	J2175	2.00	0.00	J2930	10.00	0.00
J1510	0.00	0.00	J2180	17.10	0.00	J2940	64.88	0.00
J1520	0.00	0.00	J2210	5.01	0.00	J2941	68.14	0.00

CODE	COMMERCIAL	MEDICARE	CODE	COMMERCIAL	MEDICARE	CODE	COMMERCIAL	MEDICARE
J2950	0.95	0.00	J7193	1.35	0.00	J8499	0.00	0.00
J2970	0.00	0.00	J7194	0.98	0.00	J8510	5.00	0.00
J2993	0.00	0.00	J7195	1.18	0.00	J8520	4.95	0.00
J2995	0.00	0.00	J7197	0.00	0.00	J8521	13.50	0.00
J2997	58.00	0.00	J7198	1.64	0.00	J8530	7.00	0.00
J3000	5.48	0.00	J7199	0.00	0.00	J8560	74.18	0.00
J3010	2.70	0.00	J7300	360.00	0.00	J8600	3.00	0.00
J3030	75.02	0.00	J7302	459.94	0.00	J8610	5.49	0.00
J3070	15.00	0.00	J7308	129.96	0.00	J8700	13.00	0.00
J3080	0.00	0.00	J7310	0.00	0.00	J8999	0.00	0.00
J3100	0.00	0.00	J7315	185.97	0.00	J9000	84.99	0.00
J3105	6.72	0.00	J7316	49.99	0.00	J9001	645.94	0.00
J3120	10.00	0.00	J7317	194.00	0.00	J9010	850.23	0.00
J3130	20.00	0.00	J7320	269.97	0.00	J9015	960.20	0.00
J3140	13.00	0.00	J7330	0.00	0.00	J9017	560.95	0.00
J3150	1.00	0.00	J7340	28.00	0.00	J9020	127.02	0.00
J3230	12.00	0.00	J7342	0.00	0.00	J9031	209.97	0.00
J3240	559.00	0.00	J7350	0.00	0.00	J9040	481.19	0.00
J3245	0.00	0.00	J7500	1.41	0.00	J9045	200.04	0.00
J3250	6.00	0.00	J7501	0.00	0.00	J9050	200.92	0.00
J3260	8.64	0.00	J7502	6.37	0.00	J9060	74.50	0.00
J3265	7.93	0.00	J7504	424.98	0.00	J9062	392.90	0.00
J3270	0.00	0.00	J7505	0.00	0.00	J9065	93.02	0.00
J3280	9.00	0.00	J7506	0.09	0.00	J9070	11.05	0.00
J3301	2.50	0.00	J7507	3.43	0.00	J9080	21.41	0.00
J3302	2.00	0.00	J7508	17.12	0.00	J9090	45.01	0.00
J3303	5.00	0.00	J7509	0.65	0.00	J9091	93.02	0.00
J3305	199.98	0.00	J7510	0.18	0.00	J9092	160.00	0.00
J3310	13.00	0.00	J7511	0.00	0.00	J9093	12.90	0.00
J3315	0.00	0.00	J7513	606.38	0.00	J9094	26.00	0.00
J3320	40.00	0.00	J7515	1.61	0.00	J9095	51.00	0.00
J3350	0.00	0.00	J7516	59.99	0.00	J9096	110.00	0.00
J3360	3.00	0.00	J7517	2.88	0.00	J9097	205.97	0.00
J3364	0.00	0.00	J7520	8.13	0.00	J9100	14.25	0.00
J3365	0.00	0.00	J7525	0.00	0.00	J9110	53.01	0.00
J3370	26.00	0.00	J7599	0.00	0.00	J9120	31.00	0.00
J3390	0.00	0.00	J7608	10.60	0.00	J9130	25.00	0.00
J3395	1535.61	0.00	J7618	0.30	0.00	J9140	50.00	0.00
J3400	16.30	0.00	J7619	0.60	0.00	J9150	170.19	0.00
J3410	1.50	0.00	J7622	5.30	0.00	J9151	179.99	0.00
J3420	10.00	0.00	J7624	1.40	0.00	J9160	2199.64	0.00
J3430	4.00	0.00	J7626	4.89	0.00	J9165	30.00	0.00
J3450	25.00	0.00	J7628	0.20	0.00	J9170	510.42	0.00
J3470	30.00	0.00	J7629	0.50	0.00	J9180	1148.13	0.00
J3475	1.00	0.00	J7631	0.55	0.00	J9181	23.00	0.00
J3480	0.20	0.00	J7633	0.00	0.00	J9182	220.02	0.00
J3485	6.15	0.00	J7635	0.20	0.00	J9185	458.95	0.00
J3487	354.10	0.00	J7636	0.50	0.00	J9190	5.50	0.00
J3490	0.00	0.00	J7637	0.30	0.00	J9200	239.97	0.00
J3520	0.00	0.00	J7638	0.40	0.00	J9201	182.99	0.00
J3530	0.00	0.00	J7639	52.63	0.00	J9202	566.80	0.00
J3535	2.30	0.00	J7641	1.80	0.00	J9206	229.64	0.00
J3570	0.00	0.00	J7642	7.10	0.00	J9208	335.34	0.00
J3590	0.00	0.00	J7643	16.00	0.00	J9209	80.61	0.00
J7030	20.00	0.00	J7644	4.30	0.00	J9211	650.06	0.00
J7040	20.00	0.00	J7648	0.00	0.00	J9212	33.00	0.00
J7042	16.00	0.00	J7649	0.90	0.00	J9213	54.99	0.00
J7050	20.00	0.00	J7658	0.00	0.00	J9214	21.00	0.00
J7051	2.00	0.00	J7659	0.00	0.00	J9215	13.90	0.00
J7060	20.00	0.00	J7668	0.10	0.00	J9216	355.50	0.00
J7070	28.80	0.00	J7669	1.60	0.00	J9217	649.00	0.00
J7100	130.04	0.00	J7680	29.80	0.00	J9218	109.70	0.00
J7110	0.00	0.00	J7681	2.30	0.00	J9219	5998.55	0.00
J7120	22.17	0.00	J7682	129.72	0.00	J9230	22.00	0.00
J7130	6.50	0.00	J7683	0.10	0.00	J9245	843.57	0.00
J7190	0.81	0.00	J7684	0.20	0.00	J9250	1.00	0.00
J7191	0.00	0.00	J7699	0.00	0.00	J9260	10.00	0.00
J7192	1.63	0.00	J7799	0.00	0.00	J9265	329.99	0.00

CODE		COMMERCIAL	MEDICARE	CODE		COMMERCIAL	MEDICARE	CODE		COMMERCIAL	MEDICARE
J9266		1089.00	0.00	K0020	RR	0.00	4.30	K0043	NU	21.96	18.07
J9268		3656.33	0.00	K0020	NU	0.00	42.98	K0044	UE	0.00	11.55
J9270		0.00	0.00	K0021	UE	0.00	45.61	K0044	RR	0.00	1.55
J9280		206.00	0.00	K0021	RR	8.48	7.03	K0044	NU	0.00	15.39
J9290		600.10	0.00	K0021	NU	80.01	60.82	K0045	UE	0.00	39.29
J9291		1000.24	0.00	K0022	UE	0.00	34.84	K0045	RR	5.64	5.40
J9293		420.09	0.00	K0022	RR	0.00	4.63	K0045	NU	0.00	52.38
J9300		3299.33	0.00	K0022	NU	0.00	46.46	K0046	UE	0.00	13.56
J9310		772.13	0.00	K0023	UE	0.00	65.29	K0046	RR	0.00	1.81
J9320		190.02	0.00	K0023	RR	0.00	8.70	K0046	NU	0.00	18.07
J9340		144.96	0.00	K0023	NU	0.00	87.04	K0047	UE	0.00	53.04
J9350		1097.22	0.00	K0024	UE	0.00	77.30	K0047	RR	0.00	7.10
J9355		103.00	0.00	K0024	RR	0.00	10.32	K0047	NU	0.00	70.75
J9357		550.08	0.00	K0024	NU	0.00	103.04	K0048	UE	0.00	84.87
J9360		9.00	0.00	K0025	UE	0.00	49.51	K0048	RR	19.10	12.23
J9370		63.03	0.00	K0025	RR	0.00	6.51	K0048	NU	180.02	108.63
J9375		121.98	0.00	K0025	NU	84.98	66.02	K0049	UE	0.00	21.07
J9380		250.00	0.00	K0026	UE	0.00	32.41	K0049	RR	0.00	2.82
J9390		149.98	0.00	K0026	RR	0.00	4.29	K0049	NU	0.00	28.12
J9600		0.00	0.00	K0026	NU	0.00	43.02	K0050	UE	0.00	22.56
J9999		0.00	0.00	K0027	UE	0.00	32.41	K0050	RR	0.00	3.00
K0001	UE	0.00	0.00	K0027	RR	0.00	4.29	K0050	NU	0.00	30.07
K0001	RR	65.02	50.53	K0027	NU	0.00	43.02	K0051	UE	0.00	36.48
K0001	NU	0.00	0.00	K0028	UE	0.00	378.51	K0051	RR	0.00	4.90
K0002	UE	0.00	0.00	K0028	RR	57.55	51.95	K0051	NU	0.00	48.67
K0002	RR	91.89	75.70	K0028	NU	550.06	504.73	K0052	UE	0.00	64.12
K0002	NU	0.00	0.00	K0029	UE	0.00	34.53	K0052	RR	10.51	8.55
K0003	UE	0.00	0.00	K0029	RR	0.00	4.57	K0052	NU	109.95	85.51
K0003	RR	100.04	82.87	K0029	NU	0.00	46.02	K0053	UE	0.00	70.77
K0003	NU	0.00	0.00	K0030		92.94	0.00	K0053	RR	14.57	9.43
K0004	UE	0.00	0.00	K0031	UE	0.00	29.29	K0053	NU	0.00	94.36
K0004	RR	141.25	123.62	K0031	RR	5.00	3.96	K0054	UE	0.00	72.59
K0004	NU	1395.07	0.00	K0031	NU	50.18	39.50	K0054	RR	10.80	9.68
K0005	UE	0.00	1282.56	K0032	UE	0.00	32.00	K0054	NU	0.00	96.79
K0005	RR	195.94	171.00	K0032	RR	0.00	4.07	K0055	UE	0.00	65.99
K0005	NU	2186.15	1710.11	K0032	NU	0.00	42.44	K0055	RR	10.00	8.80
K0006	UE	0.00	0.00	K0033	UE	0.00	32.00	K0055	NU	108.02	87.97
K0006	RR	135.05	116.01	K0033	RR	0.00	4.07	K0056	UE	0.00	65.99
K0006	NU	0.00	0.00	K0033	NU	0.00	42.44	K0056	RR	11.70	8.80
K0007	UE	0.00	0.00	K0034	UE	0.00	13.07	K0056	NU	0.00	87.97
K0007	RR	190.03	165.12	K0034	RR	2.06	1.81	K0057	UE	0.00	86.16
K0007	NU	0.00	0.00	K0034	NU	21.99	17.42	K0057	RR	15.00	11.50
K0008		0.00	0.00	K0035	UE	0.00	17.99	K0057	NU	0.00	114.89
K0009		2837.00	0.00	K0035	RR	0.00	2.41	K0058	UE	0.00	41.88
K0010	UE	0.00	0.00	K0035	NU	0.00	23.96	K0058	RR	0.00	5.59
K0010	RR	0.00	394.04	K0036	UE	0.00	13.07	K0058	NU	77.00	55.84
K0010	NU	0.00	0.00	K0036	RR	0.00	1.82	K0059	UE	0.00	22.01
K0011	RR	599.88	489.93	K0036	NU	0.00	17.42	K0059	RR	0.00	2.93
K0011	NU	6199.38	0.00	K0037	UE	0.00	33.42	K0059	NU	0.00	29.34
K0012		0.00	0.00	K0037	RR	0.00	3.98	K0060	UE	0.00	19.24
K0013		0.00	0.00	K0037	NU	0.00	44.55	K0060	RR	0.00	2.57
K0014		0.00	0.00	K0038	UE	0.00	16.84	K0060	NU	0.00	25.67
K0015	UE	0.00	126.05	K0038	RR	0.00	2.25	K0061	UE	0.00	27.33
K0015	RR	19.91	16.82	K0038	NU	0.00	22.44	K0061	RR	0.00	3.65
K0015	NU	0.00	168.08	K0039	UE	0.00	37.38	K0061	NU	0.00	36.42
K0016	UE	0.00	79.77	K0039	RR	0.00	5.00	K0062	UE	0.00	42.32
K0016	RR	12.00	10.13	K0039	NU	0.00	49.84	K0062	RR	0.00	5.66
K0016	NU	118.04	106.35	K0040	UE	0.00	51.79	K0062	NU	0.00	56.44
K0017	UE	0.00	35.46	K0040	RR	0.00	6.89	K0063	UE	0.00	56.50
K0017	RR	0.00	4.73	K0040	NU	85.00	69.07	K0063	RR	0.00	7.54
K0017	NU	0.00	47.28	K0041	UE	0.00	36.72	K0063	NU	0.00	75.35
K0018	UE	0.00	19.83	K0041	RR	0.00	4.91	K0064	UE	0.00	21.08
K0018	RR	0.00	2.63	K0041	NU	0.00	48.95	K0064	RR	6.50	2.82
K0018	NU	0.00	26.41	K0042	UE	0.00	25.27	K0064	NU	62.51	28.13
K0019	UE	0.00	11.96	K0042	RR	0.00	3.36	K0065	UE	0.00	30.84
K0019	RR	0.00	1.59	K0042	NU	0.00	33.70	K0065	RR	0.00	4.12
K0019	NU	22.00	15.95	K0043	UE	0.00	13.56	K0065	NU	0.00	41.13
K0020	UE	0.00	32.22	K0043	RR	0.00	1.81	K0066	UE	0.00	20.18

CODE		COMMERCIAL	MEDICARE	CODE		COMMERCIAL	MEDICARE	CODE		COMMERCIAL	MEDICARE
K0066	RR	0.00	2.55	K0096	UE	0.00	190.29	K0538	RR	0.00	1587.73
K0066	NU	32.49	26.38	K0096	RR	0.00	25.37	K0539		35.00	25.37
K0067	UE	0.00	27.11	K0096	NU	0.00	253.72	K0540		37.80	22.69
K0067	RR	6.50	3.71	K0097	UE	0.00	43.76	K0541		0.00	0.00
K0067	NU	42.90	37.84	K0097	RR	0.00	5.84	K0542		0.00	0.00
K0068	UE	0.00	4.09	K0097	NU	75.01	58.36	K0543		0.00	0.00
K0068	NU	7.35	5.44	K0098	UE	0.00	18.86	K0544		0.00	0.00
K0069	UE	0.00	69.32	K0098	RR	0.00	2.52	K0545		0.00	0.00
K0069	NU	0.00	92.43	K0098	NU	0.00	25.17	K0546		0.00	0.00
K0070	UE	0.00	127.07	K0099	UE	0.00	56.13	K0547		200.00	0.00
K0070	NU	0.00	169.43	K0099	RR	0.00	7.50	K0548		2.68	0.00
K0071	UE	0.00	75.78	K0099	NU	0.00	74.84	K0549	UE	0.00	0.00
K0071	NU	0.00	101.06	K0100	UE	0.00	61.90	K0549	RR	0.00	281.18
K0072	UE	0.00	45.62	K0100	RR	9.50	8.22	K0549	NU	0.00	0.00
K0072	NU	0.00	60.83	K0100	NU	0.00	81.79	K0550	UE	0.00	0.00
K0073	UE	0.00	24.15	K0101	UE	0.00	0.00	K0550	RR	2.40	712.87
K0073	RR	0.00	3.22	K0101	RR	0.00	40.36	K0550	NU	0.00	0.00
K0073	NU	0.00	32.19	K0101	NU	0.00	0.00	K0551		0.00	0.00
K0074	UE	0.00	24.97	K0102	UE	0.00	30.07	K0552		0.00	0.00
K0074	RR	0.00	3.67	K0102	RR	0.00	4.02	K0556		836.00	625.20
K0074	NU	0.00	33.30	K0102	NU	0.00	40.10	K0557		0.00	520.99
K0075	UE	0.00	29.04	K0103	UE	0.00	37.34	K0558		0.50	1106.10
K0075	RR	0.00	4.37	K0103	RR	0.00	5.19	K0559		0.00	1106.10
K0075	NU	0.00	38.71	K0103	NU	57.98	50.99	K0560		0.00	0.00
K0076	UE	0.00	17.74	K0104	UE	0.00	82.41	K0561		6.10	3.15
K0076	RR	0.00	2.39	K0104	RR	14.56	10.98	K0562		7.00	5.31
K0076	NU	0.00	23.64	K0104	NU	145.95	109.87	K0563		12.50	8.11
K0077	UE	0.00	40.82	K0105	UE	0.00	68.98	K0564		8.70	9.13
K0077	RR	0.00	5.44	K0105	RR	0.00	9.19	K0565		8.90	5.76
K0077	NU	0.00	54.44	K0105	NU	0.00	91.98	K0566		8.90	8.36
K0078	UE	0.00	6.64	K0106	UE	0.00	74.35	K0567		3.33	1.91
K0078	RR	0.00	0.88	K0106	RR	0.00	9.94	K0568		2.98	3.50
K0078	NU	0.00	8.88	K0106	NU	112.04	99.13	K0569		4.40	5.09
K0079	UE	0.00	27.49	K0107	UE	0.00	72.12	K0570		6.80	4.56
K0079	RR	7.00	5.76	K0107	RR	0.00	9.63	K0571		7.20	5.55
K0079	NU	59.19	55.06	K0107	NU	0.00	96.16	K0572		0.10	0.09
K0080	UE	0.00	109.61	K0108		0.00	0.00	K0573		0.50	0.34
K0080	RR	22.82	15.39	K0112		0.00	249.22	K0574		0.50	0.44
K0080	NU	0.00	145.05	K0113		0.00	152.02	K0575		0.30	0.26
K0081	UE	0.00	28.22	K0114	UE	0.00	526.00	K0576		0.30	0.26
K0081	NU	50.00	37.63	K0114	RR	0.00	70.15	K0577		5.60	0.26
K0082		128.04	0.00	K0114	NU	0.00	701.34	K0578		0.60	0.50
K0083		160.92	0.00	K0115	UE	0.00	603.14	K0579		0.20	0.11
K0084		0.00	0.00	K0115	RR	0.00	80.44	K0580		0.00	0.33
K0085		204.42	0.00	K0115	NU	0.00	804.18	K0581		4.40	2.55
K0086		115.02	0.00	K0116	UE	0.00	1258.90	K0582		0.00	3.44
K0087		123.95	0.00	K0116	RR	0.00	167.85	K0583		0.00	1.68
K0088		0.00	0.00	K0116	NU	0.00	1678.51	K0584		0.00	1.61
K0089	UE	0.00	290.74	K0183		108.99	0.00	K0585		0.00	0.00
K0089	NU	0.00	387.65	K0184		32.35	0.00	K0586		0.00	0.00
K0090	UE	0.00	52.86	K0185		49.51	0.00	K0587		0.00	4.40
K0090	RR	0.00	7.06	K0186		24.11	0.00	K0588		0.00	3.31
K0090	NU	0.00	70.47	K0187		48.98	0.00	K0589		0.00	2.19
K0091	UE	0.00	14.40	K0188		6.17	0.00	K0590		0.00	0.00
K0091	RR	0.00	1.92	K0189		18.33	0.00	K0591		0.00	6.02
K0091	NU	0.00	19.21	K0195		69.96	0.00	K0592		0.00	6.96
K0092	UE	0.00	168.68	K0268		112.30	0.00	K0593		0.00	7.88
K0092	RR	0.00	22.48	K0415		0.00	0.00	K0594		0.00	4.70
K0092	NU	0.00	224.90	K0452		8.00	0.00	K0595		0.00	3.32
K0093	UE	0.00	105.37	K0455		900.00	0.00	K0596		0.00	3.09
K0093	RR	0.00	14.05	K0460		0.00	0.00	K0597		0.00	3.48
K0093	NU	186.97	140.49	K0461		0.00	0.00	K0600		0.00	0.00
K0094	UE	0.00	34.33	K0462		0.00	0.00	K0601		0.00	0.00
K0094	RR	0.00	4.59	K0531		49.50	0.00	K0602		0.00	0.00
K0094	NU	0.00	45.79	K0532		305.00	0.00	K0603		0.00	0.00
K0095	UE	0.00	34.33	K0533		652.00	0.00	K0604		0.00	0.00
K0095	RR	0.00	4.59	K0534		14.90	0.00	K0605		0.00	0.00
K0095	NU	0.00	45.79					K0606		0.00	0.00

CODE	COMMERCIAL	MEDICARE	CODE	COMMERCIAL	MEDICARE	CODE	COMMERCIAL	MEDICARE
K0607	0.00	0.00	L0486	0.00	1655.83	L1500	0.00	1668.15
K0608	0.00	0.00	L0488	0.00	1176.75	L1510	0.00	1055.34
K0609	0.00	0.00	L0490	0.00	983.88	L1520	0.00	2003.53
K0610	0.00	0.00	L0500	134.99	119.10	L1600	0.00	113.17
K0611	0.00	0.00	L0510	270.07	242.06	L1610	0.00	38.56
K0612	0.00	0.00	L0515	179.99	255.64	L1620	120.00	117.67
K0613	0.00	0.00	L0520	0.00	361.89	L1630	0.00	148.82
K0614	0.00	0.00	L0530	450.00	363.84	L1640	0.00	405.24
K0615	0.00	0.00	L0540	0.00	391.86	L1650	233.96	203.33
K0616	0.00	0.00	L0550	1499.77	1161.60	L1652	0.00	299.10
K0617	0.00	0.00	L0560	1482.75	1269.07	L1660	171.95	150.29
K0618	0.00	0.00	L0561	0.00	289.64	L1680	0.00	1070.04
K0619	0.00	0.00	L0565	1187.61	984.82	L1685	1200.35	1044.62
K0620	0.00	0.00	L0600	77.68	80.98	L1686	1035.01	801.11
K0621	0.00	0.00	L0610	0.00	226.88	L1690	1775.00	1622.49
L0100	761.88	505.64	L0620	0.00	371.83	L1700	0.00	1341.13
L0110	149.95	126.17	L0700	0.00	1775.49	L1710	0.00	1569.94
L0120	10.00	23.30	L0710	0.00	1834.16	L1720	0.00	1157.24
L0130	170.95	143.28	L0810	0.00	2265.28	L1730	0.00	993.96
L0140	60.00	56.22	L0820	0.00	1897.02	L1750	0.00	172.79
L0150	33.00	94.91	L0830	0.00	2753.90	L1755	0.00	1390.43
L0160	168.95	137.55	L0860	0.00	1069.87	L1800	59.98	58.42
L0170	0.00	566.37	L0900	151.79	140.61	L1810	95.01	86.49
L0172	136.60	111.50	L0910	0.00	305.34	L1815	90.02	85.08
L0174	275.09	241.26	L0920	144.99	149.05	L1820	125.04	113.87
L0180	198.96	325.41	L0930	0.00	332.27	L1825	40.00	48.29
L0190	495.08	435.04	L0940	148.36	138.86	L1830	79.00	76.83
L0200	639.92	453.52	L0950	0.00	302.33	L1832	545.76	533.93
L0210	39.92	38.89	L0960	70.02	60.67	L1834	0.00	681.72
L0220	0.00	107.56	L0970	117.02	100.37	L1836	0.00	111.95
L0300	178.03	152.64	L0972	108.03	90.38	L1840	975.32	807.50
L0310	340.05	289.50	L0974	183.65	157.24	L1843	851.00	752.84
L0315	260.95	230.94	L0976	158.04	140.42	L1844	1500.23	1396.42
L0317	0.00	313.31	L0978	0.00	169.05	L1845	805.04	717.82
L0320	0.00	328.12	L0980	0.00	15.34	L1846	1099.99	932.40
L0321	0.00	459.15	L0982	0.00	14.30	L1847	500.00	482.59
L0330	487.86	402.56	L0984	57.98	52.57	L1850	240.00	252.79
L0331	0.00	533.60	L0986	145.00	116.53	L1855	1091.28	965.06
L0340	0.00	573.32	L0999	0.00	0.00	L1858	1147.24	1052.33
L0350	0.00	840.63	L1000	0.00	1782.99	L1860	0.00	942.38
L0360	0.00	1244.43	L1005	0.00	2685.47	L1870	0.00	919.07
L0370	425.06	355.10	L1010	72.00	58.94	L1880	567.03	621.60
L0380	0.00	546.50	L1020	92.03	75.91	L1885	949.75	873.80
L0390	1615.85	1250.53	L1025	0.00	109.52	L1900	215.05	236.92
L0391	0.00	669.39	L1030	44.97	55.87	L1901	0.00	14.84
L0400	1568.20	1361.86	L1040	77.44	68.52	L1902	73.02	70.11
L0410	1699.94	1560.71	L1050	83.95	73.12	L1904	436.40	412.98
L0420	1900.08	1655.83	L1060	105.00	83.99	L1906	85.51	105.62
L0430	1504.21	1176.75	L1070	0.00	79.02	L1910	0.00	234.86
L0440	1042.62	983.88	L1080	0.00	48.60	L1920	249.89	307.02
L0450	0.00	152.64	L1085	0.00	135.18	L1930	225.02	207.76
L0452	0.00	289.50	L1090	0.00	80.50	L1940	499.80	434.32
L0454	0.00	320.98	L1100	0.00	139.66	L1945	1040.38	812.96
L0456	0.00	320.98	L1110	0.00	224.29	L1950	706.15	654.14
L0458	0.00	638.32	L1120	41.99	34.88	L1960	604.76	486.79
L0460	0.00	638.32	L1200	1756.01	1376.01	L1970	748.08	624.91
L0462	0.00	638.32	L1210	263.84	229.80	L1980	349.94	322.32
L0464	0.00	638.32	L1220	236.01	194.56	L1990	449.98	391.47
L0466	0.00	328.12	L1230	0.00	499.23	L2000	0.00	890.76
L0468	0.00	402.56	L1240	82.01	68.19	L2010	0.00	812.01
L0470	0.00	559.91	L1250	82.20	63.45	L2020	1236.68	1025.45
L0472	0.00	355.10	L1260	84.42	66.44	L2030	0.00	889.67
L0474	0.00	546.50	L1270	73.57	68.04	L2035	0.00	146.27
L0476	0.00	840.63	L1280	123.98	75.76	L2036	1948.91	1629.38
L0478	0.00	1244.43	L1290	84.02	69.03	L2037	1889.78	1462.76
L0480	0.00	1250.53	L1300	1777.78	1467.00	L2038	0.00	1255.62
L0482	0.00	1361.86	L1310	0.00	1509.55	L2039	0.00	1864.67
L0484	0.00	1560.71	L1499	0.00	0.00	L2040	0.00	155.93

CODE	COMMERCIAL	MEDICARE	CODE	COMMERCIAL	MEDICARE	CODE	COMMERCIAL	MEDICARE
L2050	495.14	418.35	L2600	0.00	180.37	L3225	75.60	59.41
L2060	0.00	509.88	L2610	270.08	213.28	L3230	280.05	0.00
L2070	0.00	118.11	L2620	277.94	234.82	L3250	350.12	0.00
L2080	0.00	315.88	L2622	304.34	269.32	L3251	0.00	0.00
L2090	0.00	385.09	L2624	376.09	290.82	L3252	282.44	0.00
L2102	398.99	0.00	L2627	0.00	1505.52	L3253	71.98	0.00
L2104	400.02	0.00	L2628	0.00	1471.35	L3254	25.00	0.00
L2106	505.90	597.11	L2630	0.00	217.47	L3255	20.00	0.00
L2108	1038.71	938.34	L2640	380.48	295.13	L3257	24.99	0.00
L2112	384.99	409.74	L2650	0.00	105.40	L3260	26.00	0.00
L2114	463.91	509.75	L2660	0.00	163.68	L3265	24.99	0.00
L2116	550.80	625.21	L2670	0.00	149.81	L3300	36.20	0.00
L2122	0.00	0.00	L2680	0.00	137.43	L3310	66.00	0.00
L2124	0.00	0.00	L2750	94.97	73.41	L3320	100.97	0.00
L2126	0.00	1051.63	L2755	130.00	109.63	L3330	0.00	0.00
L2128	0.00	1505.90	L2760	63.99	53.36	L3332	15.00	0.00
L2132	921.11	708.44	L2768	0.00	109.33	L3334	12.01	0.00
L2134	0.00	849.39	L2770	64.98	54.23	L3340	45.90	0.00
L2136	0.00	1038.58	L2780	71.98	59.43	L3350	20.00	0.00
L2180	125.05	102.84	L2785	33.00	27.84	L3360	25.01	0.00
L2182	98.97	80.49	L2795	72.00	74.62	L3370	29.99	0.00
L2184	114.97	108.79	L2800	107.04	93.68	L3380	0.00	0.00
L2186	156.77	132.22	L2810	85.00	68.59	L3390	46.99	0.00
L2188	0.00	263.02	L2820	90.00	76.27	L3400	50.01	0.00
L2190	0.00	76.70	L2830	99.67	82.51	L3410	79.98	0.00
L2192	0.00	313.14	L2840	47.84	38.37	L3420	38.00	0.00
L2200	54.00	41.76	L2850	59.99	54.38	L3430	70.02	0.00
L2210	70.08	59.04	L2860	350.00	0.00	L3440	0.00	0.00
L2220	89.13	71.92	L2999	0.00	0.00	L3450	44.00	0.00
L2230	81.97	67.39	L3000	210.00	0.00	L3455	24.00	0.00
L2240	0.00	73.44	L3001	125.05	0.00	L3460	20.00	0.00
L2250	342.10	312.06	L3002	144.00	0.00	L3465	14.99	0.00
L2260	219.38	176.05	L3003	167.44	0.00	L3470	0.00	0.00
L2265	129.03	103.43	L3010	187.43	0.00	L3480	35.01	0.00
L2270	60.00	47.17	L3020	187.40	0.00	L3485	25.00	0.00
L2275	137.01	110.15	L3030	200.01	0.00	L3500	26.99	0.00
L2280	474.95	397.67	L3040	34.98	0.00	L3510	25.01	0.00
L2300	0.00	236.45	L3050	30.02	0.00	L3520	0.00	0.00
L2310	0.00	108.04	L3060	49.97	0.00	L3530	0.00	0.00
L2320	189.92	180.69	L3070	20.01	0.00	L3540	44.99	0.00
L2330	441.58	344.84	L3080	11.00	0.00	L3550	6.00	0.00
L2335	0.00	199.51	L3090	15.00	0.00	L3560	0.00	0.00
L2340	474.83	392.51	L3100	22.50	0.00	L3570	0.00	0.00
L2350	899.68	782.53	L3140	91.99	0.00	L3580	38.02	0.00
L2360	54.99	45.44	L3150	74.98	0.00	L3590	0.00	0.00
L2370	0.00	225.45	L3160	0.00	0.00	L3595	0.00	0.00
L2375	100.02	99.23	L3170	27.00	0.00	L3600	82.34	0.00
L2380	0.00	108.12	L3201	69.98	0.00	L3610	109.00	0.00
L2385	132.93	117.63	L3202	70.00	0.00	L3620	74.03	0.00
L2390	117.04	96.13	L3203	0.00	0.00	L3630	96.60	0.00
L2395	164.97	137.41	L3204	70.02	0.00	L3640	0.00	0.00
L2397	125.02	98.70	L3206	60.00	0.00	L3649	0.00	0.00
L2405	80.00	73.15	L3207	0.00	0.00	L3650	53.03	50.97
L2415	147.04	101.92	L3208	46.51	0.00	L3651	0.00	50.28
L2425	153.98	120.27	L3209	46.49	0.00	L3652	0.00	151.53
L2430	155.00	120.27	L3211	46.51	0.00	L3660	99.96	88.33
L2435	165.00	145.34	L3212	0.00	0.00	L3670	105.02	97.18
L2492	114.96	89.56	L3213	0.00	0.00	L3675	142.45	134.01
L2500	0.00	277.05	L3214	0.00	0.00	L3677	0.00	0.00
L2510	0.00	637.92	L3215	114.03	0.00	L3700	54.99	59.99
L2520	0.00	404.58	L3216	139.95	0.00	L3701	0.00	15.55
L2525	1110.89	1070.54	L3217	0.00	0.00	L3710	131.99	106.24
L2526	0.00	601.53	L3218	25.00	0.00	L3720	635.51	562.10
L2530	250.00	206.35	L3219	134.99	0.00	L3730	945.09	774.69
L2540	419.77	371.30	L3221	149.99	0.00	L3740	995.36	918.46
L2550	326.10	252.23	L3222	162.50	0.00	L3760	381.50	381.88
L2570	0.00	418.31	L3223	30.00	0.00	L3762	0.00	82.11
L2580	0.00	407.59	L3224	75.00	51.64	L3800	145.01	171.84

CODE	COMMERCIAL	MEDICARE	CODE	COMMERCIAL	MEDICARE	CODE	COMMERCIAL	MEDICARE
L3805	279.89	274.95	L4020	0.00	756.43	L5595	0.00	3767.32
L3807	176.90	190.94	L4030	0.00	443.40	L5600	0.00	4160.24
L3810	64.79	55.70	L4040	0.00	358.49	L5610	0.00	1937.12
L3815	0.00	51.71	L4045	324.90	288.09	L5611	1650.54	1507.47
L3820	96.96	88.81	L4050	0.00	362.57	L5613	0.00	2292.95
L3825	68.01	55.73	L4055	265.41	234.77	L5614	0.00	1418.61
L3830	84.67	72.75	L4060	0.00	279.10	L5616	0.00	1270.74
L3835	0.00	78.87	L4070	298.05	247.16	L5617	0.00	473.39
L3840	0.00	54.02	L4080	0.00	88.83	L5618	346.06	263.13
L3845	71.00	69.77	L4090	0.00	79.31	L5620	335.13	260.12
L3850	100.96	99.65	L4100	121.00	91.60	L5622	420.72	339.19
L3855	109.55	100.45	L4110	96.02	74.48	L5624	440.12	340.16
L3860	155.04	137.50	L4130	0.00	435.72	L5626	0.00	446.10
L3890	350.00	0.00	L4205	26.00	0.00	L5628	0.00	451.74
L3900	1294.99	1112.00	L4210	32.00	0.00	L5629	383.96	297.35
L3901	0.00	1381.04	L4350	73.02	78.51	L5630	0.00	419.91
L3902	0.00	2093.34	L4360	250.07	243.17	L5631	518.93	411.10
L3904	0.00	2516.64	L4370	182.53	165.80	L5632	279.95	207.75
L3906	313.15	339.57	L4380	64.99	94.33	L5634	0.00	284.61
L3907	475.20	436.54	L4386	0.00	133.04	L5636	0.00	238.40
L3908	49.00	51.50	L4392	25.01	19.72	L5637	370.86	270.30
L3909	0.00	10.79	L4394	0.00	14.39	L5638	0.00	455.34
L3910	324.96	322.35	L4396	149.95	140.56	L5639	0.00	1049.01
L3911	0.00	0.00	L4398	94.59	64.70	L5640	0.00	598.28
L3912	70.00	81.50	L5000	567.85	472.74	L5642	0.00	579.69
L3914	69.99	73.67	L5010	1595.83	1139.08	L5643	0.00	1456.26
L3916	95.04	109.15	L5020	2540.09	1854.19	L5644	0.00	552.63
L3918	73.02	67.35	L5050	2901.73	2147.24	L5645	904.54	746.53
L3920	0.00	84.17	L5060	0.00	2584.22	L5646	0.00	512.65
L3922	0.00	84.04	L5100	2820.29	2174.55	L5647	931.04	744.26
L3923	37.40	29.72	L5105	0.00	3250.33	L5648	0.00	616.00
L3924	102.00	91.64	L5150	0.00	3285.64	L5649	2313.51	1781.38
L3926	0.00	79.78	L5160	0.00	3573.73	L5650	566.81	456.76
L3928	36.00	50.02	L5200	0.00	3090.83	L5651	1452.27	1123.62
L3930	54.86	52.88	L5210	0.00	2270.38	L5652	500.15	407.92
L3932	39.01	40.39	L5220	0.00	2580.70	L5653	0.00	544.53
L3934	39.75	41.41	L5230	0.00	3559.30	L5654	0.00	310.29
L3936	71.96	76.55	L5250	0.00	4854.56	L5655	316.25	248.17
L3938	80.99	80.16	L5270	0.00	4812.04	L5656	0.00	347.08
L3940	87.98	92.39	L5280	0.00	4763.92	L5658	0.00	340.19
L3942	58.51	63.90	L5300	3521.99	0.00	L5660	649.88	539.40
L3944	0.00	84.40	L5301	2844.35	2148.24	L5661	0.00	569.37
L3946	45.02	76.16	L5310	0.00	0.00	L5662	627.88	494.63
L3948	50.02	47.36	L5311	0.00	3086.17	L5663	812.17	644.73
L3950	0.00	128.87	L5320	5014.39	0.00	L5664	800.12	621.17
L3952	85.04	143.03	L5321	4104.91	3075.14	L5665	559.32	479.07
L3954	94.32	94.91	L5330	0.00	0.00	L5666	85.02	65.50
L3956	58.00	0.00	L5331	0.00	4351.44	L5667	1838.18	0.00
L3960	699.72	631.58	L5340	0.00	0.00	L5668	122.48	94.48
L3962	580.11	616.60	L5341	0.00	4728.63	L5669	1340.83	0.00
L3963	890.50	1433.72	L5400	0.00	1126.07	L5670	298.94	253.88
L3964	0.00	0.00	L5410	0.00	390.93	L5671	570.10	465.39
L3965	0.00	0.00	L5420	0.00	1422.18	L5672	0.00	279.00
L3966	0.00	0.00	L5430	0.00	470.82	L5674	74.99	59.80
L3968	0.00	0.00	L5450	473.89	381.19	L5675	100.00	81.06
L3969	0.00	0.00	L5460	0.00	510.18	L5676	412.05	339.05
L3970	0.00	0.00	L5500	0.00	1201.66	L5677	0.00	461.32
L3972	0.00	0.00	L5505	0.00	1627.36	L5678	45.99	37.15
L3974	0.00	0.00	L5510	0.00	1362.16	L5680	364.91	284.78
L3980	289.55	265.68	L5520	0.00	1345.49	L5682	0.00	585.14
L3982	341.00	320.82	L5530	2119.94	1616.06	L5684	58.01	45.03
L3984	315.00	295.79	L5535	0.00	1586.65	L5686	0.00	47.80
L3985	423.94	502.29	L5540	2188.20	1693.46	L5688	73.99	57.15
L3986	490.80	481.69	L5560	0.00	1818.48	L5690	0.00	91.55
L3995	34.99	28.11	L5570	0.00	1890.57	L5692	0.00	124.32
L3999	0.00	0.00	L5580	2803.61	2207.11	L5694	217.06	169.74
L4000	0.00	1119.77	L5585	0.00	2393.87	L5695	189.96	152.59
L4010	0.00	589.39	L5590	2774.89	2249.20	L5696	224.01	173.11

CODE	COMMERCIAL	MEDICARE	CODE	COMMERCIAL	MEDICARE	CODE	COMMERCIAL	MEDICARE
L5697	95.98	75.11	L5987	7107.00	6047.63	L6672	0.00	157.76
L5698	137.64	97.60	L5988	1950.00	1679.42	L6675	136.03	112.36
L5699	0.00	174.45	L5989	3500.00	2604.03	L6676	0.00	113.47
L5700	3027.24	2562.27	L5990	0.00	1525.16	L6680	291.04	217.08
L5701	3848.78	3181.26	L5995	0.00	0.00	L6682	314.97	240.01
L5702	0.00	4064.99	L5999	0.00	0.00	L6684	0.00	326.14
L5704	623.92	492.66	L6000	0.00	1243.17	L6686	0.00	552.36
L5705	1116.29	869.13	L6010	0.00	1383.44	L6687	0.00	539.68
L5706	0.00	852.68	L6020	0.00	1289.84	L6688	0.00	495.65
L5707	0.00	1157.42	L6025	0.00	6727.43	L6689	0.00	630.43
L5710	0.00	336.51	L6050	0.00	1777.35	L6690	0.00	643.35
L5711	0.00	488.55	L6055	0.00	2477.16	L6691	0.00	322.97
L5712	0.00	403.16	L6100	0.00	1800.72	L6692	0.00	523.24
L5714	0.00	391.35	L6110	1619.55	1909.97	L6693	0.00	2386.69
L5716	0.00	681.93	L6120	0.00	2225.80	L6700	0.00	485.35
L5718	0.00	852.33	L6130	0.00	2422.08	L6705	0.00	284.94
L5722	0.00	844.76	L6200	0.00	2552.48	L6710	0.00	322.92
L5724	0.00	1412.25	L6205	0.00	3407.16	L6715	0.00	320.76
L5726	0.00	1627.60	L6250	0.00	2512.49	L6720	0.00	798.20
L5728	0.00	2226.33	L6300	0.00	3485.81	L6725	0.00	386.44
L5780	0.00	1071.21	L6310	0.00	2839.26	L6730	0.00	597.88
L5781	0.00	3363.70	L6320	0.00	1598.93	L6735	0.00	278.80
L5782	0.00	0.00	L6350	0.00	3664.79	L6740	0.00	363.48
L5785	622.56	486.11	L6360	0.00	2980.15	L6745	0.00	332.57
L5790	865.09	672.74	L6370	0.00	1900.34	L6750	0.00	328.73
L5795	0.00	1004.58	L6380	0.00	1076.23	L6755	0.00	327.80
L5810	585.00	455.53	L6382	0.00	1385.36	L6765	0.00	342.47
L5811	771.56	682.37	L6384	0.00	1783.88	L6770	0.00	330.15
L5812	638.82	528.91	L6386	0.00	375.74	L6775	0.00	391.18
L5814	3590.80	3122.17	L6388	0.00	411.32	L6780	0.00	418.14
L5816	0.00	795.70	L6400	0.00	2171.03	L6790	0.00	422.78
L5818	0.00	898.51	L6450	0.00	2884.63	L6795	0.00	1157.95
L5822	0.00	1593.29	L6500	0.00	2886.99	L6800	0.00	948.00
L5824	0.00	1434.85	L6550	0.00	3567.79	L6805	0.00	318.34
L5826	0.00	2641.82	L6570	0.00	4095.13	L6806	0.00	1359.65
L5828	3319.92	2642.16	L6580	0.00	1462.54	L6807	0.00	1232.92
L5830	0.00	1775.39	L6582	0.00	1287.71	L6808	0.00	1052.79
L5840	0.00	3171.23	L6584	0.00	1915.05	L6809	0.00	347.17
L5845	2052.00	1506.81	L6586	0.00	1762.19	L6810	0.00	174.53
L5846	5881.20	4586.24	L6588	0.00	2644.58	L6825	0.00	965.32
L5847	0.00	13020.15	L6590	0.00	2461.56	L6830	0.00	1267.02
L5848	904.00	904.00	L6600	0.00	175.50	L6835	0.00	1103.70
L5850	141.96	119.69	L6605	0.00	173.29	L6840	0.00	766.77
L5855	0.00	288.95	L6610	0.00	155.77	L6845	0.00	711.80
L5910	410.98	338.86	L6615	0.00	162.53	L6850	0.00	644.66
L5920	602.97	496.43	L6616	0.00	60.69	L6855	0.00	819.93
L5925	0.00	314.38	L6620	0.00	283.69	L6860	0.00	621.85
L5930	3581.60	2847.78	L6623	0.00	600.17	L6865	0.00	304.67
L5940	580.61	469.32	L6625	0.00	497.62	L6867	0.00	898.88
L5950	876.26	727.93	L6628	0.00	448.21	L6868	0.00	224.32
L5960	0.00	901.99	L6629	0.00	136.89	L6870	0.00	222.39
L5962	645.03	549.96	L6630	0.00	201.65	L6872	0.00	881.19
L5964	1085.58	876.24	L6632	0.00	60.79	L6873	0.00	437.69
L5966	0.00	1116.54	L6635	0.00	164.79	L6875	0.00	727.22
L5968	0.00	3054.96	L6637	0.00	343.55	L6880	0.00	471.79
L5970	254.88	190.03	L6638	0.00	2102.31	L6881	0.00	3436.90
L5972	410.55	329.75	L6640	0.00	262.08	L6882	0.00	2607.06
L5974	278.00	218.03	L6641	0.00	150.10	L6890	211.95	159.14
L5975	550.00	389.74	L6642	0.00	203.45	L6895	675.20	522.45
L5976	636.10	523.98	L6645	0.00	298.68	L6900	0.00	1413.23
L5978	336.06	273.05	L6646	0.00	2651.49	L6905	0.00	1373.70
L5979	2463.23	2134.88	L6647	0.00	436.52	L6910	0.00	1338.27
L5980	4247.47	3469.05	L6648	0.00	2734.64	L6915	0.00	585.73
L5981	3518.16	2694.78	L6650	0.00	316.70	L6920	0.00	6244.14
L5982	0.00	540.90	L6655	0.00	70.28	L6925	0.00	7208.77
L5984	688.97	533.01	L6660	110.97	85.88	L6930	0.00	6282.86
L5985	312.94	238.91	L6665	49.37	43.10	L6935	0.00	7343.72
L5986	761.21	592.89	L6670	0.00	44.87	L6940	0.00	8208.97

CODE	COMMERCIAL	MEDICARE	CODE	COMMERCIAL	MEDICARE	CODE	COMMERCIAL	MEDICARE
L6945	0.00	9550.17	L8210	101.72	0.00	P9023	0.00	0.00
L6950	0.00	9330.64	L8220	27.90	0.00	P9031	0.00	0.00
L6955	0.00	11174.72	L8230	0.00	0.00	P9032	0.00	0.00
L6960	0.00	11270.55	L8239	0.00	0.00	P9033	0.00	0.00
L6965	0.00	13260.33	L8300	84.98	78.93	P9034	566.20	0.00
L6970	0.00	13646.10	L8310	135.05	124.61	P9035	690.00	0.00
L6975	0.00	14951.79	L8320	0.00	50.02	P9036	0.00	0.00
L7010	0.00	3417.25	L8330	0.00	46.19	P9037	790.00	0.00
L7015	0.00	5430.27	L8400	19.01	14.73	P9038	0.00	0.00
L7020	0.00	3183.87	L8410	24.64	19.38	P9039	0.00	0.00
L7025	0.00	3212.99	L8415	25.00	20.06	P9040	450.00	0.00
L7030	0.00	4913.16	L8417	79.90	63.20	P9041	40.51	0.00
L7035	0.00	3290.48	L8420	23.99	18.20	P9042	103.00	0.00
L7040	0.00	2637.71	L8430	26.42	20.71	P9043	0.00	0.00
L7045	0.00	1512.29	L8435	25.01	19.67	P9044	0.00	0.00
L7170	0.00	5486.08	L8440	51.01	39.13	P9045	94.54	0.00
L7180	0.00	30564.31	L8460	75.02	62.36	P9046	0.00	0.00
L7185	0.00	5555.39	L8465	62.01	45.64	P9047	189.02	0.00
L7186	0.00	8276.16	L8470	8.00	6.25	P9048	0.00	0.00
L7190	0.00	7068.17	L8480	10.00	8.61	P9050	0.00	0.00
L7191	0.00	8648.11	L8485	12.00	10.41	P9603	0.80	0.00
L7260	0.00	1841.35	L8490	129.03	124.32	P9604	24.00	0.00
L7261	0.00	3351.95	L8499	0.00	0.00	P9612	36.99	0.00
L7266	0.00	926.35	L8500	525.00	617.48	P9615	15.00	0.00
L7272	0.00	1888.81	L8501	134.96	113.03	Q0035	0.00	0.00
L7274	0.00	5373.88	L8505	29.00	0.00	Q0081	104.99	0.00
L7360	0.00	212.77	L8507	39.00	35.22	Q0083	139.27	0.00
L7362	0.00	234.42	L8509	199.00	91.81	Q0084	233.05	0.00
L7364	0.00	372.83	L8510	0.00	212.44	Q0085	400.00	0.00
L7366	0.00	502.21	L8600	999.75	584.26	Q0086	78.00	0.00
L7367	0.00	327.30	L8603	450.00	368.95	Q0091	40.00	0.00
L7368	0.00	424.29	L8606	300.00	185.01	Q0092	20.00	0.00
L7499	0.00	0.00	L8610	409.50	547.64	Q0111	18.00	0.00
L7500	90.00	0.00	L8612	700.00	568.90	Q0112	20.00	0.00
L7510	35.00	0.00	L8613	0.00	240.59	Q0113	0.00	0.00
L7520	27.50	0.00	L8614	0.00	16260.69	Q0114	15.00	0.00
L7900	474.95	450.85	L8619	0.00	6979.72	Q0115	60.00	0.00
L8000	39.99	34.16	L8630	0.00	315.22	Q0136	25.00	0.00
L8001	0.00	105.44	L8641	280.00	327.51	Q0144	24.47	0.00
L8002	0.00	138.70	L8642	0.00	265.65	Q0160	1.18	0.00
L8010	67.59	0.00	L8658	0.00	285.56	Q0161	1.06	0.00
L8015	62.00	50.51	L8670	0.00	468.73	Q0163	0.00	0.00
L8020	183.16	187.70	L8699	0.00	0.00	Q0164	0.84	0.00
L8030	298.93	295.18	L9900	0.00	0.00	Q0165	1.10	0.00
L8035	2400.00	3079.93	M0064	49.99	0.00	Q0166	70.02	0.00
L8039	0.00	0.00	M0075	0.00	0.00	Q0167	0.00	0.00
L8040	5.50	2082.16	M0076	37.70	0.00	Q0168	0.00	0.00
L8041	0.00	2509.70	M0100	0.00	0.00	Q0169	0.00	0.00
L8042	70.00	2819.89	M0300	90.00	0.00	Q0170	0.00	0.00
L8043	0.00	3158.28	M0301	0.00	0.00	Q0171	0.00	0.00
L8044	0.00	3496.66	M0302	125.00	0.00	Q0172	0.00	0.00
L8045	0.00	2300.81	P2028	0.00	0.00	Q0173	0.00	0.00
L8046	0.00	2255.91	P2029	0.00	0.00	Q0174	0.00	0.00
L8047	0.00	1156.16	P2031	0.00	0.00	Q0175	0.00	0.00
L8048	0.00	0.00	P2033	0.00	0.00	Q0176	0.00	0.00
L8049	0.00	0.00	P2038	0.00	0.00	Q0177	0.00	0.00
L8100	33.00	0.00	P3000	32.00	0.00	Q0178	0.00	0.00
L8110	35.00	0.00	P3001	36.00	0.00	Q0179	81.02	0.00
L8120	36.00	0.00	P7001	45.01	0.00	Q0180	118.23	0.00
L8130	45.00	0.00	P9010	0.00	0.00	Q0181	0.00	0.00
L8140	53.25	0.00	P9011	0.00	0.00	Q0183	0.00	0.00
L8150	47.94	0.00	P9012	0.00	0.00	Q0184	16.00	0.00
L8160	57.49	0.00	P9016	300.00	0.00	Q0185	44.40	0.00
L8170	60.00	0.00	P9017	114.00	0.00	Q0187	23.80	0.00
L8180	59.46	0.00	P9019	85.00	0.00	Q1001	50.00	0.00
L8190	125.01	0.00	P9020	0.00	0.00	Q1002	94.50	0.00
L8195	139.10	0.00	P9021	260.00	0.00	Q1003	0.00	0.00
L8200	139.05	0.00	P9022	95.00	0.00	Q1004	0.00	0.00

CODE	COMMERCIAL	MEDICARE	CODE	COMMERCIAL	MEDICARE	CODE	COMMERCIAL	MEDICARE
Q1005	0.00	0.00	Q4021	35.00	0.00	S0030	25.00	0.00
Q2001	0.00	0.00	Q4022	67.99	0.00	S0032	10.63	0.00
Q2002	0.00	0.00	Q4023	0.00	0.00	S0034	0.00	0.00
Q2003	0.00	0.00	Q4024	30.00	0.00	S0039	0.00	0.00
Q2004	0.00	0.00	Q4025	0.00	0.00	S0040	33.46	0.00
Q2005	0.00	0.00	Q4026	0.00	0.00	S0071	3.90	0.00
Q2006	0.00	0.00	Q4027	0.00	0.00	S0072	0.00	0.00
Q2007	0.00	0.00	Q4028	0.00	0.00	S0073	25.00	0.00
Q2008	0.00	0.00	Q4029	0.00	0.00	S0074	0.00	0.00
Q2009	31.00	0.00	Q4030	114.95	0.00	S0077	12.93	0.00
Q2010	41.19	0.00	Q4031	0.00	0.00	S0078	0.00	0.00
Q2011	26.00	0.00	Q4032	81.98	0.00	S0079	0.00	0.00
Q2012	0.00	0.00	Q4033	0.00	0.00	S0080	0.00	0.00
Q2013	0.00	0.00	Q4034	0.00	0.00	S0081	2.40	0.00
Q2014	0.00	0.00	Q4035	0.00	0.00	S0085	0.00	0.00
Q2015	207.36	0.00	Q4036	0.00	0.00	S0086	0.00	0.00
Q2016	68.14	0.00	Q4037	74.97	0.00	S0087	0.00	0.00
Q2017	0.00	0.00	Q4038	135.98	0.00	S0088	17.50	0.00
Q2018	0.00	0.00	Q4039	49.99	0.00	S0090	0.00	0.00
Q2019	0.00	0.00	Q4040	70.75	0.00	S0091	0.00	0.00
Q2020	0.00	0.00	Q4041	0.00	0.00	S0092	0.00	0.00
Q2021	0.00	0.00	Q4042	0.00	0.00	S0093	0.00	0.00
Q2022	1.00	0.00	Q4043	0.00	0.00	S0096	0.00	0.00
Q3000	0.00	0.00	Q4044	0.00	0.00	S0104	0.00	0.00
Q3001	53.00	0.00	Q4045	34.00	0.00	S0106	0.00	0.00
Q3002	36.00	0.00	Q4046	64.01	0.00	S0108	0.00	0.00
Q3003	0.00	0.00	Q4047	0.00	0.00	S0112	0.00	0.00
Q3004	60.00	0.00	Q4048	0.00	0.00	S0114	0.00	0.00
Q3005	264.00	0.00	Q4049	40.01	0.00	S0122	0.00	0.00
Q3006	0.00	0.00	Q4050	0.00	0.00	S0124	0.00	0.00
Q3007	0.00	0.00	Q4051	0.00	0.00	S0126	0.00	0.00
Q3008	0.00	0.00	Q4052	0.00	0.00	S0128	0.00	0.00
Q3009	49.00	0.00	Q4053	0.00	0.00	S0130	0.00	0.00
Q3010	18.00	0.00	Q9920	16.93	0.00	S0132	0.00	0.00
Q3011	0.00	0.00	Q9921	20.00	0.00	S0135	0.00	0.00
Q3012	0.00	0.00	Q9922	24.00	0.00	S0136	0.00	0.00
Q3013	0.00	0.00	Q9923	19.00	0.00	S0137	0.00	0.00
Q3014	35.00	0.00	Q9924	28.00	0.00	S0138	0.00	0.00
Q3017	0.00	0.00	Q9925	20.00	0.00	S0139	0.00	0.00
Q3019	400.00	0.00	Q9926	20.00	0.00	S0140	0.00	0.00
Q3020	372.00	0.00	Q9927	20.00	0.00	S0141	0.00	0.00
Q3021	0.00	0.00	Q9928	20.00	0.00	S0155	17.13	0.00
Q3022	0.00	0.00	Q9929	20.00	0.00	S0156	0.00	0.00
Q3023	0.00	0.00	Q9930	19.00	0.00	S0157	0.00	0.00
Q3025	0.00	0.00	Q9931	20.00	0.00	S0170	0.00	0.00
Q3026	0.00	0.00	Q9932	19.00	0.00	S0171	0.00	0.00
Q3030	56.60	0.00	Q9933	20.00	0.00	S0172	0.00	0.00
Q3031	0.00	0.00	Q9934	20.00	0.00	S0173	0.00	0.00
Q4001	0.00	0.00	Q9935	20.00	0.00	S0174	0.00	0.00
Q4002	0.00	0.00	Q9936	20.00	0.00	S0175	0.00	0.00
Q4003	0.00	0.00	Q9937	20.00	0.00	S0176	0.00	0.00
Q4004	0.00	0.00	Q9938	19.00	0.00	S0177	0.00	0.00
Q4005	0.00	0.00	Q9939	19.00	0.00	S0178	0.00	0.00
Q4006	95.98	0.00	Q9940	19.00	0.00	S0179	0.00	0.00
Q4007	0.00	0.00	R0070	125.00	0.00	S0181	0.00	0.00
Q4008	50.98	0.00	R0075	54.99	0.00	S0182	0.00	0.00
Q4009	45.01	0.00	R0076	189.98	0.00	S0183	0.00	0.00
Q4010	70.00	0.00	S0009	14.67	0.00	S0187	0.00	0.00
Q4011	27.67	0.00	S0012	0.00	0.00	S0189	0.00	0.00
Q4012	41.99	0.00	S0014	0.00	0.00	S0190	125.02	0.00
Q4013	0.00	0.00	S0016	0.00	0.00	S0191	4.00	0.00
Q4014	61.98	0.00	S0017	0.00	0.00	S0195	0.00	0.00
Q4015	0.00	0.00	S0020	8.00	0.00	S0199	700.00	0.00
Q4016	0.00	0.00	S0021	0.00	0.00	S0201	0.00	0.00
Q4017	38.01	0.00	S0023	7.00	0.00	S0206	0.00	0.00
Q4018	64.99	0.00	S0024	0.00	0.00	S0207	0.00	0.00
Q4019	0.00	0.00	S0028	8.19	0.00	S0208	0.00	0.00
Q4020	34.99	0.00	S0029	0.00	0.00	S0209	1.40	0.00

CODE	COMMERCIAL	MEDICARE	CODE	COMMERCIAL	MEDICARE	CODE	COMMERCIAL	MEDICARE
S0215	1.40	0.00	S2130	0.00	0.00	S3844	0.00	0.00
S0220	0.00	0.00	S2140	0.00	0.00	S3845	0.00	0.00
S0221	0.00	0.00	S2142	0.00	0.00	S3846	0.00	0.00
S0250	0.00	0.00	S2150	0.00	0.00	S3847	0.00	0.00
S0255	0.00	0.00	S2180	0.00	0.00	S3848	0.00	0.00
S0260	0.00	0.00	S2202	0.00	0.00	S3849	0.00	0.00
S0302	48.00	0.00	S2205	0.00	0.00	S3850	0.00	0.00
S0310	0.00	0.00	S2206	0.00	0.00	S3851	0.00	0.00
S0315	0.00	0.00	S2207	0.00	0.00	S3852	0.00	0.00
S0316	0.00	0.00	S2208	0.00	0.00	S3900	0.00	0.00
S0317	0.00	0.00	S2209	0.00	0.00	S3902	0.00	0.00
S0320	0.00	0.00	S2210	0.00	0.00	S3904	0.00	0.00
S0340	0.00	0.00	S2211	0.00	0.00	S3906	0.00	0.00
S0341	0.00	0.00	S2220	0.00	0.00	S4005	0.00	0.00
S0342	0.00	0.00	S2250	0.00	0.00	S4011	0.00	0.00
S0390	0.00	0.00	S2260	0.00	0.00	S4013	0.00	0.00
S0395	50.00	0.00	S2262	0.00	0.00	S4014	0.00	0.00
S0400	0.00	0.00	S2265	0.00	0.00	S4015	0.00	0.00
S0500	66.00	0.00	S2266	0.00	0.00	S4016	0.00	0.00
S0504	0.00	0.00	S2267	0.00	0.00	S4017	0.00	0.00
S0506	0.00	0.00	S2300	0.00	0.00	S4018	0.00	0.00
S0508	0.00	0.00	S2340	0.00	0.00	S4020	0.00	0.00
S0510	0.00	0.00	S2341	0.00	0.00	S4021	0.00	0.00
S0512	0.00	0.00	S2342	0.00	0.00	S4022	0.00	0.00
S0514	0.00	0.00	S2350	0.00	0.00	S4023	0.00	0.00
S0516	0.00	0.00	S2351	0.00	0.00	S4025	0.00	0.00
S0518	0.00	0.00	S2360	0.00	0.00	S4026	0.00	0.00
S0580	30.00	0.00	S2361	0.00	0.00	S4027	0.00	0.00
S0581	0.00	0.00	S2370	0.00	0.00	S4028	0.00	0.00
S0590	0.00	0.00	S2371	0.00	0.00	S4030	0.00	0.00
S0592	0.00	0.00	S2400	0.00	0.00	S4031	0.00	0.00
S0601	0.00	0.00	S2401	0.00	0.00	S4035	0.00	0.00
S0605	22.00	0.00	S2402	0.00	0.00	S4036	0.00	0.00
S0610	120.00	0.00	S2403	0.00	0.00	S4037	0.00	0.00
S0612	90.00	0.00	S2404	0.00	0.00	S4040	0.00	0.00
S0620	56.00	0.00	S2405	0.00	0.00	S4980	0.00	0.00
S0621	65.00	0.00	S2409	0.00	0.00	S4981	0.00	0.00
S0622	0.00	0.00	S2411	0.00	0.00	S4989	0.00	0.00
S0630	50.00	0.00	S3000	0.00	0.00	S4990	0.00	0.00
S0800	1395.00	0.00	S3600	0.00	0.00	S4991	0.00	0.00
S0810	0.00	0.00	S3601	0.00	0.00	S4993	24.30	0.00
S0812	0.00	0.00	S3620	30.00	0.00	S4995	0.00	0.00
S0820	100.00	0.00	S3625	0.00	0.00	S5000	5.20	0.00
S0830	60.00	0.00	S3630	0.00	0.00	S5001	13.90	0.00
S1001	0.00	0.00	S3645	0.00	0.00	S5002	0.00	0.00
S1002	0.00	0.00	S3650	0.00	0.00	S5003	0.00	0.00
S1015	26.50	0.00	S3652	0.00	0.00	S5010	15.00	0.00
S1016	0.00	0.00	S3655	0.00	0.00	S5011	5.80	0.00
S1025	0.00	0.00	S3700	0.00	0.00	S5012	0.00	0.00
S1030	0.00	0.00	S3701	0.00	0.00	S5013	0.00	0.00
S1031	0.00	0.00	S3708	0.00	0.00	S5014	0.00	0.00
S1040	0.00	0.00	S3818	0.00	0.00	S5016	127.30	0.00
S2052	0.00	0.00	S3819	0.00	0.00	S5017	0.00	0.00
S2053	0.00	0.00	S3820	0.00	0.00	S5018	0.00	0.00
S2054	0.00	0.00	S3822	0.00	0.00	S5019	100.00	0.00
S2055	0.00	0.00	S3823	0.00	0.00	S5020	0.00	0.00
S2060	0.00	0.00	S3828	0.00	0.00	S5021	81.80	0.00
S2061	0.00	0.00	S3829	0.00	0.00	S5022	0.00	0.00
S2065	0.00	0.00	S3830	0.00	0.00	S5025	25.00	0.00
S2080	0.00	0.00	S3831	0.00	0.00	S5035	15.00	0.00
S2090	0.00	0.00	S3833	0.00	0.00	S5036	0.00	0.00
S2091	0.00	0.00	S3834	0.00	0.00	S5100	0.00	0.00
S2102	0.00	0.00	S3835	0.00	0.00	S5101	0.00	0.00
S2103	0.00	0.00	S3837	0.00	0.00	S5102	0.00	0.00
S2107	0.00	0.00	S3840	0.00	0.00	S5105	0.00	0.00
S2112	0.00	0.00	S3841	0.00	0.00	S5108	0.00	0.00
S2115	0.00	0.00	S3842	0.00	0.00	S5109	0.00	0.00
S2120	0.00	0.00	S3843	0.00	0.00	S5110	0.00	0.00

CODE	COMMERCIAL	MEDICARE	CODE	COMMERCIAL	MEDICARE	CODE	COMMERCIAL	MEDICARE
S5111	0.00	0.00	S8200	0.00	0.00	S9145	0.00	0.00
S5115	0.00	0.00	S8205	0.00	0.00	S9150	0.00	0.00
S5116	0.00	0.00	S8210	0.00	0.00	S9200	0.00	0.00
S5120	0.00	0.00	S8260	1095.00	0.00	S9208	0.00	0.00
S5121	0.00	0.00	S8262	0.00	0.00	S9209	0.00	0.00
S5125	0.00	0.00	S8265	0.00	0.00	S9210	0.00	0.00
S5126	0.00	0.00	S8400	0.80	0.00	S9211	0.00	0.00
S5130	0.00	0.00	S8401	0.90	0.00	S9212	0.00	0.00
S5131	0.00	0.00	S8402	0.70	0.00	S9213	11.60	0.00
S5135	0.00	0.00	S8403	1.00	0.00	S9214	0.00	0.00
S5136	0.00	0.00	S8404	1.40	0.00	S9216	0.00	0.00
S5140	0.00	0.00	S8405	0.40	0.00	S9217	0.00	0.00
S5141	0.00	0.00	S8415	0.00	0.00	S9218	0.00	0.00
S5145	0.00	0.00	S8420	0.00	0.00	S9220	0.00	0.00
S5146	0.00	0.00	S8421	0.00	0.00	S9225	0.00	0.00
S5150	0.00	0.00	S8422	0.00	0.00	S9230	0.00	0.00
S5151	0.00	0.00	S8423	0.00	0.00	S9300	39.00	0.00
S5160	0.00	0.00	S8424	0.00	0.00	S9308	29.00	0.00
S5161	0.00	0.00	S8425	0.00	0.00	S9310	0.00	0.00
S5162	0.00	0.00	S8426	0.00	0.00	S9325	235.00	0.00
S5165	0.00	0.00	S8427	0.00	0.00	S9326	101.40	0.00
S5170	0.00	0.00	S8428	0.00	0.00	S9327	0.00	0.00
S5175	0.00	0.00	S8429	0.00	0.00	S9328	0.00	0.00
S5180	0.00	0.00	S8430	0.00	0.00	S9329	215.00	0.00
S5181	0.00	0.00	S8431	0.00	0.00	S9330	90.00	0.00
S5185	0.00	0.00	S8433	0.00	0.00	S9331	245.00	0.00
S5190	0.00	0.00	S8450	0.00	0.00	S9335	0.00	0.00
S5199	0.00	0.00	S8451	28.00	0.00	S9336	0.00	0.00
S5497	0.00	0.00	S8452	0.00	0.00	S9338	126.00	0.00
S5498	15.00	0.00	S8460	0.00	0.00	S9339	0.00	0.00
S5501	23.00	0.00	S8470	0.00	0.00	S9340	33.00	0.00
S5502	12.00	0.00	S8490	0.30	0.00	S9341	0.00	0.00
S5503	0.00	0.00	S8945	0.00	0.00	S9342	30.00	0.00
S5517	0.00	0.00	S8950	0.00	0.00	S9343	11.00	0.00
S5518	0.00	0.00	S8990	0.00	0.00	S9345	0.00	0.00
S5520	0.00	0.00	S8999	0.00	0.00	S9346	0.00	0.00
S5521	47.00	0.00	S9001	100.00	0.00	S9347	65.00	0.00
S5522	0.00	0.00	S9007	0.00	0.00	S9348	0.00	0.00
S5523	0.00	0.00	S9015	87.50	0.00	S9349	200.30	0.00
S8001	0.00	0.00	S9022	0.00	0.00	S9351	0.00	0.00
S8002	0.00	0.00	S9023	0.00	0.00	S9353	0.00	0.00
S8003	0.00	0.00	S9024	0.00	0.00	S9355	4.70	0.00
S8004	0.00	0.00	S9025	0.00	0.00	S9357	0.00	0.00
S8030	0.00	0.00	S9034	0.00	0.00	S9359	0.00	0.00
S8035	0.00	0.00	S9035	40.00	0.00	S9361	0.00	0.00
S8037	0.00	0.00	S9055	0.00	0.00	S9363	0.00	0.00
S8040	0.00	0.00	S9056	0.00	0.00	S9364	650.00	0.00
S8042	0.00	0.00	S9061	0.00	0.00	S9365	650.00	0.00
S8049	0.00	0.00	S9075	0.00	0.00	S9366	650.00	0.00
S8055	0.00	0.00	S9083	106.00	0.00	S9367	455.00	0.00
S8080	0.00	0.00	S9085	0.00	0.00	S9368	0.00	0.00
S8085	475.00	0.00	S9088	90.00	0.00	S9370	285.00	0.00
S8092	495.00	0.00	S9090	65.00	0.00	S9372	26.50	0.00
S8095	400.00	0.00	S9092	0.00	0.00	S9373	163.00	0.00
S8096	25.00	0.00	S9098	0.00	0.00	S9374	100.00	0.00
S8097	0.00	0.00	S9109	0.00	0.00	S9375	26.40	0.00
S8100	0.00	0.00	S9117	0.00	0.00	S9376	365.00	0.00
S8101	0.00	0.00	S9122	17.50	0.00	S9377	11.10	0.00
S8105	310.00	0.00	S9123	39.10	0.00	S9379	0.00	0.00
S8110	15.00	0.00	S9124	45.00	0.00	S9381	0.00	0.00
S8180	0.00	0.00	S9125	0.00	0.00	S9395	0.00	0.00
S8181	5.80	0.00	S9126	144.00	0.00	S9401	0.00	0.00
S8182	0.00	0.00	S9127	200.00	0.00	S9420	0.00	0.00
S8183	0.00	0.00	S9128	98.40	0.00	S9423	0.00	0.00
S8185	0.00	0.00	S9129	127.00	0.00	S9425	0.00	0.00
S8186	33.50	0.00	S9131	128.00	0.00	S9430	60.00	0.00
S8189	17.50	0.00	S9140	30.00	0.00	S9434	0.00	0.00
S8190	0.00	0.00	S9141	0.00	0.00	S9435	11.00	0.00

CODE	COMMERCIAL	MEDICARE	CODE	COMMERCIAL	MEDICARE	CODE	COMMERCIAL	MEDICARE
S9436	0.00	0.00	S9990	0.00	0.00	V2116	0.00	61.53
S9437	0.00	0.00	S9991	0.00	0.00	V2117	69.46	71.53
S9438	0.00	0.00	S9992	22.80	0.00	V2118	0.00	68.61
S9439	0.00	0.00	S9994	60.00	0.00	V2199	112.50	0.00
S9441	0.00	0.00	S9996	0.00	0.00	V2200	59.98	47.97
S9442	0.00	0.00	S9999	0.00	0.00	V2201	52.52	52.28
S9443	0.00	0.00	T1000	0.00	0.00	V2202	60.51	61.52
S9444	0.00	0.00	T1001	0.00	0.00	V2203	50.02	48.39
S9445	0.00	0.00	T1002	15.00	0.00	V2204	55.01	50.59
S9446	0.00	0.00	T1003	0.00	0.00	V2205	54.98	54.71
S9447	0.00	0.00	T1004	0.00	0.00	V2206	70.01	58.77
S9449	0.00	0.00	T1005	0.00	0.00	V2207	56.72	53.46
S9451	0.00	0.00	T1006	0.00	0.00	V2208	65.02	56.11
S9452	0.00	0.00	T1007	0.00	0.00	V2209	57.48	60.41
S9453	0.00	0.00	T1008	180.00	0.00	V2210	70.75	66.63
S9454	0.00	0.00	T1009	0.00	0.00	V2211	75.00	69.10
S9455	43.80	0.00	T1010	0.00	0.00	V2212	92.04	71.35
S9460	75.00	0.00	T1011	0.00	0.00	V2213	70.00	72.08
S9465	31.40	0.00	T1012	0.00	0.00	V2214	94.00	78.35
S9470	47.00	0.00	T1013	82.50	0.00	V2215	81.53	79.53
S9472	0.00	0.00	T1014	0.00	0.00	V2216	70.04	86.13
S9473	0.00	0.00	T1015	10.00	0.00	V2217	89.51	81.40
S9474	0.00	0.00	T1016	0.00	0.00	V2218	0.00	94.64
S9475	0.00	0.00	T1017	0.00	0.00	V2219	53.05	41.66
S9480	150.00	0.00	T1018	0.00	0.00	V2220	42.50	33.79
S9484	0.00	0.00	T1019	0.00	0.00	V2299	82.00	0.00
S9485	0.00	0.00	T1020	0.00	0.00	V2300	99.50	61.06
S9490	0.00	0.00	T1021	0.00	0.00	V2301	93.04	71.98
S9494	10.80	0.00	T1022	0.00	0.00	V2302	98.99	76.73
S9497	220.50	0.00	T1023	0.00	0.00	V2303	82.49	60.09
S9500	139.00	0.00	T1024	0.00	0.00	V2304	77.50	62.87
S9501	180.00	0.00	T1025	0.00	0.00	V2305	85.03	72.85
S9502	200.00	0.00	T1026	0.00	0.00	V2306	87.99	75.01
S9503	311.80	0.00	T1027	0.00	0.00	V2307	90.03	71.02
S9504	251.80	0.00	T1028	0.00	0.00	V2308	100.03	74.43
S9524	95.00	0.00	T1029	0.00	0.00	V2309	97.02	81.08
S9526	140.00	0.00	T1030	0.00	0.00	V2310	0.00	80.12
S9527	0.00	0.00	T1031	0.00	0.00	V2311	119.97	83.36
S9528	0.00	0.00	T1500	0.00	0.00	V2312	117.98	83.84
S9529	150.00	0.00	T1502	0.00	0.00	V2313	0.00	93.64
S9533	0.00	0.00	T1999	0.00	0.00	V2314	107.02	100.56
S9535	36.50	0.00	T2001	0.00	0.00	V2315	40.00	111.64
S9537	66.60	0.00	T2002	0.00	0.00	V2316	0.00	104.67
S9538	0.00	0.00	T2003	0.00	0.00	V2317	130.98	112.65
S9539	206.30	0.00	T2004	0.00	0.00	V2318	0.00	137.25
S9542	0.00	0.00	T2005	0.00	0.00	V2319	74.52	46.46
S9543	80.00	0.00	T2006	0.00	0.00	V2320	82.51	49.02
S9545	0.00	0.00	T2007	0.00	0.00	V2399	100.00	0.00
S9546	0.00	0.00	T2010	0.00	0.00	V2410	47.48	83.90
S9550	50.00	0.00	T2011	0.00	0.00	V2430	104.00	101.11
S9555	0.00	0.00	V2020	91.99	58.67	V2499	50.00	0.00
S9558	4.00	0.00	V2025	100.00	0.00	V2500	87.46	76.05
S9559	125.00	0.00	V2100	46.26	36.65	V2501	90.04	115.84
S9560	0.00	0.00	V2101	41.97	38.62	V2502	99.96	142.70
S9562	0.00	0.00	V2102	47.50	54.33	V2503	0.00	131.43
S9590	0.00	0.00	V2103	34.99	31.83	V2510	83.32	103.81
S9800	40.00	0.00	V2104	43.18	35.25	V2511	129.98	149.16
S9802	0.00	0.00	V2105	43.02	38.37	V2512	160.08	176.26
S9803	0.00	0.00	V2106	43.11	42.58	V2513	100.03	147.98
S9806	0.00	0.00	V2107	43.00	40.50	V2520	74.96	97.58
S9810	0.00	0.00	V2108	46.00	41.93	V2521	119.95	169.88
S9900	0.00	0.00	V2109	44.48	46.39	V2522	133.99	165.33
S9970	0.00	0.00	V2110	63.00	45.78	V2523	99.98	140.89
S9975	0.00	0.00	V2111	54.99	47.72	V2530	160.02	208.68
S9981	0.00	0.00	V2112	47.48	52.09	V2531	0.00	458.11
S9982	0.50	0.00	V2113	58.99	58.71	V2599	42.50	0.00
S9986	0.00	0.00	V2114	71.76	63.60	V2600	0.00	0.00
S9989	0.00	0.00	V2115	87.48	69.22	V2610	250.00	0.00

CODE	COMMERCIAL	MEDICARE	CODE	COMMERCIAL	MEDICARE	CODE	COMMERCIAL	MEDICARE
V2615	0.00	0.00	V5251	2509.00	0.00			
V2623	1750.09	839.86	V5252	3939.00	0.00			
V2624	60.01	56.96	V5253	2356.10	0.00			
V2625	450.02	346.30	V5254	2695.00	0.00			
V2626	249.94	186.67	V5255	2056.00	0.00			
V2627	1849.43	1205.59	V5256	1770.00	0.00			
V2628	355.04	284.67	V5257	2036.30	0.00			
V2629	0.00	0.00	V5258	3939.00	0.00			
V2630	137.50	0.00	V5259	3500.00	0.00			
V2631	0.00	0.00	V5260	3300.00	0.00			
V2632	425.00	0.00	V5261	2500.00	0.00			
V2700	47.52	40.99	V5262	0.00	0.00			
V2710	69.02	59.99	V5263	0.00	0.00			
V2715	11.99	10.88	V5264	50.00	0.00			
V2718	30.00	26.72	V5265	0.00	0.00			
V2730	28.50	19.73	V5266	1.30	0.00			
V2740	12.00	9.82	V5267	18.00	0.00			
V2741	10.00	9.42	V5268	0.00	0.00			
V2742	12.00	9.37	V5269	0.00	0.00			
V2743	17.50	11.99	V5270	0.00	0.00			
V2744	31.80	15.35	V5271	0.00	0.00			
V2750	30.01	17.86	V5272	0.00	0.00			
V2755	13.01	15.54	V5273	0.00	0.00			
V2760	14.99	14.99	V5274	0.00	0.00			
V2770	0.00	18.26	V5275	30.00	0.00			
V2780	10.00	11.73	V5298	0.00	0.00			
V2781	97.80	0.00	V5299	0.00	0.00			
V2785	2282.00	0.00	V5336	0.00	0.00			
V2790	0.00	0.00	V5362	0.00	0.00			
V2799	0.00	0.00	V5363	0.00	0.00			
V5008	26.01	0.00	V5364	0.00	0.00			
V5010	109.98	0.00						
V5011	111.96	0.00						
V5014	175.05	0.00						
V5020	74.99	0.00						
V5030	1407.69	0.00						
V5040	0.00	0.00						
V5050	1038.23	0.00						
V5060	945.00	0.00						
V5070	0.00	0.00						
V5080	0.00	0.00						
V5090	300.09	0.00						
V5095	0.00	0.00						
V5100	1899.43	0.00						
V5110	399.96	0.00						
V5120	0.00	0.00						
V5130	1727.50	0.00						
V5140	1600.30	0.00						
V5150	0.00	0.00						
V5160	350.05	0.00						
V5170	0.00	0.00						
V5180	0.00	0.00						
V5190	0.00	0.00						
V5200	0.00	0.00						
V5210	0.00	0.00						
V5220	0.00	0.00						
V5230	0.00	0.00						
V5240	0.00	0.00						
V5241	350.00	0.00						
V5242	0.00	0.00						
V5243	825.00	0.00						
V5244	0.00	0.00						
V5245	1570.00	0.00						
V5246	1400.00	0.00						
V5247	1500.00	0.00						
V5248	0.00	0.00						
V5249	1298.00	0.00						
V5250	3500.00	0.00						